THE BATMAN ADVENTURES

VOLUME 1

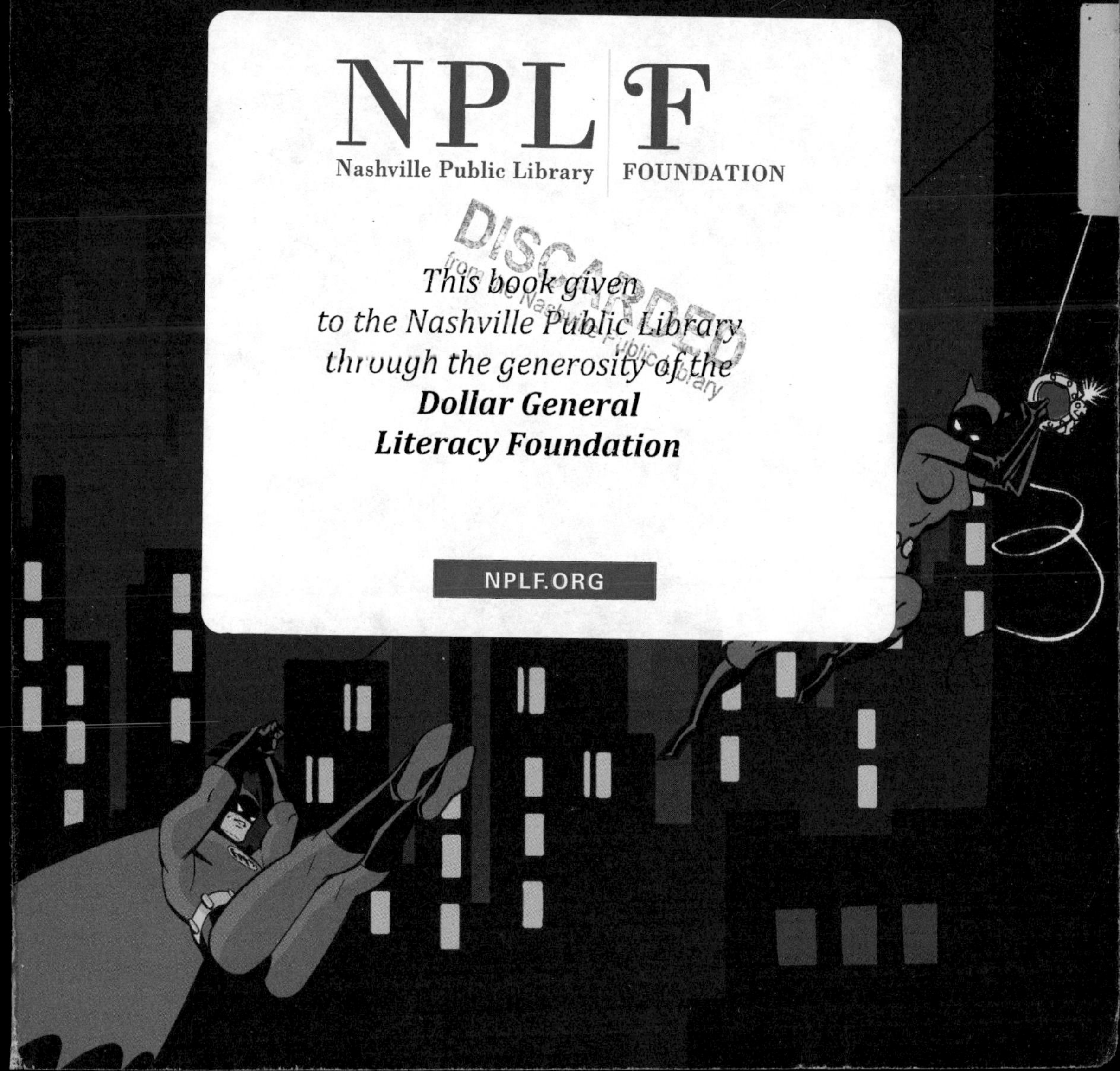

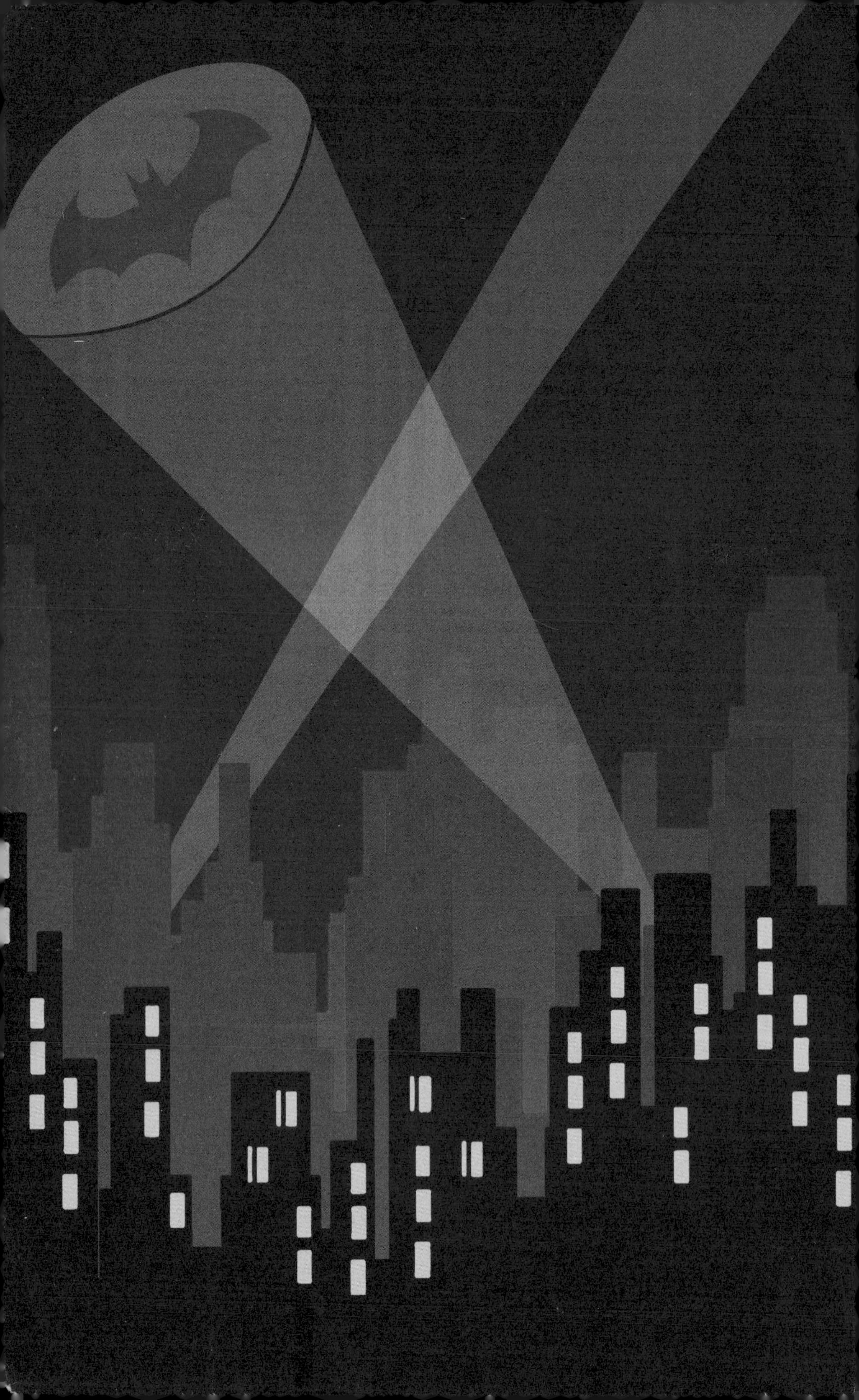

THE
BATMAN
ADVENTURES
VOLUME 1

KELLEY PUCKETT   MARTIN PASKO
writers

TY TEMPLETON   RICK BURCHETT
BRAD RADER   MIKE PAROBECK
artists

RICK TAYLOR
colorist

TIM HARKINS
letterer

TY TEMPLETON
collection cover artist

BATMAN created by **BOB KANE**

Scott Peterson	Editor—Original Series
Rachel Pinnelas	Editor
Robbin Brosterman	Design Director—Books
Sarabeth Kett	Publication Design
Bob Harras	Senior VP—Editor-in-Chief, DC Comics
Diane Nelson	President
Dan DiDio and Jim Lee	Co-Publishers
Geoff Johns	Chief Creative Officer
Amit Desai	Senior VP—Marketing & Franchise Management
Amy Genkins	Senior VP—Business & Legal Affairs
Nairi Gardiner	Senior VP—Finance
Jeff Boison	VP—Publishing Planning
Mark Chiarello	VP—Art Direction & Design
John Cunningham	VP—Marketing
Terri Cunningham	VP—Editorial Administration
Larry Ganem	VP—Talent Relations & Services
Alison Gill	Senior VP—Manufacturing & Operations
Hank Kanalz	Senior VP—Vertigo & Integrated Publishing
Jay Kogan	VP—Business & Legal Affairs, Publishing
Jack Mahan	VP—Business Affairs, Talent
Nick Napolitano	VP—Manufacturing Administration
Sue Pohja	VP—Book Sales
Fred Ruiz	VP—Manufacturing Operations
Courtney Simmons	Senior VP—Publicity
Bob Wayne	Senior VP—Sales

BATMAN ADVENTURES VOLUME 1

Published by DC Comics. Compilation Copyright © 2014 DC Comics. All Rights Reserved.

Originally published in single magazine form in THE BATMAN ADVENTURES 1-10. Copyright © 1992, 1993 DC Comics. All Rights Reserved. All characters, their distinctive likenesses and related elements featured in this publication are trademarks of DC Comics. The stories, characters and incidents featured in this publication are entirely fictional. DC Comics does not read or accept unsolicited ideas, stories or artwork.

DC Comics, 1700 Broadway, New York, NY 10019
A Warner Bros. Entertainment Company.
Printed by RR Donnelley, Salem, VA, USA. 10/3/14. First Printing.
ISBN: 978-1-4012-5229-8

Library of Congress Cataloging-in-Publication Data

Puckett, Kelley.
  Batman Adventures Volume 1 / Kelley Puckett, writer ; Ty Templeton, artist.
    pages cm
  ISBN 978-1-4012-5229-8 (paperback)
  1. Graphic novels. I. Templeton, Ty, illustrator. II. Title.

PN6728.B36P773 2014
741.5'973—dc23

2014033208

SUSTAINABLE FORESTRY INITIATIVE
Certified Sourcing
www.sfiprogram.org
SFI-01042
APPLIES TO TEXT STOCK ONLY

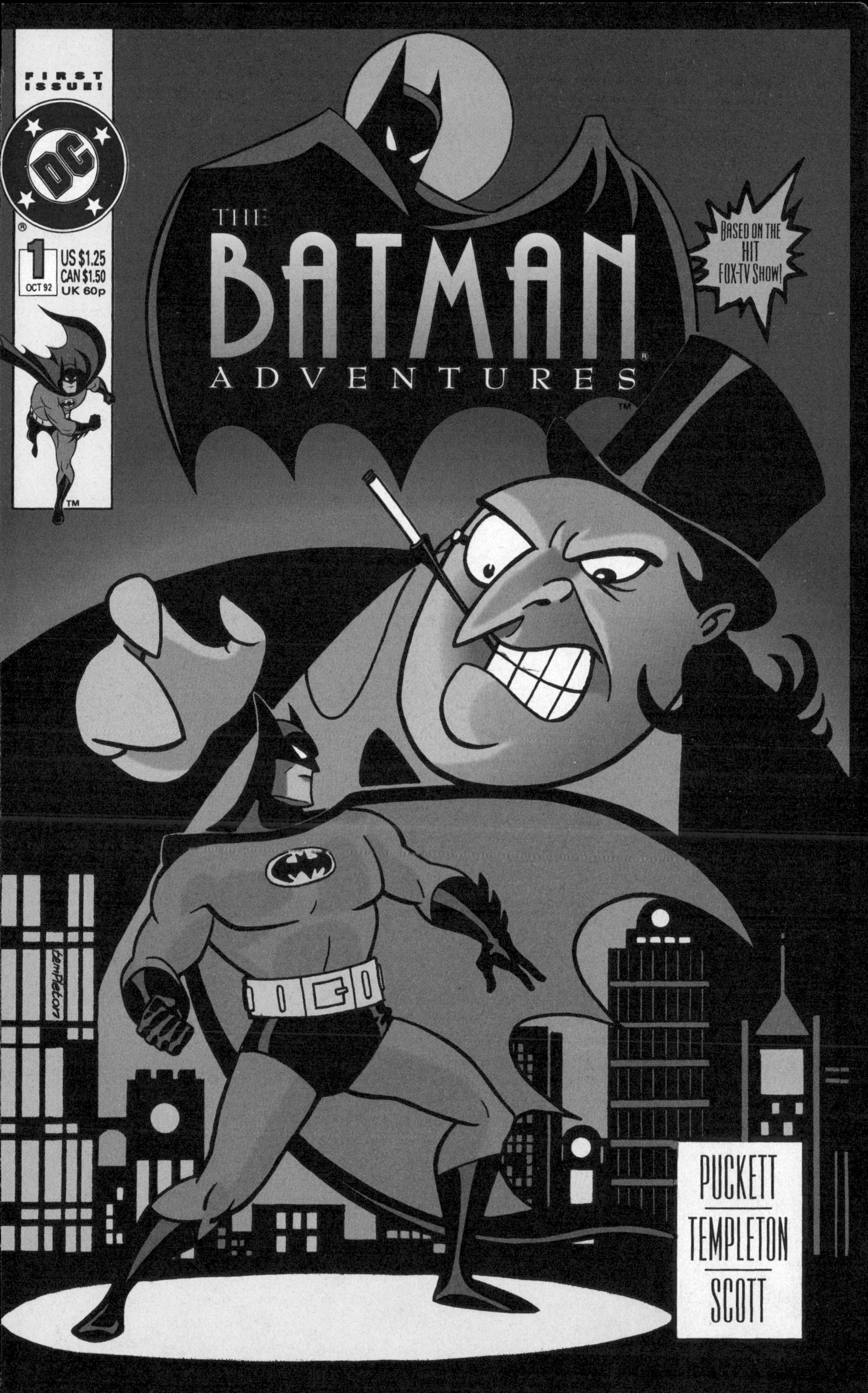

FIRST ISSUE!
DC
1
OCT 92
US $1.25
CAN $1.50
UK 60p
THE BATMAN ADVENTURES
BASED ON THE HIT FOX-TV SHOW!
PUCKETT
TEMPLETON
SCOTT

PENGUIN'S BIG SCORE

ACT ONE: CHARM SCHOOL DROPOUT!

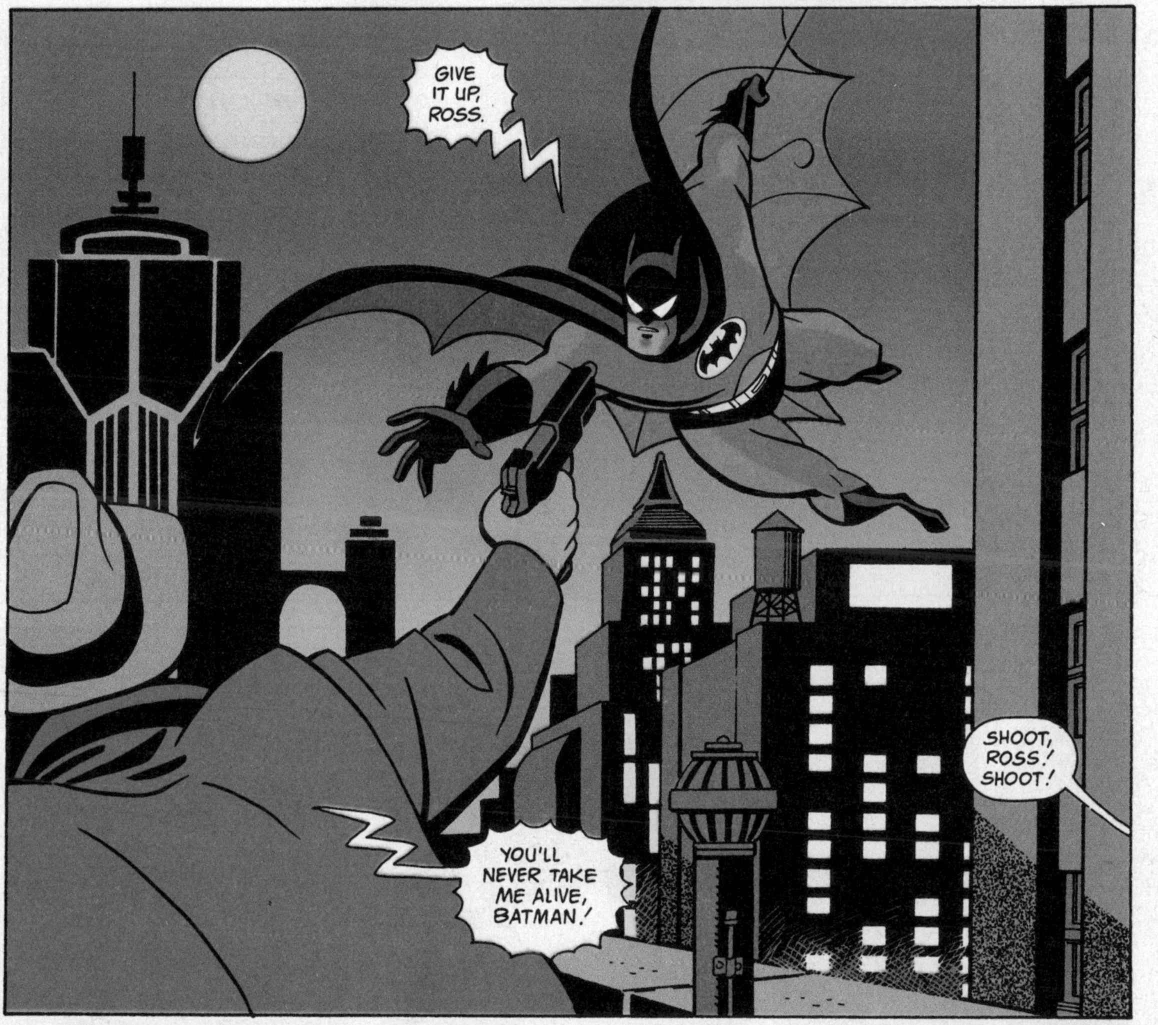
GIVE IT UP, ROSS.
YOU'LL NEVER TAKE ME ALIVE, BATMAN!
SHOOT, ROSS! SHOOT!

KELLEY PUCKETT ~ WRITER TY TEMPLETON ~ PENCILLER RICK BURCHETT ~ INKER
RICK TAYLOR ~ COLORIST TIM HARKINS ~ LETTERER SCOTT PETERSON ~ EDITOR
BATMAN CREATED BY BOB KANE *WITH SPECIAL THANKS TO SAM ARGO

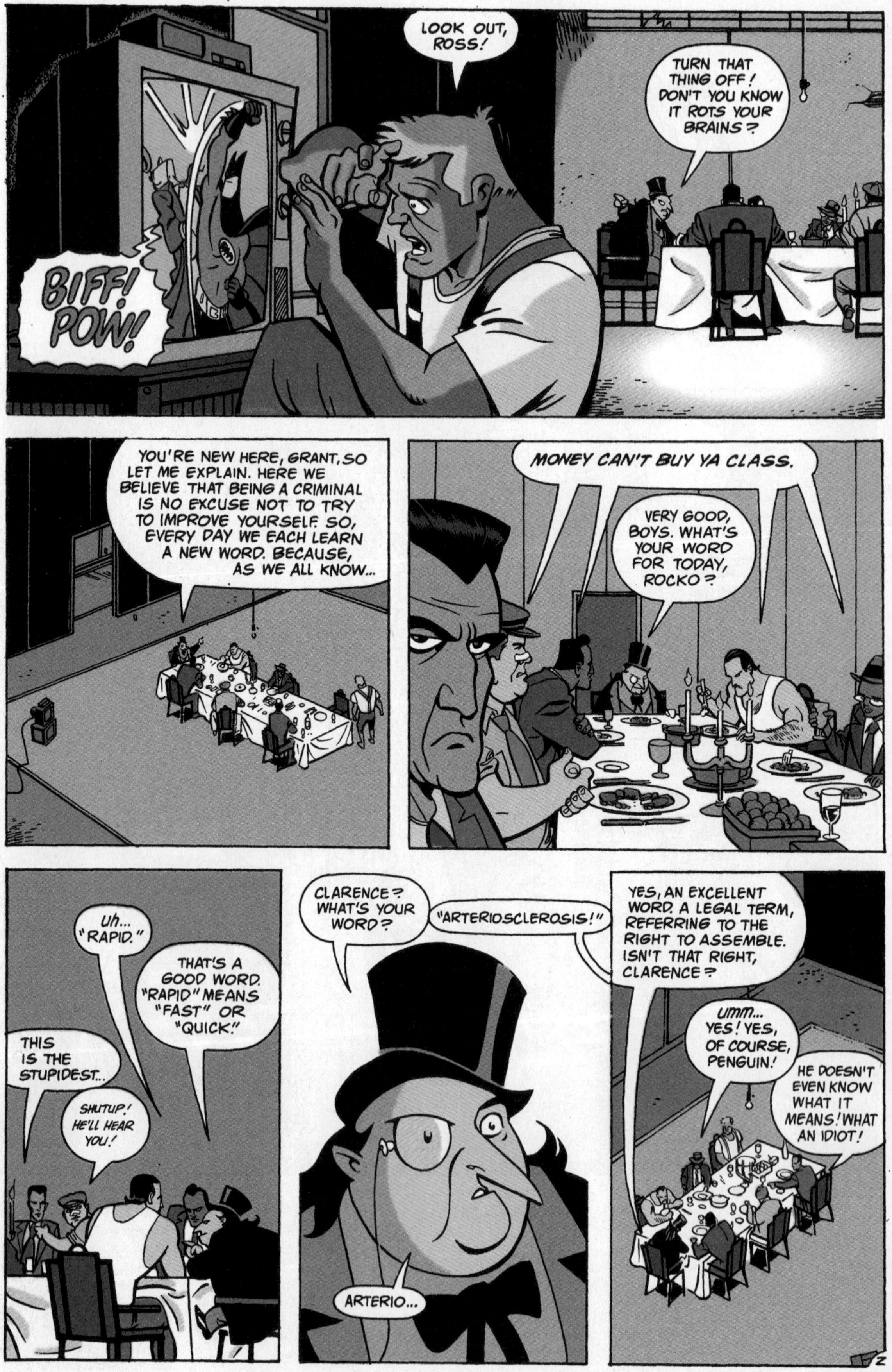
BIFF! POW!
LOOK OUT, ROSS!
TURN THAT THING OFF! DON'T YOU KNOW IT ROTS YOUR BRAINS?
YOU'RE NEW HERE, GRANT, SO LET ME EXPLAIN. HERE WE BELIEVE THAT BEING A CRIMINAL IS NO EXCUSE NOT TO TRY TO IMPROVE YOURSELF. SO, EVERY DAY WE EACH LEARN A NEW WORD. BECAUSE, AS WE ALL KNOW...
MONEY CAN'T BUY YA CLASS.
VERY GOOD, BOYS. WHAT'S YOUR WORD FOR TODAY, ROCKO?
Uh... "RAPID."
THAT'S A GOOD WORD. "RAPID" MEANS "FAST" OR "QUICK."
THIS IS THE STUPIDEST...
SHUTUP! HE'LL HEAR YOU!
CLARENCE? WHAT'S YOUR WORD?
ARTERIO...
"ARTERIOSCLEROSIS!"
YES, AN EXCELLENT WORD. A LEGAL TERM, REFERRING TO THE RIGHT TO ASSEMBLE. ISN'T THAT RIGHT, CLARENCE?
umm... YES! YES, OF COURSE, PENGUIN!
HE DOESN'T EVEN KNOW WHAT IT MEANS! WHAT AN IDIOT!

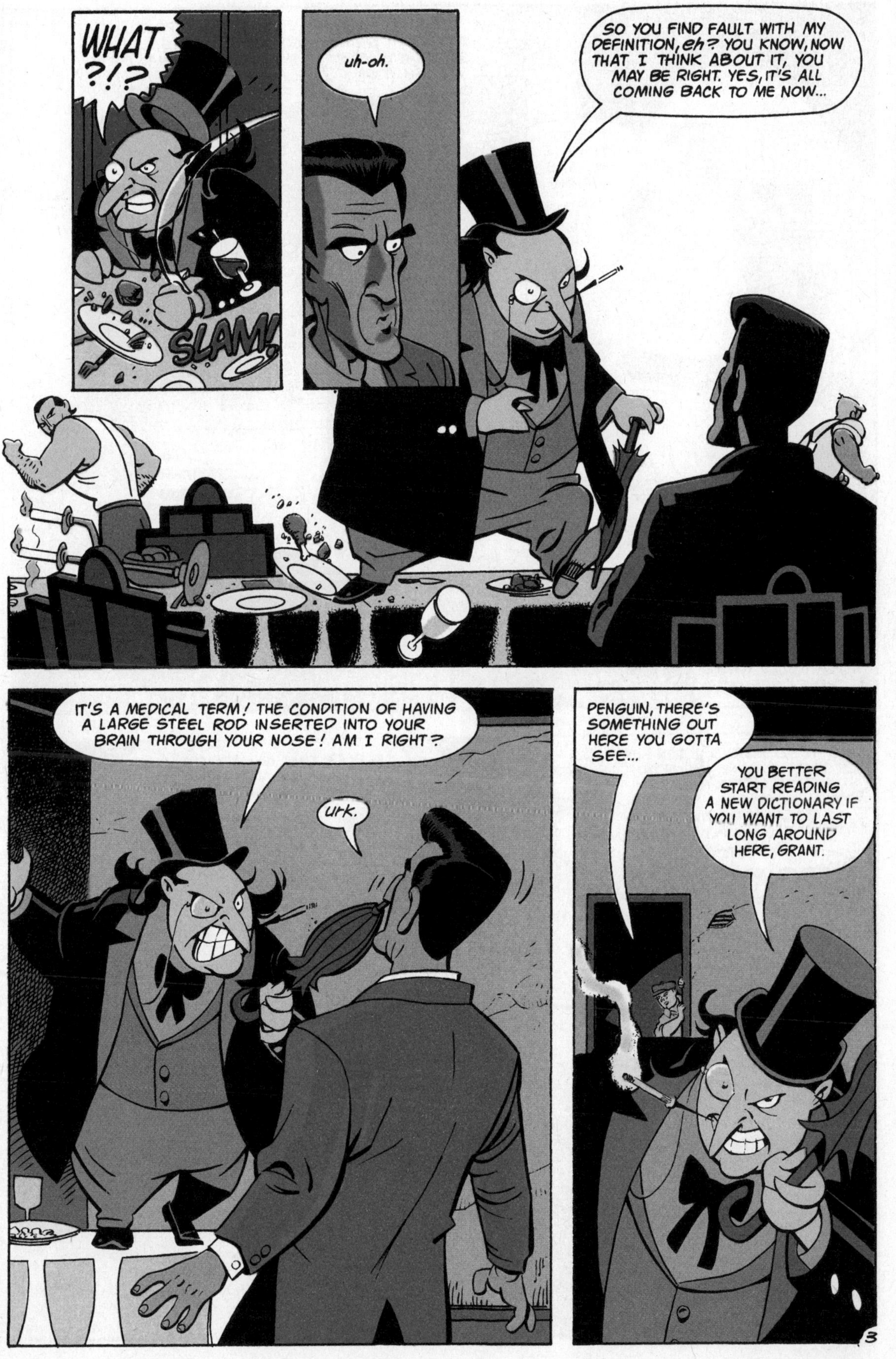
WHAT ?!?
SLAM!
uh-oh.
SO YOU FIND FAULT WITH MY DEFINITION, eh? YOU KNOW, NOW THAT I THINK ABOUT IT, YOU MAY BE RIGHT. YES, IT'S ALL COMING BACK TO ME NOW...
IT'S A MEDICAL TERM! THE CONDITION OF HAVING A LARGE STEEL ROD INSERTED INTO YOUR BRAIN THROUGH YOUR NOSE! AM I RIGHT?
urk.
PENGUIN, THERE'S SOMETHING OUT HERE YOU GOTTA SEE...
YOU BETTER START READING A NEW DICTIONARY IF YOU WANT TO LAST LONG AROUND HERE, GRANT.
3

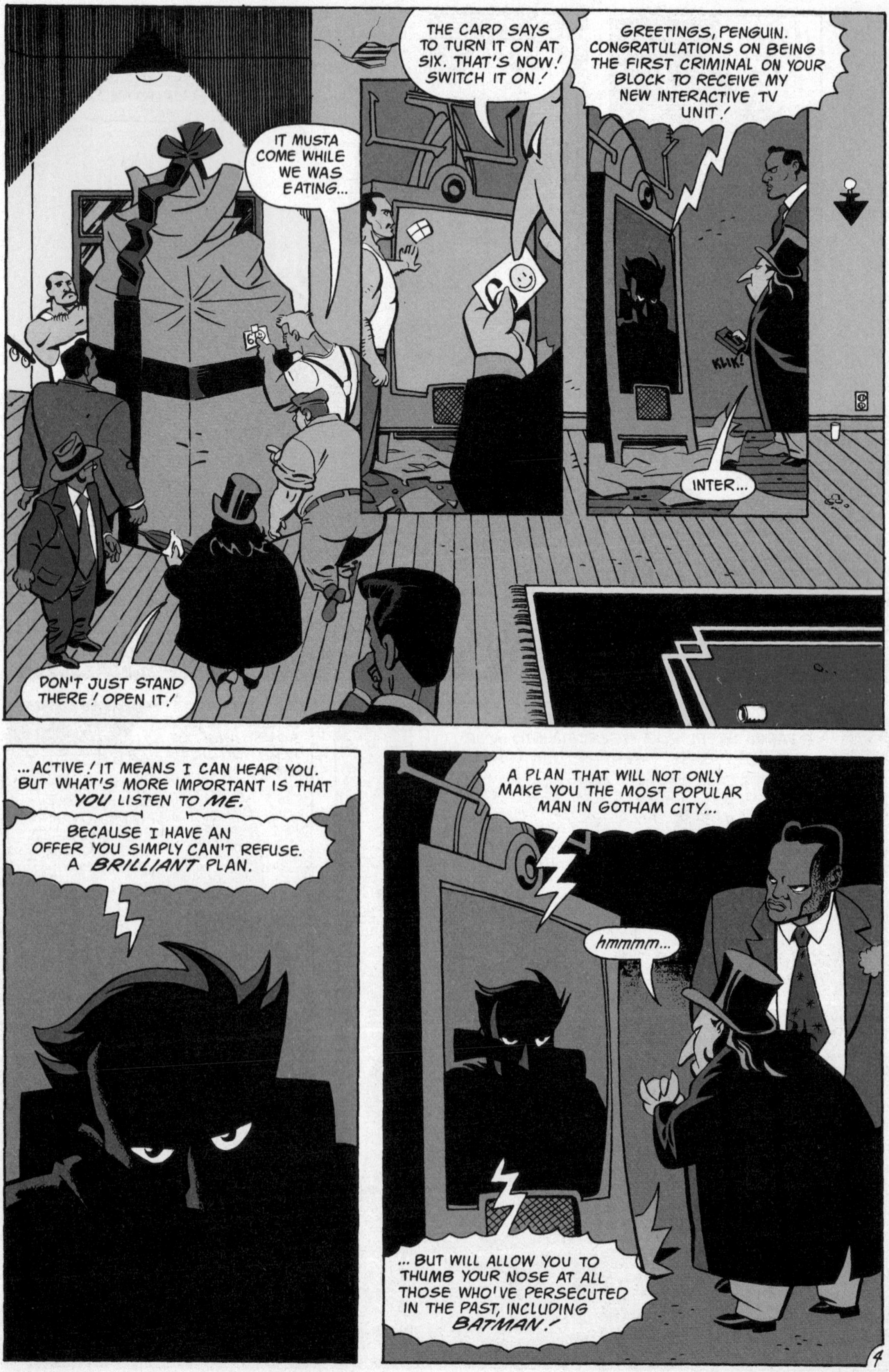

DON'T JUST STAND THERE! OPEN IT!
IT MUSTA COME WHILE WE WAS EATING...
THE CARD SAYS TO TURN IT ON AT SIX. THAT'S NOW! SWITCH IT ON!
GREETINGS, PENGUIN. CONGRATULATIONS ON BEING THE FIRST CRIMINAL ON YOUR BLOCK TO RECEIVE MY NEW INTERACTIVE TV UNIT!
KLIK!
INTER...
...ACTIVE! IT MEANS I CAN HEAR YOU. BUT WHAT'S MORE IMPORTANT IS THAT YOU LISTEN TO ME.
BECAUSE I HAVE AN OFFER YOU SIMPLY CAN'T REFUSE. A BRILLIANT PLAN.
A PLAN THAT WILL NOT ONLY MAKE YOU THE MOST POPULAR MAN IN GOTHAM CITY...
hmmmm...
... BUT WILL ALLOW YOU TO THUMB YOUR NOSE AT ALL THOSE WHO'VE PERSECUTED IN THE PAST, INCLUDING BATMAN!
4

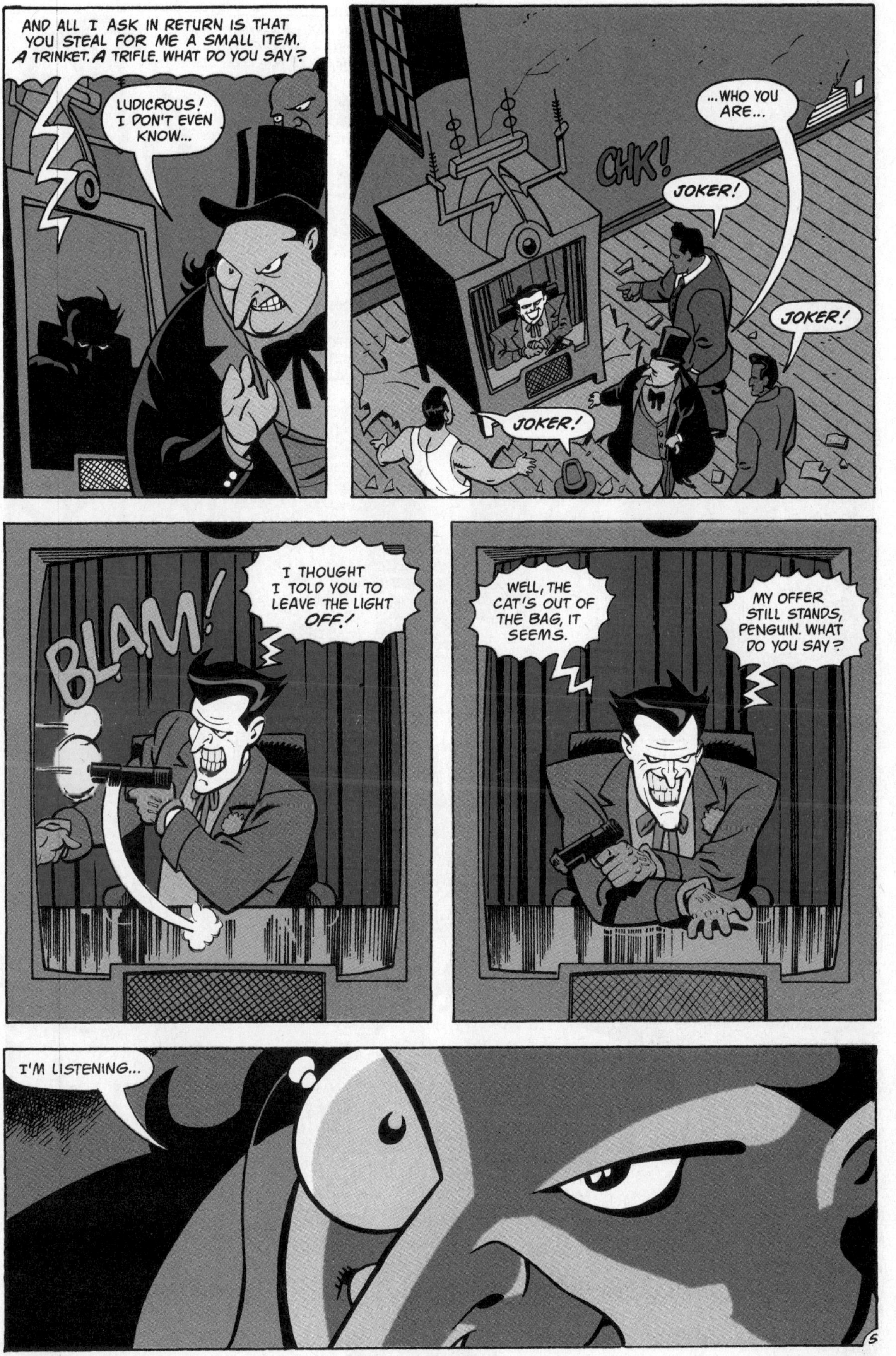
AND ALL I ASK IN RETURN IS THAT YOU STEAL FOR ME A SMALL ITEM. A TRINKET. A TRIFLE. WHAT DO YOU SAY?
LUDICROUS! I DON'T EVEN KNOW...
...WHO YOU ARE...
CHK!
JOKER!
JOKER!
JOKER!
BLAM!
I THOUGHT I TOLD YOU TO LEAVE THE LIGHT OFF!
WELL, THE CAT'S OUT OF THE BAG, IT SEEMS.
MY OFFER STILL STANDS, PENGUIN. WHAT DO YOU SAY?
I'M LISTENING...
5

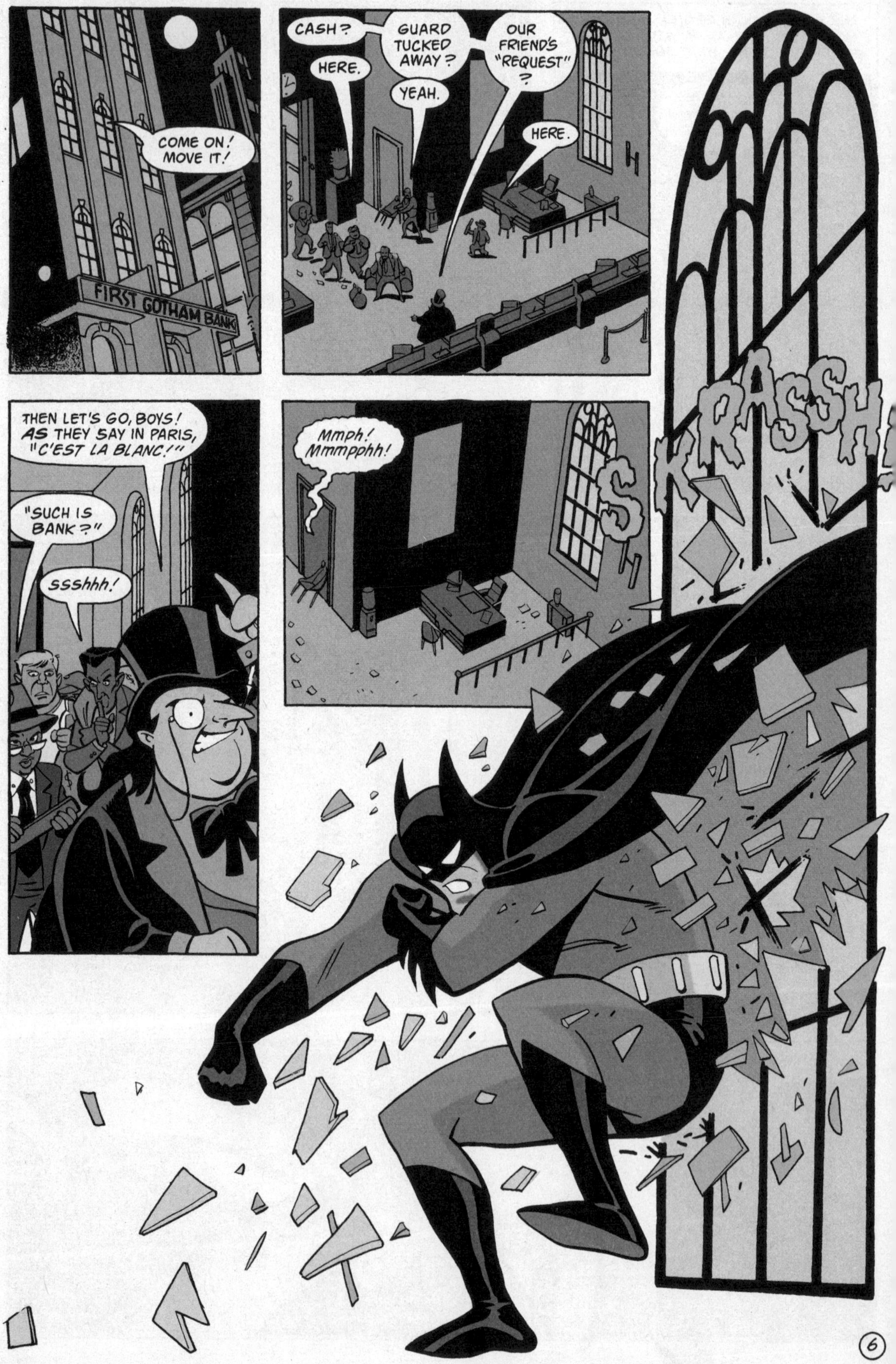
COME ON! MOVE IT!
CASH?
HERE.
GUARD TUCKED AWAY?
YEAH.
OUR FRIEND'S "REQUEST"?
HERE.
FIRST GOTHAM BANK
THEN LET'S GO, BOYS! AS THEY SAY IN PARIS, "C'EST LA BLANC!"
"SUCH IS BANK?"
SSSHHH!
Mmph! Mmmpphh!
SKRASSH!
6

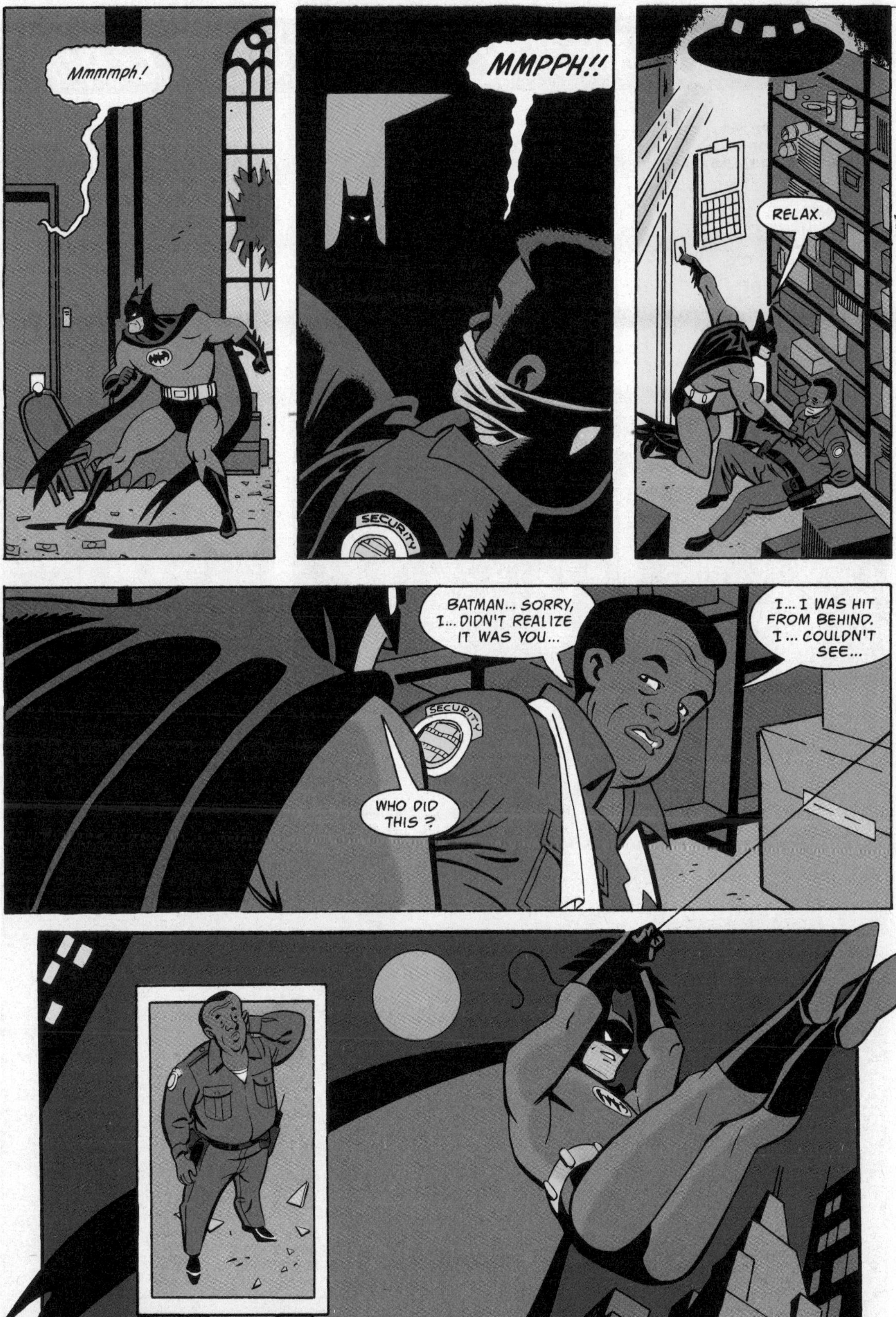
Mmmmph!
MMPPH!!
RELAX.
BATMAN... SORRY, I... DIDN'T REALIZE IT WAS YOU...
I... I WAS HIT FROM BEHIND. I... COULDN'T SEE...
WHO DID THIS?
SECURITY
7

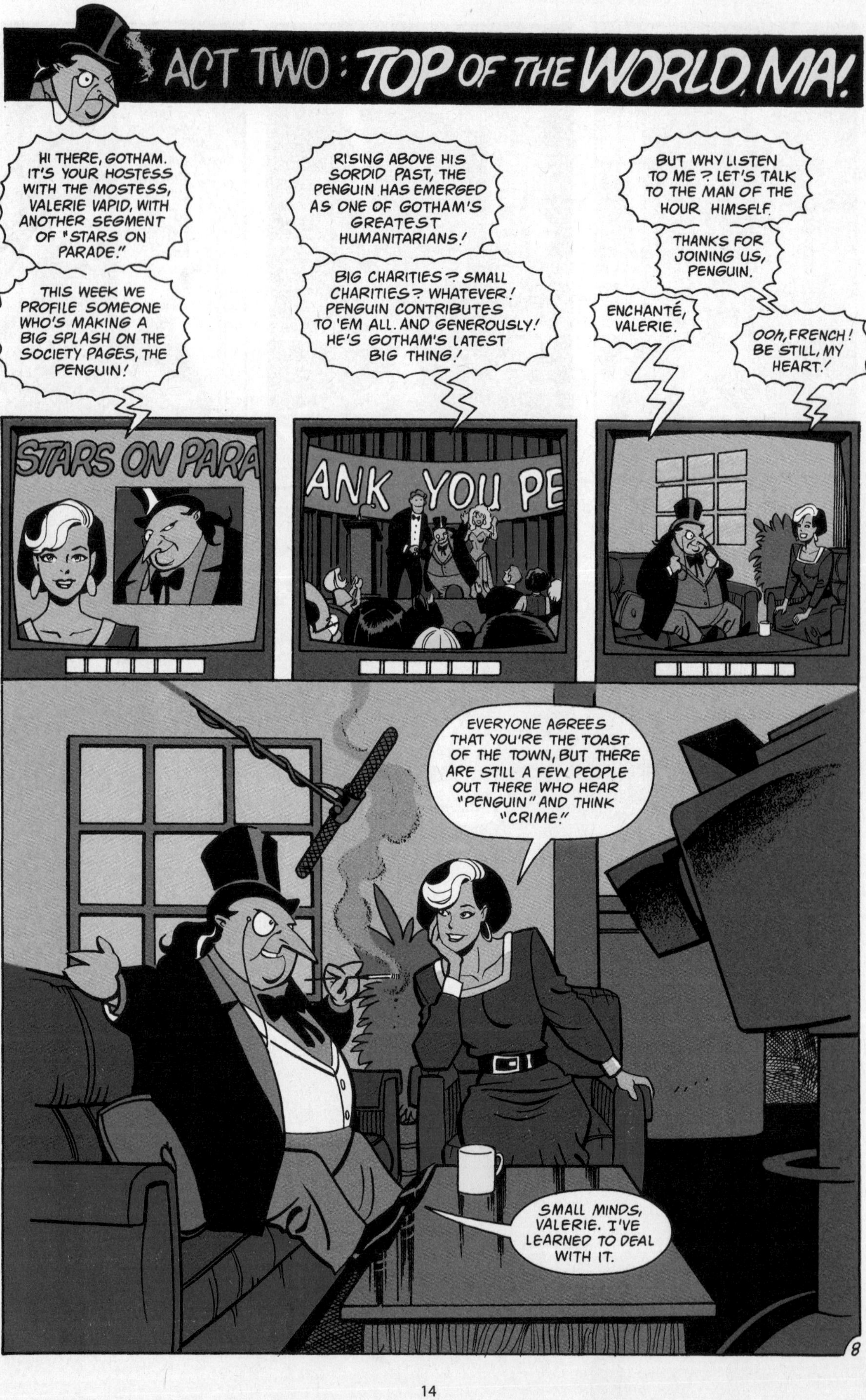

ACT TWO: TOP OF THE WORLD, MA!
HI THERE, GOTHAM. IT'S YOUR HOSTESS WITH THE MOSTESS, VALERIE VAPID, WITH ANOTHER SEGMENT OF "STARS ON PARADE."
THIS WEEK WE PROFILE SOMEONE WHO'S MAKING A BIG SPLASH ON THE SOCIETY PAGES, THE PENGUIN!
RISING ABOVE HIS SORDID PAST, THE PENGUIN HAS EMERGED AS ONE OF GOTHAM'S GREATEST HUMANITARIANS!
BIG CHARITIES? SMALL CHARITIES? WHATEVER! PENGUIN CONTRIBUTES TO 'EM ALL. AND GENEROUSLY! HE'S GOTHAM'S LATEST BIG THING!
BUT WHY LISTEN TO ME? LET'S TALK TO THE MAN OF THE HOUR HIMSELF.
THANKS FOR JOINING US, PENGUIN.
ENCHANTÉ, VALERIE.
OOH, FRENCH! BE STILL, MY HEART!
STARS ON PARA
ANK YOU PE
EVERYONE AGREES THAT YOU'RE THE TOAST OF THE TOWN, BUT THERE ARE STILL A FEW PEOPLE OUT THERE WHO HEAR "PENGUIN" AND THINK "CRIME."
SMALL MINDS, VALERIE. I'VE LEARNED TO DEAL WITH IT.
8

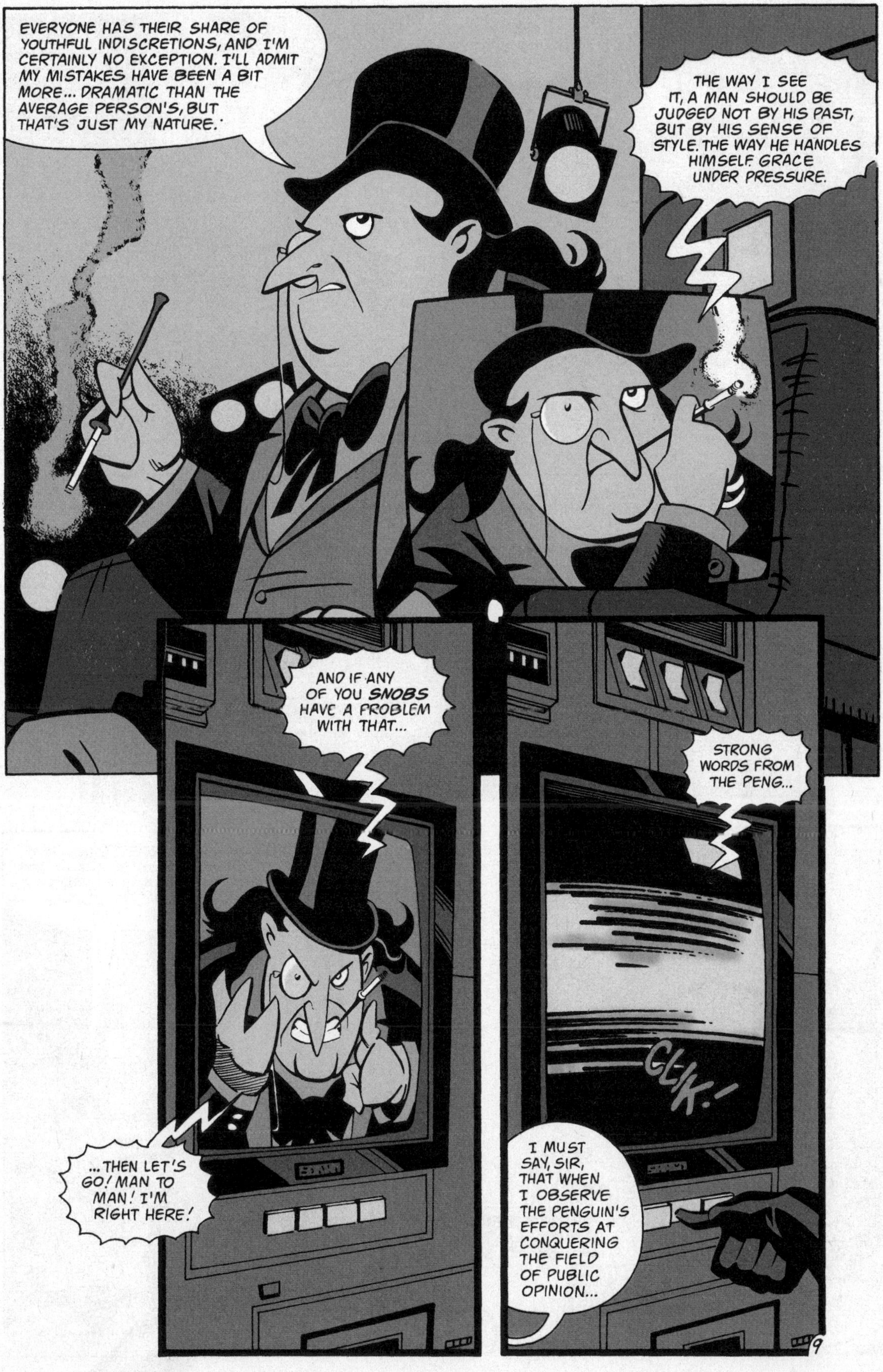
EVERYONE HAS THEIR SHARE OF YOUTHFUL INDISCRETIONS, AND I'M CERTAINLY NO EXCEPTION. I'LL ADMIT MY MISTAKES HAVE BEEN A BIT MORE... DRAMATIC THAN THE AVERAGE PERSON'S, BUT THAT'S JUST MY NATURE.
THE WAY I SEE IT, A MAN SHOULD BE JUDGED NOT BY HIS PAST, BUT BY HIS SENSE OF STYLE. THE WAY HE HANDLES HIMSELF. GRACE UNDER PRESSURE.
AND IF ANY OF YOU SNOBS HAVE A PROBLEM WITH THAT...
...THEN LET'S GO! MAN TO MAN! I'M RIGHT HERE!
STRONG WORDS FROM THE PENG...
CLIK!
I MUST SAY, SIR, THAT WHEN I OBSERVE THE PENGUIN'S EFFORTS AT CONQUERING THE FIELD OF PUBLIC OPINION...
9

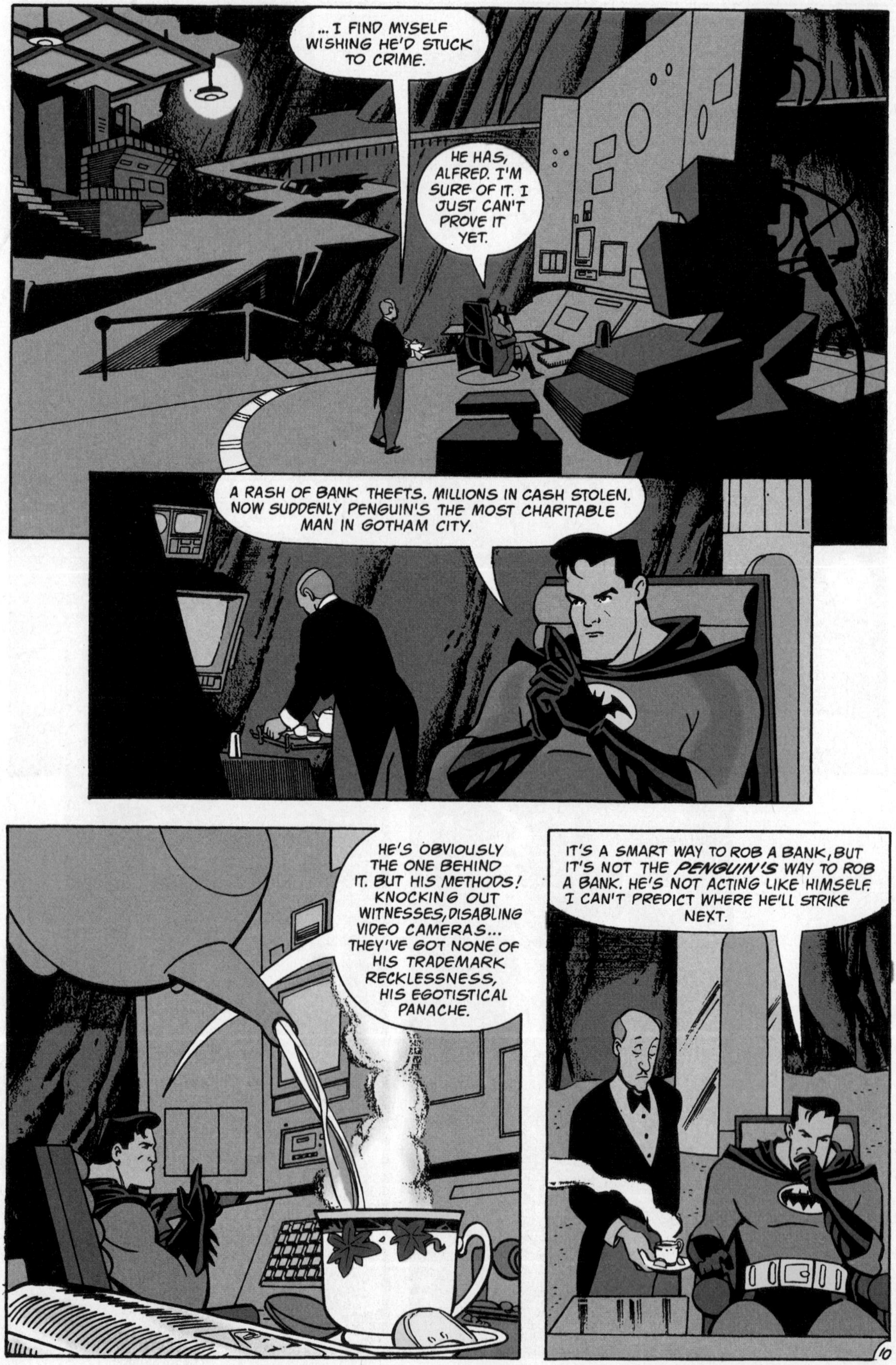
...I FIND MYSELF WISHING HE'D STUCK TO CRIME.
HE HAS, ALFRED. I'M SURE OF IT. I JUST CAN'T PROVE IT YET.
A RASH OF BANK THEFTS. MILLIONS IN CASH STOLEN. NOW SUDDENLY PENGUIN'S THE MOST CHARITABLE MAN IN GOTHAM CITY.
HE'S OBVIOUSLY THE ONE BEHIND IT. BUT HIS METHODS! KNOCKING OUT WITNESSES, DISABLING VIDEO CAMERAS... THEY'VE GOT NONE OF HIS TRADEMARK RECKLESSNESS, HIS EGOTISTICAL PANACHE.
IT'S A SMART WAY TO ROB A BANK, BUT IT'S NOT THE *PENGUIN'S* WAY TO ROB A BANK. HE'S NOT ACTING LIKE HIMSELF. I CAN'T PREDICT WHERE HE'LL STRIKE NEXT.
10

TCH! SEEMS THE THEATER COUNCIL HAS INVITED HIM ON THE BOARD FOR RESTORING THE FUNDING THAT CARNEGIE WITHDREW...

LELAND CARNEGIE WAS A MAJOR SPONSOR OF THE THEATER?

THE MAJOR SPONSOR, BUT RECENTLY HE...

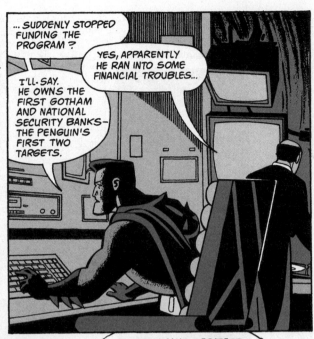

... SUDDENLY STOPPED FUNDING THE PROGRAM?

YES, APPARENTLY HE RAN INTO SOME FINANCIAL TROUBLES...

I'LL SAY. HE OWNS THE FIRST GOTHAM AND NATIONAL SECURITY BANKS— THE PENGUIN'S FIRST TWO TARGETS.

TAKE A LOOK AT THE LIST OF BANK OWNERS, ALFRED. ANY NAMES RING A BELL?

SIR?

GOOD LORD! J.P. STANFORD... ANDREW MORGAN...

YES. GOTHAM'S GREATEST PHILANTHROPISTS. PENGUIN'S BEEN BANKRUPTING THEM AND USING THE MONEY TO TAKE THEIR PLACE IN HIGH SOCIETY. CLEVER.

DON'T CANCEL MY INVITATION TO TONIGHT'S CHARITY GALA, ALFRED. I THINK BRUCE WAYNE WILL BE ATTENDING AFTER ALL...

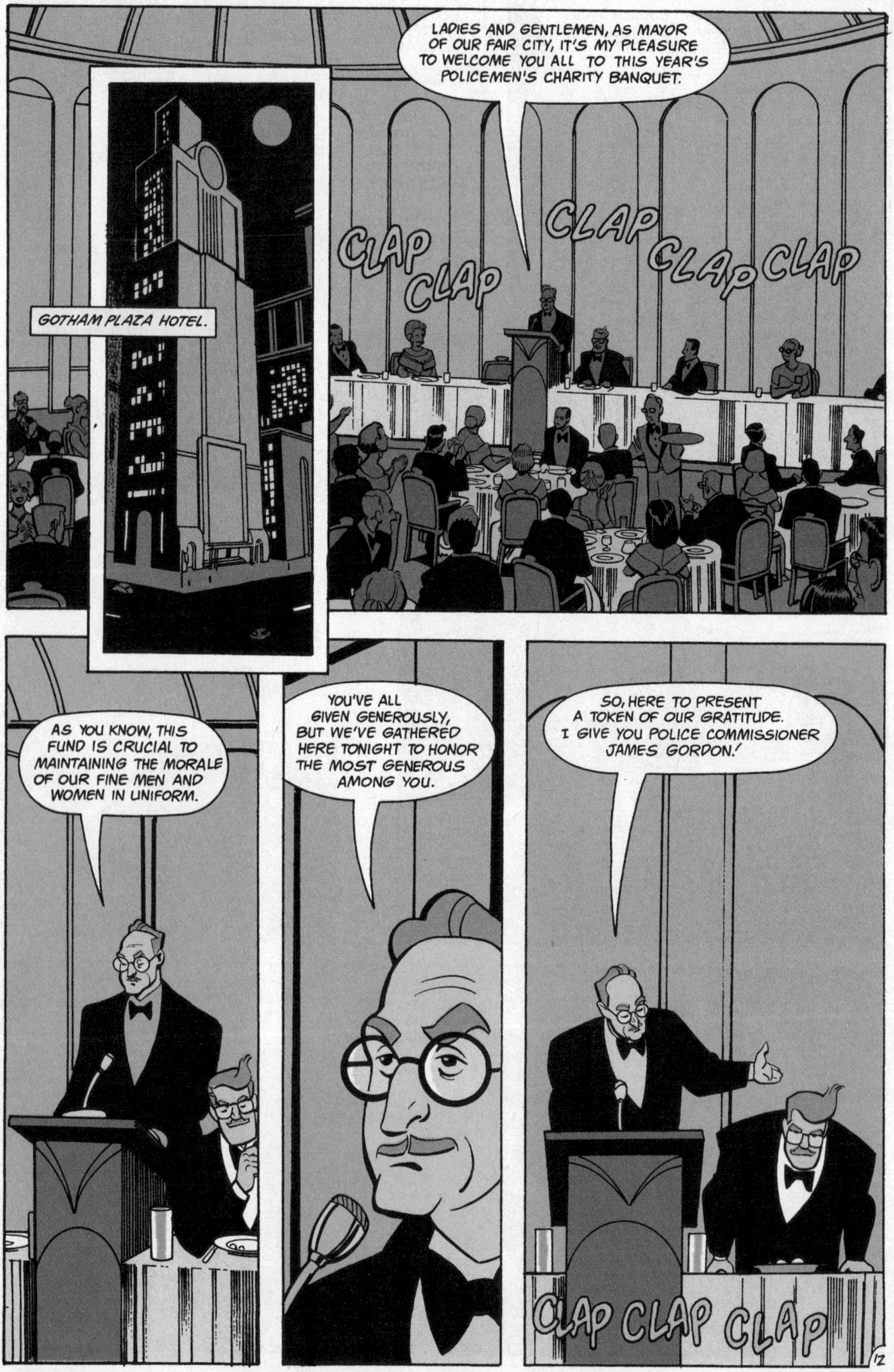
GOTHAM PLAZA HOTEL.
LADIES AND GENTLEMEN, AS MAYOR OF OUR FAIR CITY, IT'S MY PLEASURE TO WELCOME YOU ALL TO THIS YEAR'S POLICEMEN'S CHARITY BANQUET.
CLAP CLAP
CLAP CLAP CLAP
AS YOU KNOW, THIS FUND IS CRUCIAL TO MAINTAINING THE MORALE OF OUR FINE MEN AND WOMEN IN UNIFORM.
YOU'VE ALL GIVEN GENEROUSLY, BUT WE'VE GATHERED HERE TONIGHT TO HONOR THE MOST GENEROUS AMONG YOU.
SO, HERE TO PRESENT A TOKEN OF OUR GRATITUDE. I GIVE YOU POLICE COMMISSIONER JAMES GORDON!
CLAP CLAP CLAP

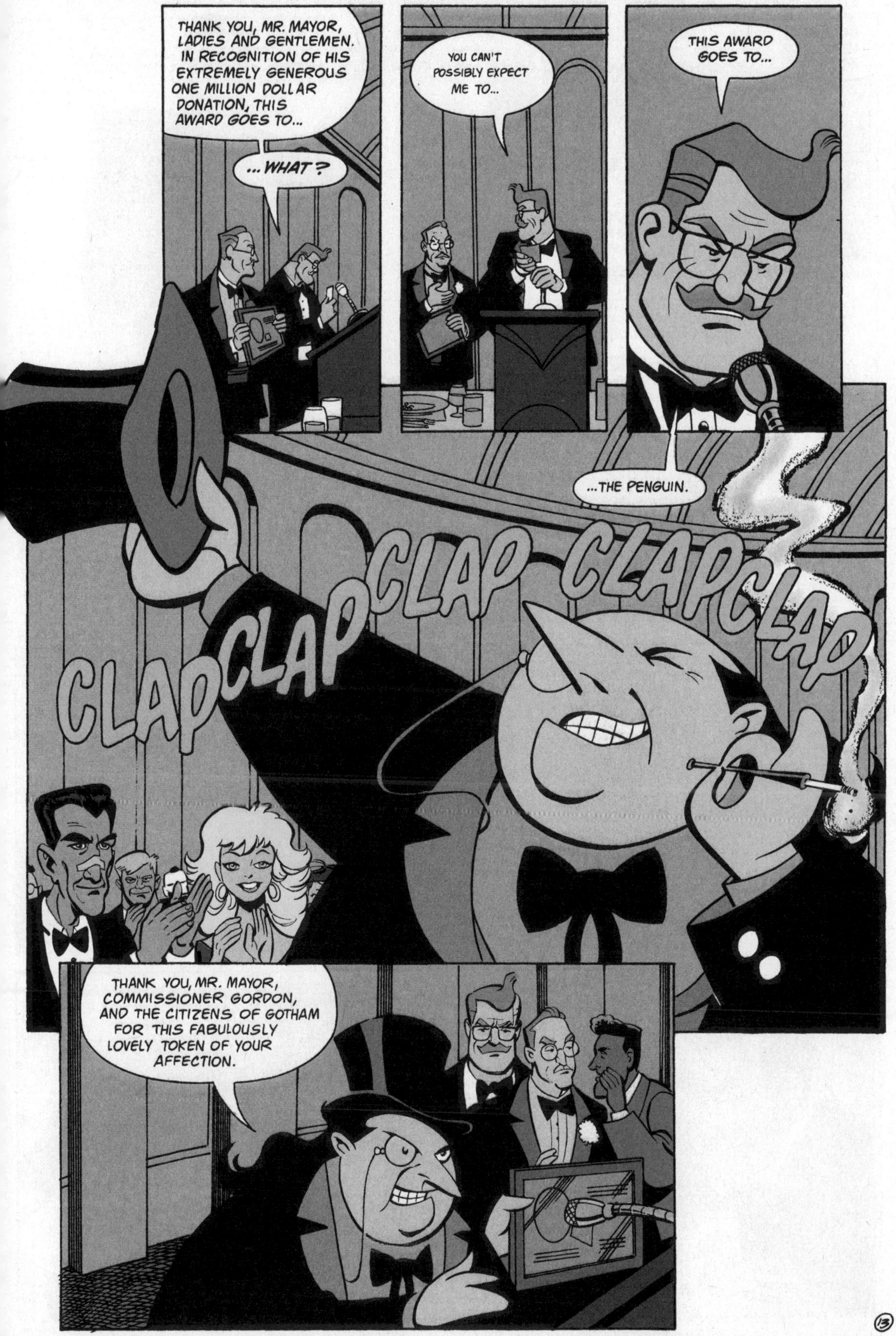
THANK YOU, MR. MAYOR, LADIES AND GENTLEMEN. IN RECOGNITION OF HIS EXTREMELY GENEROUS ONE MILLION DOLLAR DONATION, THIS AWARD GOES TO...
...WHAT?
YOU CAN'T POSSIBLY EXPECT ME TO...
THIS AWARD GOES TO...
...THE PENGUIN.
CLAPCLAPCLAP CLAPCLAP
THANK YOU, MR. MAYOR, COMMISSIONER GORDON, AND THE CITIZENS OF GOTHAM FOR THIS FABULOUSLY LOVELY TOKEN OF YOUR AFFECTION.
13

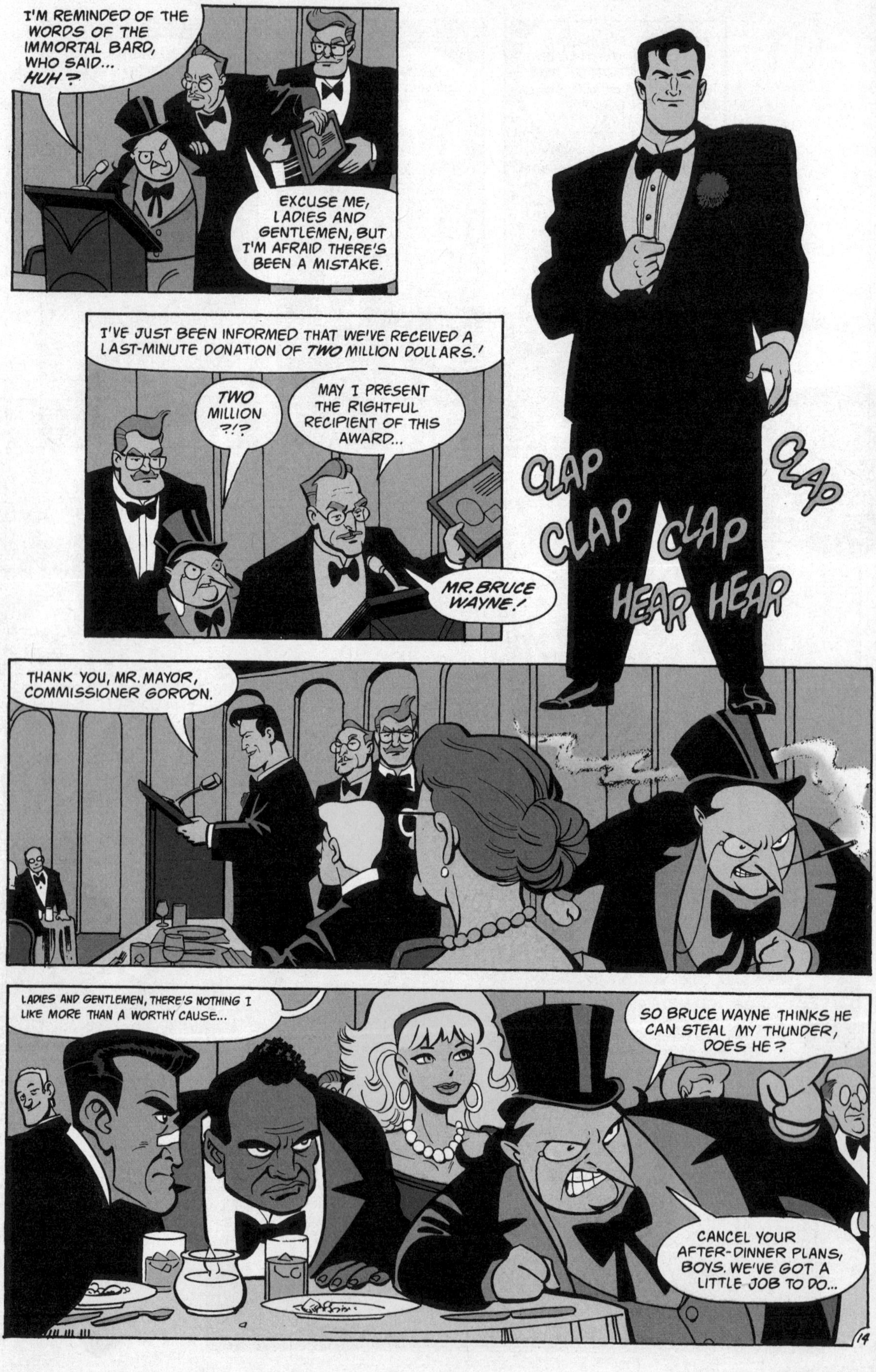
I'M REMINDED OF THE WORDS OF THE IMMORTAL BARD, WHO SAID... HUH?
EXCUSE ME, LADIES AND GENTLEMEN, BUT I'M AFRAID THERE'S BEEN A MISTAKE.
I'VE JUST BEEN INFORMED THAT WE'VE RECEIVED A LAST-MINUTE DONATION OF TWO MILLION DOLLARS.!
TWO MILLION ?!?
MAY I PRESENT THE RIGHTFUL RECIPIENT OF THIS AWARD...
MR. BRUCE WAYNE.!
CLAP
CLAP
CLAP
CLAP
HEAR HEAR
THANK YOU, MR. MAYOR, COMMISSIONER GORDON.
LADIES AND GENTLEMEN, THERE'S NOTHING I LIKE MORE THAN A WORTHY CAUSE...
SO BRUCE WAYNE THINKS HE CAN STEAL MY THUNDER, DOES HE?
CANCEL YOUR AFTER-DINNER PLANS, BOYS. WE'VE GOT A LITTLE JOB TO DO...
14

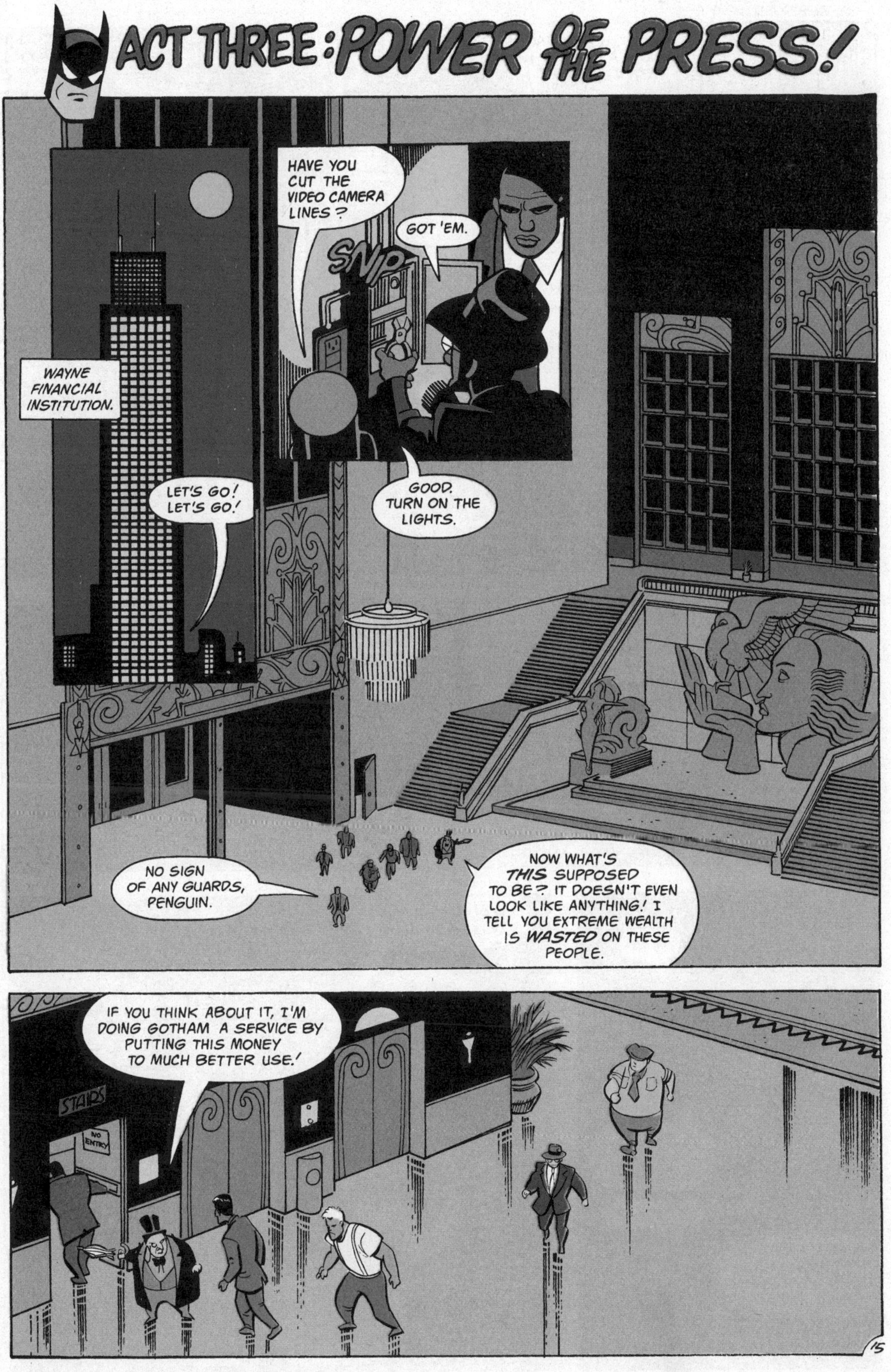
ACT THREE: POWER OF THE PRESS!
WAYNE FINANCIAL INSTITUTION.
LET'S GO! LET'S GO!
HAVE YOU CUT THE VIDEO CAMERA LINES?
GOT 'EM.
SNIP
GOOD. TURN ON THE LIGHTS.
NO SIGN OF ANY GUARDS, PENGUIN.
NOW WHAT'S THIS SUPPOSED TO BE? IT DOESN'T EVEN LOOK LIKE ANYTHING! I TELL YOU EXTREME WEALTH IS WASTED ON THESE PEOPLE.
IF YOU THINK ABOUT IT, I'M DOING GOTHAM A SERVICE BY PUTTING THIS MONEY TO MUCH BETTER USE!
STAIRS
NO ENTRY
15

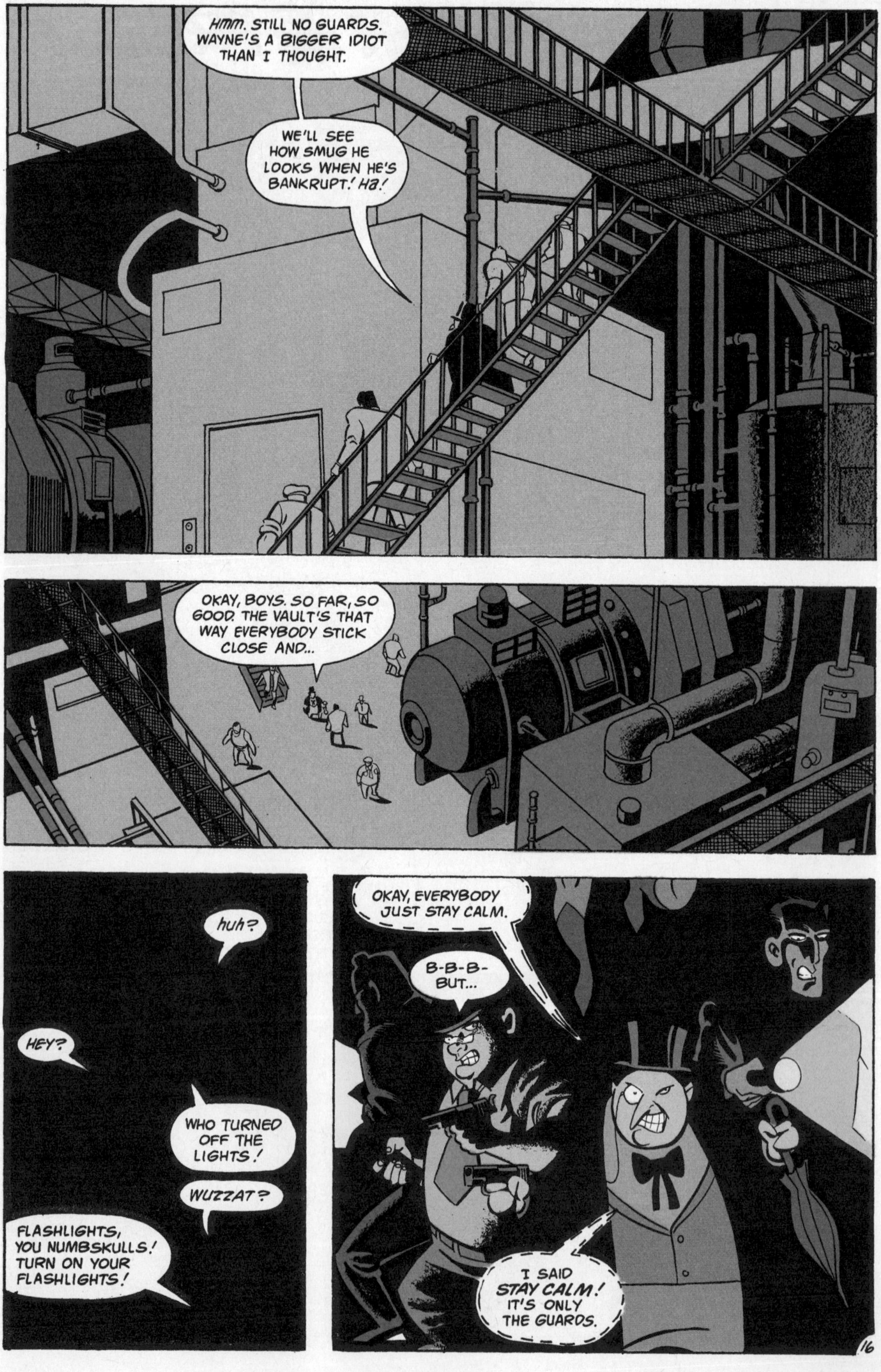
HMM. STILL NO GUARDS. WAYNE'S A BIGGER IDIOT THAN I THOUGHT.
WE'LL SEE HOW SMUG HE LOOKS WHEN HE'S BANKRUPT! HA!
OKAY, BOYS. SO FAR, SO GOOD. THE VAULT'S THAT WAY. EVERYBODY STICK CLOSE AND...
huh?
HEY?
WHO TURNED OFF THE LIGHTS!
WUZZAT?
FLASHLIGHTS, YOU NUMBSKULLS! TURN ON YOUR FLASHLIGHTS!
OKAY, EVERYBODY JUST STAY CALM.
B-B-B-BUT...
I SAID STAY CALM! IT'S ONLY THE GUARDS.
16

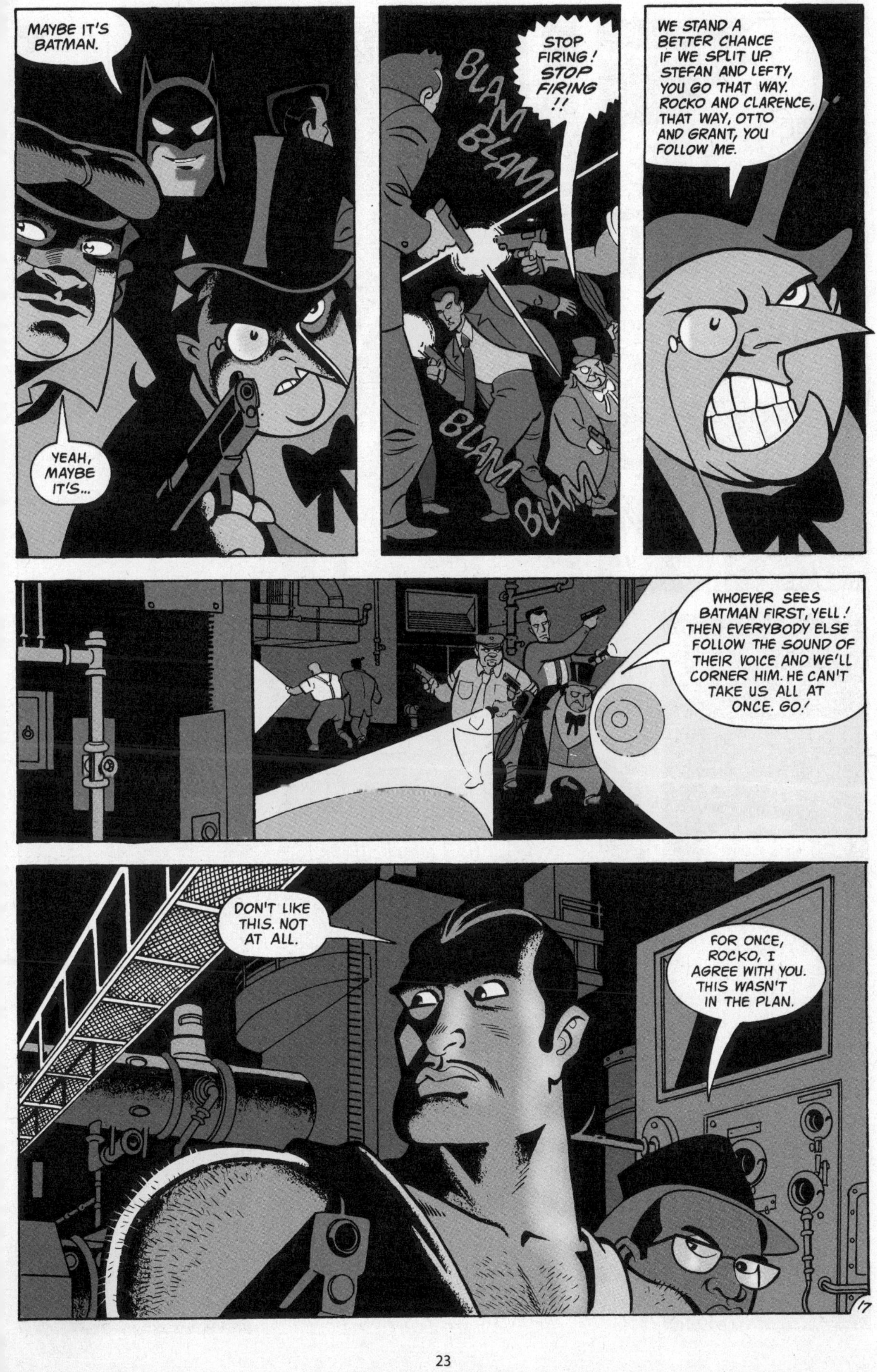
MAYBE IT'S BATMAN.
YEAH, MAYBE IT'S...
BLAM BLAM BLAM
STOP FIRING! STOP FIRING!!
BLAM BLAM
WE STAND A BETTER CHANCE IF WE SPLIT UP. STEFAN AND LEFTY, YOU GO THAT WAY. ROCKO AND CLARENCE, THAT WAY, OTTO AND GRANT, YOU FOLLOW ME.
WHOEVER SEES BATMAN FIRST, YELL! THEN EVERYBODY ELSE FOLLOW THE SOUND OF THEIR VOICE AND WE'LL CORNER HIM. HE CAN'T TAKE US ALL AT ONCE. GO!
DON'T LIKE THIS. NOT AT ALL.
FOR ONCE, ROCKO, I AGREE WITH YOU. THIS WASN'T IN THE PLAN.
17

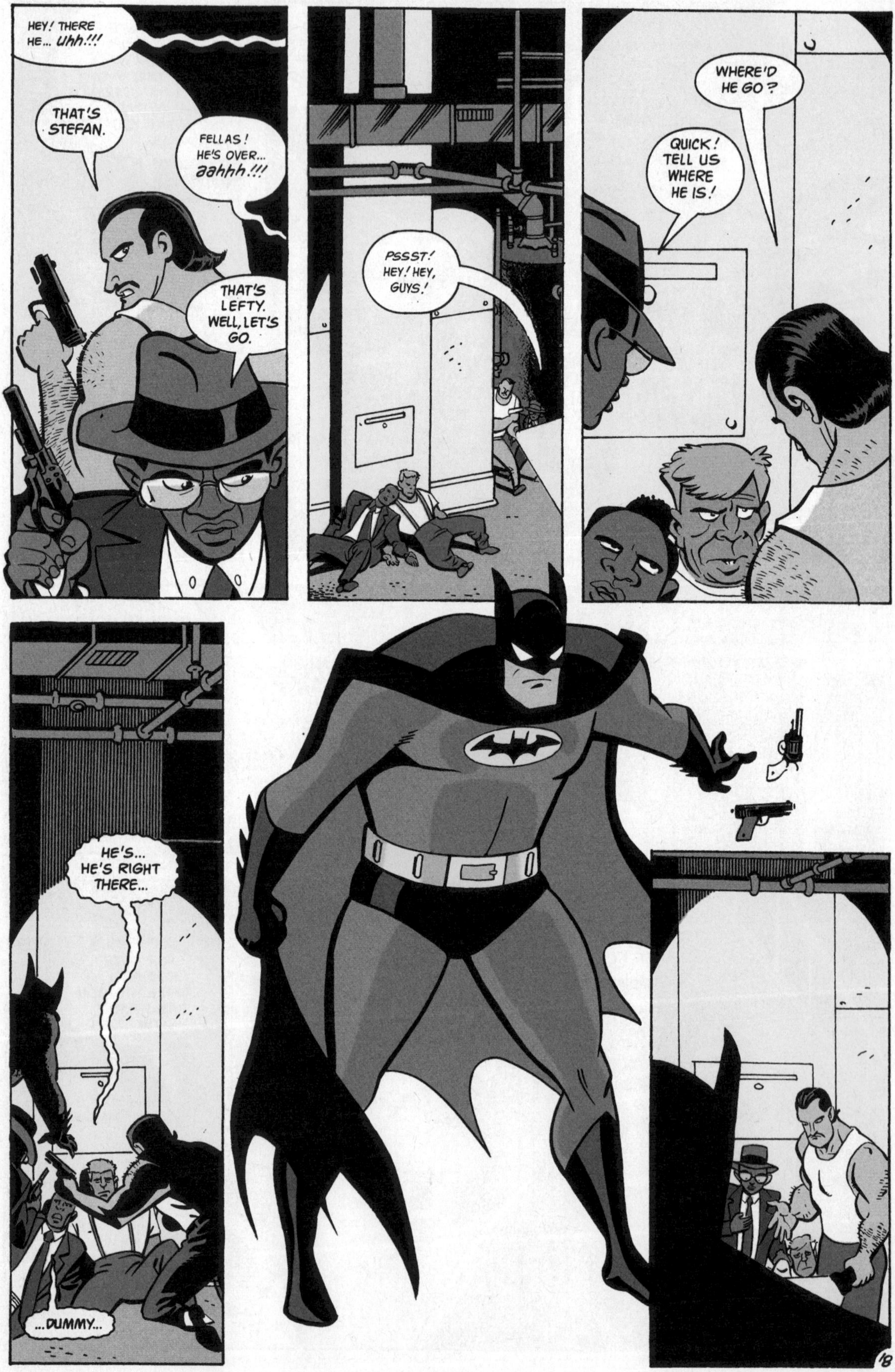
HEY! THERE HE... UHH!!!
THAT'S STEFAN.
FELLAS! HE'S OVER... AAHHH!!!
THAT'S LEFTY. WELL, LET'S GO.
PSSST! HEY! HEY, GUYS!
WHERE'D HE GO?
QUICK! TELL US WHERE HE IS!
HE'S... HE'S RIGHT THERE...
...DUMMY...
18

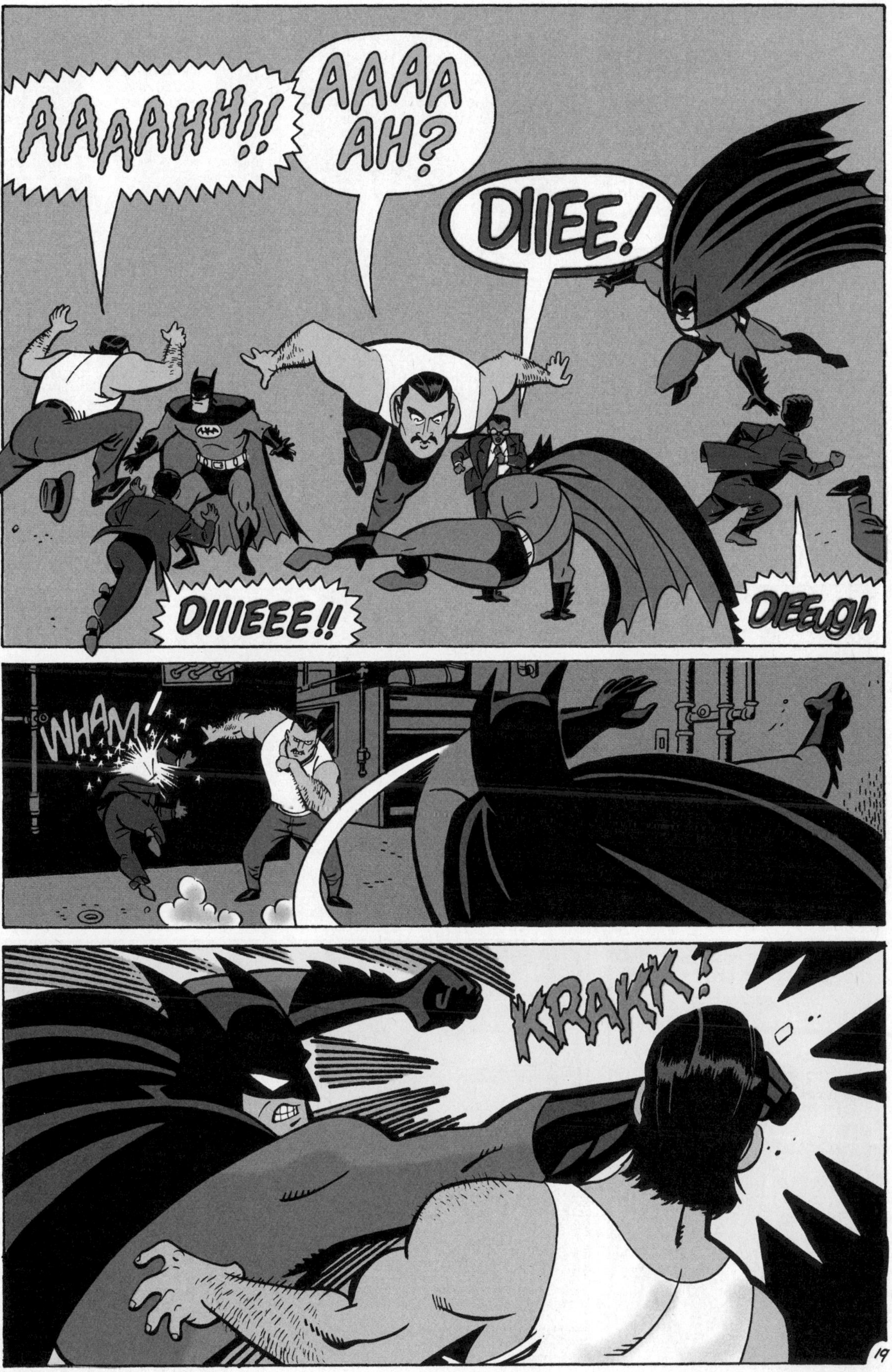
AAAAHH!!
AAAA AH?
DIIEE!
DIIIEEE!!
DIEEugh
WHAM!
KRAKK!
19

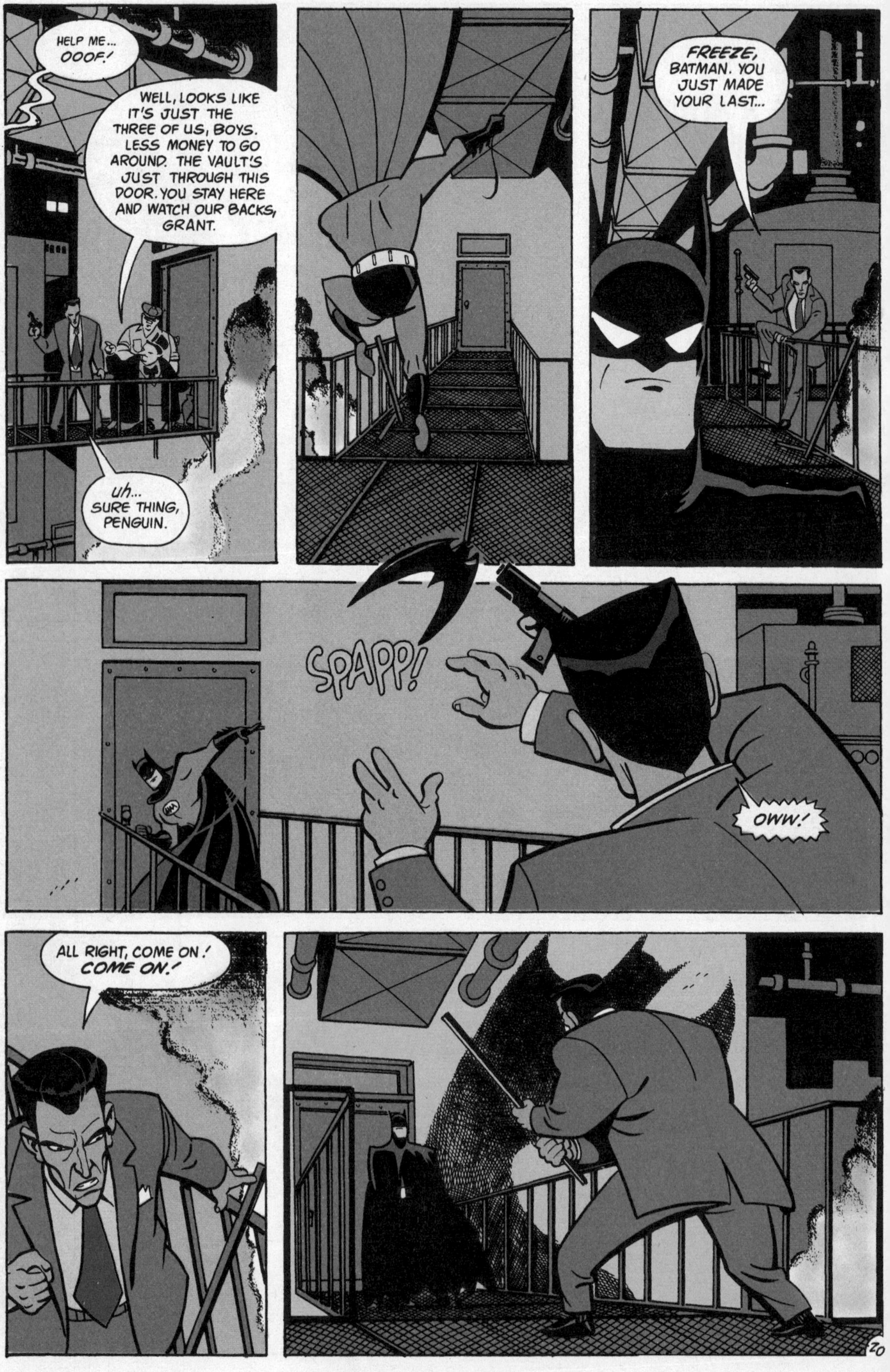
HELP ME... OOOF!
WELL, LOOKS LIKE IT'S JUST THE THREE OF US, BOYS. LESS MONEY TO GO AROUND. THE VAULT'S JUST THROUGH THIS DOOR. YOU STAY HERE AND WATCH OUR BACKS, GRANT.
uh... SURE THING, PENGUIN.
FREEZE, BATMAN. YOU JUST MADE YOUR LAST...
SPAPP!
OWW!
ALL RIGHT, COME ON! COME ON!
20

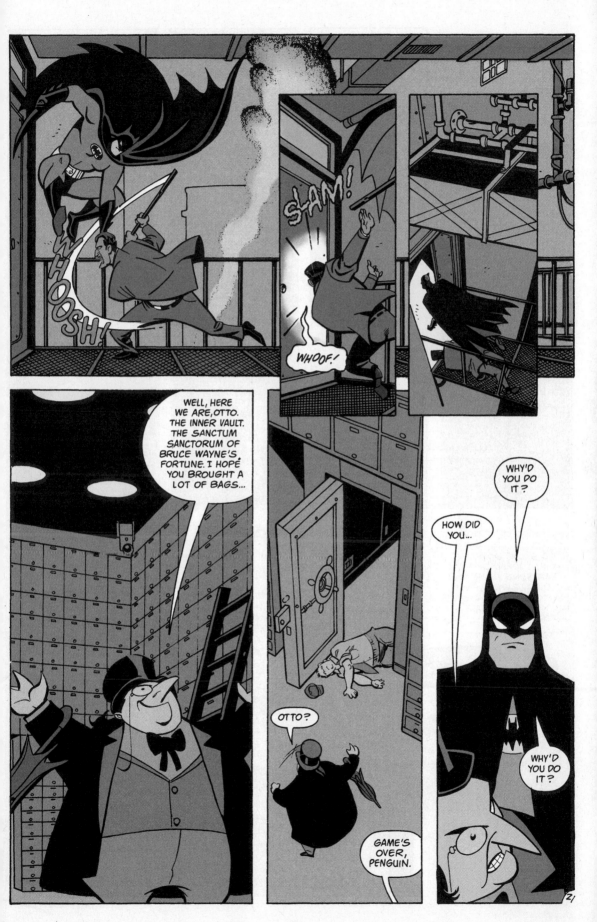

WHOOSH!

SLAM!

WHOOF!

WELL, HERE WE ARE, OTTO. THE INNER VAULT. THE SANCTUM SANCTORUM OF BRUCE WAYNE'S FORTUNE. I HOPE YOU BROUGHT A LOT OF BAGS...

OTTO?

GAME'S OVER, PENGUIN.

HOW DID YOU...

WHY'D YOU DO IT?

WHY'D YOU DO IT?

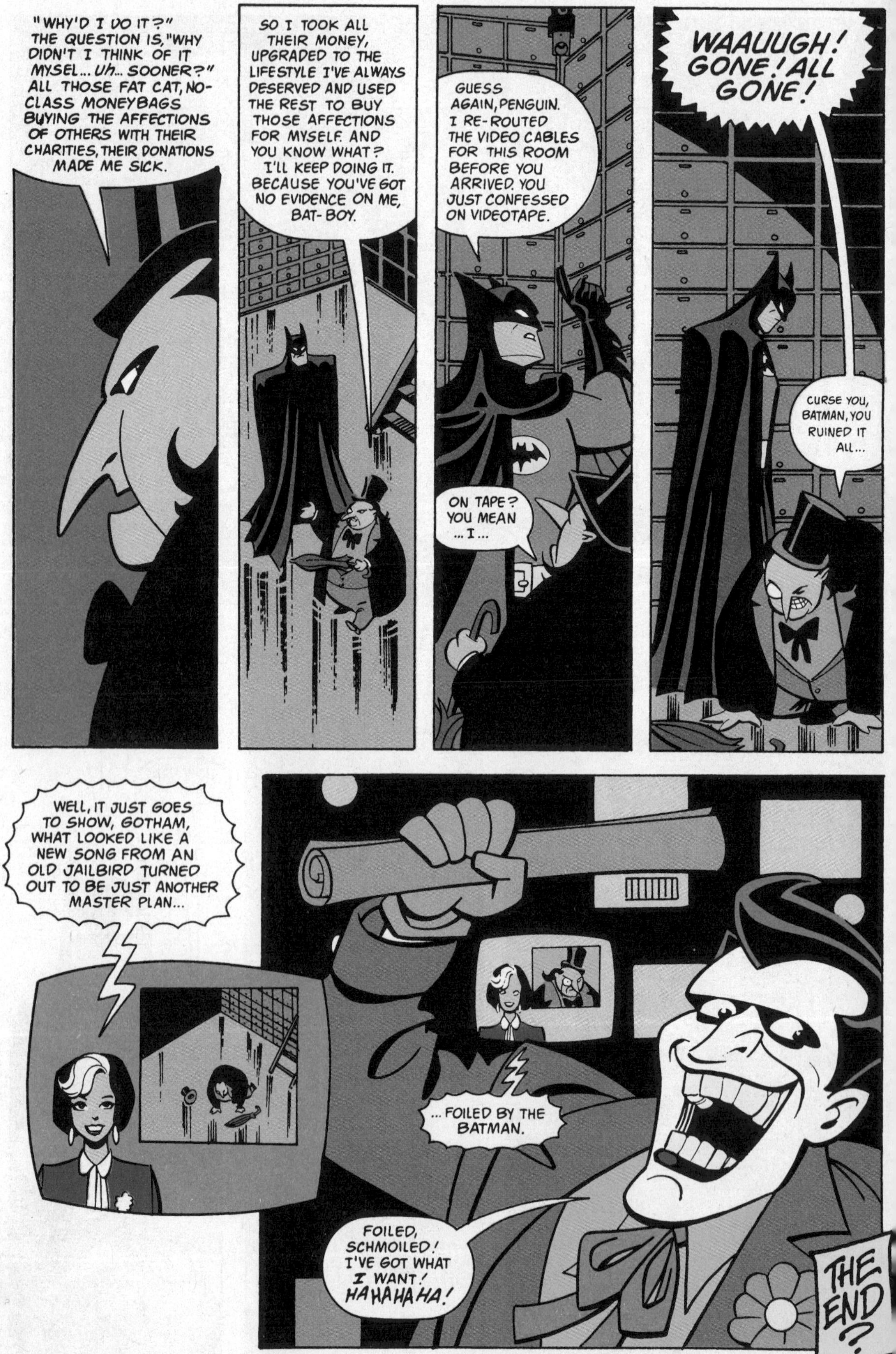
"WHY'D I DO IT?" THE QUESTION IS, "WHY DIDN'T I THINK OF IT MYSEL... Uh... SOONER?" ALL THOSE FAT CAT, NO-CLASS MONEYBAGS BUYING THE AFFECTIONS OF OTHERS WITH THEIR CHARITIES, THEIR DONATIONS MADE ME SICK.
SO I TOOK ALL THEIR MONEY, UPGRADED TO THE LIFESTYLE I'VE ALWAYS DESERVED AND USED THE REST TO BUY THOSE AFFECTIONS FOR MYSELF. AND YOU KNOW WHAT? I'LL KEEP DOING IT. BECAUSE YOU'VE GOT NO EVIDENCE ON ME, BAT-BOY.
GUESS AGAIN, PENGUIN. I RE-ROUTED THE VIDEO CABLES FOR THIS ROOM BEFORE YOU ARRIVED. YOU JUST CONFESSED ON VIDEOTAPE.
ON TAPE? YOU MEAN ...I...
WAAUUGH! GONE! ALL GONE!
CURSE YOU, BATMAN, YOU RUINED IT ALL...
WELL, IT JUST GOES TO SHOW, GOTHAM, WHAT LOOKED LIKE A NEW SONG FROM AN OLD JAILBIRD TURNED OUT TO BE JUST ANOTHER MASTER PLAN...
...FOILED BY THE BATMAN.
FOILED, SCHMOILED! I'VE GOT WHAT I WANT! HAHAHAHA!
THE END?

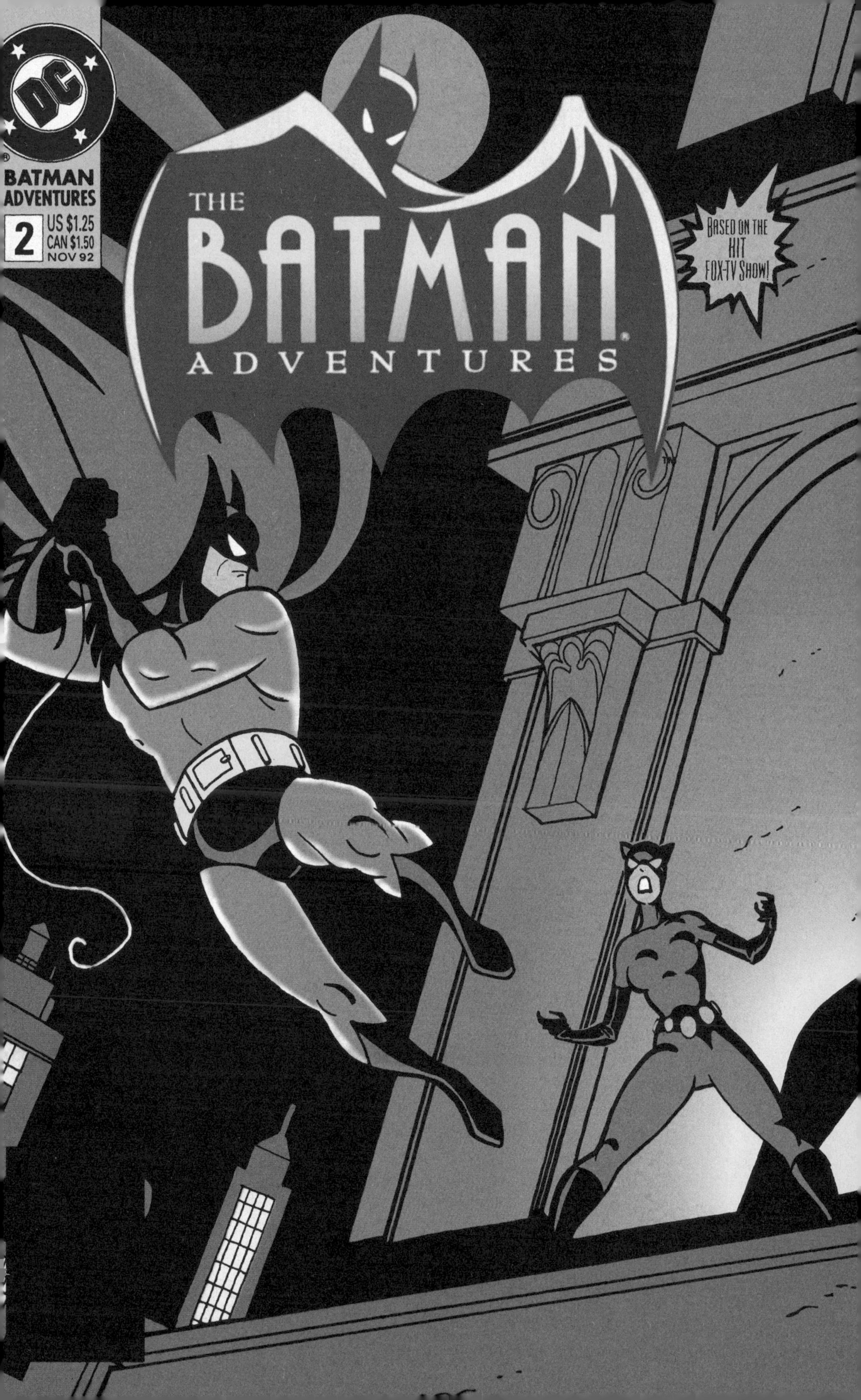

DC
BATMAN ADVENTURES
2
US $1.25
CAN $1.50
NOV 92
THE BATMAN ADVENTURES
BASED ON THE HIT FOX-TV SHOW!

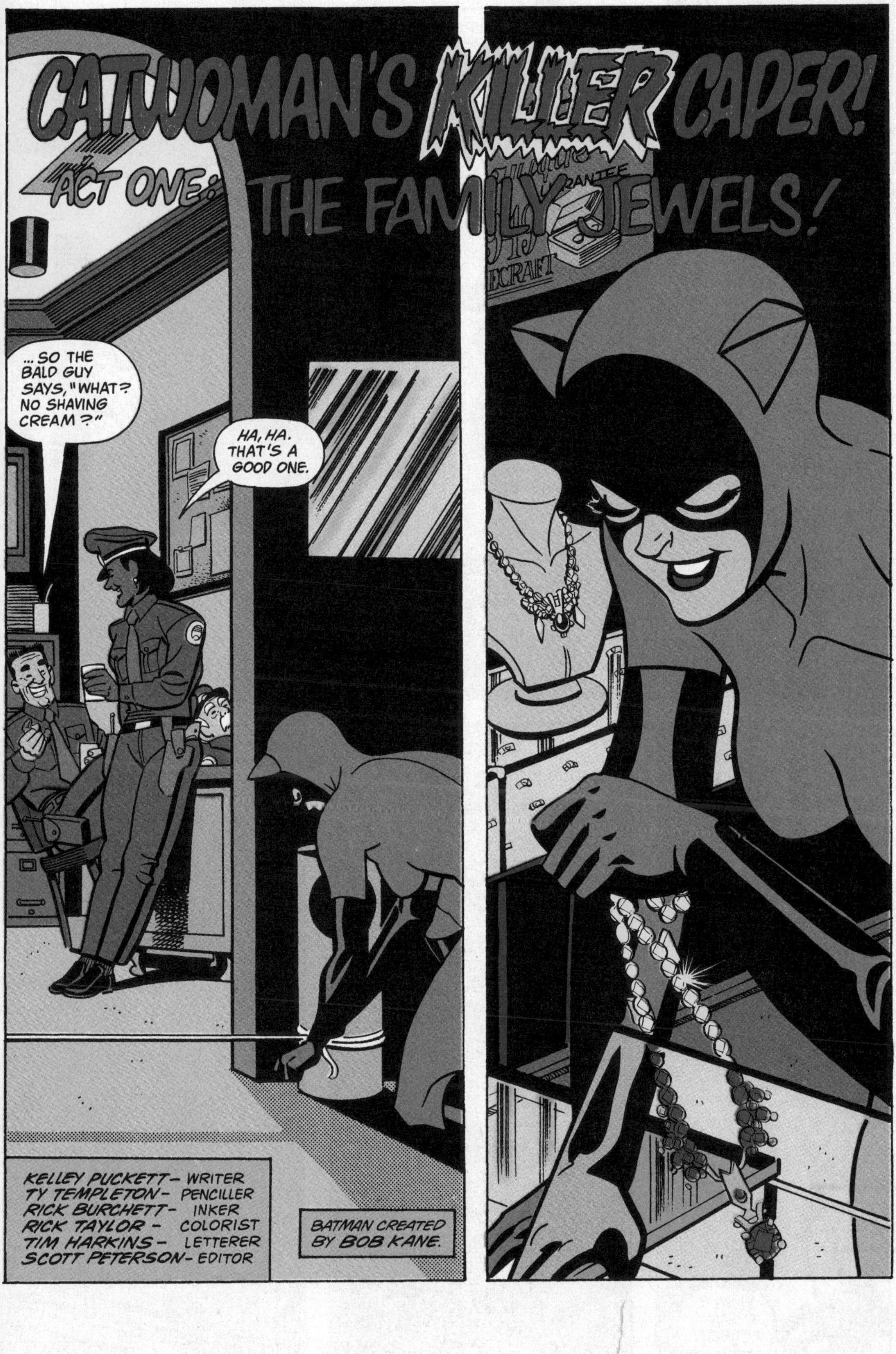
CATWOMAN'S KILLER CAPER!
ACT ONE: THE FAMILY JEWELS!
...SO THE BALD GUY SAYS, "WHAT? NO SHAVING CREAM?"
HA, HA. THAT'S A GOOD ONE.
KELLEY PUCKETT- WRITER
TY TEMPLETON- PENCILLER
RICK BURCHETT- INKER
RICK TAYLOR - COLORIST
TIM HARKINS- LETTERER
SCOTT PETERSON- EDITOR
BATMAN CREATED BY BOB KANE.

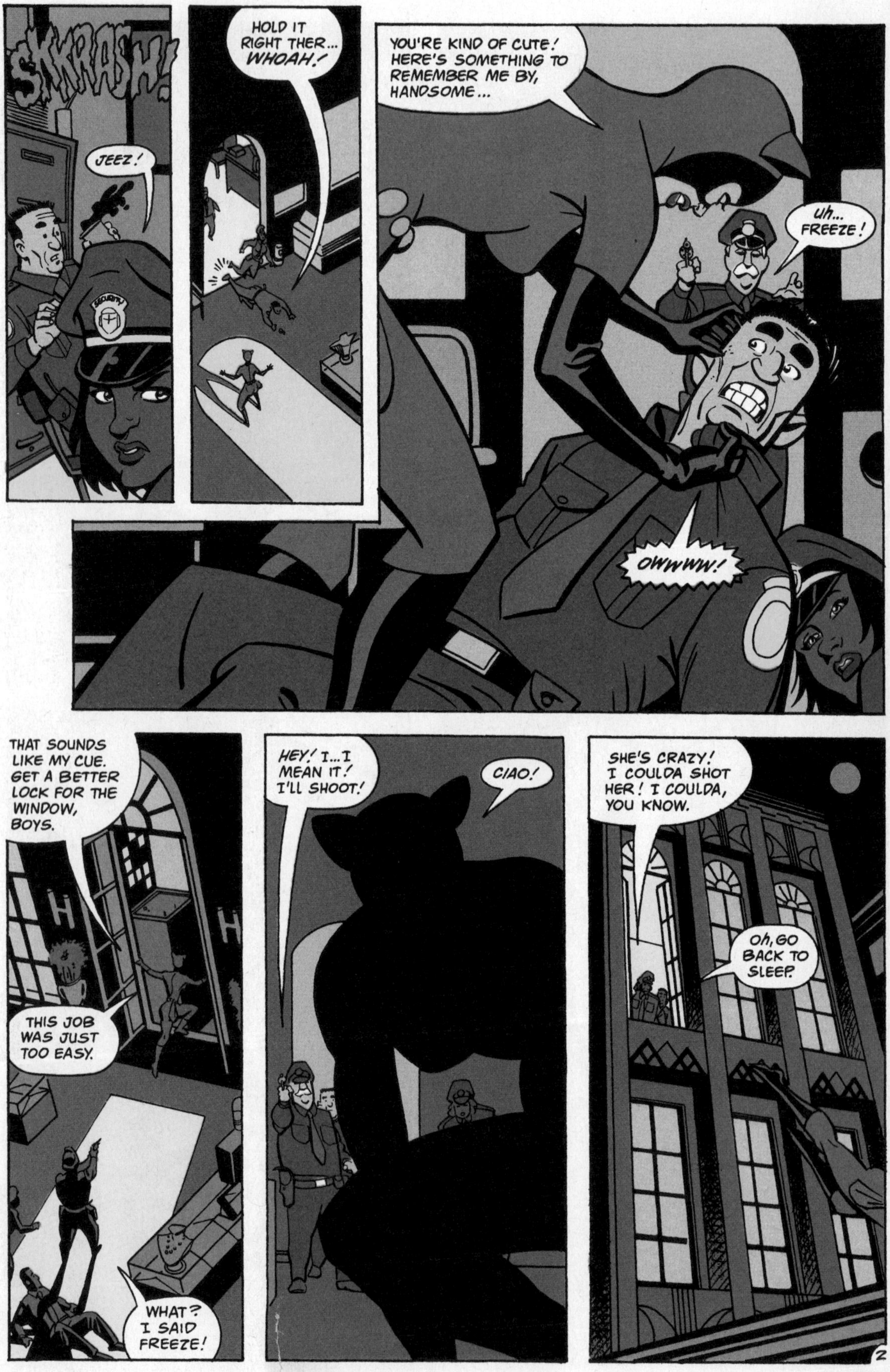
SKKRASH!
JEEZ!
HOLD IT RIGHT THER... WHOAH!
YOU'RE KIND OF CUTE! HERE'S SOMETHING TO REMEMBER ME BY, HANDSOME...
uh... FREEZE!
OWWWW!
THAT SOUNDS LIKE MY CUE. GET A BETTER LOCK FOR THE WINDOW, BOYS.
THIS JOB WAS JUST TOO EASY.
WHAT? I SAID FREEZE!
HEY! I...I MEAN IT! I'LL SHOOT!
CIAO!
SHE'S CRAZY! I COULDA SHOT HER! I COULDA, YOU KNOW.
Oh, GO BACK TO SLEEP.
2

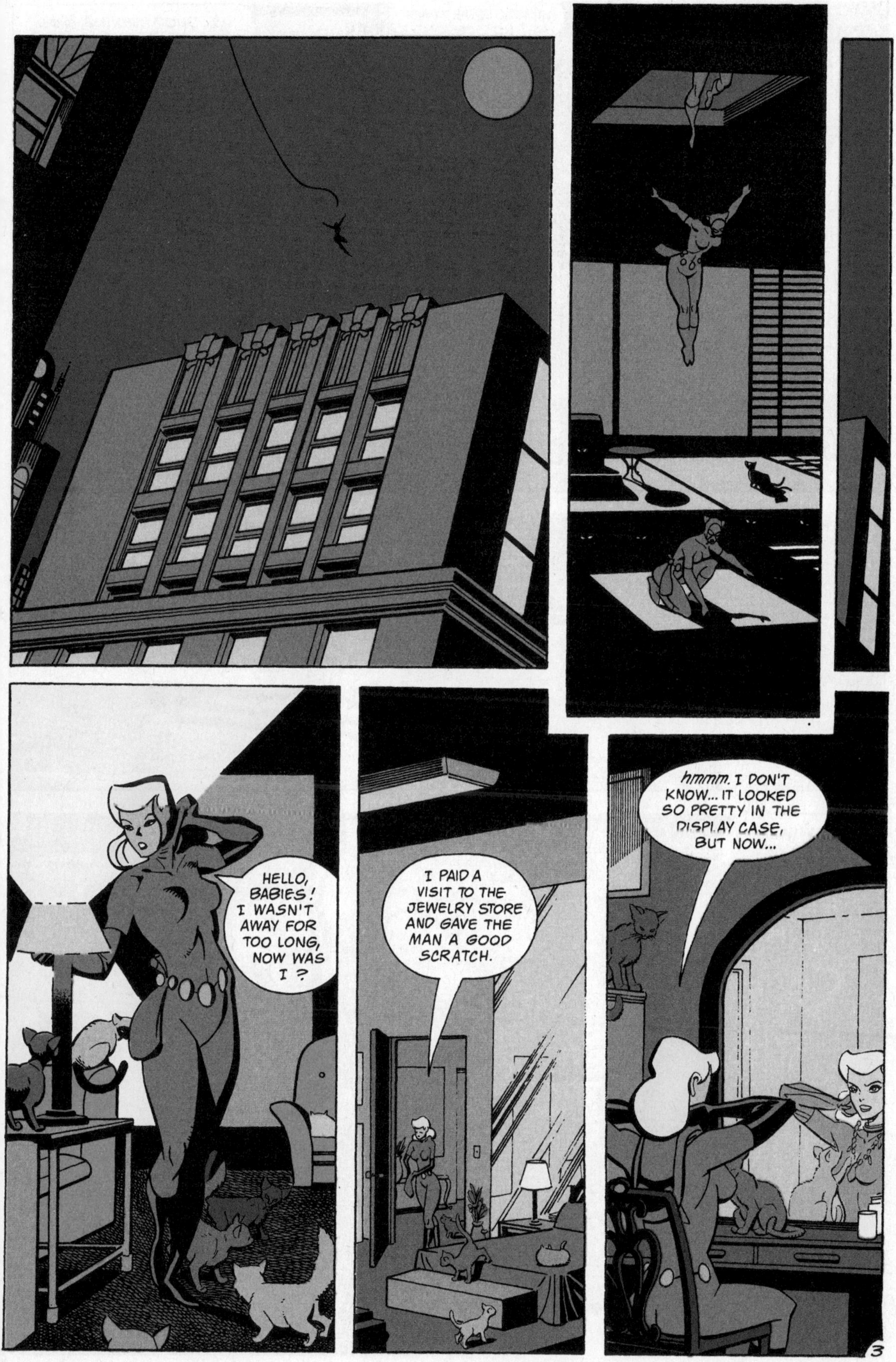

HELLO, BABIES! I WASN'T AWAY FOR TOO LONG, NOW WAS I?
I PAID A VISIT TO THE JEWELRY STORE AND GAVE THE MAN A GOOD SCRATCH.
hmmm. I DON'T KNOW... IT LOOKED SO PRETTY IN THE DISPLAY CASE, BUT NOW...
3

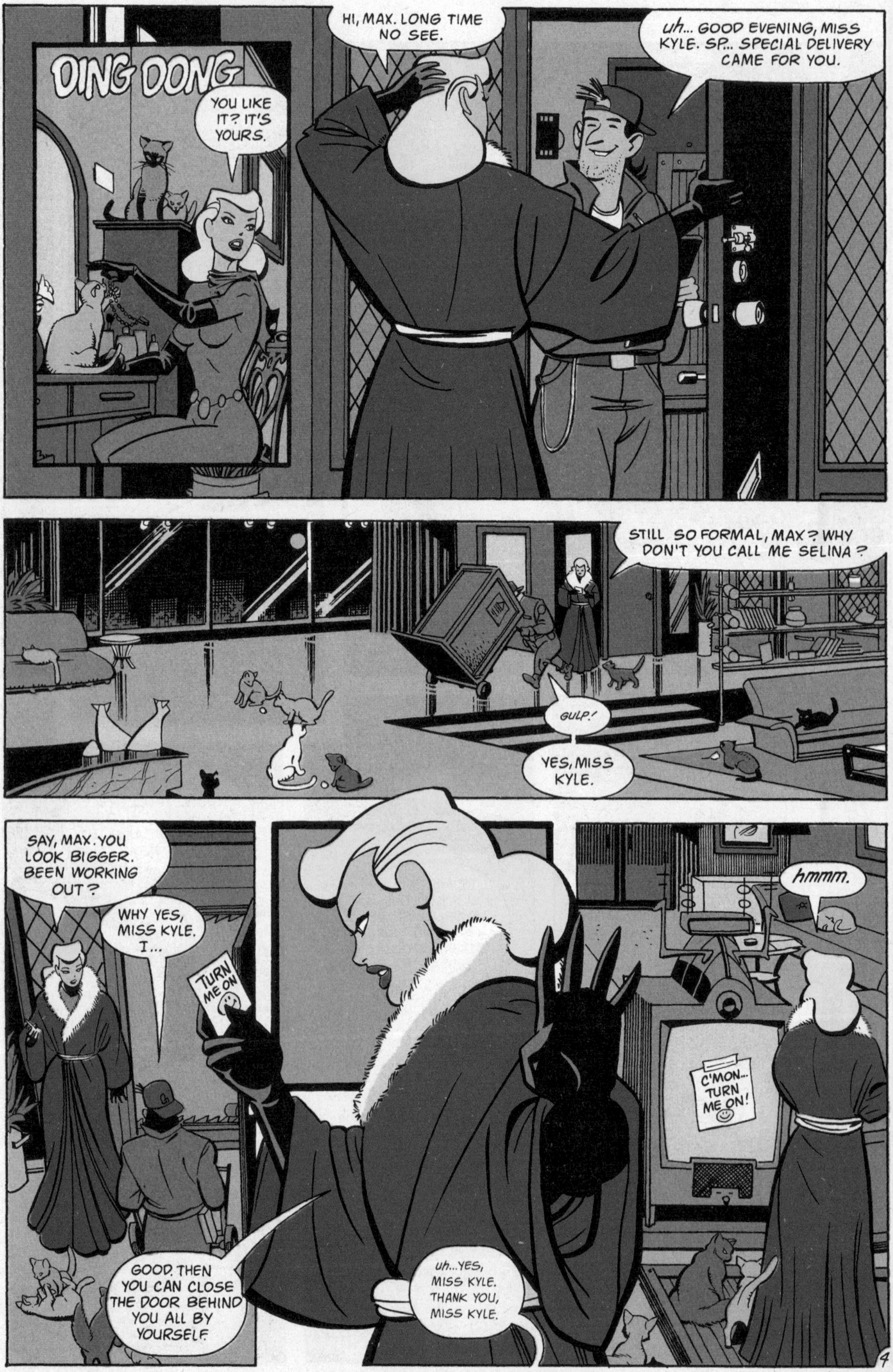
DING DONG
YOU LIKE IT? IT'S YOURS.
HI, MAX. LONG TIME NO SEE.
uh... GOOD EVENING, MISS KYLE. SP... SPECIAL DELIVERY CAME FOR YOU.
STILL SO FORMAL, MAX? WHY DON'T YOU CALL ME SELINA?
GULP!
YES, MISS KYLE.
SAY, MAX. YOU LOOK BIGGER. BEEN WORKING OUT?
WHY YES, MISS KYLE. I...
TURN ME ON
GOOD. THEN YOU CAN CLOSE THE DOOR BEHIND YOU ALL BY YOURSELF.
uh...YES, MISS KYLE. THANK YOU, MISS KYLE.
hmmm.
C'MON... TURN ME ON!
4

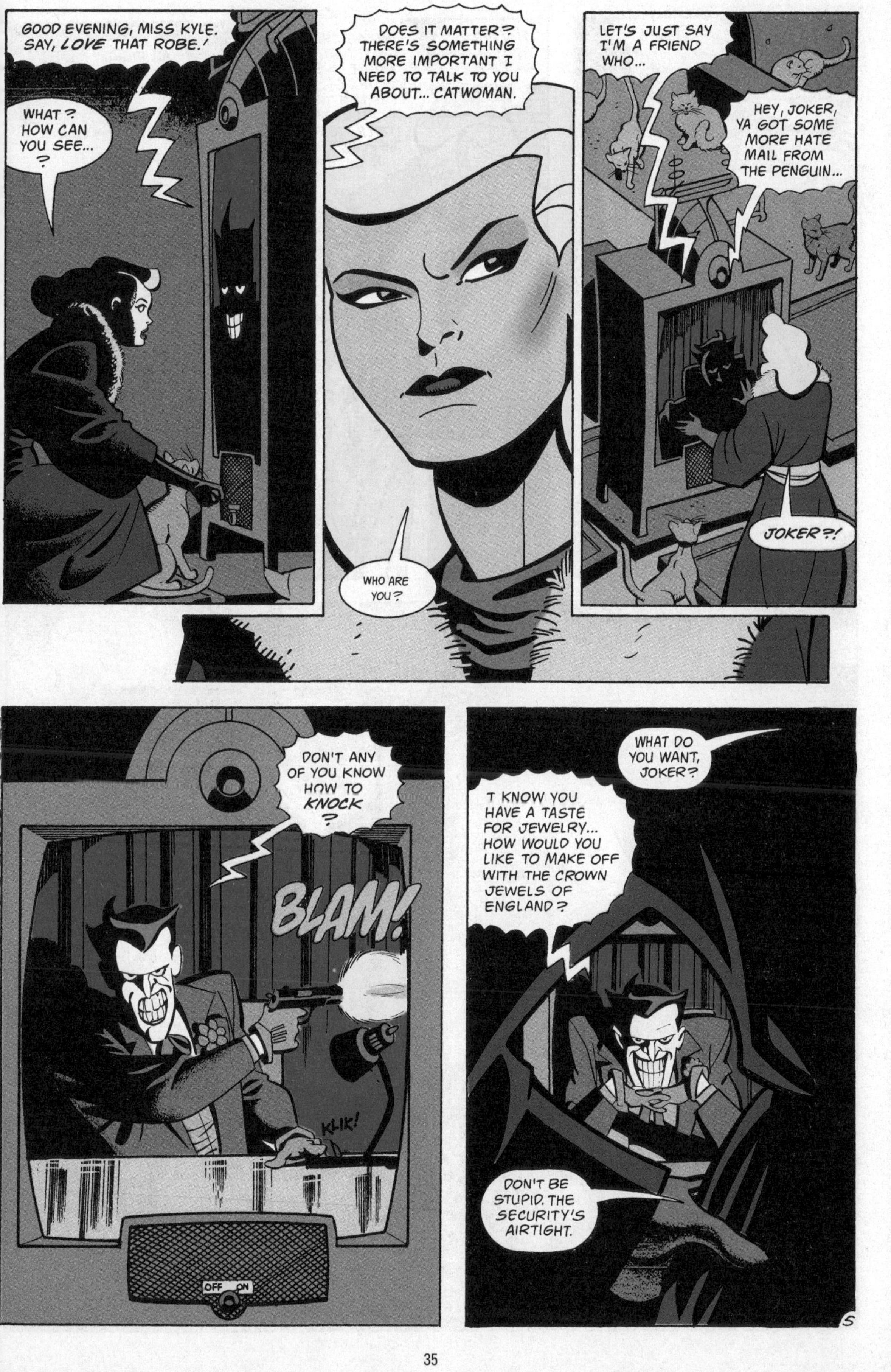
GOOD EVENING, MISS KYLE. SAY, LOVE THAT ROBE.!
WHAT? HOW CAN YOU SEE...?
DOES IT MATTER? THERE'S SOMETHING MORE IMPORTANT I NEED TO TALK TO YOU ABOUT... CATWOMAN.
WHO ARE YOU?
LET'S JUST SAY I'M A FRIEND WHO...
HEY, JOKER, YA GOT SOME MORE HATE MAIL FROM THE PENGUIN...
JOKER?!
DON'T ANY OF YOU KNOW HOW TO KNOCK?
BLAM!
KLIK!
OFF ON
WHAT DO YOU WANT, JOKER?
I KNOW YOU HAVE A TASTE FOR JEWELRY... HOW WOULD YOU LIKE TO MAKE OFF WITH THE CROWN JEWELS OF ENGLAND?
DON'T BE STUPID. THE SECURITY'S AIRTIGHT.
5

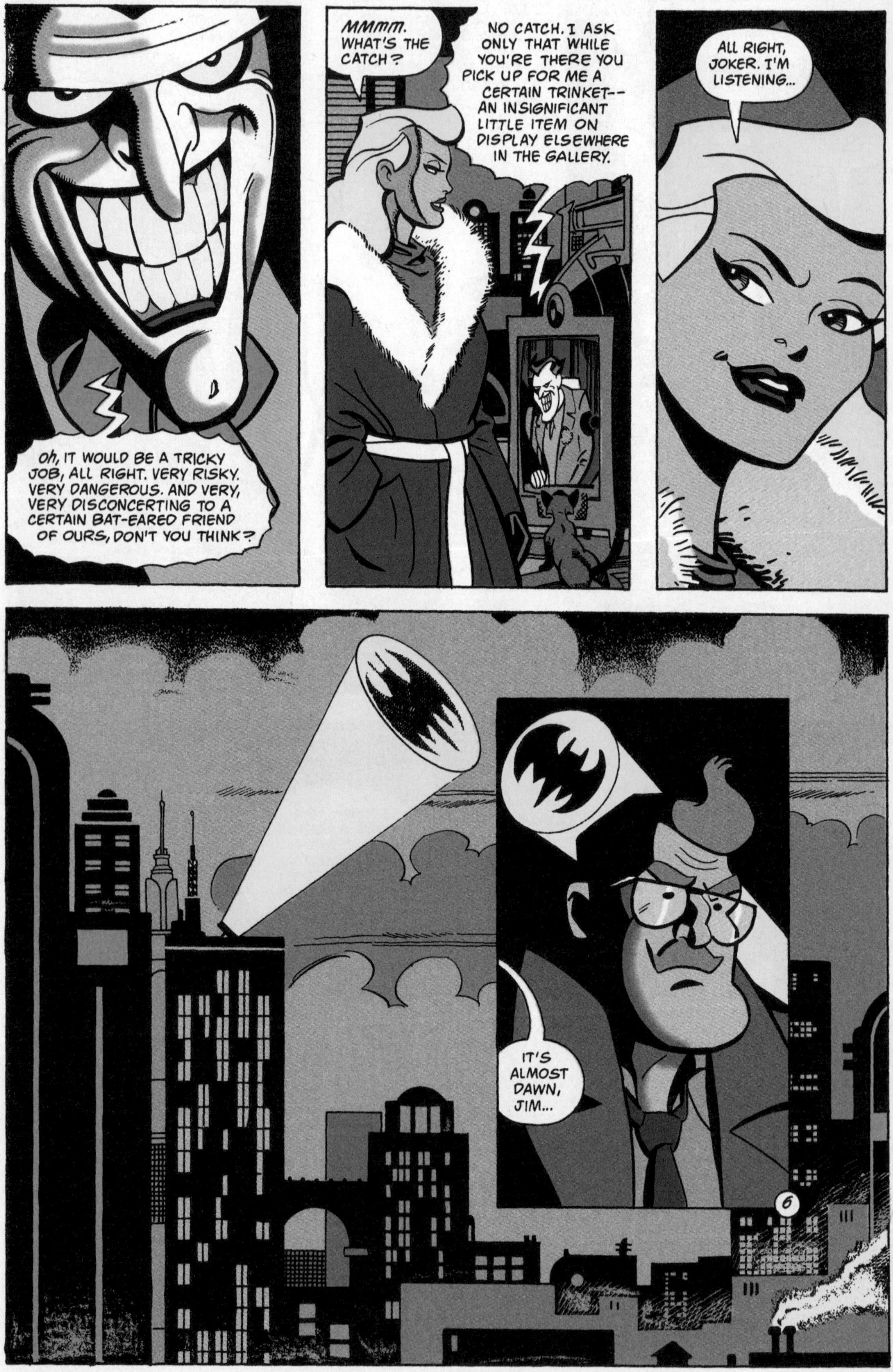
Oh, IT WOULD BE A TRICKY JOB, ALL RIGHT. VERY RISKY. VERY DANGEROUS. AND VERY, VERY DISCONCERTING TO A CERTAIN BAT-EARED FRIEND OF OURS, DON'T YOU THINK?
MMMM. WHAT'S THE CATCH?
NO CATCH. I ASK ONLY THAT WHILE YOU'RE THERE YOU PICK UP FOR ME A CERTAIN TRINKET-- AN INSIGNIFICANT LITTLE ITEM ON DISPLAY ELSEWHERE IN THE GALLERY.
ALL RIGHT, JOKER. I'M LISTENING...
IT'S ALMOST DAWN, JIM...
6

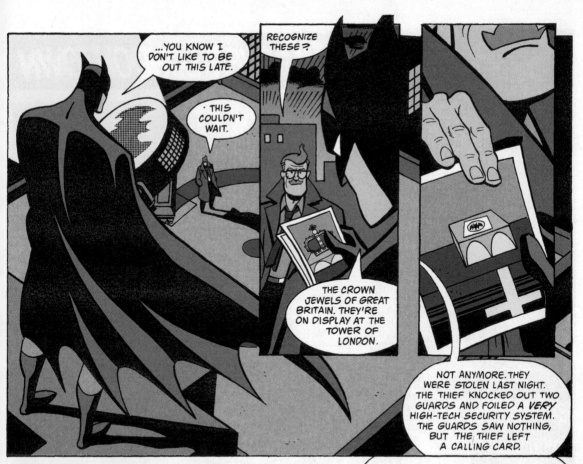

...YOU KNOW I DON'T LIKE TO BE OUT THIS LATE.

RECOGNIZE THESE?

· THIS COULDN'T WAIT.

THE CROWN JEWELS OF GREAT BRITAIN. THEY'RE ON DISPLAY AT THE TOWER OF LONDON.

NOT ANYMORE. THEY WERE STOLEN LAST NIGHT. THE THIEF KNOCKED OUT TWO GUARDS AND FOILED A *VERY* HIGH-TECH SECURITY SYSTEM. THE GUARDS SAW NOTHING, BUT THE THIEF LEFT A CALLING CARD.

CATWOMAN.

I THOUGHT SO, TOO. I TOLD THE BRITISH AUTHORITIES TO BE ON THE LOOKOUT FOR HER.

CERTAINLY A STEP UP FROM THAT JEWELRY HEIST LAST WEEK...

I ALSO TOLD THEM YOU'D PROBABLY BE IN LONDON BEFORE I HAD A CHANCE TO TURN YOU OVER TO THEM FOR QUESTIONING.

THANKS, JIM. YOU KEEP STICKING YOUR NECK OUT FOR ME.

YOU KEEP MAKING IT WORTH MY WHILE.

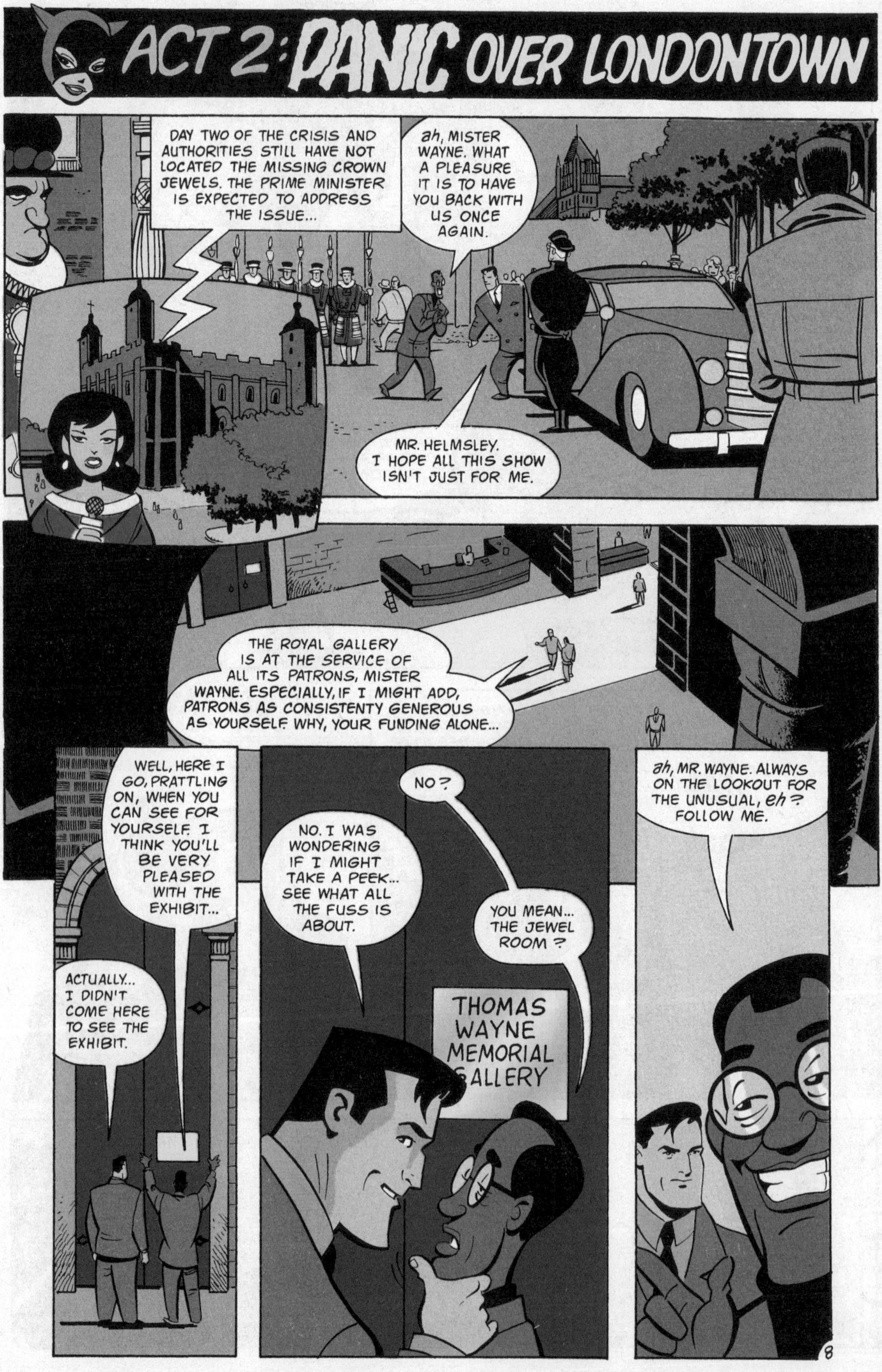
ACT 2: PANIC OVER LONDONTOWN
DAY TWO OF THE CRISIS AND AUTHORITIES STILL HAVE NOT LOCATED THE MISSING CROWN JEWELS. THE PRIME MINISTER IS EXPECTED TO ADDRESS THE ISSUE...
ah, MISTER WAYNE. WHAT A PLEASURE IT IS TO HAVE YOU BACK WITH US ONCE AGAIN.
MR. HELMSLEY. I HOPE ALL THIS SHOW ISN'T JUST FOR ME.
THE ROYAL GALLERY IS AT THE SERVICE OF ALL ITS PATRONS, MISTER WAYNE. ESPECIALLY, IF I MIGHT ADD, PATRONS AS CONSISTENTY GENEROUS AS YOURSELF. WHY, YOUR FUNDING ALONE...
WELL, HERE I GO, PRATTLING ON, WHEN YOU CAN SEE FOR YOURSELF. I THINK YOU'LL BE VERY PLEASED WITH THE EXHIBIT...
ACTUALLY... I DIDN'T COME HERE TO SEE THE EXHIBIT.
NO?
NO. I WAS WONDERING IF I MIGHT TAKE A PEEK... SEE WHAT ALL THE FUSS IS ABOUT.
YOU MEAN... THE JEWEL ROOM?
THOMAS WAYNE MEMORIAL GALLERY
ah, MR. WAYNE. ALWAYS ON THE LOOKOUT FOR THE UNUSUAL, eh? FOLLOW ME.
8

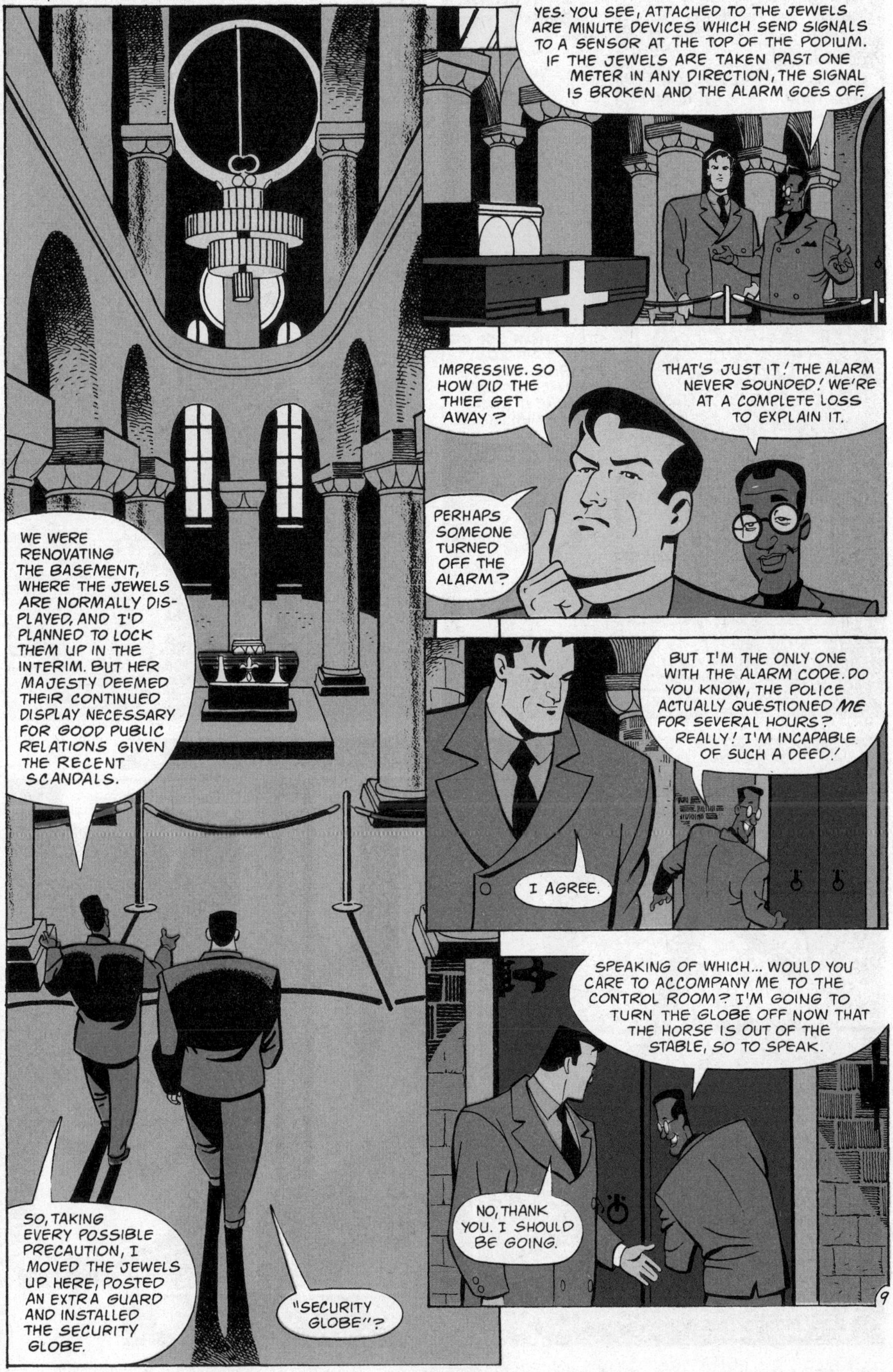
YES. YOU SEE, ATTACHED TO THE JEWELS ARE MINUTE DEVICES WHICH SEND SIGNALS TO A SENSOR AT THE TOP OF THE PODIUM. IF THE JEWELS ARE TAKEN PAST ONE METER IN ANY DIRECTION, THE SIGNAL IS BROKEN AND THE ALARM GOES OFF.
IMPRESSIVE. SO HOW DID THE THIEF GET AWAY?
THAT'S JUST IT! THE ALARM NEVER SOUNDED! WE'RE AT A COMPLETE LOSS TO EXPLAIN IT.
PERHAPS SOMEONE TURNED OFF THE ALARM?
BUT I'M THE ONLY ONE WITH THE ALARM CODE. DO YOU KNOW, THE POLICE ACTUALLY QUESTIONED ME FOR SEVERAL HOURS? REALLY! I'M INCAPABLE OF SUCH A DEED!
I AGREE.
SPEAKING OF WHICH... WOULD YOU CARE TO ACCOMPANY ME TO THE CONTROL ROOM? I'M GOING TO TURN THE GLOBE OFF NOW THAT THE HORSE IS OUT OF THE STABLE, SO TO SPEAK.
NO, THANK YOU. I SHOULD BE GOING.
WE WERE RENOVATING THE BASEMENT, WHERE THE JEWELS ARE NORMALLY DISPLAYED, AND I'D PLANNED TO LOCK THEM UP IN THE INTERIM. BUT HER MAJESTY DEEMED THEIR CONTINUED DISPLAY NECESSARY FOR GOOD PUBLIC RELATIONS GIVEN THE RECENT SCANDALS.
SO, TAKING EVERY POSSIBLE PRECAUTION, I MOVED THE JEWELS UP HERE, POSTED AN EXTRA GUARD AND INSTALLED THE SECURITY GLOBE.
"SECURITY GLOBE"?
9

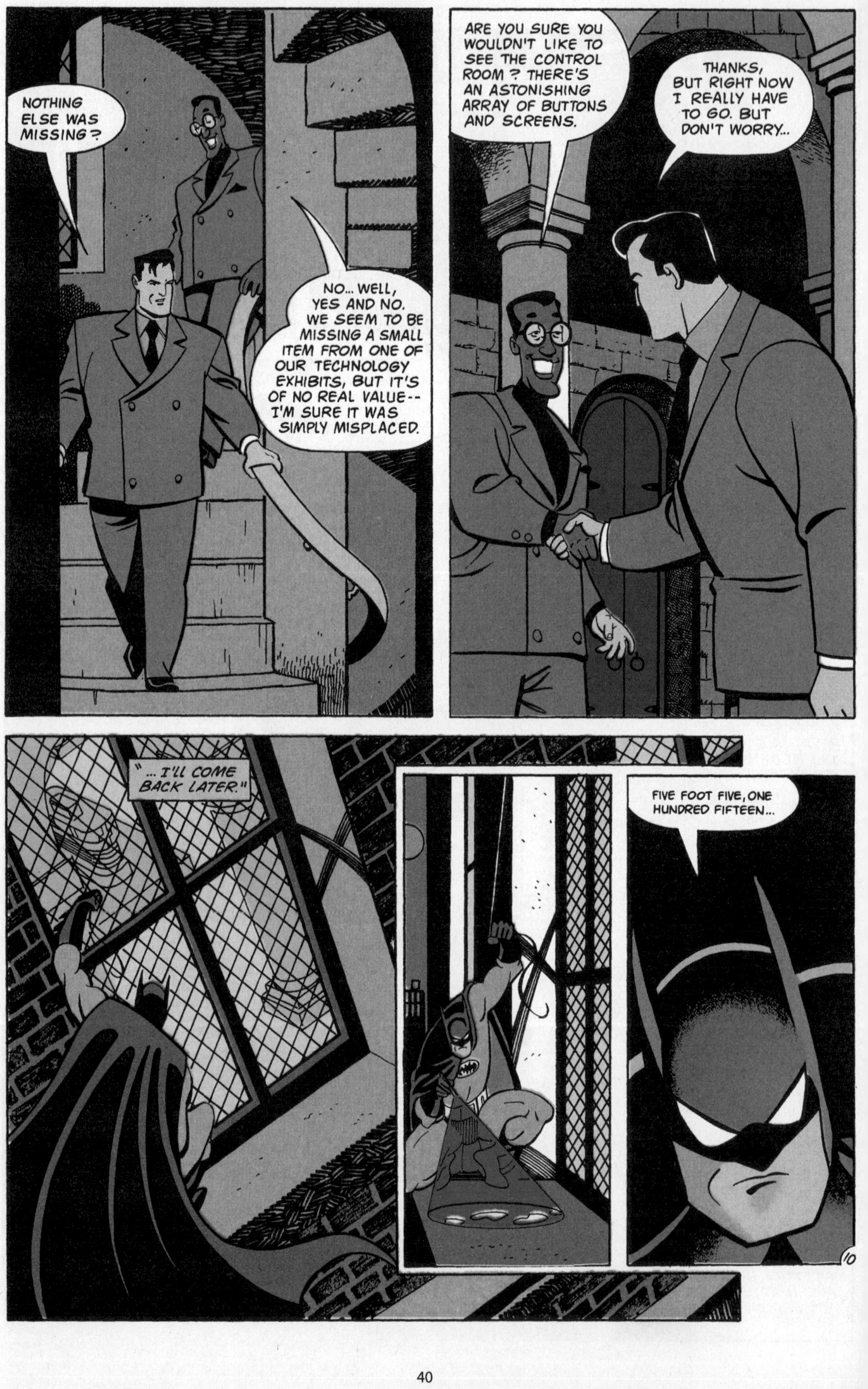
NOTHING ELSE WAS MISSING?
NO... WELL, YES AND NO. WE SEEM TO BE MISSING A SMALL ITEM FROM ONE OF OUR TECHNOLOGY EXHIBITS, BUT IT'S OF NO REAL VALUE-- I'M SURE IT WAS SIMPLY MISPLACED.
ARE YOU SURE YOU WOULDN'T LIKE TO SEE THE CONTROL ROOM? THERE'S AN ASTONISHING ARRAY OF BUTTONS AND SCREENS.
THANKS, BUT RIGHT NOW I REALLY HAVE TO GO. BUT DON'T WORRY...
"...I'LL COME BACK LATER."
FIVE FOOT FIVE, ONE HUNDRED FIFTEEN...
10

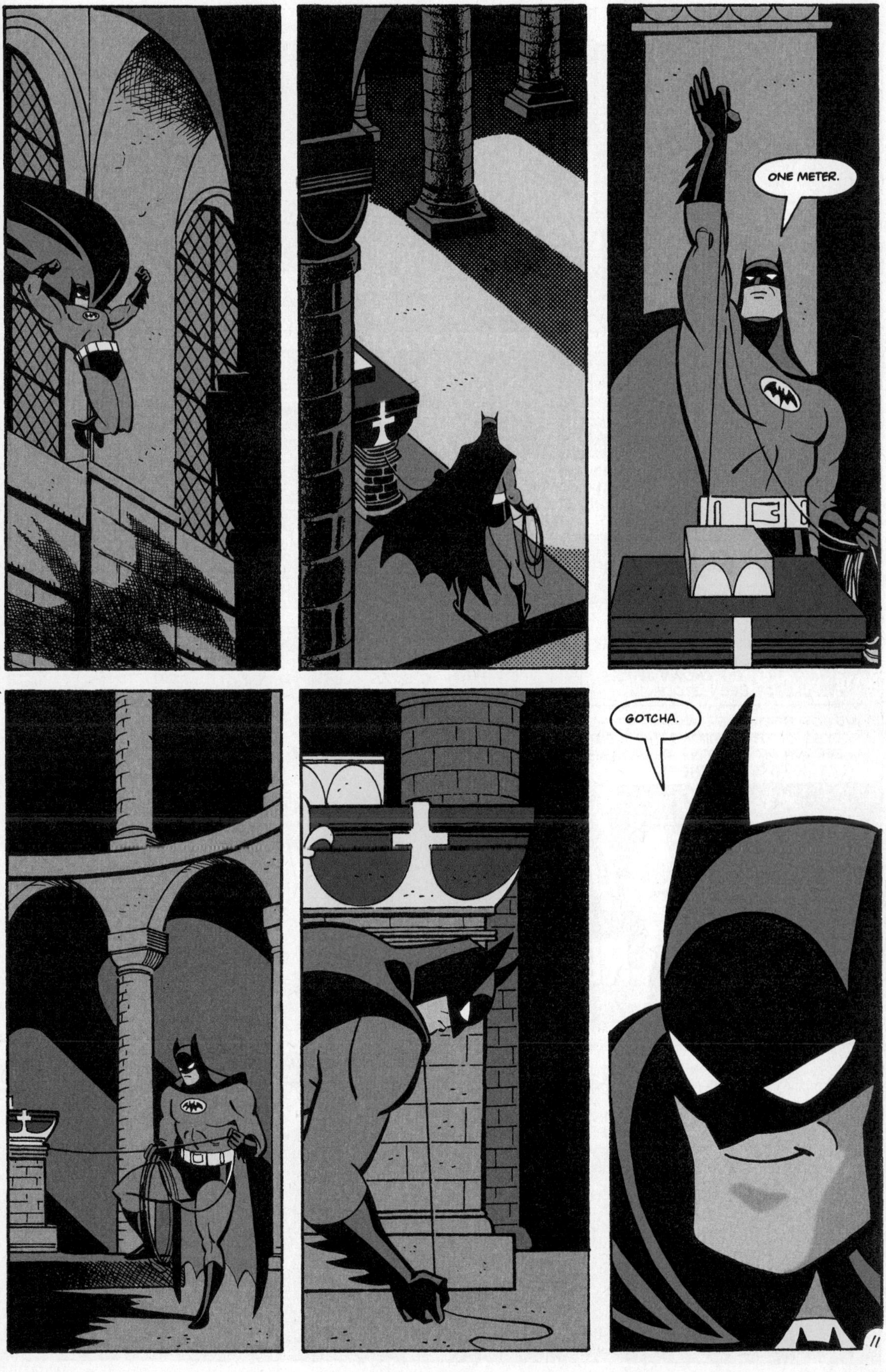
ONE METER.
GOTCHA.
11

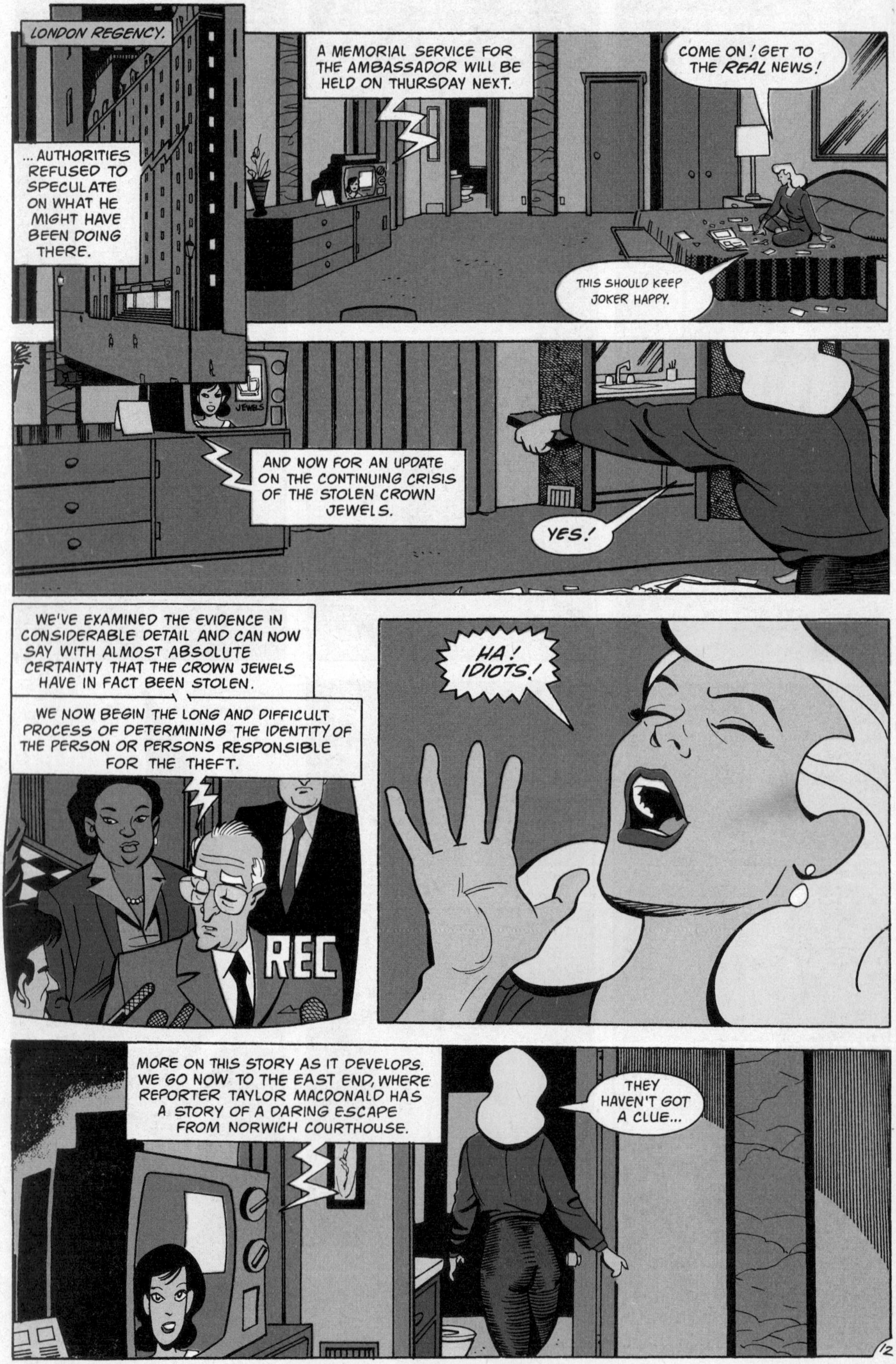
LONDON REGENCY.
...AUTHORITIES REFUSED TO SPECULATE ON WHAT HE MIGHT HAVE BEEN DOING THERE.
A MEMORIAL SERVICE FOR THE AMBASSADOR WILL BE HELD ON THURSDAY NEXT.
COME ON! GET TO THE REAL NEWS!
THIS SHOULD KEEP JOKER HAPPY.
JEWELS
AND NOW FOR AN UPDATE ON THE CONTINUING CRISIS OF THE STOLEN CROWN JEWELS.
YES!
WE'VE EXAMINED THE EVIDENCE IN CONSIDERABLE DETAIL AND CAN NOW SAY WITH ALMOST ABSOLUTE CERTAINTY THAT THE CROWN JEWELS HAVE IN FACT BEEN STOLEN.
WE NOW BEGIN THE LONG AND DIFFICULT PROCESS OF DETERMINING THE IDENTITY OF THE PERSON OR PERSONS RESPONSIBLE FOR THE THEFT.
REC
HA! IDIOTS!
MORE ON THIS STORY AS IT DEVELOPS. WE GO NOW TO THE EAST END, WHERE REPORTER TAYLOR MACDONALD HAS A STORY OF A DARING ESCAPE FROM NORWICH COURTHOUSE.
THEY HAVEN'T GOT A CLUE...
12

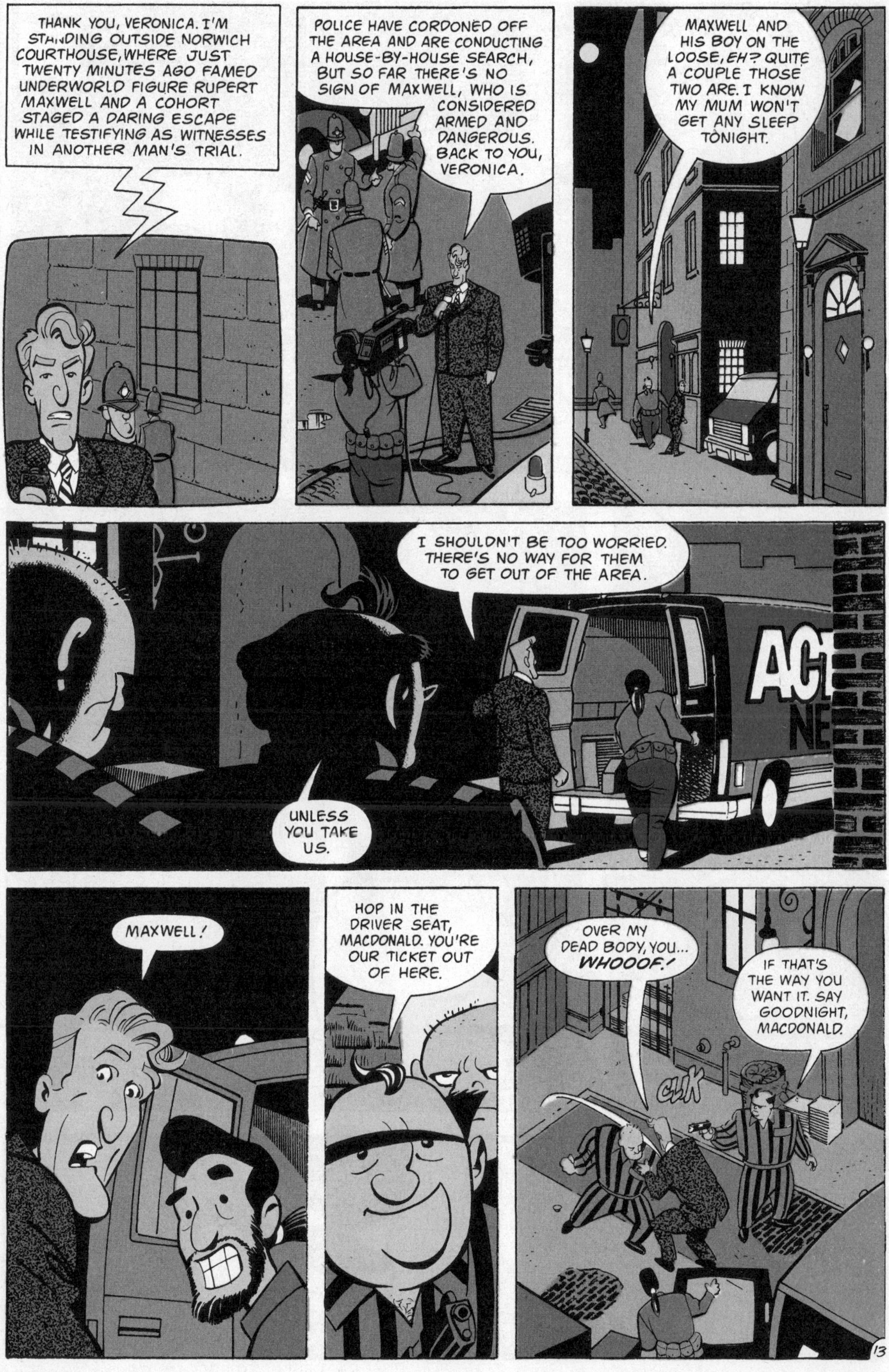
THANK YOU, VERONICA. I'M STANDING OUTSIDE NORWICH COURTHOUSE, WHERE JUST TWENTY MINUTES AGO FAMED UNDERWORLD FIGURE RUPERT MAXWELL AND A COHORT STAGED A DARING ESCAPE WHILE TESTIFYING AS WITNESSES IN ANOTHER MAN'S TRIAL.
POLICE HAVE CORDONED OFF THE AREA AND ARE CONDUCTING A HOUSE-BY-HOUSE SEARCH, BUT SO FAR THERE'S NO SIGN OF MAXWELL, WHO IS CONSIDERED ARMED AND DANGEROUS. BACK TO YOU, VERONICA.
MAXWELL AND HIS BOY ON THE LOOSE, *EH?* QUITE A COUPLE THOSE TWO ARE. I KNOW MY MUM WON'T GET ANY SLEEP TONIGHT.
I SHOULDN'T BE TOO WORRIED. THERE'S NO WAY FOR THEM TO GET OUT OF THE AREA.
ACT
NE
UNLESS YOU TAKE US.
MAXWELL!
HOP IN THE DRIVER SEAT, MACDONALD. YOU'RE OUR TICKET OUT OF HERE.
OVER MY DEAD BODY, YOU... **WHOOOF!**
CLIK
IF THAT'S THE WAY YOU WANT IT. SAY GOODNIGHT, MACDONALD.
13

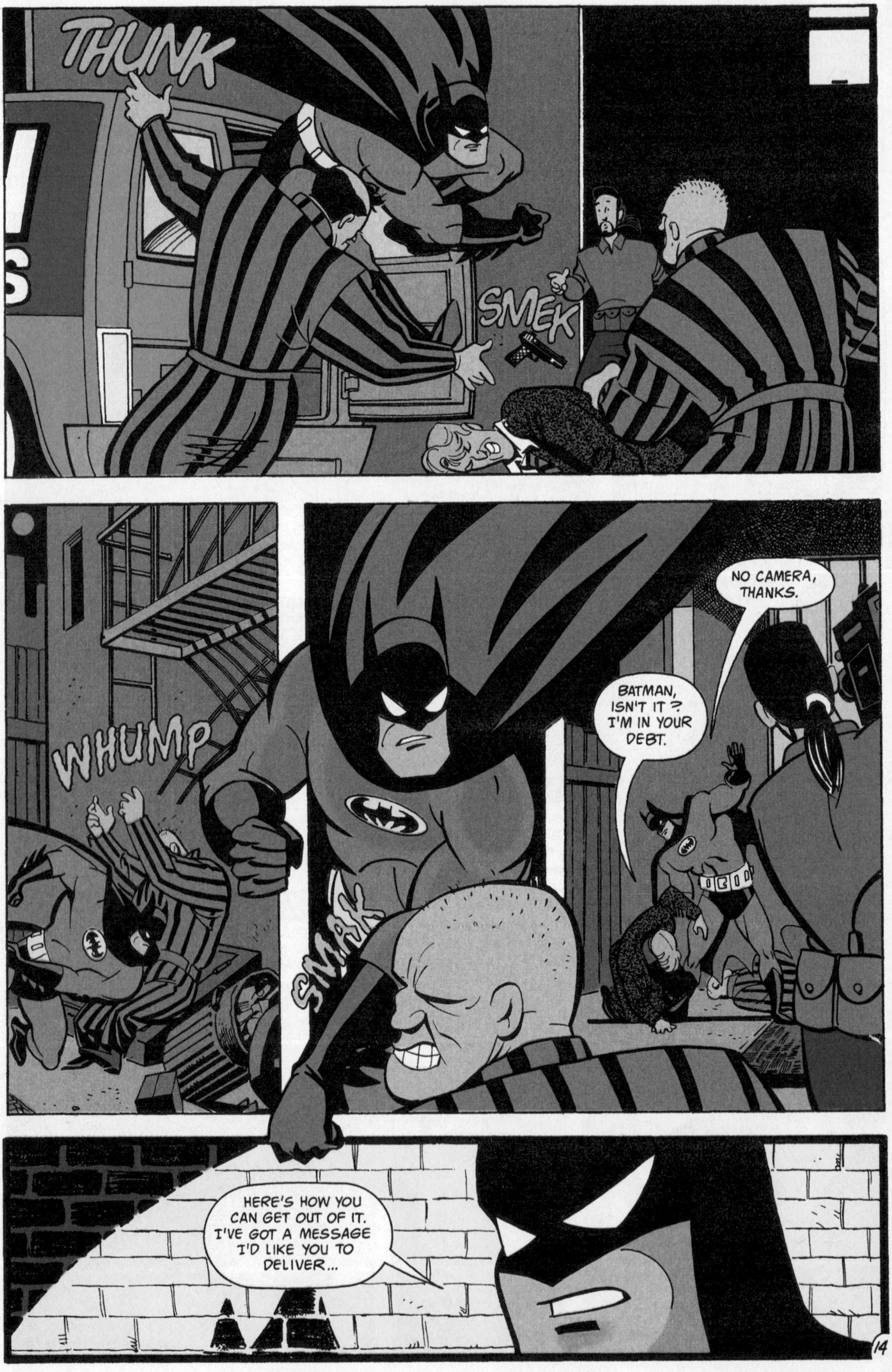
THUNK
SMEK
WHUMP
SMAK
BATMAN, ISN'T IT? I'M IN YOUR DEBT.
NO CAMERA, THANKS.
HERE'S HOW YOU CAN GET OUT OF IT. I'VE GOT A MESSAGE I'D LIKE YOU TO DELIVER...
14

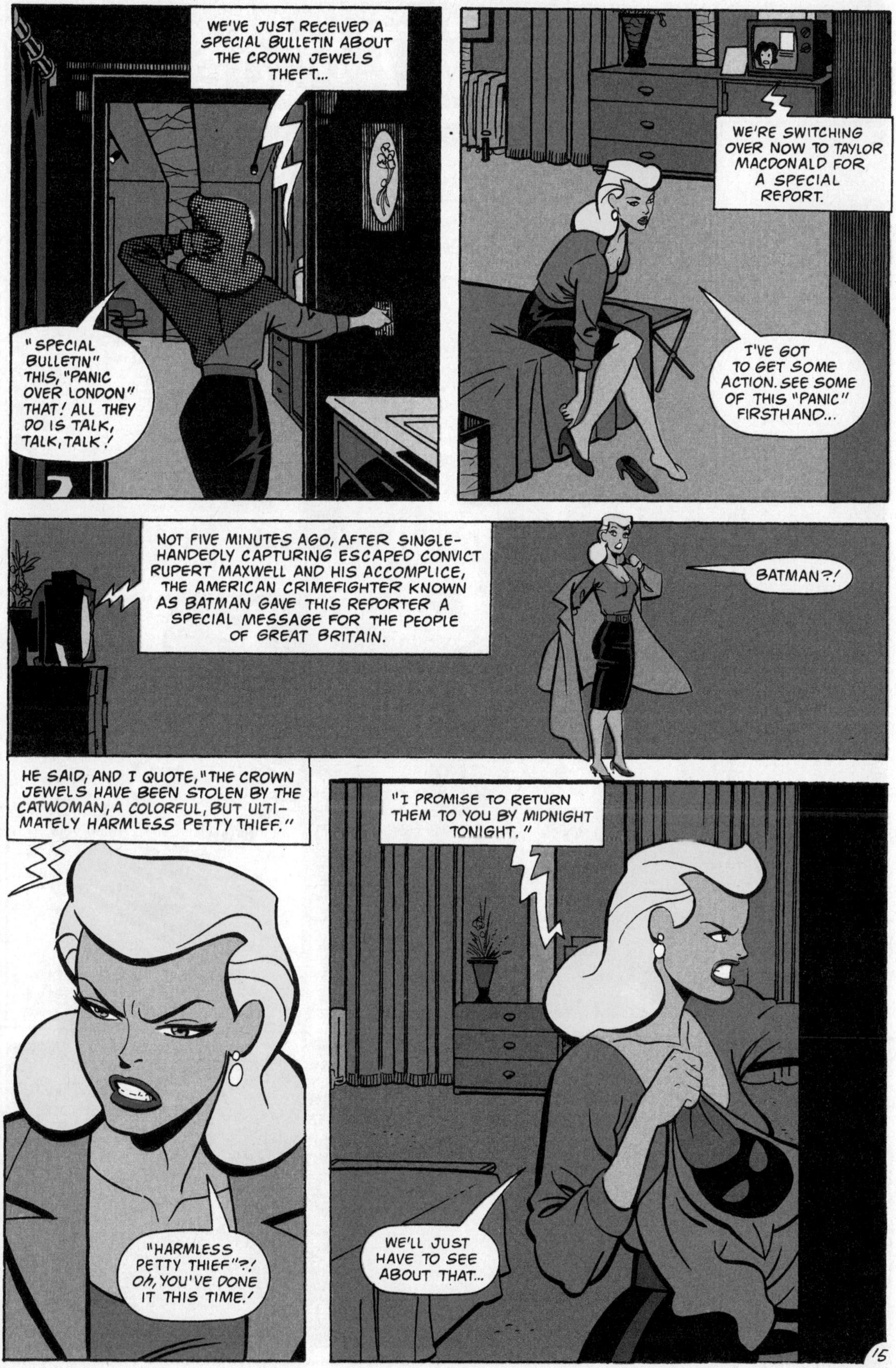
WE'VE JUST RECEIVED A SPECIAL BULLETIN ABOUT THE CROWN JEWELS THEFT...
"SPECIAL BULLETIN" THIS, "PANIC OVER LONDON" THAT! ALL THEY DO IS TALK, TALK, TALK!
WE'RE SWITCHING OVER NOW TO TAYLOR MACDONALD FOR A SPECIAL REPORT.
I'VE GOT TO GET SOME ACTION. SEE SOME OF THIS "PANIC" FIRSTHAND...
NOT FIVE MINUTES AGO, AFTER SINGLE-HANDEDLY CAPTURING ESCAPED CONVICT RUPERT MAXWELL AND HIS ACCOMPLICE, THE AMERICAN CRIMEFIGHTER KNOWN AS BATMAN GAVE THIS REPORTER A SPECIAL MESSAGE FOR THE PEOPLE OF GREAT BRITAIN.
BATMAN?!
HE SAID, AND I QUOTE, "THE CROWN JEWELS HAVE BEEN STOLEN BY THE CATWOMAN, A COLORFUL, BUT ULTI-MATELY HARMLESS PETTY THIEF."
"HARMLESS PETTY THIEF"?! Oh, YOU'VE DONE IT THIS TIME!
"I PROMISE TO RETURN THEM TO YOU BY MIDNIGHT TONIGHT."
WE'LL JUST HAVE TO SEE ABOUT THAT...
15

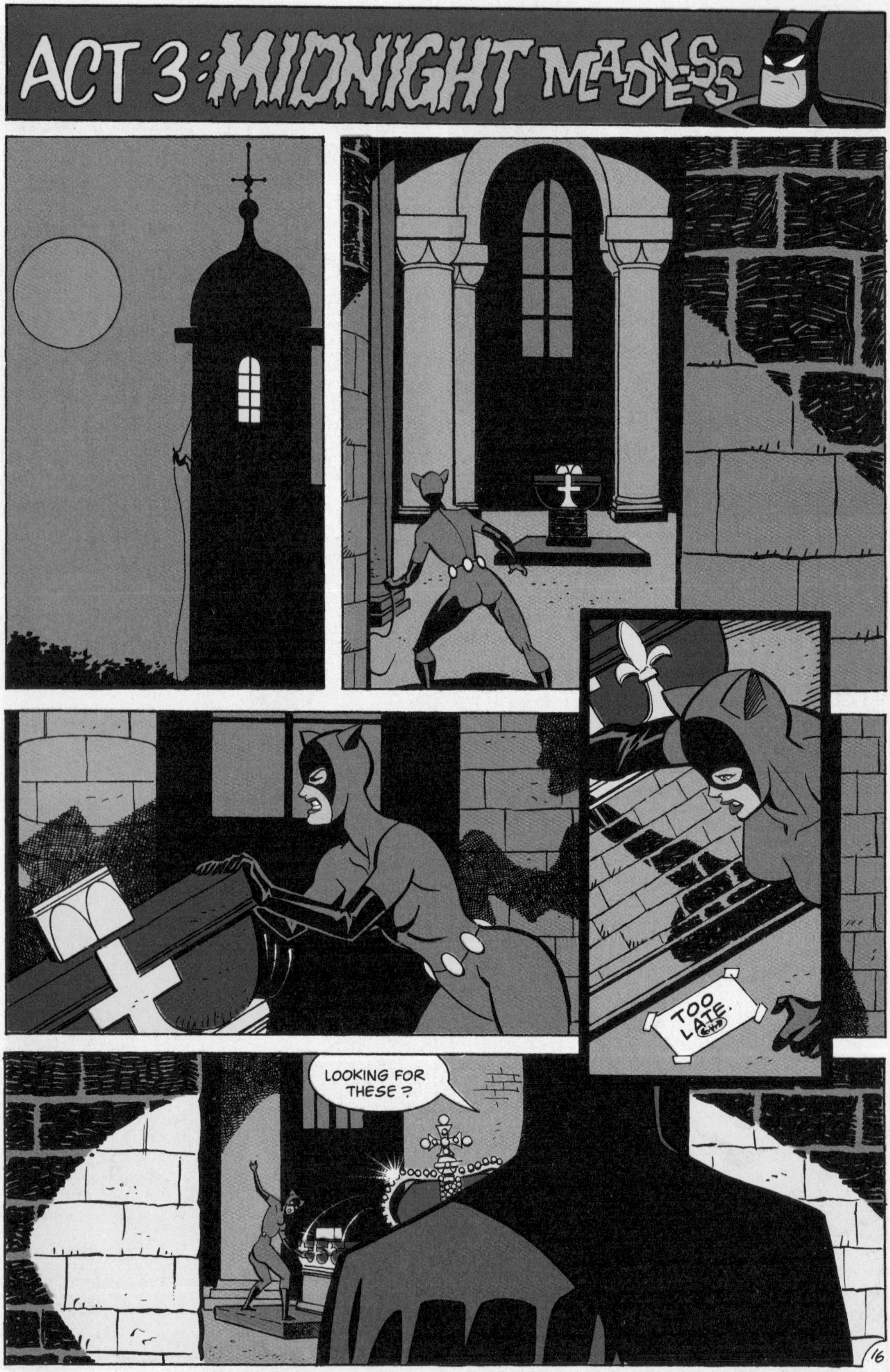
ACT 3: MIDNIGHT MADNESS
TOO LATE.
LOOKING FOR THESE?
16

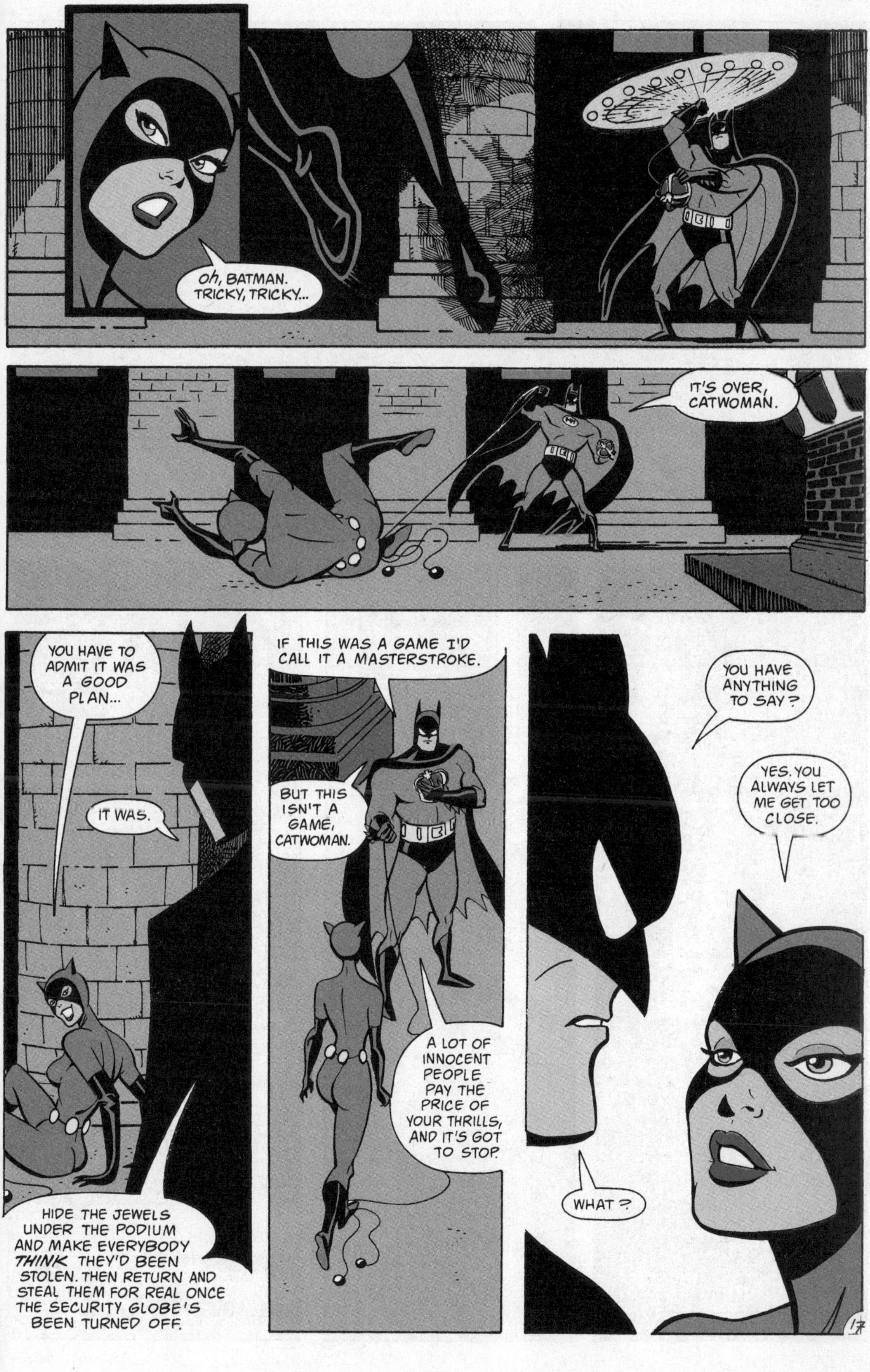
Oh, BATMAN. TRICKY, TRICKY...
IT'S OVER, CATWOMAN.
YOU HAVE TO ADMIT IT WAS A GOOD PLAN...
IT WAS.
HIDE THE JEWELS UNDER THE PODIUM AND MAKE EVERYBODY THINK THEY'D BEEN STOLEN. THEN RETURN AND STEAL THEM FOR REAL ONCE THE SECURITY GLOBE'S BEEN TURNED OFF.
IF THIS WAS A GAME I'D CALL IT A MASTERSTROKE.
BUT THIS ISN'T A GAME, CATWOMAN.
A LOT OF INNOCENT PEOPLE PAY THE PRICE OF YOUR THRILLS, AND IT'S GOT TO STOP.
YOU HAVE ANYTHING TO SAY?
YES. YOU ALWAYS LET ME GET TOO CLOSE.
WHAT?
17

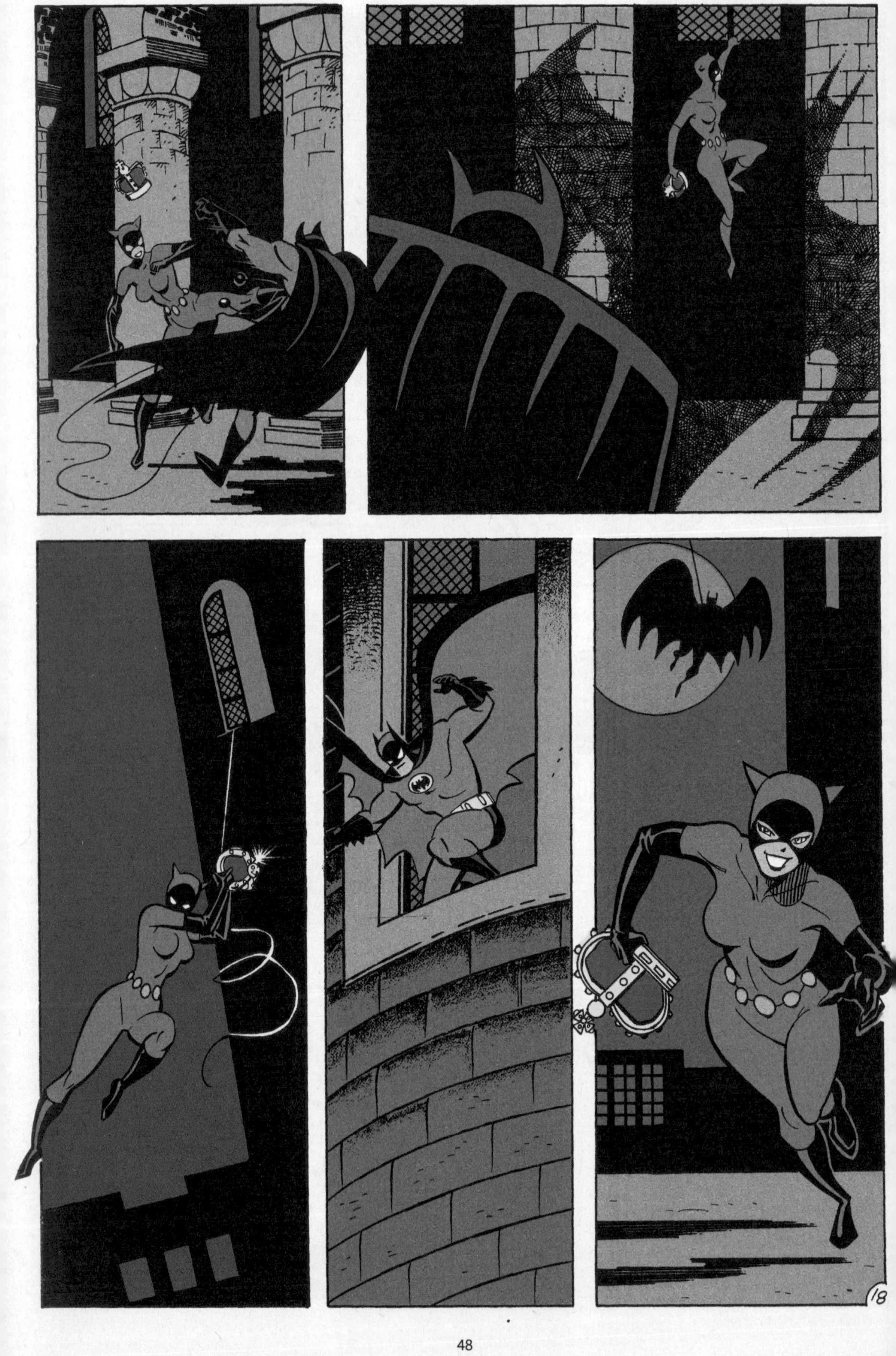
18

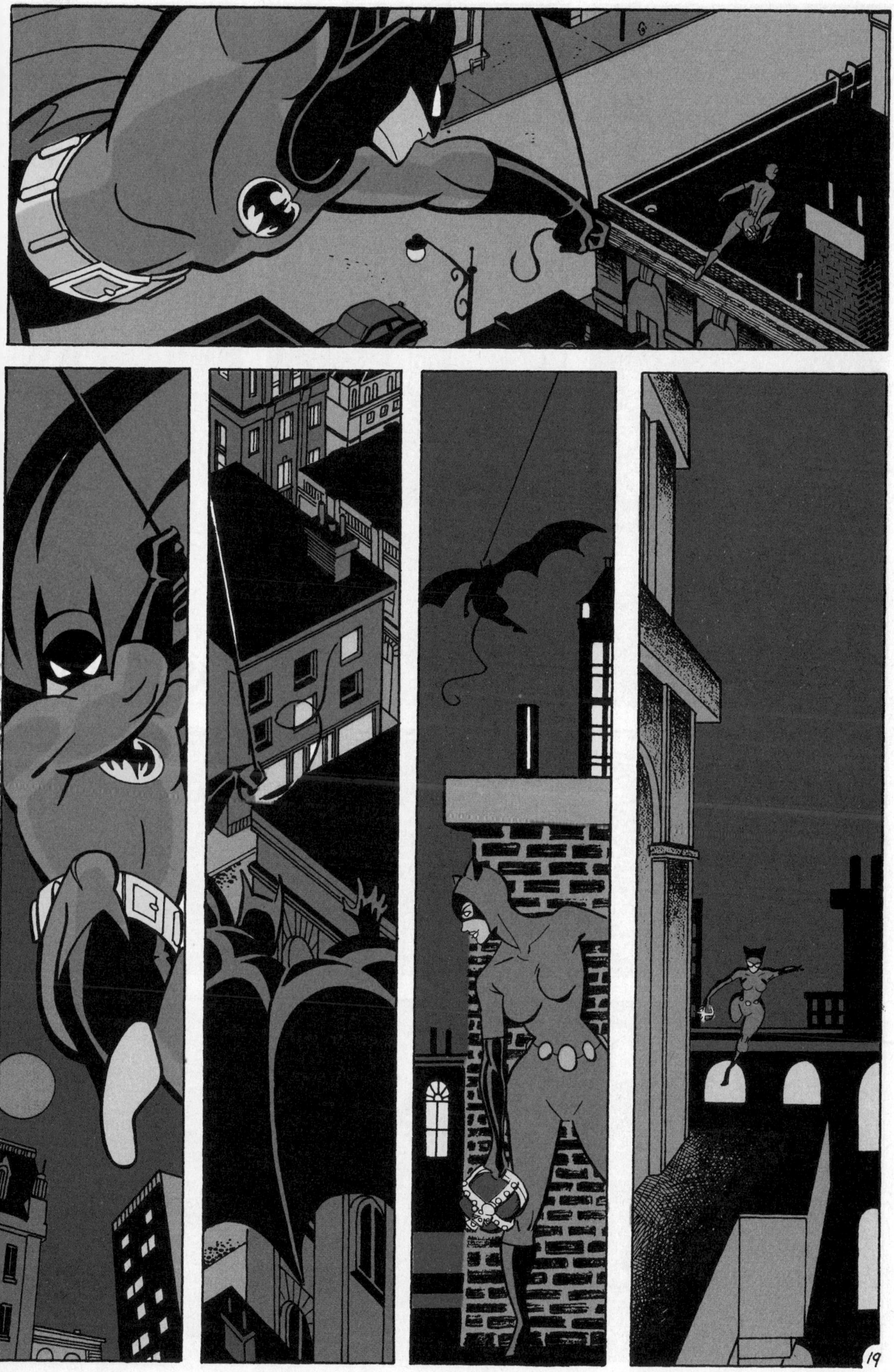
19

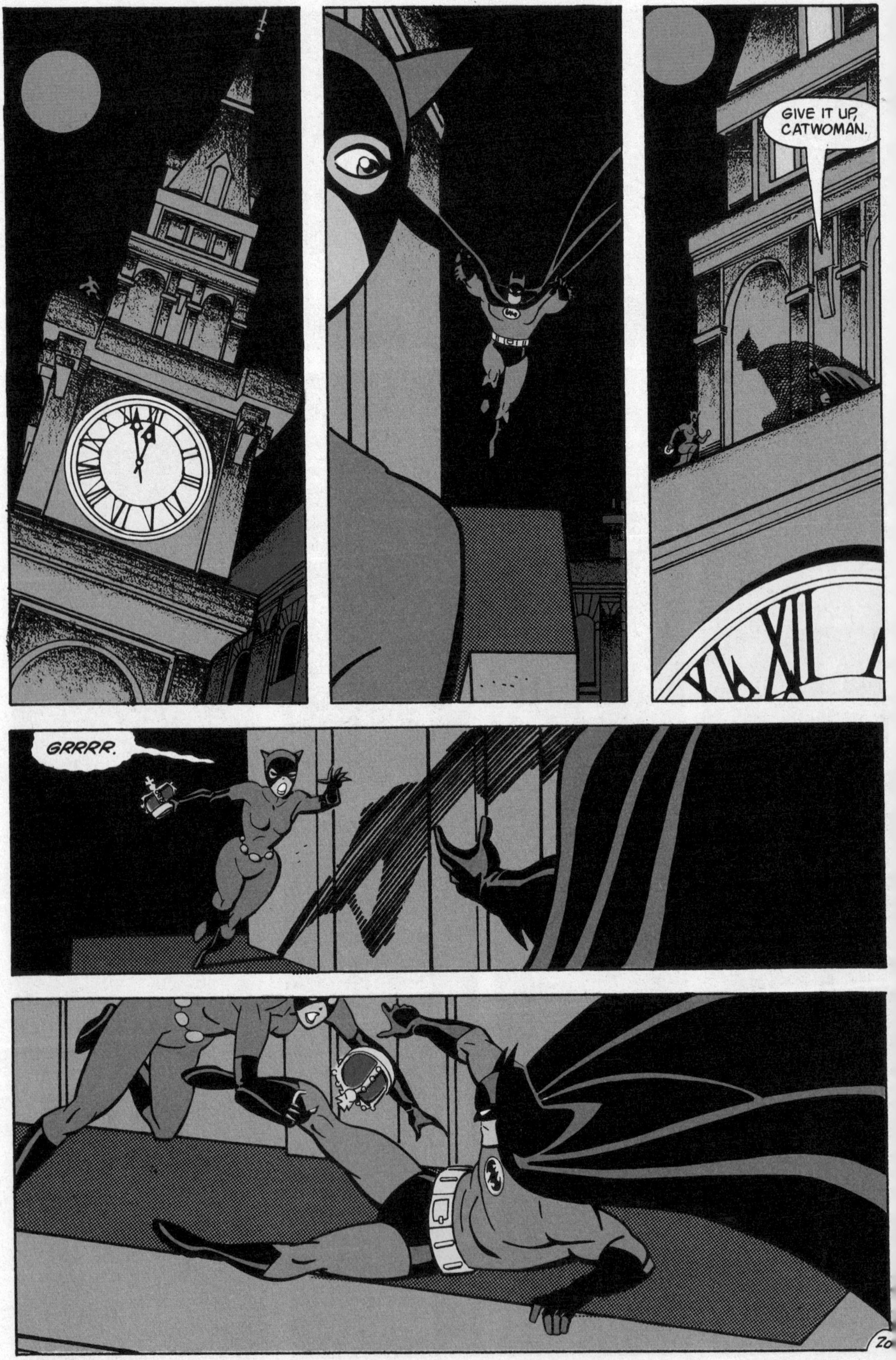
GIVE IT UP, CATWOMAN.
GRRRR.

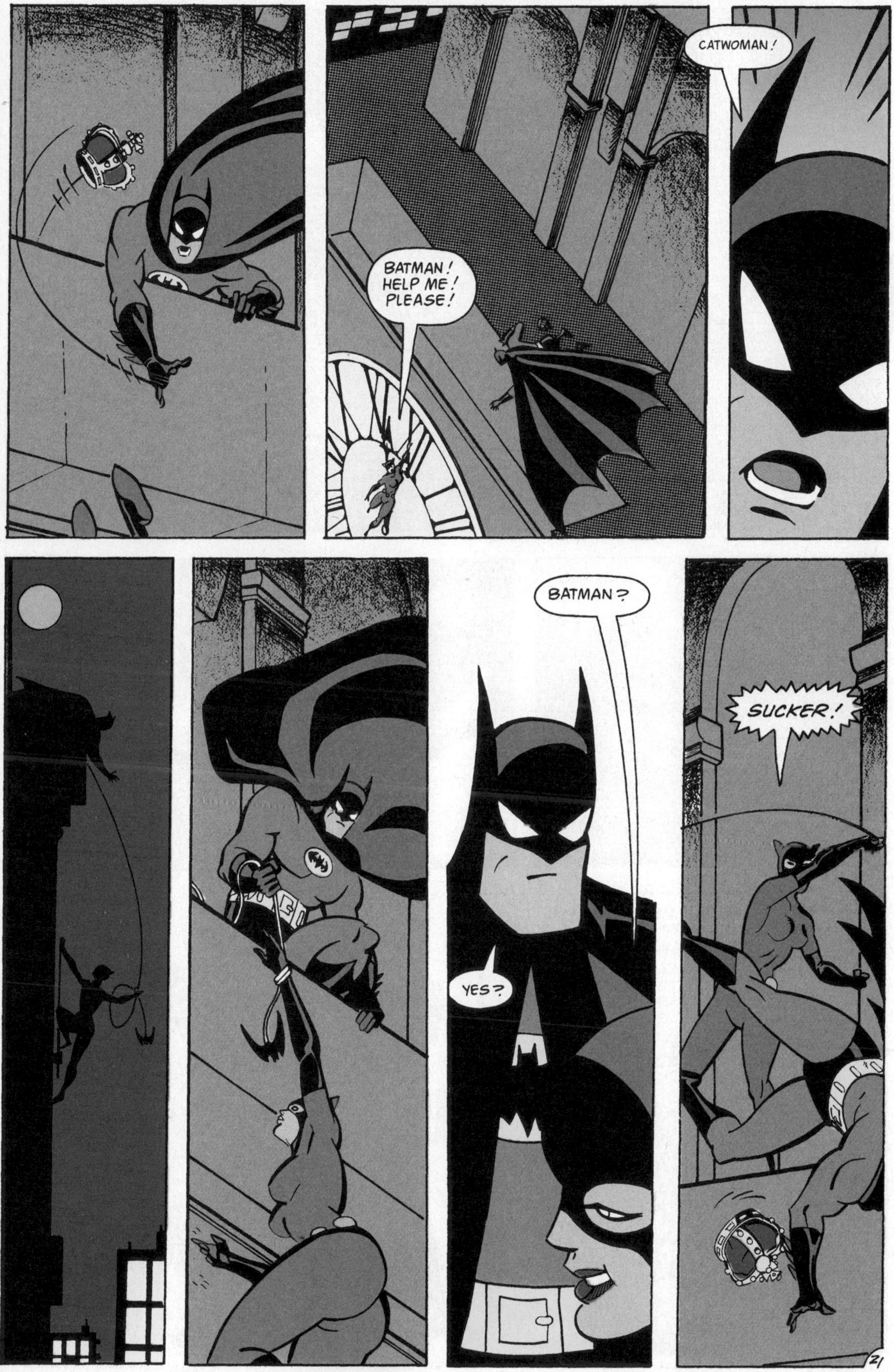
BATMAN! HELP ME! PLEASE!
CATWOMAN!
BATMAN?
YES?
SUCKER!
21

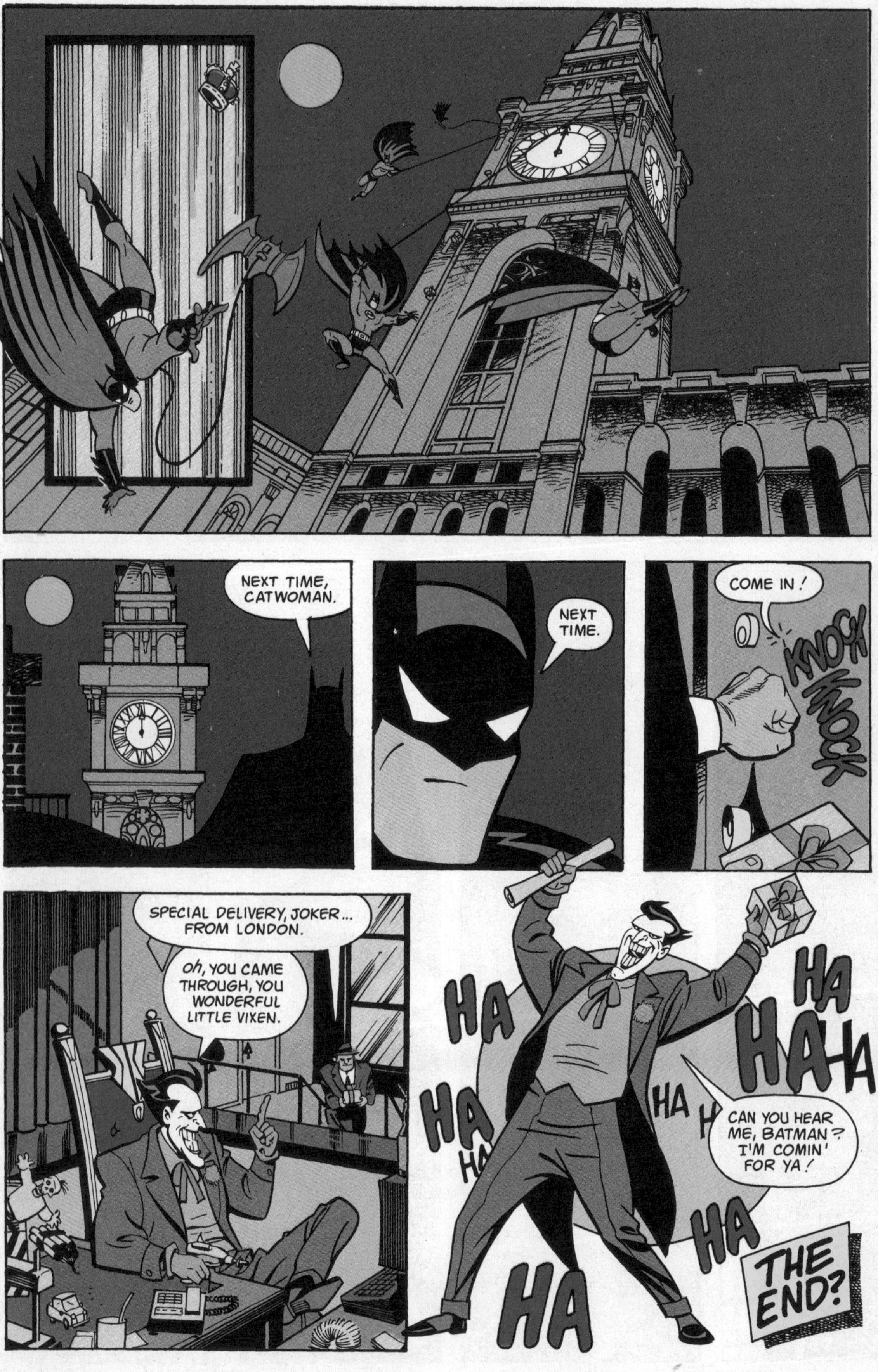
NEXT TIME, CATWOMAN.
NEXT TIME.
COME IN!
KNOCK KNOCK
SPECIAL DELIVERY, JOKER... FROM LONDON.
OH, YOU CAME THROUGH, YOU WONDERFUL LITTLE VIXEN.
HA
HA
HA HA
HA
HA HA
HA
CAN YOU HEAR ME, BATMAN? I'M COMIN' FOR YA!
HA
HA
THE END?

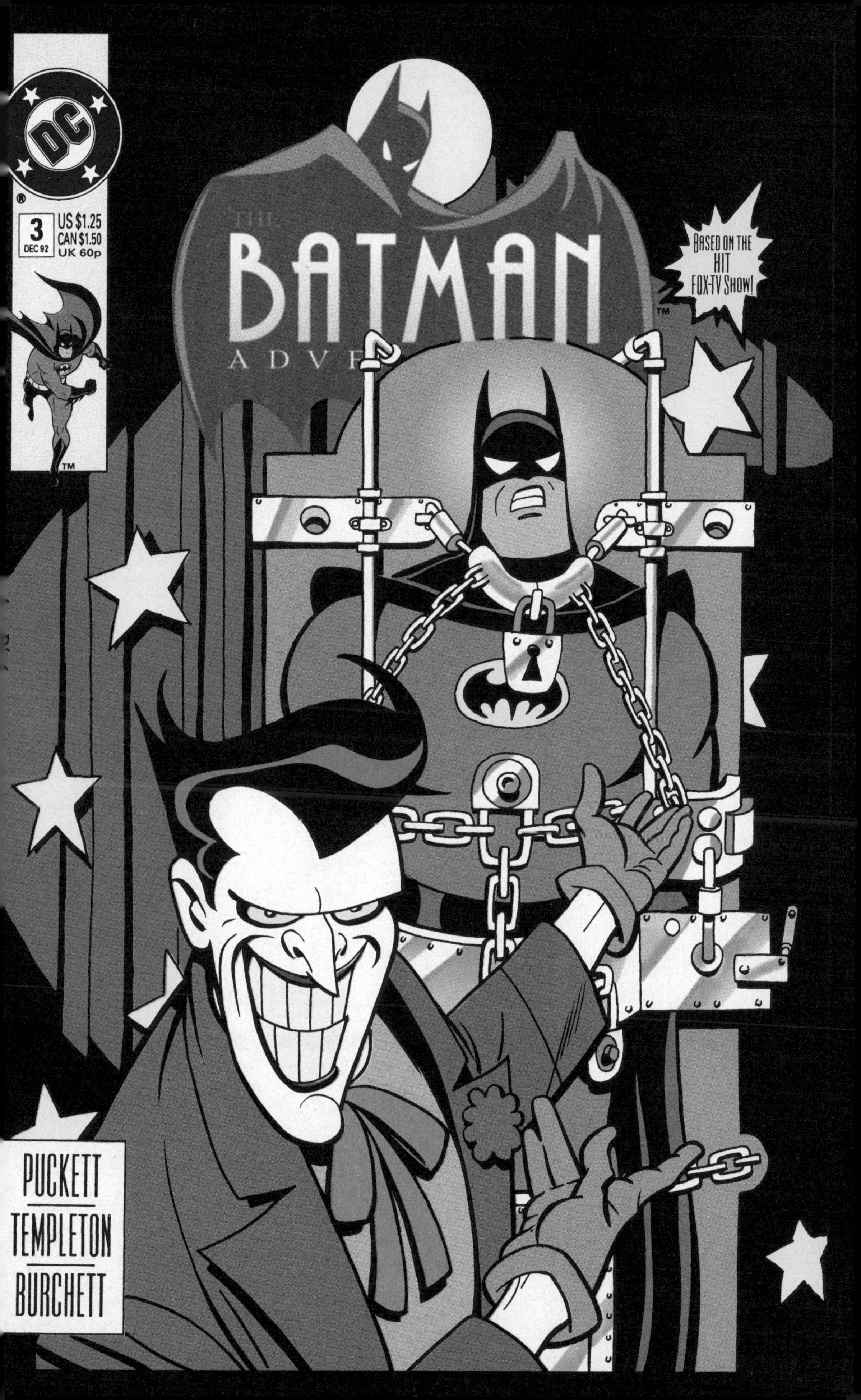

DC
3
DEC 92
US $1.25
CAN $1.50
UK 60p
THE
BATMAN
ADVE
BASED ON THE HIT FOX-TV SHOW!
PUCKETT
TEMPLETON
BURCHETT

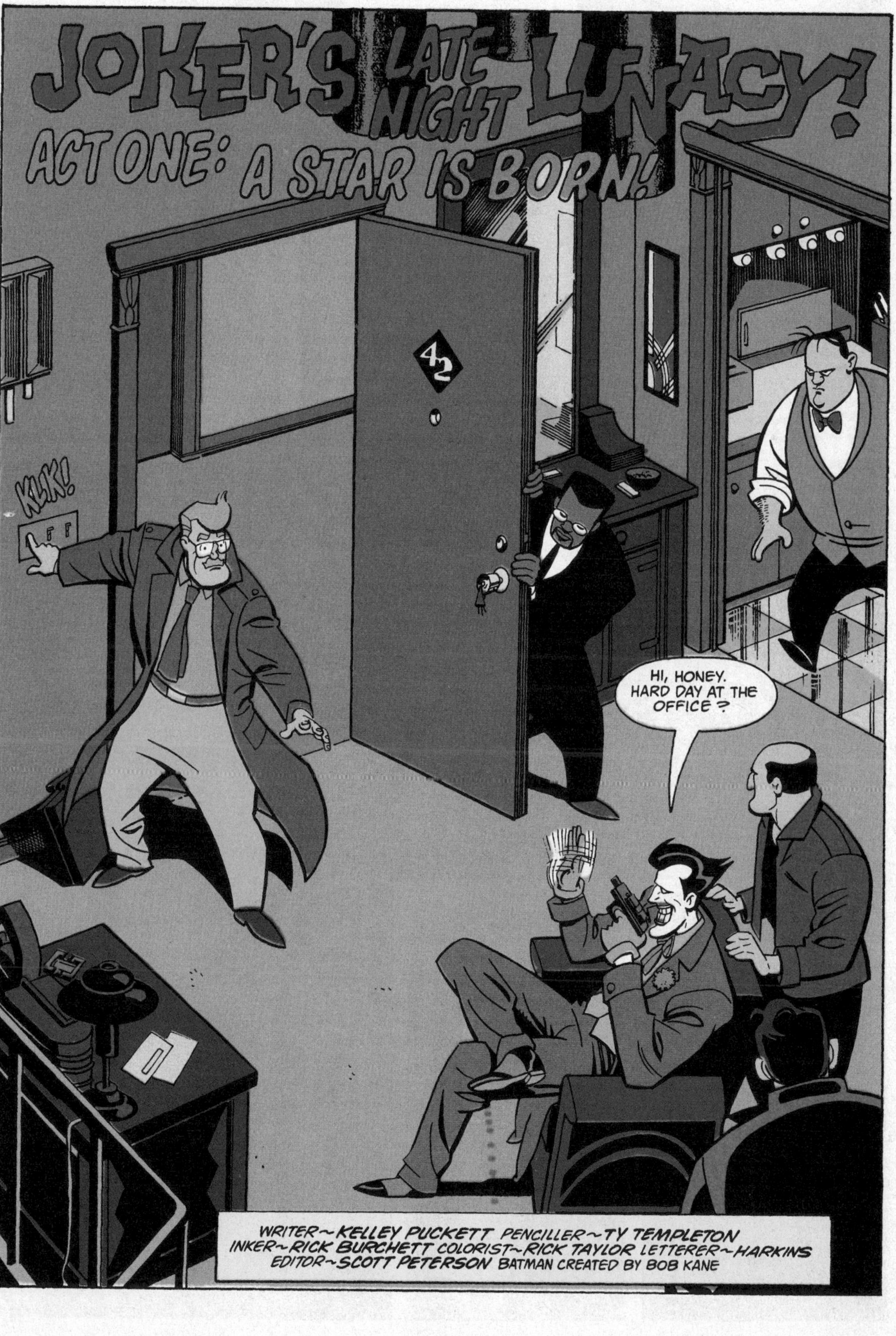
JOKER'S LATE-NIGHT LUNACY!
ACT ONE: A STAR IS BORN!
42
KLIK!
HI, HONEY. HARD DAY AT THE OFFICE?
WRITER~KELLEY PUCKETT PENCILLER~TY TEMPLETON
INKER~RICK BURCHETT COLORIST~RICK TAYLOR LETTERER~HARKINS
EDITOR~SCOTT PETERSON BATMAN CREATED BY BOB KANE

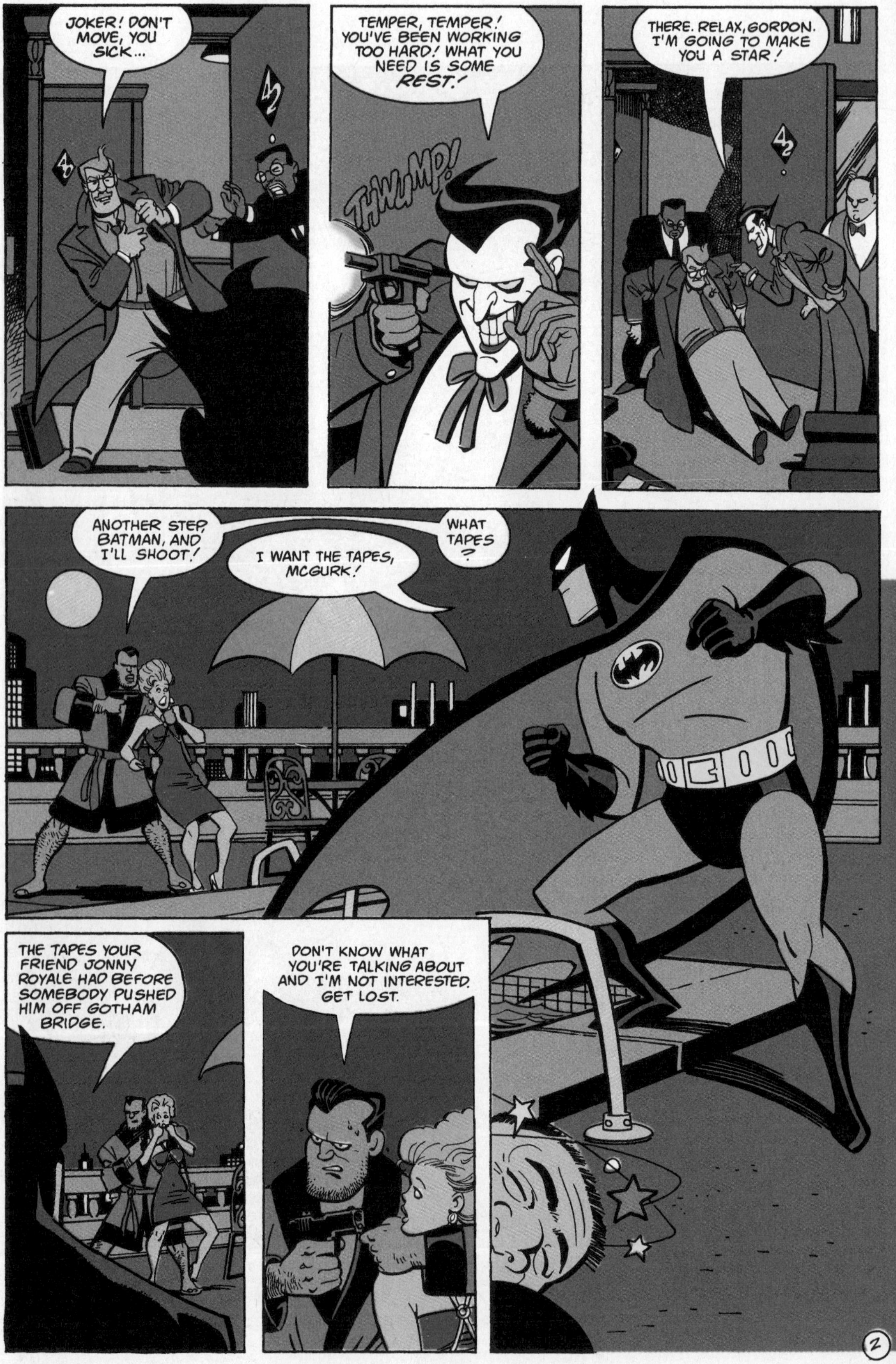
JOKER! DON'T MOVE, YOU SICK...
TEMPER, TEMPER! YOU'VE BEEN WORKING TOO HARD! WHAT YOU NEED IS SOME REST!
THWUMP!
THERE. RELAX, GORDON. I'M GOING TO MAKE YOU A STAR!
ANOTHER STEP, BATMAN, AND I'LL SHOOT!
I WANT THE TAPES, MCGURK!
WHAT TAPES?
THE TAPES YOUR FRIEND JONNY ROYALE HAD BEFORE SOMEBODY PUSHED HIM OFF GOTHAM BRIDGE.
DON'T KNOW WHAT YOU'RE TALKING ABOUT AND I'M NOT INTERESTED. GET LOST.
2

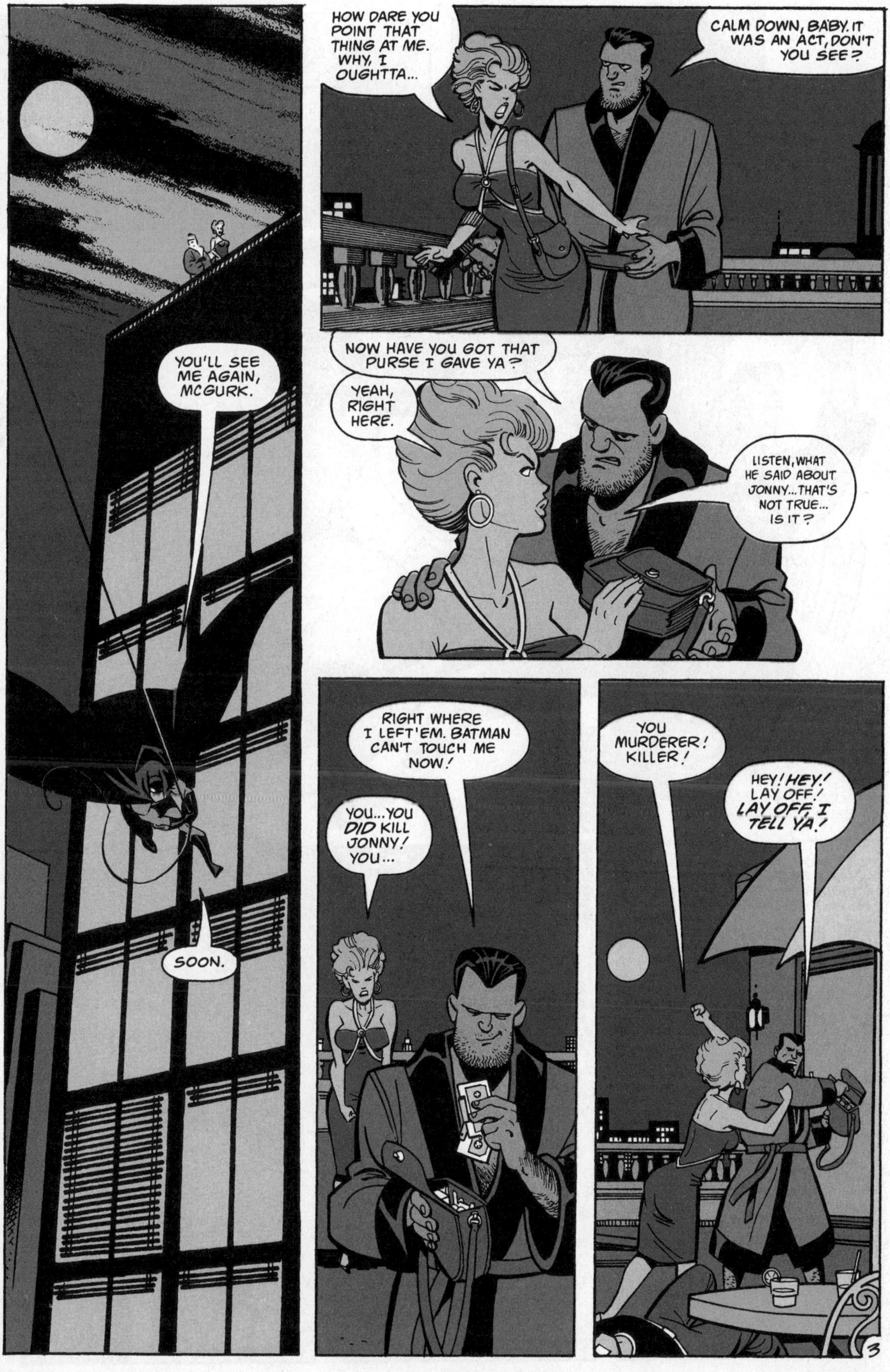
HOW DARE YOU POINT THAT THING AT ME. WHY, I OUGHTTA...
CALM DOWN, BABY. IT WAS AN ACT, DON'T YOU SEE?
YOU'LL SEE ME AGAIN, MCGURK.
SOON.
NOW HAVE YOU GOT THAT PURSE I GAVE YA?
YEAH, RIGHT HERE.
LISTEN, WHAT HE SAID ABOUT JONNY...THAT'S NOT TRUE... IS IT?
RIGHT WHERE I LEFT'EM. BATMAN CAN'T TOUCH ME NOW!
YOU...YOU DID KILL JONNY! YOU...
YOU MURDERER! KILLER!
HEY! HEY! LAY OFF! LAY OFF, I TELL YA!
3

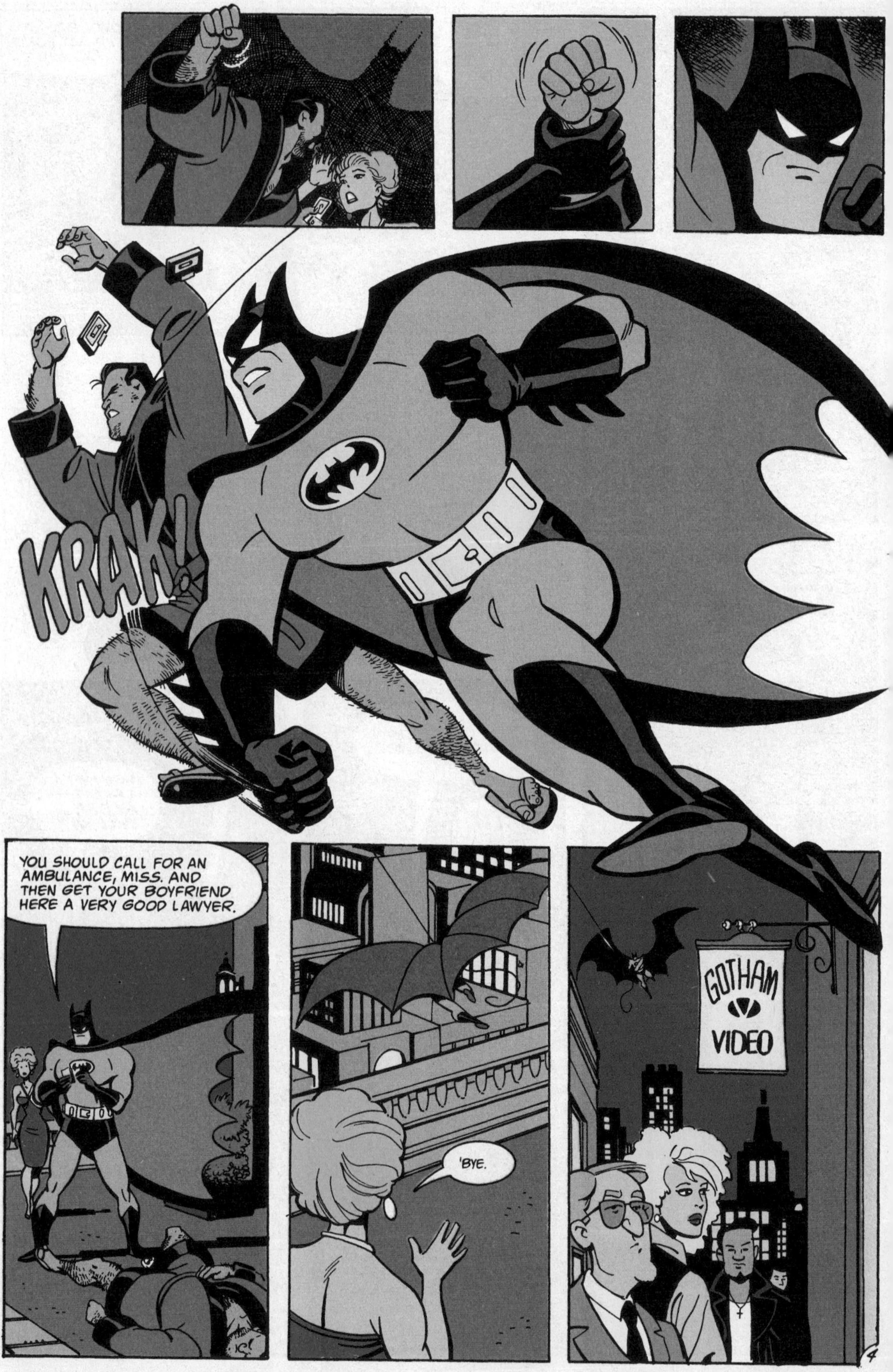

KRAK!
YOU SHOULD CALL FOR AN AMBULANCE, MISS. AND THEN GET YOUR BOYFRIEND HERE A VERY GOOD LAWYER.
'BYE.
GOTHAM VIDEO

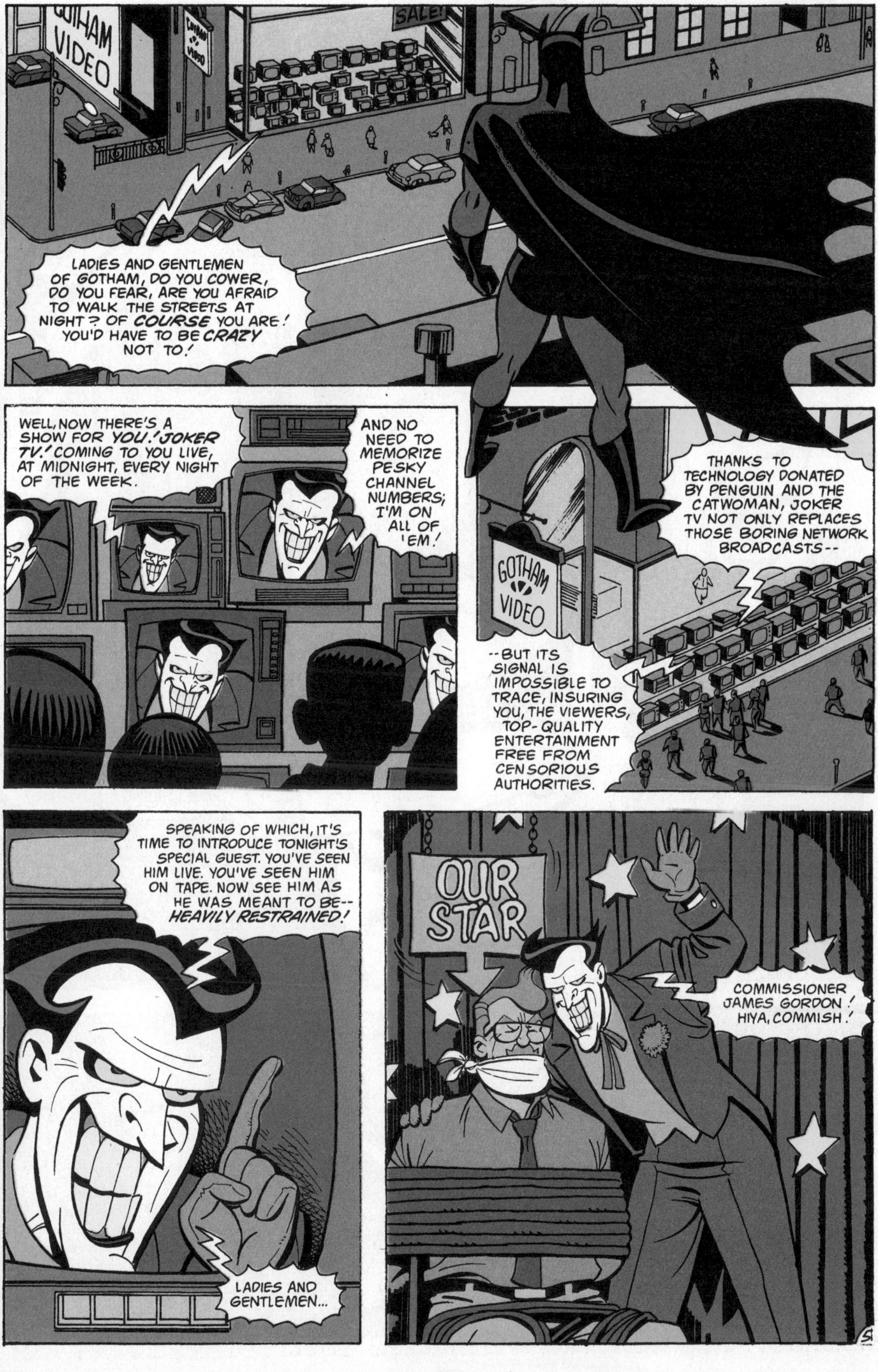
GOTHAM VIDEO
SALE!
LADIES AND GENTLEMEN OF GOTHAM, DO YOU COWER, DO YOU FEAR, ARE YOU AFRAID TO WALK THE STREETS AT NIGHT? OF COURSE YOU ARE! YOU'D HAVE TO BE CRAZY NOT TO!
WELL, NOW THERE'S A SHOW FOR YOU! 'JOKER TV!' COMING TO YOU LIVE, AT MIDNIGHT, EVERY NIGHT OF THE WEEK.
AND NO NEED TO MEMORIZE PESKY CHANNEL NUMBERS; I'M ON ALL OF 'EM!
THANKS TO TECHNOLOGY DONATED BY PENGUIN AND THE CATWOMAN, JOKER TV NOT ONLY REPLACES THOSE BORING NETWORK BROADCASTS--
GOTHAM VIDEO
--BUT ITS SIGNAL IS IMPOSSIBLE TO TRACE, INSURING YOU, THE VIEWERS, TOP-QUALITY ENTERTAINMENT FREE FROM CENSORIOUS AUTHORITIES.
SPEAKING OF WHICH, IT'S TIME TO INTRODUCE TONIGHT'S SPECIAL GUEST. YOU'VE SEEN HIM LIVE. YOU'VE SEEN HIM ON TAPE. NOW SEE HIM AS HE WAS MEANT TO BE--HEAVILY RESTRAINED!
LADIES AND GENTLEMEN...
OUR STAR
COMMISSIONER JAMES GORDON! HIYA, COMMISH!

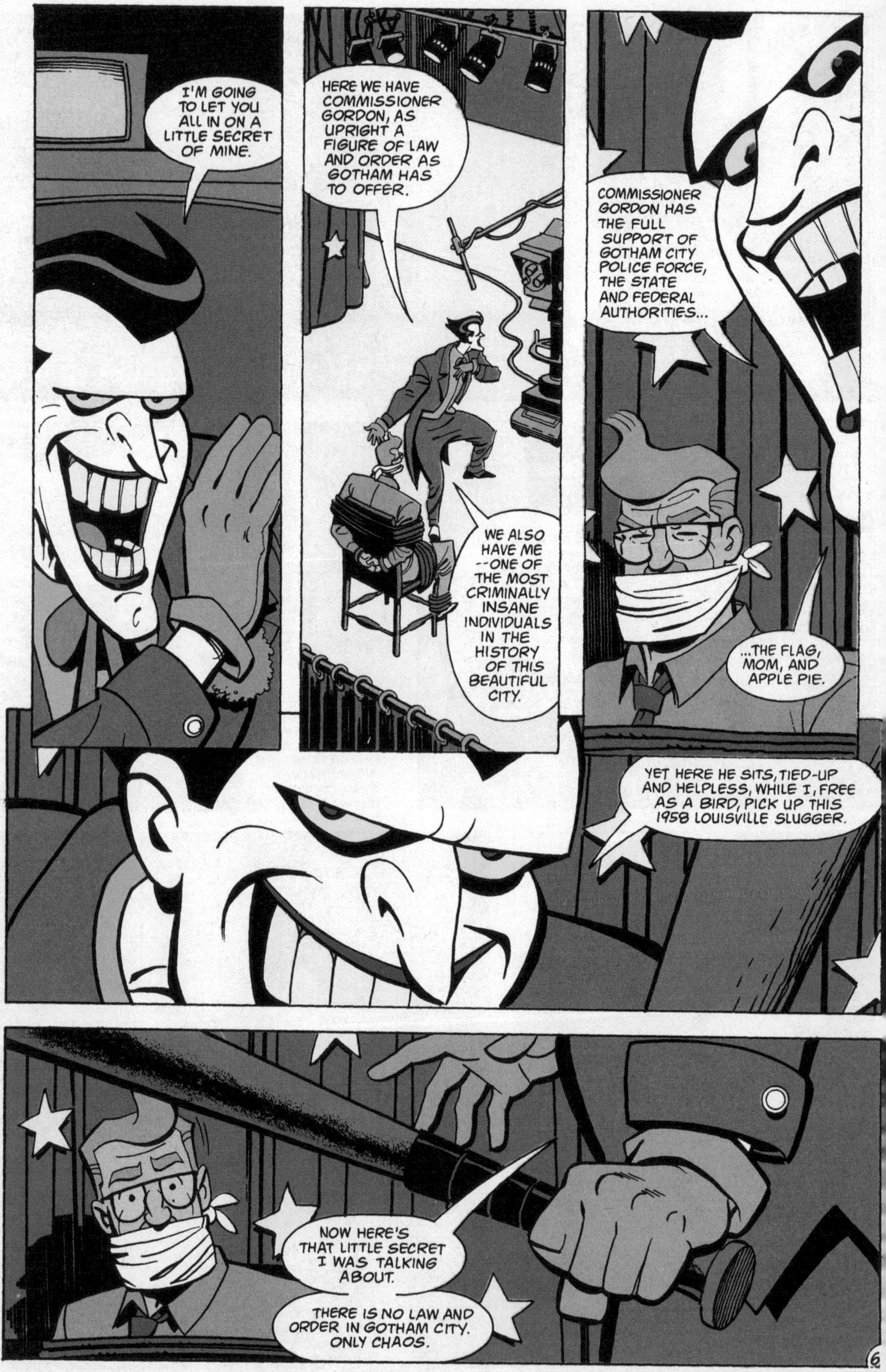

I'M GOING TO LET YOU ALL IN ON A LITTLE SECRET OF MINE.
HERE WE HAVE COMMISSIONER GORDON, AS UPRIGHT A FIGURE OF LAW AND ORDER AS GOTHAM HAS TO OFFER.
WE ALSO HAVE ME --ONE OF THE MOST CRIMINALLY INSANE INDIVIDUALS IN THE HISTORY OF THIS BEAUTIFUL CITY.
COMMISSIONER GORDON HAS THE FULL SUPPORT OF GOTHAM CITY POLICE FORCE, THE STATE AND FEDERAL AUTHORITIES...
...THE FLAG, MOM, AND APPLE PIE.
YET HERE HE SITS, TIED-UP AND HELPLESS, WHILE I, FREE AS A BIRD, PICK UP THIS 1958 LOUISVILLE SLUGGER.
NOW HERE'S THAT LITTLE SECRET I WAS TALKING ABOUT.
THERE IS NO LAW AND ORDER IN GOTHAM CITY. ONLY CHAOS.
6

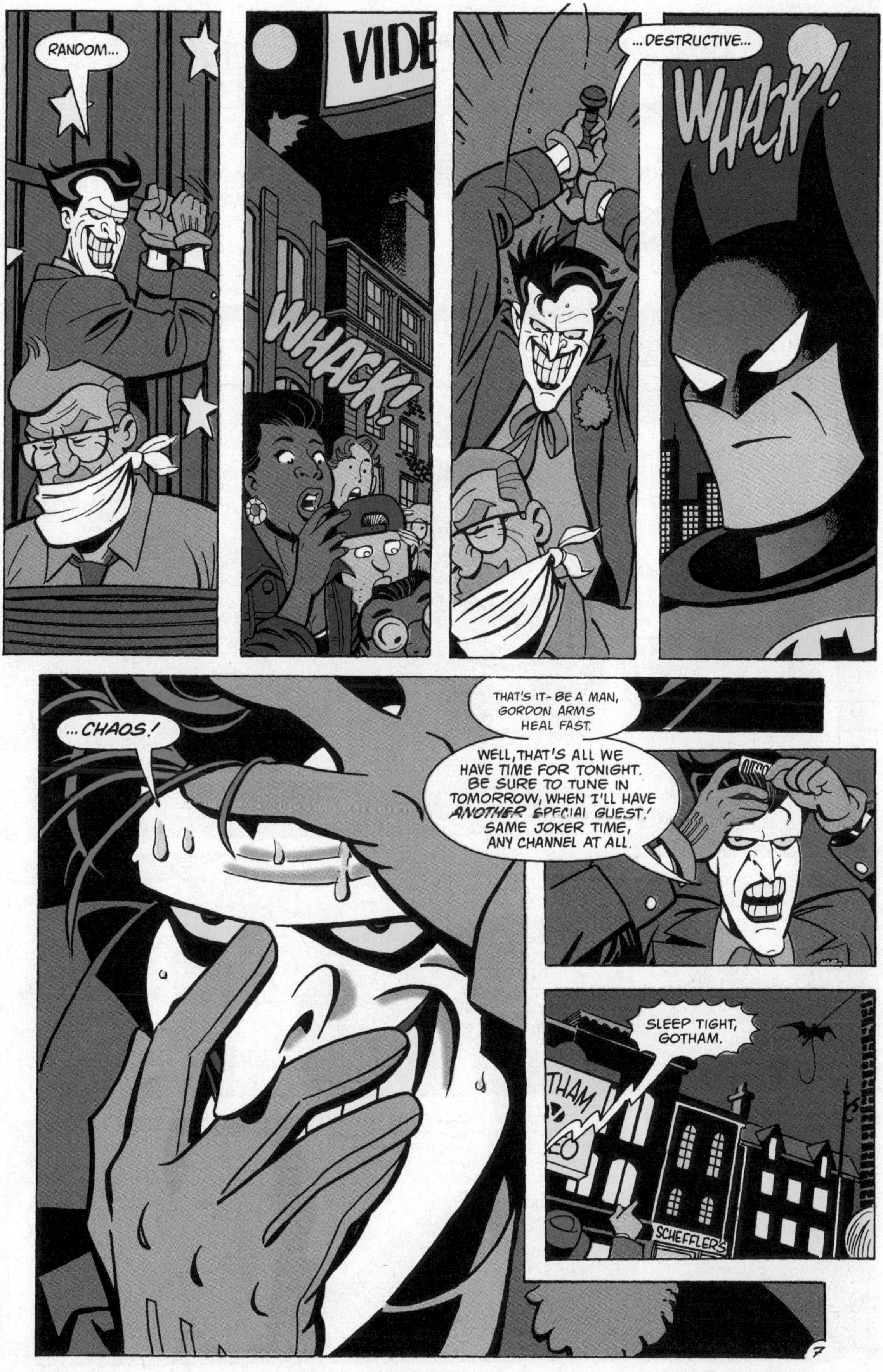
RANDOM...
VIDE
WHACK!
...DESTRUCTIVE...
WHACK!
...CHAOS!
THAT'S IT- BE A MAN, GORDON ARMS HEAL FAST.
WELL, THAT'S ALL WE HAVE TIME FOR TONIGHT. BE SURE TO TUNE IN TOMORROW, WHEN I'LL HAVE ANOTHER SPECIAL GUEST! SAME JOKER TIME, ANY CHANNEL AT ALL.
SLEEP TIGHT, GOTHAM.
THAM
SCHEFFLERS
7

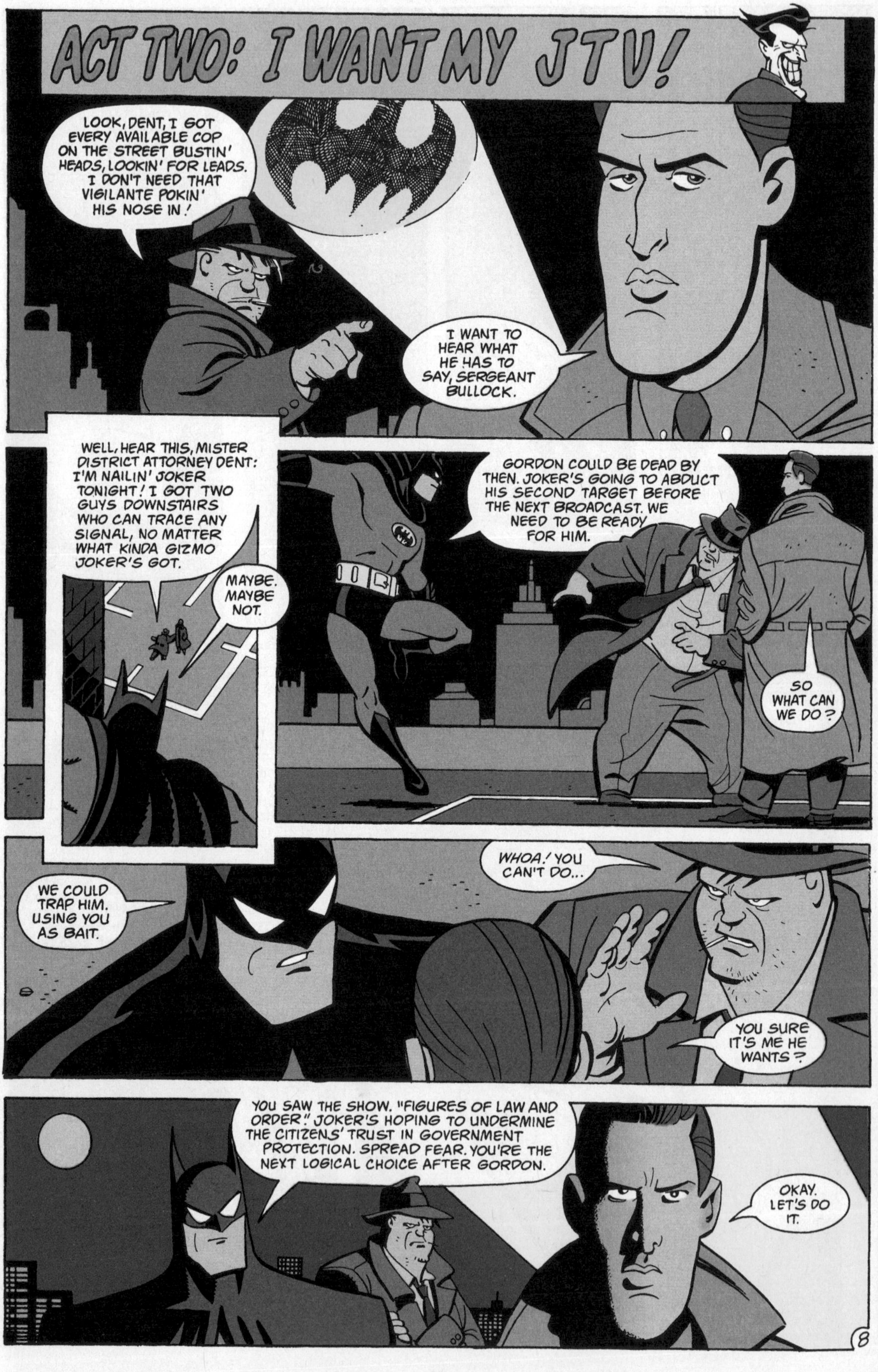
ACT TWO: I WANT MY JTV!
LOOK, DENT, I GOT EVERY AVAILABLE COP ON THE STREET BUSTIN' HEADS, LOOKIN' FOR LEADS. I DON'T NEED THAT VIGILANTE POKIN' HIS NOSE IN!
I WANT TO HEAR WHAT HE HAS TO SAY, SERGEANT BULLOCK.
WELL, HEAR THIS, MISTER DISTRICT ATTORNEY DENT: I'M NAILIN' JOKER TONIGHT! I GOT TWO GUYS DOWNSTAIRS WHO CAN TRACE ANY SIGNAL, NO MATTER WHAT KINDA GIZMO JOKER'S GOT.
MAYBE. MAYBE NOT.
GORDON COULD BE DEAD BY THEN. JOKER'S GOING TO ABDUCT HIS SECOND TARGET BEFORE THE NEXT BROADCAST. WE NEED TO BE READY FOR HIM.
SO WHAT CAN WE DO?
WE COULD TRAP HIM. USING YOU AS BAIT.
WHOA! YOU CAN'T DO...
YOU SURE IT'S ME HE WANTS?
YOU SAW THE SHOW. "FIGURES OF LAW AND ORDER." JOKER'S HOPING TO UNDERMINE THE CITIZENS' TRUST IN GOVERNMENT PROTECTION. SPREAD FEAR. YOU'RE THE NEXT LOGICAL CHOICE AFTER GORDON.
OKAY. LET'S DO IT.
8

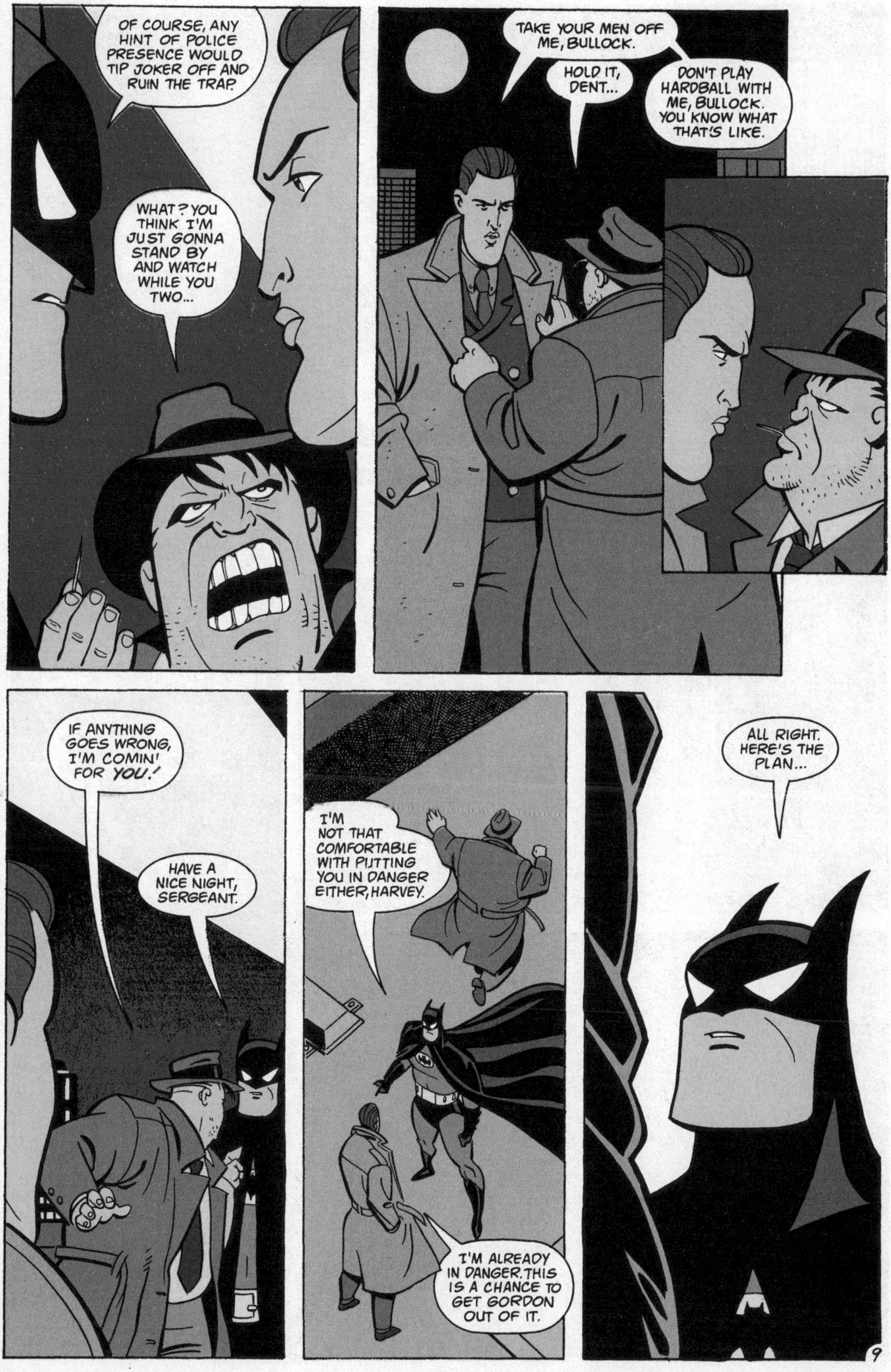
OF COURSE, ANY HINT OF POLICE PRESENCE WOULD TIP JOKER OFF AND RUIN THE TRAP.
WHAT? YOU THINK I'M JUST GONNA STAND BY AND WATCH WHILE YOU TWO...
TAKE YOUR MEN OFF ME, BULLOCK.
HOLD IT, DENT...
DON'T PLAY HARDBALL WITH ME, BULLOCK. YOU KNOW WHAT THAT'S LIKE.
IF ANYTHING GOES WRONG, I'M COMIN' FOR YOU!
HAVE A NICE NIGHT, SERGEANT.
I'M NOT THAT COMFORTABLE WITH PUTTING YOU IN DANGER EITHER, HARVEY.
I'M ALREADY IN DANGER. THIS IS A CHANCE TO GET GORDON OUT OF IT.
ALL RIGHT. HERE'S THE PLAN...
9

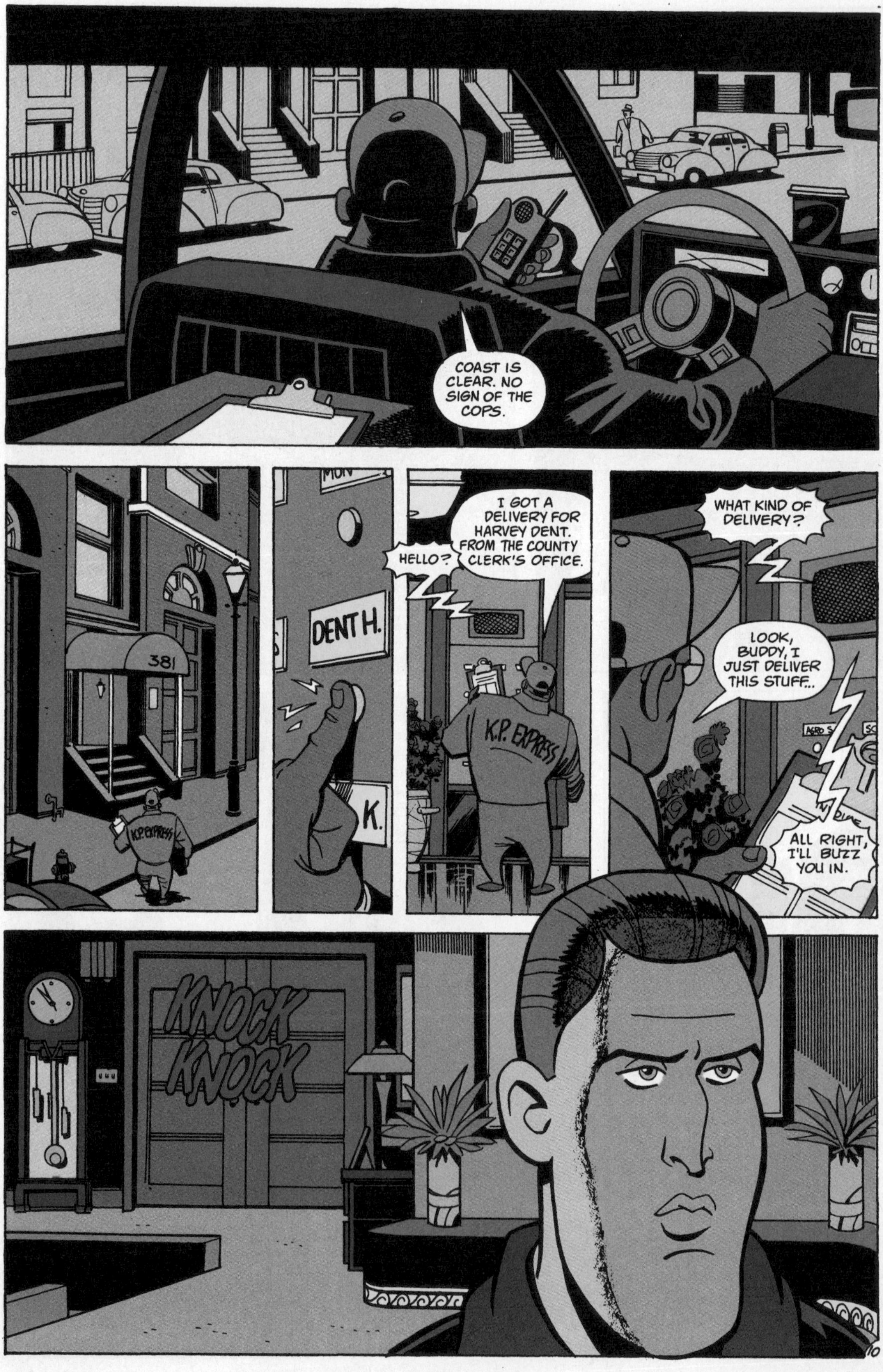
COAST IS CLEAR. NO SIGN OF THE COPS.
381
DENT H.
K.
K.P. EXPRESS
HELLO?
I GOT A DELIVERY FOR HARVEY DENT. FROM THE COUNTY CLERK'S OFFICE.
WHAT KIND OF DELIVERY?
LOOK, BUDDY, I JUST DELIVER THIS STUFF...
ALL RIGHT, I'LL BUZZ YOU IN.
KNOCK KNOCK
10

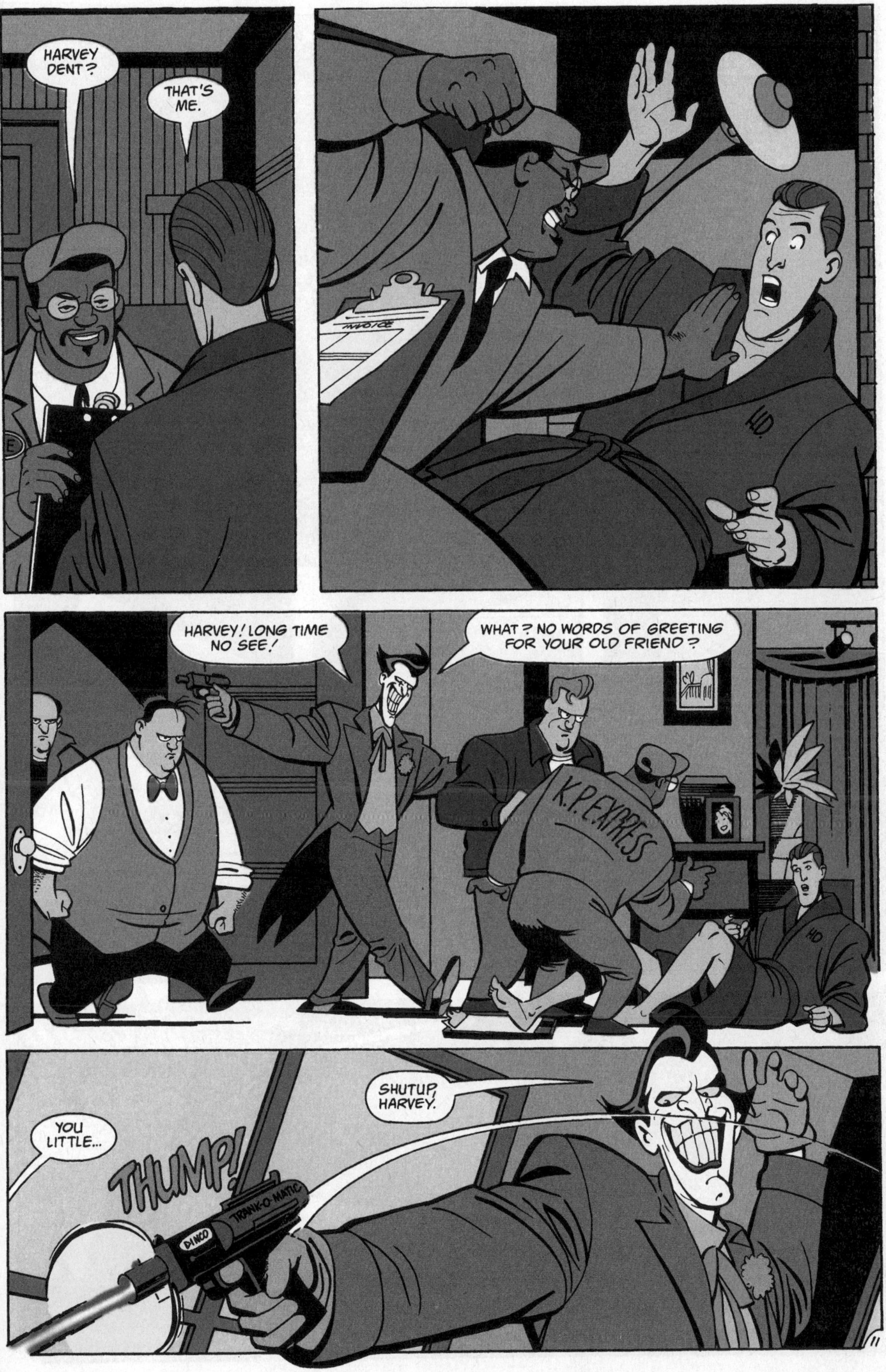
HARVEY DENT?
THAT'S ME.
INVOICE
H.D.
HARVEY! LONG TIME NO SEE!
WHAT? NO WORDS OF GREETING FOR YOUR OLD FRIEND?
K.P.E. EXPRESS
HD
YOU LITTLE...
SHUTUP, HARVEY.
THUMP!
DINCO
TRANK-O-MATIC

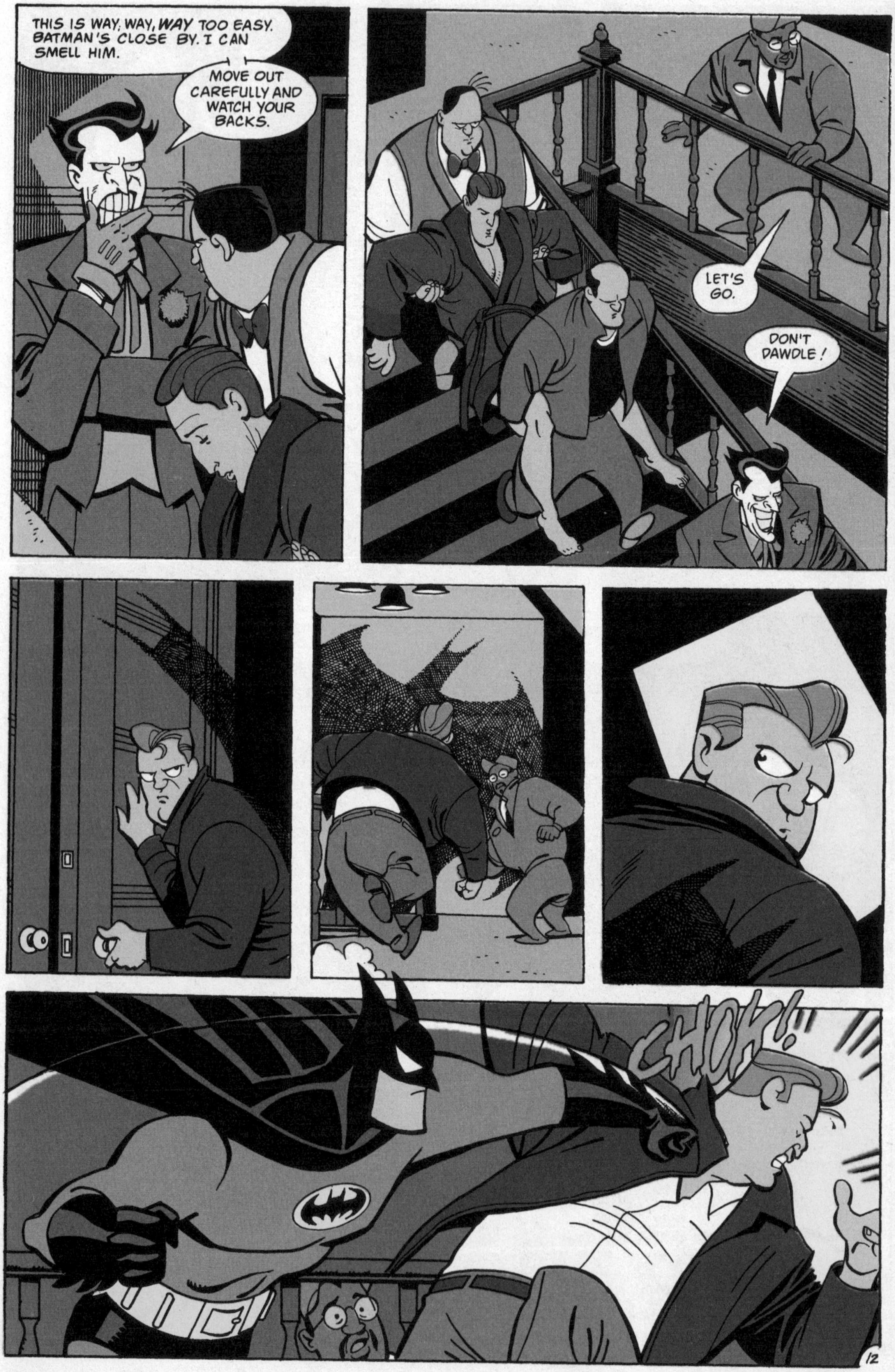
THIS IS WAY, WAY, WAY TOO EASY. BATMAN'S CLOSE BY. I CAN SMELL HIM.
MOVE OUT CAREFULLY AND WATCH YOUR BACKS.
LET'S GO.
DON'T DAWDLE!
CHOK!
12

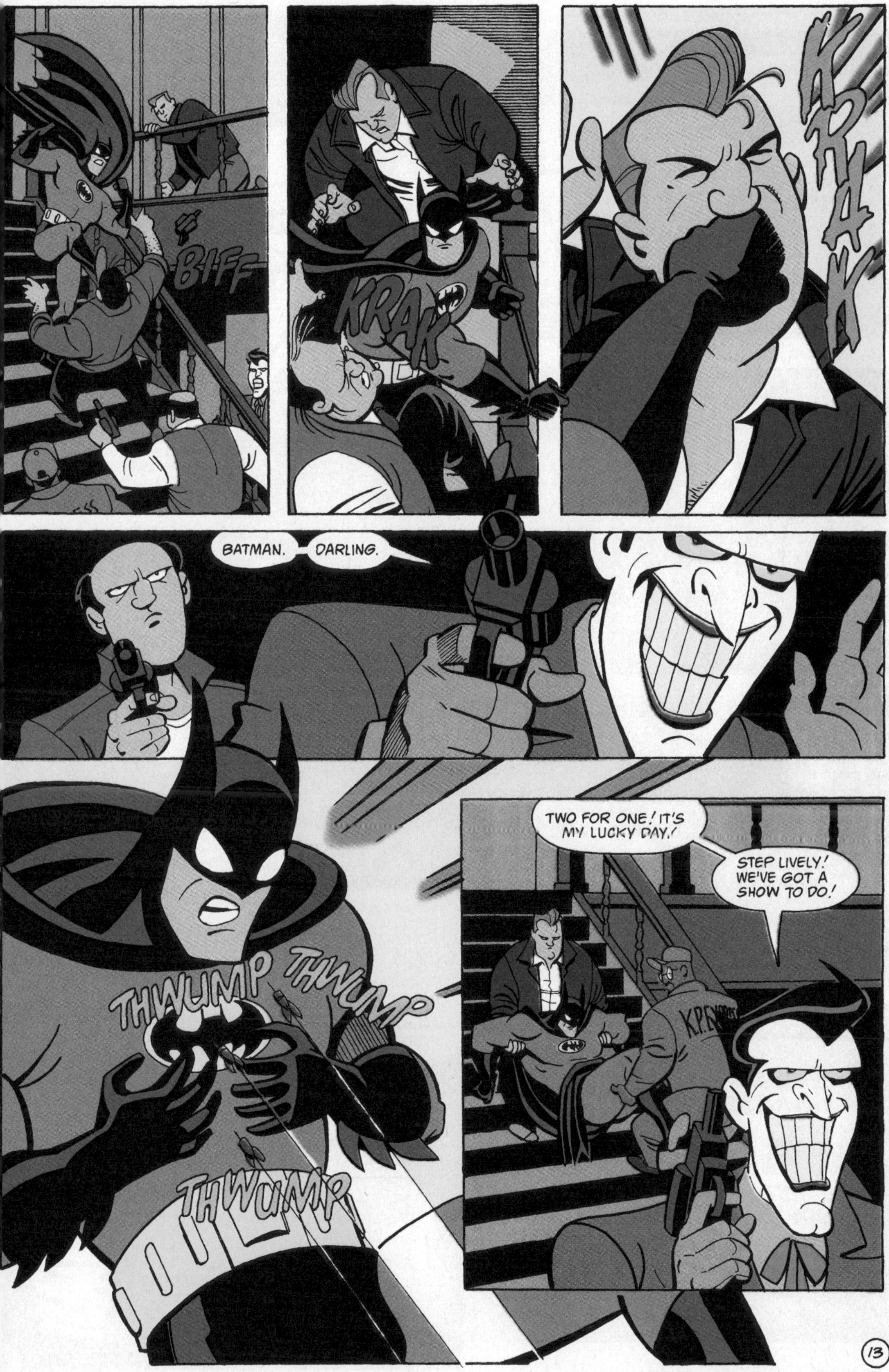
BIFF
KRAK
KRAK
BATMAN.
DARLING.
THWUMP
THWUMP
THWUMP
TWO FOR ONE! IT'S MY LUCKY DAY!
STEP LIVELY! WE'VE GOT A SHOW TO DO!
13

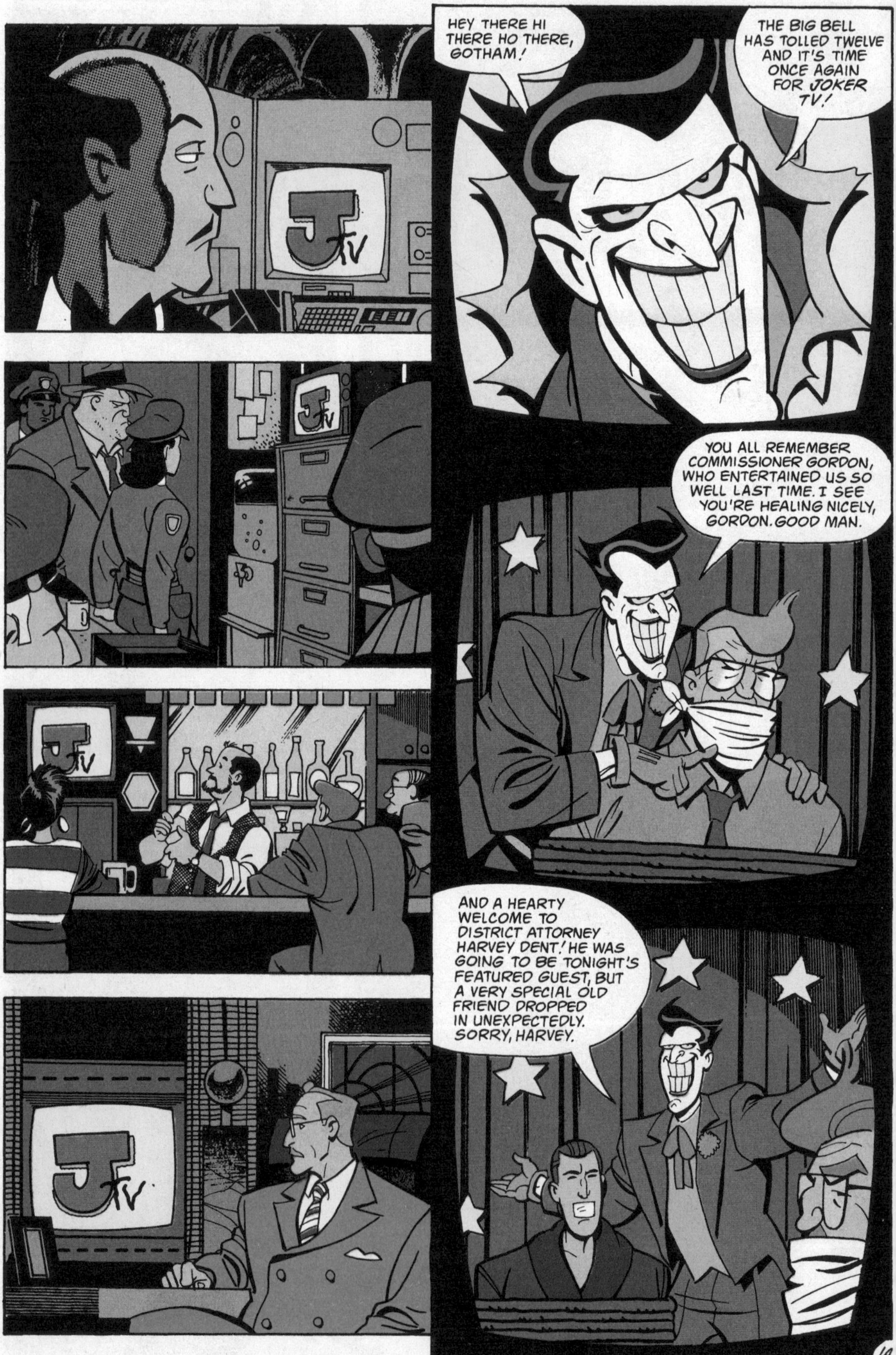
HEY THERE HI THERE HO THERE, GOTHAM!
THE BIG BELL HAS TOLLED TWELVE AND IT'S TIME ONCE AGAIN FOR JOKER TV!
YOU ALL REMEMBER COMMISSIONER GORDON, WHO ENTERTAINED US SO WELL LAST TIME. I SEE YOU'RE HEALING NICELY, GORDON. GOOD MAN.
AND A HEARTY WELCOME TO DISTRICT ATTORNEY HARVEY DENT! HE WAS GOING TO BE TONIGHT'S FEATURED GUEST, BUT A VERY SPECIAL OLD FRIEND DROPPED IN UNEXPECTEDLY. SORRY, HARVEY.
14

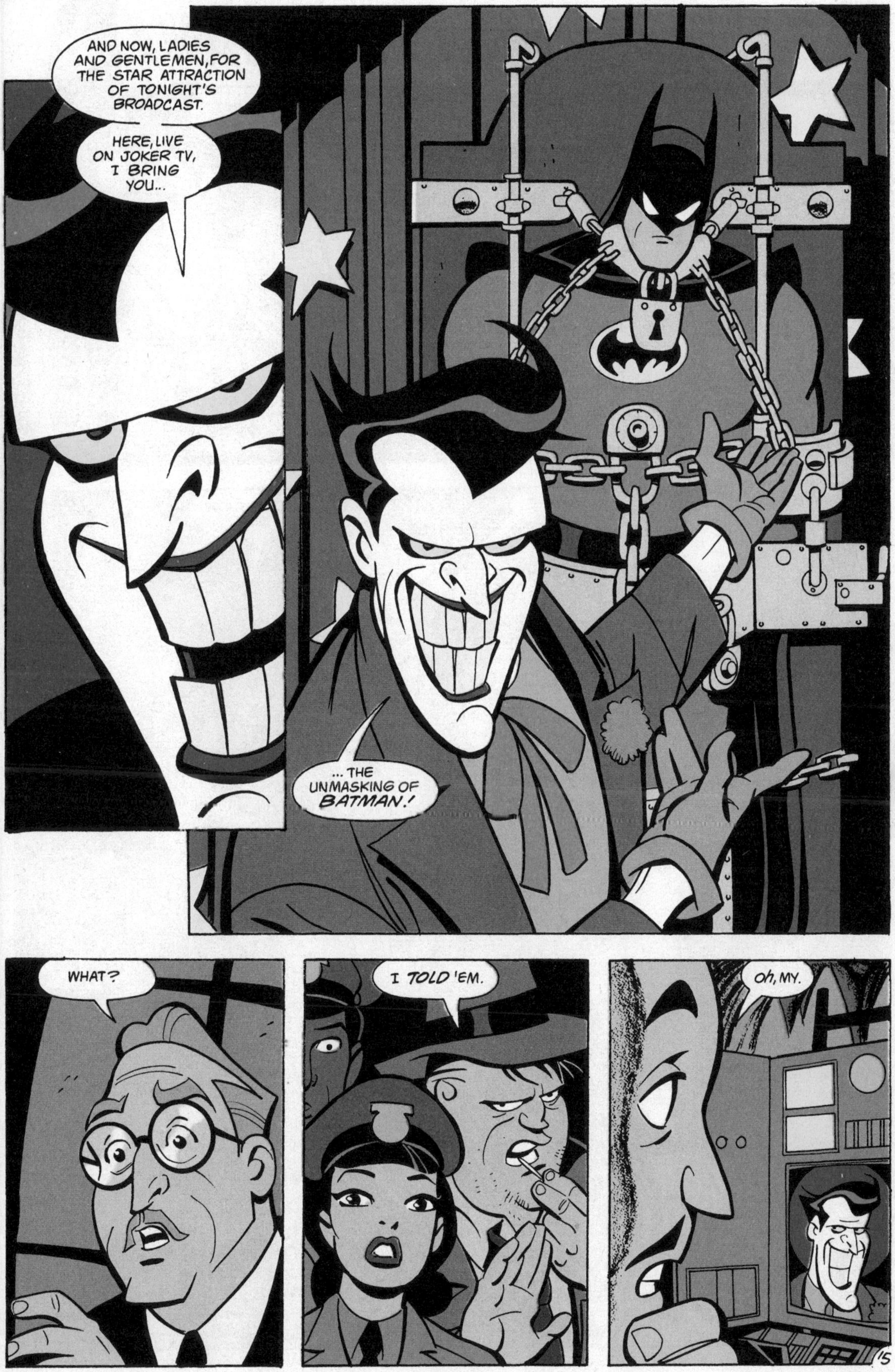
AND NOW, LADIES AND GENTLEMEN, FOR THE STAR ATTRACTION OF TONIGHT'S BROADCAST.
HERE, LIVE ON JOKER TV, I BRING YOU...
... THE UNMASKING OF BATMAN!
WHAT?
I TOLD 'EM.
Oh, MY.
15

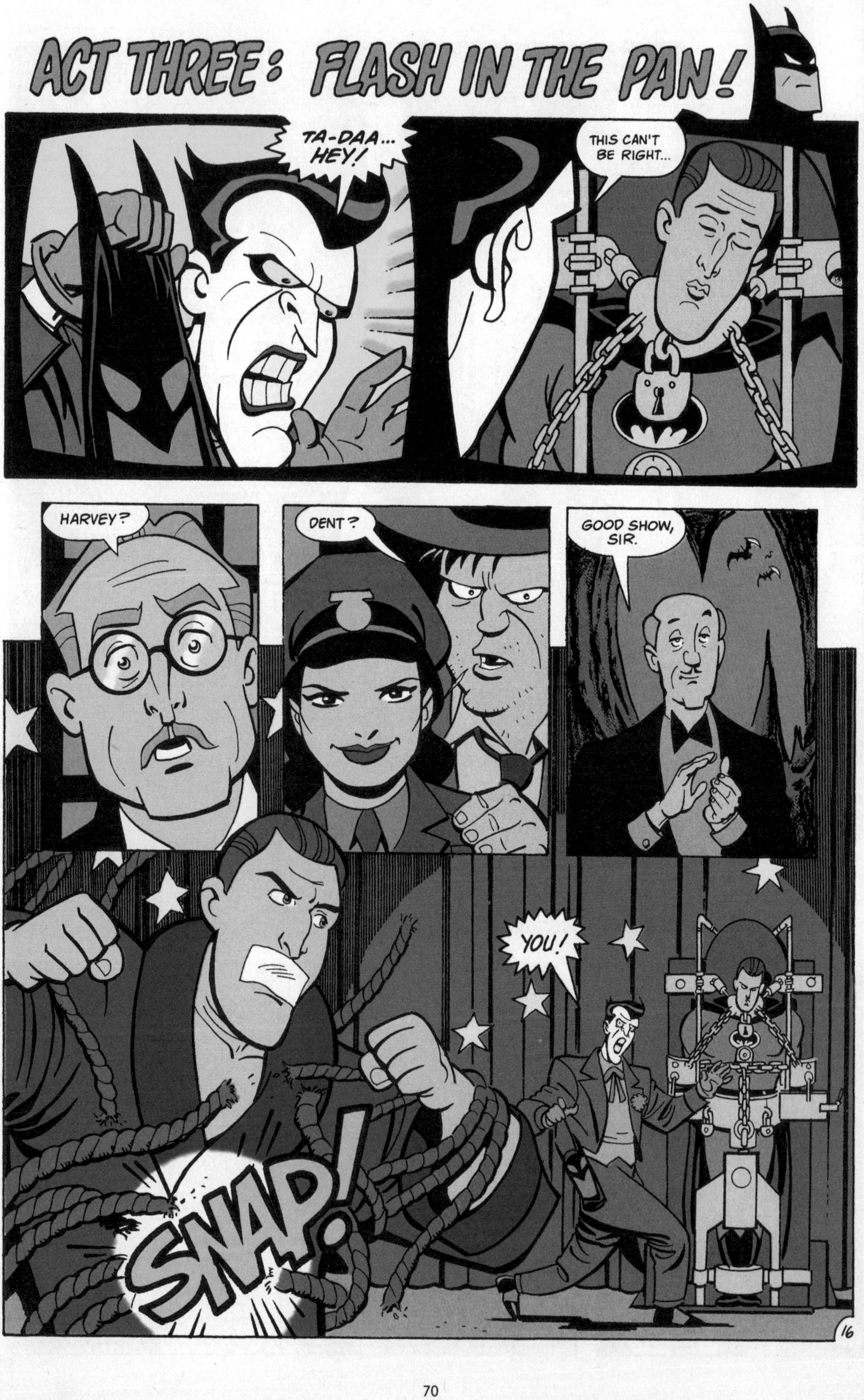
ACT THREE: FLASH IN THE PAN!
TA-DAA... HEY!
THIS CAN'T BE RIGHT...
HARVEY?
DENT?
GOOD SHOW, SIR.
YOU!
SNAP!
16

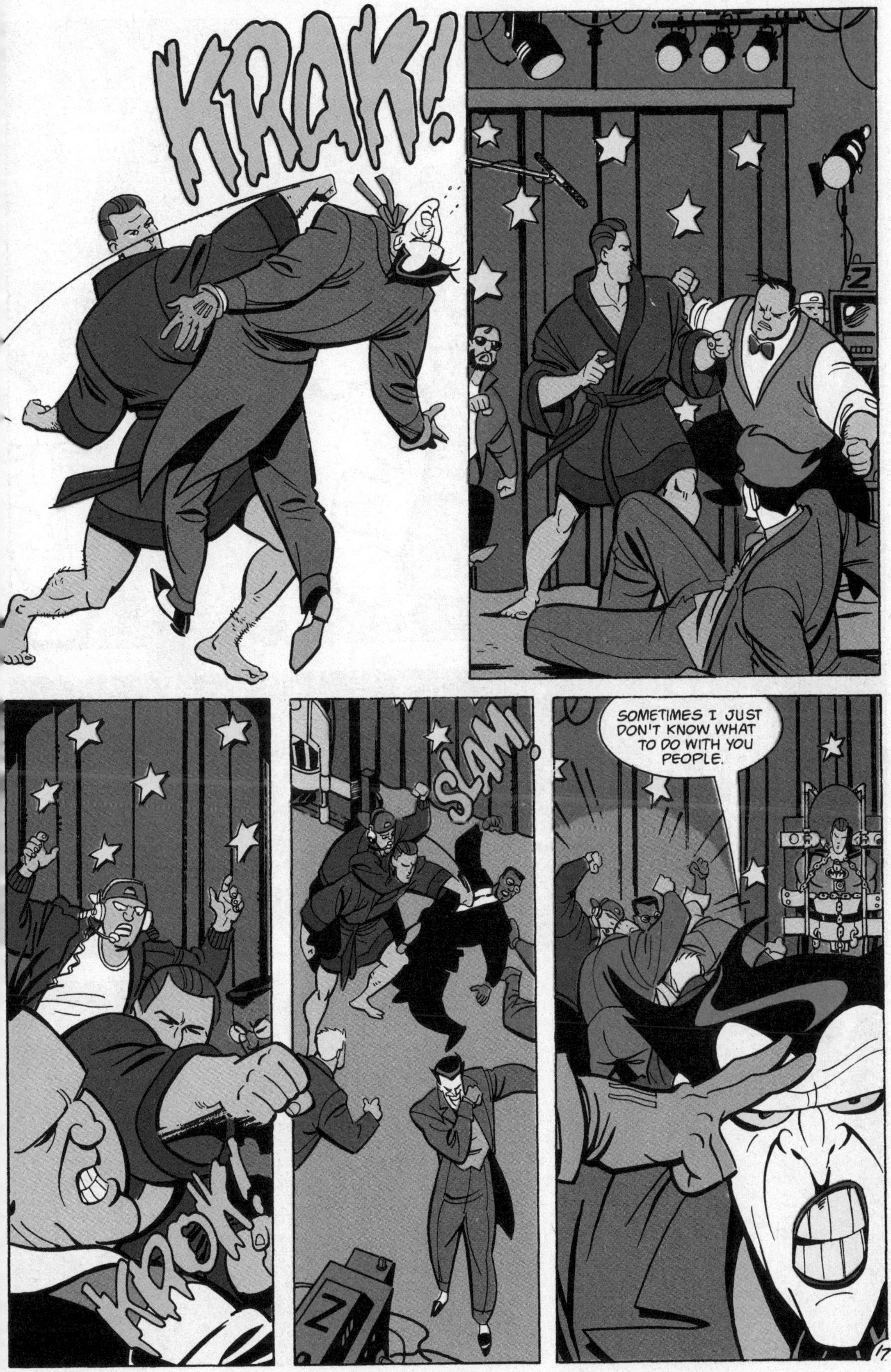
KRAK!
SLAM!
SOMETIMES I JUST DON'T KNOW WHAT TO DO WITH YOU PEOPLE.
17

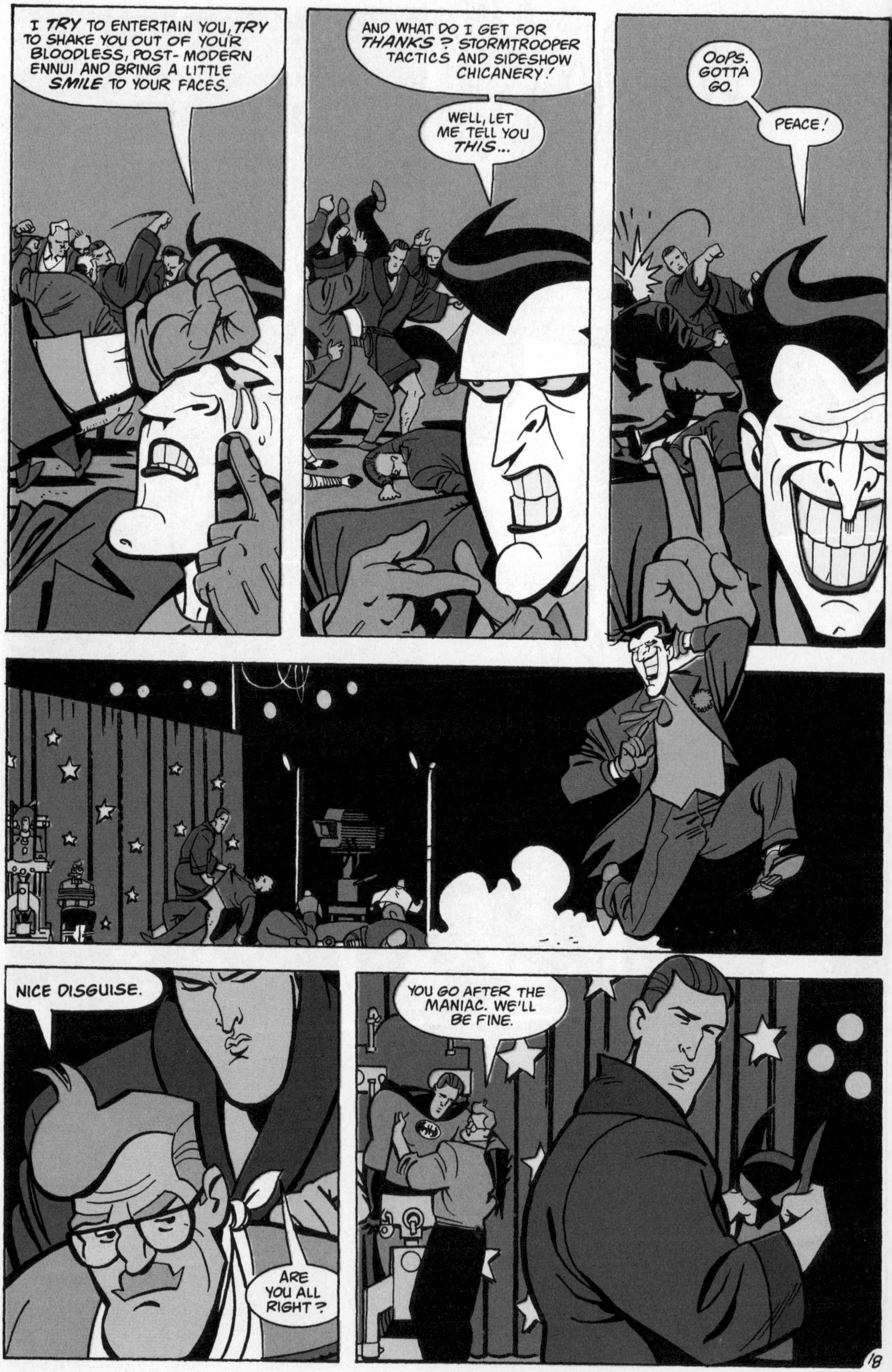
I TRY TO ENTERTAIN YOU, TRY TO SHAKE YOU OUT OF YOUR BLOODLESS, POST-MODERN ENNUI AND BRING A LITTLE SMILE TO YOUR FACES.
AND WHAT DO I GET FOR THANKS? STORMTROOPER TACTICS AND SIDESHOW CHICANERY!
WELL, LET ME TELL YOU THIS...
OOPS. GOTTA GO.
PEACE!
NICE DISGUISE.
ARE YOU ALL RIGHT?
YOU GO AFTER THE MANIAC. WE'LL BE FINE.
18

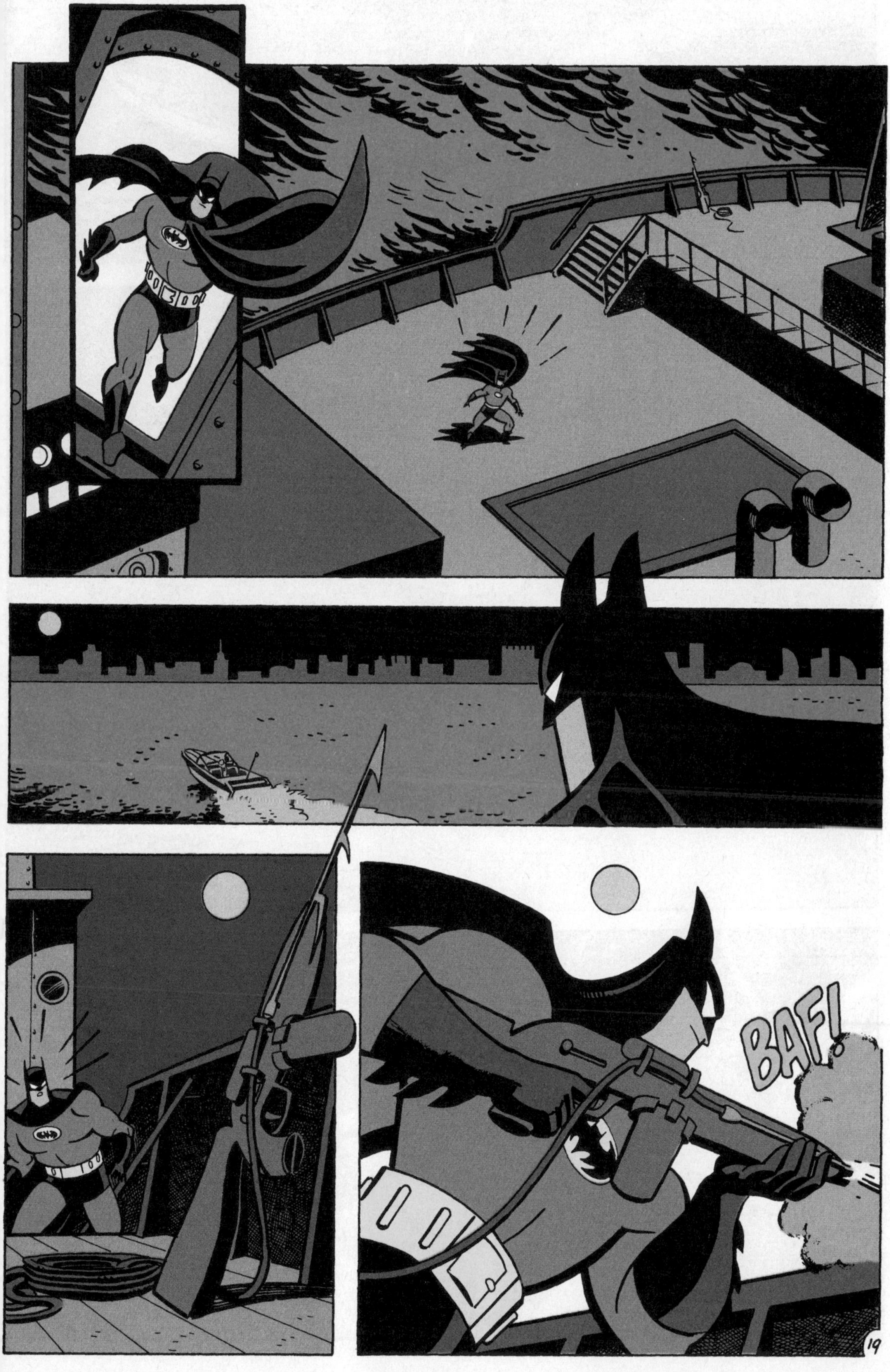
BAF!
19

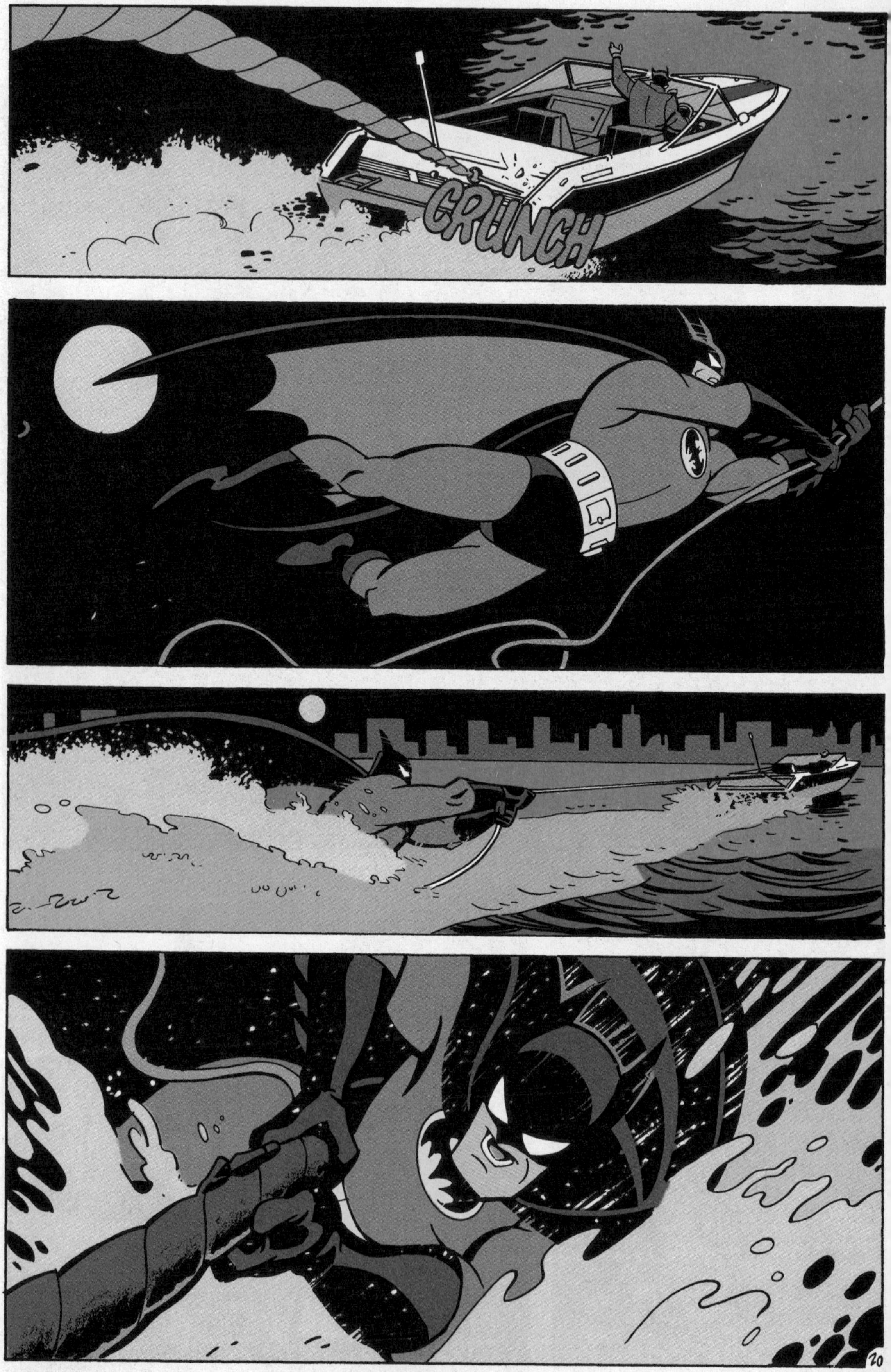
CRUNCH
20

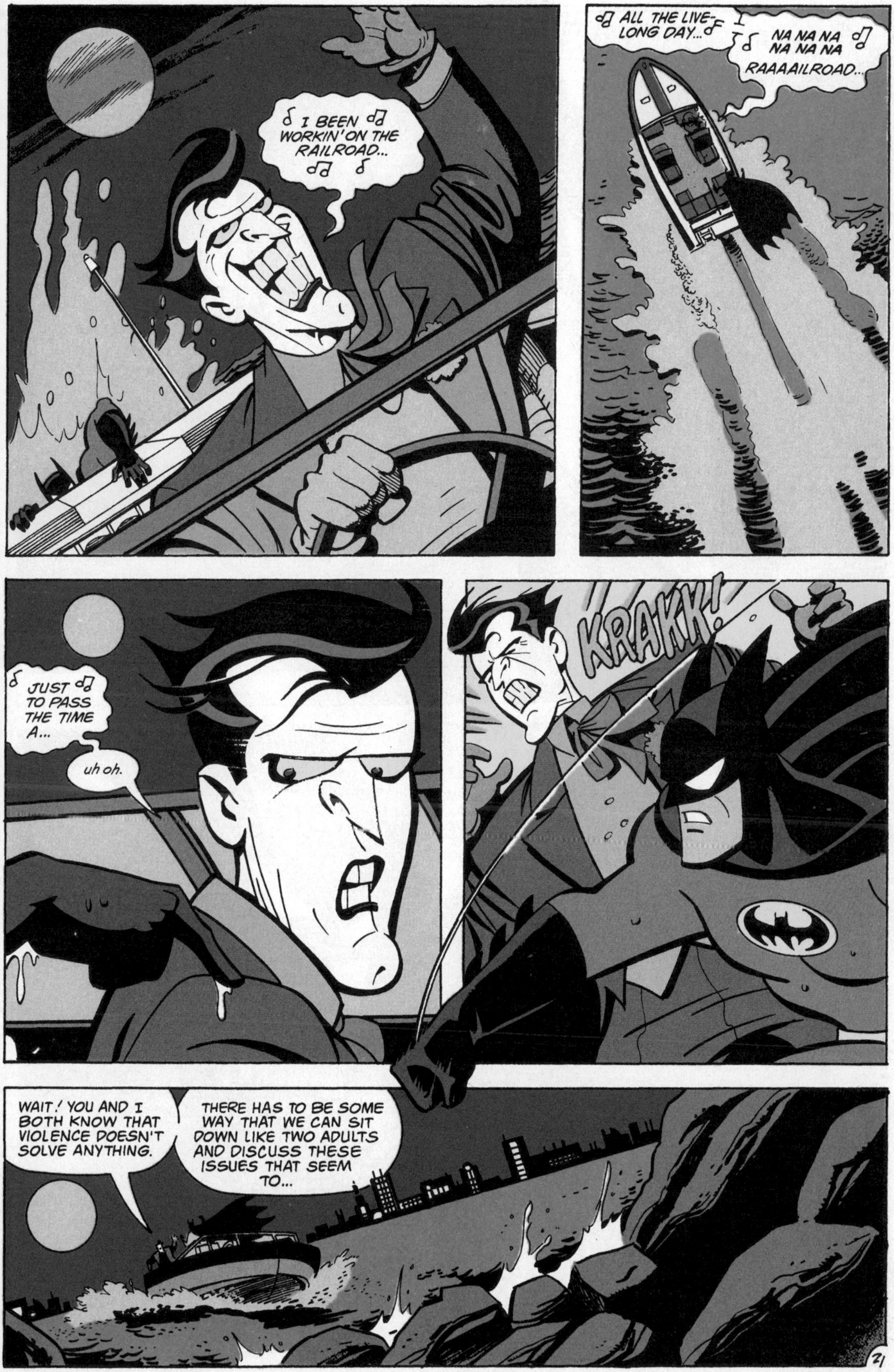
I BEEN WORKIN' ON THE RAILROAD...
ALL THE LIVE-LONG DAY...
NA NA NA NA NA NA RAAAAILROAD...
JUST TO PASS THE TIME A...
uh oh.
KRAKK!
WAIT! YOU AND I BOTH KNOW THAT VIOLENCE DOESN'T SOLVE ANYTHING.
THERE HAS TO BE SOME WAY THAT WE CAN SIT DOWN LIKE TWO ADULTS AND DISCUSS THESE ISSUES THAT SEEM TO...
21

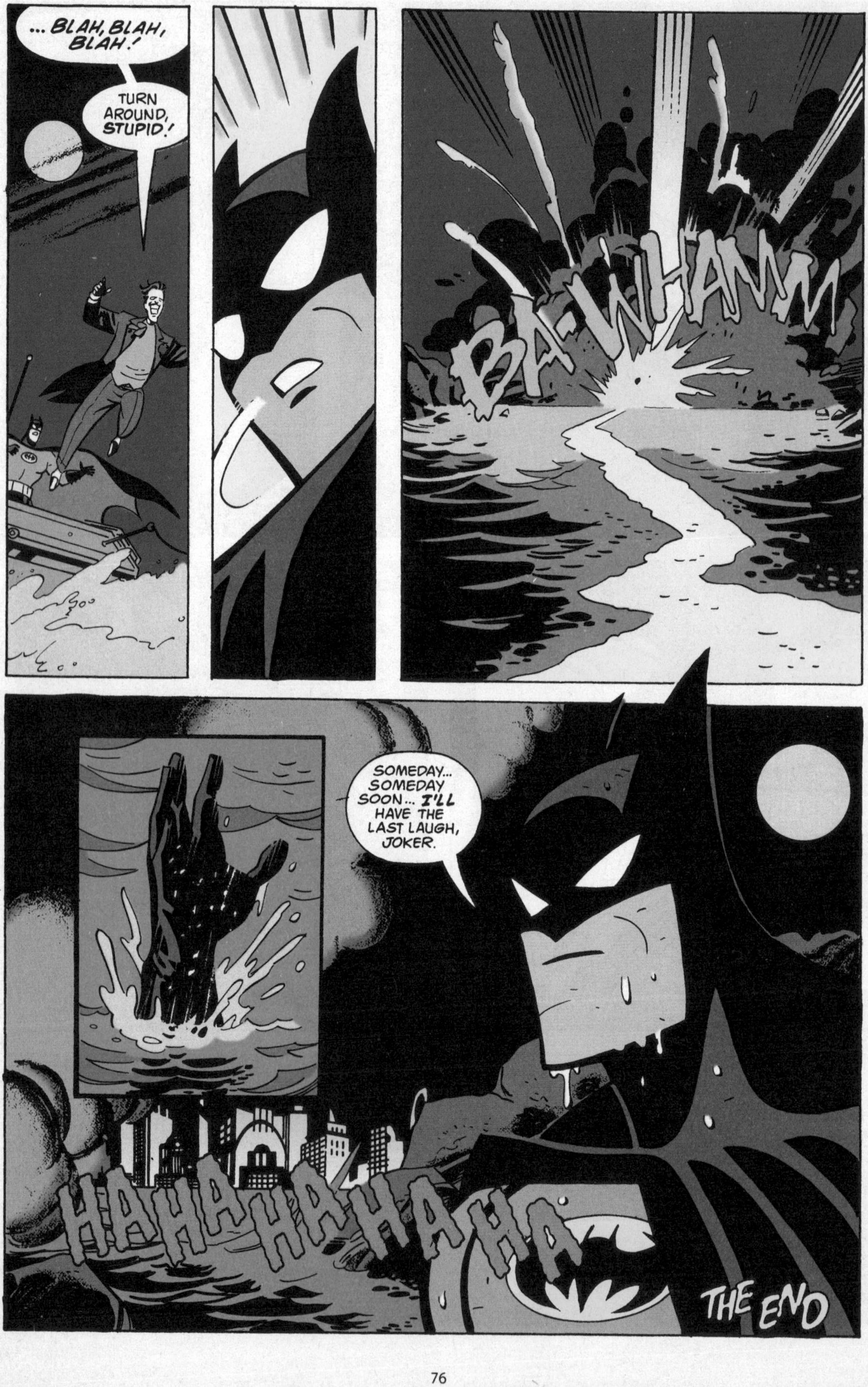
...BLAH, BLAH, BLAH!
TURN AROUND, STUPID!
BA-WHAMM
SOMEDAY... SOMEDAY SOON... I'LL HAVE THE LAST LAUGH, JOKER.
HAHAHAHAHAHA
THE END

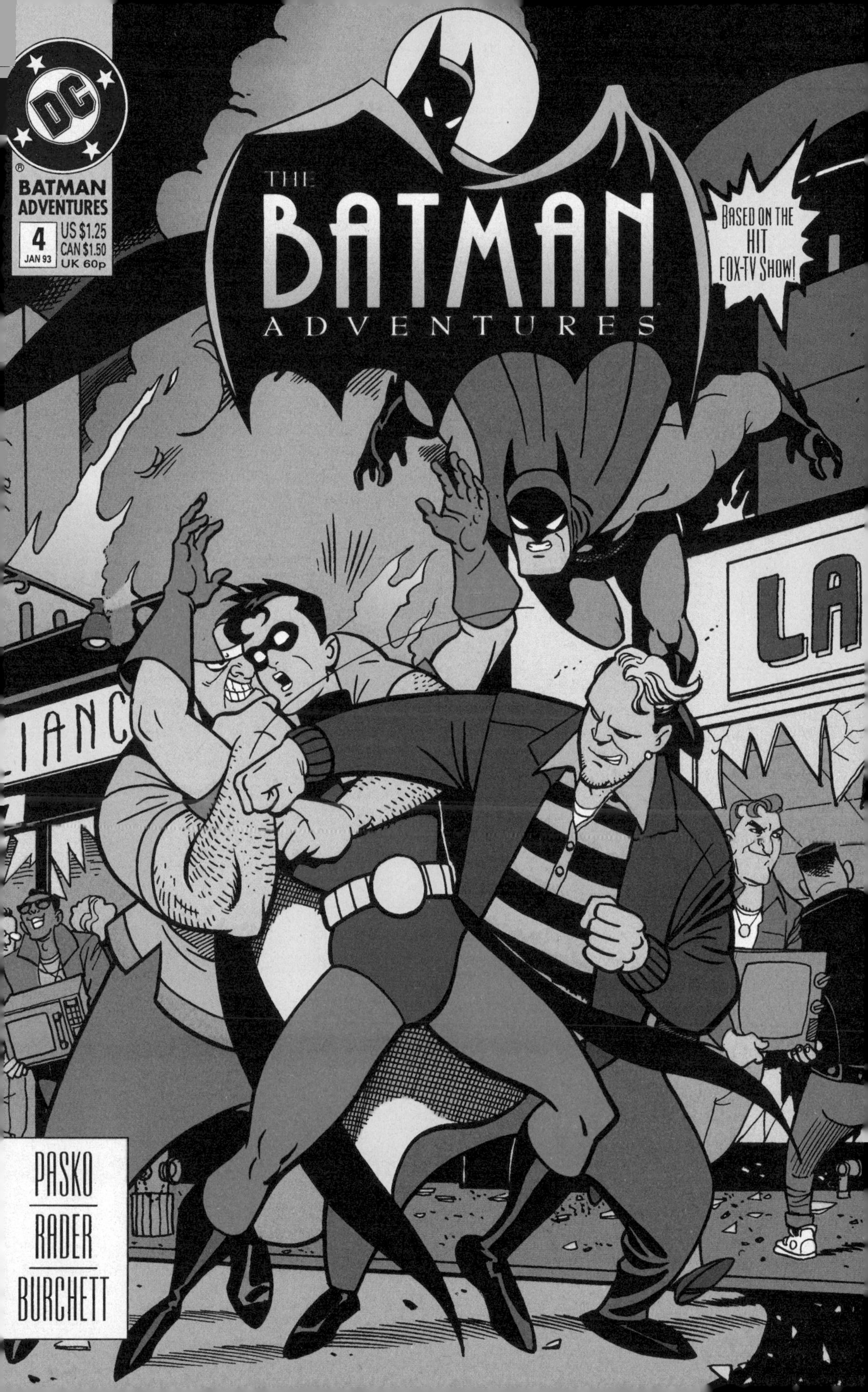
DC
BATMAN ADVENTURES
4
JAN 93
US $1.25
CAN $1.50
UK 60p
THE BATMAN ADVENTURES
BASED ON THE HIT FOX-TV SHOW!
LA
IANC
PASKO
RADER
BURCHETT

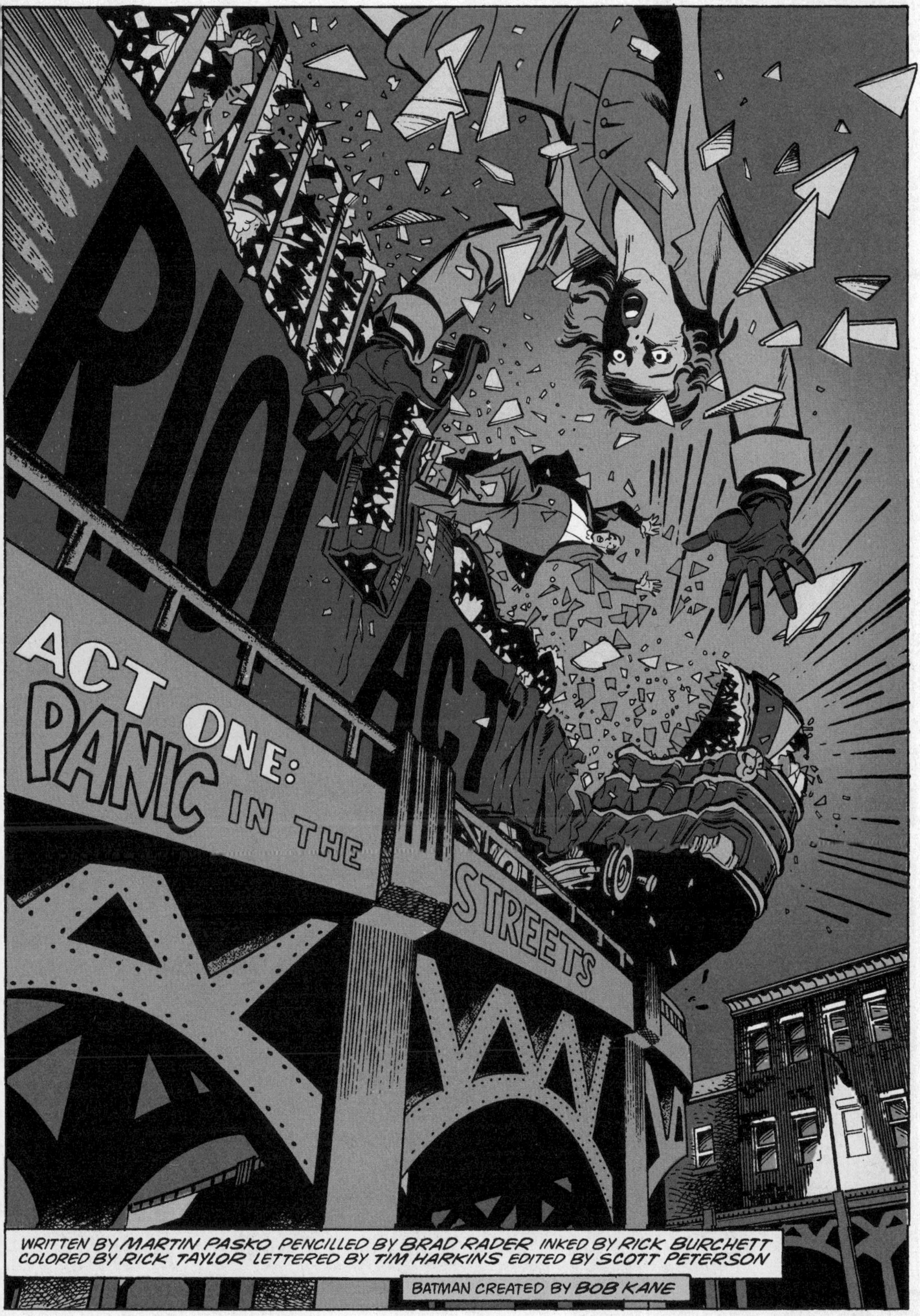
RIOT ACT
ACT ONE:
PANIC IN THE STREETS
WRITTEN BY MARTIN PASKO PENCILLED BY BRAD RADER INKED BY RICK BURCHETT
COLORED BY RICK TAYLOR LETTERED BY TIM HARKINS EDITED BY SCOTT PETERSON
BATMAN CREATED BY BOB KANE

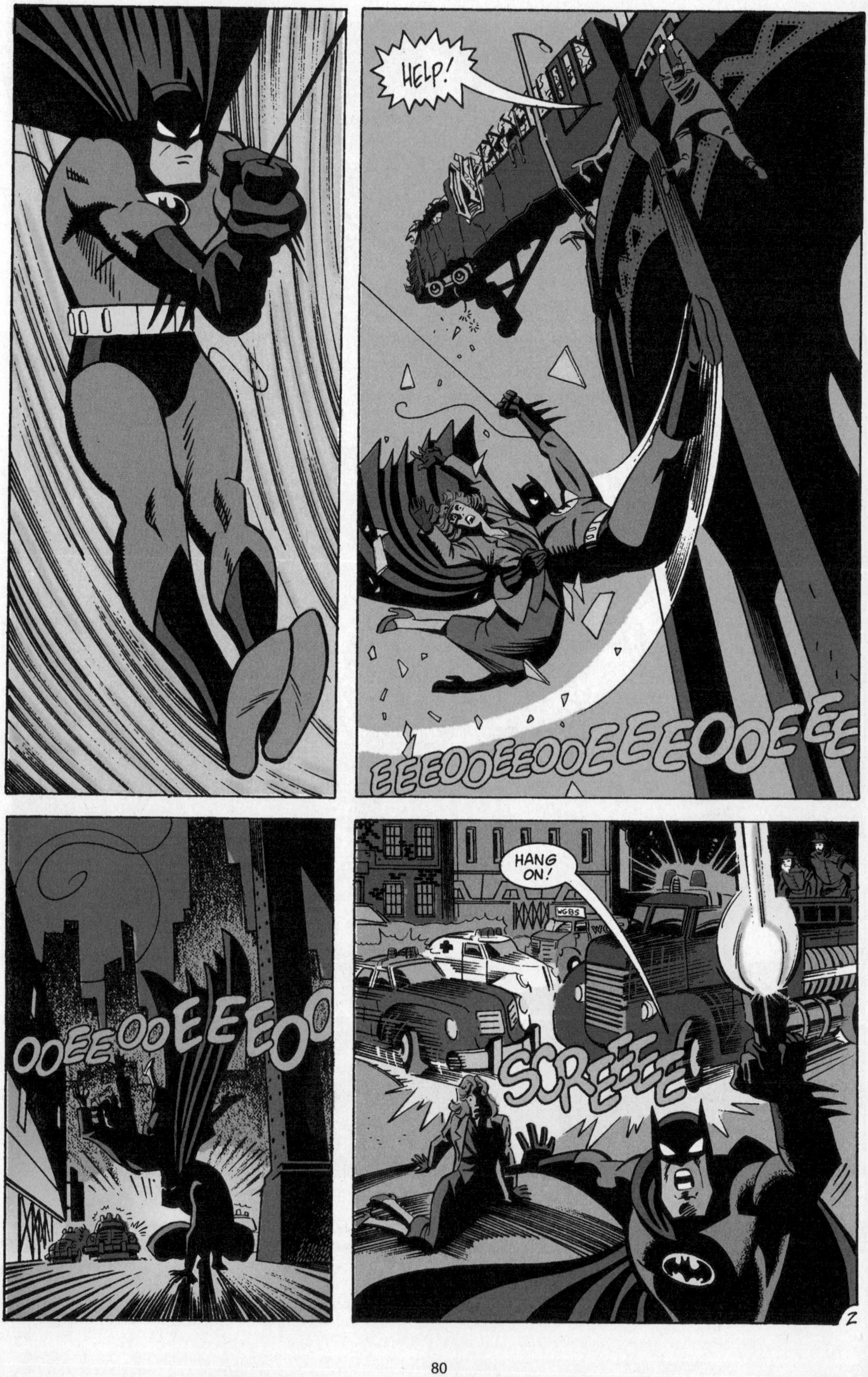
HELP!
EEEOOEEOOEEEEOOEEE
OOEEOOEEEOO
HANG ON!
WGBS
SCREEEEE
2

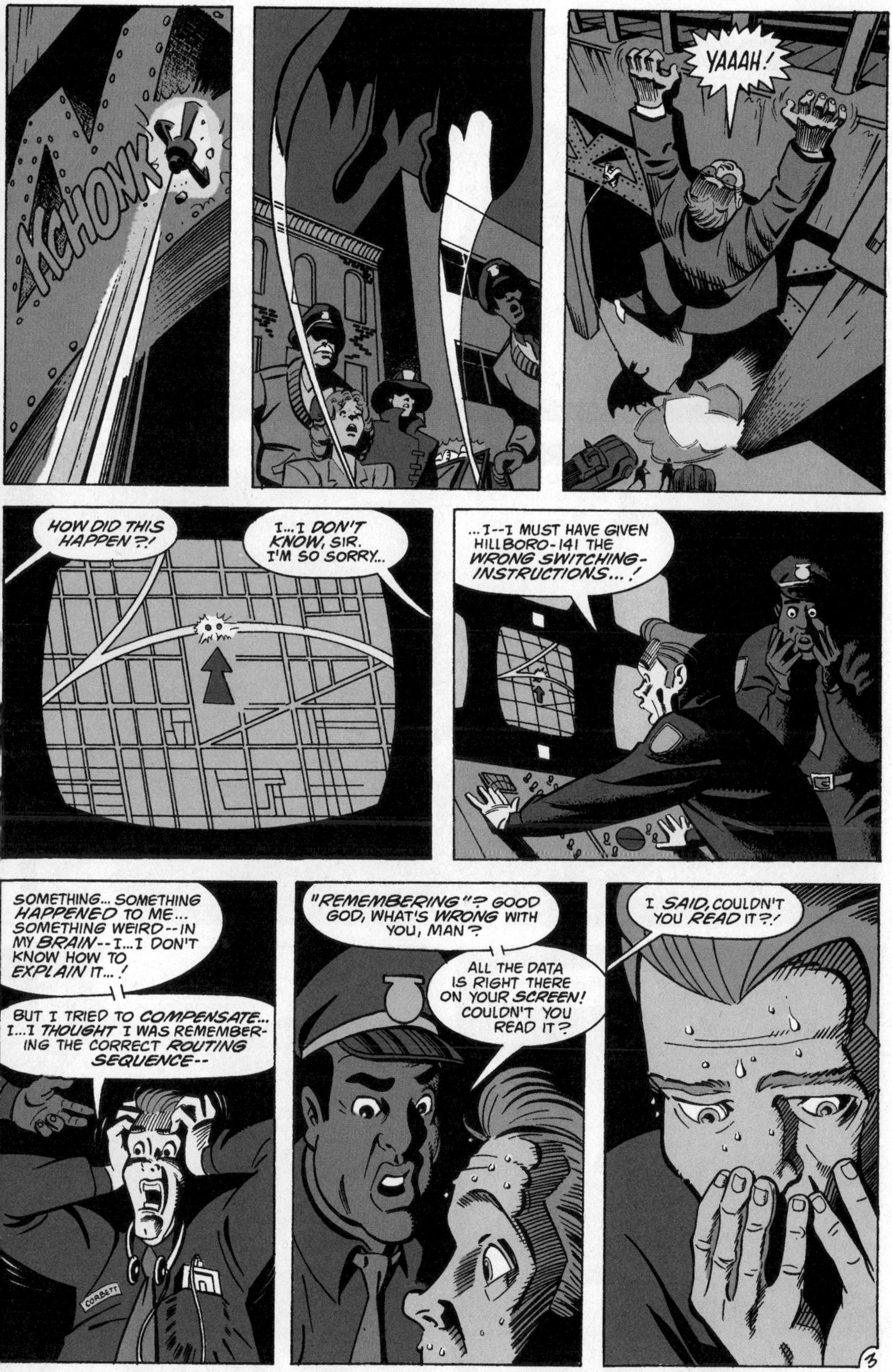
KCHONK
YAAAH!
HOW DID THIS HAPPEN?!
I...I DON'T KNOW, SIR. I'M SO SORRY...
...I--I MUST HAVE GIVEN HILLBORO-141 THE WRONG SWITCHING-INSTRUCTIONS...!
SOMETHING... SOMETHING HAPPENED TO ME... SOMETHING WEIRD--IN MY BRAIN--I...I DON'T KNOW HOW TO EXPLAIN IT...!
BUT I TRIED TO COMPENSATE... I...I THOUGHT I WAS REMEMBERING THE CORRECT ROUTING SEQUENCE--
CORBETT
"REMEMBERING"? GOOD GOD, WHAT'S WRONG WITH YOU, MAN?
ALL THE DATA IS RIGHT THERE ON YOUR SCREEN! COULDN'T YOU READ IT?
I SAID, COULDN'T YOU READ IT?!
3

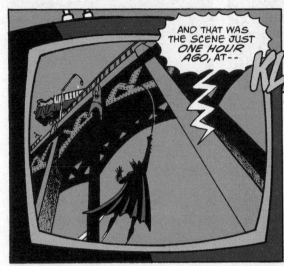

AND THAT WAS THE SCENE JUST *ONE HOUR AGO*, AT--

KLIK

MARIO...THIS FRIEND OF YOURS -- THIS MISTER...

CORBETT, PROFESSOR. BARNEY CORBETT.

WHATEVER. YOU *DID* GIVE THIS CORBETT FELLOW THE *GIFT*, DIDN'T YOU?

YESSIR.

AND YOU'RE *SURE* HE TOOK IT TO WORK WITH HIM?

YES, PROFESSOR.

THEN WE CAN ASSUME IT'S *SAFE* TO CALL OUR TEST OF THE *DYSLEXUS DEVICE* A *SUCCESS.*

IN THAT CASE... SET *PHASE ONE* OF OUR PLAN IN MOTION *IMMEDIATELY.*

4

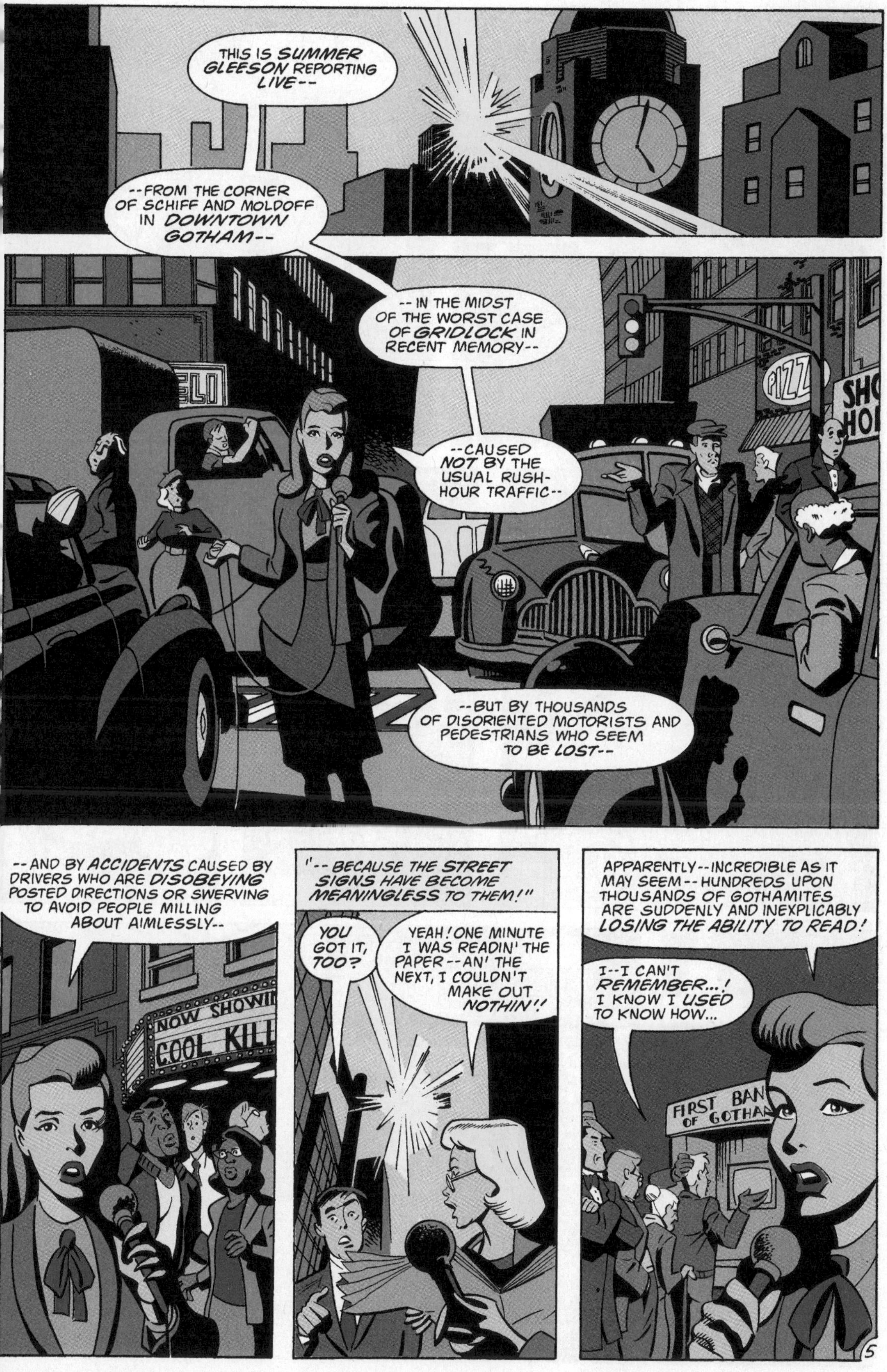
THIS IS SUMMER GLEESON REPORTING LIVE--
--FROM THE CORNER OF SCHIFF AND MOLDOFF IN DOWNTOWN GOTHAM--
--IN THE MIDST OF THE WORST CASE OF GRIDLOCK IN RECENT MEMORY--
ELI
PIZZ
SHO HOI
--CAUSED NOT BY THE USUAL RUSH-HOUR TRAFFIC--
--BUT BY THOUSANDS OF DISORIENTED MOTORISTS AND PEDESTRIANS WHO SEEM TO BE LOST--
--AND BY ACCIDENTS CAUSED BY DRIVERS WHO ARE DISOBEYING POSTED DIRECTIONS OR SWERVING TO AVOID PEOPLE MILLING ABOUT AIMLESSLY--
NOW SHOWI
COOL KIL
"--BECAUSE THE STREET SIGNS HAVE BECOME MEANINGLESS TO THEM!"
YOU GOT IT, TOO?
YEAH! ONE MINUTE I WAS READIN' THE PAPER--AN' THE NEXT, I COULDN'T MAKE OUT NOTHIN'!
APPARENTLY--INCREDIBLE AS IT MAY SEEM--HUNDREDS UPON THOUSANDS OF GOTHAMITES ARE SUDDENLY AND INEXPLICABLY LOSING THE ABILITY TO READ!
I--I CAN'T REMEMBER...! I KNOW I USED TO KNOW HOW...
FIRST BAN OF GOTHA
5

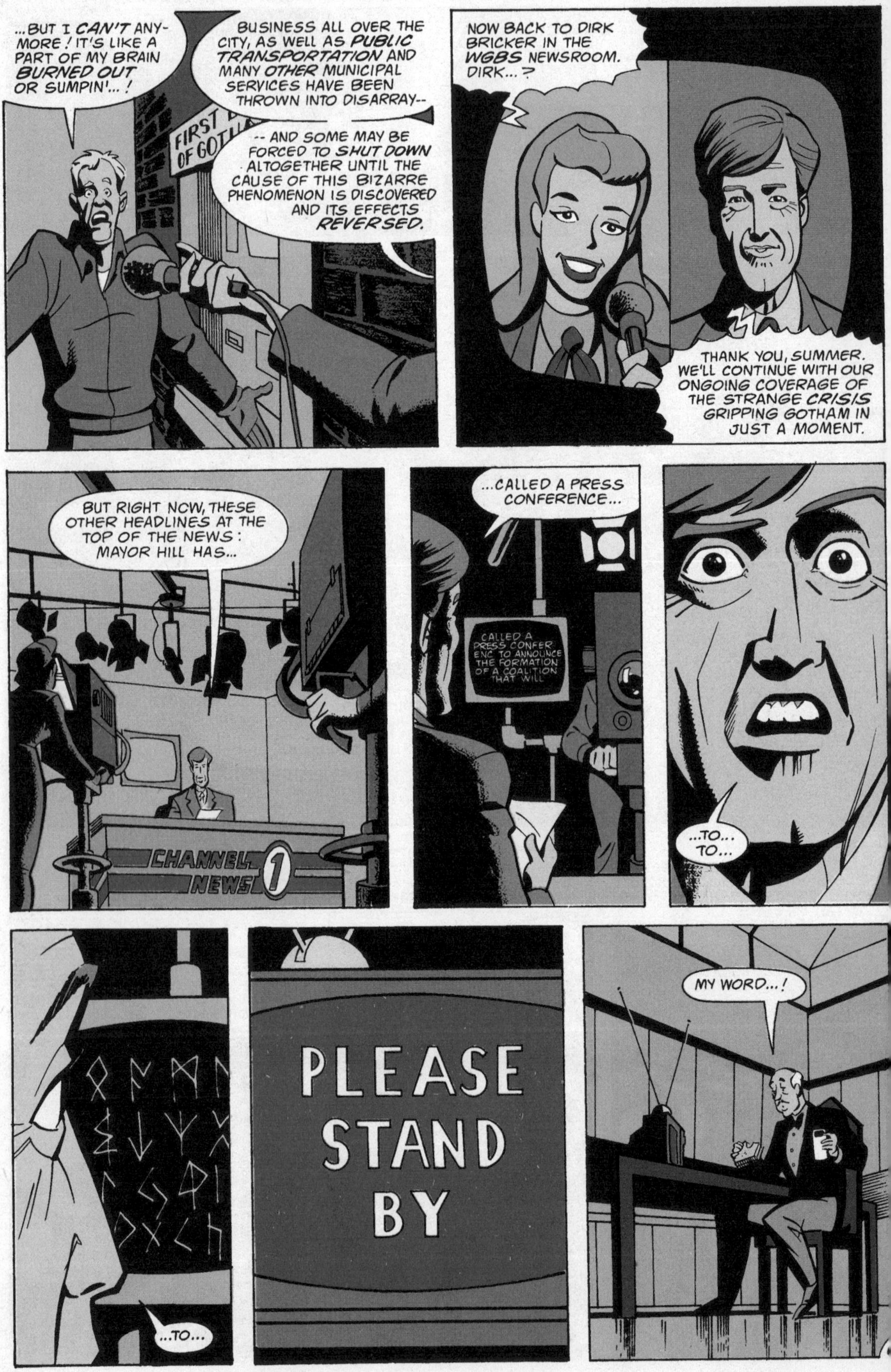
...BUT I CAN'T ANY-MORE! IT'S LIKE A PART OF MY BRAIN BURNED OUT OR SUMPIN'...!
BUSINESS ALL OVER THE CITY, AS WELL AS PUBLIC TRANSPORTATION AND MANY OTHER MUNICIPAL SERVICES HAVE BEEN THROWN INTO DISARRAY--
FIRST
OF GOTH
-- AND SOME MAY BE FORCED TO SHUT DOWN ALTOGETHER UNTIL THE CAUSE OF THIS BIZARRE PHENOMENON IS DISCOVERED AND ITS EFFECTS REVERSED.
NOW BACK TO DIRK BRICKER IN THE WGBS NEWSROOM. DIRK...?
THANK YOU, SUMMER. WE'LL CONTINUE WITH OUR ONGOING COVERAGE OF THE STRANGE CRISIS GRIPPING GOTHAM IN JUST A MOMENT.
BUT RIGHT NOW, THESE OTHER HEADLINES AT THE TOP OF THE NEWS: MAYOR HILL HAS...
CHANNEL NEWS 1
...CALLED A PRESS CONFERENCE...
CALLED A PRESS CONFER ENC TO ANNOUNCE THE FORMATION OF A COALITION THAT WILL
...TO... TO...
...TO...
PLEASE STAND BY
MY WORD...!

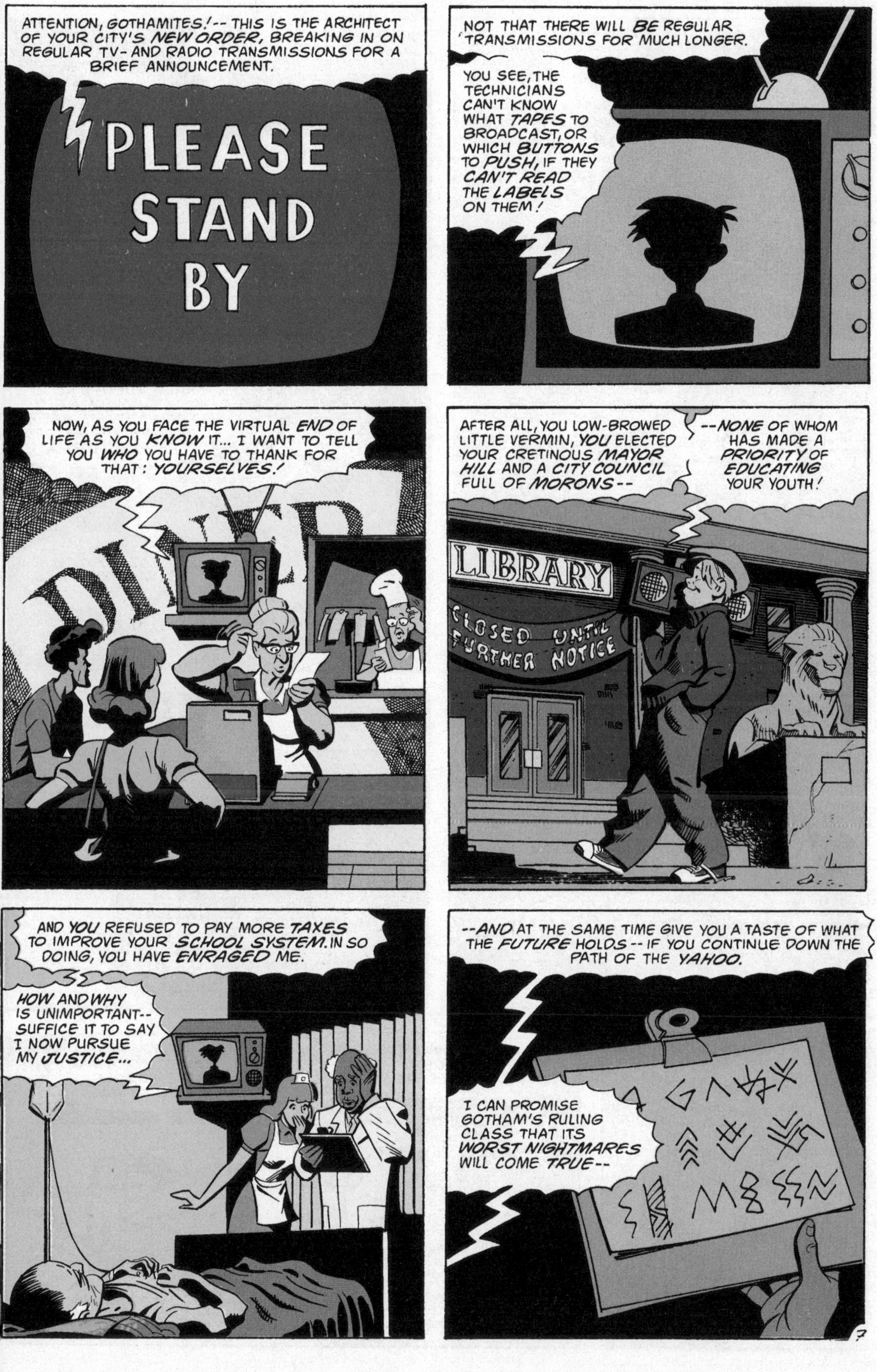
ATTENTION, GOTHAMITES!-- THIS IS THE ARCHITECT OF YOUR CITY'S NEW ORDER, BREAKING IN ON REGULAR TV- AND RADIO TRANSMISSIONS FOR A BRIEF ANNOUNCEMENT.
PLEASE STAND BY
NOT THAT THERE WILL BE REGULAR TRANSMISSIONS FOR MUCH LONGER.
YOU SEE, THE TECHNICIANS CAN'T KNOW WHAT TAPES TO BROADCAST, OR WHICH BUTTONS TO PUSH, IF THEY CAN'T READ THE LABELS ON THEM!
NOW, AS YOU FACE THE VIRTUAL END OF LIFE AS YOU KNOW IT... I WANT TO TELL YOU WHO YOU HAVE TO THANK FOR THAT: YOURSELVES!
AFTER ALL, YOU LOW-BROWED LITTLE VERMIN, YOU ELECTED YOUR CRETINOUS MAYOR HILL AND A CITY COUNCIL FULL OF MORONS--
--NONE OF WHOM HAS MADE A PRIORITY OF EDUCATING YOUR YOUTH!
LIBRARY
CLOSED UNTIL FURTHER NOTICE
AND YOU REFUSED TO PAY MORE TAXES TO IMPROVE YOUR SCHOOL SYSTEM. IN SO DOING, YOU HAVE ENRAGED ME.
HOW AND WHY IS UNIMPORTANT-- SUFFICE IT TO SAY I NOW PURSUE MY JUSTICE...
--AND AT THE SAME TIME GIVE YOU A TASTE OF WHAT THE FUTURE HOLDS-- IF YOU CONTINUE DOWN THE PATH OF THE YAHOO.
I CAN PROMISE GOTHAM'S RULING CLASS THAT ITS WORST NIGHTMARES WILL COME TRUE--
7

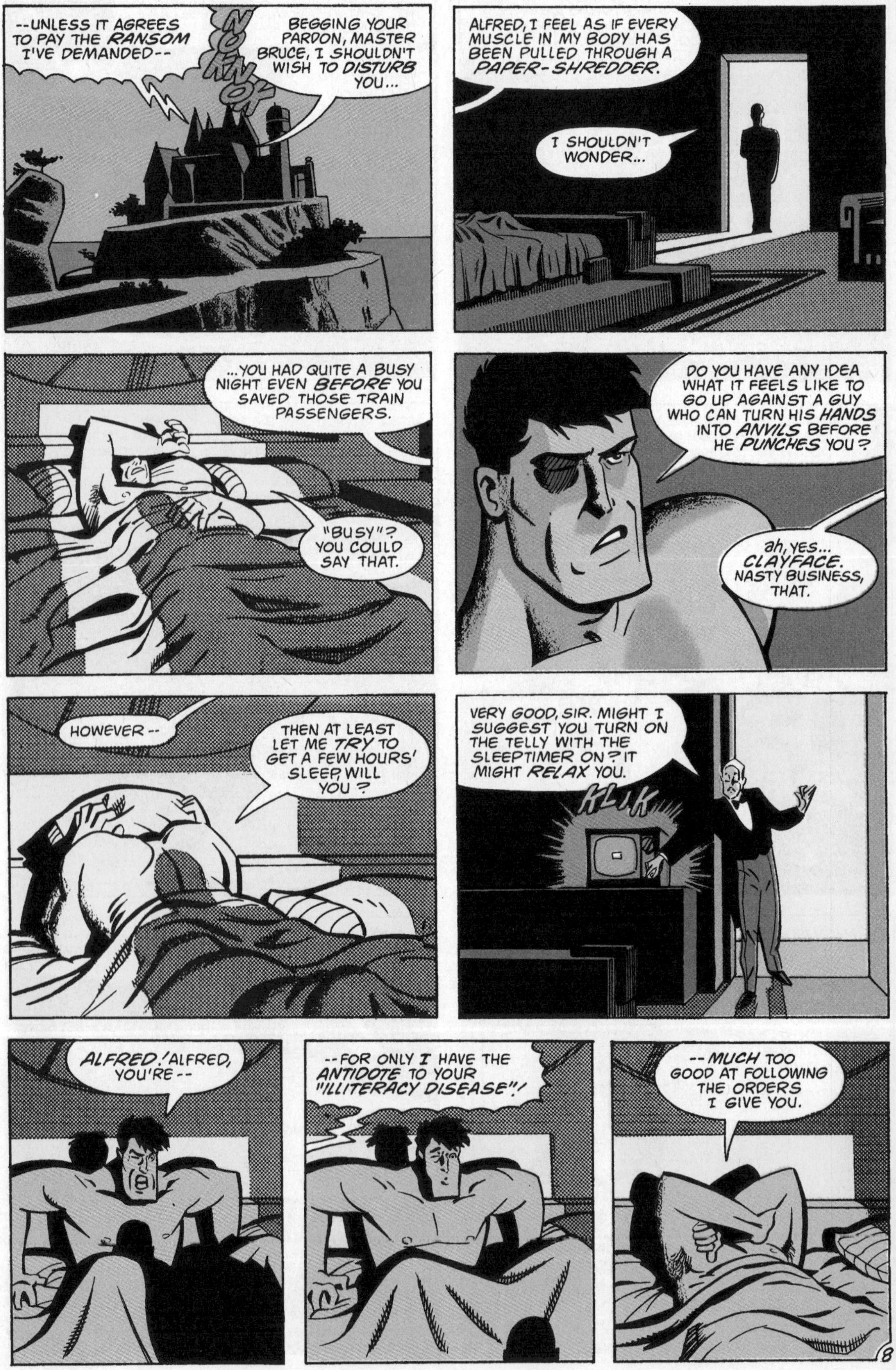
--UNLESS IT AGREES TO PAY THE RANSOM I'VE DEMANDED--
NOK NOK
BEGGING YOUR PARDON, MASTER BRUCE, I SHOULDN'T WISH TO DISTURB YOU...
ALFRED, I FEEL AS IF EVERY MUSCLE IN MY BODY HAS BEEN PULLED THROUGH A PAPER-SHREDDER.
I SHOULDN'T WONDER...
...YOU HAD QUITE A BUSY NIGHT EVEN BEFORE YOU SAVED THOSE TRAIN PASSENGERS.
"BUSY"? YOU COULD SAY THAT.
DO YOU HAVE ANY IDEA WHAT IT FEELS LIKE TO GO UP AGAINST A GUY WHO CAN TURN HIS HANDS INTO ANVILS BEFORE HE PUNCHES YOU?
ah, YES... CLAYFACE. NASTY BUSINESS, THAT.
HOWEVER--
THEN AT LEAST LET ME TRY TO GET A FEW HOURS' SLEEP, WILL YOU?
VERY GOOD, SIR. MIGHT I SUGGEST YOU TURN ON THE TELLY WITH THE SLEEPTIMER ON? IT MIGHT RELAX YOU.
KLIK
ALFRED! ALFRED, YOU'RE--
--FOR ONLY I HAVE THE ANTIDOTE TO YOUR "ILLITERACY DISEASE"!
--MUCH TOO GOOD AT FOLLOWING THE ORDERS I GIVE YOU.
8

"I'VE ALREADY DELIVERED MY INSTRUCTIONS TO YOUR MAYOR HILL--ON AUDIO CASSETTE, OF COURSE...

ARE THE EFFECTS PERMANENT?

YES.

REEEEEEEE KLIK

THE DAMAGE THIS THING'LL DO IS INCALCULABLE.

WHOK WHOK

TELL ME ABOUT IT! I'VE GOT EVERY AVAILABLE MAN ON THE STREET, HAMILTON--AND NOT ONLY MY RESOURCES--

--BUT ALSO THE FIRE DEPARTMENT'S ARE BEING STRETCHED TO THE LIMIT JUST COPING WITH ALL THE ACCIDENTS!

THE MINUTE THE CRIMINAL ELEMENT SEES THAT THE FORCE IS VULNERABLE, IT'LL BE A FREE-FOR-ALL OUT THERE!

WHOKWHOKWHOK

I AGREE. THE AMOUNT THIS GUY'S ASKING FOR IS NOTHING COMPARED TO THE COST OF POTENTIAL DAMAGE--

--OR OF TRYING TO REEDUCATE OUR KEY PERSONNEL... AND THE EXTORTIONIST KNOWS IT.

REEEEEEEE

DO YOU HAVE TO DO THAT NOW?

REEEEEE

SORREE, MISTA MAYOR... ALL I KNOW'S I GOT A WORK ORDER TO FIX THIS THING. BUT DON'T SWEAT IT-- I'M DONE.

AS I WAS SAYING, GENTLEMEN... I'M RECOMMENDING THAT SOMEHOW WE FIND THE MONEY TO PAY THE RANSOM...

...BEFORE MASS HYSTERIA AND RIOTING REDUCE OUR CITY TO RUBBLE!

9

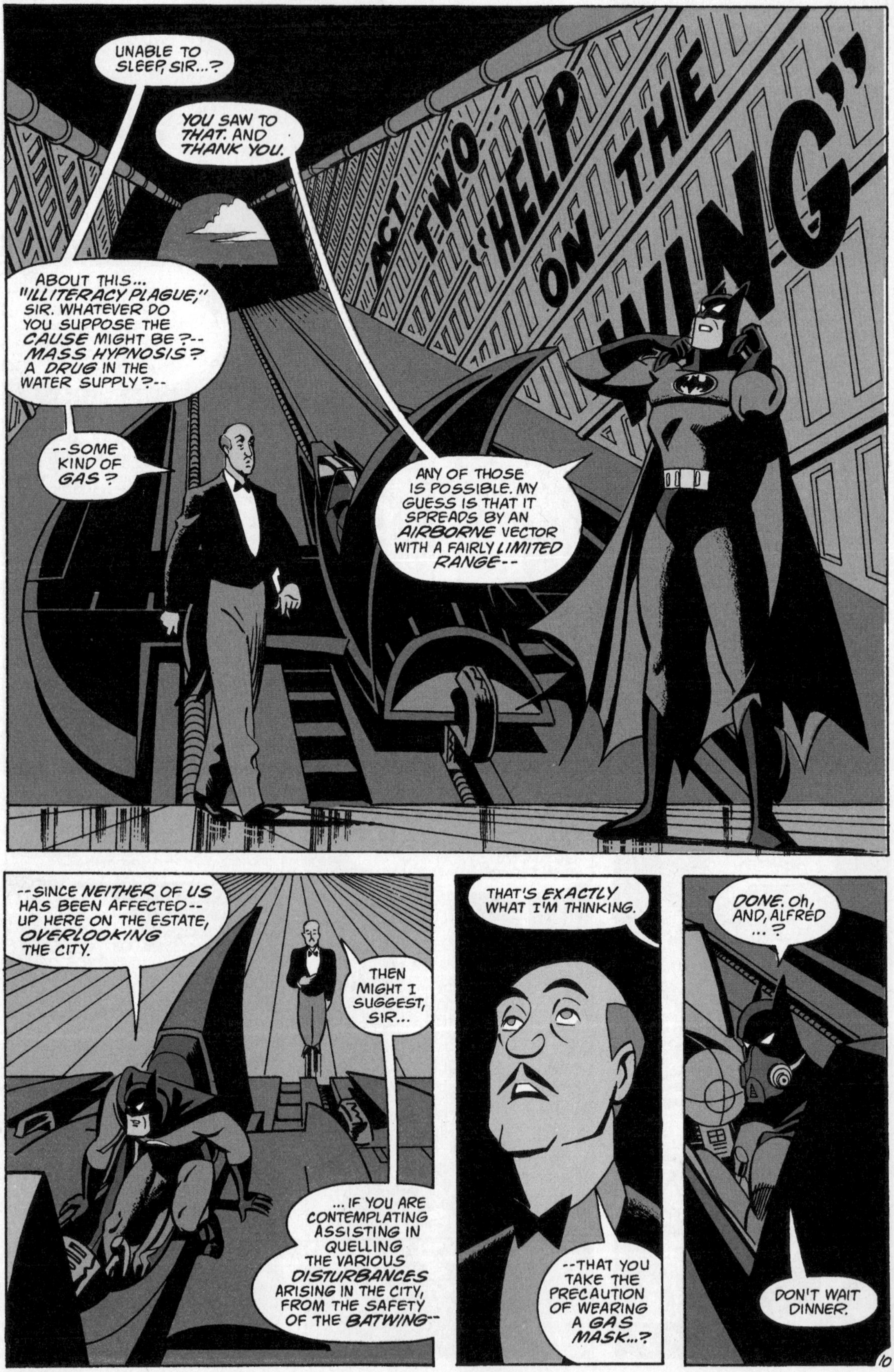
UNABLE TO SLEEP, SIR...?
YOU SAW TO THAT. AND THANK YOU.
ACT TWO "HELP ON THE WING"
ABOUT THIS... "ILLITERACY PLAGUE," SIR. WHATEVER DO YOU SUPPOSE THE CAUSE MIGHT BE?-- MASS HYPNOSIS? A DRUG IN THE WATER SUPPLY?--
--SOME KIND OF GAS?
ANY OF THOSE IS POSSIBLE. MY GUESS IS THAT IT SPREADS BY AN AIRBORNE VECTOR WITH A FAIRLY LIMITED RANGE--
--SINCE NEITHER OF US HAS BEEN AFFECTED-- UP HERE ON THE ESTATE, OVERLOOKING THE CITY.
THEN MIGHT I SUGGEST, SIR...
...IF YOU ARE CONTEMPLATING ASSISTING IN QUELLING THE VARIOUS DISTURBANCES ARISING IN THE CITY, FROM THE SAFETY OF THE BATWING--
THAT'S EXACTLY WHAT I'M THINKING.
--THAT YOU TAKE THE PRECAUTION OF WEARING A GAS MASK...?
DONE. Oh, AND, ALFRED ...?
DON'T WAIT DINNER.
10

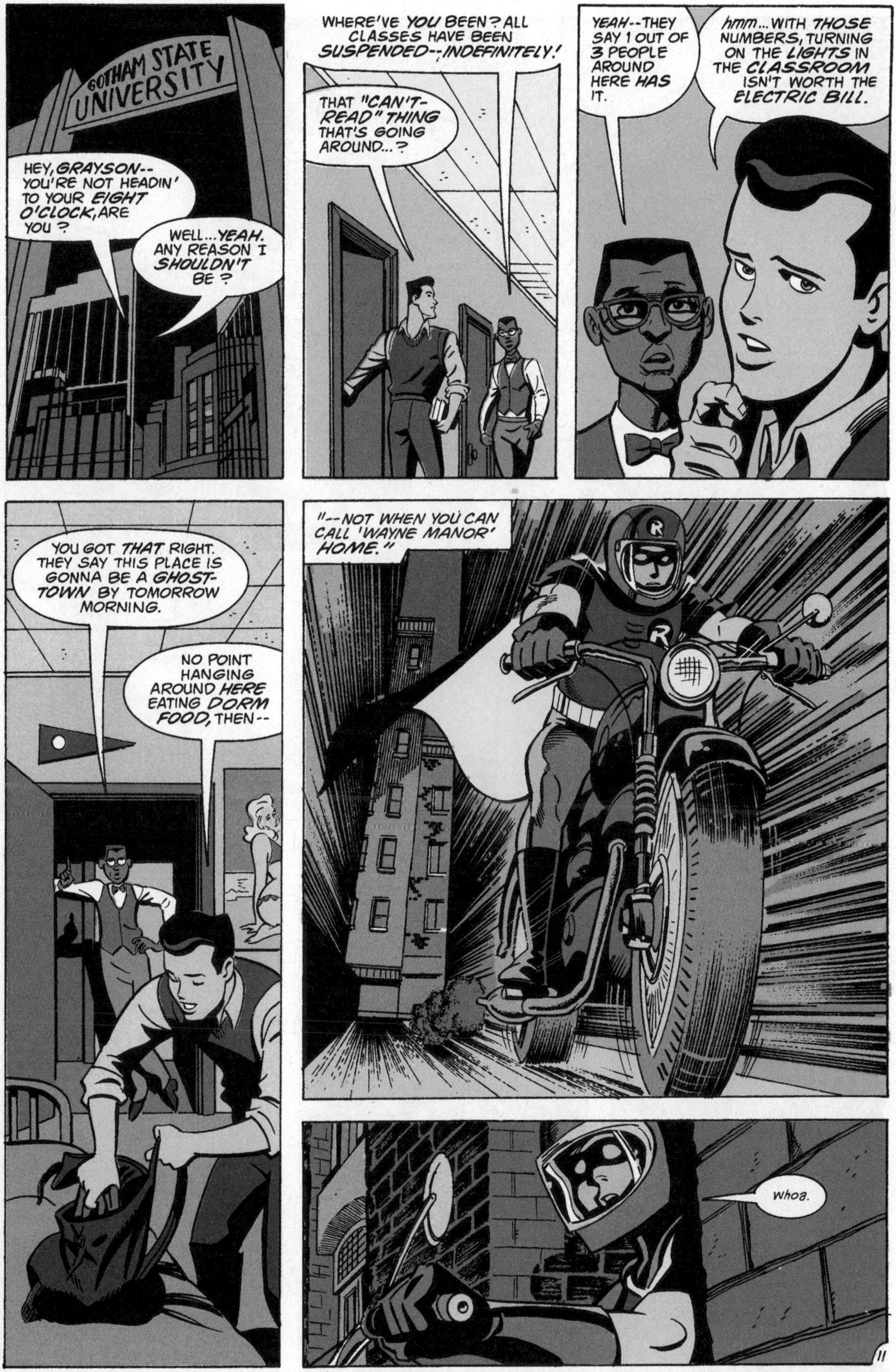
GOTHAM STATE UNIVERSITY
HEY, GRAYSON-- YOU'RE NOT HEADIN' TO YOUR EIGHT O'CLOCK, ARE YOU?
WELL... YEAH. ANY REASON I SHOULDN'T BE?
WHERE'VE YOU BEEN? ALL CLASSES HAVE BEEN SUSPENDED--INDEFINITELY!
THAT "CAN'T-READ" THING THAT'S GOING AROUND...?
YEAH--THEY SAY 1 OUT OF 3 PEOPLE AROUND HERE HAS IT.
hmm... WITH THOSE NUMBERS, TURNING ON THE LIGHTS IN THE CLASSROOM ISN'T WORTH THE ELECTRIC BILL.
YOU GOT THAT RIGHT. THEY SAY THIS PLACE IS GONNA BE A GHOST-TOWN BY TOMORROW MORNING.
NO POINT HANGING AROUND HERE EATING DORM FOOD, THEN--
"--NOT WHEN YOU CAN CALL 'WAYNE MANOR' HOME."
whoa.
11

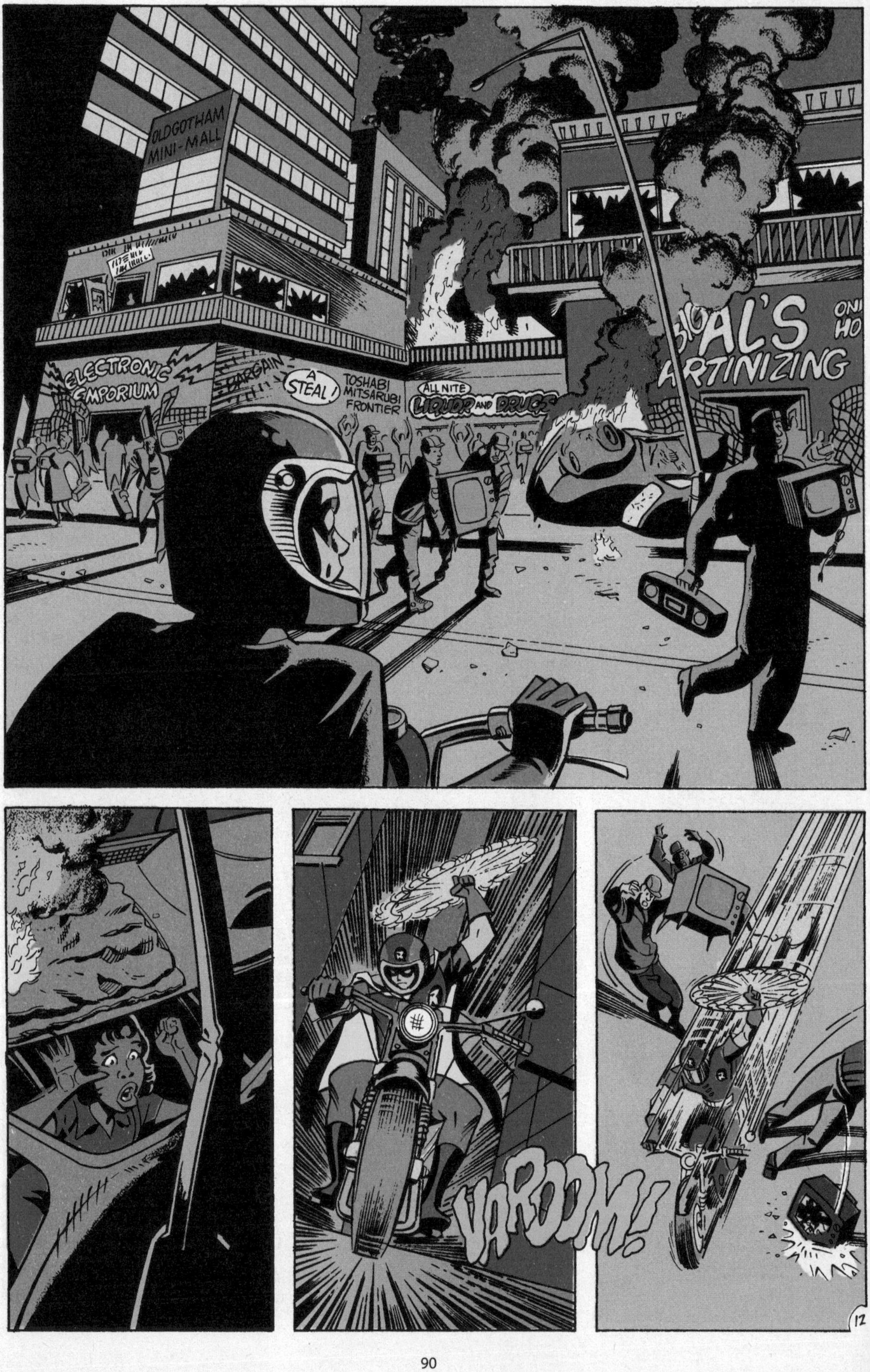

OLDGOTHAM
MINI-MALL
ELECTRONIC EMPORIUM
BARGAIN
A STEAL!
TOSHABI
MITSARUBI
FRONTIER
ALL NITE
LIQUOR AND DRUGS
BIG AL'S
ARTINIZING
VAROOM!
12

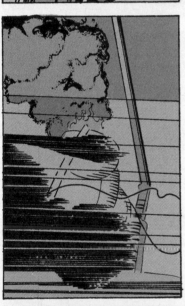

KRREUMP

BWAAROOM

"THE WORST FEARS OF LAW ENFORCEMENT OFFICIALS ARE BEING REALIZED AT THIS HOUR--

13

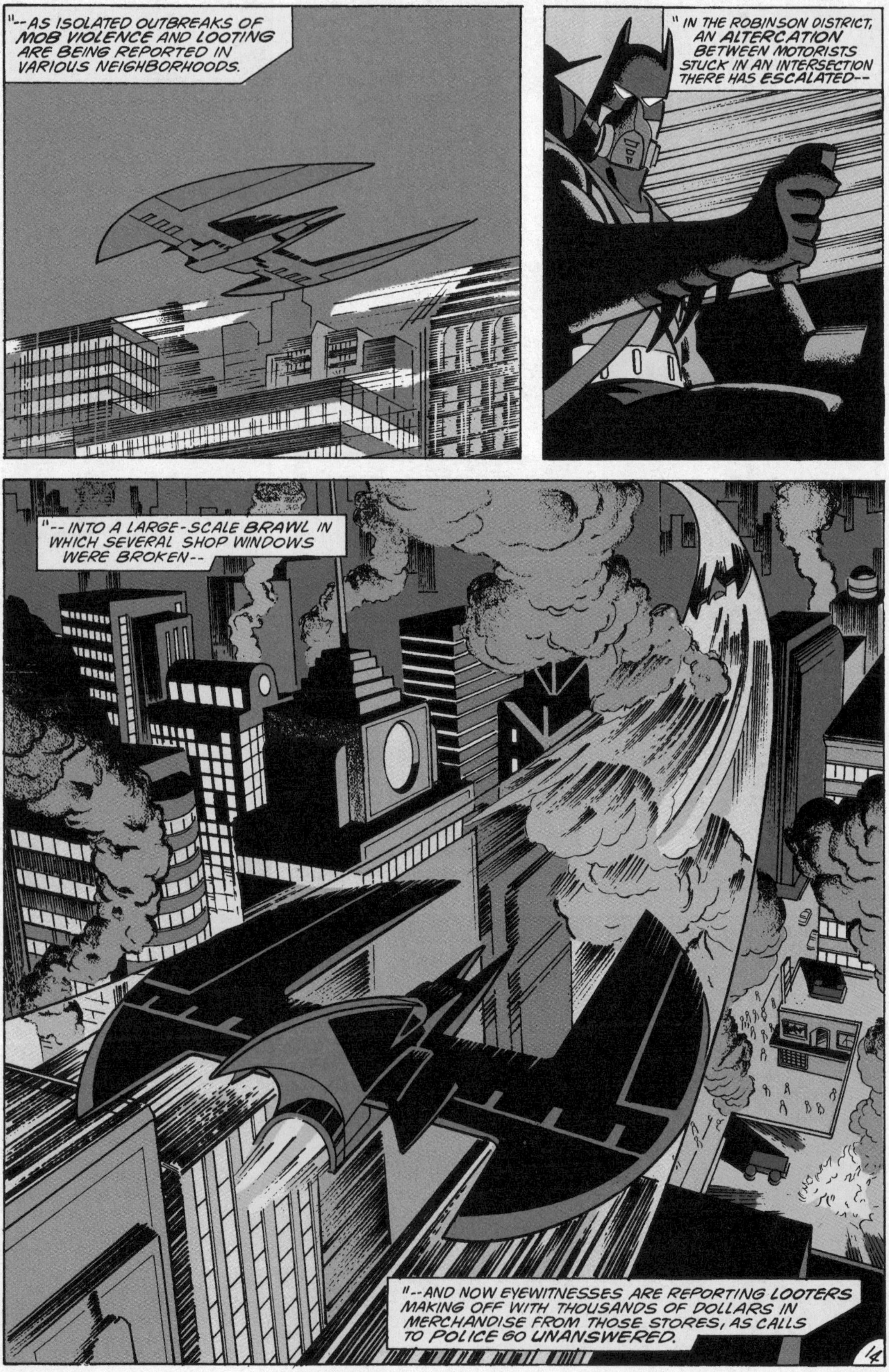
"--AS ISOLATED OUTBREAKS OF MOB VIOLENCE AND LOOTING ARE BEING REPORTED IN VARIOUS NEIGHBORHOODS.
" IN THE ROBINSON DISTRICT, AN ALTERCATION BETWEEN MOTORISTS STUCK IN AN INTERSECTION THERE HAS ESCALATED--
"-- INTO A LARGE-SCALE BRAWL IN WHICH SEVERAL SHOP WINDOWS WERE BROKEN--
"--AND NOW EYEWITNESSES ARE REPORTING LOOTERS MAKING OFF WITH THOUSANDS OF DOLLARS IN MERCHANDISE FROM THOSE STORES, AS CALLS TO POLICE GO UNANSWERED.
14

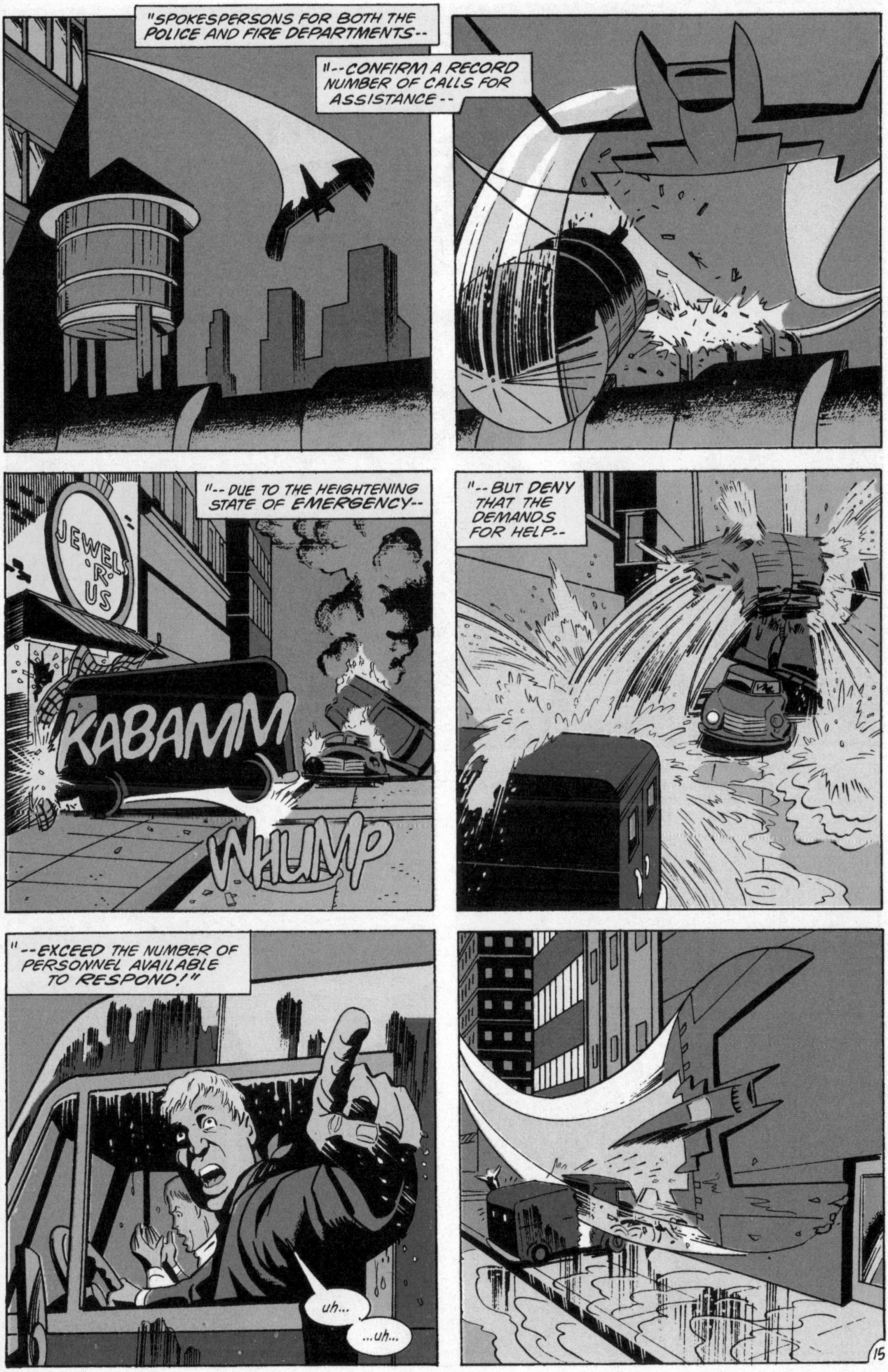
"SPOKESPERSONS FOR BOTH THE POLICE AND FIRE DEPARTMENTS--
"--CONFIRM A RECORD NUMBER OF CALLS FOR ASSISTANCE--
"--DUE TO THE HEIGHTENING STATE OF EMERGENCY--
JEWELS 'R' US
KABAMM
WHUMP
"--BUT DENY THAT THE DEMANDS FOR HELP--
"--EXCEED THE NUMBER OF PERSONNEL AVAILABLE TO RESPOND!"
uh...
...uh...
15

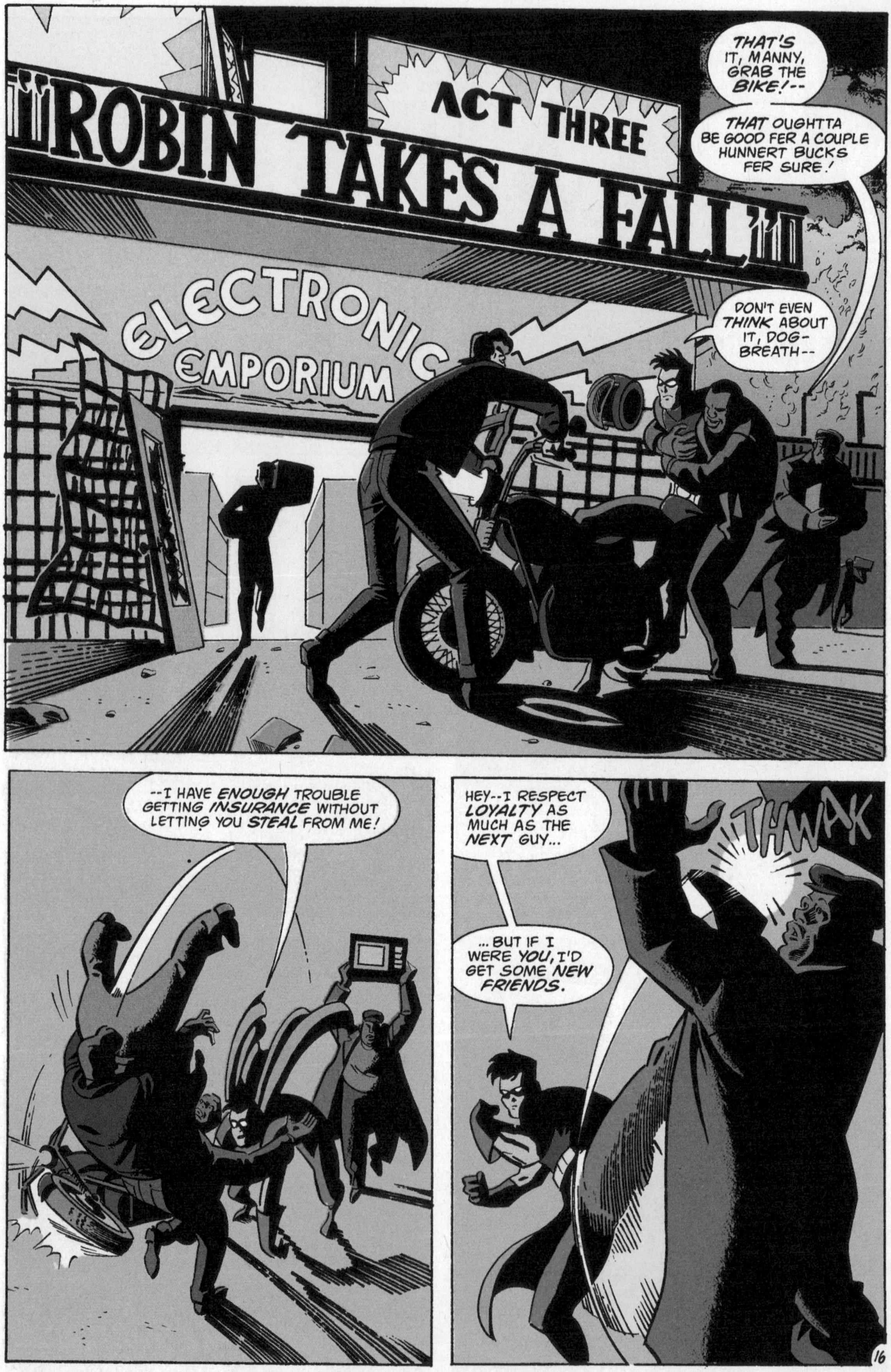

ACT THREE
"ROBIN TAKES A FALL"
ELECTRONIC EMPORIUM
THAT'S IT, MANNY, GRAB THE BIKE!--
THAT OUGHTTA BE GOOD FER A COUPLE HUNNERT BUCKS FER SURE!
DON'T EVEN THINK ABOUT IT, DOG-BREATH--
--I HAVE ENOUGH TROUBLE GETTING INSURANCE WITHOUT LETTING YOU STEAL FROM ME!
HEY--I RESPECT LOYALTY AS MUCH AS THE NEXT GUY...
...BUT IF I WERE YOU, I'D GET SOME NEW FRIENDS.
THWAK
16

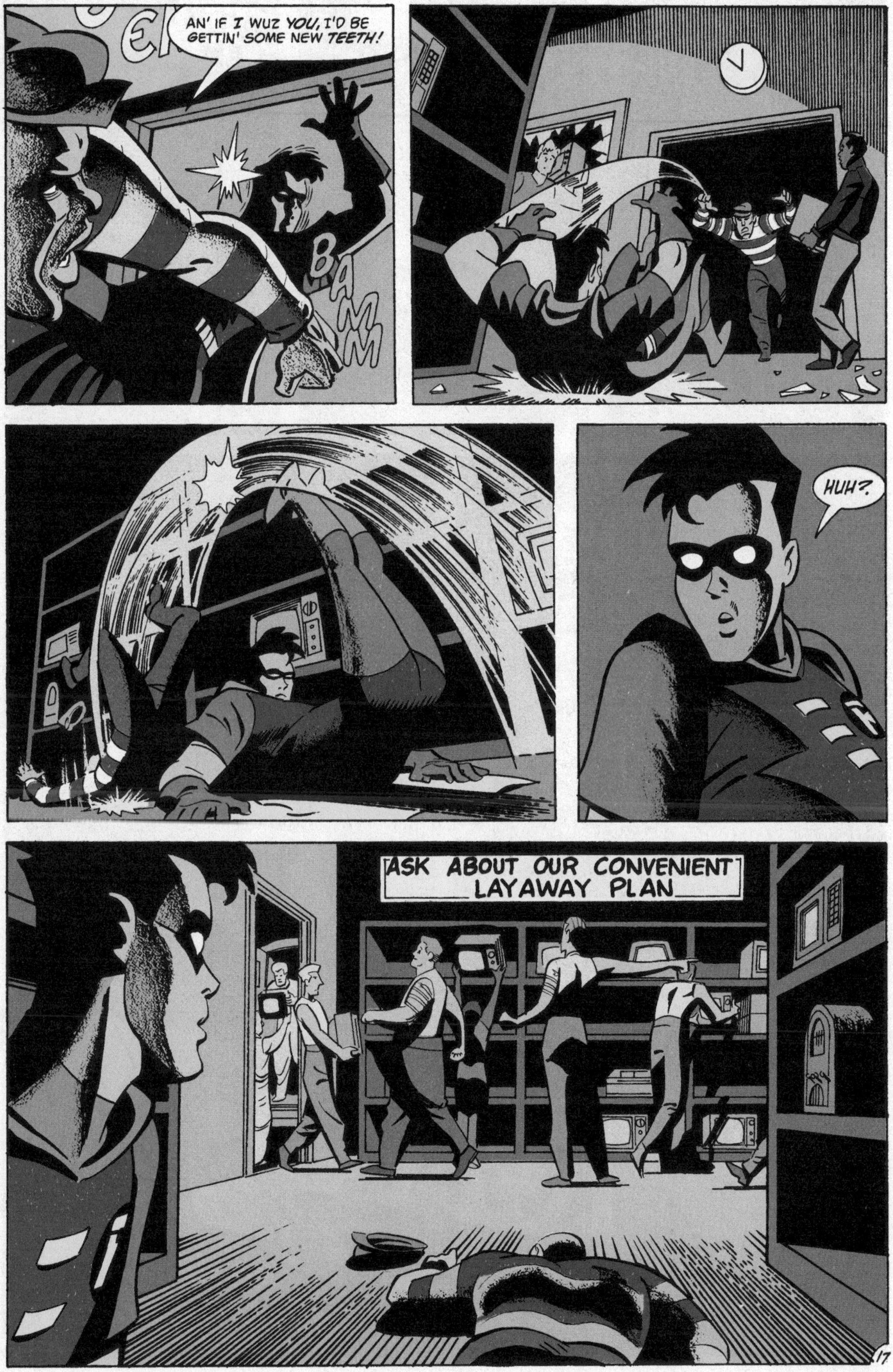
AN' IF I WUZ YOU, I'D BE GETTIN' SOME NEW TEETH!
BAMM
HUH?
ASK ABOUT OUR CONVENIENT LAYAWAY PLAN
17

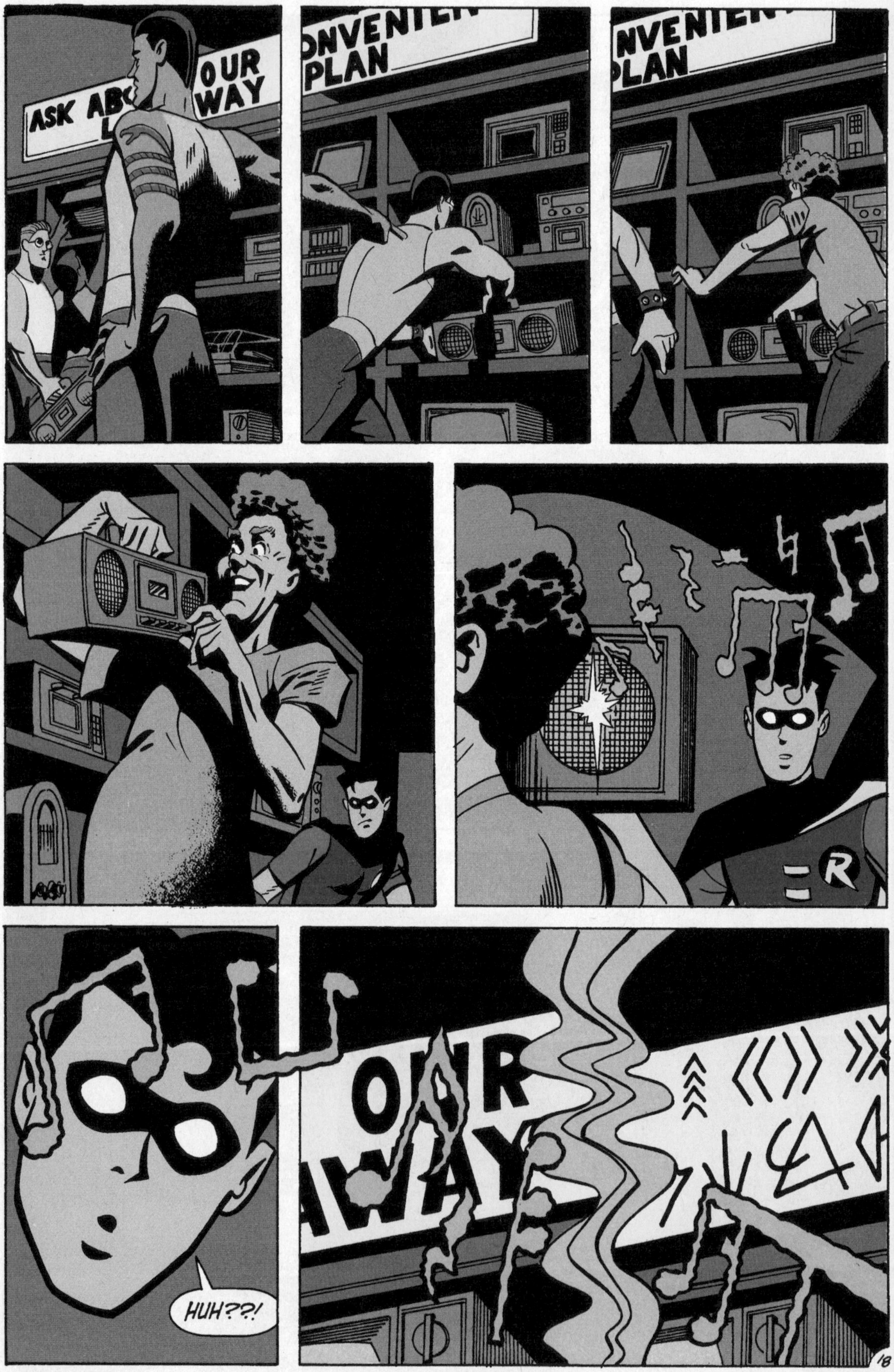
ASK ABO
OUR
WAY
ONVENIEN
PLAN
NVENIEN
PLAN
HUH??!
OUR
AWAY
18

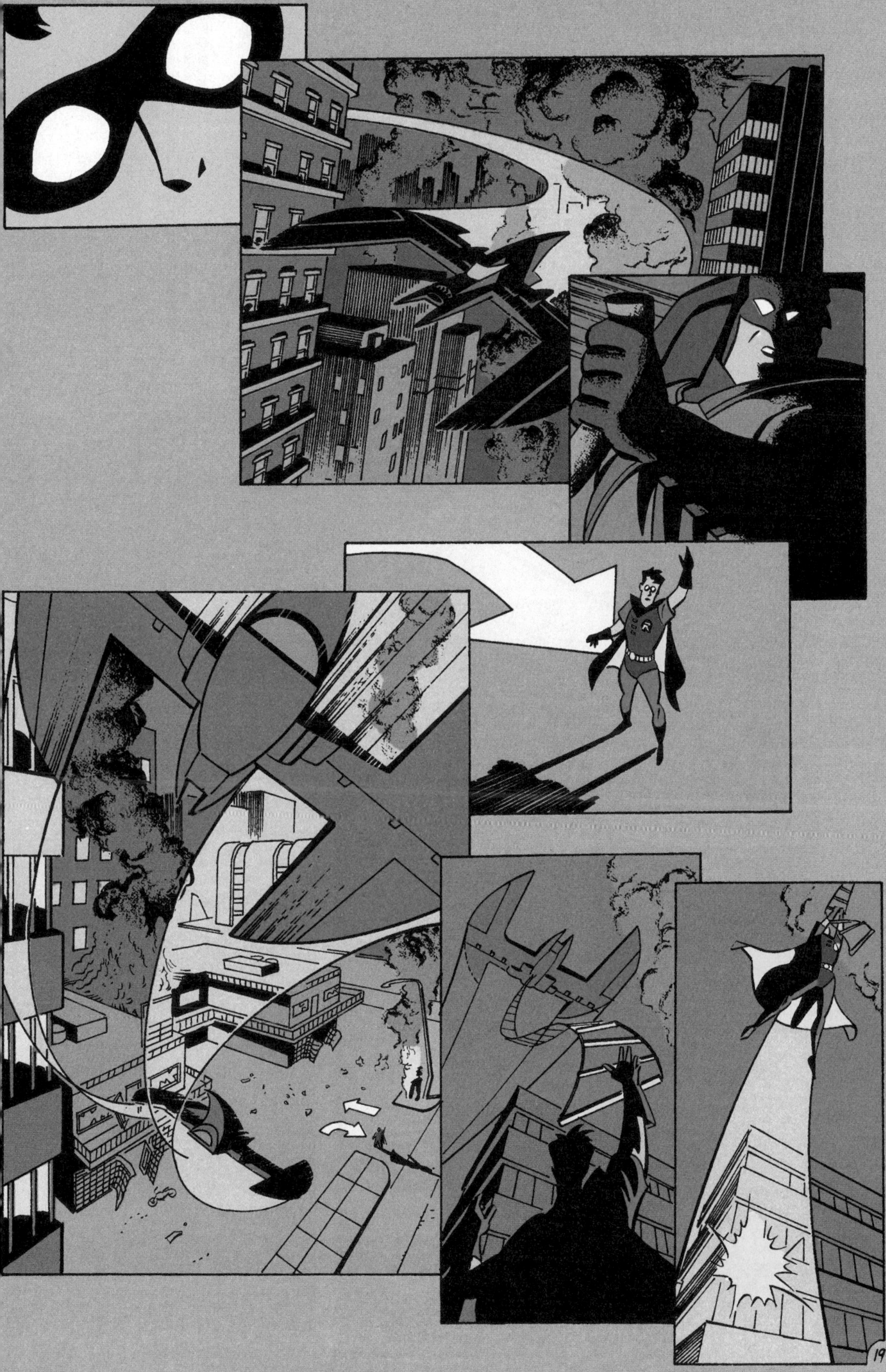
19

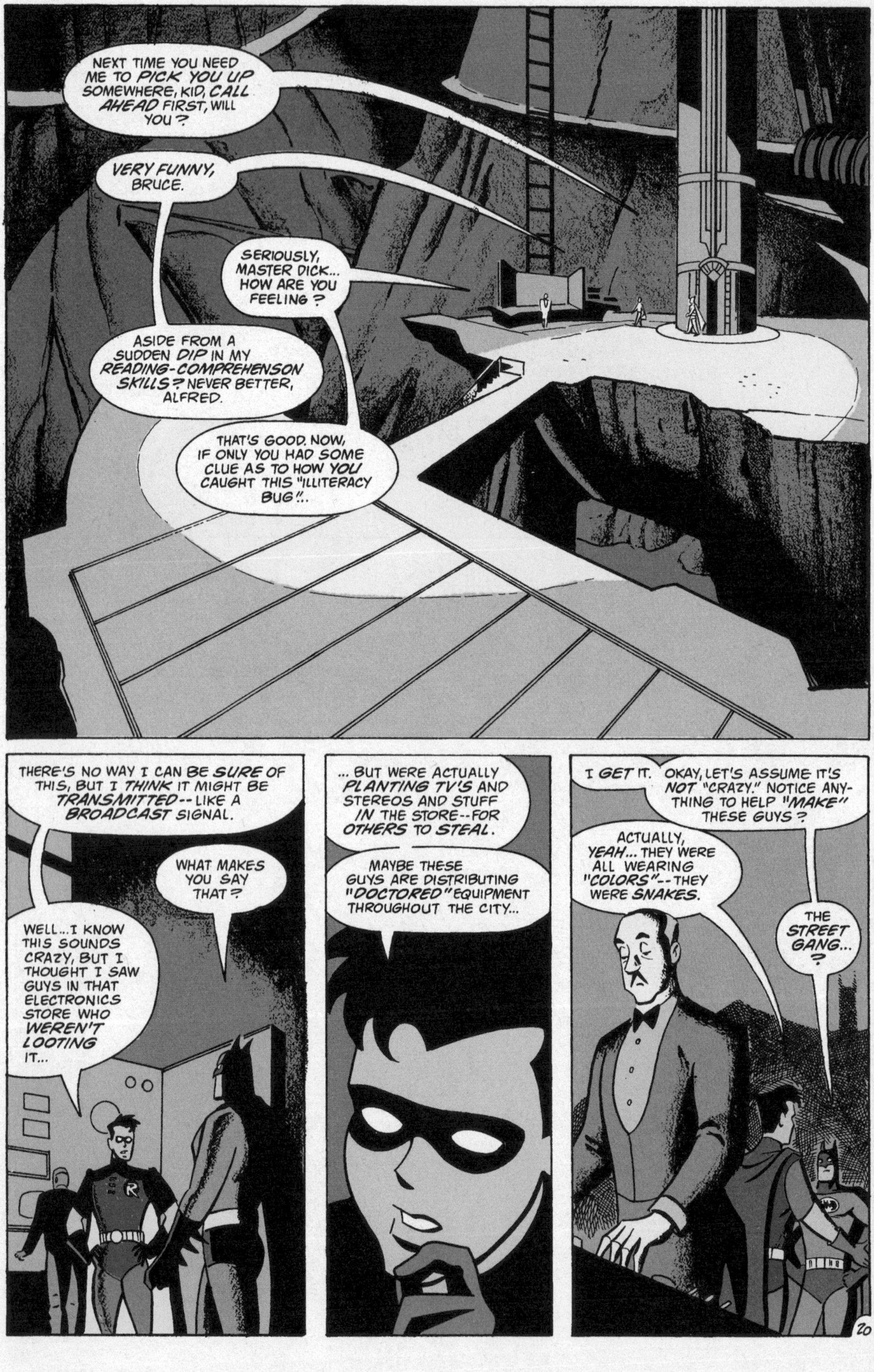
NEXT TIME YOU NEED ME TO PICK YOU UP SOMEWHERE, KID, CALL AHEAD FIRST, WILL YOU?
VERY FUNNY, BRUCE.
SERIOUSLY, MASTER DICK... HOW ARE YOU FEELING?
ASIDE FROM A SUDDEN DIP IN MY READING-COMPREHENSON SKILLS? NEVER BETTER, ALFRED.
THAT'S GOOD. NOW, IF ONLY YOU HAD SOME CLUE AS TO HOW YOU CAUGHT THIS "ILLITERACY BUG"...
THERE'S NO WAY I CAN BE SURE OF THIS, BUT I THINK IT MIGHT BE TRANSMITTED--LIKE A BROADCAST SIGNAL.
WHAT MAKES YOU SAY THAT?
WELL...I KNOW THIS SOUNDS CRAZY, BUT I THOUGHT I SAW GUYS IN THAT ELECTRONICS STORE WHO WEREN'T LOOTING IT...
...BUT WERE ACTUALLY PLANTING TV'S AND STEREOS AND STUFF IN THE STORE--FOR OTHERS TO STEAL.
MAYBE THESE GUYS ARE DISTRIBUTING "DOCTORED" EQUIPMENT THROUGHOUT THE CITY...
I GET IT.
OKAY, LET'S ASSUME IT'S NOT "CRAZY." NOTICE ANYTHING TO HELP "MAKE" THESE GUYS?
ACTUALLY, YEAH... THEY WERE ALL WEARING "COLORS"--THEY WERE SNAKES.
THE STREET GANG...?
20

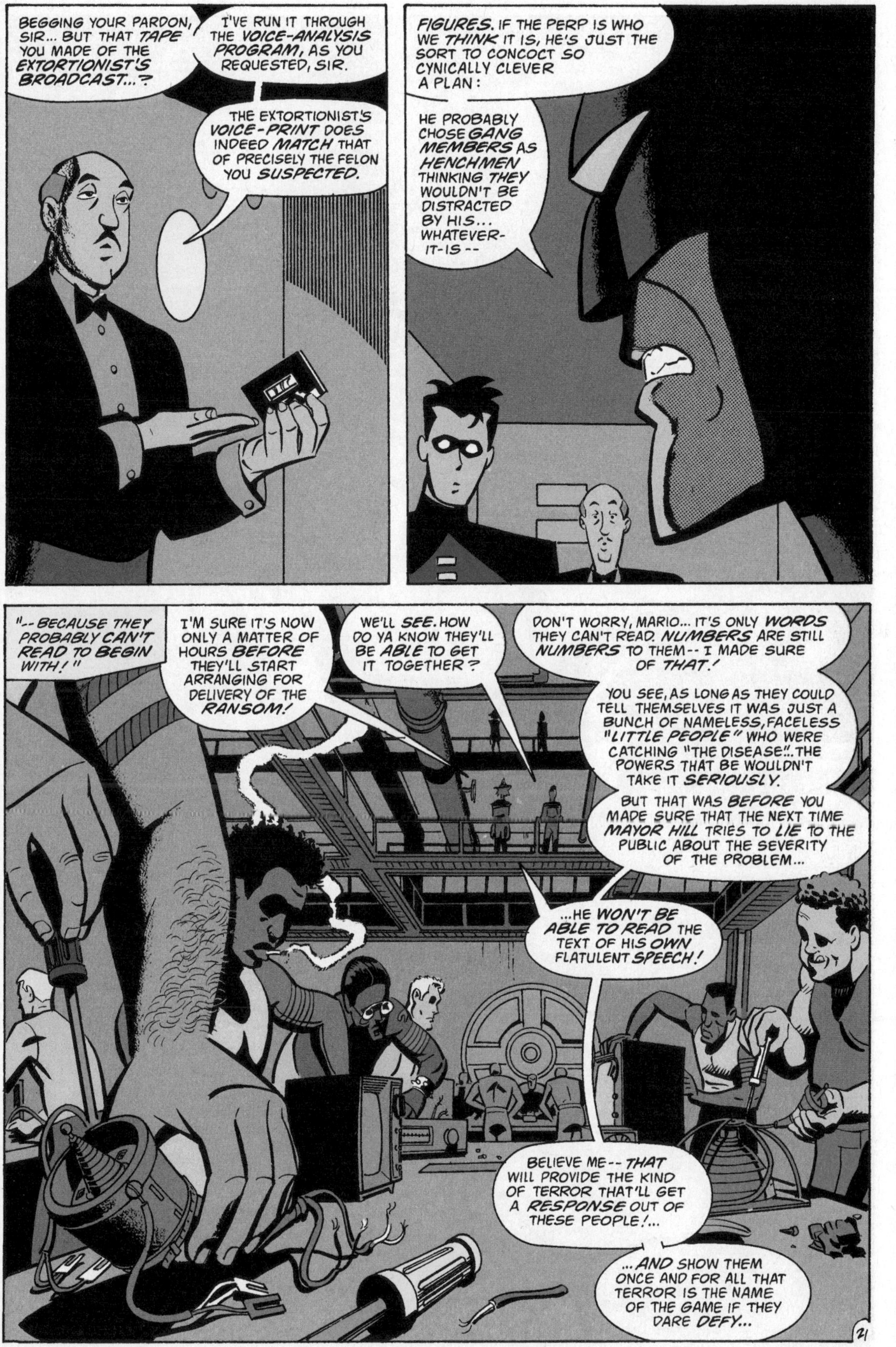
BEGGING YOUR PARDON, SIR... BUT THAT TAPE YOU MADE OF THE EXTORTIONIST'S BROADCAST...?
I'VE RUN IT THROUGH THE VOICE-ANALYSIS PROGRAM, AS YOU REQUESTED, SIR.
THE EXTORTIONIST'S VOICE-PRINT DOES INDEED MATCH THAT OF PRECISELY THE FELON YOU SUSPECTED.
FIGURES. IF THE PERP IS WHO WE THINK IT IS, HE'S JUST THE SORT TO CONCOCT SO CYNICALLY CLEVER A PLAN:
HE PROBABLY CHOSE GANG MEMBERS AS HENCHMEN THINKING THEY WOULDN'T BE DISTRACTED BY HIS... WHATEVER-IT-IS --
"-- BECAUSE THEY PROBABLY CAN'T READ TO BEGIN WITH!"
I'M SURE IT'S NOW ONLY A MATTER OF HOURS BEFORE THEY'LL START ARRANGING FOR DELIVERY OF THE RANSOM!
WE'LL SEE. HOW DO YA KNOW THEY'LL BE ABLE TO GET IT TOGETHER?
DON'T WORRY, MARIO... IT'S ONLY WORDS THEY CAN'T READ. NUMBERS ARE STILL NUMBERS TO THEM -- I MADE SURE OF THAT.!
YOU SEE, AS LONG AS THEY COULD TELL THEMSELVES IT WAS JUST A BUNCH OF NAMELESS, FACELESS "LITTLE PEOPLE" WHO WERE CATCHING "THE DISEASE"... THE POWERS THAT BE WOULDN'T TAKE IT SERIOUSLY.
BUT THAT WAS BEFORE YOU MADE SURE THAT THE NEXT TIME MAYOR HILL TRIES TO LIE TO THE PUBLIC ABOUT THE SEVERITY OF THE PROBLEM...
...HE WON'T BE ABLE TO READ THE TEXT OF HIS OWN FLATULENT SPEECH!
BELIEVE ME -- THAT WILL PROVIDE THE KIND OF TERROR THAT'LL GET A RESPONSE OUT OF THESE PEOPLE!...
...AND SHOW THEM ONCE AND FOR ALL THAT TERROR IS THE NAME OF THE GAME IF THEY DARE DEFY...
21

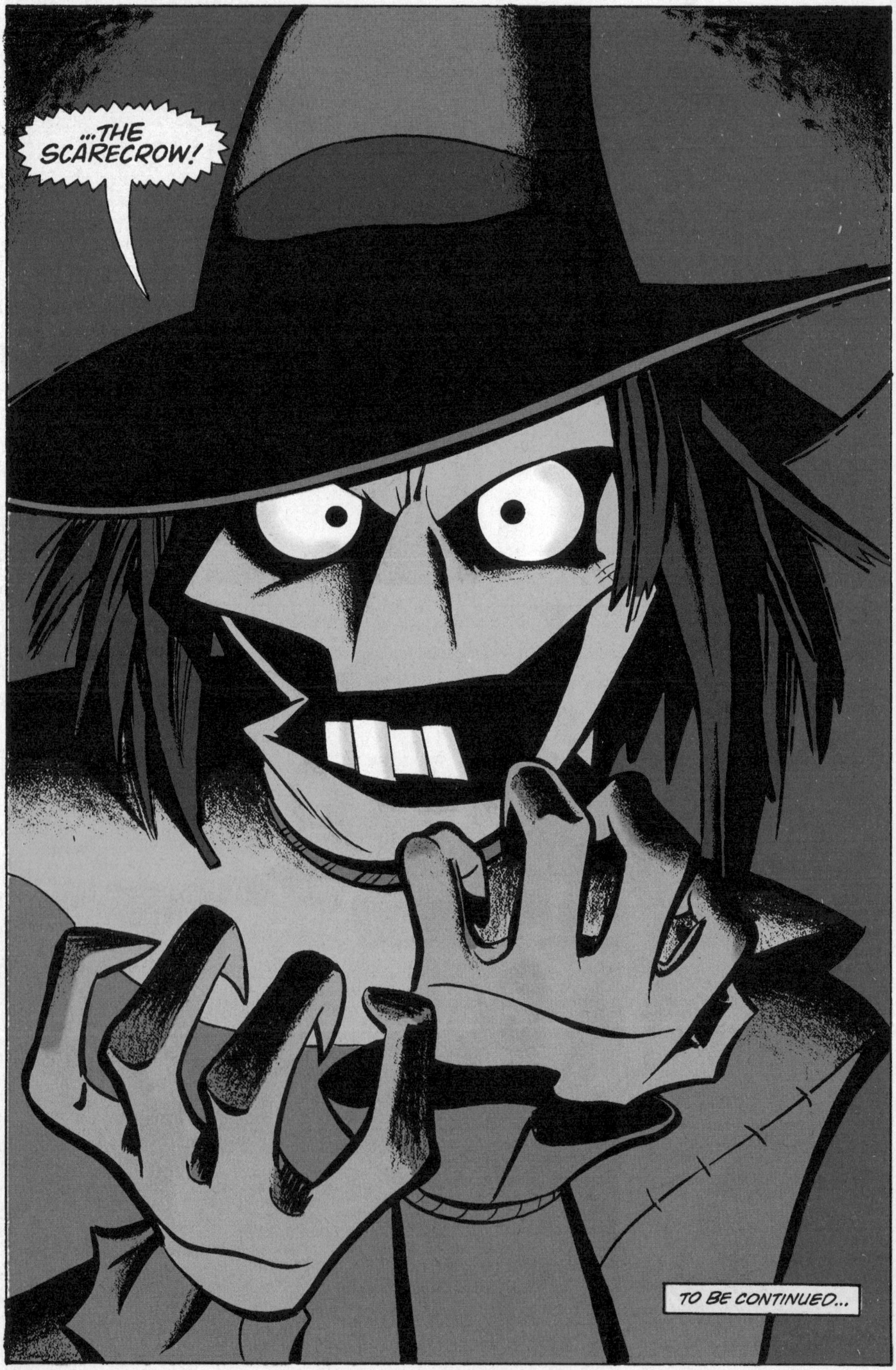
...THE SCARECROW!
TO BE CONTINUED...

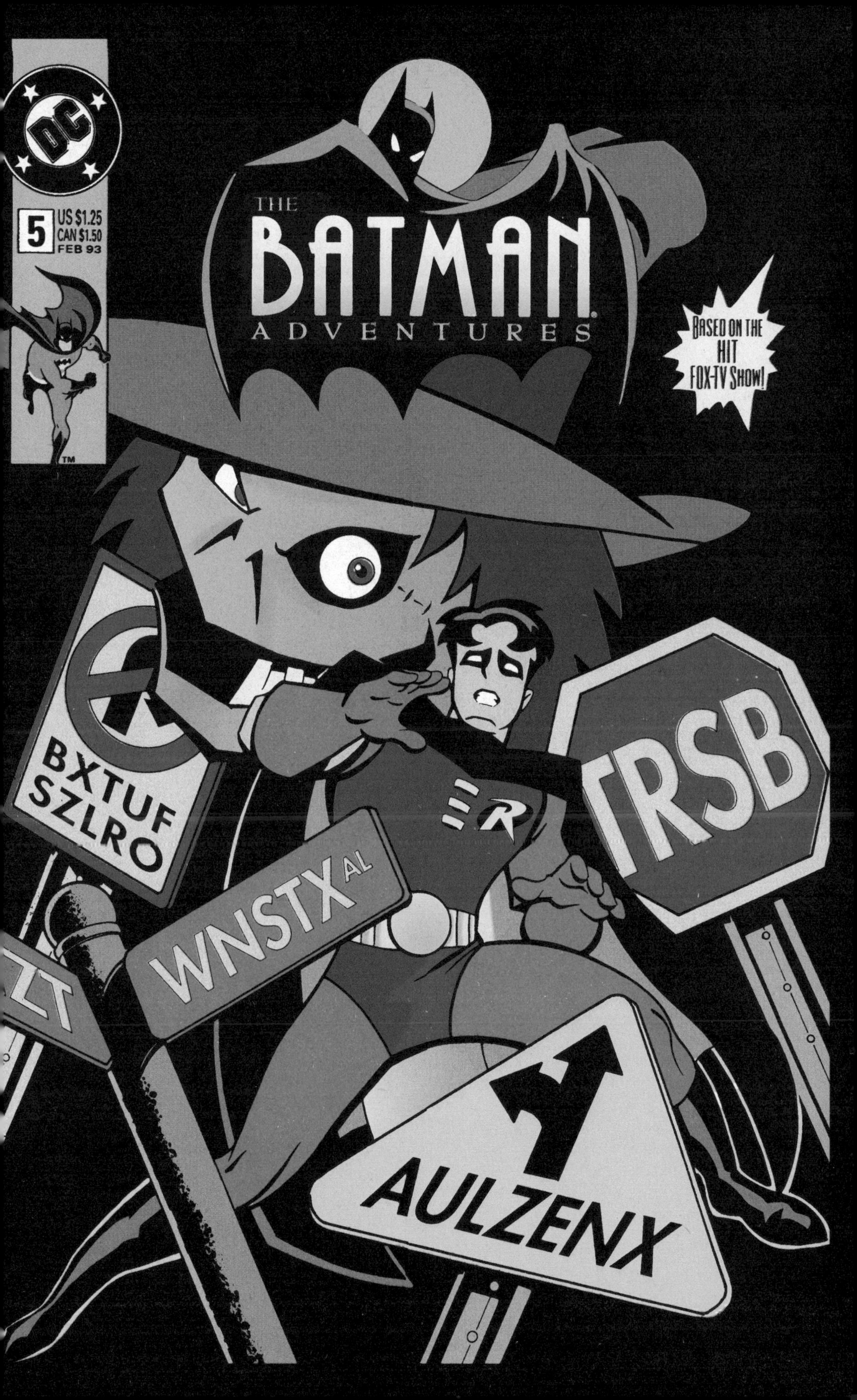
DC
5
US $1.25
CAN $1.50
FEB 93
TM
THE BATMAN ADVENTURES
BASED ON THE HIT FOX-TV SHOW!
BXTUF SZLRO
TRSB
WNSTX AL
ZT
AULZENX

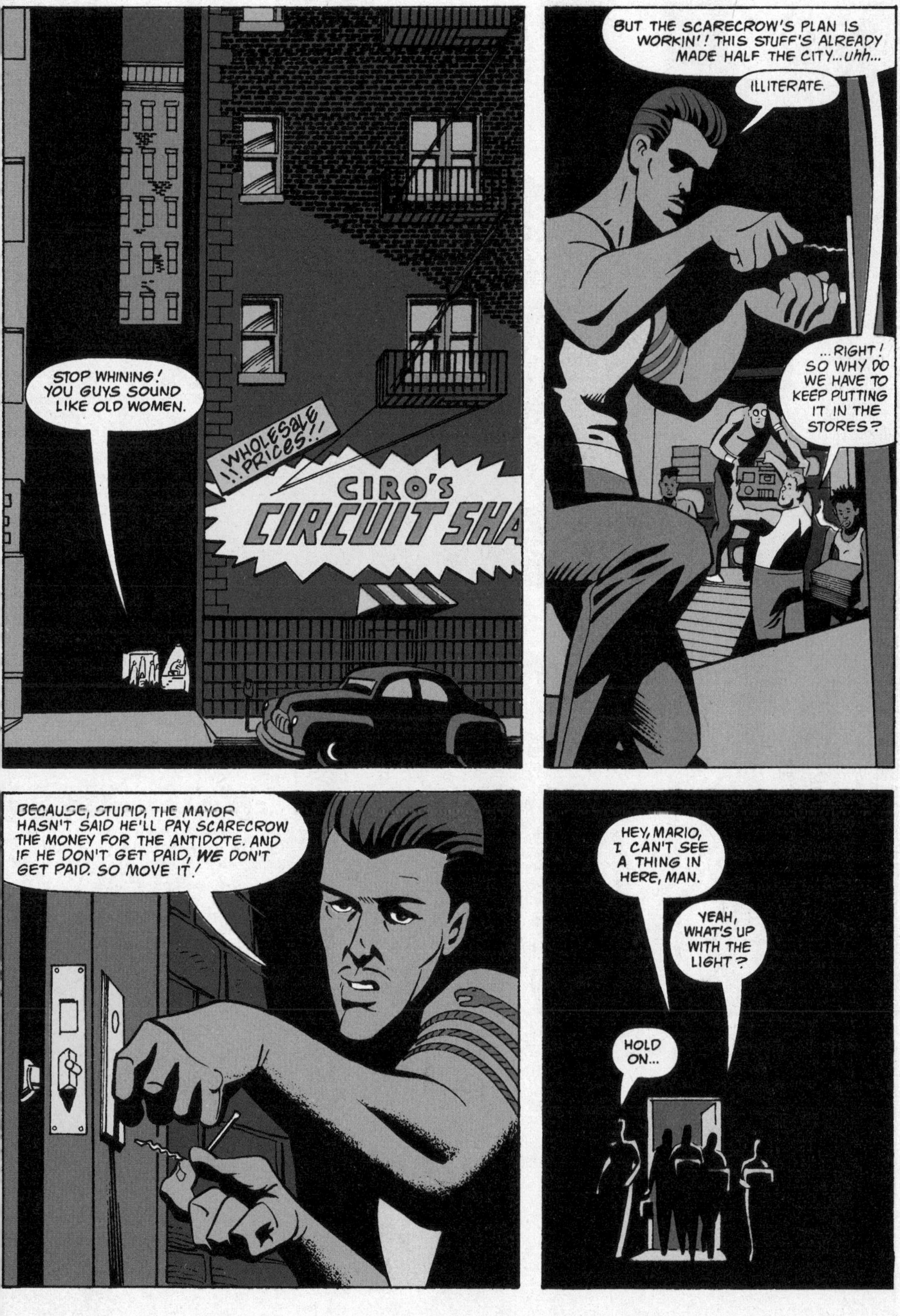

STOP WHINING! YOU GUYS SOUND LIKE OLD WOMEN.
WHOLESALE !! PRICES !!
CIRO'S CIRCUIT SHA
BUT THE SCARECROW'S PLAN IS WORKIN'! THIS STUFF'S ALREADY MADE HALF THE CITY...uhh...
ILLITERATE.
...RIGHT! SO WHY DO WE HAVE TO KEEP PUTTING IT IN THE STORES?
BECAUSE, STUPID, THE MAYOR HASN'T SAID HE'LL PAY SCARECROW THE MONEY FOR THE ANTIDOTE. AND IF HE DON'T GET PAID, WE DON'T GET PAID. SO MOVE IT!
HEY, MARIO, I CAN'T SEE A THING IN HERE, MAN.
YEAH, WHAT'S UP WITH THE LIGHT?
HOLD ON...

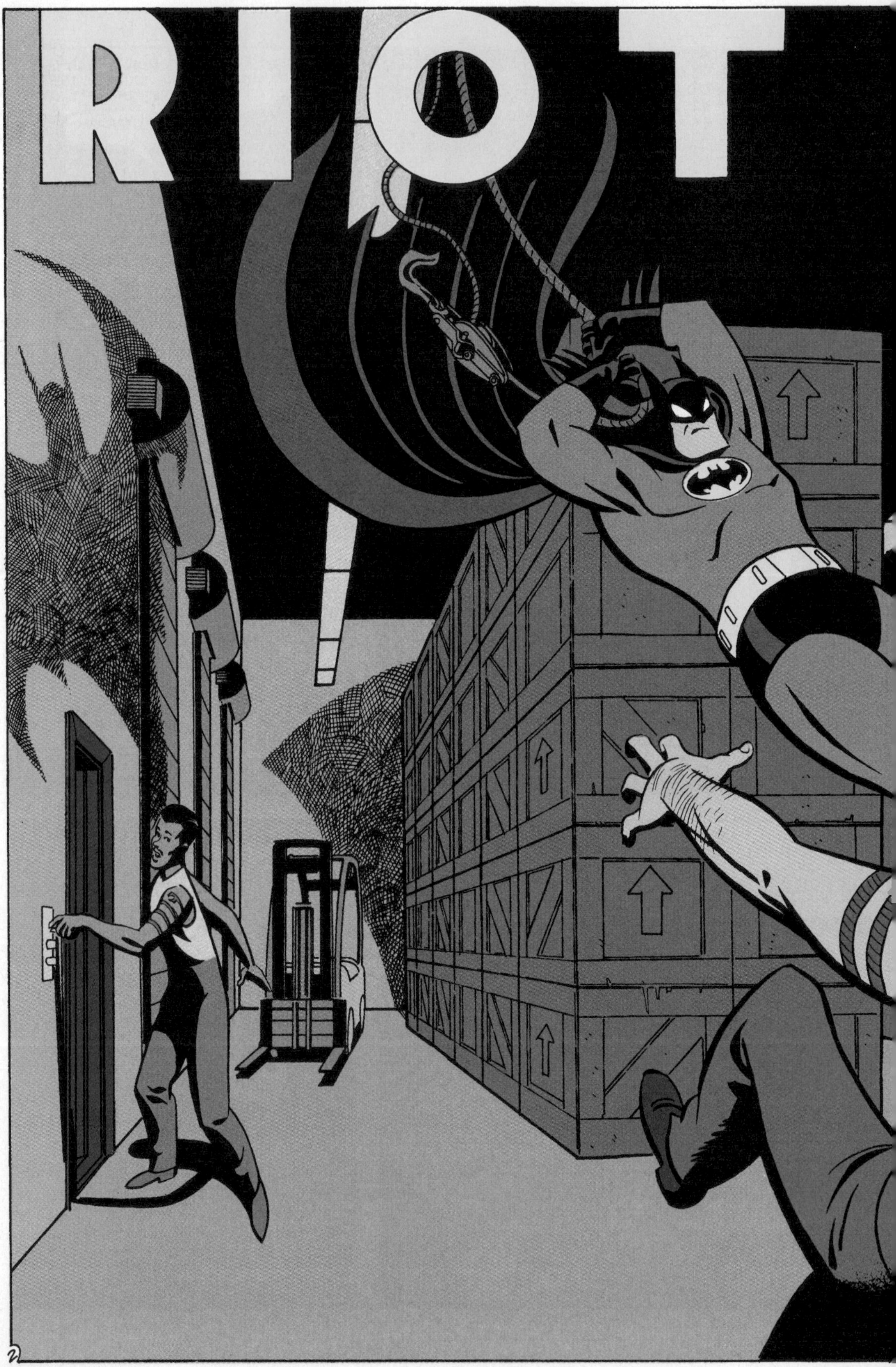
RIOT

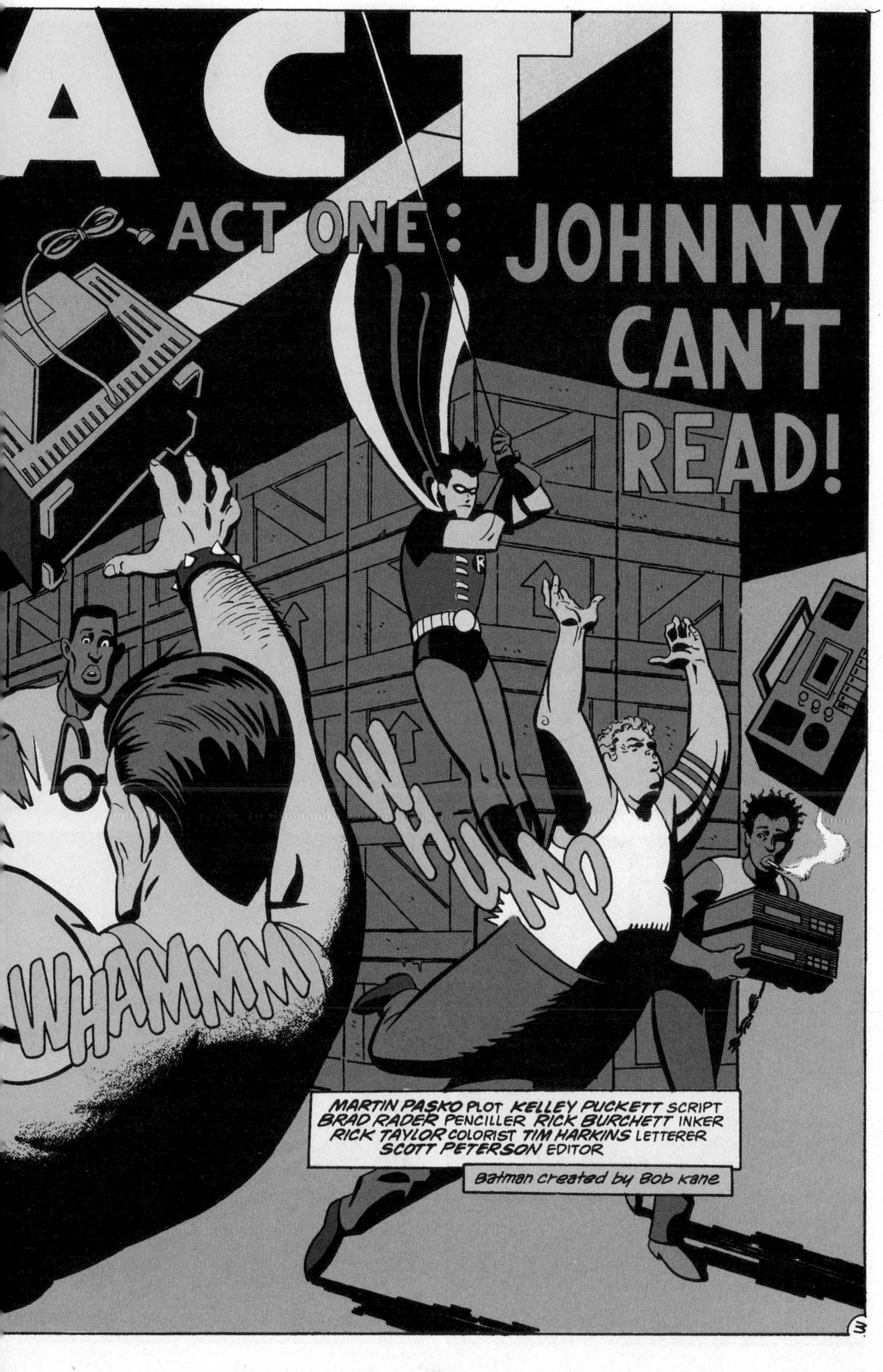
ACT II
ACT ONE: JOHNNY CAN'T READ!
WHAMMM
WHUMP
MARTIN PASKO PLOT KELLEY PUCKETT SCRIPT
BRAD RADER PENCILLER RICK BURCHETT INKER
RICK TAYLOR COLORIST TIM HARKINS LETTERER
SCOTT PETERSON EDITOR
Batman created by Bob Kane
3

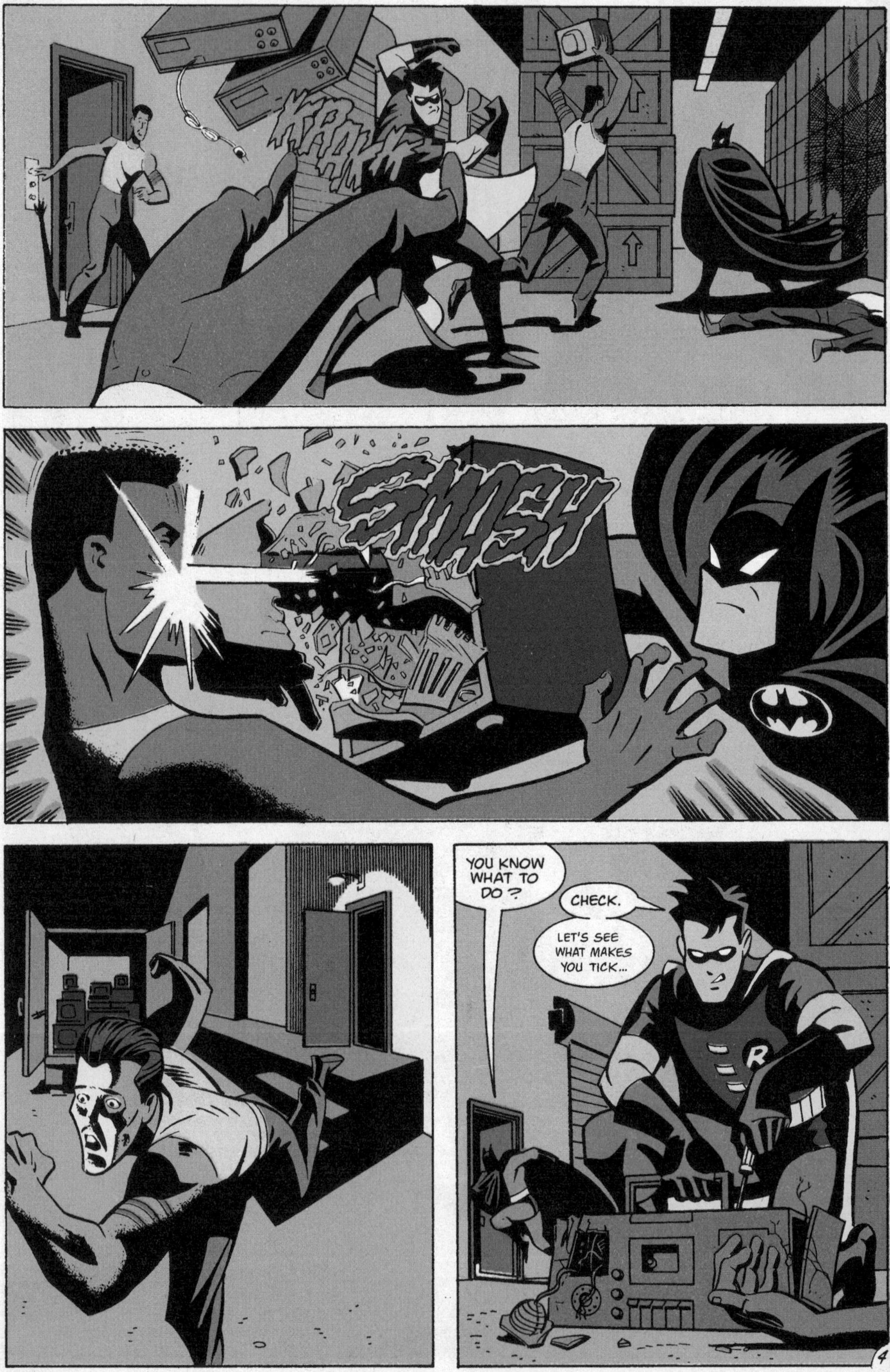
KRAKK
SMASH
YOU KNOW WHAT TO DO ?
CHECK.
LET'S SEE WHAT MAKES YOU TICK...
4

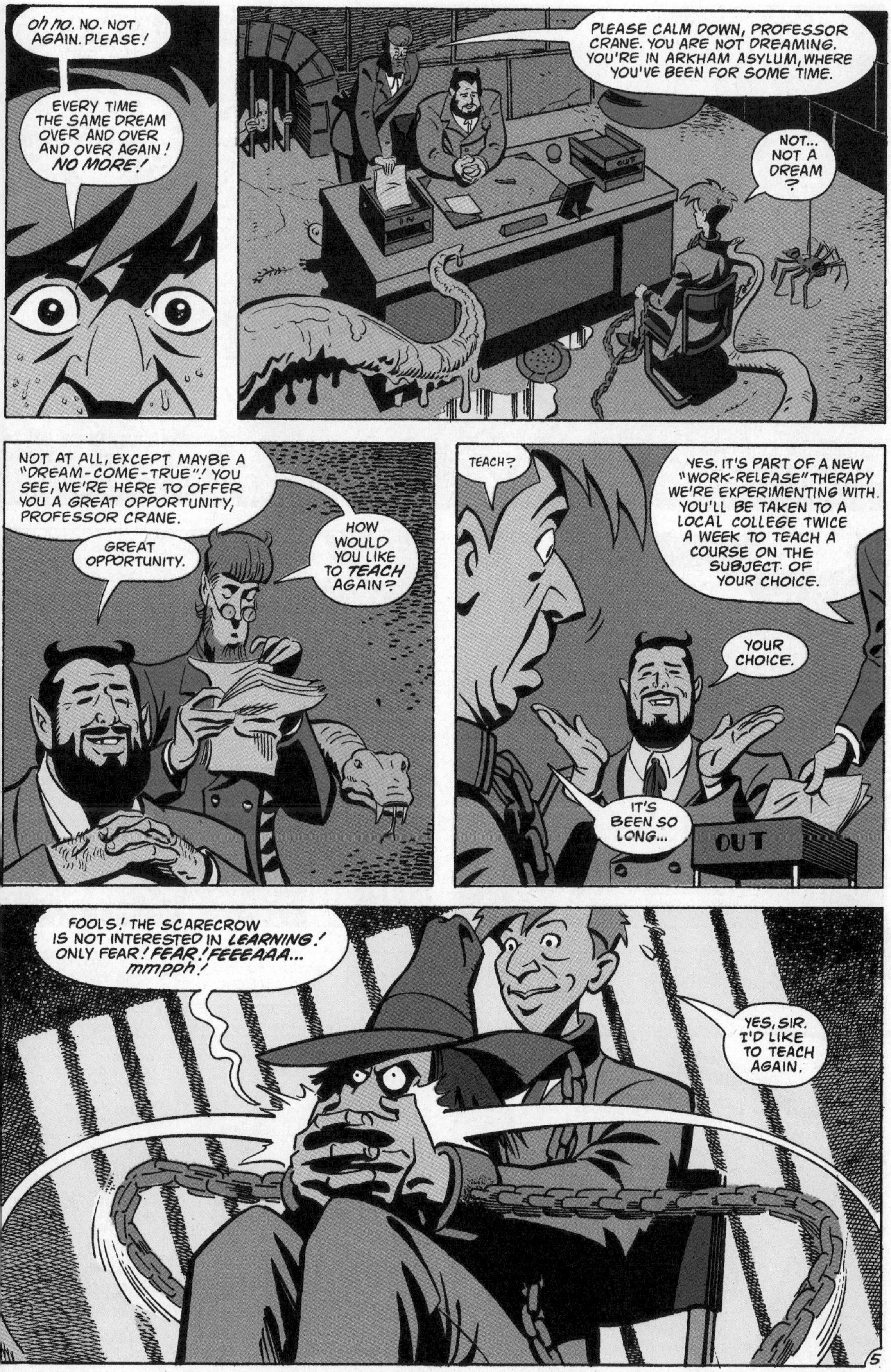
oh no. NO. NOT AGAIN. PLEASE!
EVERY TIME THE SAME DREAM OVER AND OVER AND OVER AGAIN! NO MORE!
PLEASE CALM DOWN, PROFESSOR CRANE. YOU ARE NOT DREAMING. YOU'RE IN ARKHAM ASYLUM, WHERE YOU'VE BEEN FOR SOME TIME.
OUT
NOT... NOT A DREAM?
NOT AT ALL, EXCEPT MAYBE A "DREAM-COME-TRUE"! YOU SEE, WE'RE HERE TO OFFER YOU A GREAT OPPORTUNITY, PROFESSOR CRANE.
GREAT OPPORTUNITY.
HOW WOULD YOU LIKE TO TEACH AGAIN?
TEACH?
YES. IT'S PART OF A NEW "WORK-RELEASE" THERAPY WE'RE EXPERIMENTING WITH. YOU'LL BE TAKEN TO A LOCAL COLLEGE TWICE A WEEK TO TEACH A COURSE ON THE SUBJECT OF YOUR CHOICE.
YOUR CHOICE.
IT'S BEEN SO LONG...
OUT
FOOLS! THE SCARECROW IS NOT INTERESTED IN LEARNING! ONLY FEAR! FEAR! FEEEAAA... mmpph!
YES, SIR. I'D LIKE TO TEACH AGAIN.
5

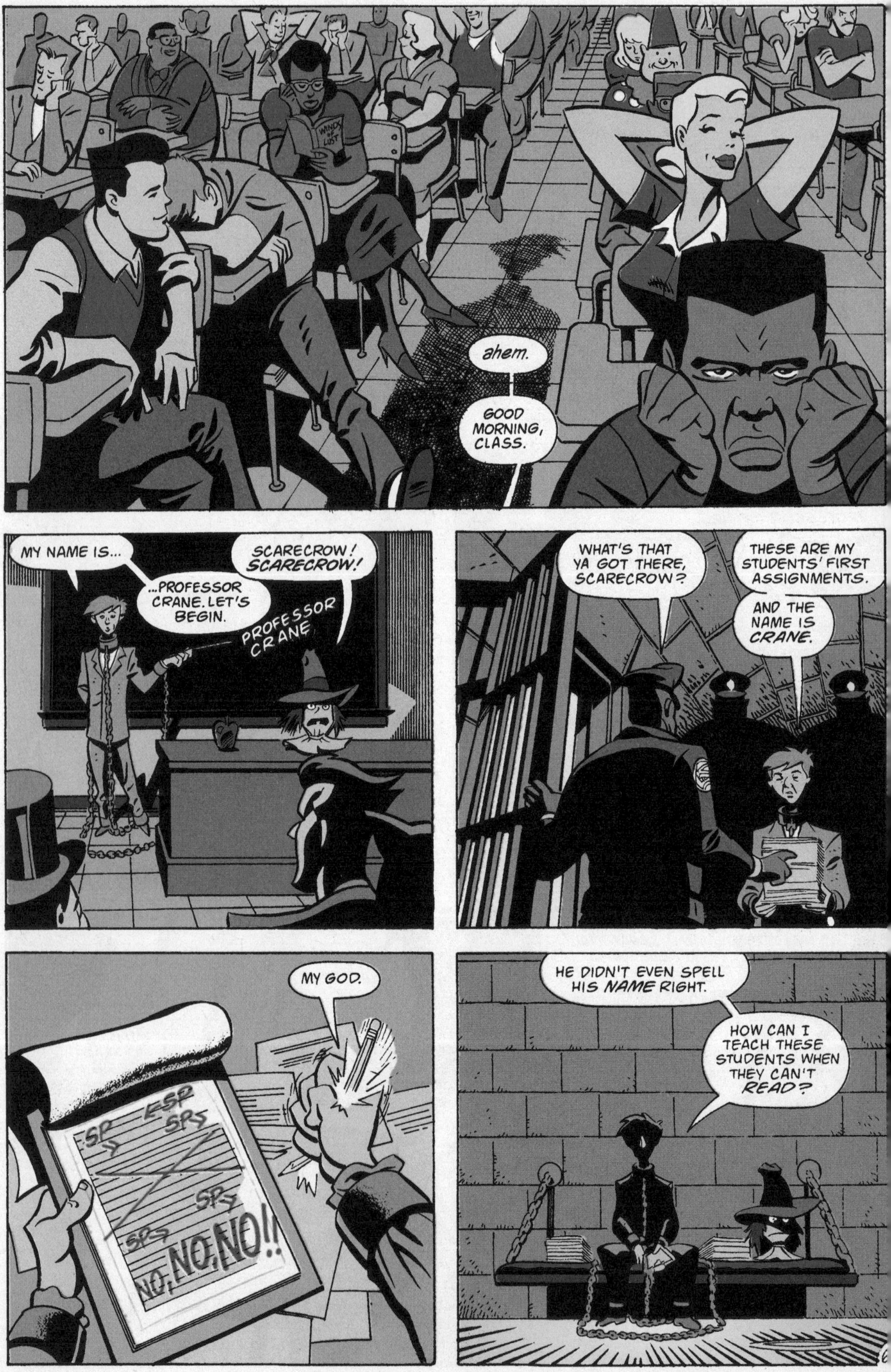
ahem.
GOOD MORNING, CLASS.
MY NAME IS...
...PROFESSOR CRANE. LET'S BEGIN.
SCARECROW! *SCARECROW!*
PROFESSOR CRANE
WHAT'S THAT YA GOT THERE, SCARECROW?
THESE ARE MY STUDENTS' FIRST ASSIGNMENTS.
AND THE NAME IS *CRANE*.
MY GOD.
NO, NO, NO!!
HE DIDN'T EVEN SPELL HIS *NAME* RIGHT.
HOW CAN I TEACH THESE STUDENTS WHEN THEY CAN'T *READ*?

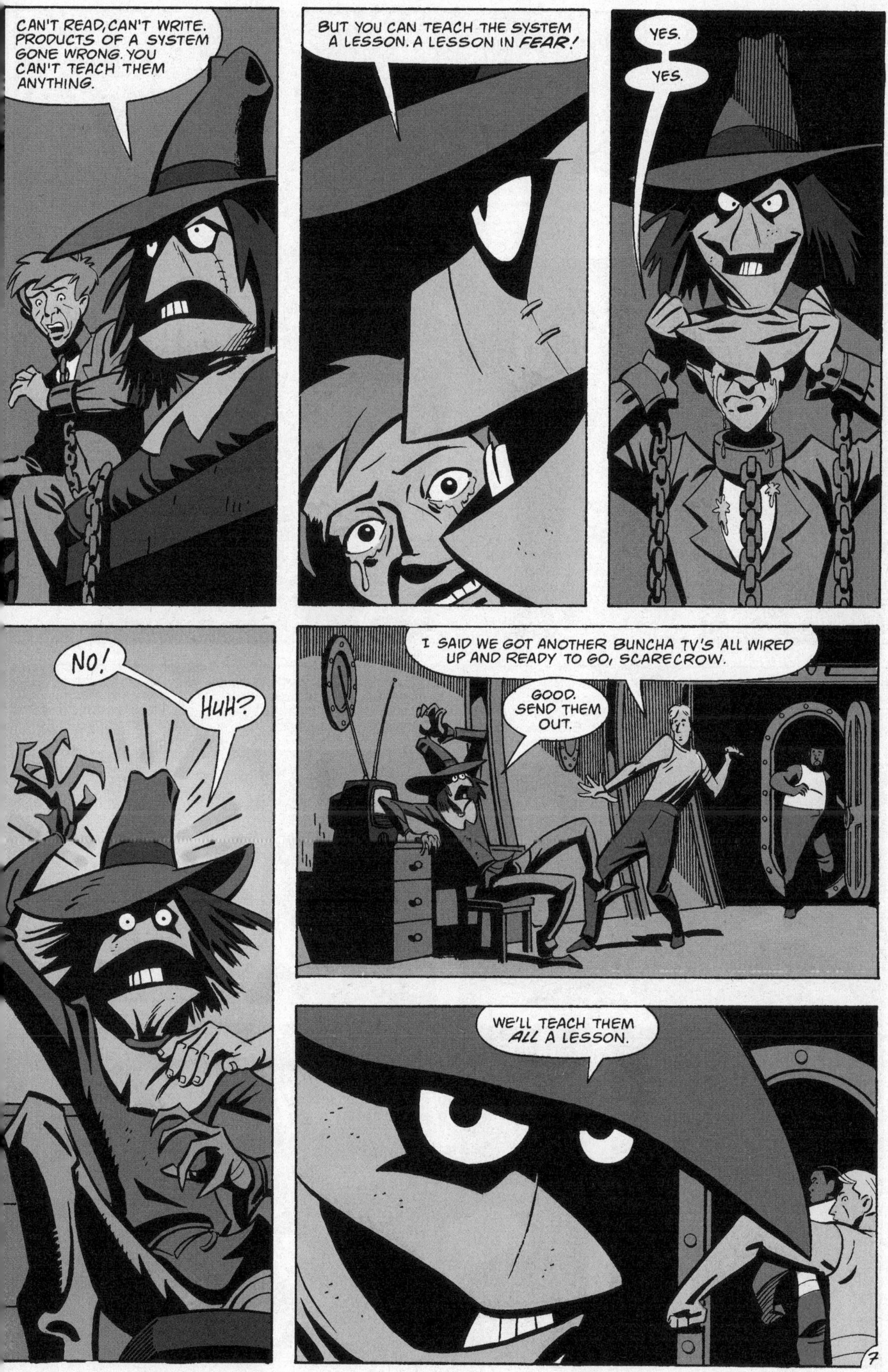

CAN'T READ, CAN'T WRITE. PRODUCTS OF A SYSTEM GONE WRONG. YOU CAN'T TEACH THEM ANYTHING.
BUT YOU CAN TEACH THE SYSTEM A LESSON. A LESSON IN FEAR!
YES.
YES.
NO!
HUH?
I SAID WE GOT ANOTHER BUNCHA TV'S ALL WIRED UP AND READY TO GO, SCARECROW.
GOOD. SEND THEM OUT.
WE'LL TEACH THEM ALL A LESSON.
7

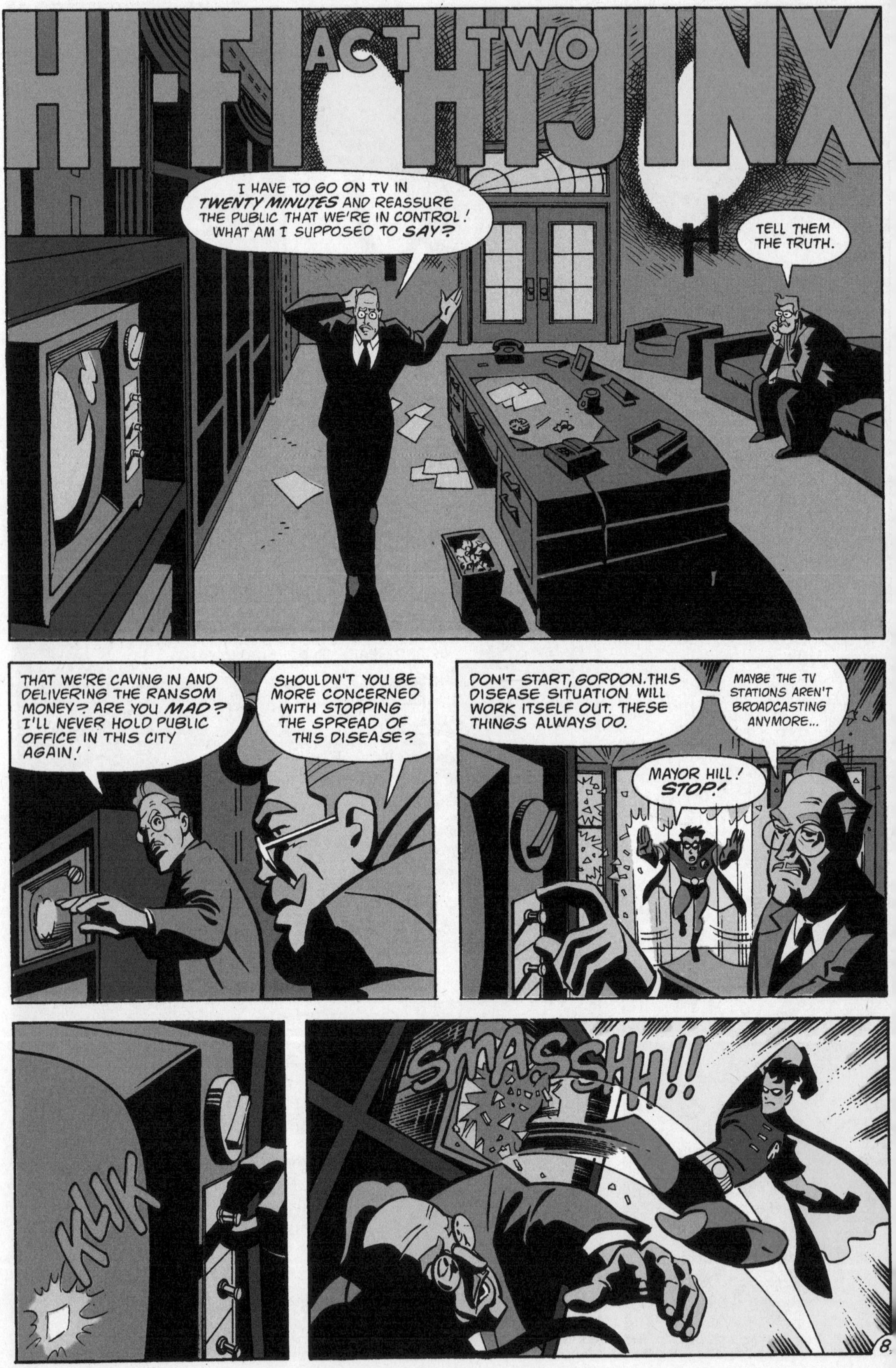
HI-FI HIJINX
ACT TWO
I HAVE TO GO ON TV IN TWENTY MINUTES AND REASSURE THE PUBLIC THAT WE'RE IN CONTROL! WHAT AM I SUPPOSED TO SAY?
TELL THEM THE TRUTH.
THAT WE'RE CAVING IN AND DELIVERING THE RANSOM MONEY? ARE YOU MAD? I'LL NEVER HOLD PUBLIC OFFICE IN THIS CITY AGAIN!
SHOULDN'T YOU BE MORE CONCERNED WITH STOPPING THE SPREAD OF THIS DISEASE?
DON'T START, GORDON. THIS DISEASE SITUATION WILL WORK ITSELF OUT. THESE THINGS ALWAYS DO.
MAYBE THE TV STATIONS AREN'T BROADCASTING ANYMORE...
MAYOR HILL! STOP!
KLIK
SMASSHH!!
8

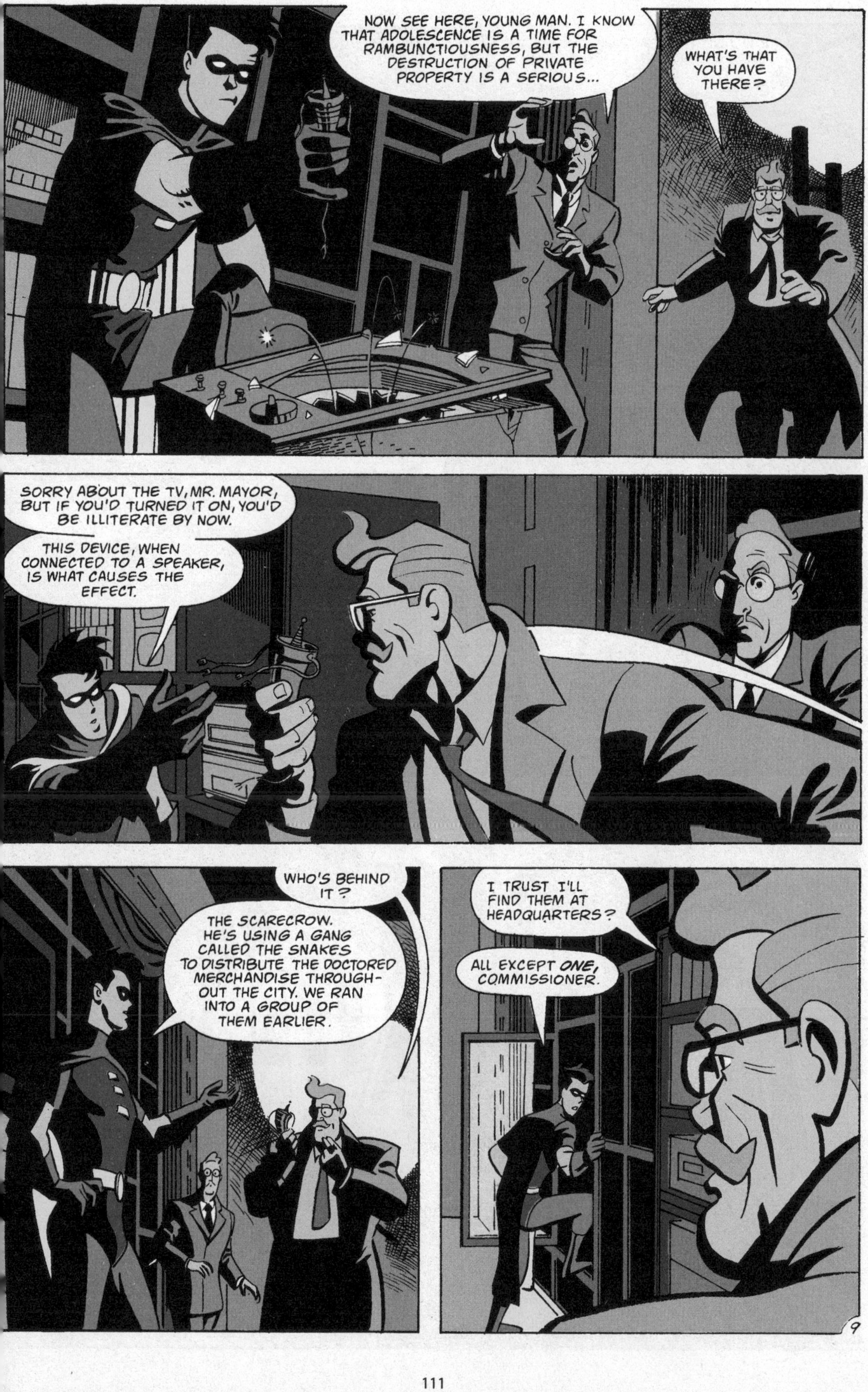
NOW SEE HERE, YOUNG MAN. I KNOW THAT ADOLESCENCE IS A TIME FOR RAMBUNCTIOUSNESS, BUT THE DESTRUCTION OF PRIVATE PROPERTY IS A SERIOUS...
WHAT'S THAT YOU HAVE THERE?
SORRY ABOUT THE TV, MR. MAYOR, BUT IF YOU'D TURNED IT ON, YOU'D BE ILLITERATE BY NOW.
THIS DEVICE, WHEN CONNECTED TO A SPEAKER, IS WHAT CAUSES THE EFFECT.
WHO'S BEHIND IT?
THE SCARECROW. HE'S USING A GANG CALLED THE SNAKES TO DISTRIBUTE THE DOCTORED MERCHANDISE THROUGH-OUT THE CITY. WE RAN INTO A GROUP OF THEM EARLIER.
I TRUST I'LL FIND THEM AT HEADQUARTERS?
ALL EXCEPT ONE, COMMISSIONER.
9

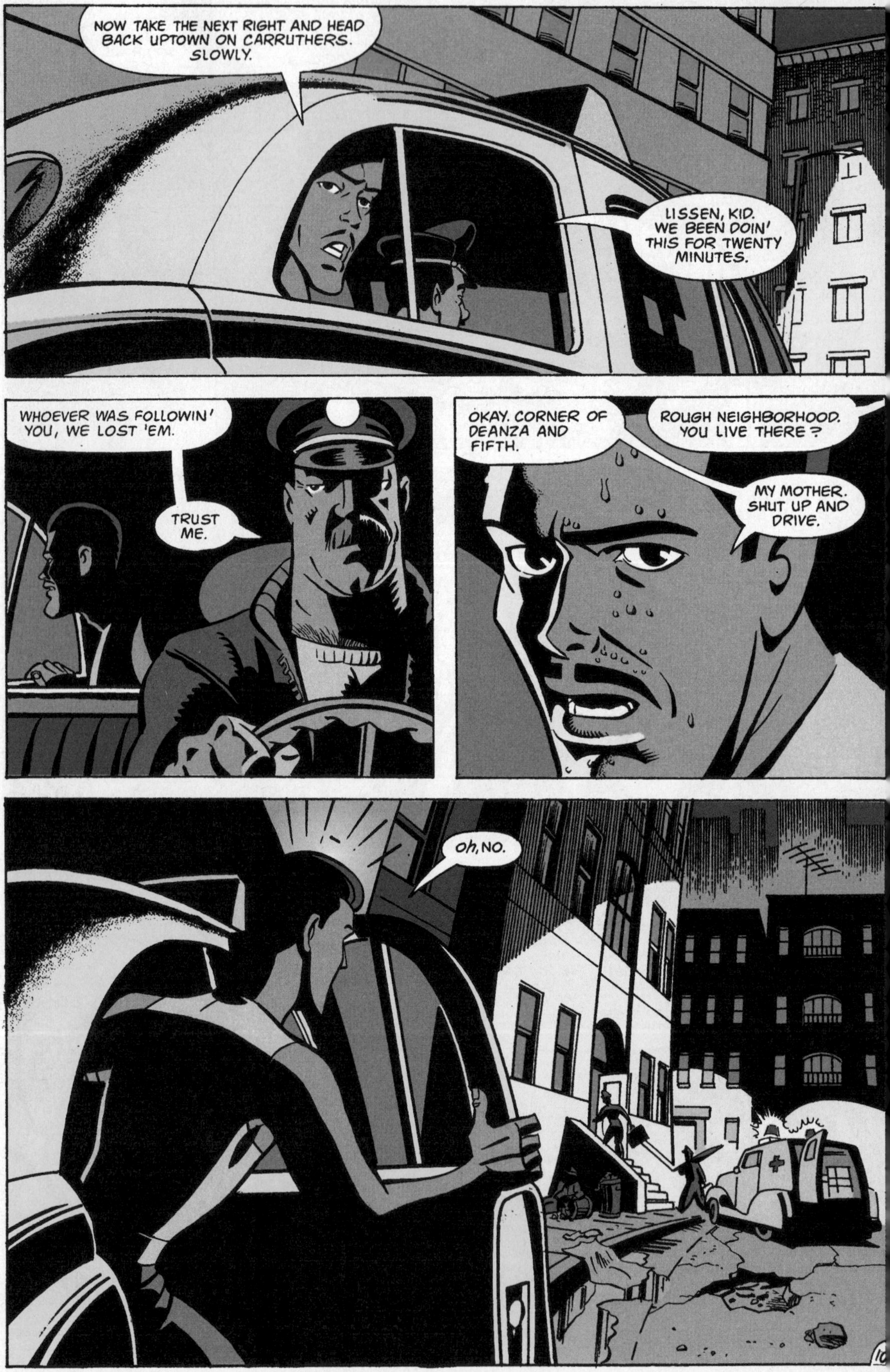
NOW TAKE THE NEXT RIGHT AND HEAD BACK UPTOWN ON CARRUTHERS. SLOWLY.
LISSEN, KID. WE BEEN DOIN' THIS FOR TWENTY MINUTES.
WHOEVER WAS FOLLOWIN' YOU, WE LOST 'EM.
TRUST ME.
OKAY. CORNER OF DEANZA AND FIFTH.
ROUGH NEIGHBORHOOD. YOU LIVE THERE?
MY MOTHER. SHUT UP AND DRIVE.
Oh, NO.
10

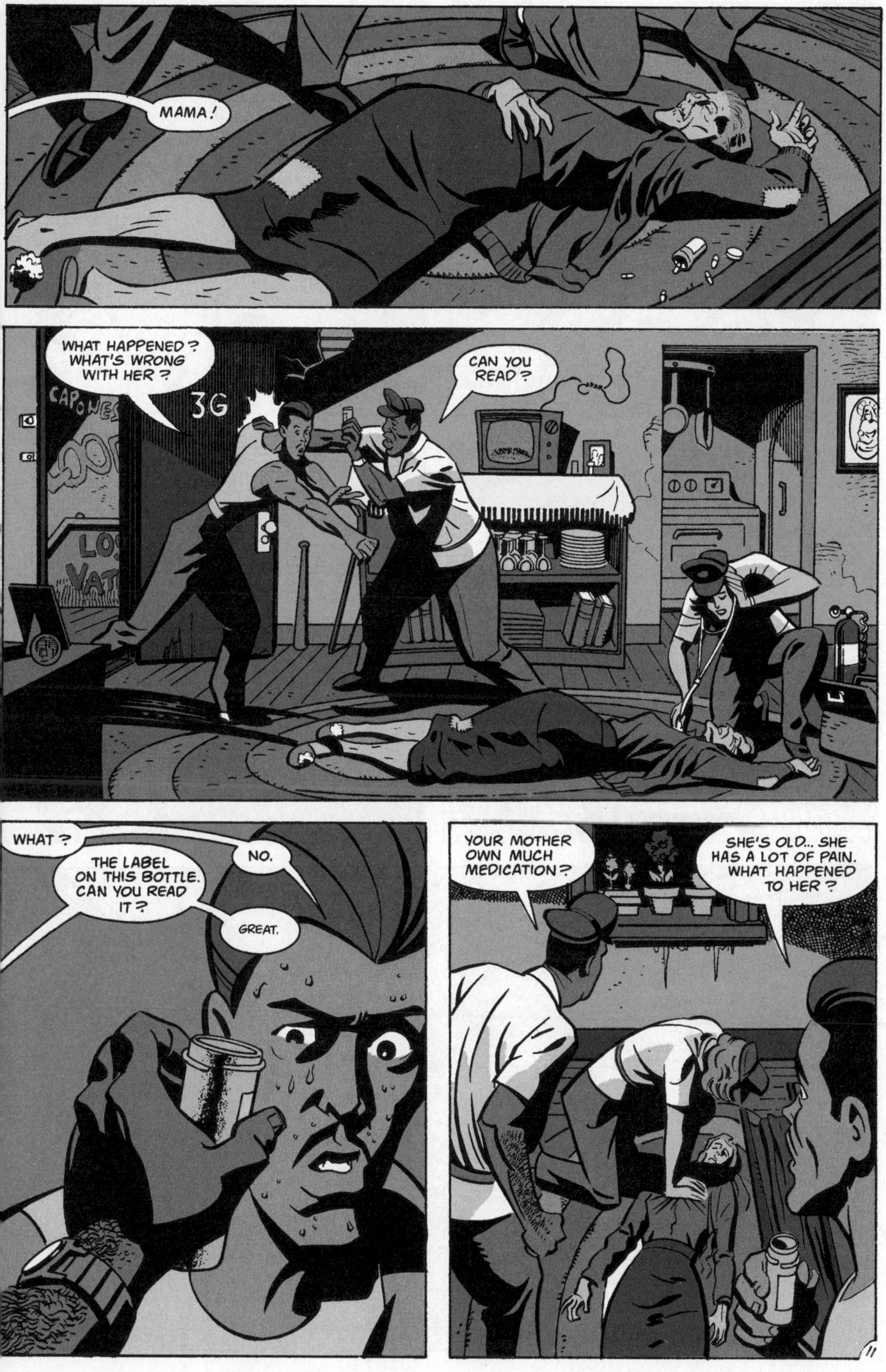
MAMA!
WHAT HAPPENED? WHAT'S WRONG WITH HER?
CAN YOU READ?
3G
WHAT?
THE LABEL ON THIS BOTTLE. CAN YOU READ IT?
NO.
GREAT.
YOUR MOTHER OWN MUCH MEDICATION?
SHE'S OLD... SHE HAS A LOT OF PAIN. WHAT HAPPENED TO HER?
11

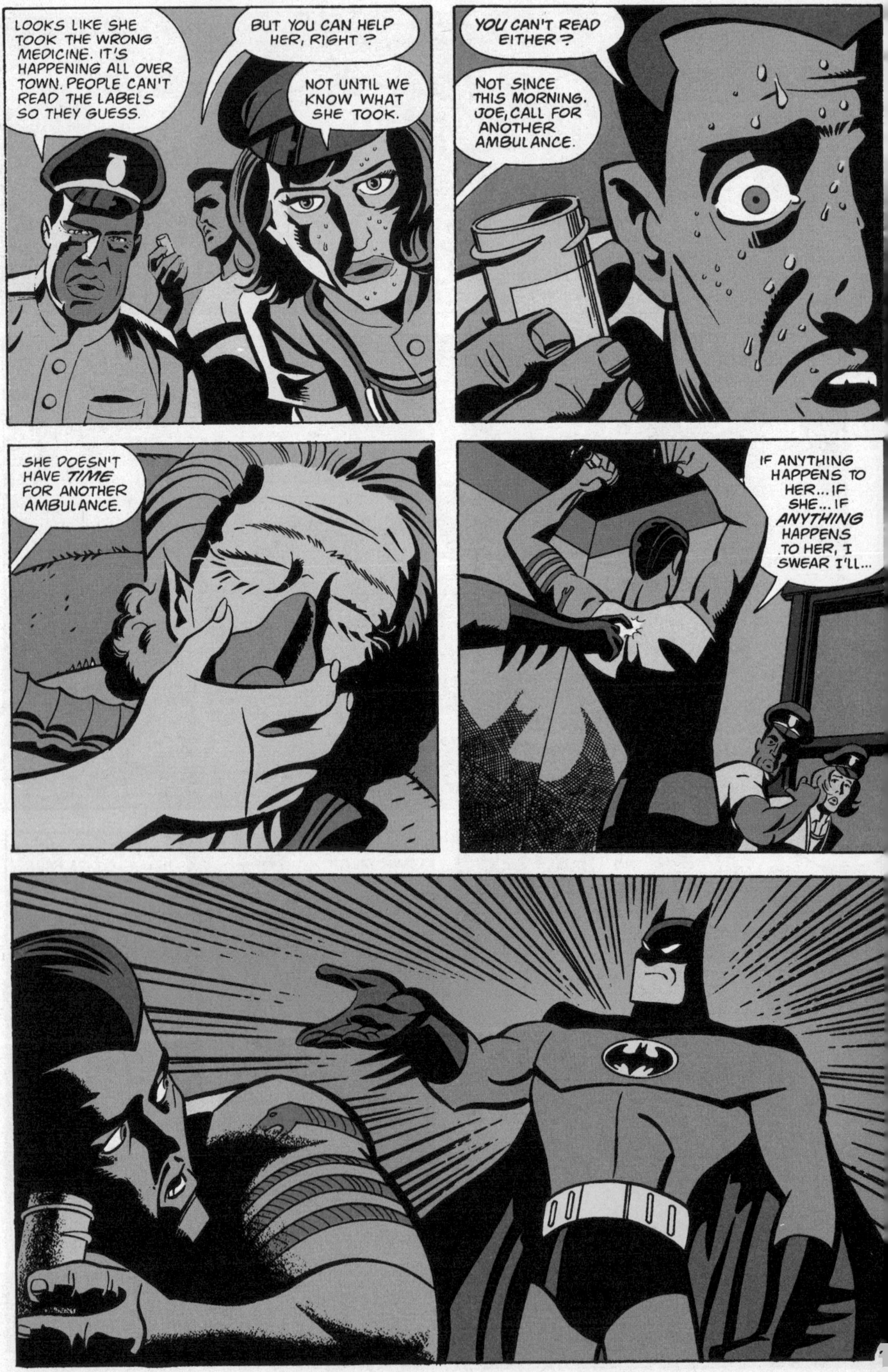
LOOKS LIKE SHE TOOK THE WRONG MEDICINE. IT'S HAPPENING ALL OVER TOWN. PEOPLE CAN'T READ THE LABELS SO THEY GUESS.
BUT YOU CAN HELP HER, RIGHT?
NOT UNTIL WE KNOW WHAT SHE TOOK.
YOU CAN'T READ EITHER?
NOT SINCE THIS MORNING. JOE, CALL FOR ANOTHER AMBULANCE.
SHE DOESN'T HAVE TIME FOR ANOTHER AMBULANCE.
IF ANYTHING HAPPENS TO HER... IF SHE... IF ANYTHING HAPPENS TO HER, I SWEAR I'LL...

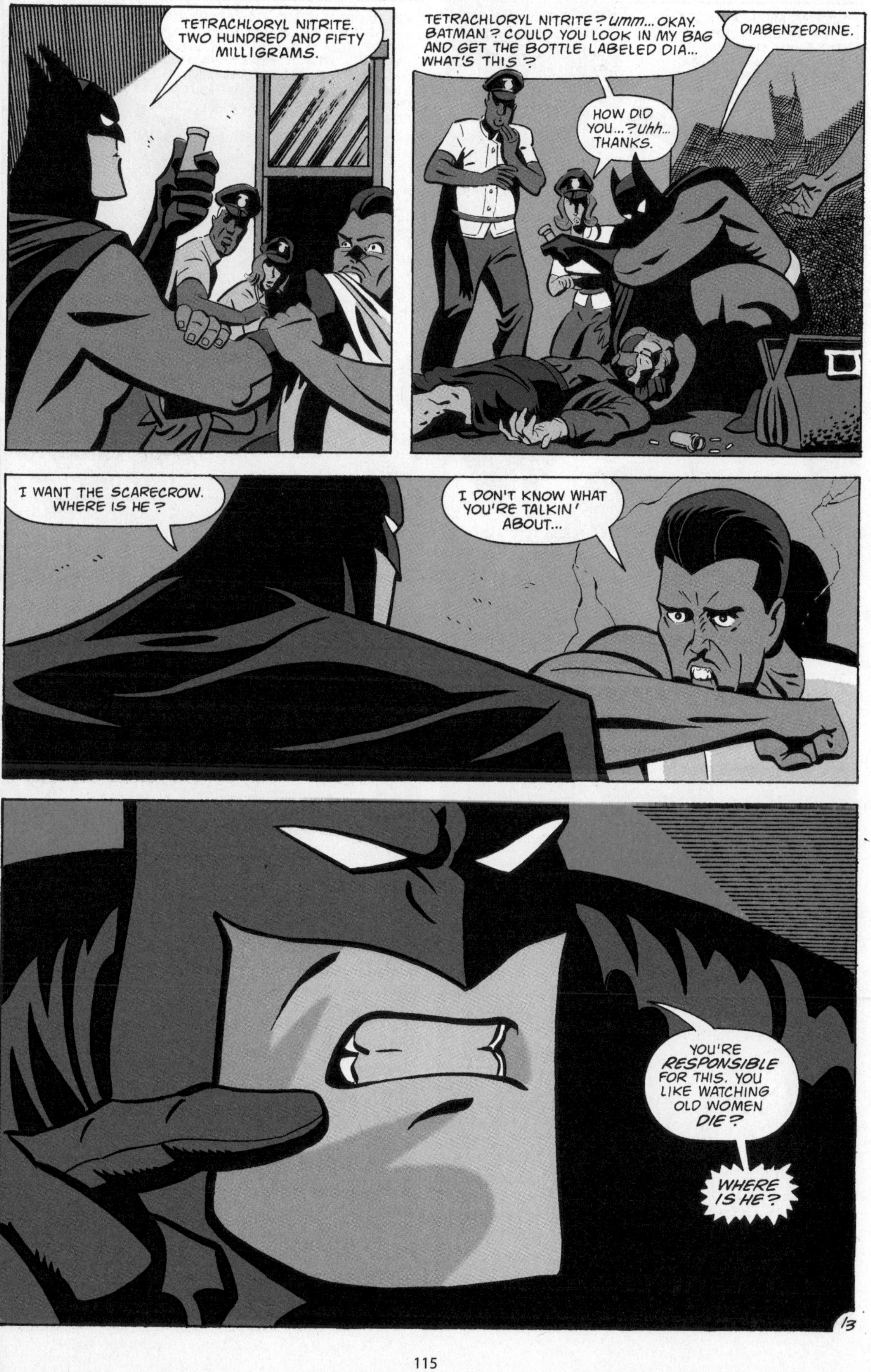
TETRACHLORYL NITRITE. TWO HUNDRED AND FIFTY MILLIGRAMS.
TETRACHLORYL NITRITE? UMM... OKAY. BATMAN? COULD YOU LOOK IN MY BAG AND GET THE BOTTLE LABELED DIA... WHAT'S THIS?
DIABENZEDRINE.
HOW DID YOU...? UHH... THANKS.
I WANT THE SCARECROW. WHERE IS HE?
I DON'T KNOW WHAT YOU'RE TALKIN' ABOUT...
YOU'RE RESPONSIBLE FOR THIS. YOU LIKE WATCHING OLD WOMEN DIE?
WHERE IS HE?
13

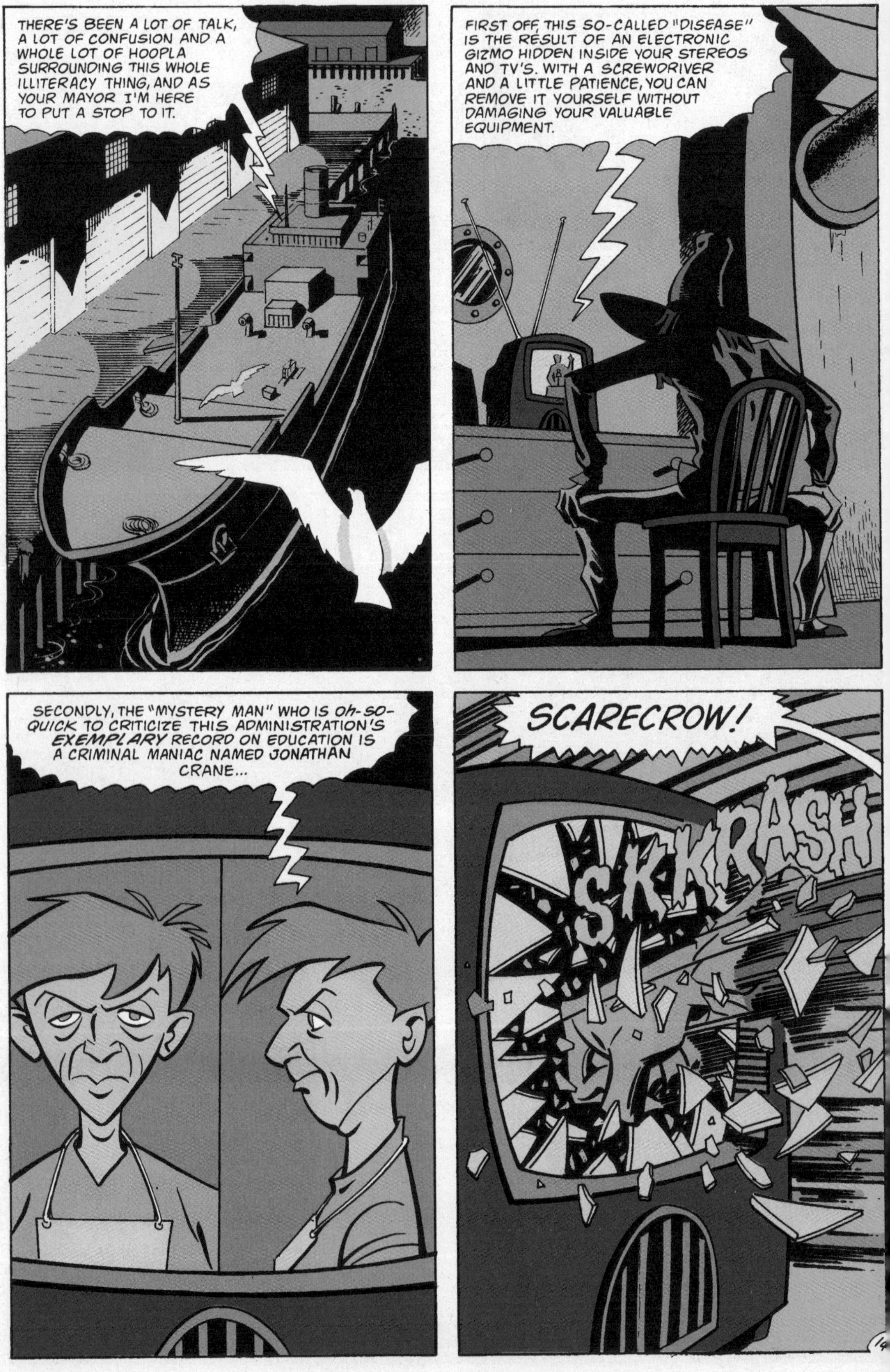
THERE'S BEEN A LOT OF TALK, A LOT OF CONFUSION AND A WHOLE LOT OF HOOPLA SURROUNDING THIS WHOLE ILLITERACY THING, AND AS YOUR MAYOR I'M HERE TO PUT A STOP TO IT.
FIRST OFF, THIS SO-CALLED "DISEASE" IS THE RESULT OF AN ELECTRONIC GIZMO HIDDEN INSIDE YOUR STEREOS AND TV'S. WITH A SCREWDRIVER AND A LITTLE PATIENCE, YOU CAN REMOVE IT YOURSELF WITHOUT DAMAGING YOUR VALUABLE EQUIPMENT.
SECONDLY, THE "MYSTERY MAN" WHO IS *oh-so-quick* TO CRITICIZE THIS ADMINISTRATION'S *EXEMPLARY* RECORD ON EDUCATION IS A CRIMINAL MANIAC NAMED JONATHAN CRANE...
SCARECROW!
SKKRASH

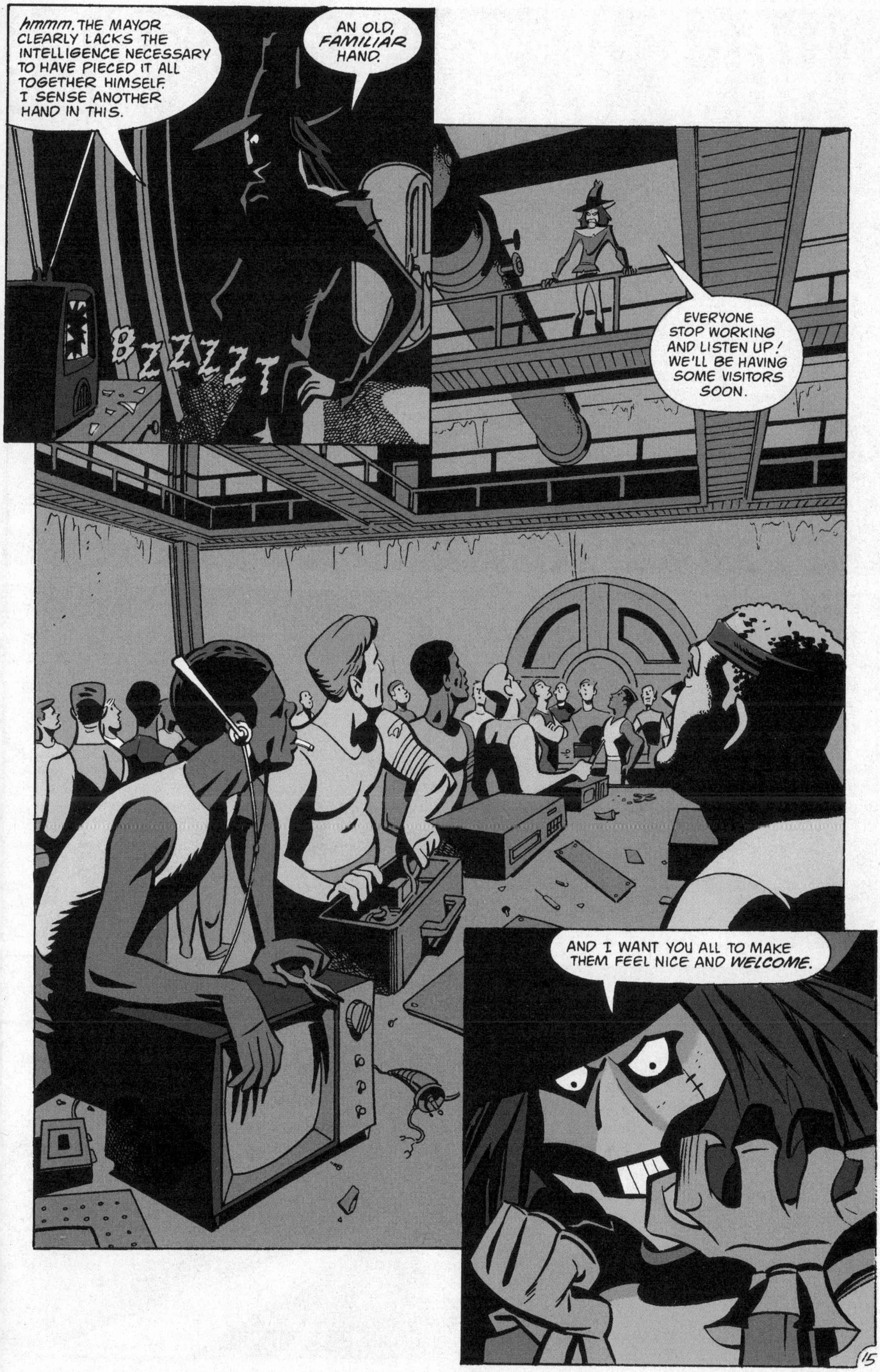
hmmm. THE MAYOR CLEARLY LACKS THE INTELLIGENCE NECESSARY TO HAVE PIECED IT ALL TOGETHER HIMSELF. I SENSE ANOTHER HAND IN THIS.
AN OLD, *FAMILIAR* HAND.
BZZZZZT
EVERYONE STOP WORKING AND LISTEN UP! WE'LL BE HAVING SOME VISITORS SOON.
AND I WANT YOU ALL TO MAKE THEM FEEL NICE AND *WELCOME*.
15

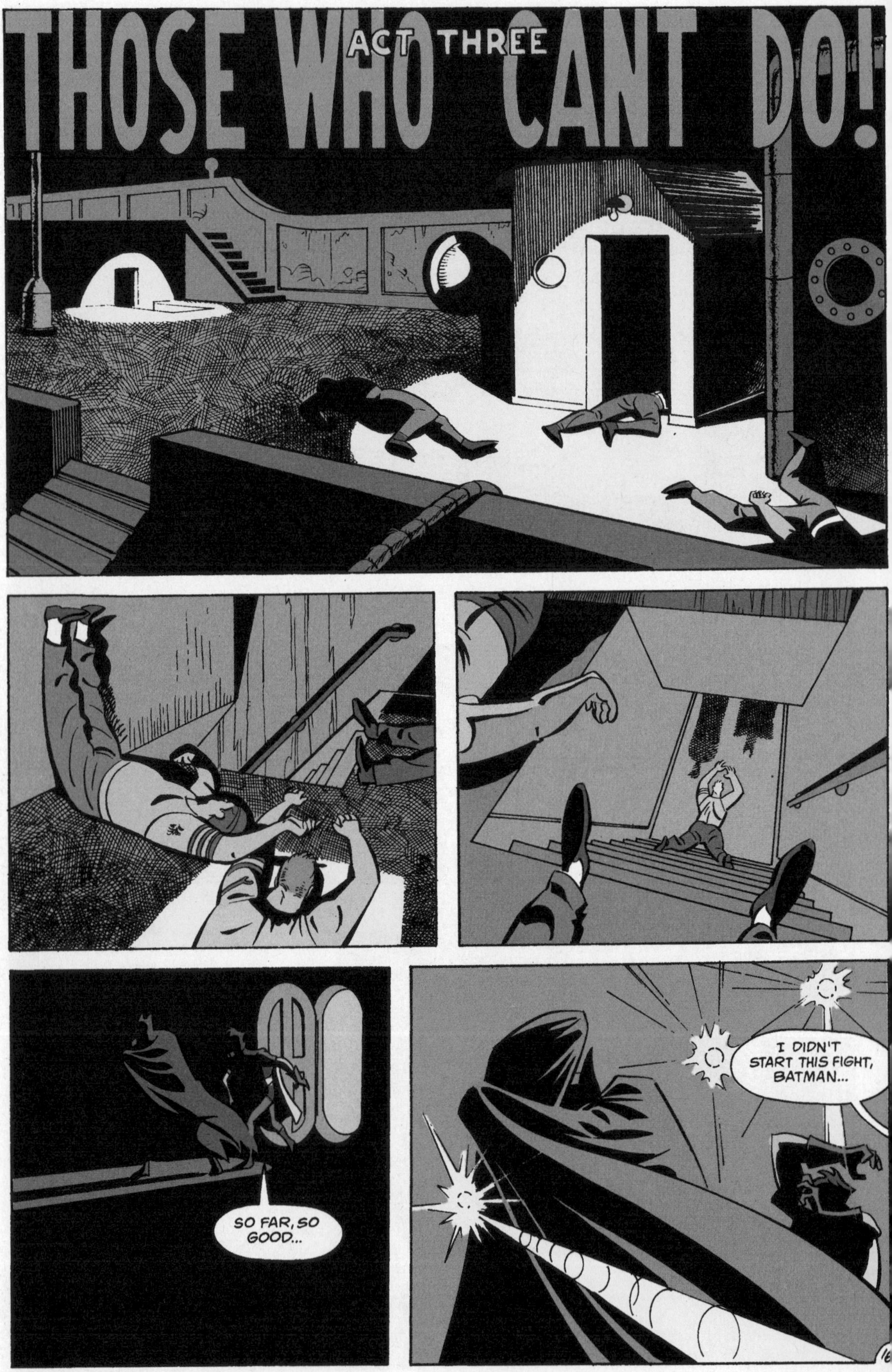
ACT THREE
THOSE WHO CANT DO!
SO FAR, SO GOOD...
I DIDN'T START THIS FIGHT, BATMAN...

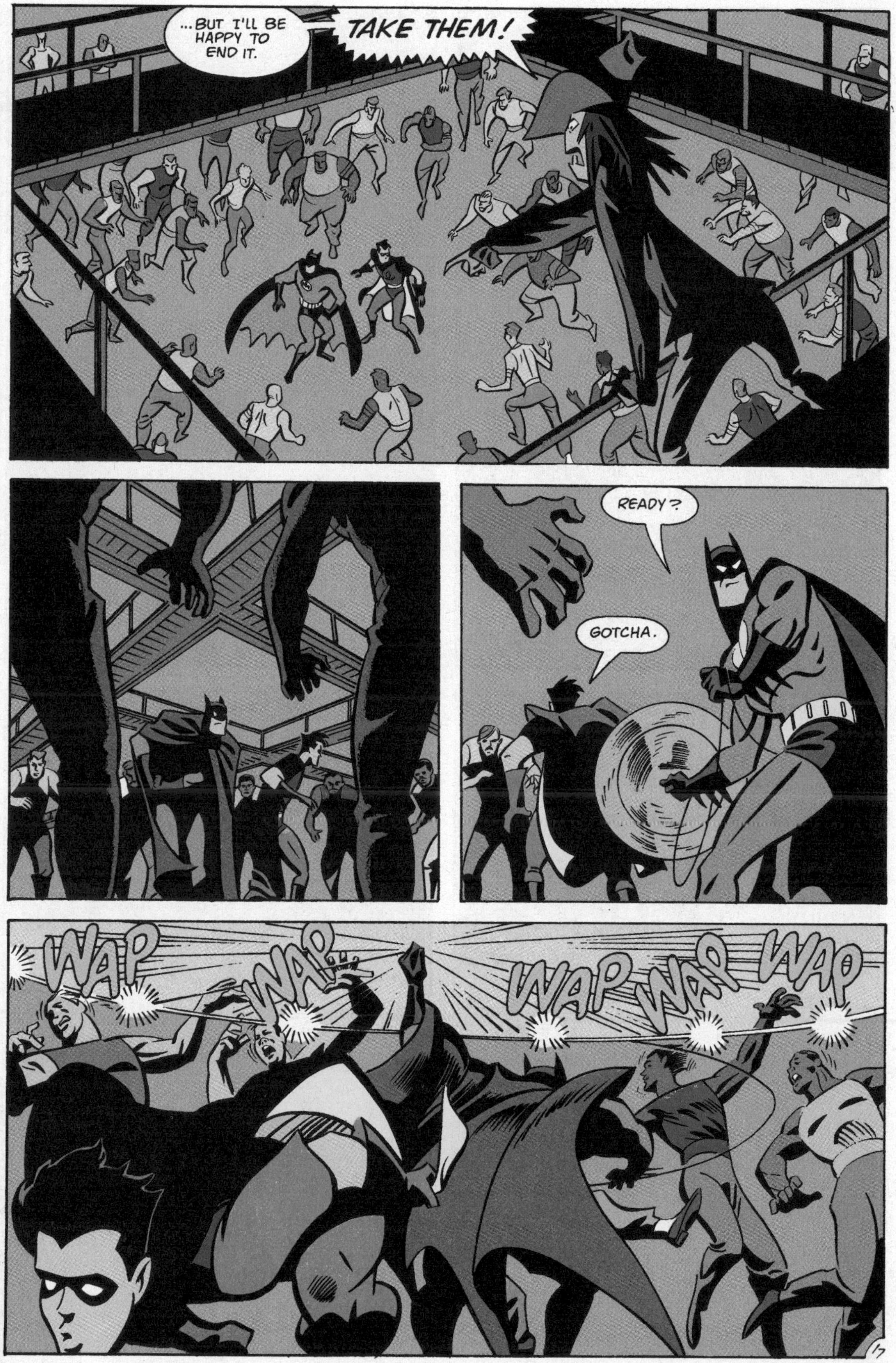
...BUT I'LL BE HAPPY TO END IT.
TAKE THEM!
READY?
GOTCHA.
WAP
WAP...
WAP
WAP
WAP
17

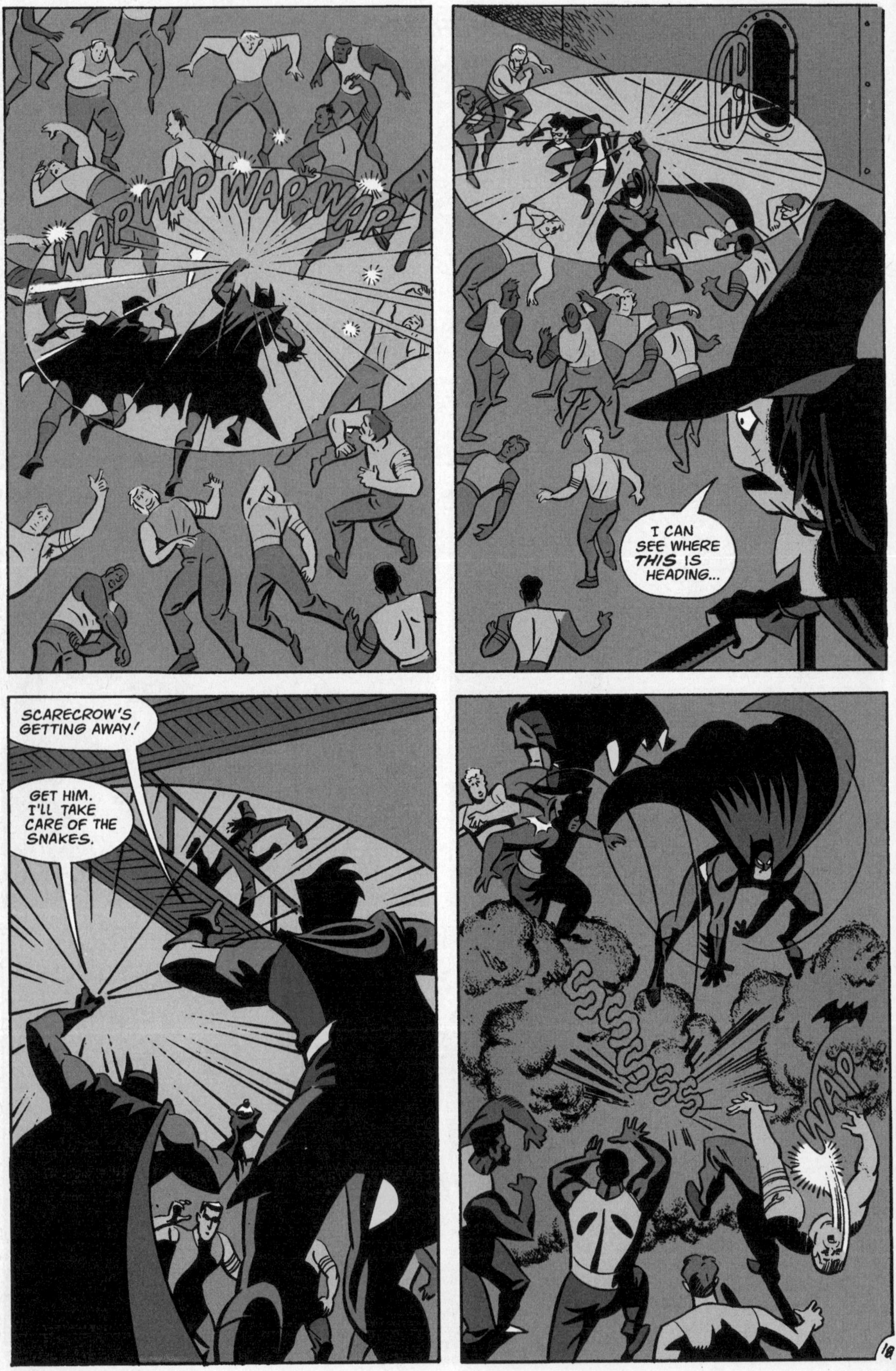
WAP WAP WAP WAP
I CAN SEE WHERE THIS IS HEADING...
SCARECROW'S GETTING AWAY!
GET HIM. I'LL TAKE CARE OF THE SNAKES.
SSSSSSS
WAP
18

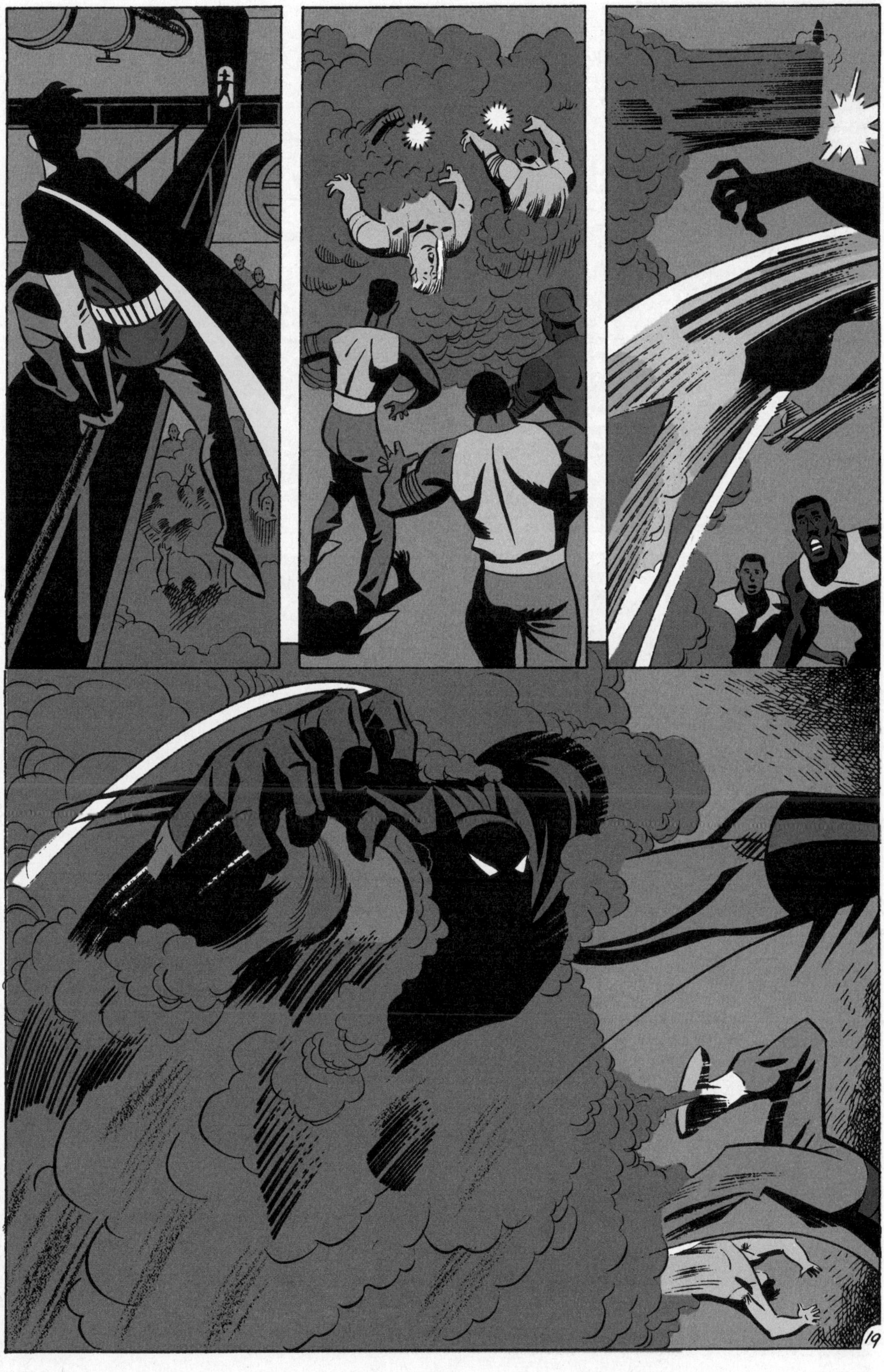
19

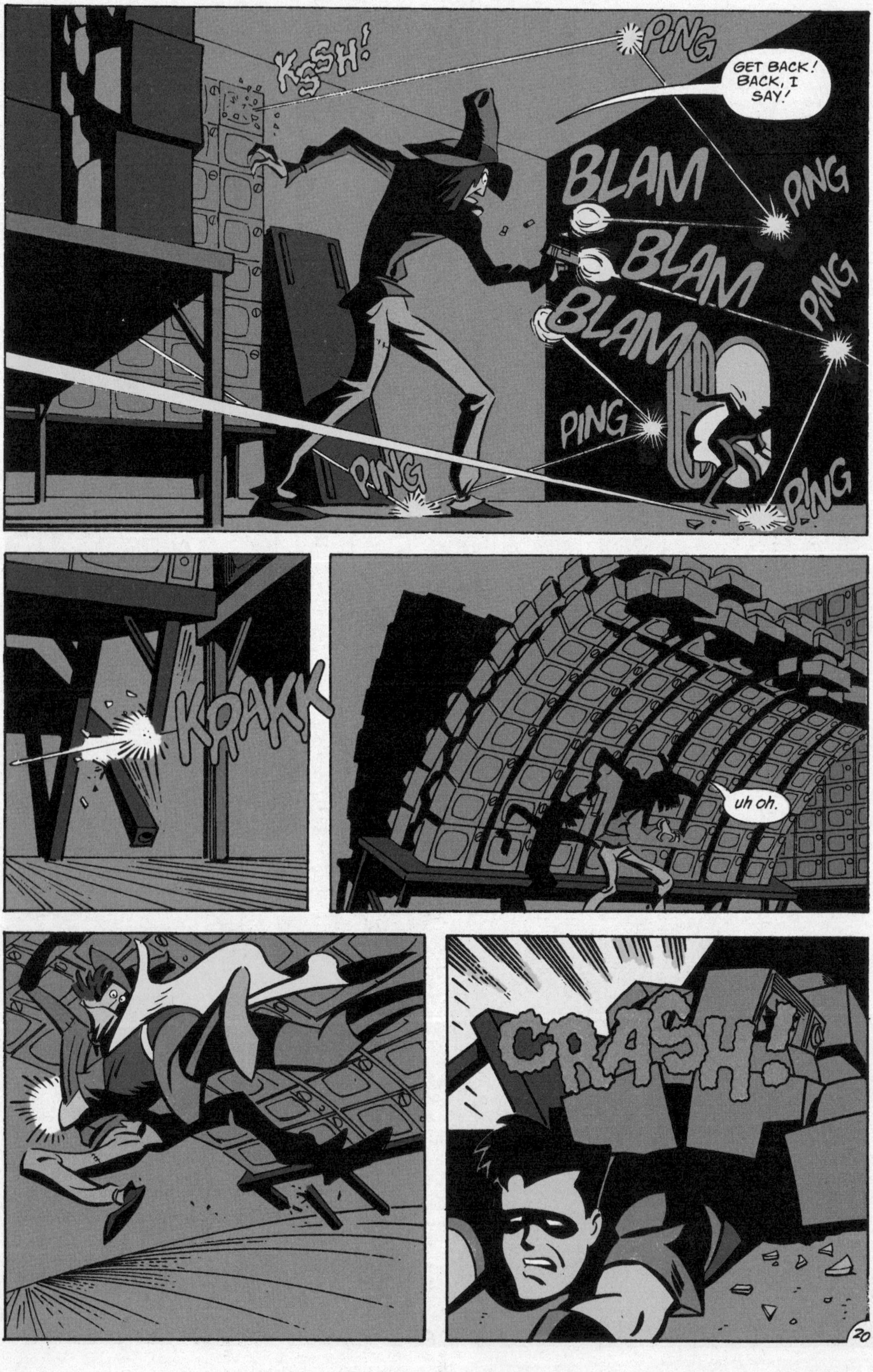
KSSH!
PING
GET BACK! BACK, I SAY!
BLAM
PING
BLAM
PING
BLAM
PING
PING
PING
KRAKK
uh oh.
CRASH!
20

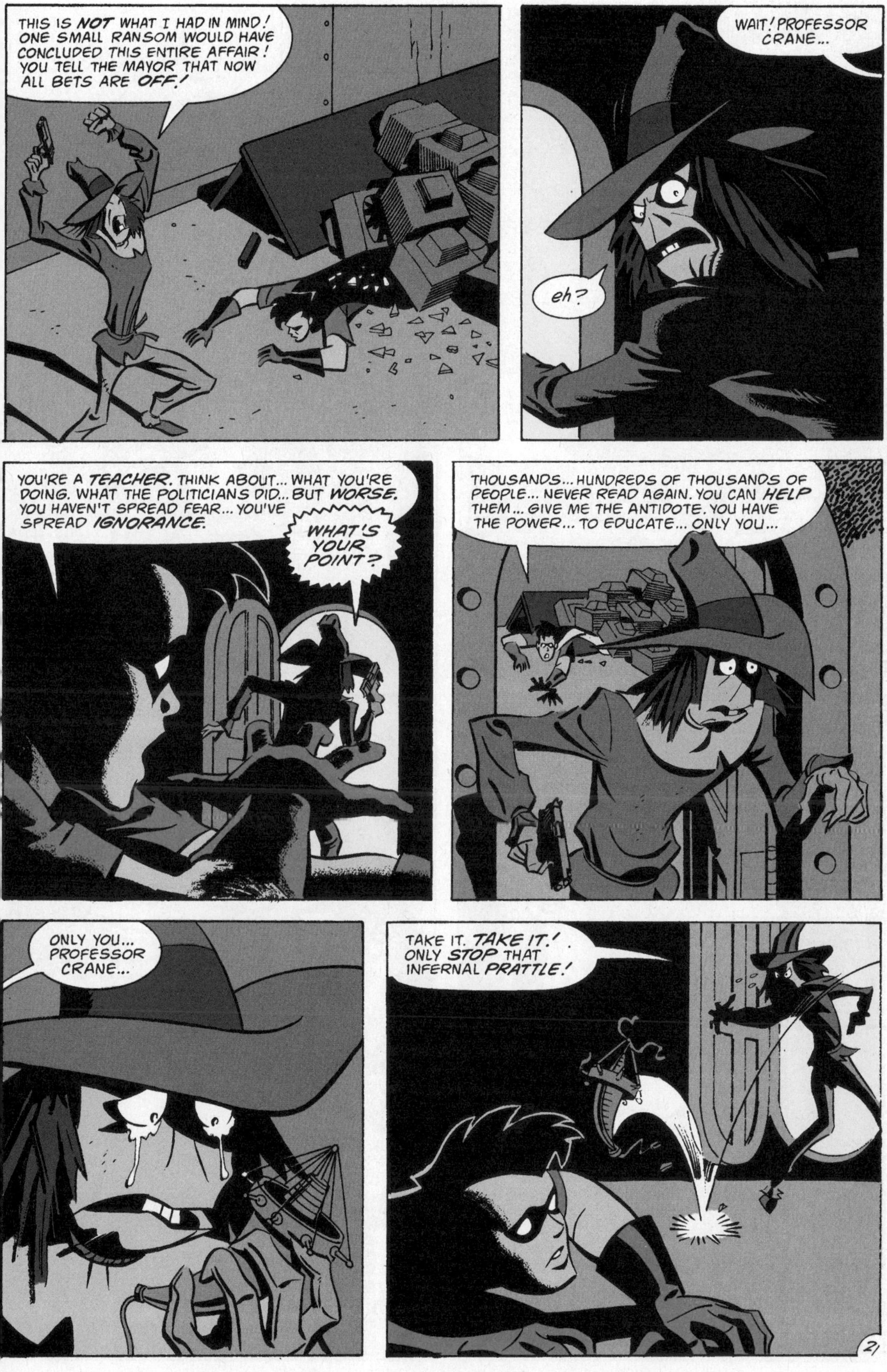
THIS IS NOT WHAT I HAD IN MIND! ONE SMALL RANSOM WOULD HAVE CONCLUDED THIS ENTIRE AFFAIR! YOU TELL THE MAYOR THAT NOW ALL BETS ARE OFF!
WAIT! PROFESSOR CRANE...
eh?
YOU'RE A TEACHER. THINK ABOUT... WHAT YOU'RE DOING. WHAT THE POLITICIANS DID... BUT WORSE. YOU HAVEN'T SPREAD FEAR... YOU'VE SPREAD IGNORANCE.
WHAT'S YOUR POINT?
THOUSANDS... HUNDREDS OF THOUSANDS OF PEOPLE... NEVER READ AGAIN. YOU CAN HELP THEM... GIVE ME THE ANTIDOTE. YOU HAVE THE POWER... TO EDUCATE... ONLY YOU...
ONLY YOU... PROFESSOR CRANE...
TAKE IT. TAKE IT! ONLY STOP THAT INFERNAL PRATTLE!
21

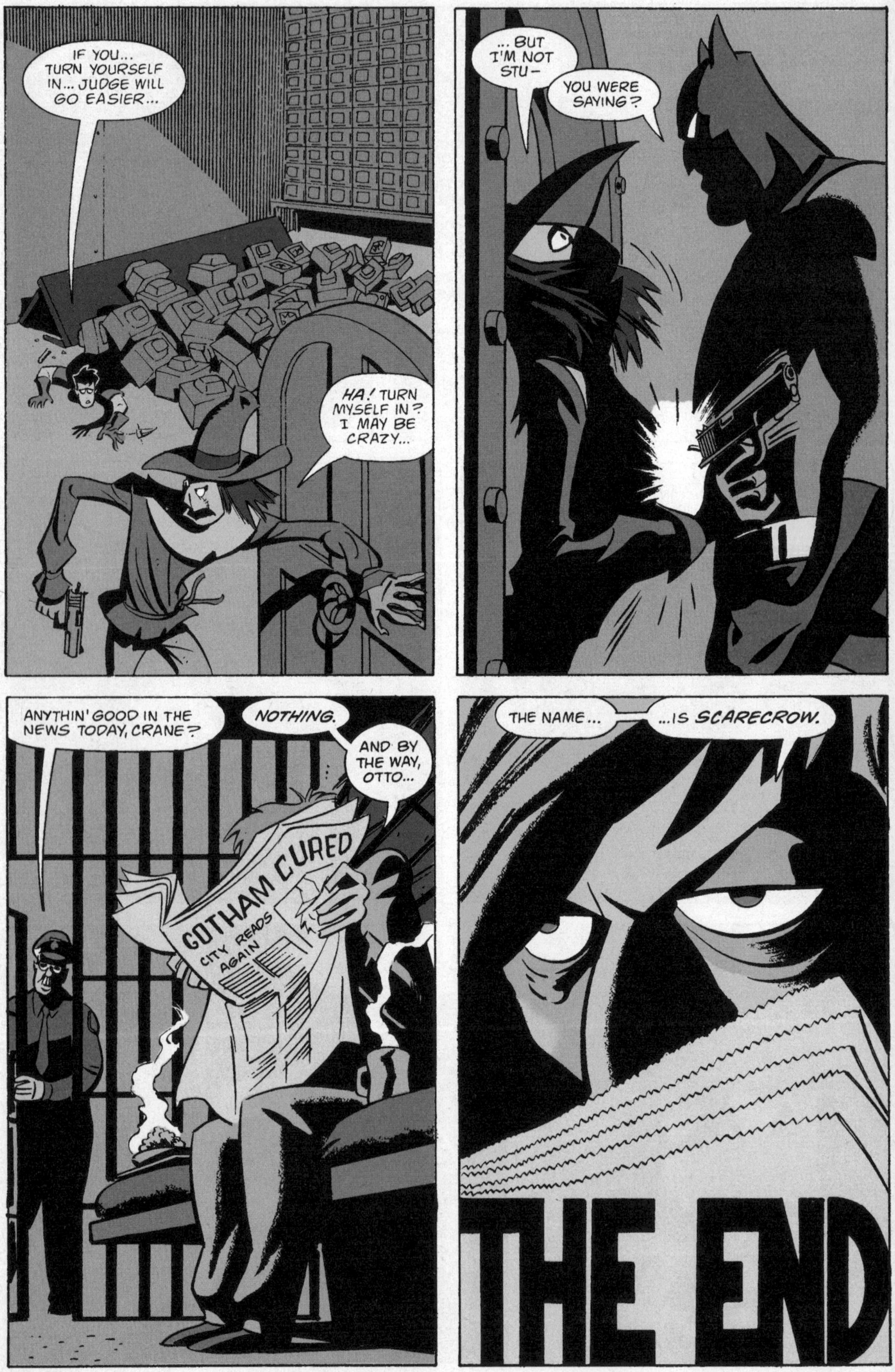

IF YOU... TURN YOURSELF IN... JUDGE WILL GO EASIER...
HA! TURN MYSELF IN? I MAY BE CRAZY...
... BUT I'M NOT STU-
YOU WERE SAYING?
ANYTHIN' GOOD IN THE NEWS TODAY, CRANE?
NOTHING.
AND BY THE WAY, OTTO...
GOTHAM CURED
CITY READS AGAIN
THE NAME...
...IS SCARECROW.
THE END

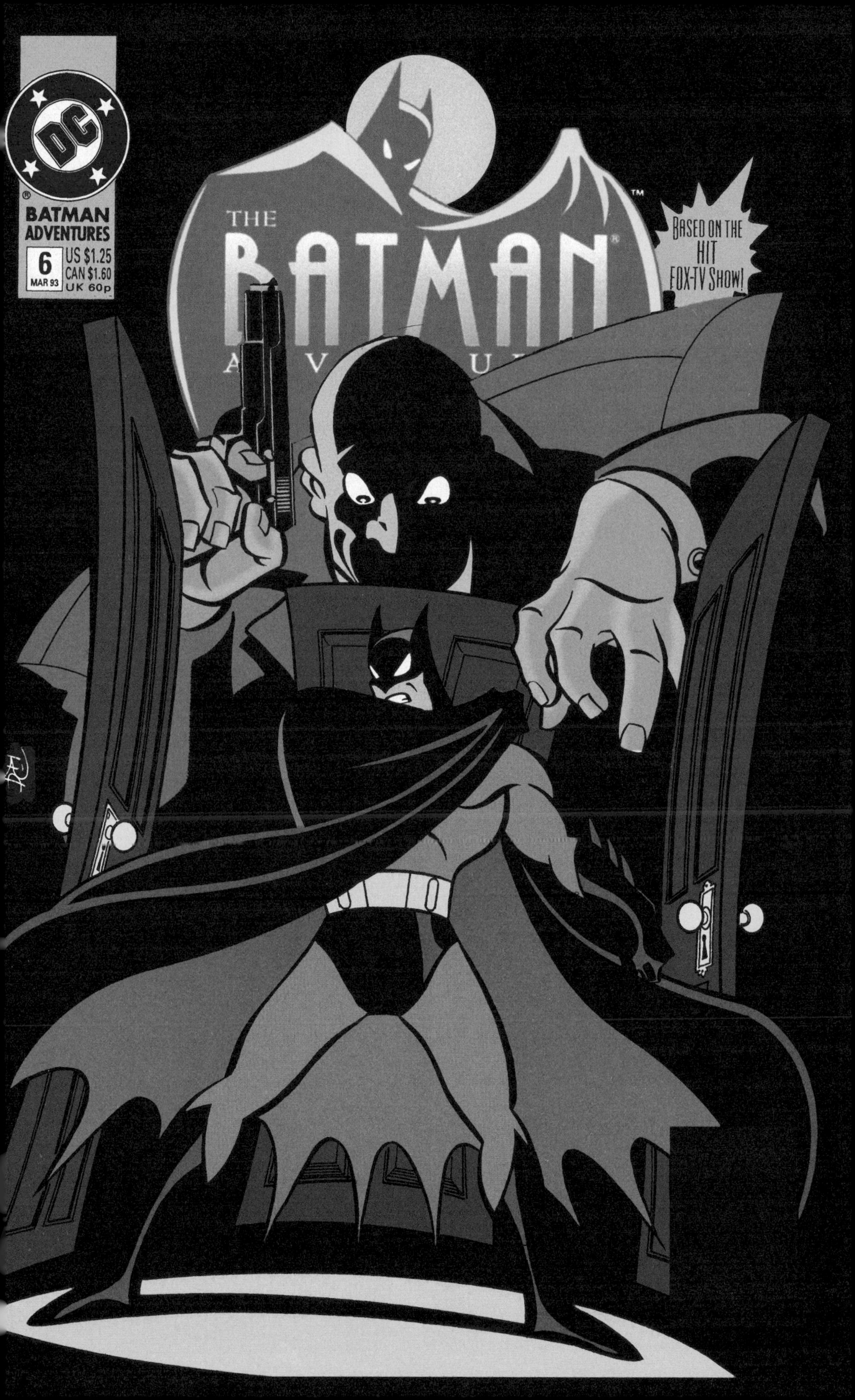

BATMAN ADVENTURES
6
MAR 93
US $1.25
CAN $1.60
UK 60p
THE BATMAN ADVENTURES
BASED ON THE HIT FOX-TV SHOW!

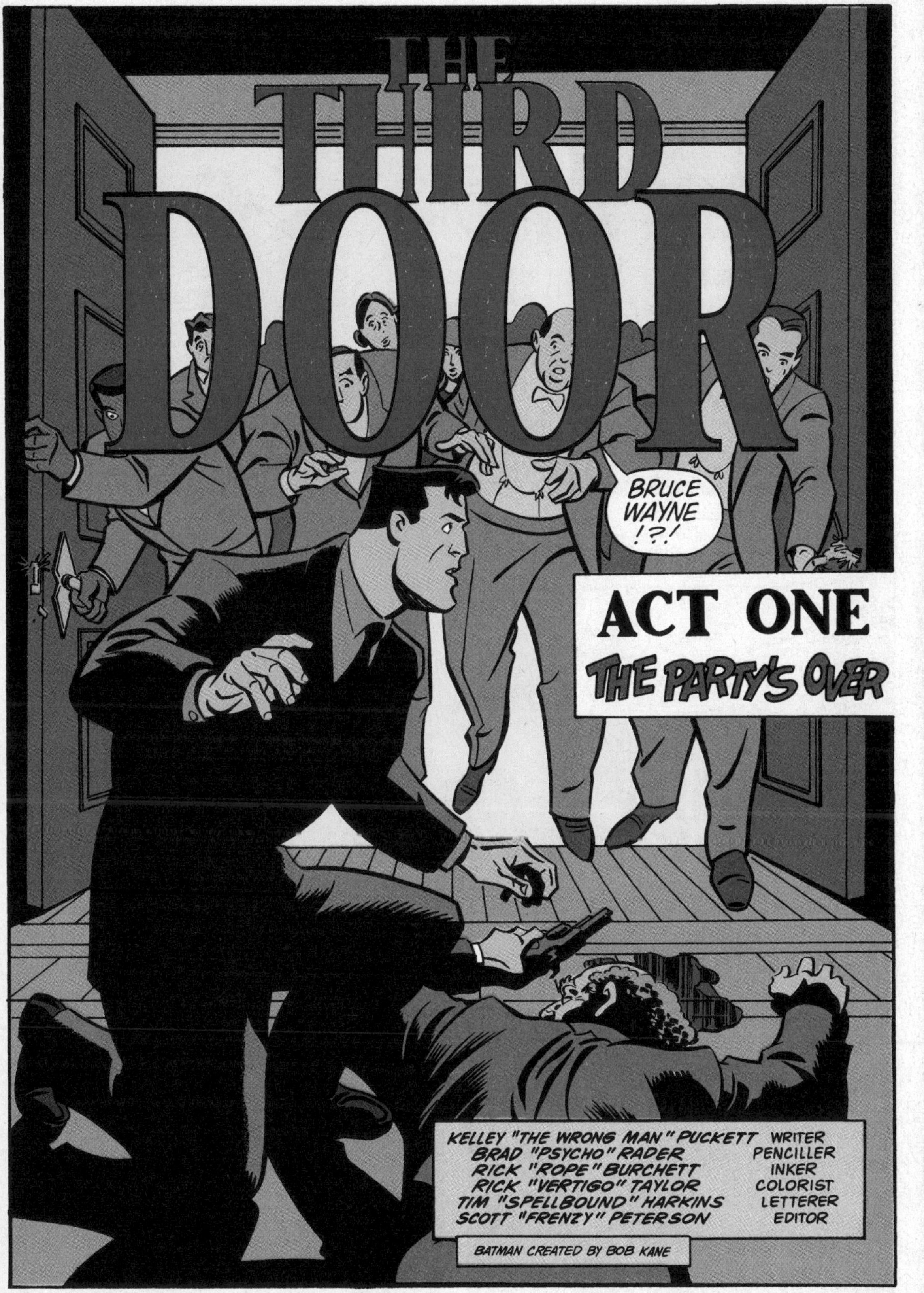
THE THIRD DOOR
BRUCE WAYNE !?!
ACT ONE
THE PARTY'S OVER
KELLEY "THE WRONG MAN" PUCKETT WRITER
BRAD "PSYCHO" RADER PENCILLER
RICK "ROPE" BURCHETT INKER
RICK "VERTIGO" TAYLOR COLORIST
TIM "SPELLBOUND" HARKINS LETTERER
SCOTT "FRENZY" PETERSON EDITOR
BATMAN CREATED BY BOB KANE

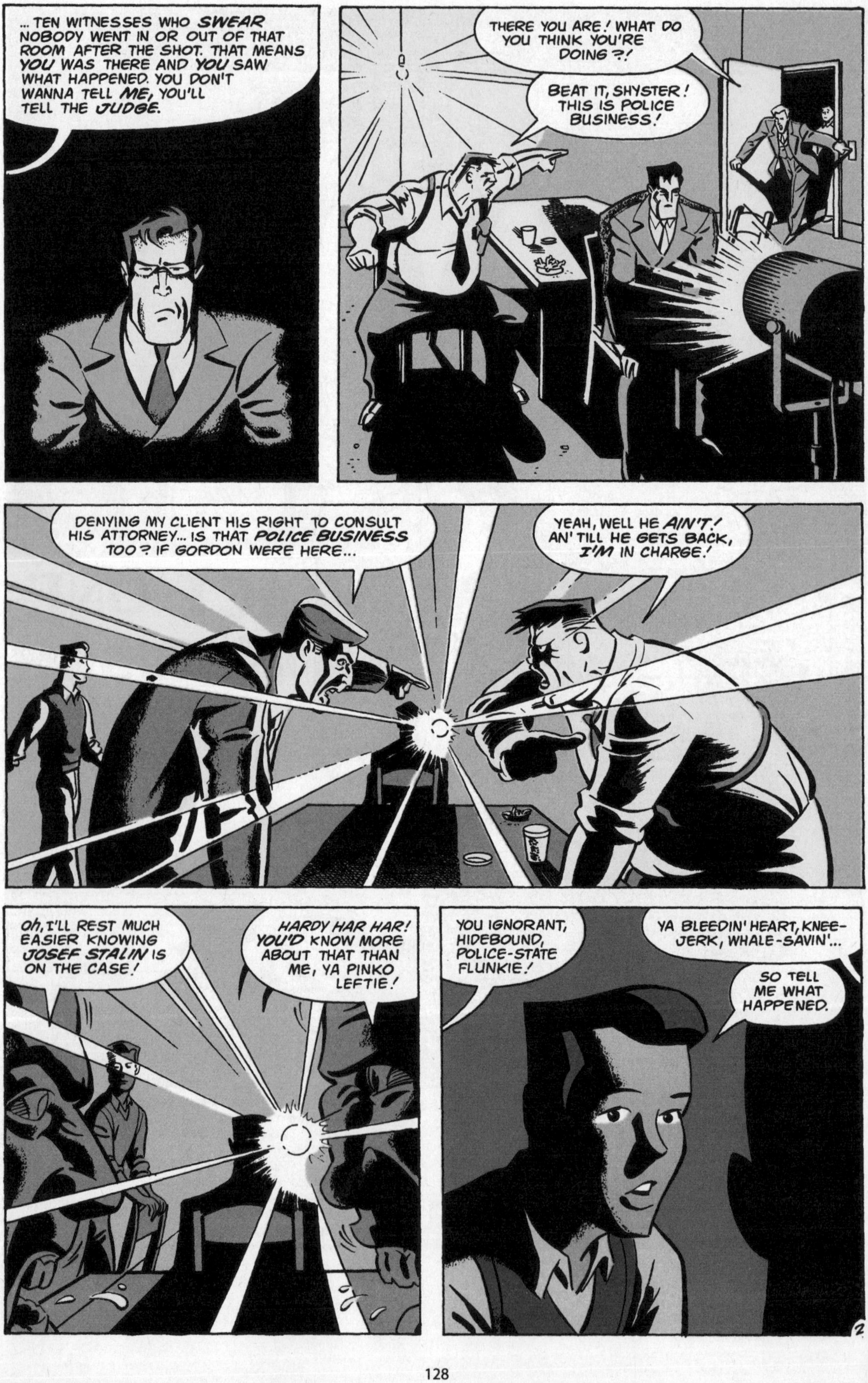
... TEN WITNESSES WHO SWEAR NOBODY WENT IN OR OUT OF THAT ROOM AFTER THE SHOT. THAT MEANS YOU WAS THERE AND YOU SAW WHAT HAPPENED. YOU DON'T WANNA TELL ME, YOU'LL TELL THE JUDGE.
THERE YOU ARE! WHAT DO YOU THINK YOU'RE DOING ?!
BEAT IT, SHYSTER! THIS IS POLICE BUSINESS!
DENYING MY CLIENT HIS RIGHT TO CONSULT HIS ATTORNEY... IS THAT POLICE BUSINESS TOO? IF GORDON WERE HERE...
YEAH, WELL HE AIN'T! AN' TILL HE GETS BACK, I'M IN CHARGE!
OH, I'LL REST MUCH EASIER KNOWING JOSEF STALIN IS ON THE CASE!
HARDY HAR HAR! YOU'D KNOW MORE ABOUT THAT THAN ME, YA PINKO LEFTIE!
YOU IGNORANT, HIDEBOUND, POLICE-STATE FLUNKIE!
YA BLEEDIN' HEART, KNEE-JERK, WHALE-SAVIN'...
SO TELL ME WHAT HAPPENED.
2

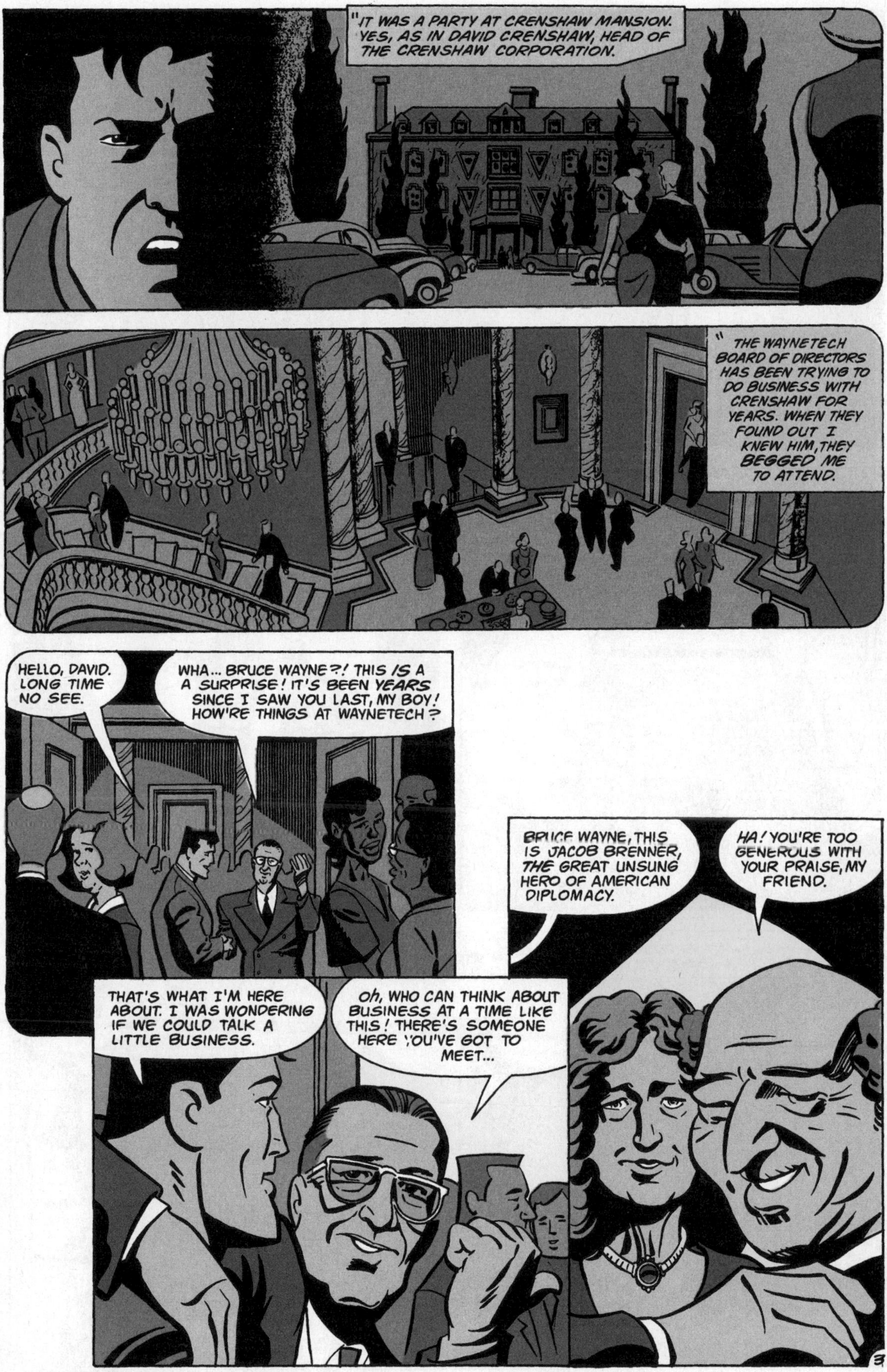
"IT WAS A PARTY AT CRENSHAW MANSION. YES, AS IN DAVID CRENSHAW, HEAD OF THE CRENSHAW CORPORATION.
"THE WAYNETECH BOARD OF DIRECTORS HAS BEEN TRYING TO DO BUSINESS WITH CRENSHAW FOR YEARS. WHEN THEY FOUND OUT I KNEW HIM, THEY BEGGED ME TO ATTEND.
HELLO, DAVID. LONG TIME NO SEE.
WHA... BRUCE WAYNE?! THIS IS A SURPRISE! IT'S BEEN YEARS SINCE I SAW YOU LAST, MY BOY! HOW'RE THINGS AT WAYNETECH?
THAT'S WHAT I'M HERE ABOUT. I WAS WONDERING IF WE COULD TALK A LITTLE BUSINESS.
Oh, WHO CAN THINK ABOUT BUSINESS AT A TIME LIKE THIS! THERE'S SOMEONE HERE YOU'VE GOT TO MEET...
BRUCE WAYNE, THIS IS JACOB BRENNER, THE GREAT UNSUNG HERO OF AMERICAN DIPLOMACY.
HA! YOU'RE TOO GENEROUS WITH YOUR PRAISE, MY FRIEND.
3

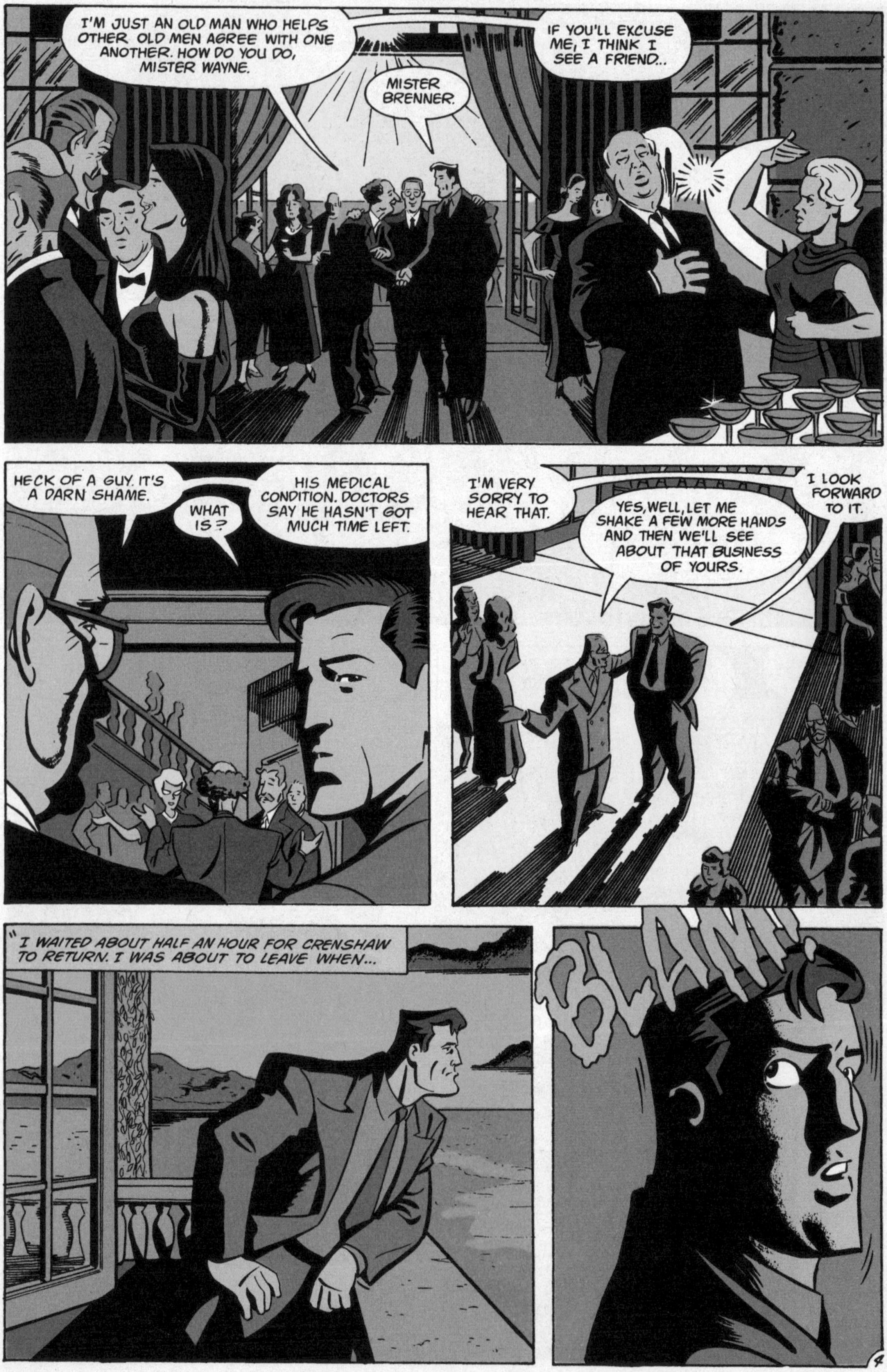
I'M JUST AN OLD MAN WHO HELPS OTHER OLD MEN AGREE WITH ONE ANOTHER. HOW DO YOU DO, MISTER WAYNE.
MISTER BRENNER.
IF YOU'LL EXCUSE ME, I THINK I SEE A FRIEND...
HECK OF A GUY. IT'S A DARN SHAME.
WHAT IS?
HIS MEDICAL CONDITION. DOCTORS SAY HE HASN'T GOT MUCH TIME LEFT.
I'M VERY SORRY TO HEAR THAT.
YES, WELL, LET ME SHAKE A FEW MORE HANDS AND THEN WE'LL SEE ABOUT THAT BUSINESS OF YOURS.
I LOOK FORWARD TO IT.
"I WAITED ABOUT HALF AN HOUR FOR CRENSHAW TO RETURN. I WAS ABOUT TO LEAVE WHEN...
BLAM!!
4

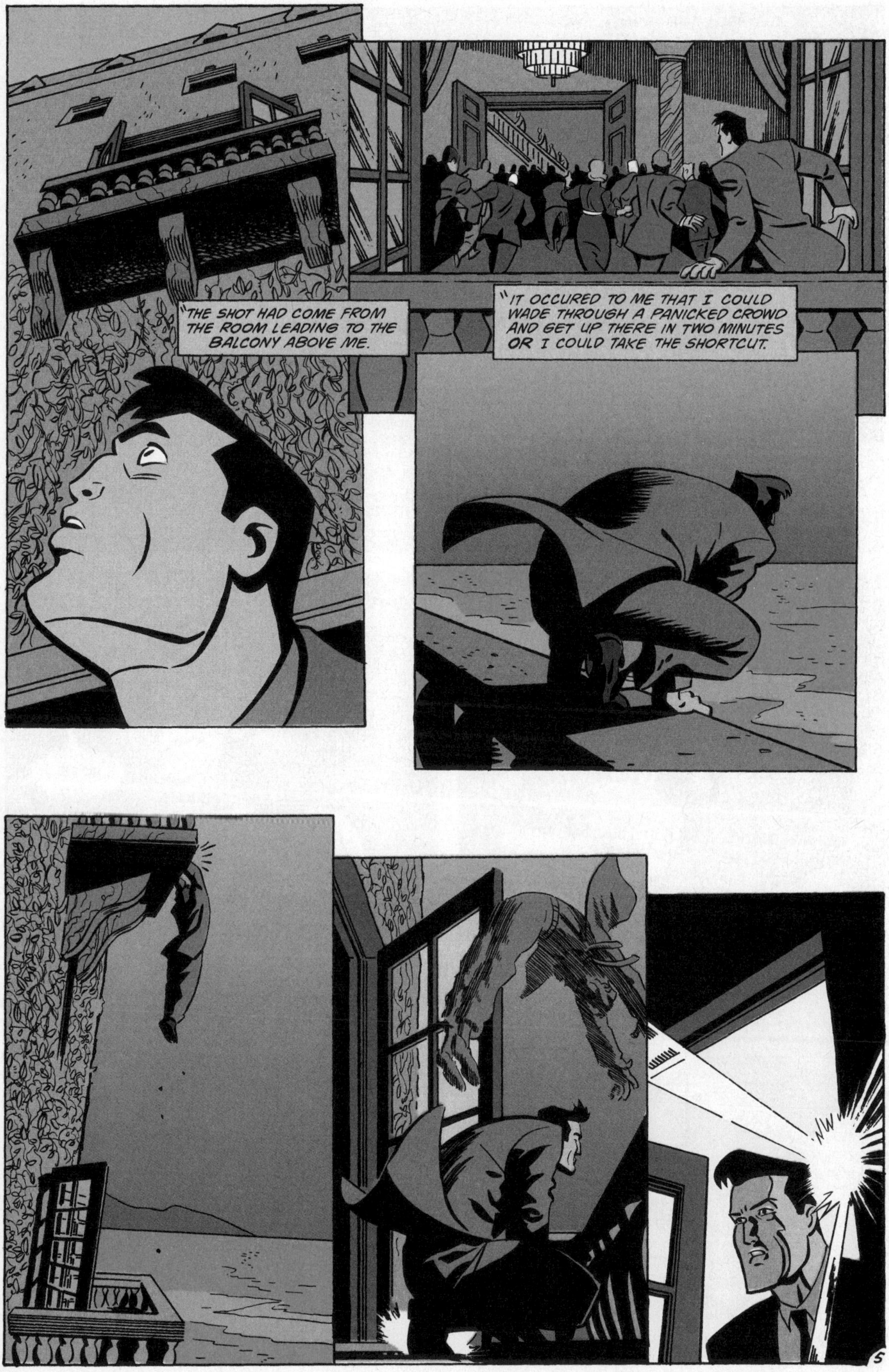
"THE SHOT HAD COME FROM THE ROOM LEADING TO THE BALCONY ABOVE ME.
"IT OCCURED TO ME THAT I COULD WADE THROUGH A PANICKED CROWD AND GET UP THERE IN TWO MINUTES OR I COULD TAKE THE SHORTCUT.

"I DID WHAT I COULD, BUT I WAS TOO LATE.

ROSE...

"I SUPPOSE HE WAS DELIRIOUS, CALLING FOR HIS WIFE, BUT HE SEEMED TO BE POINTING TO THE DOOR...

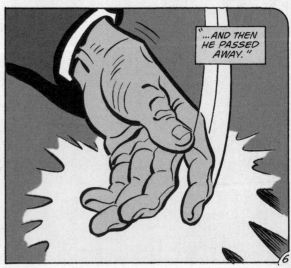

...AND THEN HE PASSED AWAY."

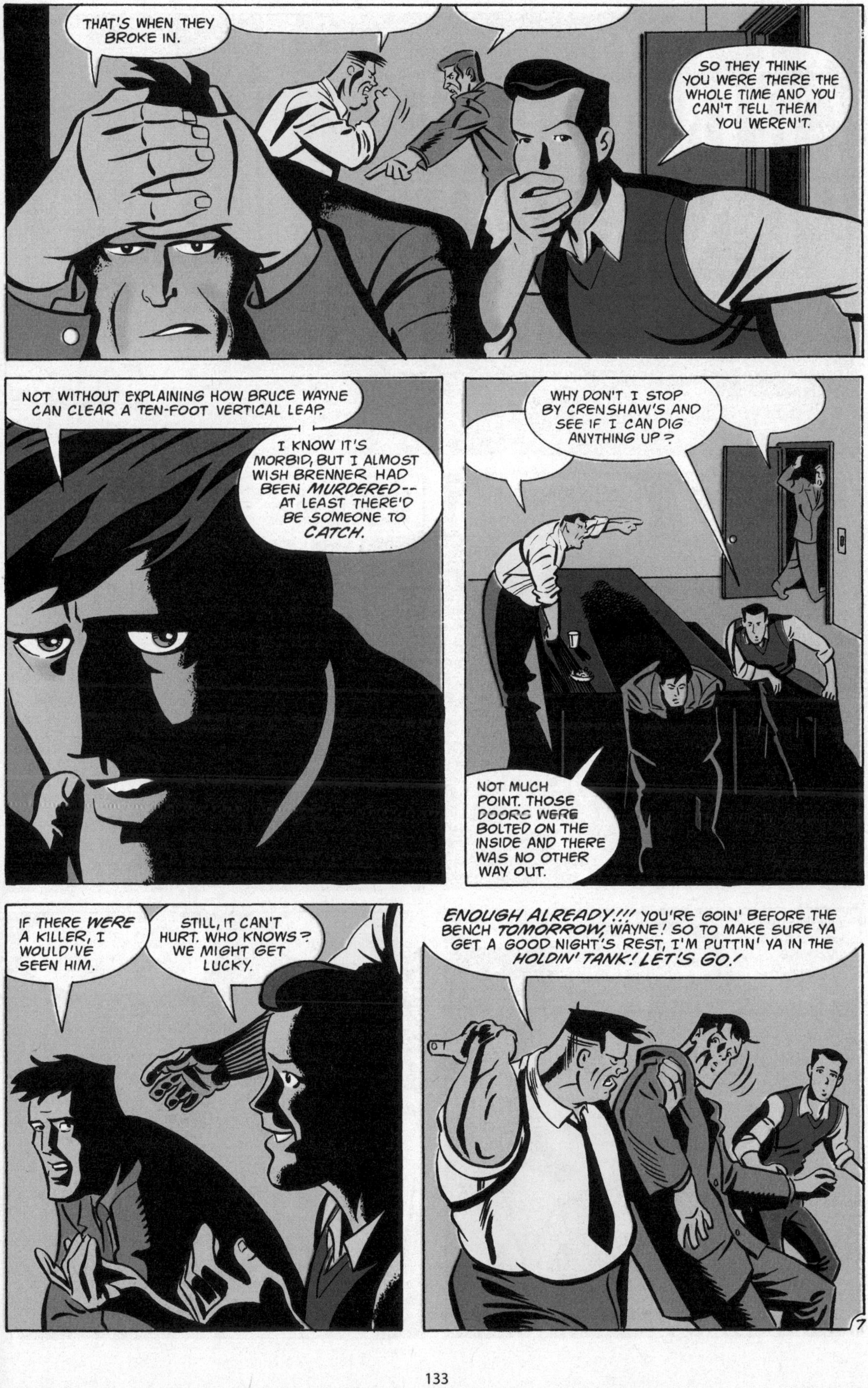
THAT'S WHEN THEY BROKE IN.
SO THEY THINK YOU WERE THERE THE WHOLE TIME AND YOU CAN'T TELL THEM YOU WEREN'T.
NOT WITHOUT EXPLAINING HOW BRUCE WAYNE CAN CLEAR A TEN-FOOT VERTICAL LEAP.
I KNOW IT'S MORBID, BUT I ALMOST WISH BRENNER HAD BEEN MURDERED-- AT LEAST THERE'D BE SOMEONE TO CATCH.
WHY DON'T I STOP BY CRENSHAW'S AND SEE IF I CAN DIG ANYTHING UP?
NOT MUCH POINT. THOSE DOORS WERE BOLTED ON THE INSIDE AND THERE WAS NO OTHER WAY OUT.
IF THERE WERE A KILLER, I WOULD'VE SEEN HIM.
STILL, IT CAN'T HURT. WHO KNOWS? WE MIGHT GET LUCKY.
ENOUGH ALREADY!!! YOU'RE GOIN' BEFORE THE BENCH TOMORROW, WAYNE! SO TO MAKE SURE YA GET A GOOD NIGHT'S REST, I'M PUTTIN' YA IN THE HOLDIN' TANK! LET'S GO!
7

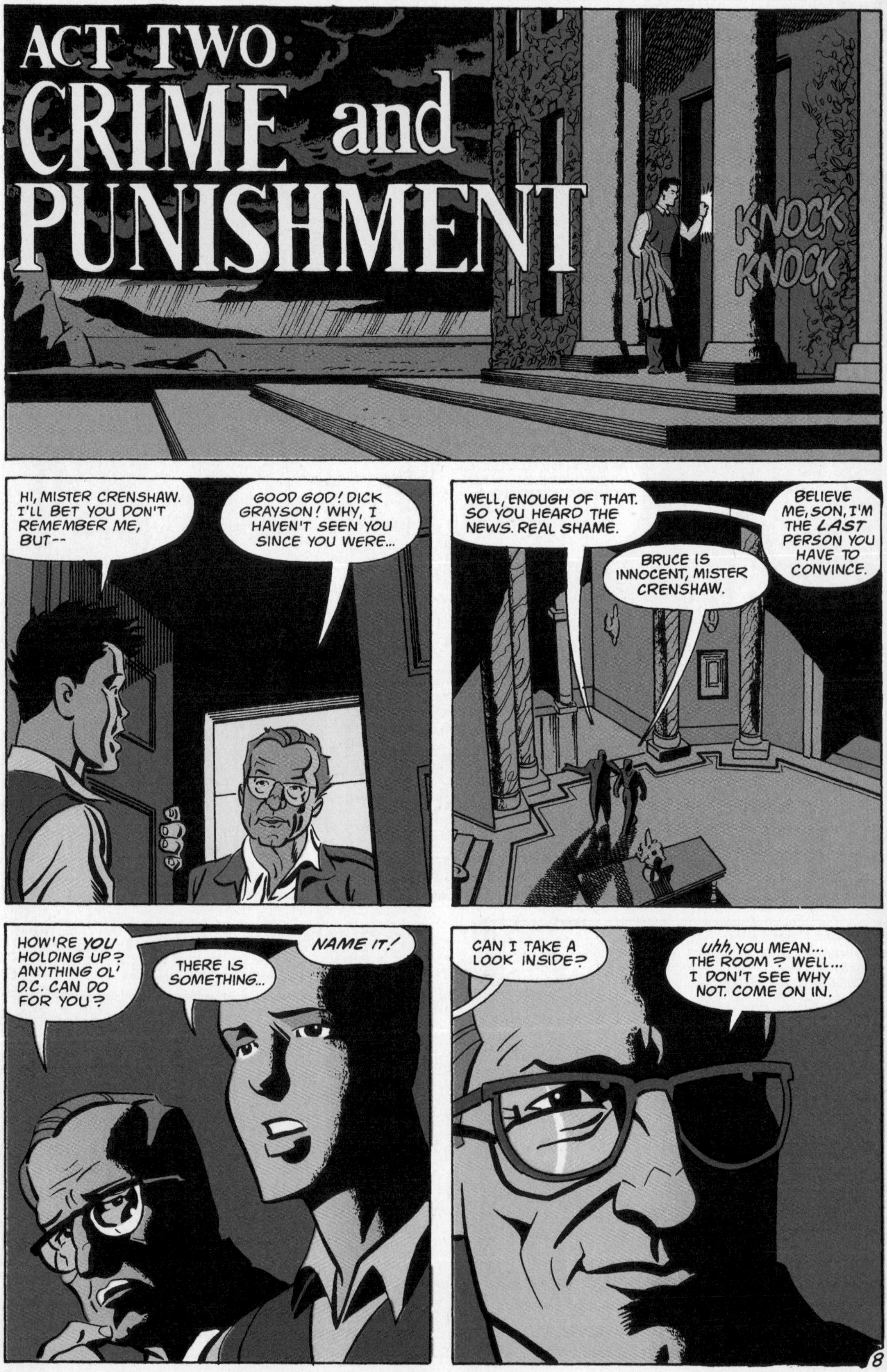

ACT TWO:
CRIME and PUNISHMENT
KNOCK KNOCK
HI, MISTER CRENSHAW. I'LL BET YOU DON'T REMEMBER ME, BUT--
GOOD GOD! DICK GRAYSON! WHY, I HAVEN'T SEEN YOU SINCE YOU WERE...
WELL, ENOUGH OF THAT. SO YOU HEARD THE NEWS. REAL SHAME.
BRUCE IS INNOCENT, MISTER CRENSHAW.
BELIEVE ME, SON, I'M THE LAST PERSON YOU HAVE TO CONVINCE.
HOW'RE YOU HOLDING UP? ANYTHING OL' D.C. CAN DO FOR YOU?
THERE IS SOMETHING...
NAME IT!
CAN I TAKE A LOOK INSIDE?
uhh, YOU MEAN... THE ROOM? WELL... I DON'T SEE WHY NOT. COME ON IN.
8

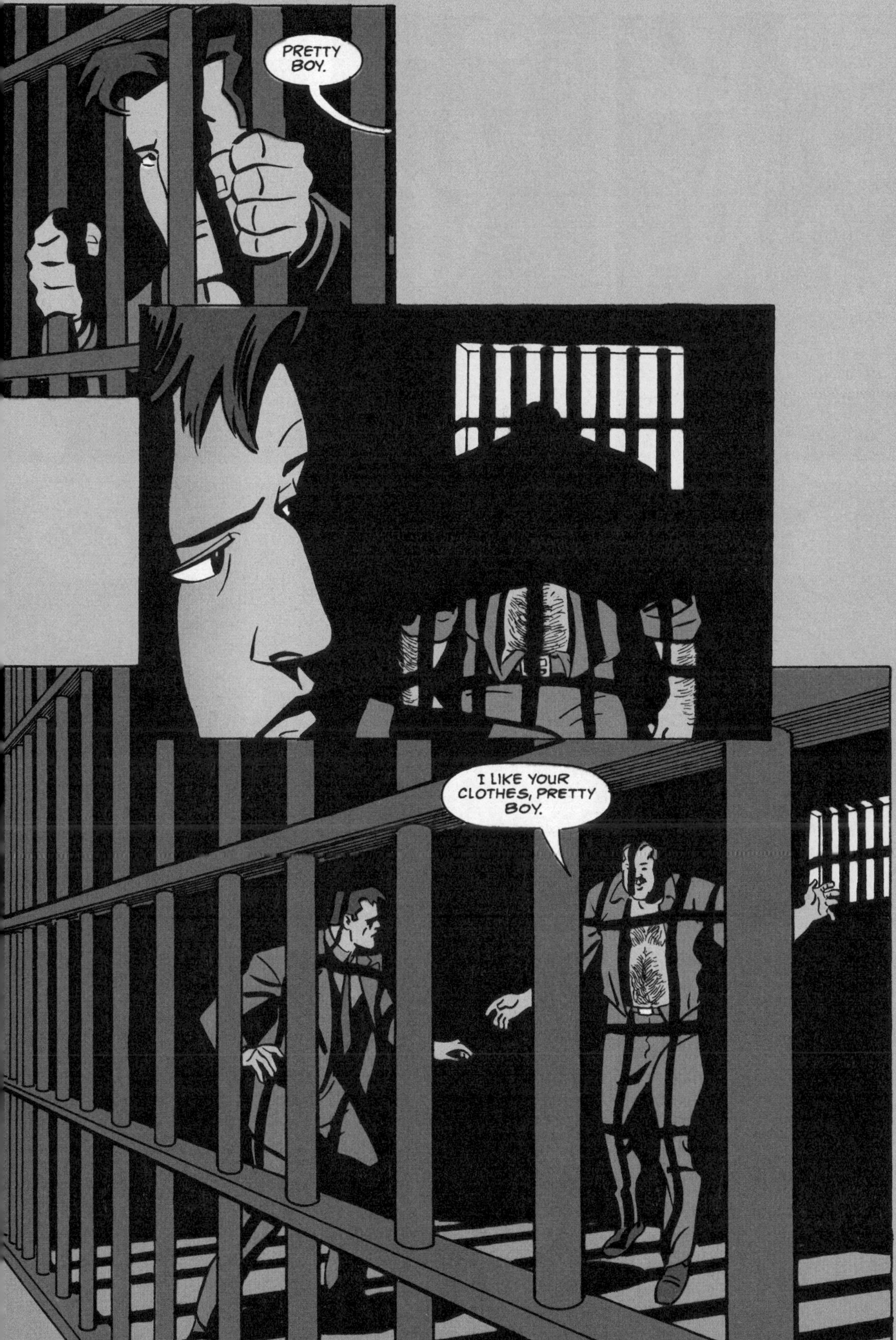
PRETTY BOY.
I LIKE YOUR CLOTHES, PRETTY BOY.
9

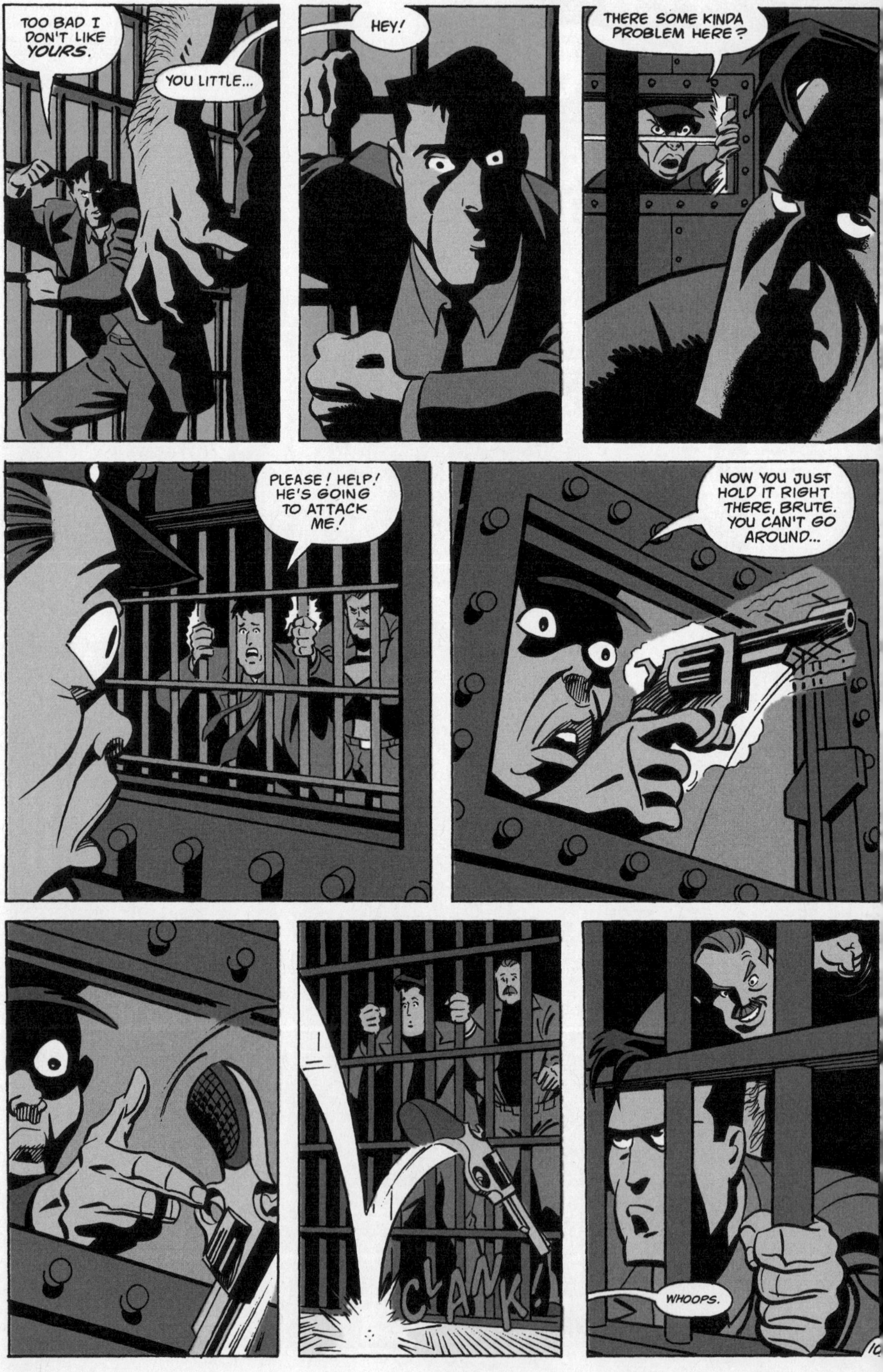
TOO BAD I DON'T LIKE *YOURS*.
YOU LITTLE...
HEY!
THERE SOME KINDA PROBLEM HERE?
PLEASE! HELP! HE'S GOING TO ATTACK ME!
NOW YOU JUST HOLD IT RIGHT THERE, BRUTE. YOU CAN'T GO AROUND...
CLANK!
WHOOPS.
10

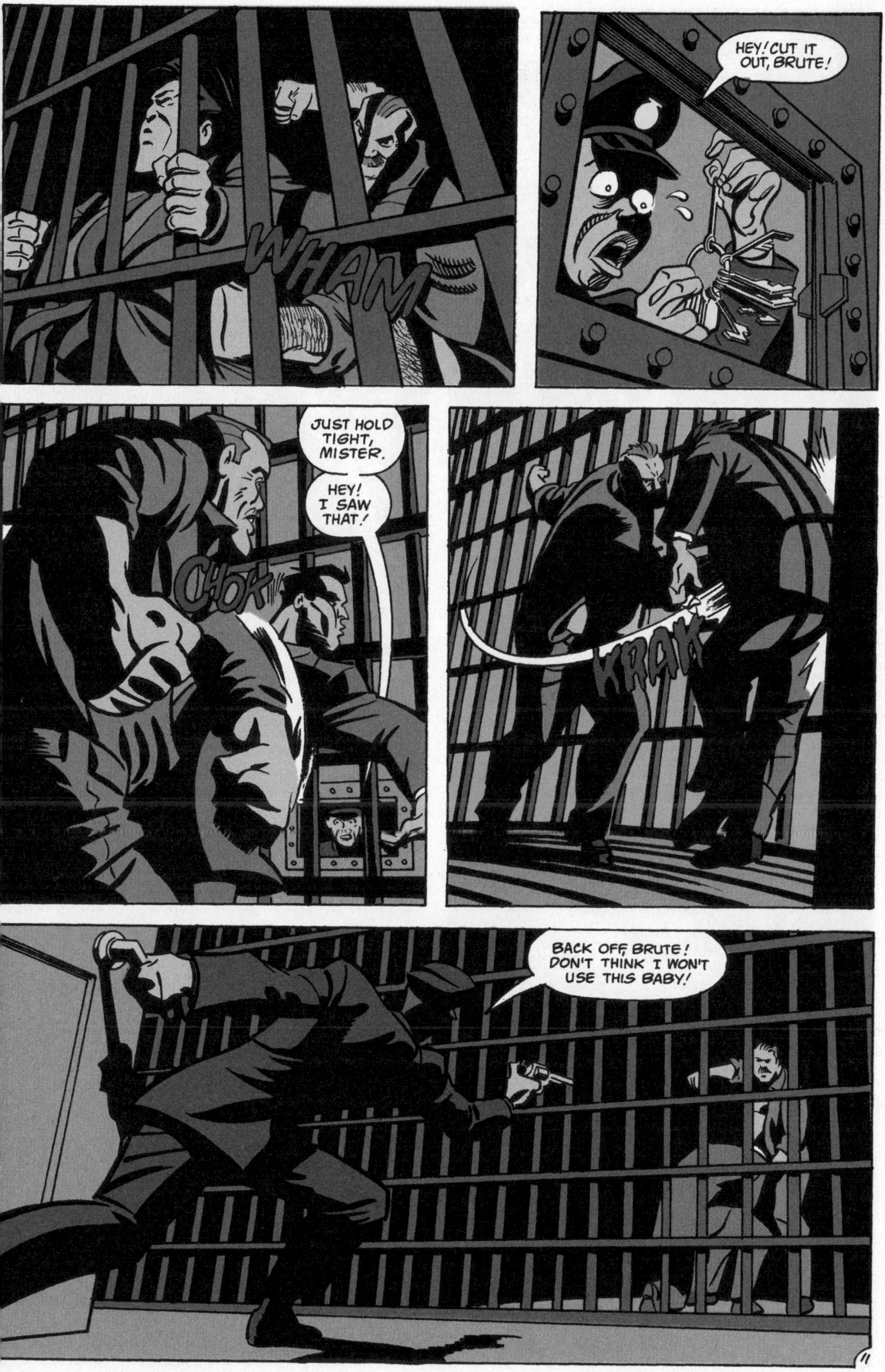
WHAM
HEY! CUT IT OUT, BRUTE!
JUST HOLD TIGHT, MISTER.
CHOK
HEY! I SAW THAT!
KRAK
BACK OFF, BRUTE! DON'T THINK I WON'T USE THIS BABY!
11

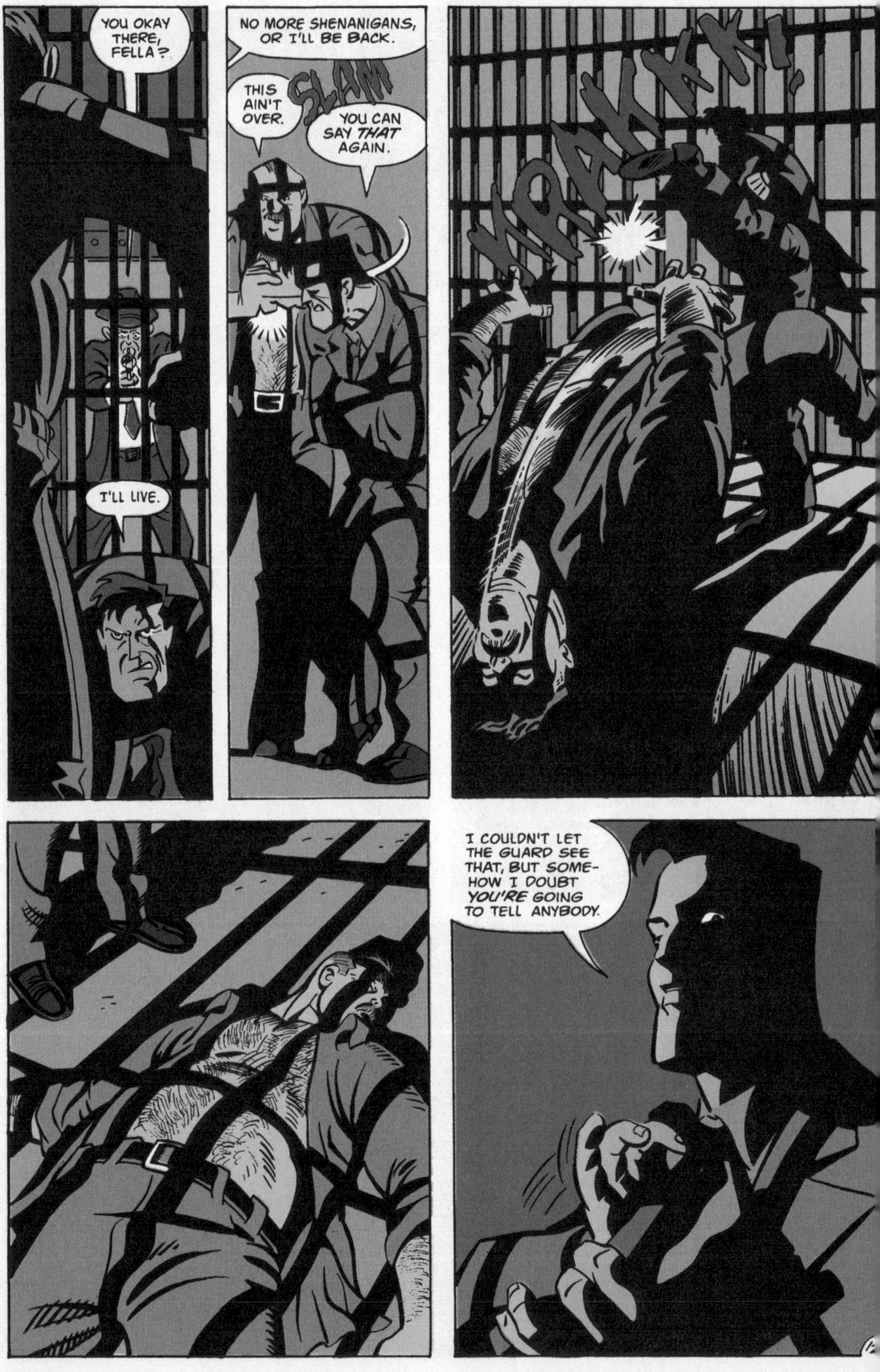

YOU OKAY THERE, FELLA?
I'LL LIVE.
NO MORE SHENANIGANS, OR I'LL BE BACK.
THIS AIN'T OVER.
SLAM
YOU CAN SAY *THAT* AGAIN.
KRAKKK!
I COULDN'T LET THE GUARD SEE THAT, BUT SOMEHOW I DOUBT *YOU'RE* GOING TO TELL ANYBODY.

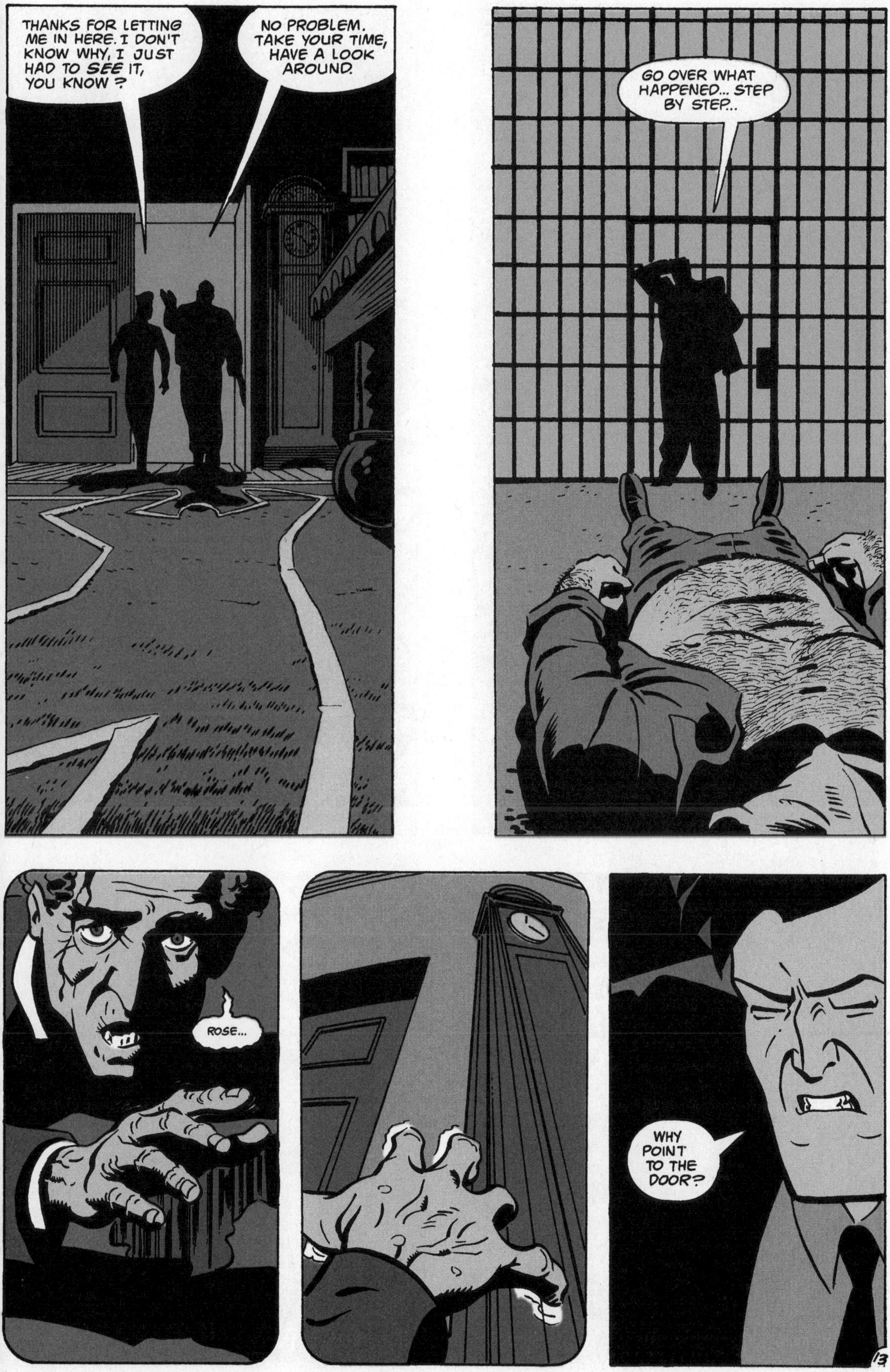
THANKS FOR LETTING ME IN HERE. I DON'T KNOW WHY, I JUST HAD TO SEE IT, YOU KNOW ?
NO PROBLEM. TAKE YOUR TIME, HAVE A LOOK AROUND.
GO OVER WHAT HAPPENED... STEP BY STEP...
ROSE...
WHY POINT TO THE DOOR?
13

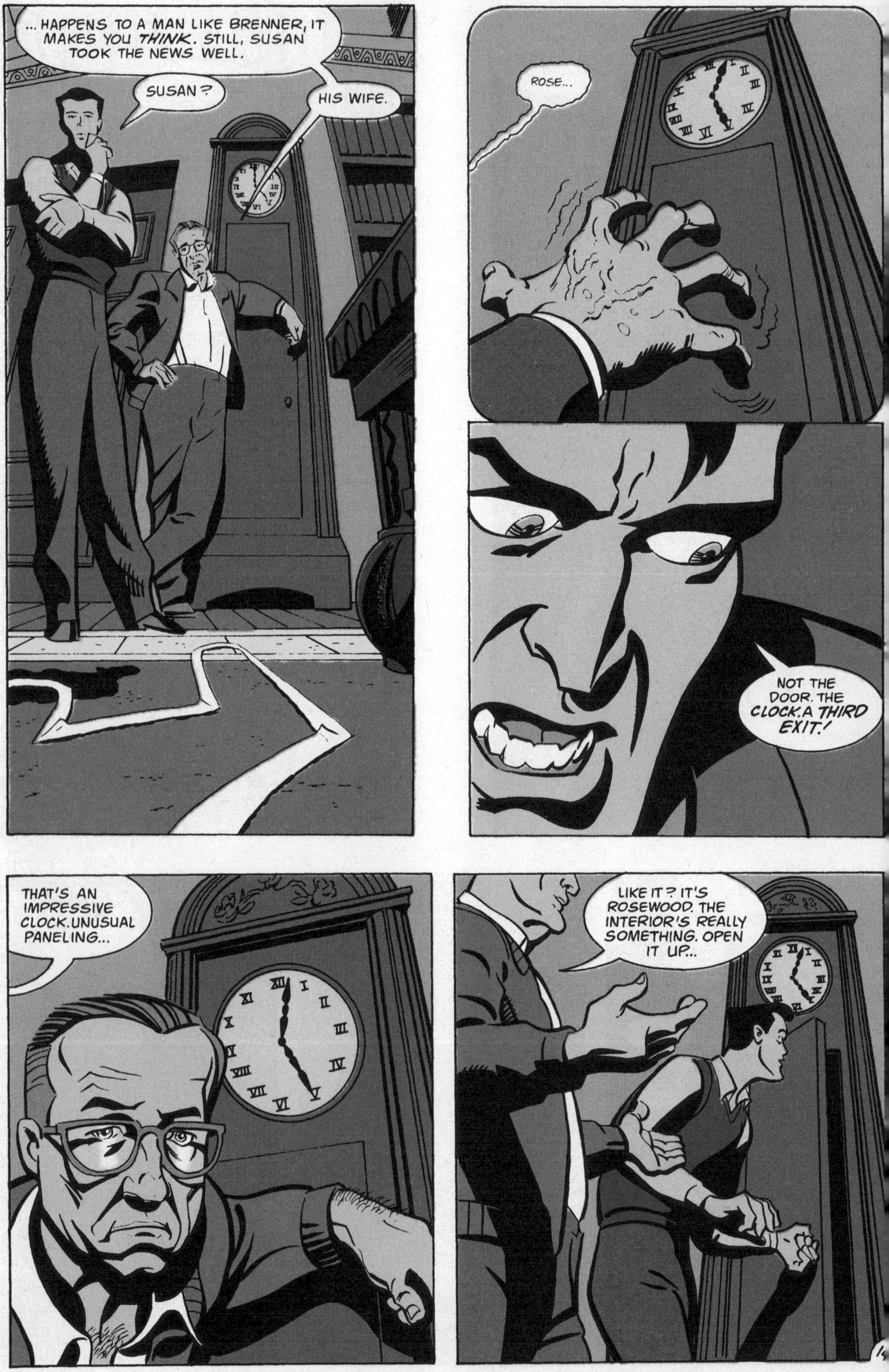
... HAPPENS TO A MAN LIKE BRENNER, IT MAKES YOU THINK. STILL, SUSAN TOOK THE NEWS WELL.
SUSAN?
HIS WIFE.
ROSE...
NOT THE DOOR. THE CLOCK. A THIRD EXIT!
THAT'S AN IMPRESSIVE CLOCK. UNUSUAL PANELING...
LIKE IT? IT'S ROSEWOOD. THE INTERIOR'S REALLY SOMETHING. OPEN IT UP...

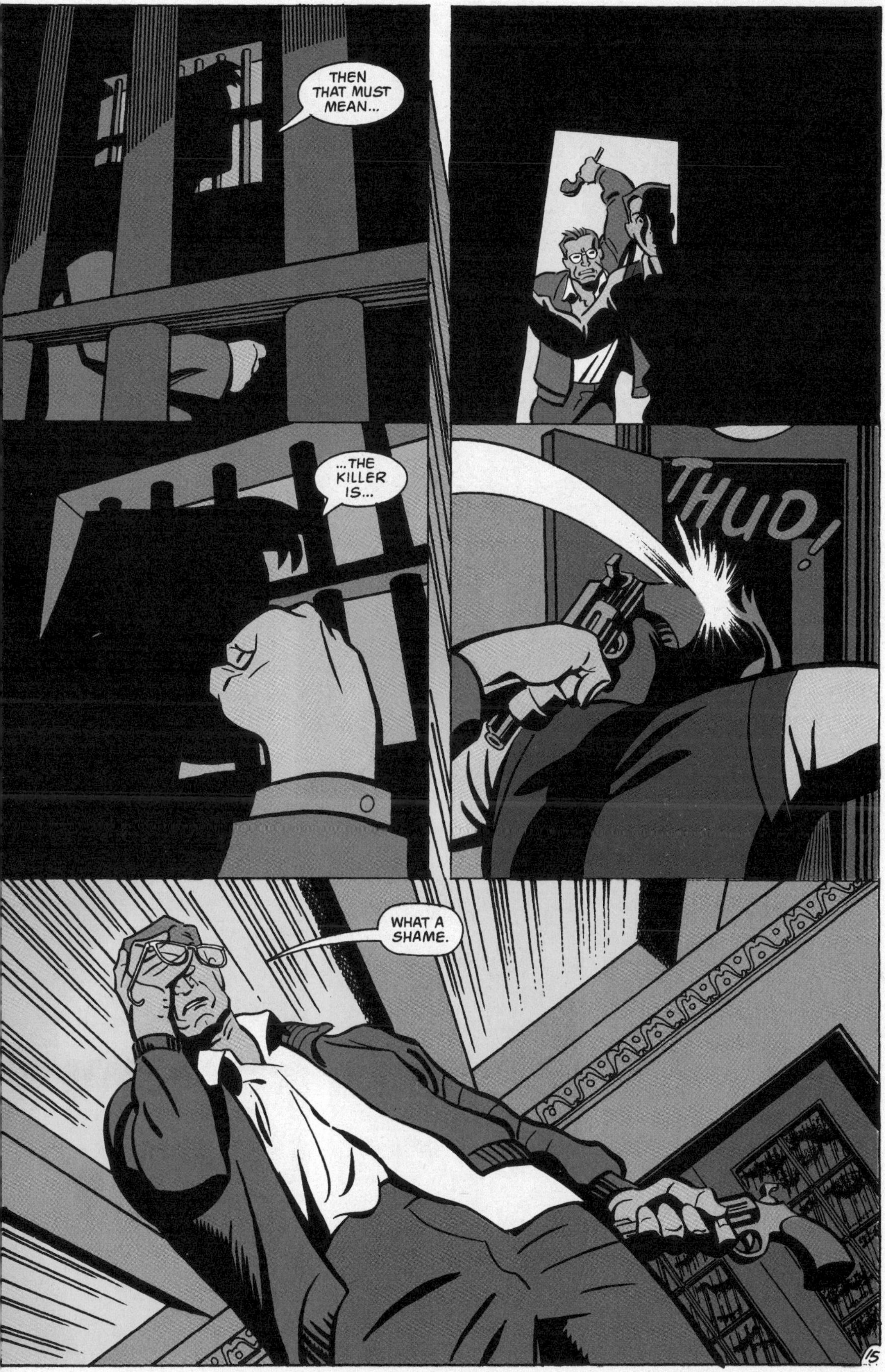
THEN THAT MUST MEAN...
...THE KILLER IS...
THUD!
WHAT A SHAME.
15

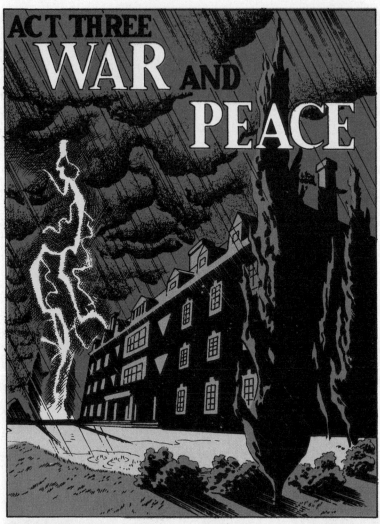

ACT THREE
WAR AND PEACE

HAVE TO STAY *CALM.* THE DRIVER WILL BE HERE *SOON.*

I'LL FLY SOUTH, RELAX, REVIEW MY OPTIONS. GET RID OF THE... *LIABILITY* ALONG THE WAY. WHAT'S NEEDED NOW IS *PATIENCE.*

WHAT'S TAKING HIM SO LONG?!?

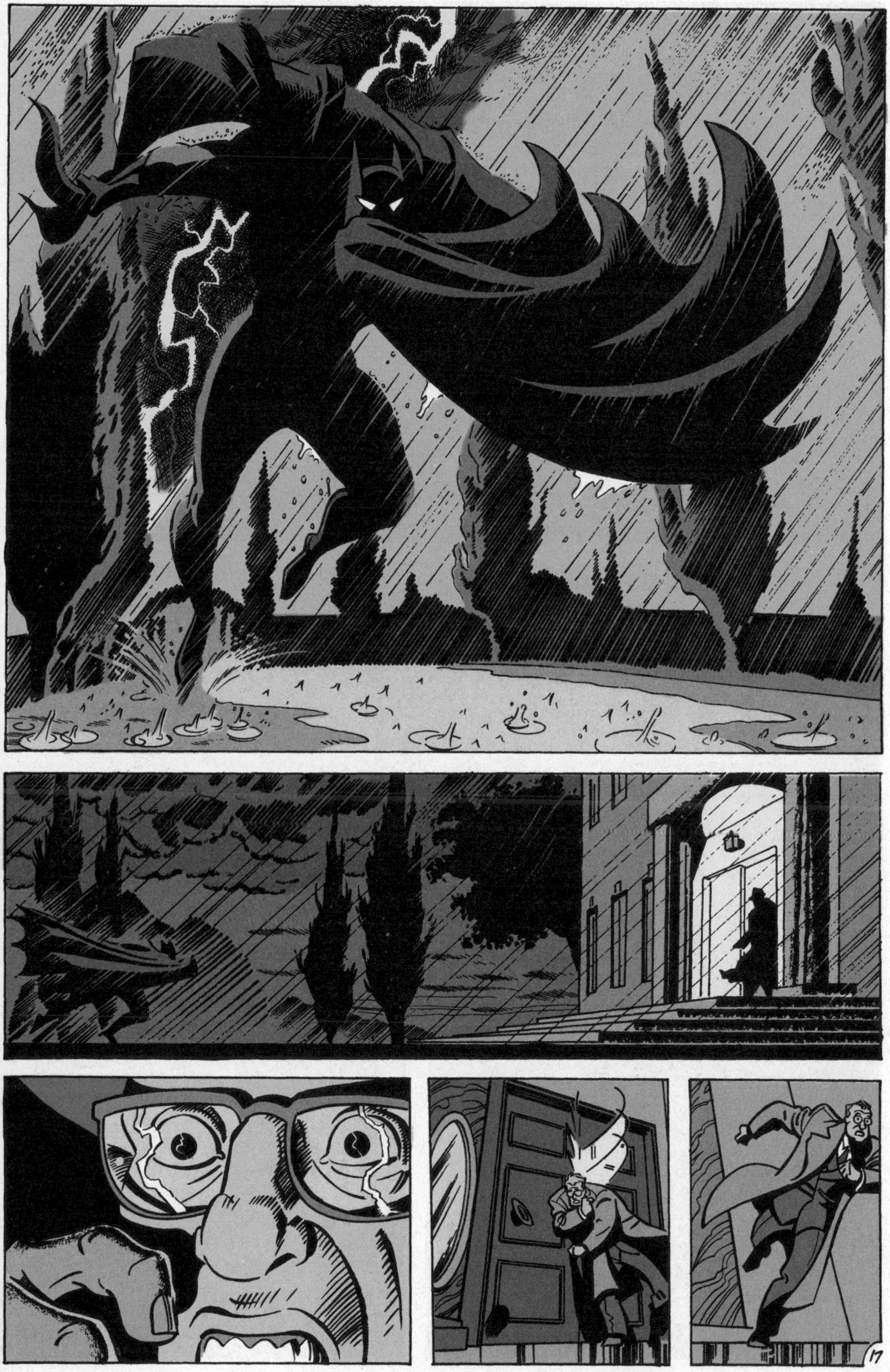
17

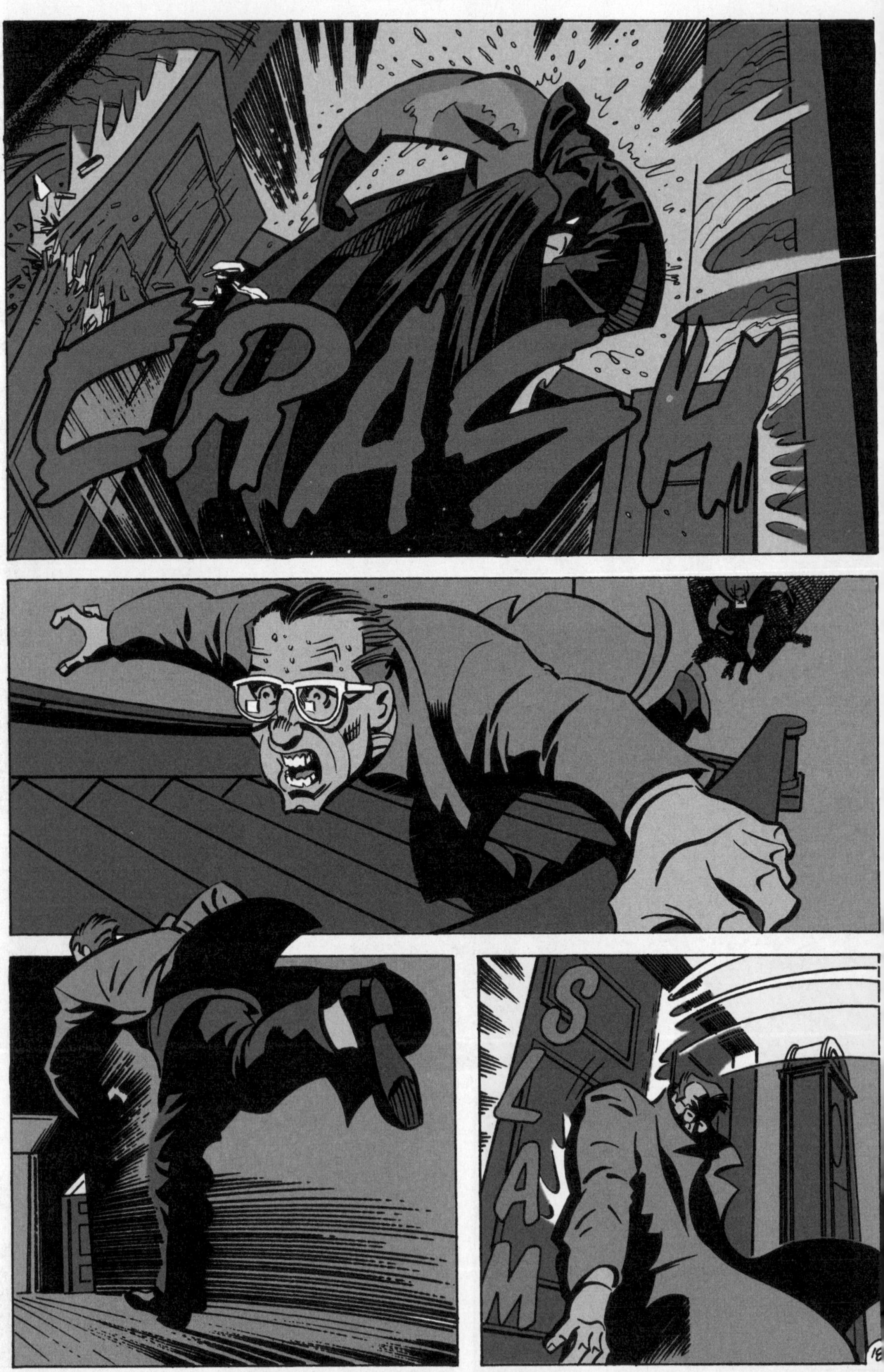
CRASH
SLAM

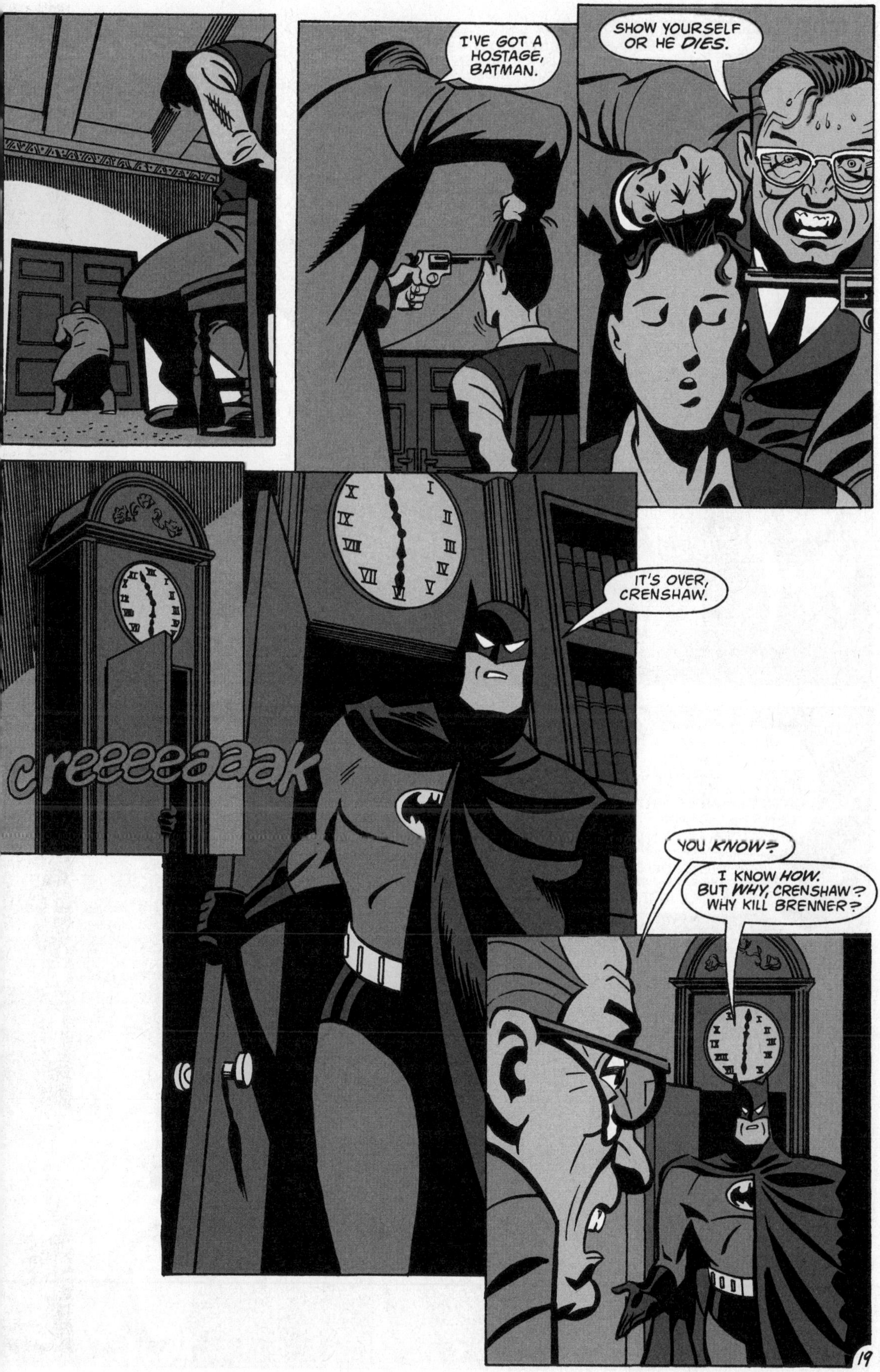
I'VE GOT A HOSTAGE, BATMAN.
SHOW YOURSELF OR HE *DIES*.
IT'S OVER, CRENSHAW.
creeeeaaak
YOU *KNOW*?
I KNOW *HOW*. BUT *WHY*, CRENSHAW? WHY KILL BRENNER?
19

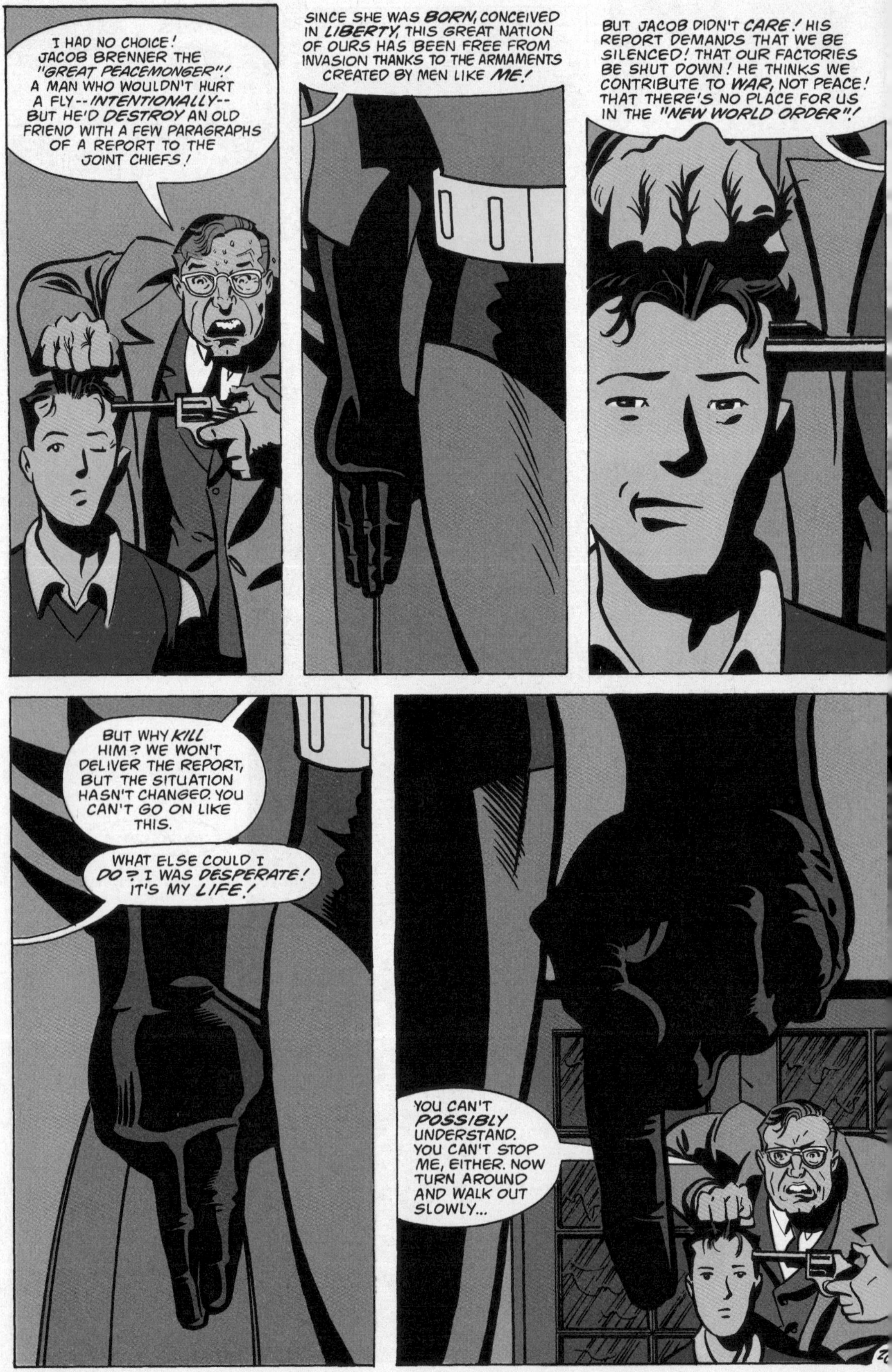
I HAD NO CHOICE! JACOB BRENNER THE "GREAT PEACEMONGER"! A MAN WHO WOULDN'T HURT A FLY--INTENTIONALLY--BUT HE'D DESTROY AN OLD FRIEND WITH A FEW PARAGRAPHS OF A REPORT TO THE JOINT CHIEFS!
SINCE SHE WAS BORN, CONCEIVED IN LIBERTY, THIS GREAT NATION OF OURS HAS BEEN FREE FROM INVASION THANKS TO THE ARMAMENTS CREATED BY MEN LIKE ME!
BUT JACOB DIDN'T CARE! HIS REPORT DEMANDS THAT WE BE SILENCED! THAT OUR FACTORIES BE SHUT DOWN! HE THINKS WE CONTRIBUTE TO WAR, NOT PEACE! THAT THERE'S NO PLACE FOR US IN THE "NEW WORLD ORDER"!
BUT WHY KILL HIM? WE WON'T DELIVER THE REPORT, BUT THE SITUATION HASN'T CHANGED. YOU CAN'T GO ON LIKE THIS.
WHAT ELSE COULD I DO? I WAS DESPERATE! IT'S MY LIFE!
YOU CAN'T POSSIBLY UNDERSTAND. YOU CAN'T STOP ME, EITHER. NOW TURN AROUND AND WALK OUT SLOWLY...

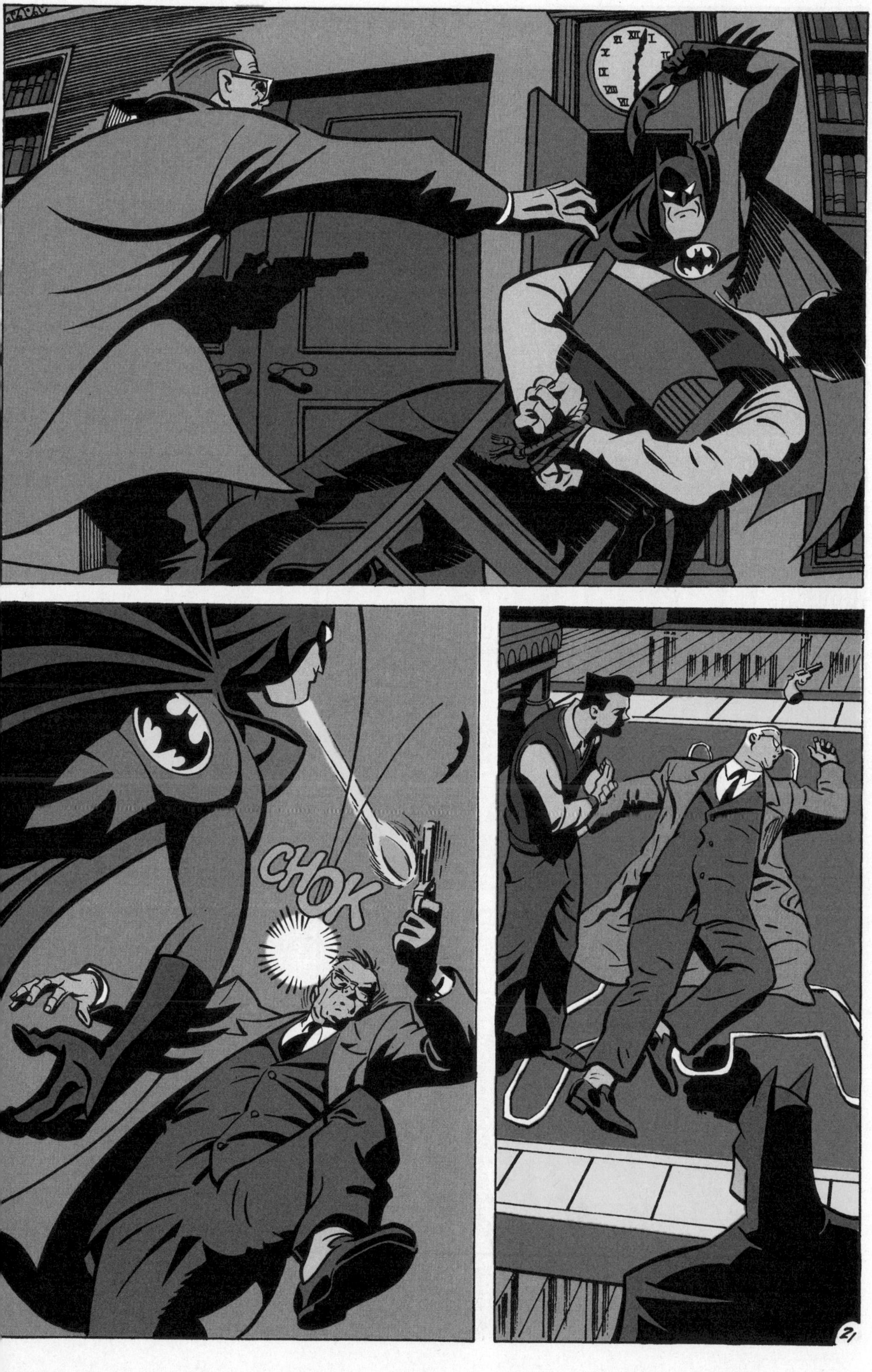
CHOK
21

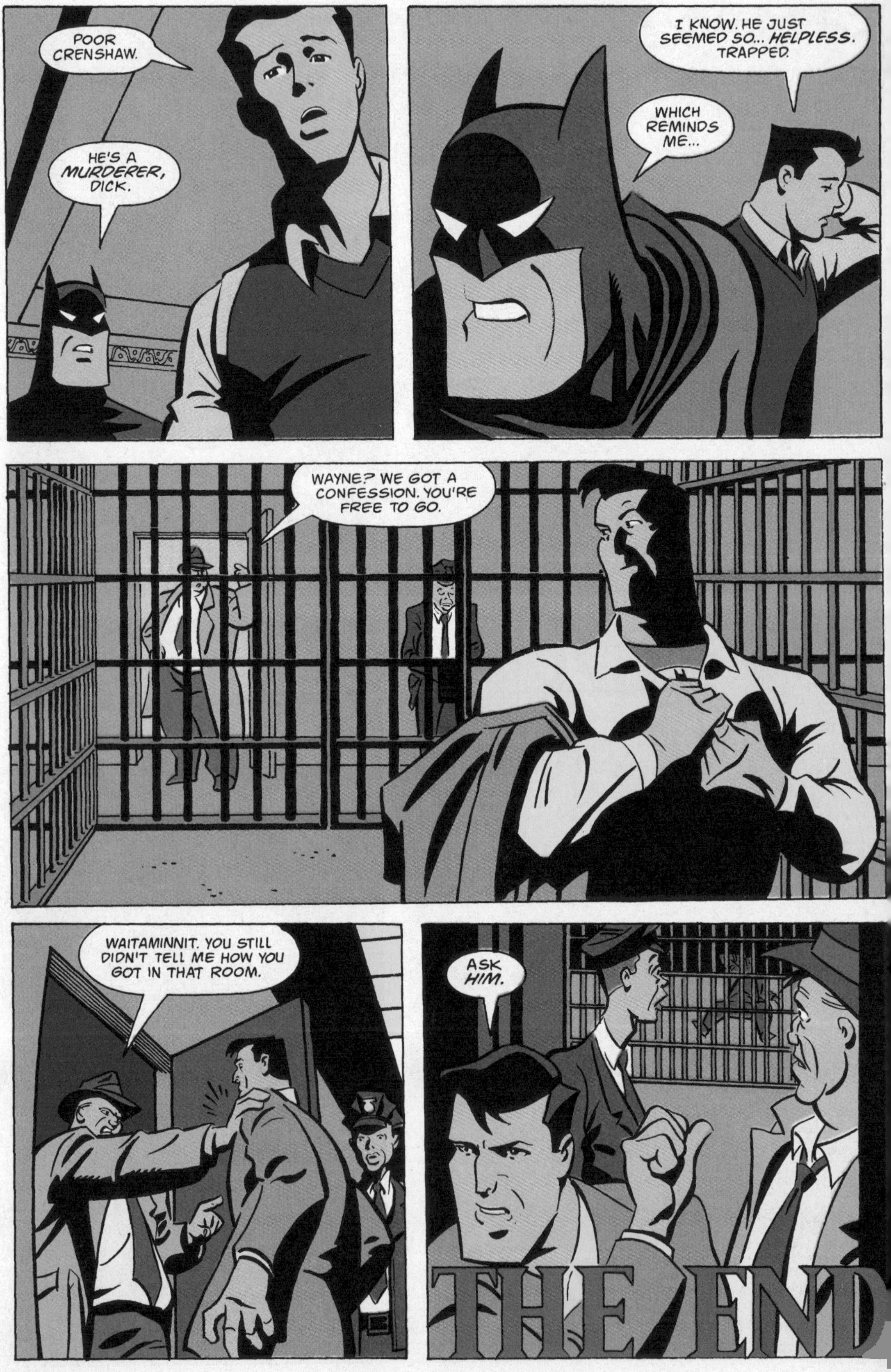
POOR CRENSHAW.
HE'S A *MURDERER*, DICK.
I KNOW. HE JUST SEEMED SO... *HELPLESS*. TRAPPED.
WHICH REMINDS ME...
WAYNE? WE GOT A CONFESSION. YOU'RE FREE TO GO.
WAITAMINNIT. YOU STILL DIDN'T TELL ME HOW YOU GOT IN THAT ROOM.
ASK *HIM*.
THE END

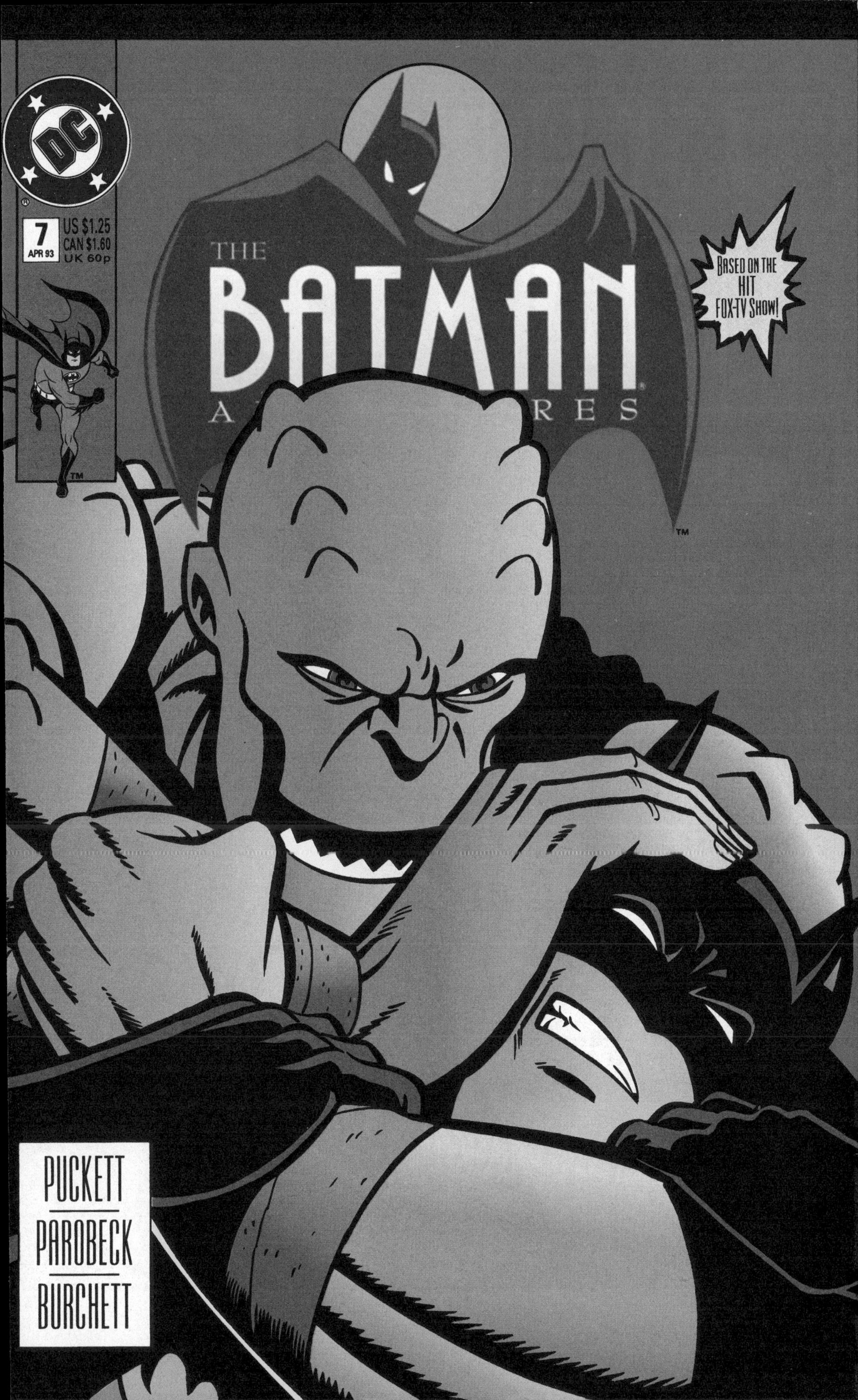
DC
7
APR 93
US $1.25
CAN $1.60
UK 60p
THE
BATMAN
BASED ON THE HIT FOX-TV SHOW!
PUCKETT
PAROBECK
BURCHETT

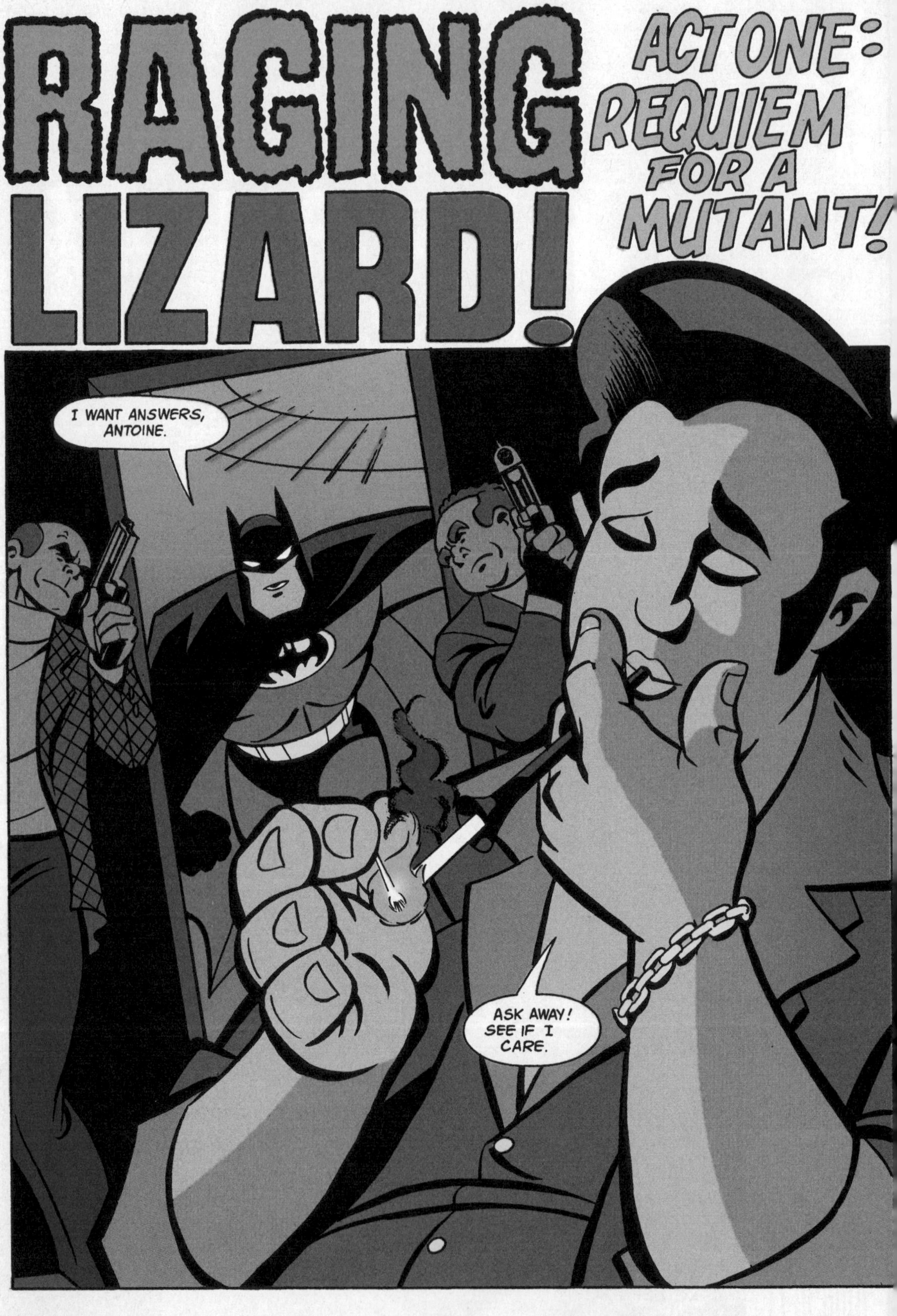
RAGING LIZARD!
ACT ONE: REQUIEM FOR A MUTANT!
I WANT ANSWERS, ANTOINE.
ASK AWAY! SEE IF I CARE.

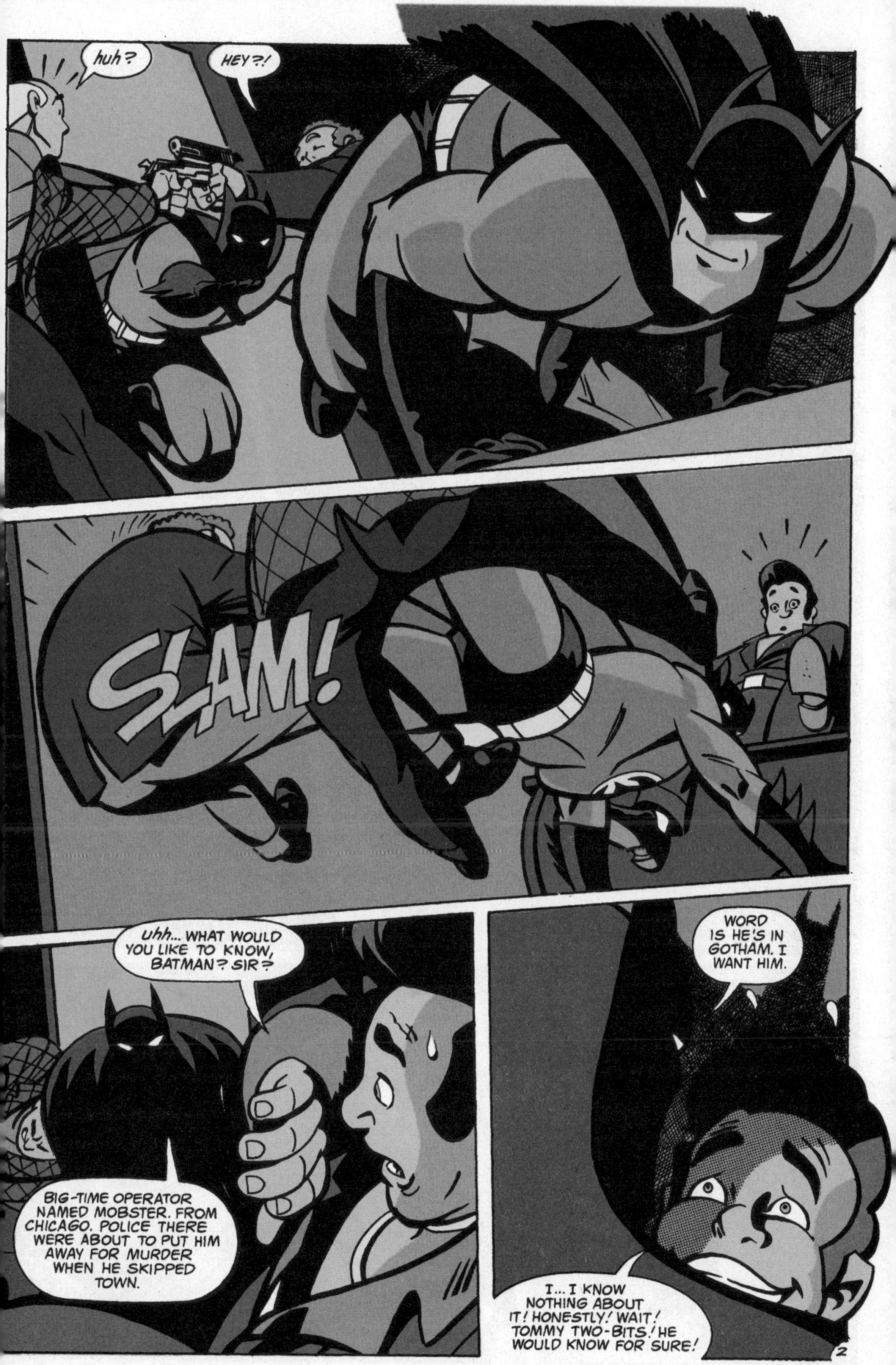

huh?
HEY?!
SLAM!
uhh... WHAT WOULD YOU LIKE TO KNOW, BATMAN? SIR?
BIG-TIME OPERATOR NAMED MOBSTER. FROM CHICAGO. POLICE THERE WERE ABOUT TO PUT HIM AWAY FOR MURDER WHEN HE SKIPPED TOWN.
WORD IS HE'S IN GOTHAM. I WANT HIM.
I... I KNOW NOTHING ABOUT IT! HONESTLY! WAIT! TOMMY TWO-BITS! HE WOULD KNOW FOR SURE!
2

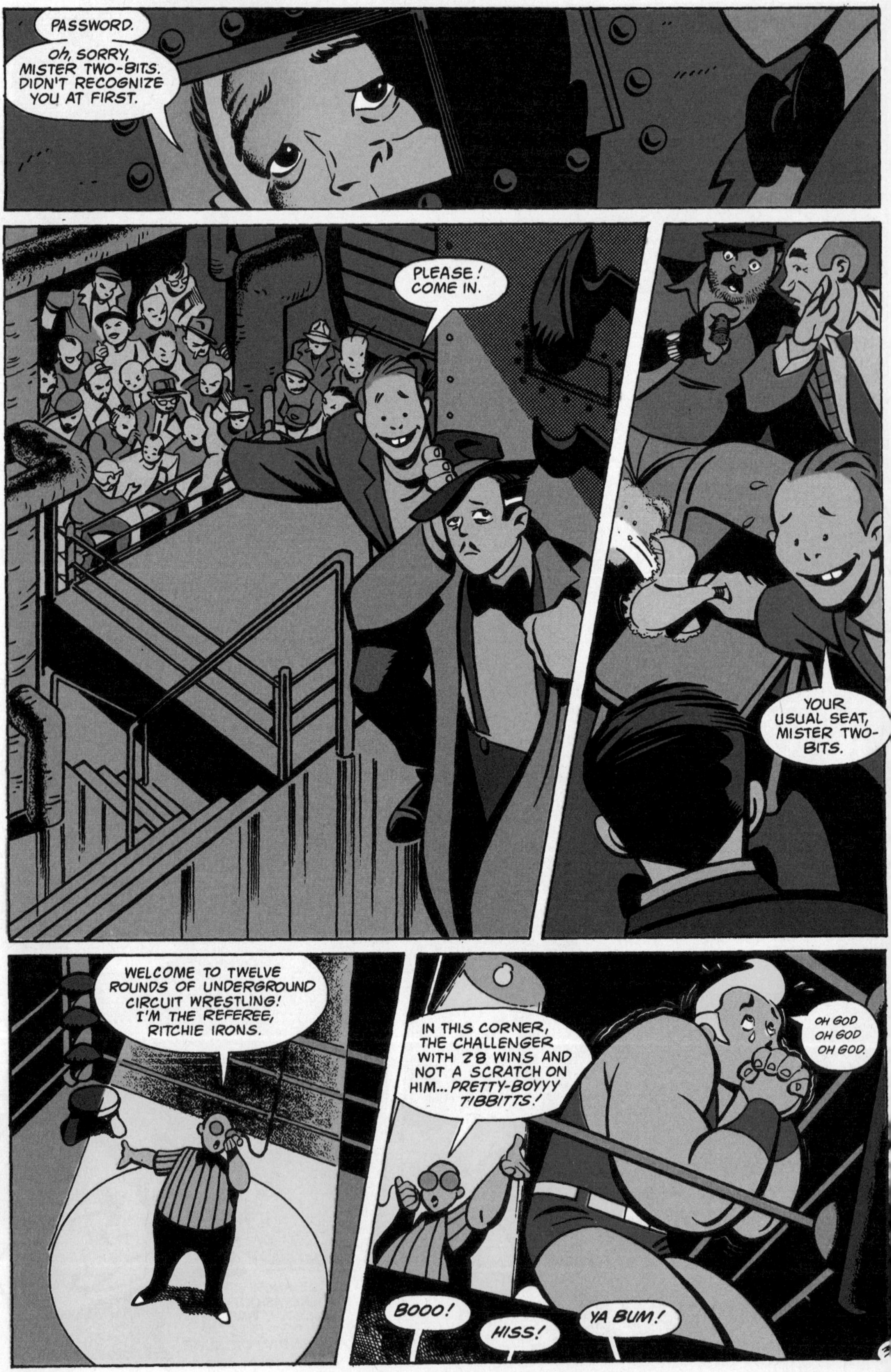
PASSWORD.
oh, SORRY, MISTER TWO-BITS. DIDN'T RECOGNIZE YOU AT FIRST.
PLEASE! COME IN.
YOUR USUAL SEAT, MISTER TWO-BITS.
WELCOME TO TWELVE ROUNDS OF UNDERGROUND CIRCUIT WRESTLING! I'M THE REFEREE, RITCHIE IRONS.
IN THIS CORNER, THE CHALLENGER WITH 28 WINS AND NOT A SCRATCH ON HIM... PRETTY-BOYYY TIBBITTS!
OH GOD OH GOD OH GOD.
BOOO!
HISS!
YA BUM!

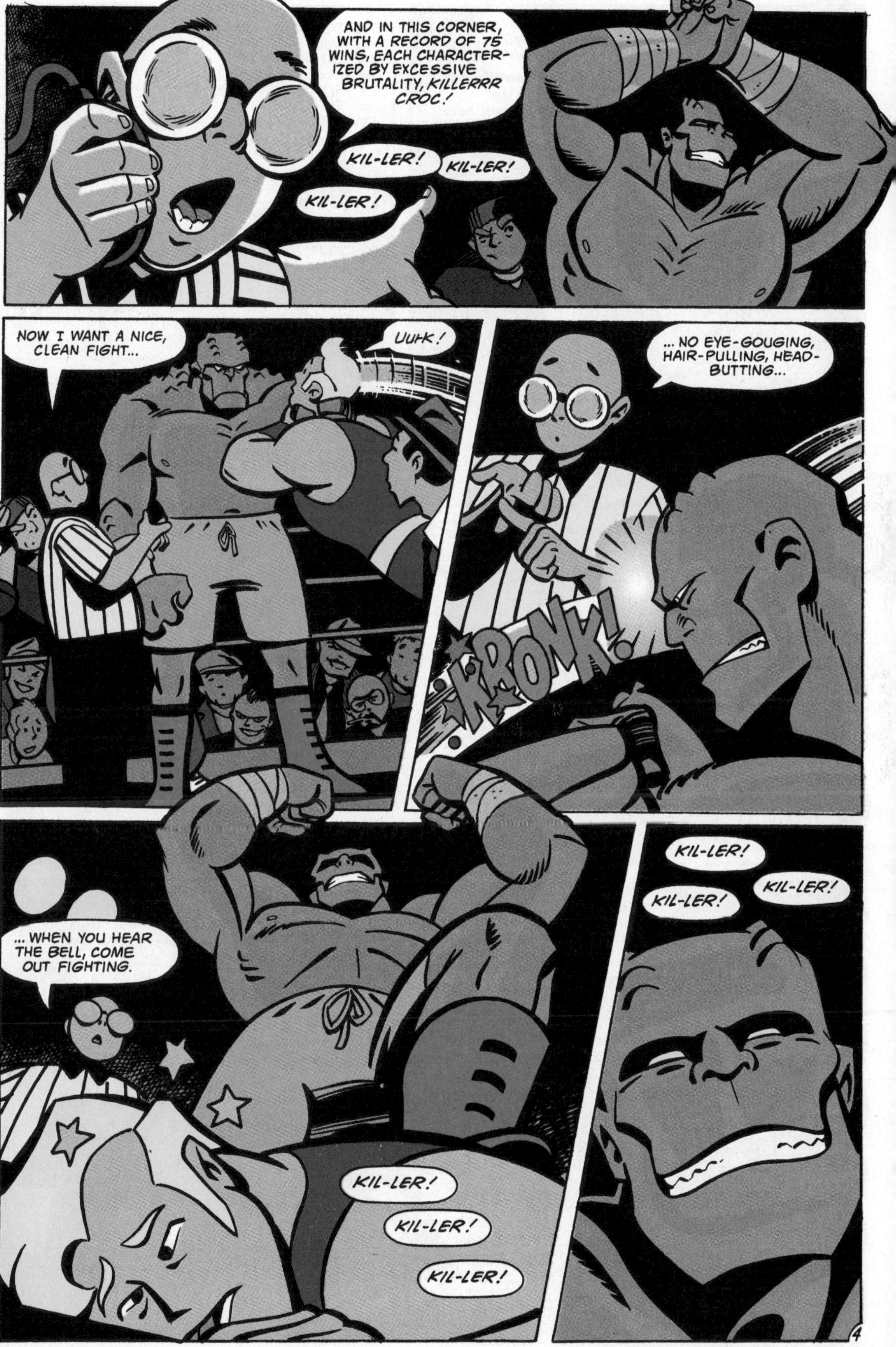
AND IN THIS CORNER, WITH A RECORD OF 75 WINS, EACH CHARACTERIZED BY EXCESSIVE BRUTALITY, KILLERRR CROC!
KIL-LER!
KIL-LER!
KIL-LER!
NOW I WANT A NICE, CLEAN FIGHT...
UUrK!
... NO EYE-GOUGING, HAIR-PULLING, HEAD-BUTTING...
KRONK!
... WHEN YOU HEAR THE BELL, COME OUT FIGHTING.
KIL-LER!
KIL-LER!
KIL-LER!
KIL-LER!
KIL-LER!
KIL-LER!
4

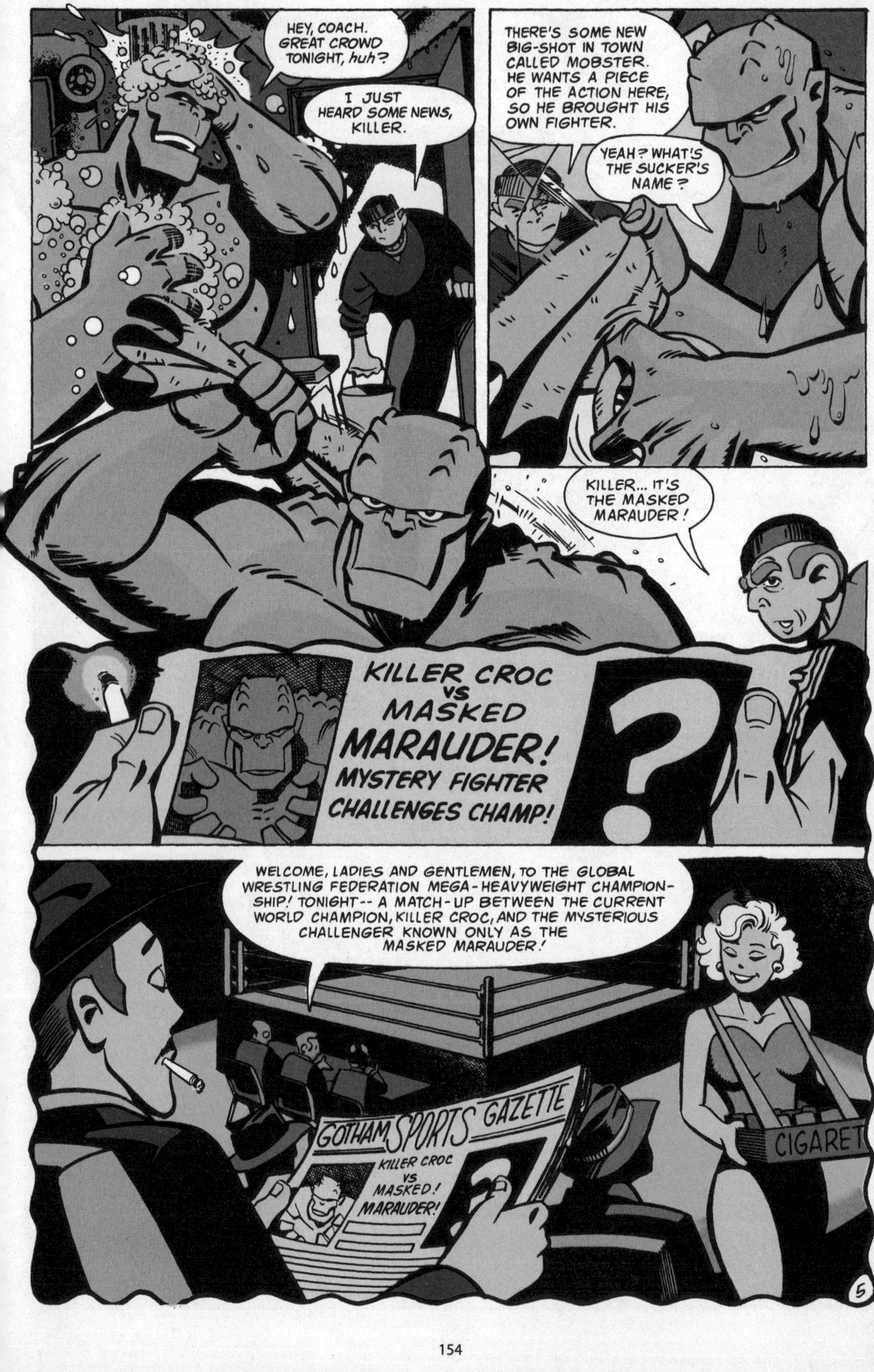
HEY, COACH. GREAT CROWD TONIGHT, huh?
I JUST HEARD SOME NEWS, KILLER.
THERE'S SOME NEW BIG-SHOT IN TOWN CALLED MOBSTER. HE WANTS A PIECE OF THE ACTION HERE, SO HE BROUGHT HIS OWN FIGHTER.
YEAH? WHAT'S THE SUCKER'S NAME?
KILLER... IT'S THE MASKED MARAUDER!
KILLER CROC VS MASKED MARAUDER! MYSTERY FIGHTER CHALLENGES CHAMP!
?
WELCOME, LADIES AND GENTLEMEN, TO THE GLOBAL WRESTLING FEDERATION MEGA-HEAVYWEIGHT CHAMPIONSHIP! TONIGHT-- A MATCH-UP BETWEEN THE CURRENT WORLD CHAMPION, KILLER CROC, AND THE MYSTERIOUS CHALLENGER KNOWN ONLY AS THE MASKED MARAUDER!
GOTHAM SPORTS GAZETTE
KILLER CROC VS MASKED! MARAUDER!
CIGARET
5

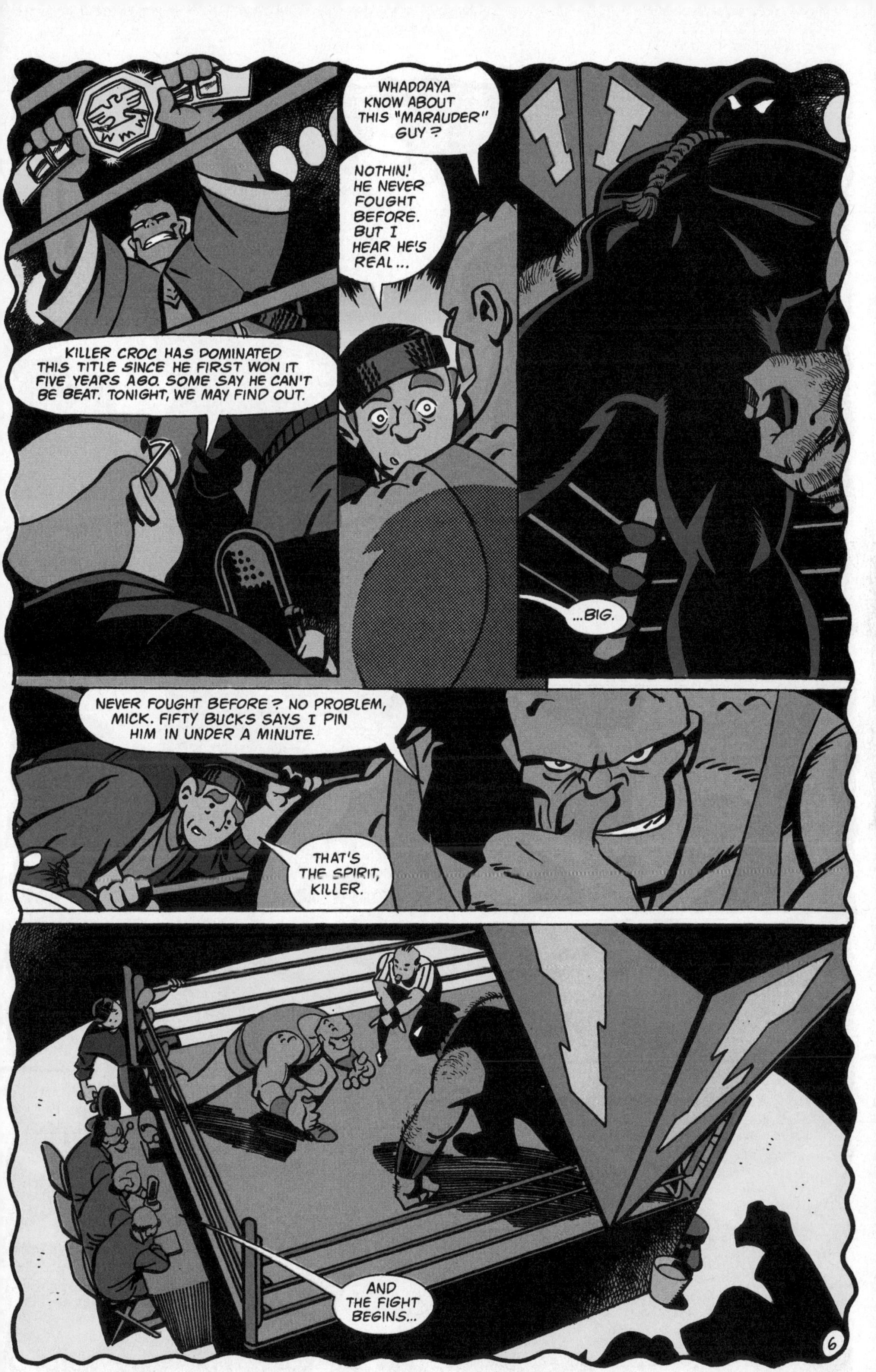
WHADDAYA KNOW ABOUT THIS "MARAUDER" GUY?
NOTHIN'! HE NEVER FOUGHT BEFORE. BUT I HEAR HE'S REAL...
KILLER CROC HAS DOMINATED THIS TITLE SINCE HE FIRST WON IT FIVE YEARS AGO. SOME SAY HE CAN'T BE BEAT. TONIGHT, WE MAY FIND OUT.
...BIG.
NEVER FOUGHT BEFORE? NO PROBLEM, MICK. FIFTY BUCKS SAYS I PIN HIM IN UNDER A MINUTE.
THAT'S THE SPIRIT, KILLER.
AND THE FIGHT BEGINS...
6

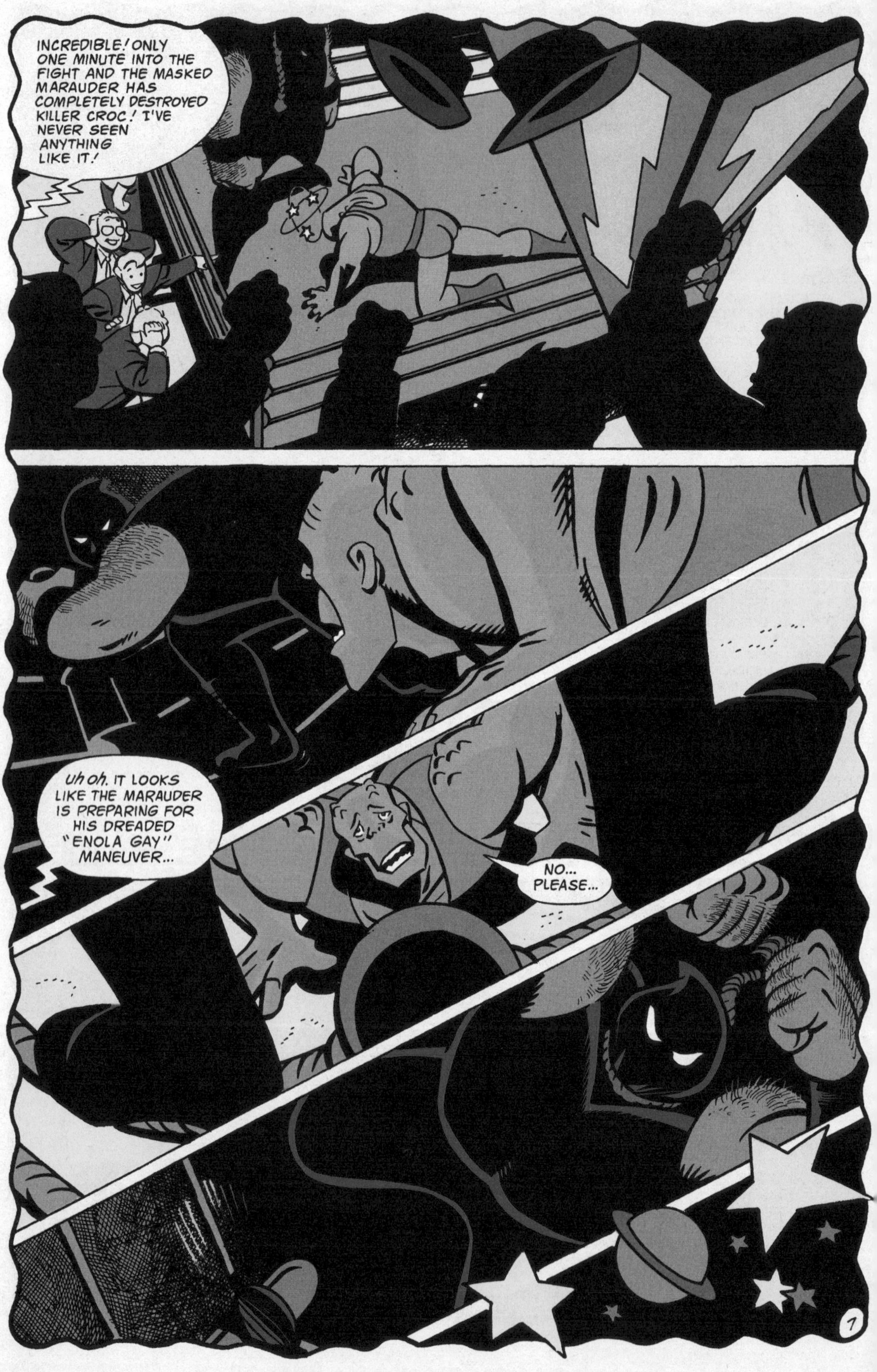
INCREDIBLE! ONLY ONE MINUTE INTO THE FIGHT AND THE MASKED MARAUDER HAS COMPLETELY DESTROYED KILLER CROC! I'VE NEVER SEEN ANYTHING LIKE IT!
UH OH. IT LOOKS LIKE THE MARAUDER IS PREPARING FOR HIS DREADED "ENOLA GAY" MANEUVER...
NO... PLEASE...
7

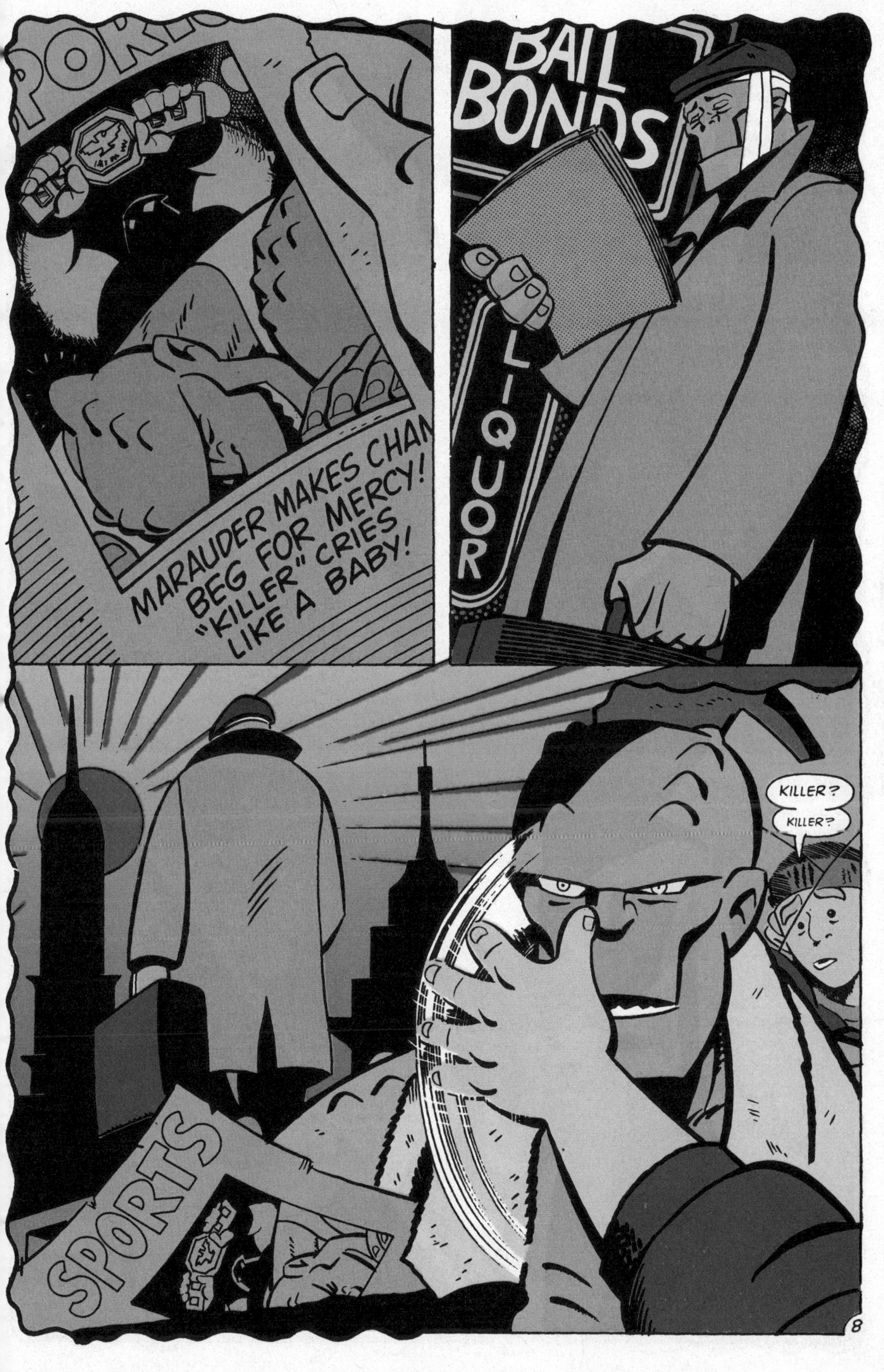
SPORTS
MARAUDER MAKES CHAM
BEG FOR MERCY!
"KILLER" CRIES
LIKE A BABY!
BAIL
BONDS
LIQUOR
KILLER?
KILLER?
SPORTS
8

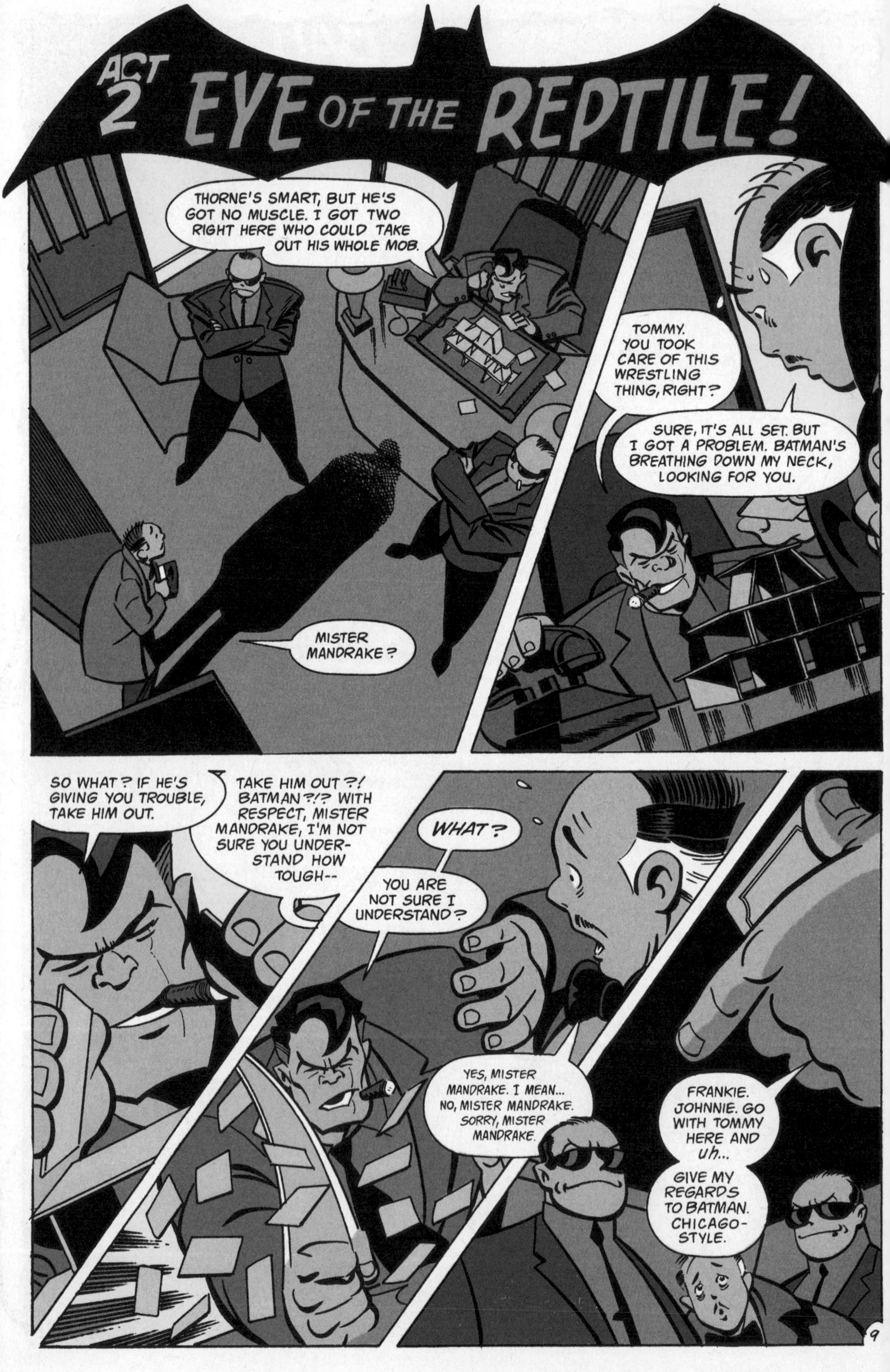

ACT 2 EYE OF THE REPTILE!
THORNE'S SMART, BUT HE'S GOT NO MUSCLE. I GOT TWO RIGHT HERE WHO COULD TAKE OUT HIS WHOLE MOB.
MISTER MANDRAKE?
TOMMY. YOU TOOK CARE OF THIS WRESTLING THING, RIGHT?
SURE, IT'S ALL SET. BUT I GOT A PROBLEM. BATMAN'S BREATHING DOWN MY NECK, LOOKING FOR YOU.
SO WHAT? IF HE'S GIVING YOU TROUBLE, TAKE HIM OUT.
TAKE HIM OUT?! BATMAN?!? WITH RESPECT, MISTER MANDRAKE, I'M NOT SURE YOU UNDER-STAND HOW TOUGH--
WHAT?
YOU ARE NOT SURE I UNDERSTAND?
YES, MISTER MANDRAKE. I MEAN... NO, MISTER MANDRAKE. SORRY, MISTER MANDRAKE.
FRANKIE. JOHNNIE. GO WITH TOMMY HERE AND uh...
GIVE MY REGARDS TO BATMAN. CHICAGO-STYLE.
9

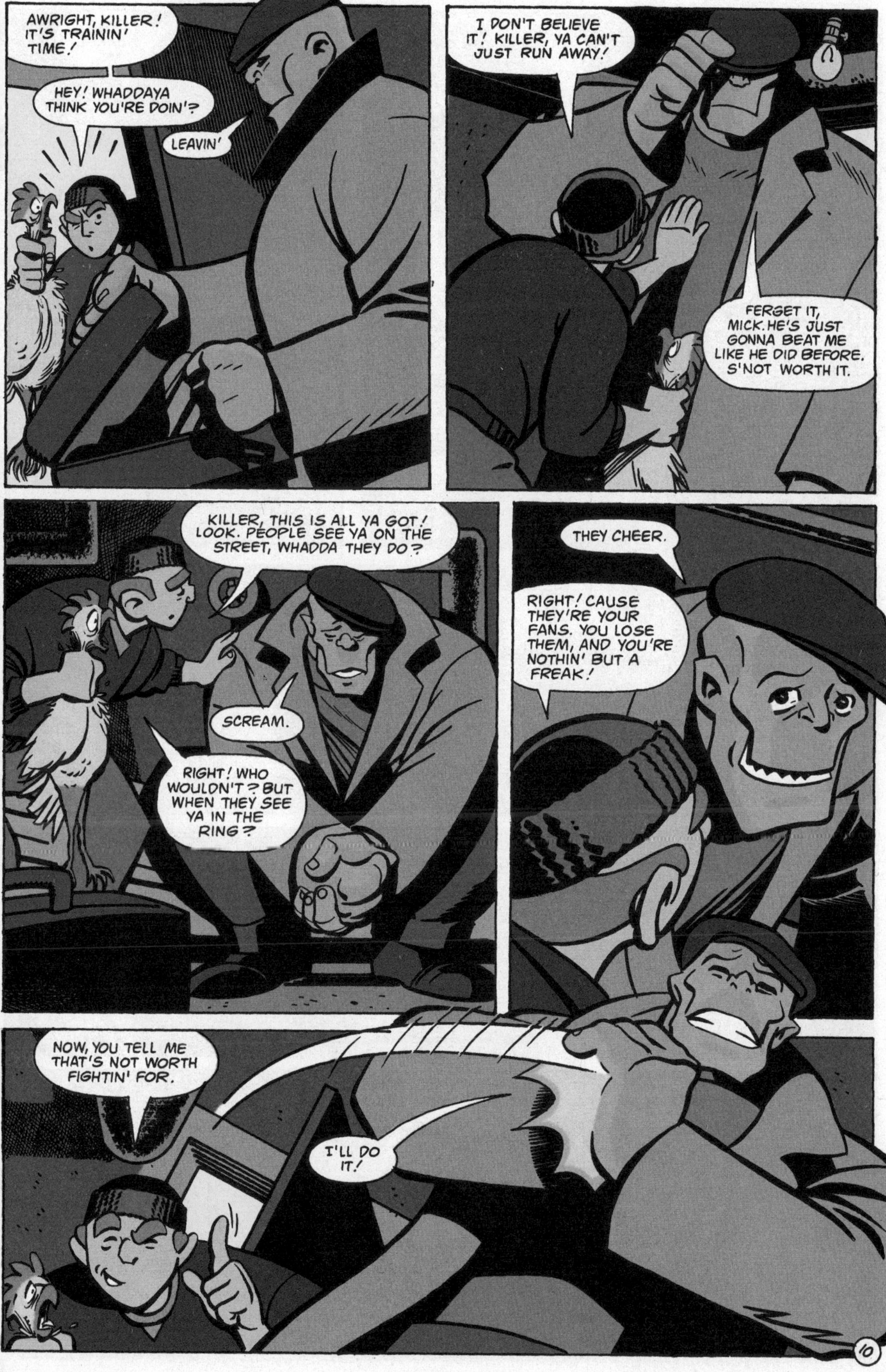
AWRIGHT, KILLER! IT'S TRAININ' TIME!
HEY! WHADDAYA THINK YOU'RE DOIN'?
LEAVIN'
I DON'T BELIEVE IT! KILLER, YA CAN'T JUST RUN AWAY!
FERGET IT, MICK. HE'S JUST GONNA BEAT ME LIKE HE DID BEFORE. S'NOT WORTH IT.
KILLER, THIS IS ALL YA GOT! LOOK. PEOPLE SEE YA ON THE STREET, WHADDA THEY DO?
SCREAM.
RIGHT! WHO WOULDN'T? BUT WHEN THEY SEE YA IN THE RING?
THEY CHEER.
RIGHT! CAUSE THEY'RE YOUR FANS. YOU LOSE THEM, AND YOU'RE NOTHIN' BUT A FREAK!
NOW, YOU TELL ME THAT'S NOT WORTH FIGHTIN' FOR.
I'LL DO IT!
10

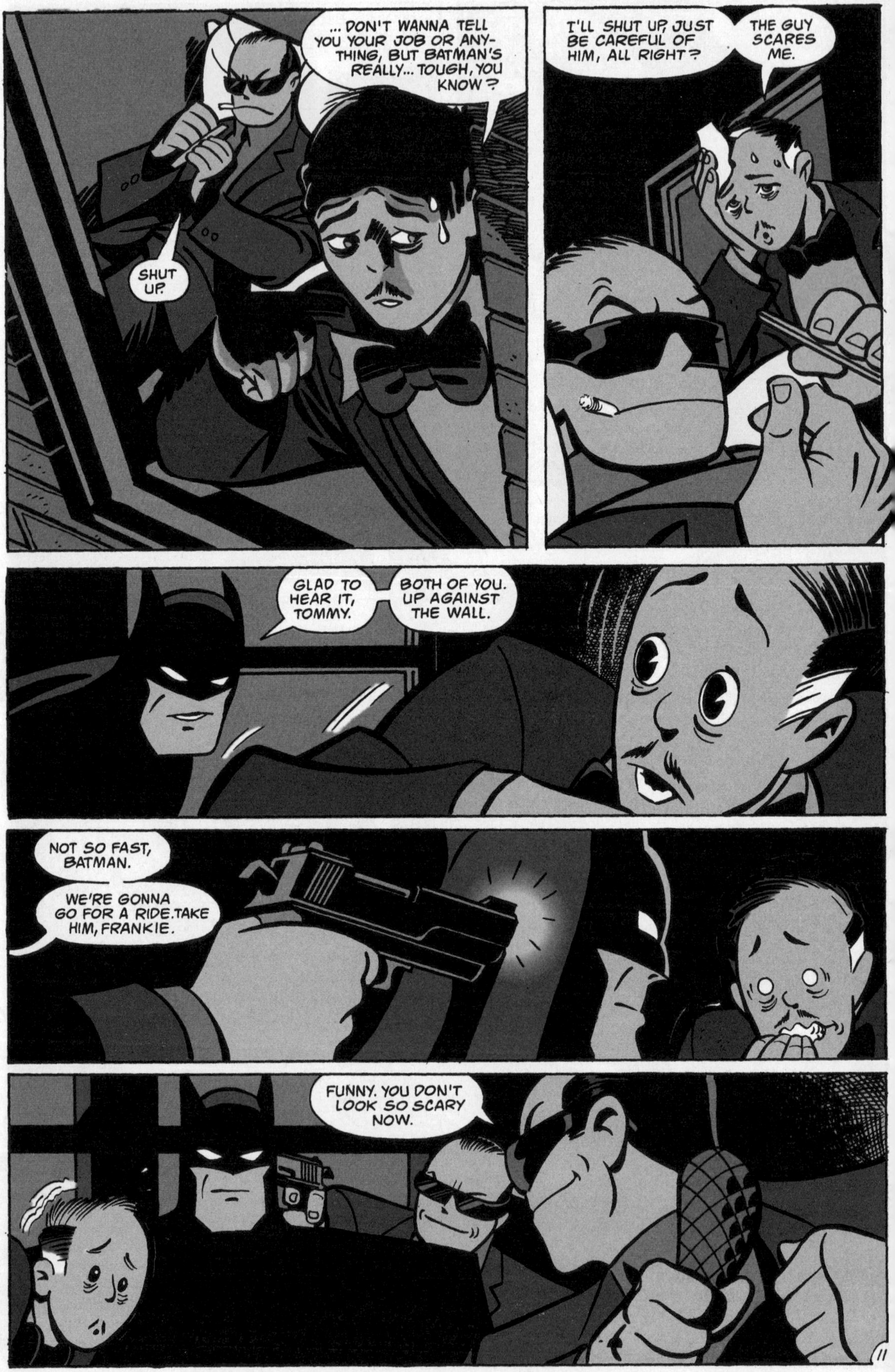

...DON'T WANNA TELL YOU YOUR JOB OR ANYTHING, BUT BATMAN'S REALLY... TOUGH, YOU KNOW?
SHUT UP.
I'LL SHUT UP, JUST BE CAREFUL OF HIM, ALL RIGHT?
THE GUY SCARES ME.
GLAD TO HEAR IT, TOMMY.
BOTH OF YOU. UP AGAINST THE WALL.
NOT SO FAST, BATMAN.
WE'RE GONNA GO FOR A RIDE. TAKE HIM, FRANKIE.
FUNNY. YOU DON'T LOOK SO SCARY NOW.
11

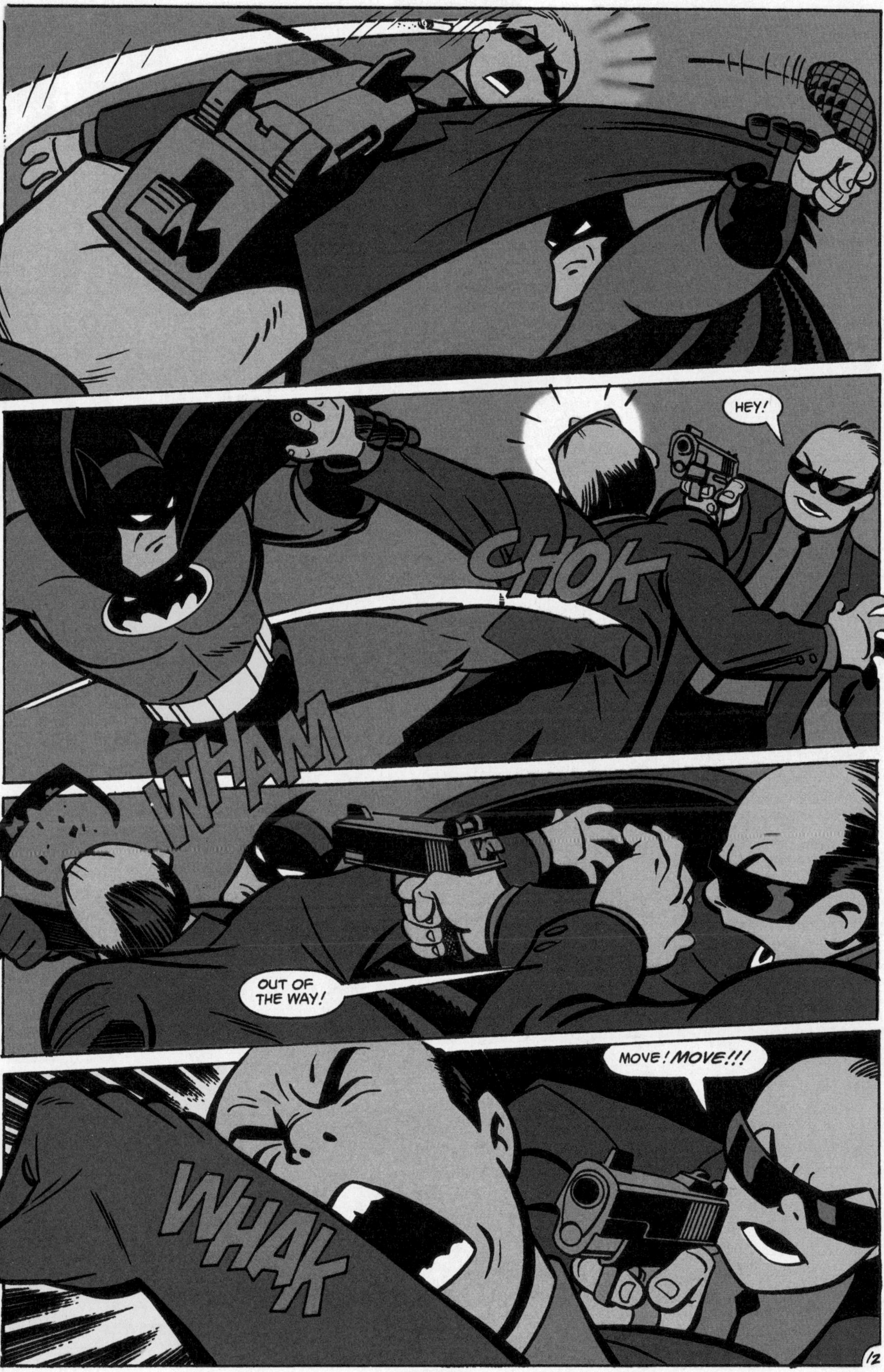

HEY!
CHOK
WHAM
OUT OF THE WAY!
MOVE! MOVE!!!
WHAK
12

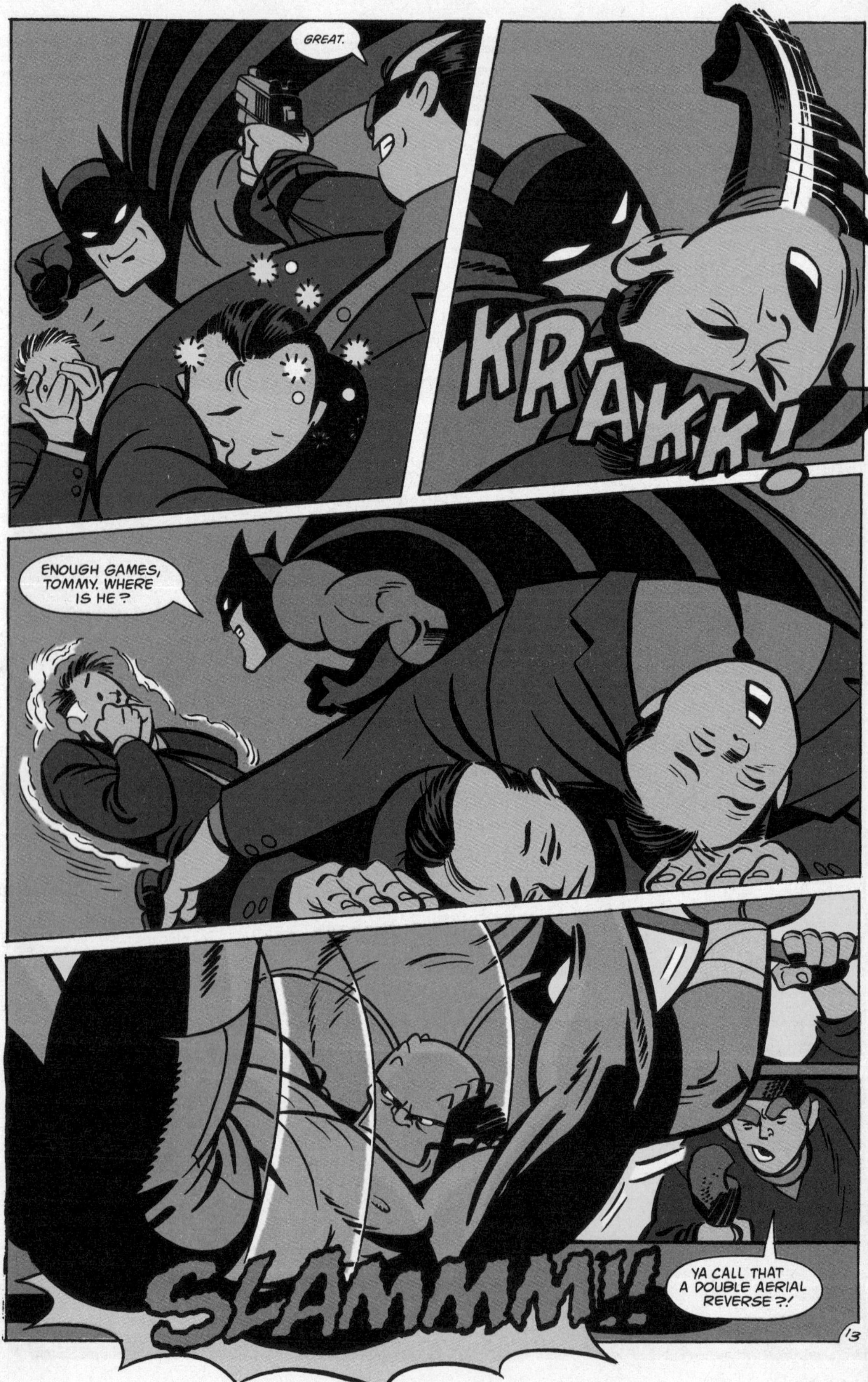
GREAT.
KRAKK!
ENOUGH GAMES, TOMMY. WHERE IS HE?
SLAMMM!!
YA CALL THAT A DOUBLE AERIAL REVERSE?!
13

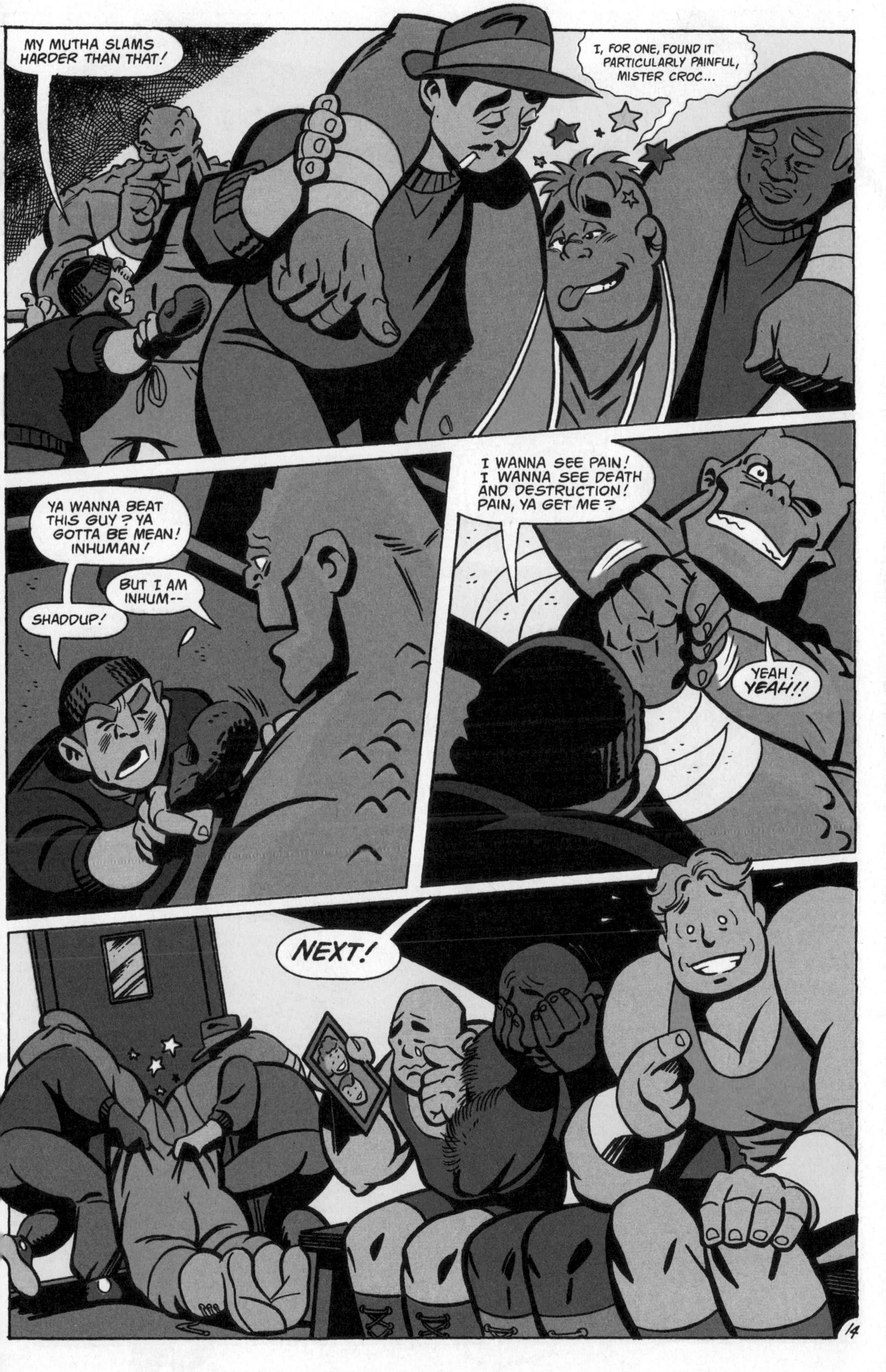
MY MUTHA SLAMS HARDER THAN THAT!
I, FOR ONE, FOUND IT PARTICULARLY PAINFUL, MISTER CROC...
YA WANNA BEAT THIS GUY? YA GOTTA BE MEAN! INHUMAN!
BUT I AM INHUM--
SHADDUP!
I WANNA SEE PAIN! I WANNA SEE DEATH AND DESTRUCTION! PAIN, YA GET ME?
YEAH! YEAH!!
NEXT!
14

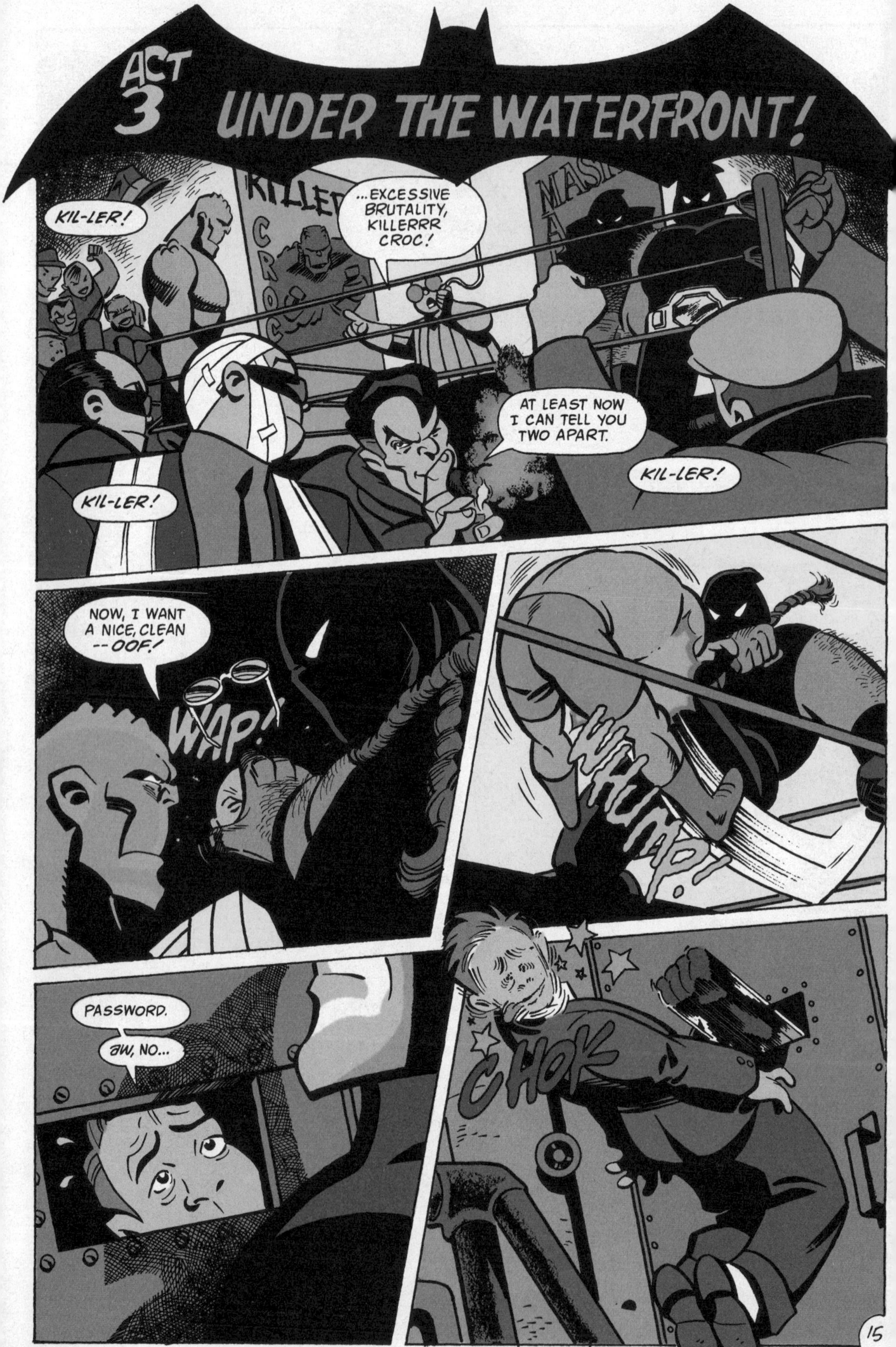
ACT 3
UNDER THE WATERFRONT!
KIL-LER!
...EXCESSIVE BRUTALITY, KILLERRR CROC!
AT LEAST NOW I CAN TELL YOU TWO APART.
KIL-LER!
KIL-LER!
NOW, I WANT A NICE, CLEAN --OOF!
WAP!
WHUMP!
PASSWORD.
aw, NO...
CHOK
15

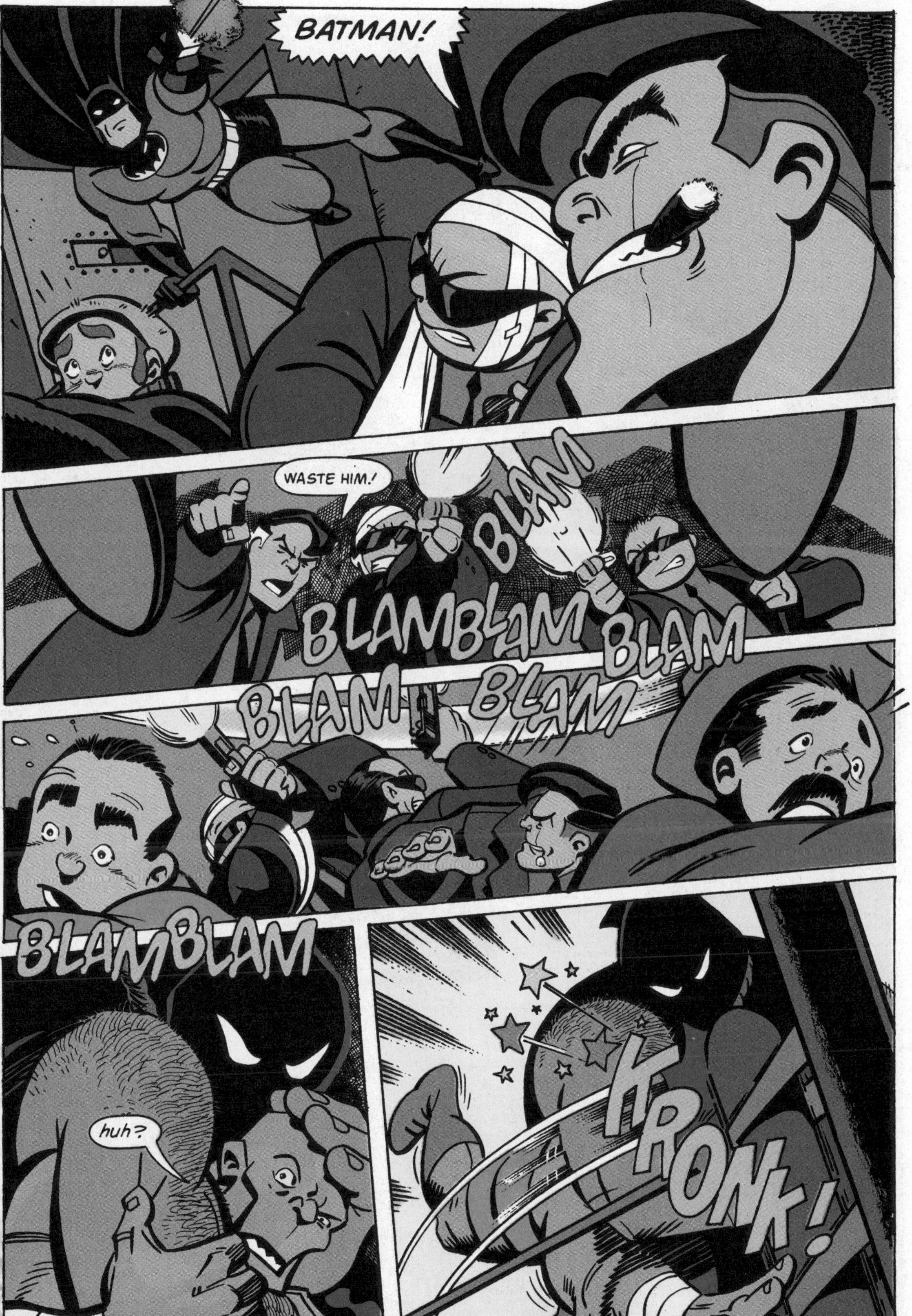
BATMAN!
WASTE HIM!
BLAM
BLAMBLAM
BLAM
BLAM
BLAM
BLAM
BLAMBLAM
huh?
KRONK!

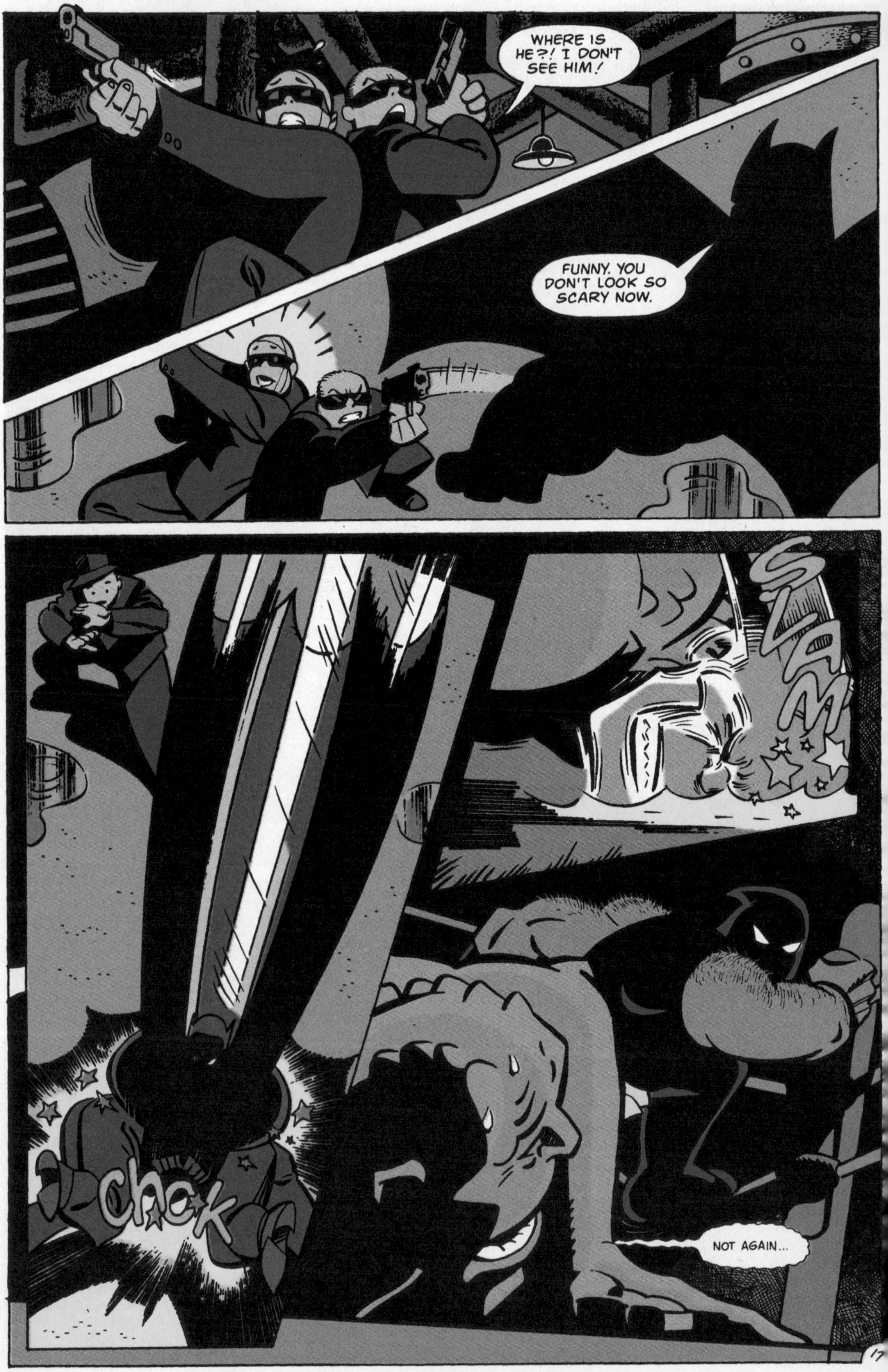
WHERE IS HE?! I DON'T SEE HIM!
FUNNY. YOU DON'T LOOK SO SCARY NOW.
SLAM
CHOK
NOT AGAIN...
17

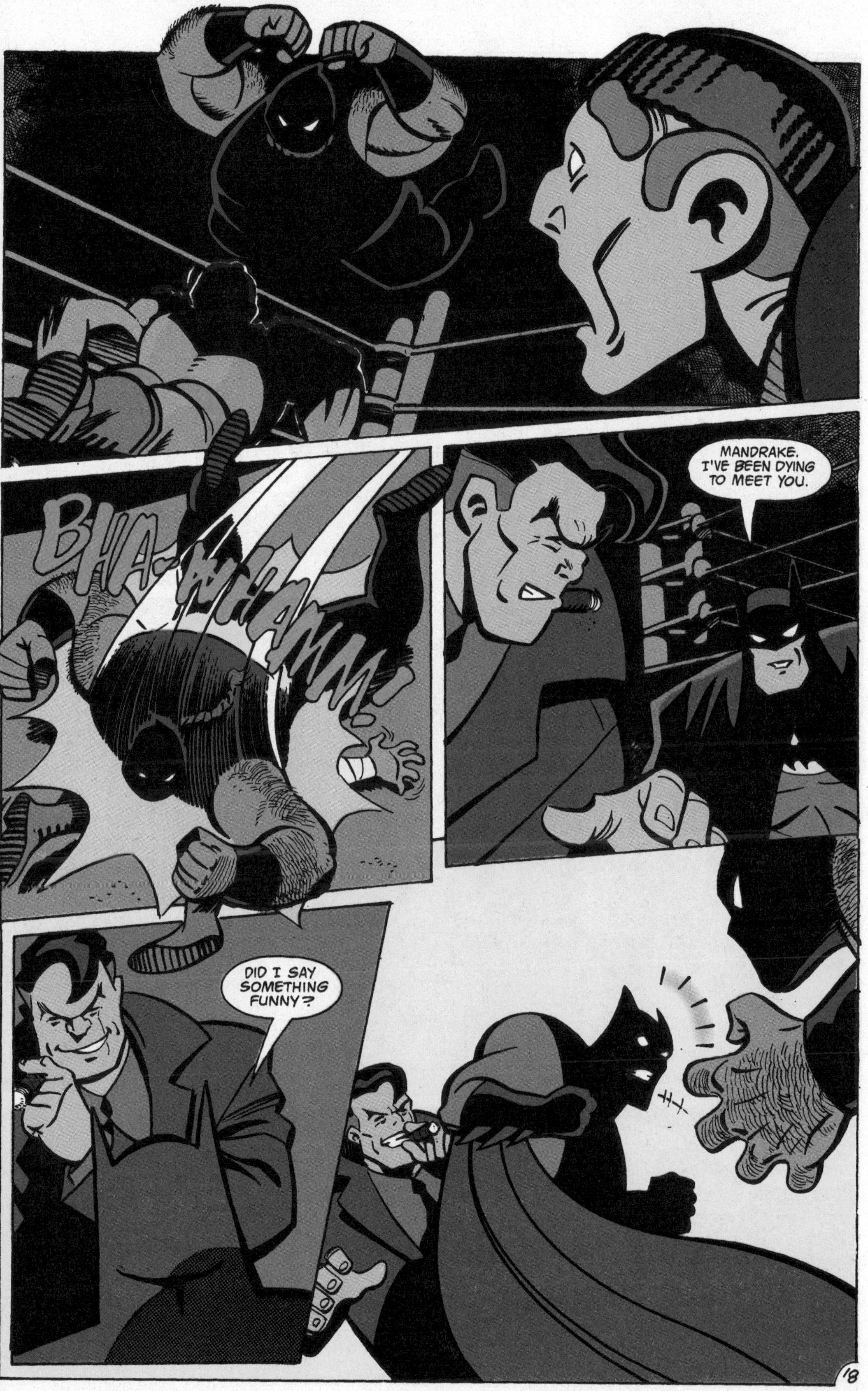
BHA-WHAMM!
MANDRAKE. I'VE BEEN DYING TO MEET YOU.
DID I SAY SOMETHING FUNNY?
18

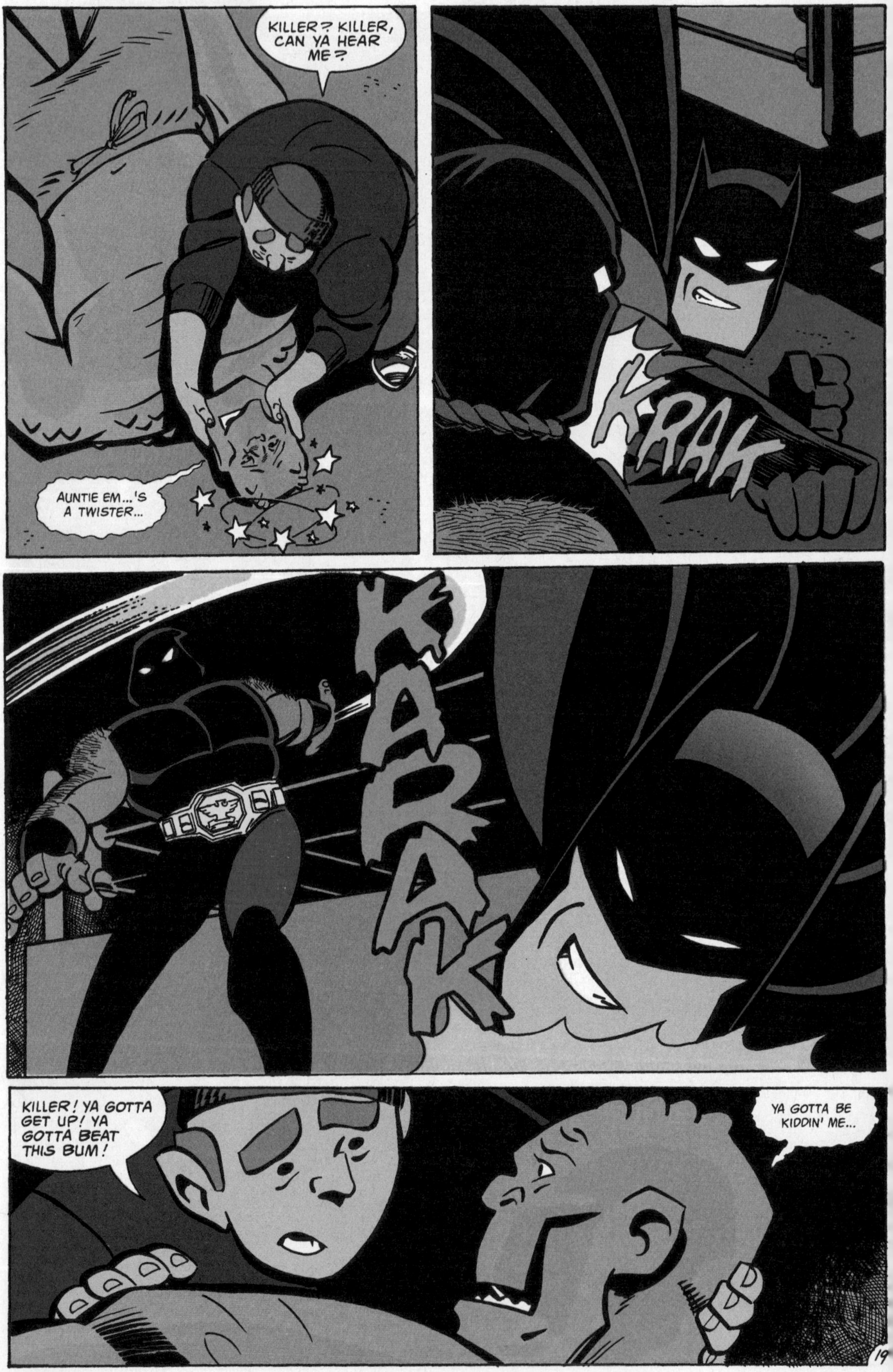
KILLER? KILLER, CAN YA HEAR ME?
AUNTIE EM...'S A TWISTER...
KRAK
KARAK
KILLER! YA GOTTA GET UP! YA GOTTA BEAT THIS BUM!
YA GOTTA BE KIDDIN' ME...
19

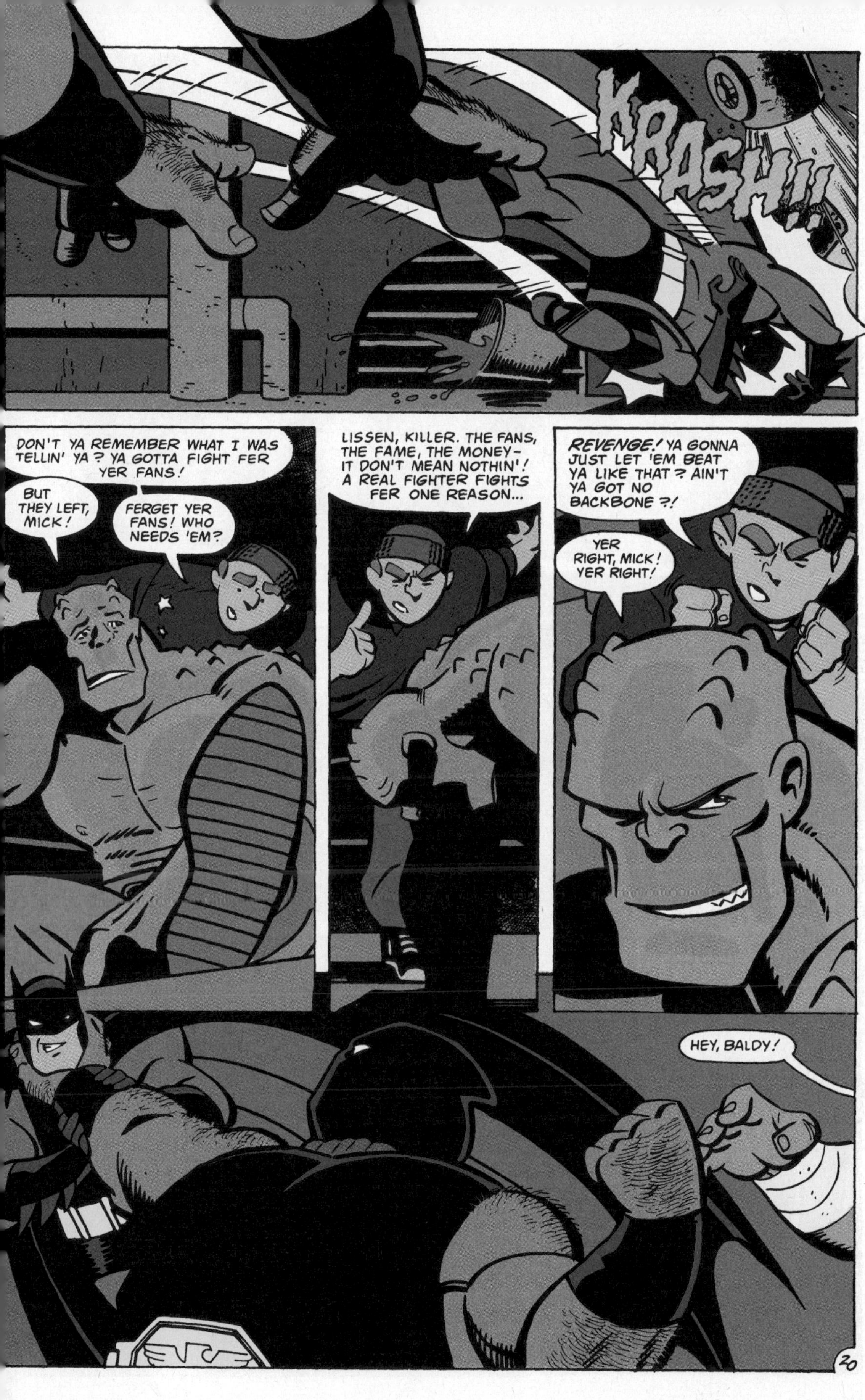
KRASH!!
DON'T YA REMEMBER WHAT I WAS TELLIN' YA? YA GOTTA FIGHT FER YER FANS!
BUT THEY LEFT, MICK!
FERGET YER FANS! WHO NEEDS 'EM?
LISSEN, KILLER. THE FANS, THE FAME, THE MONEY- IT DON'T MEAN NOTHIN'! A REAL FIGHTER FIGHTS FER ONE REASON...
REVENGE! YA GONNA JUST LET 'EM BEAT YA LIKE THAT? AIN'T YA GOT NO BACKBONE?!
YER RIGHT, MICK! YER RIGHT!
HEY, BALDY!
20

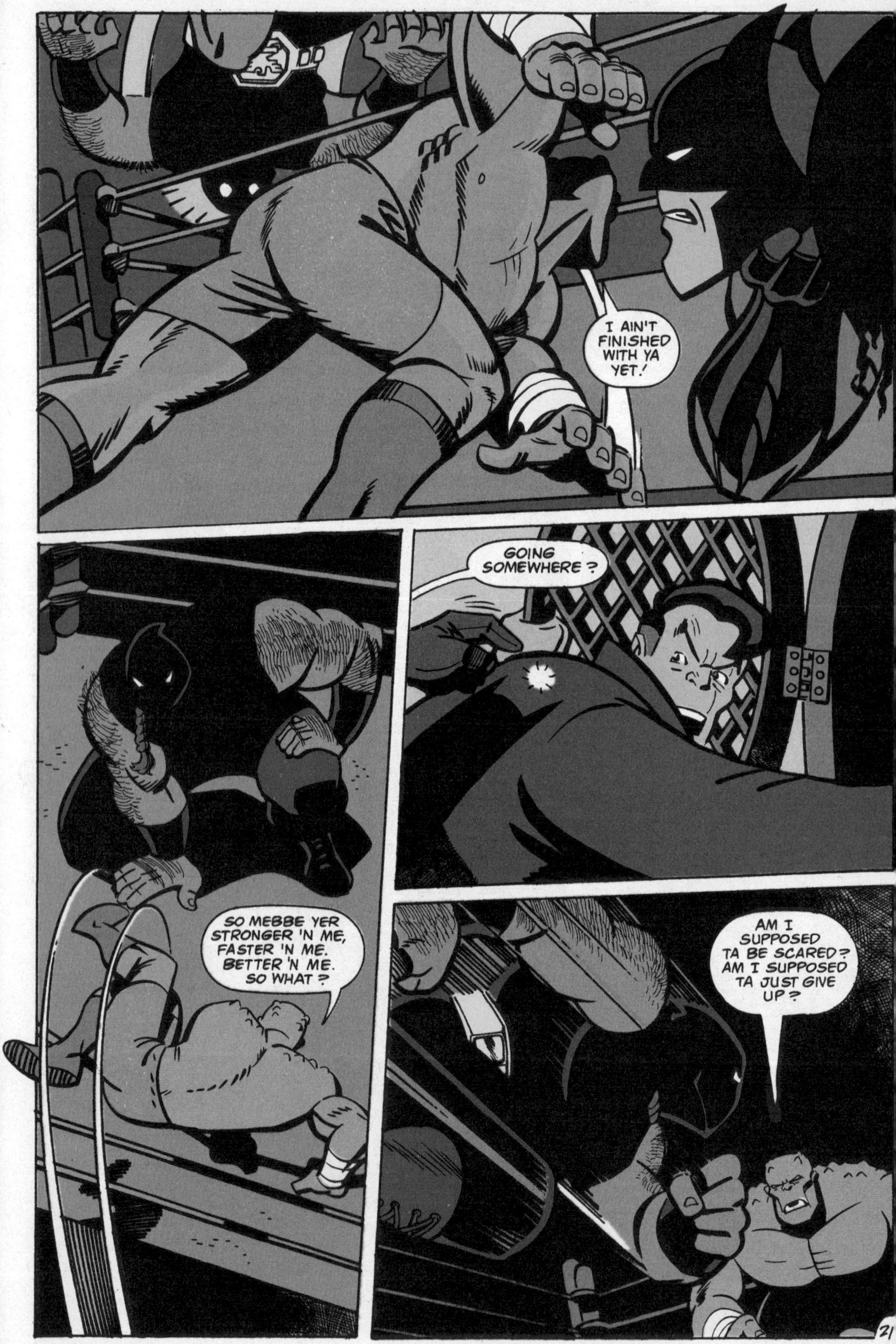
I AIN'T FINISHED WITH YA YET.!
GOING SOMEWHERE ?
SO MEBBE YER STRONGER 'N ME, FASTER 'N ME. BETTER 'N ME. SO WHAT ?
AM I SUPPOSED TA BE SCARED? AM I SUPPOSED TA JUST GIVE UP ?
21

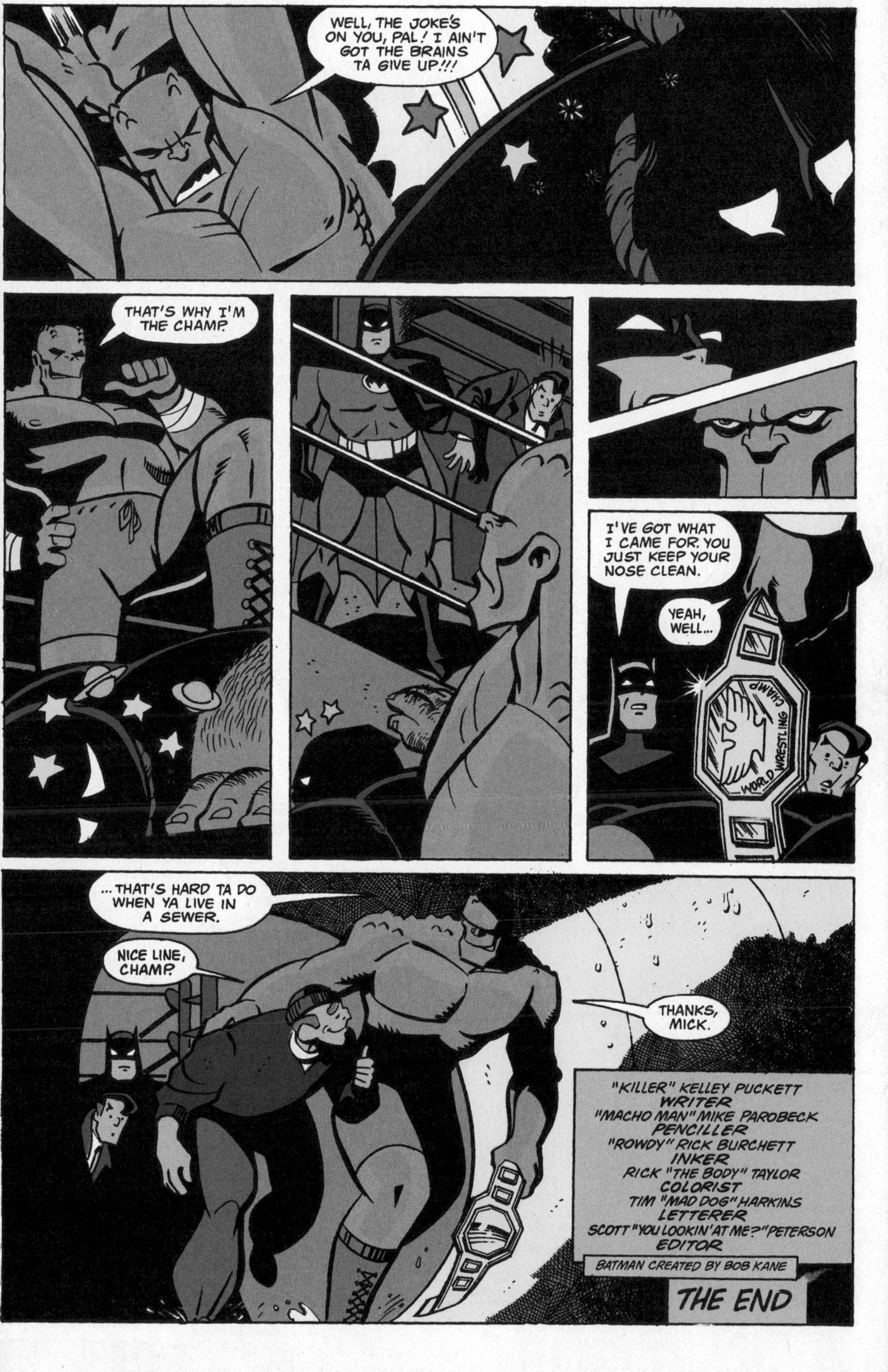
WELL, THE JOKE'S ON YOU, PAL! I AIN'T GOT THE BRAINS TA GIVE UP!!!
THAT'S WHY I'M THE CHAMP.
I'VE GOT WHAT I CAME FOR. YOU JUST KEEP YOUR NOSE CLEAN.
YEAH, WELL...
WORLD WRESTLING CHAMP
...THAT'S HARD TA DO WHEN YA LIVE IN A SEWER.
NICE LINE, CHAMP.
THANKS, MICK.
"KILLER" KELLEY PUCKETT
WRITER
"MACHO MAN" MIKE PAROBECK
PENCILLER
"ROWDY" RICK BURCHETT
INKER
RICK "THE BODY" TAYLOR
COLORIST
TIM "MAD DOG" HARKINS
LETTERER
SCOTT "YOU LOOKIN' AT ME?" PETERSON
EDITOR
BATMAN CREATED BY BOB KANE
THE END

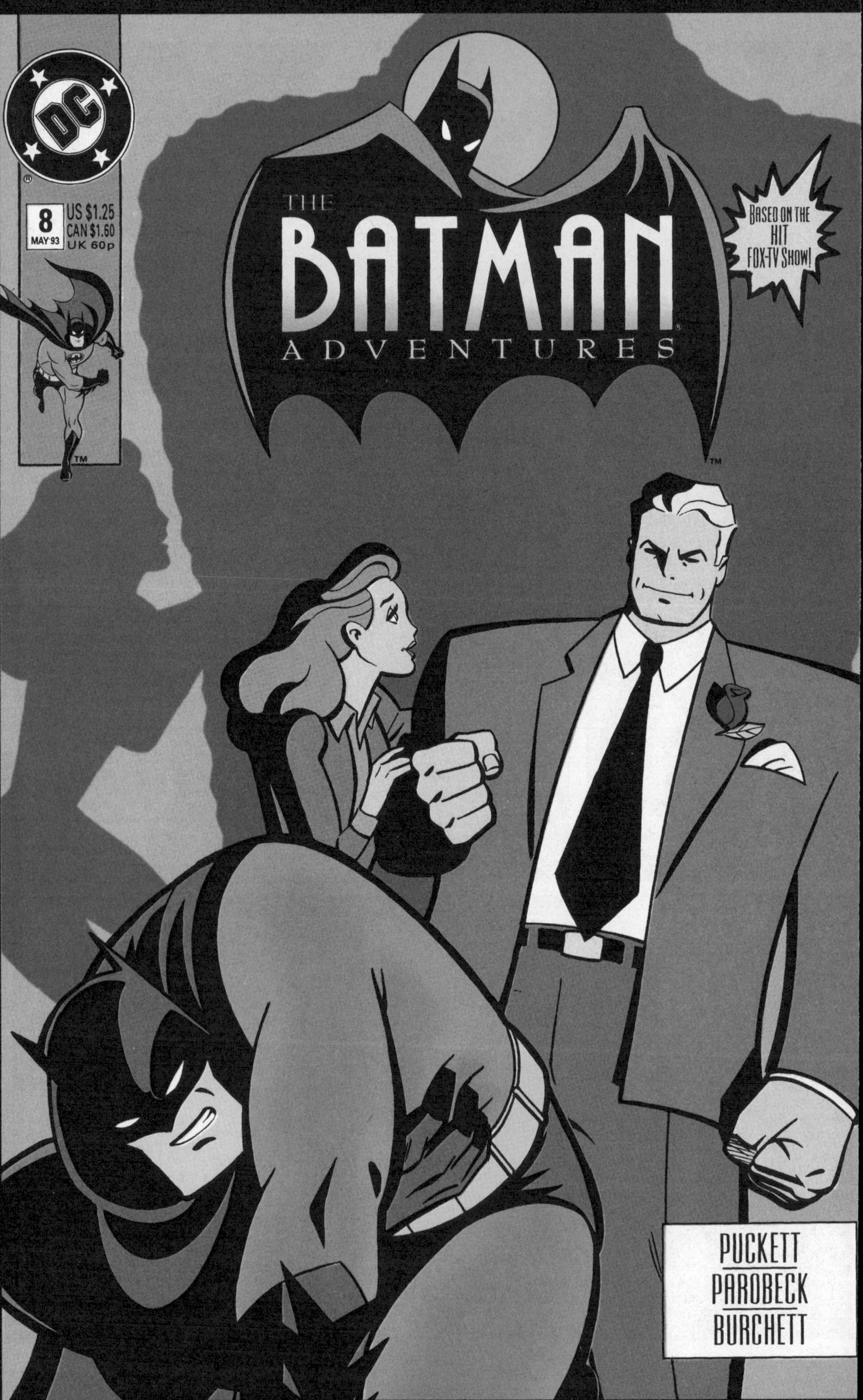
DC
8
MAY 93
US $1.25
CAN $1.60
UK 60p
THE BATMAN ADVENTURES
BASED ON THE HIT FOX-TV SHOW!
PUCKETT
PAROBECK
BURCHETT

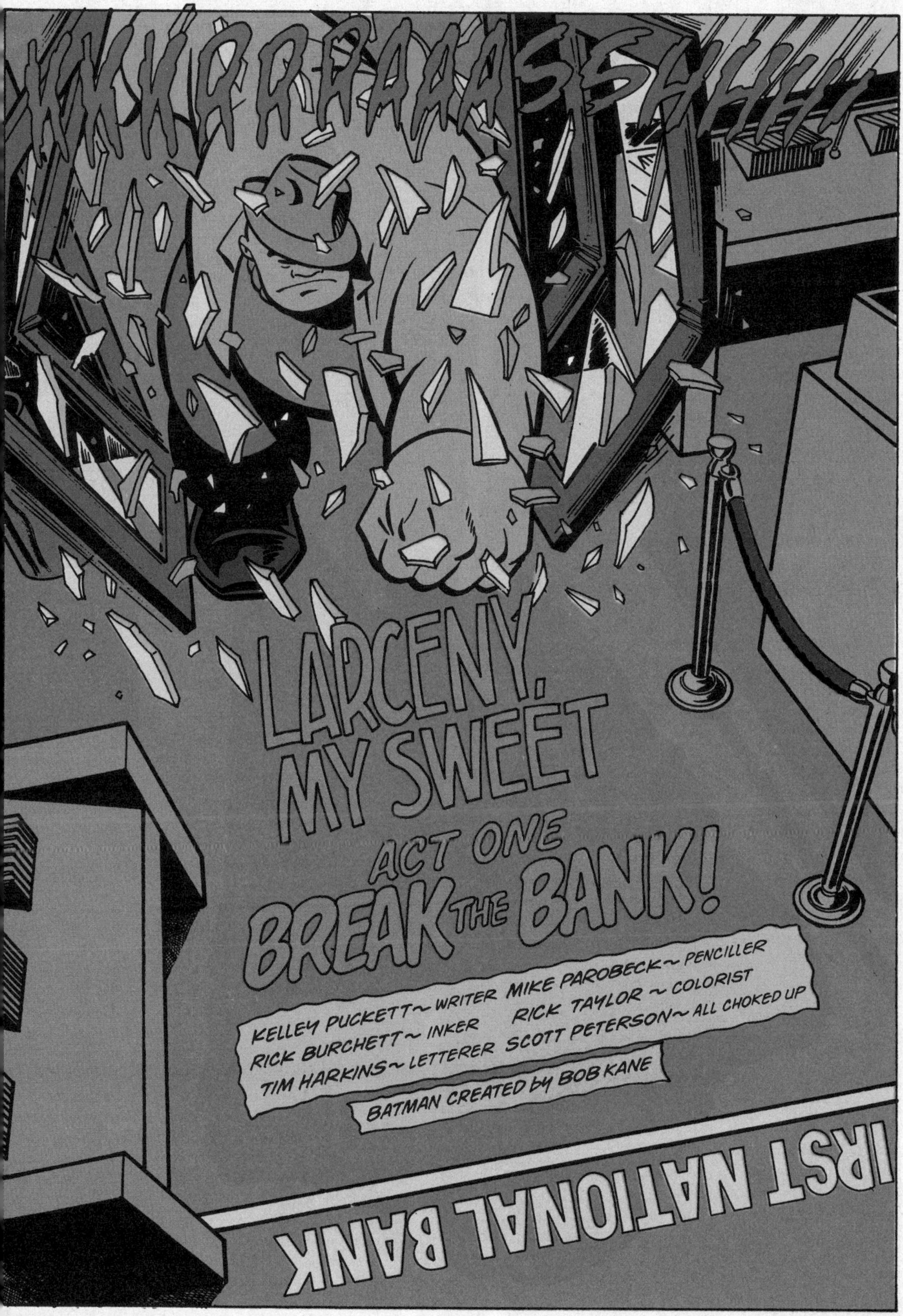
KKKRRRAAASSHHHH!
LARCENY, MY SWEET
ACT ONE
BREAK THE BANK!
KELLEY PUCKETT~ WRITER MIKE PAROBECK~ PENCILLER
RICK BURCHETT~ INKER RICK TAYLOR ~ COLORIST
TIM HARKINS~ LETTERER SCOTT PETERSON~ ALL CHOKED UP
BATMAN CREATED BY BOB KANE
IRST NATIONAL BANK

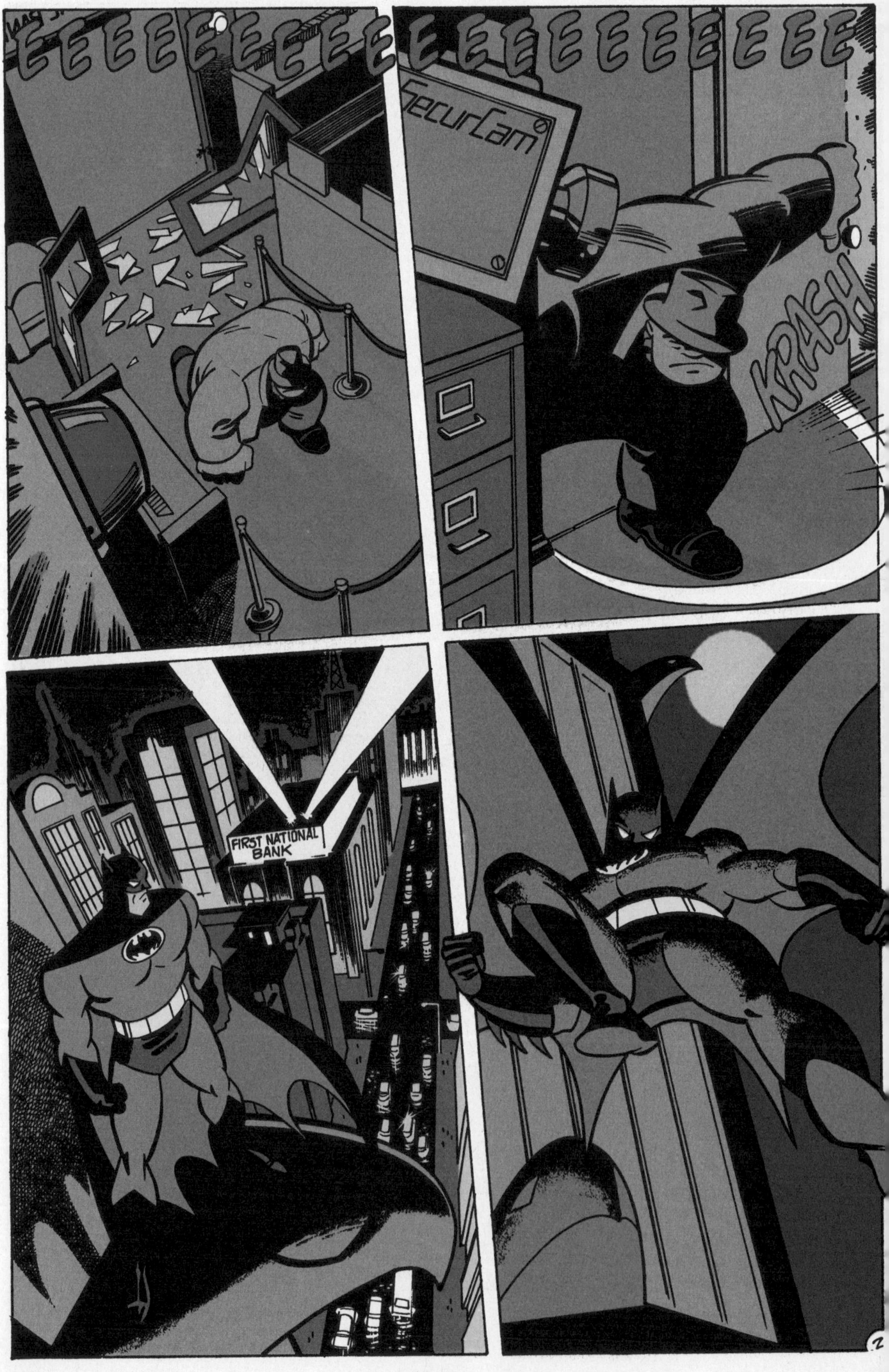
EEEEEEEEEEEEEEEEEEEEEEEE
SecurCam
KRASH
FIRST NATIONAL BANK

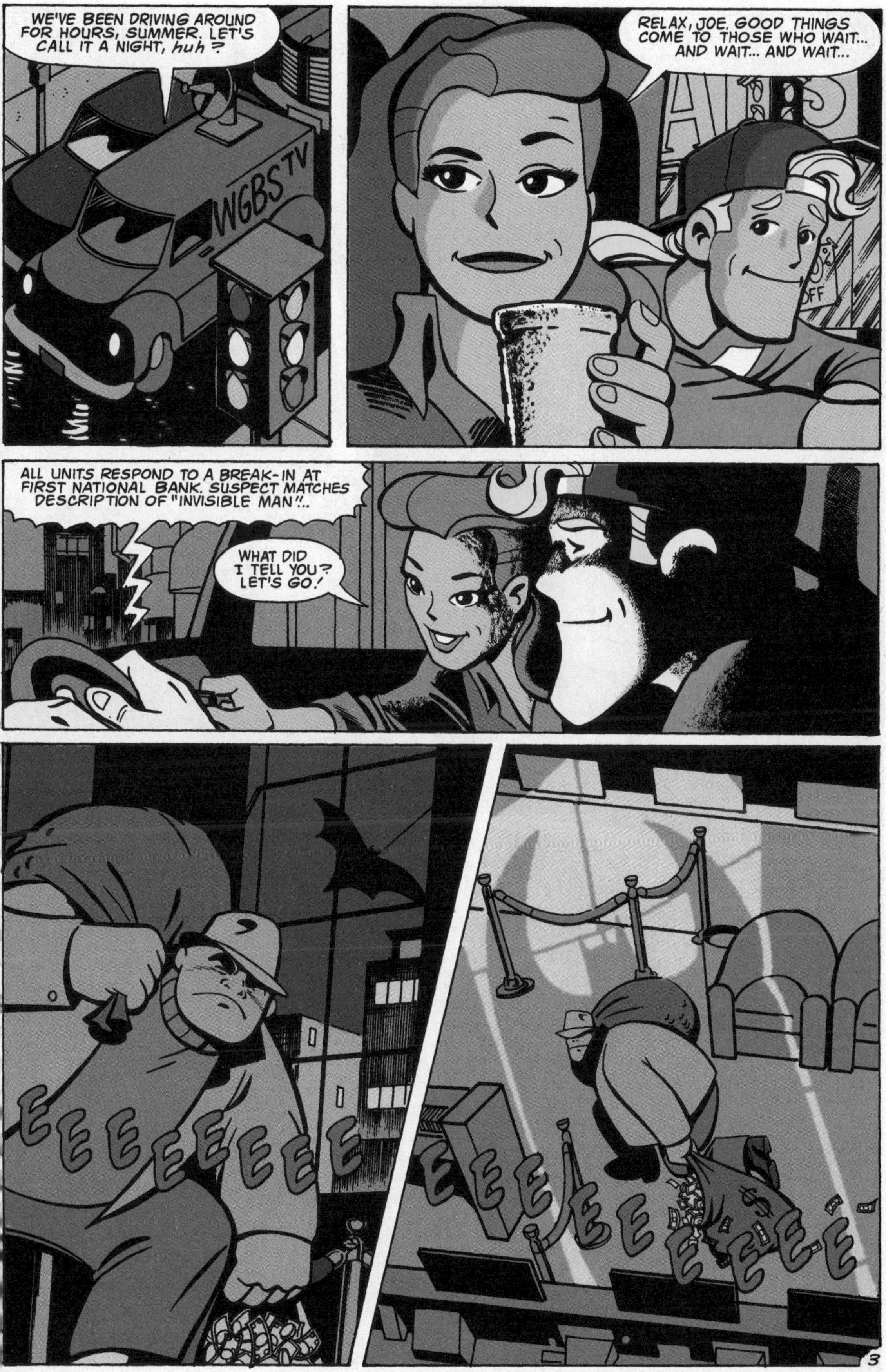
WE'VE BEEN DRIVING AROUND FOR HOURS, SUMMER. LET'S CALL IT A NIGHT, huh?
WGBS TV
RELAX, JOE. GOOD THINGS COME TO THOSE WHO WAIT... AND WAIT... AND WAIT...
ALL UNITS RESPOND TO A BREAK-IN AT FIRST NATIONAL BANK. SUSPECT MATCHES DESCRIPTION OF "INVISIBLE MAN"...
WHAT DID I TELL YOU? LET'S GO!
EEEEEEEEE
EEEEEEEEEE
3

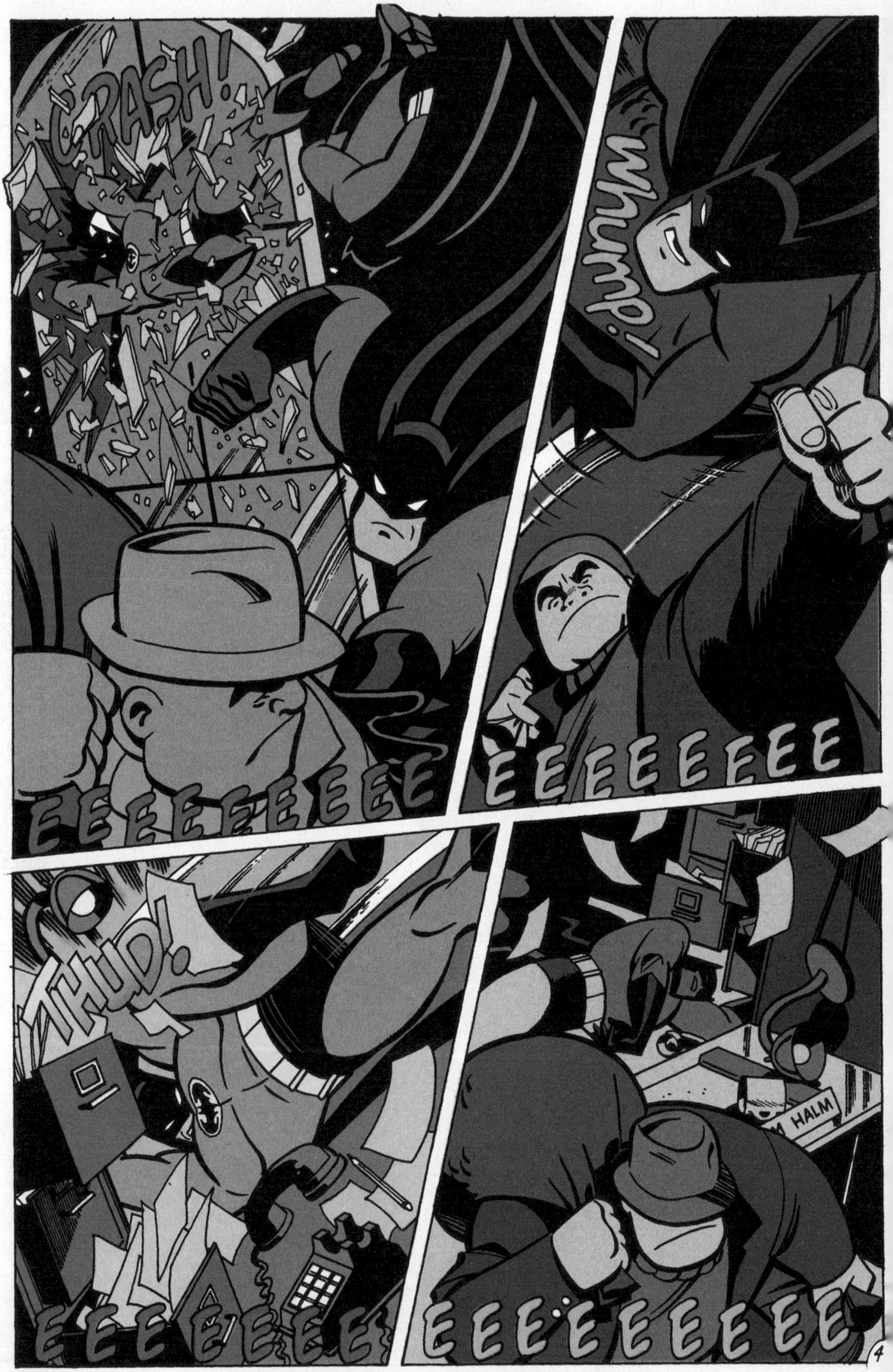
CRASH!
EEEEEEEEEEE
WHUMP!
EEEEEEEEE
THUD!
EEEEEEEEE
HALM
EEEEEEEEEE
4

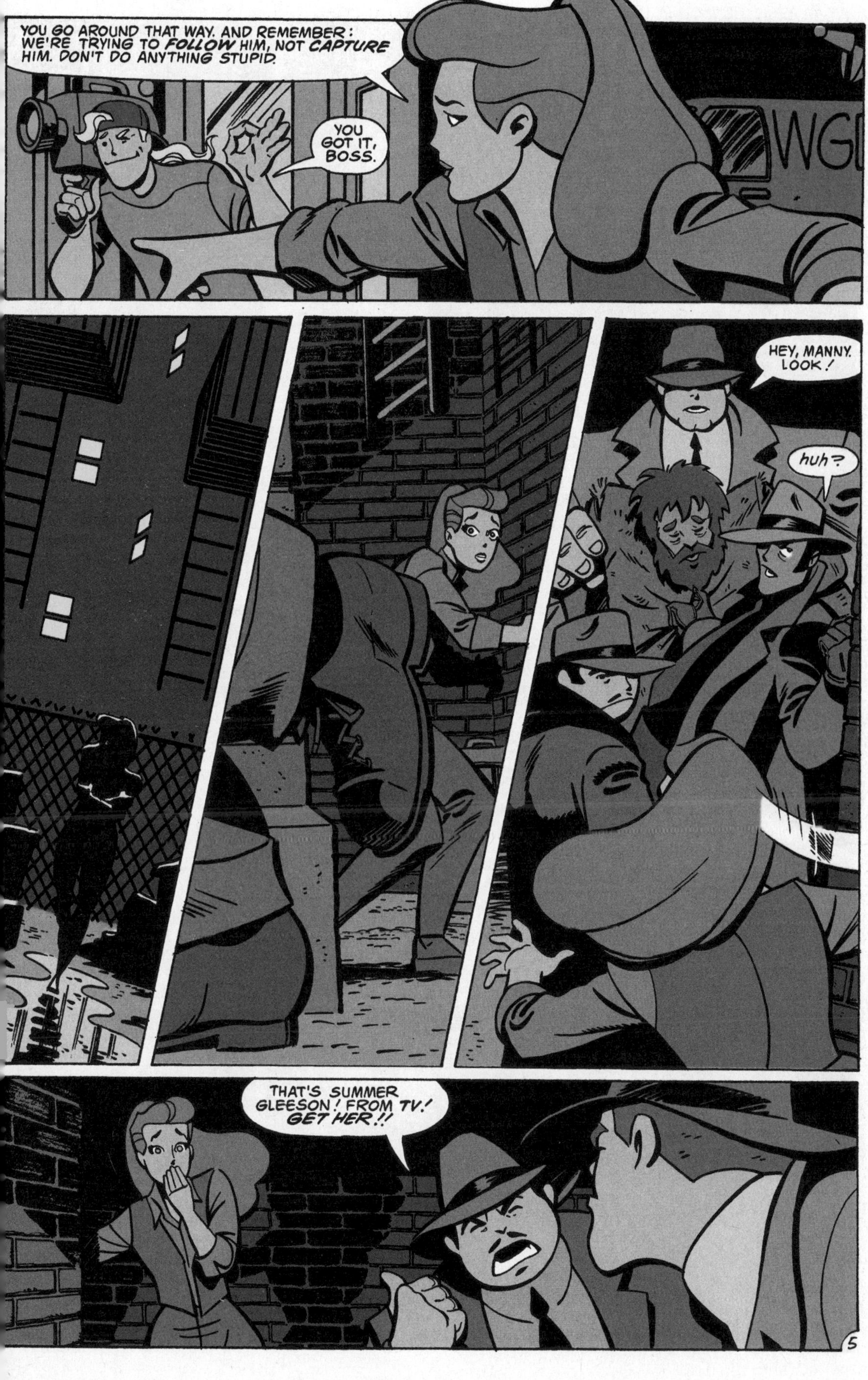
YOU GO AROUND THAT WAY. AND REMEMBER: WE'RE TRYING TO FOLLOW HIM, NOT CAPTURE HIM. DON'T DO ANYTHING STUPID.
YOU GOT IT, BOSS.
WGI
HEY, MANNY. LOOK!
huh?
THAT'S SUMMER GLEESON! FROM TV! GET HER!!
5

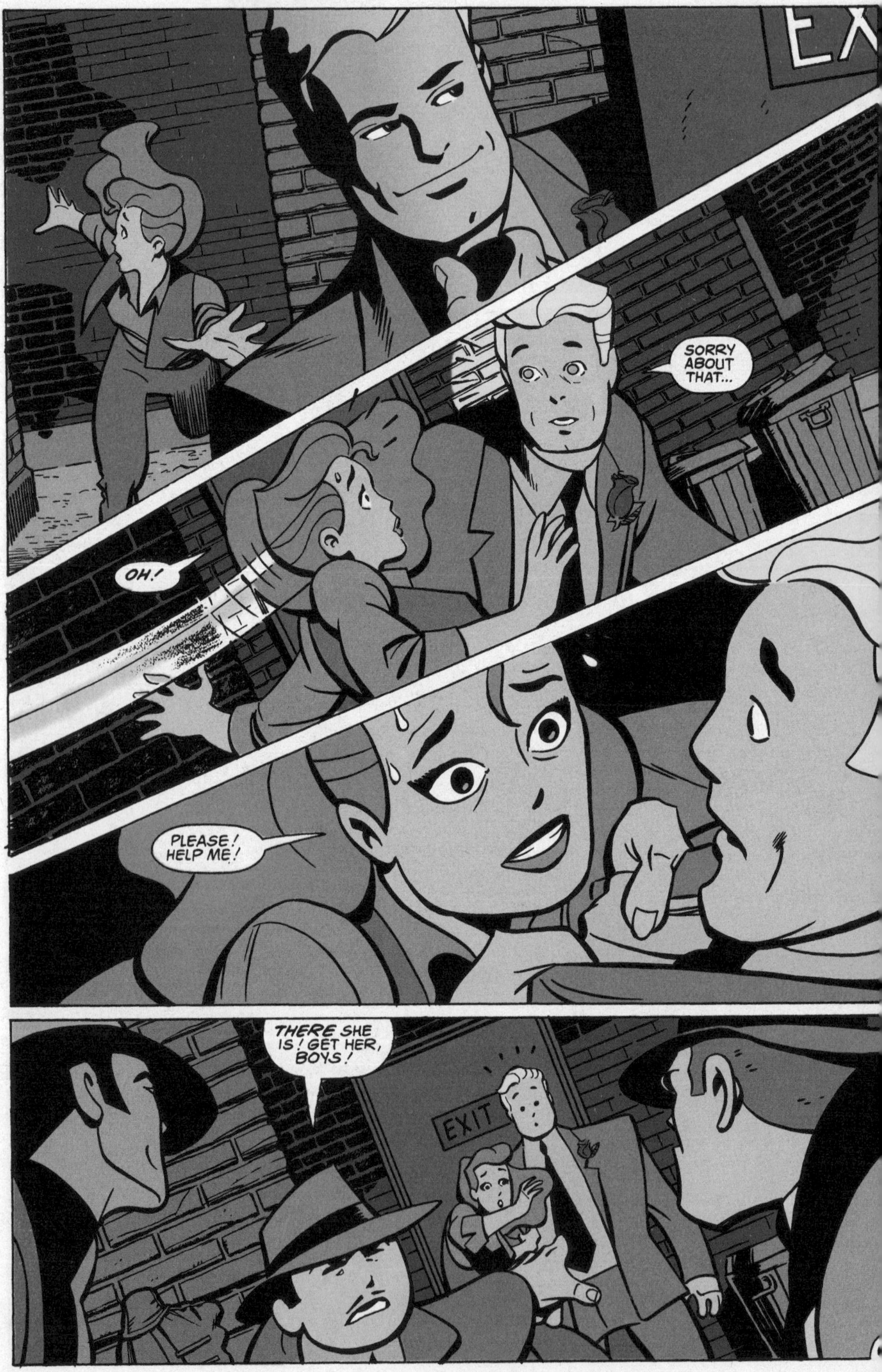
SORRY ABOUT THAT...
OH!
PLEASE! HELP ME!
THERE SHE IS! GET HER, BOYS!
EXIT

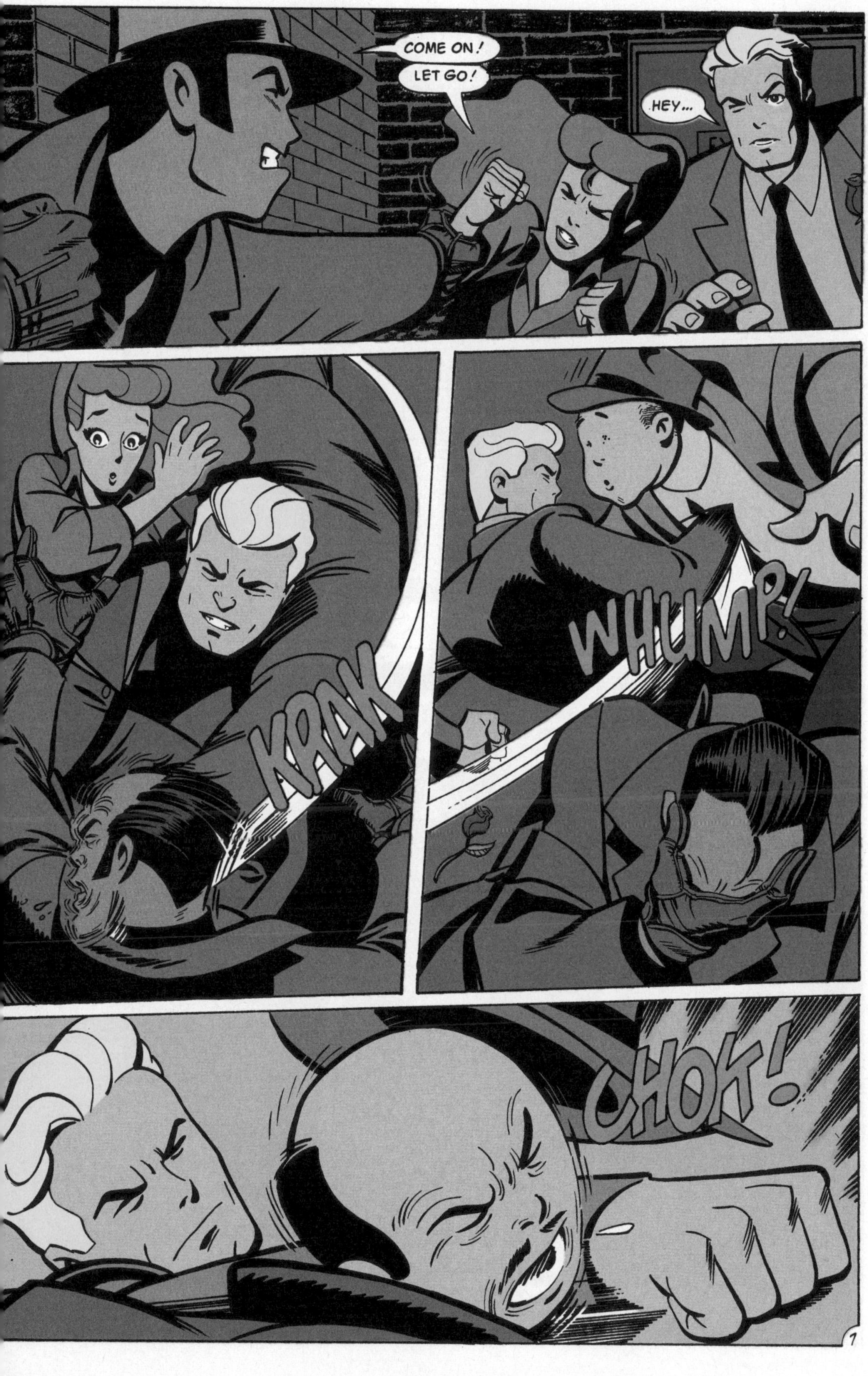
COME ON!
LET GO!
HEY...
KRAK
WHUMP!
CHOK!
7

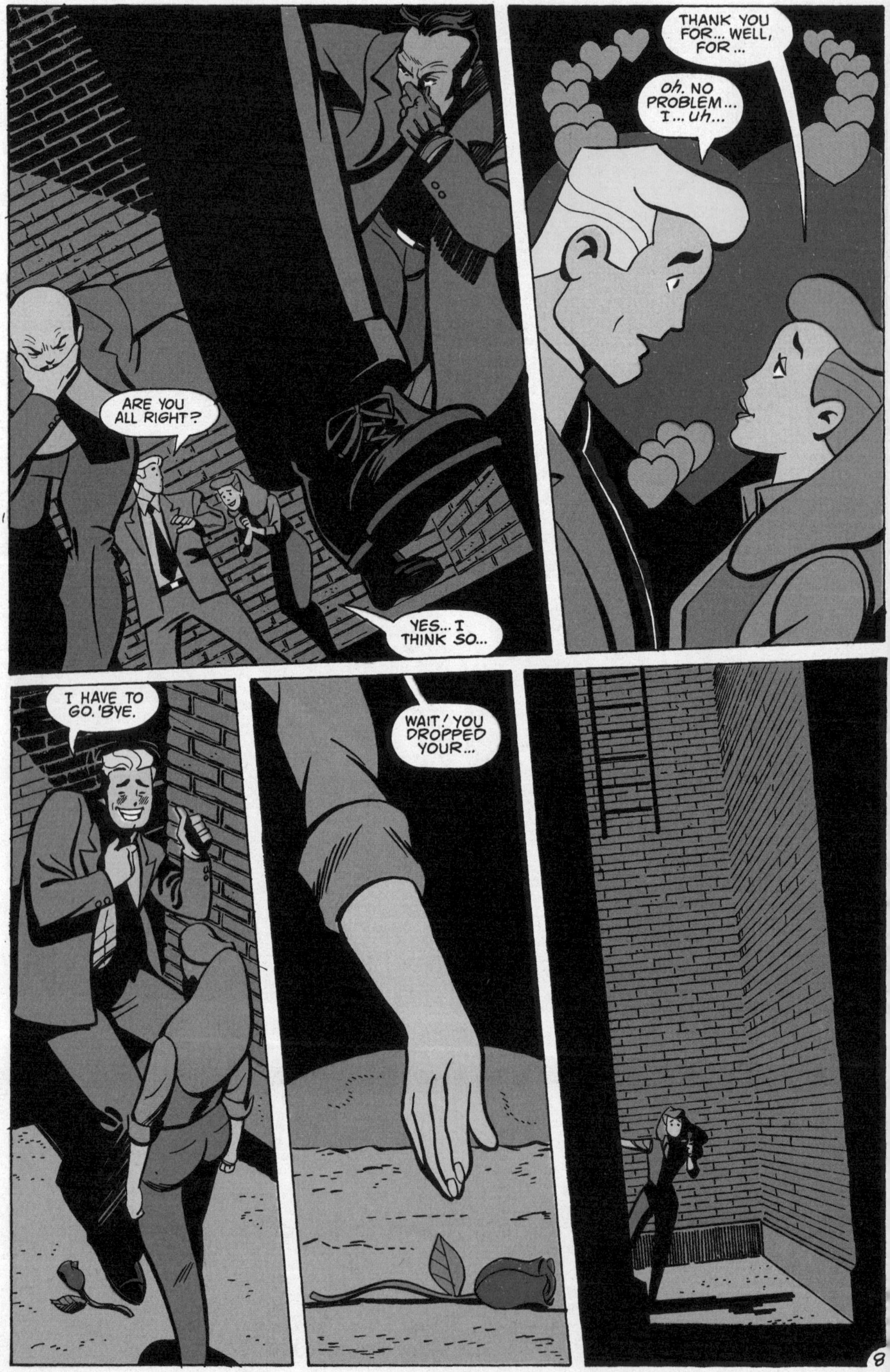
ARE YOU ALL RIGHT?
YES... I THINK SO...
THANK YOU FOR... WELL, FOR...
oh. NO PROBLEM... I... uh...
I HAVE TO GO. 'BYE.
WAIT! YOU DROPPED YOUR...
8

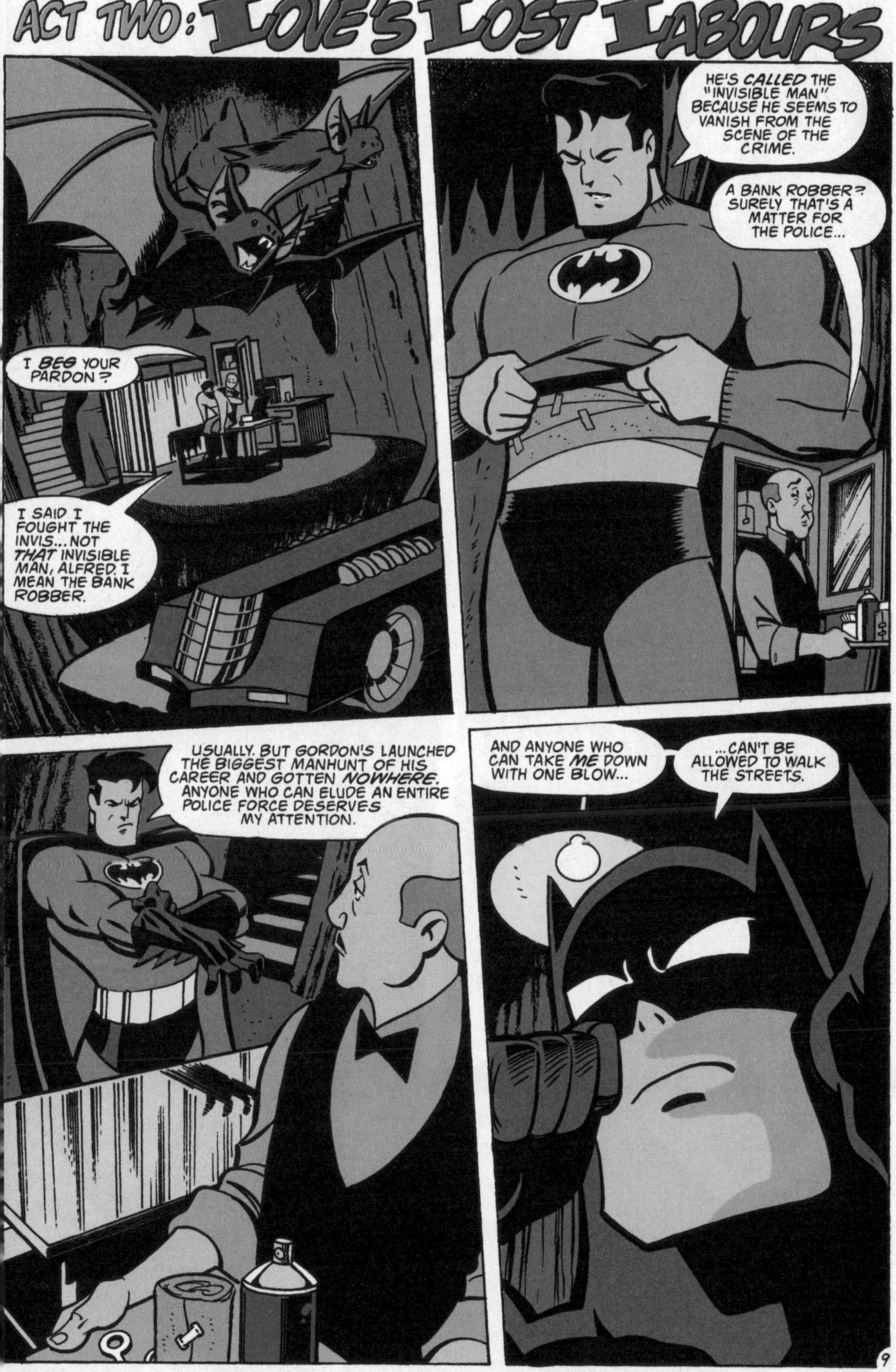
ACT TWO: LOVE'S LOST LABOURS
I BEG YOUR PARDON?
I SAID I FOUGHT THE INVIS... NOT THAT INVISIBLE MAN, ALFRED. I MEAN THE BANK ROBBER.
HE'S CALLED THE "INVISIBLE MAN" BECAUSE HE SEEMS TO VANISH FROM THE SCENE OF THE CRIME.
A BANK ROBBER? SURELY THAT'S A MATTER FOR THE POLICE...
USUALLY. BUT GORDON'S LAUNCHED THE BIGGEST MANHUNT OF HIS CAREER AND GOTTEN NOWHERE. ANYONE WHO CAN ELUDE AN ENTIRE POLICE FORCE DESERVES MY ATTENTION.
AND ANYONE WHO CAN TAKE ME DOWN WITH ONE BLOW...
...CAN'T BE ALLOWED TO WALK THE STREETS.
9

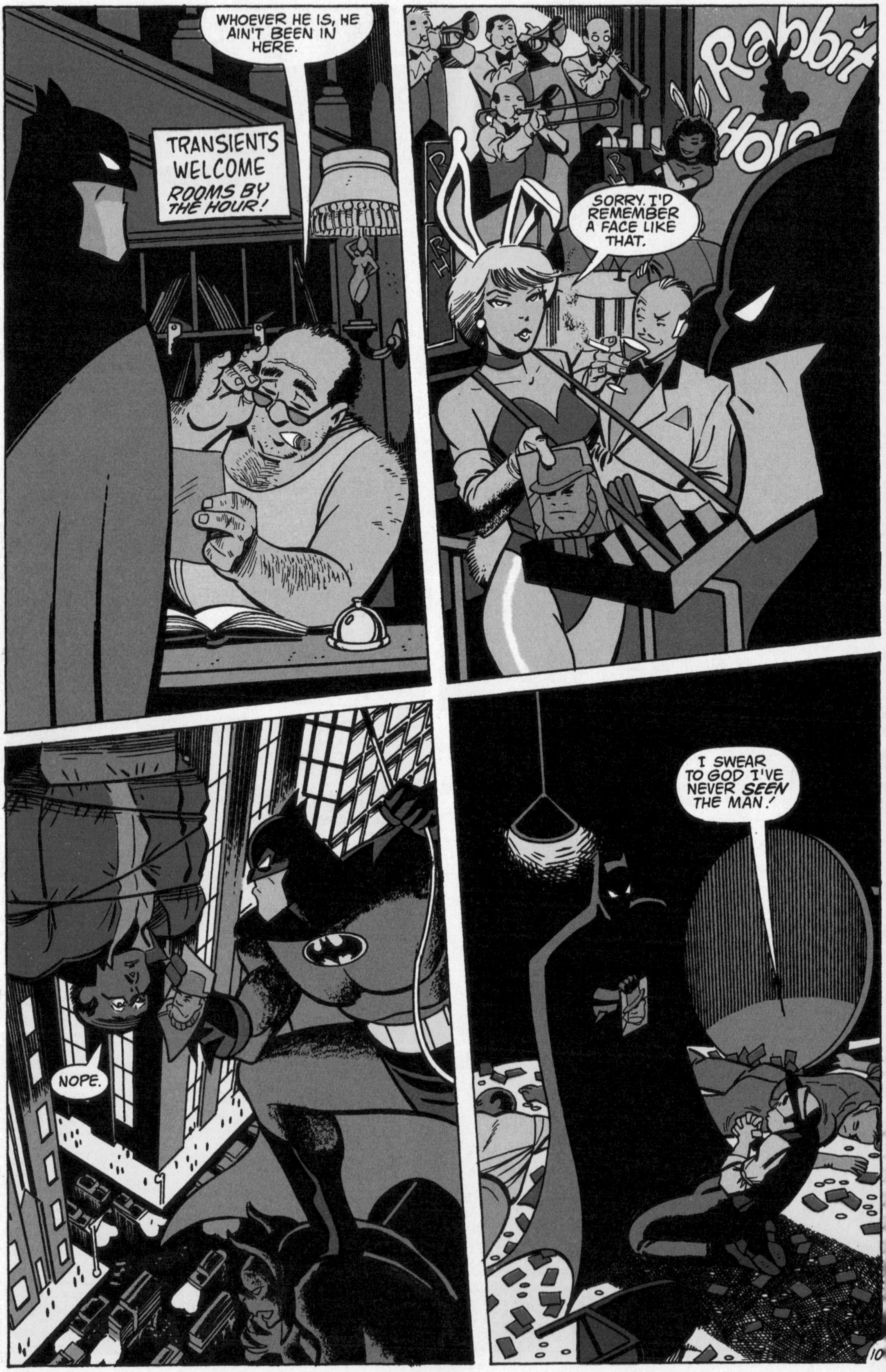
WHOEVER HE IS, HE AIN'T BEEN IN HERE.
TRANSIENTS WELCOME ROOMS BY THE HOUR!
Rabbit Hole
SORRY. I'D REMEMBER A FACE LIKE THAT.
NOPE.
I SWEAR TO GOD I'VE NEVER SEEN THE MAN!
10

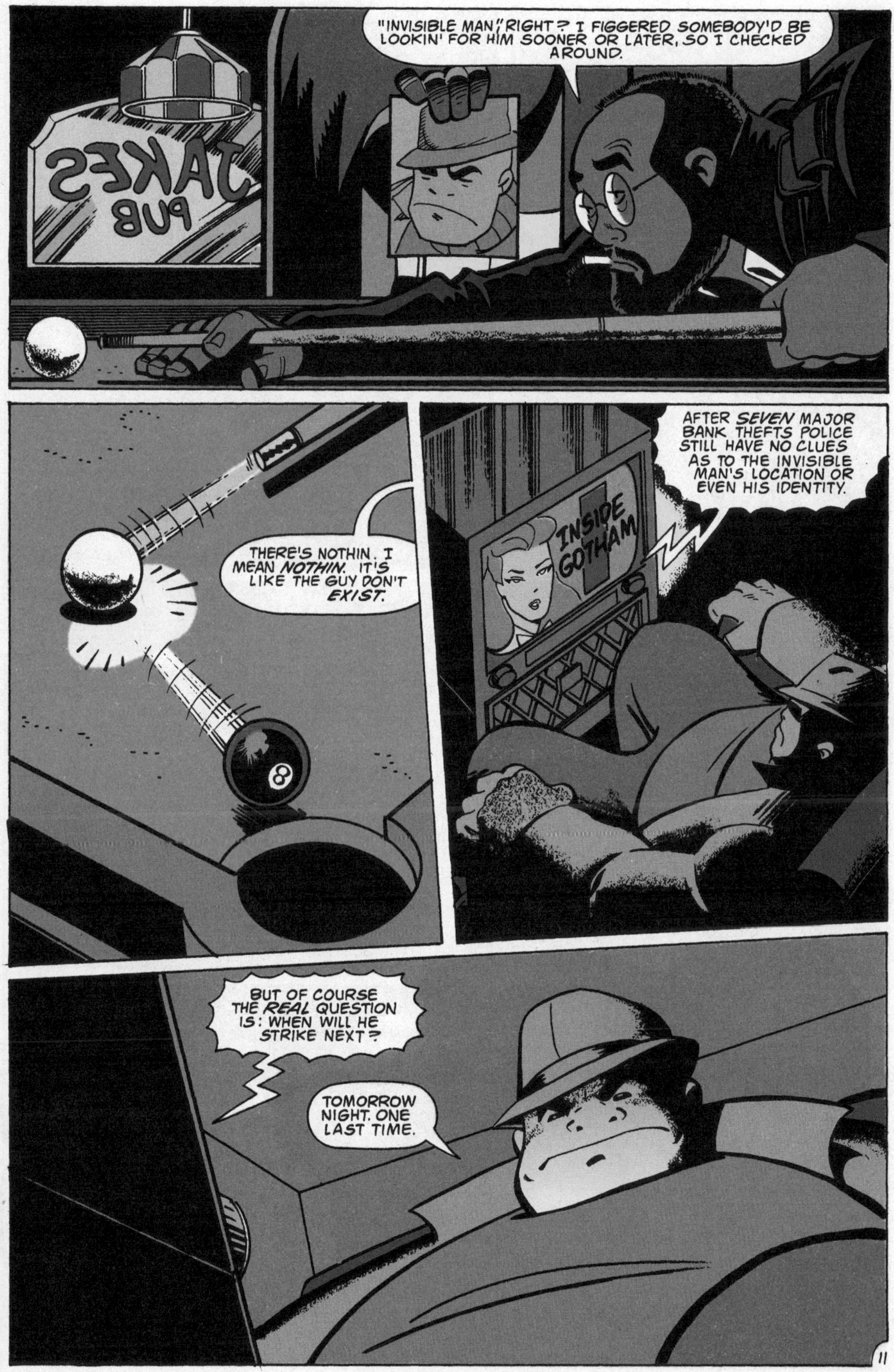
JAKES PUB
"INVISIBLE MAN," RIGHT? I FIGGERED SOMEBODY'D BE LOOKIN' FOR HIM SOONER OR LATER, SO I CHECKED AROUND.
THERE'S NOTHIN. I MEAN NOTHIN. IT'S LIKE THE GUY DON'T EXIST.
AFTER SEVEN MAJOR BANK THEFTS POLICE STILL HAVE NO CLUES AS TO THE INVISIBLE MAN'S LOCATION OR EVEN HIS IDENTITY.
INSIDE GOTHAM
BUT OF COURSE THE REAL QUESTION IS: WHEN WILL HE STRIKE NEXT?
TOMORROW NIGHT. ONE LAST TIME.
11

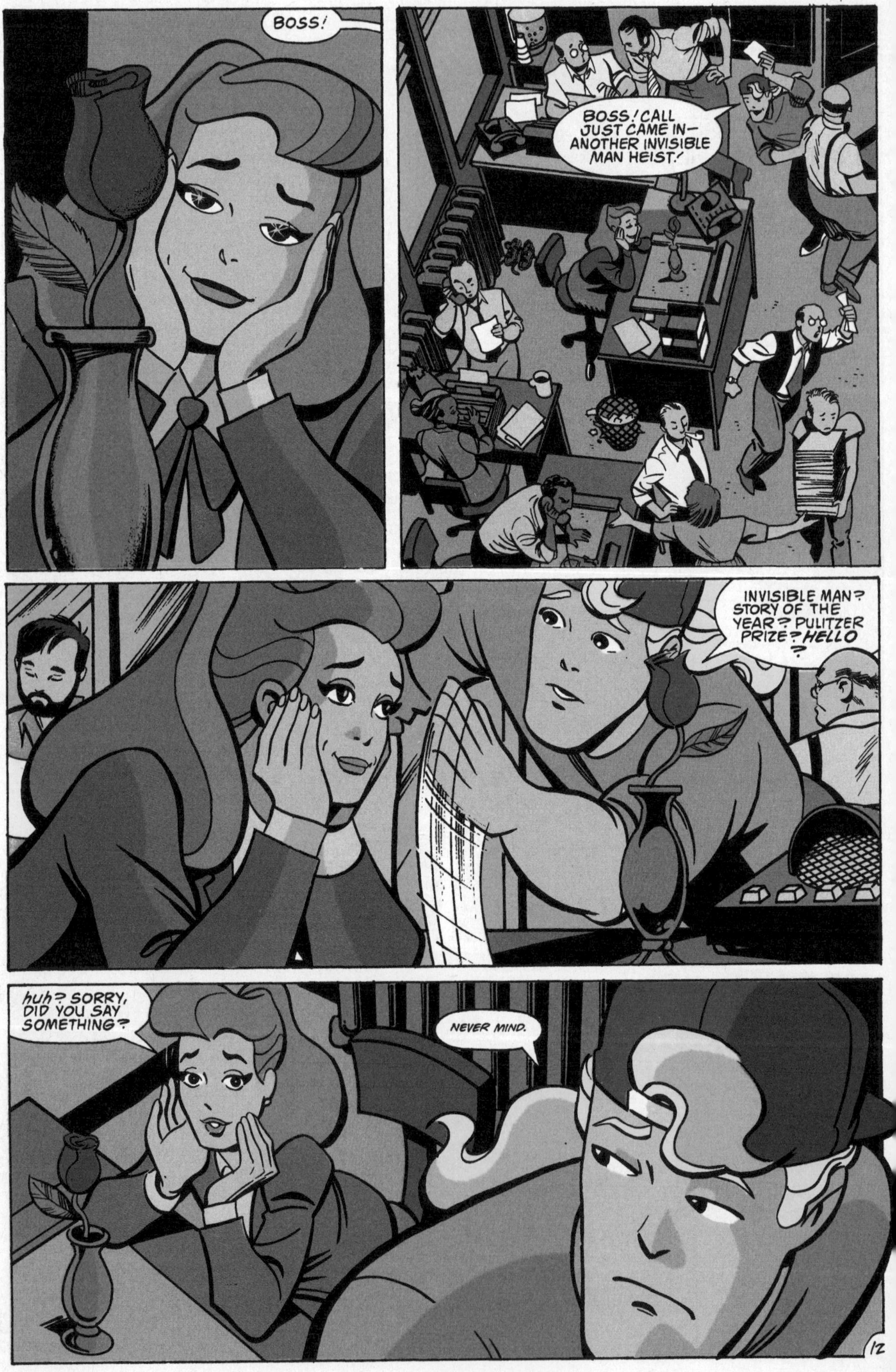
BOSS!
BOSS! CALL JUST CAME IN— ANOTHER INVISIBLE MAN HEIST!
INVISIBLE MAN? STORY OF THE YEAR? PULITZER PRIZE? HELLO?
huh? SORRY, DID YOU SAY SOMETHING?
NEVER MIND.
12

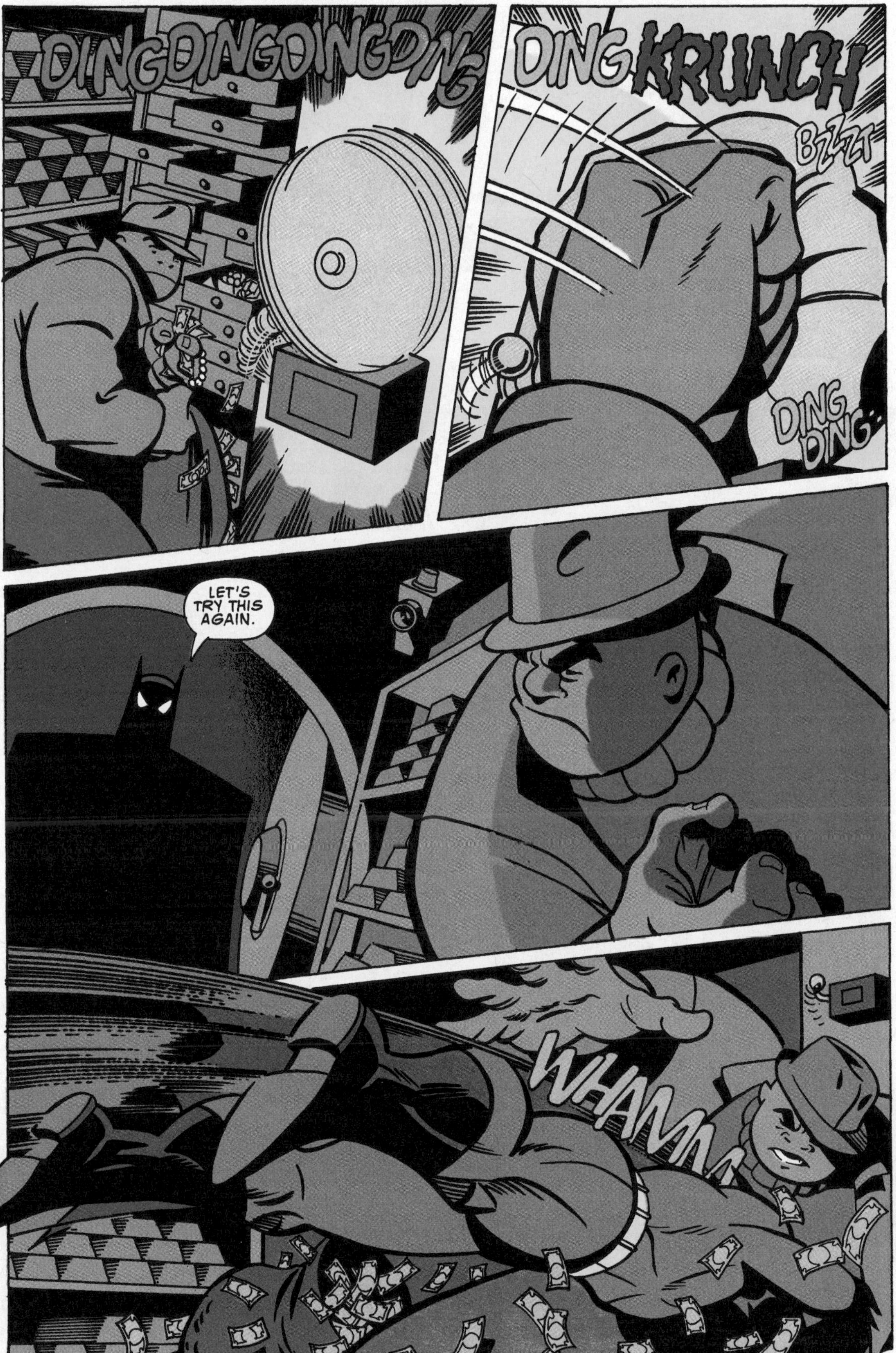

DINGDINGDINGDINGDING
DING KRUNCH
BZZZT
DING DING
LET'S TRY THIS AGAIN.
WHAMM
13

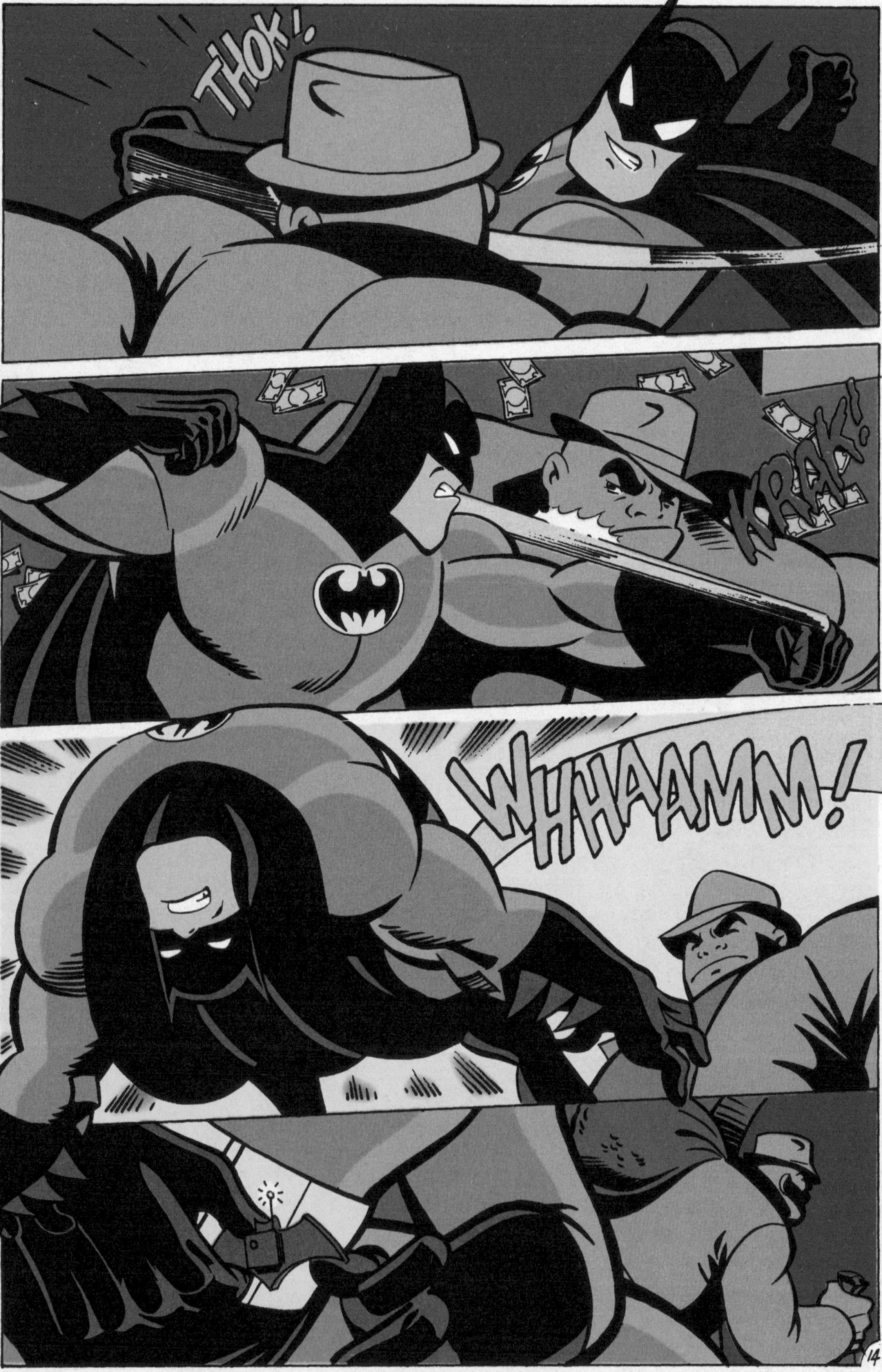
THOK!
KRAK!
WHHAAMM!
14

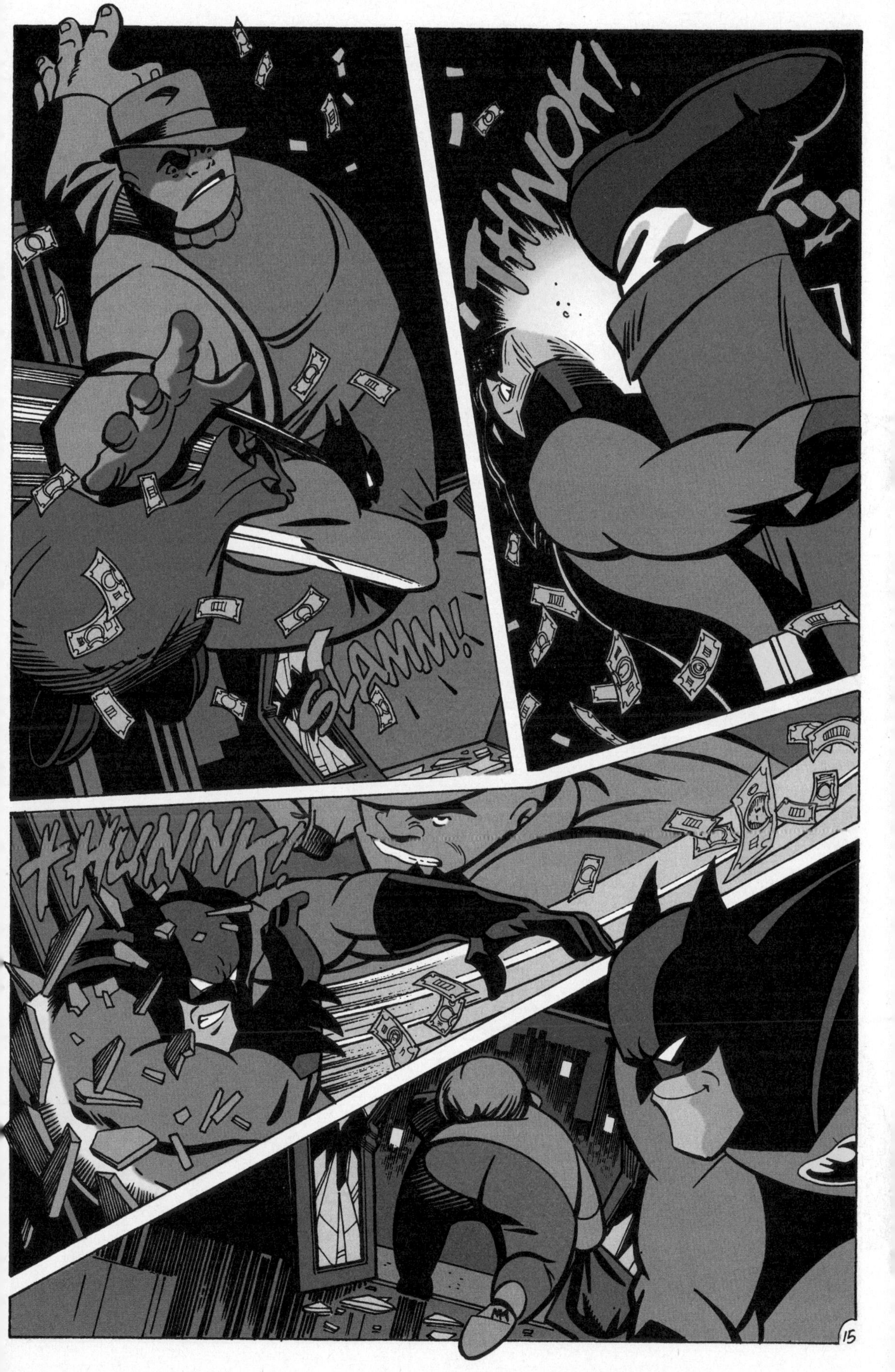
SLAMM!
THWOK!
THUNNK!
15

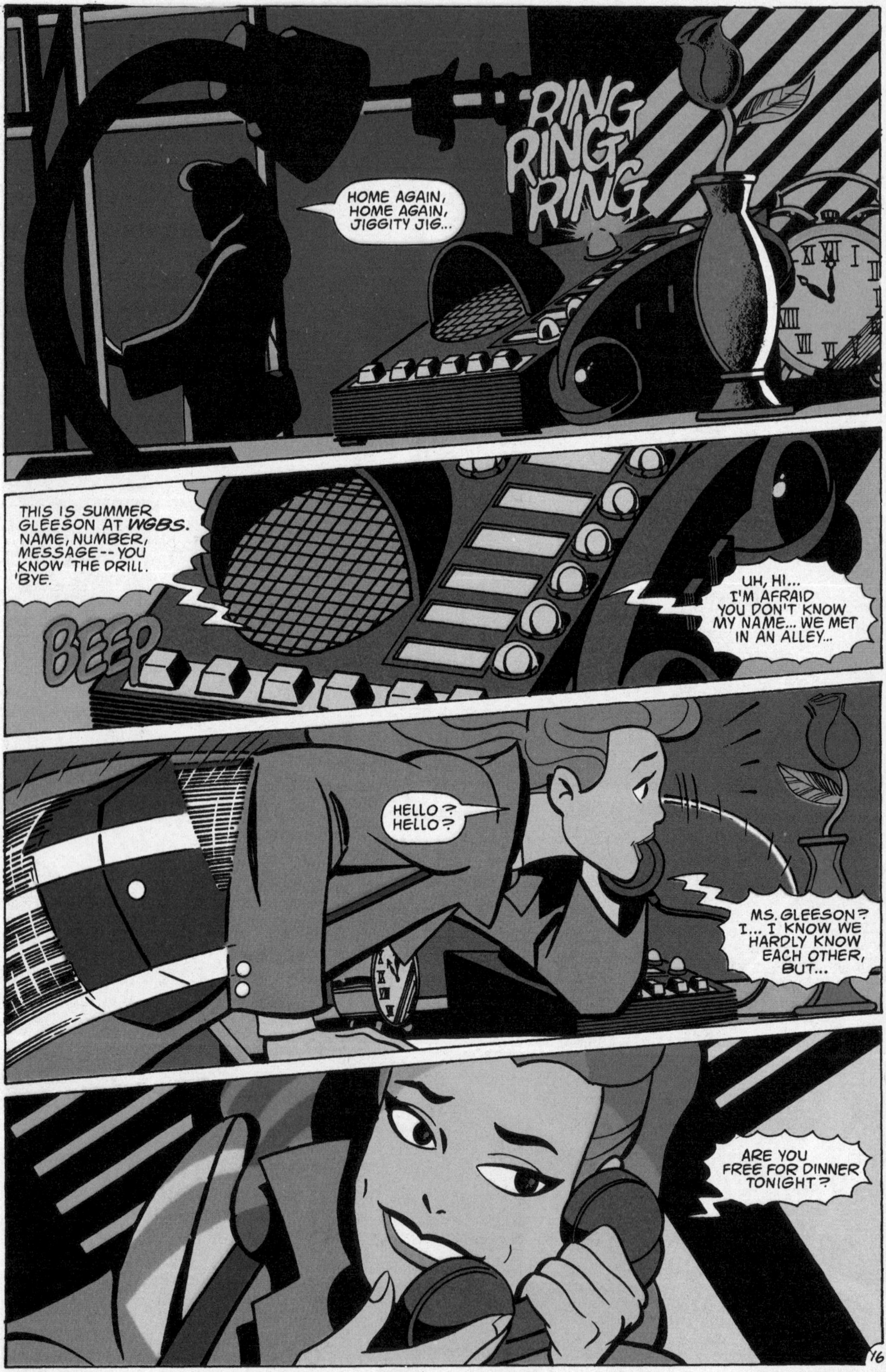
RING
RING
RING
HOME AGAIN, HOME AGAIN, JIGGITY JIG...
THIS IS SUMMER GLEESON AT WGBS. NAME, NUMBER, MESSAGE--YOU KNOW THE DRILL. 'BYE.
BEEP
UH, HI... I'M AFRAID YOU DON'T KNOW MY NAME... WE MET IN AN ALLEY...
HELLO? HELLO?
MS. GLEESON? I... I KNOW WE HARDLY KNOW EACH OTHER, BUT...
ARE YOU FREE FOR DINNER TONIGHT?
16

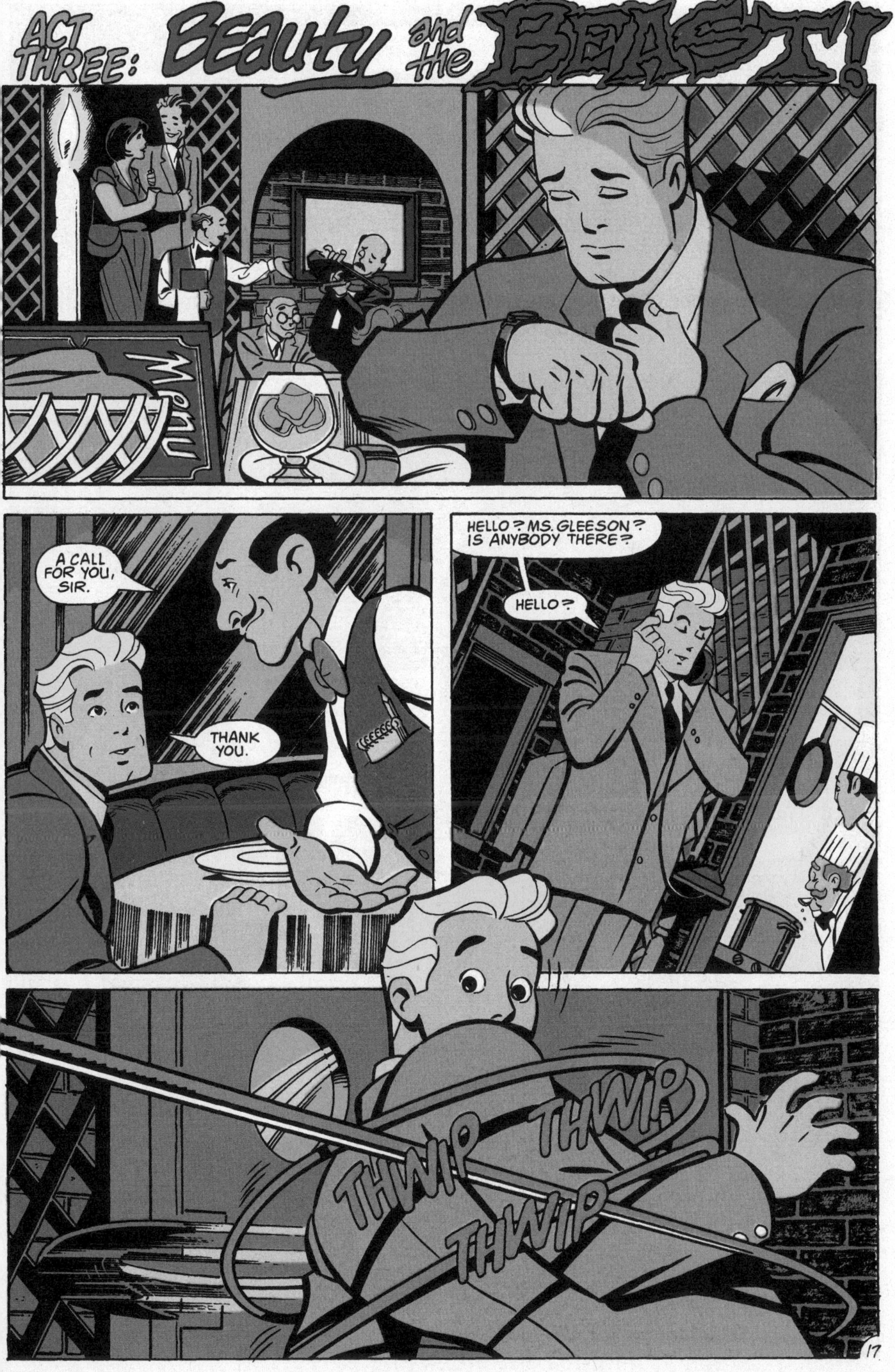
ACT THREE: Beauty and the BEAST!
Menu
A CALL FOR YOU, SIR.
THANK YOU.
HELLO? MS. GLEESON? IS ANYBODY THERE?
HELLO?
THWIP
THWIP
THWIP
THWIP
17

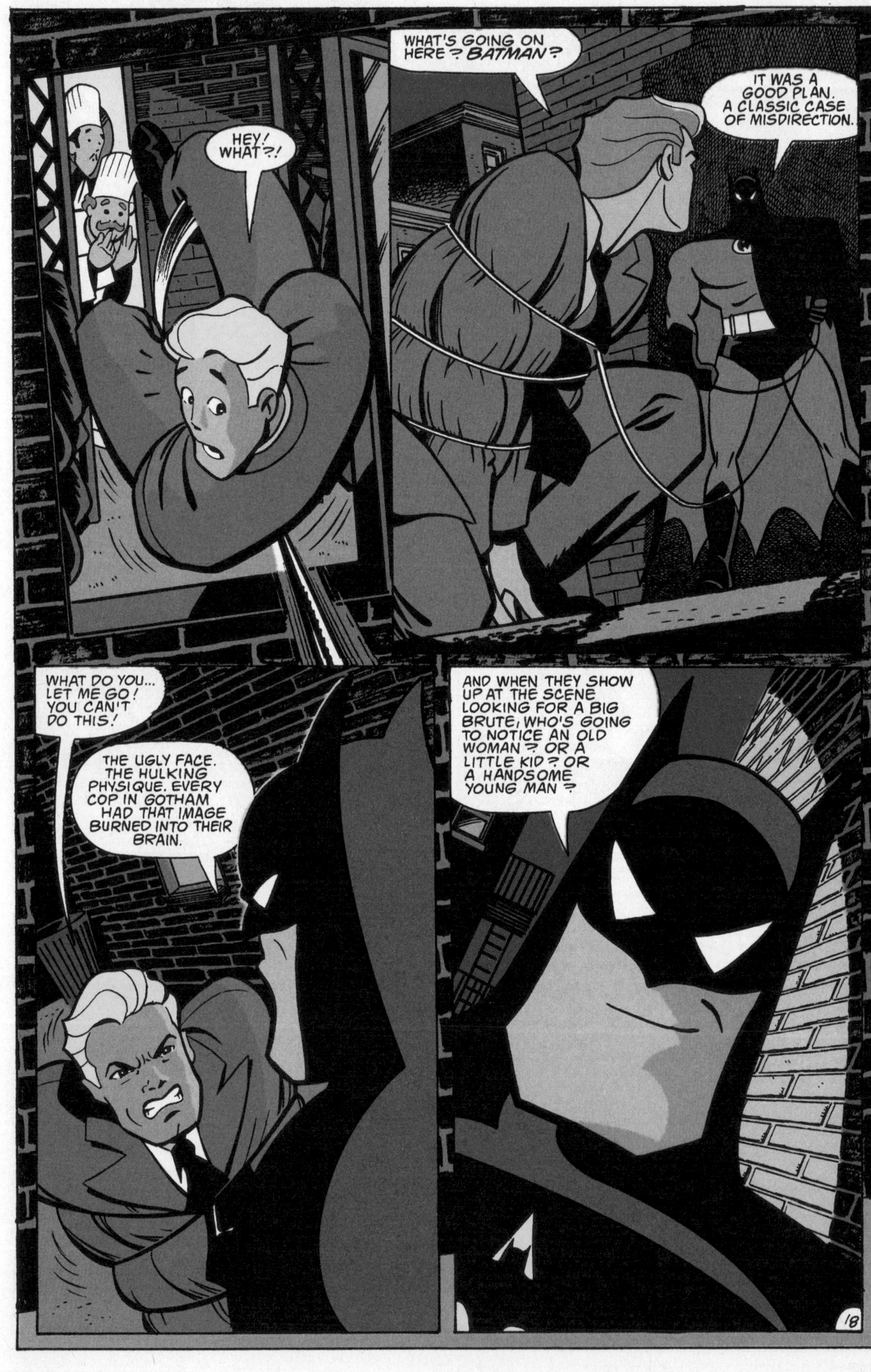
HEY! WHAT?!
WHAT'S GOING ON HERE? BATMAN?
IT WAS A GOOD PLAN. A CLASSIC CASE OF MISDIRECTION.
WHAT DO YOU... LET ME GO! YOU CAN'T DO THIS!
THE UGLY FACE. THE HULKING PHYSIQUE. EVERY COP IN GOTHAM HAD THAT IMAGE BURNED INTO THEIR BRAIN.
AND WHEN THEY SHOW UP AT THE SCENE LOOKING FOR A BIG BRUTE, WHO'S GOING TO NOTICE AN OLD WOMAN? OR A LITTLE KID? OR A HANDSOME YOUNG MAN?
18

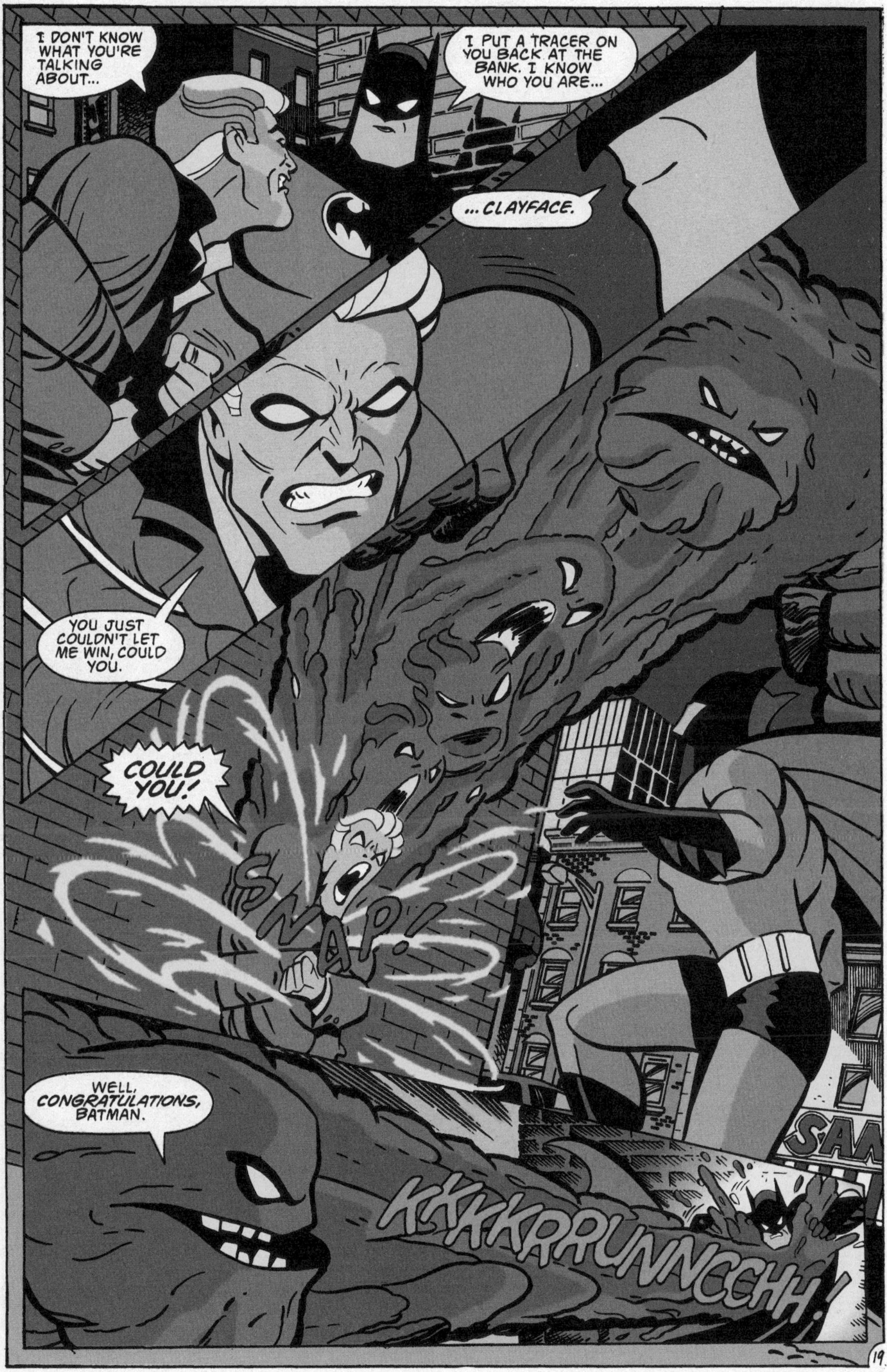
I DON'T KNOW WHAT YOU'RE TALKING ABOUT...
I PUT A TRACER ON YOU BACK AT THE BANK. I KNOW WHO YOU ARE...
...CLAYFACE.
YOU JUST COULDN'T LET ME WIN, COULD YOU.
COULD YOU!
SNAP!
WELL, CONGRATULATIONS, BATMAN.
KKKKRRUNNCCHH!
19

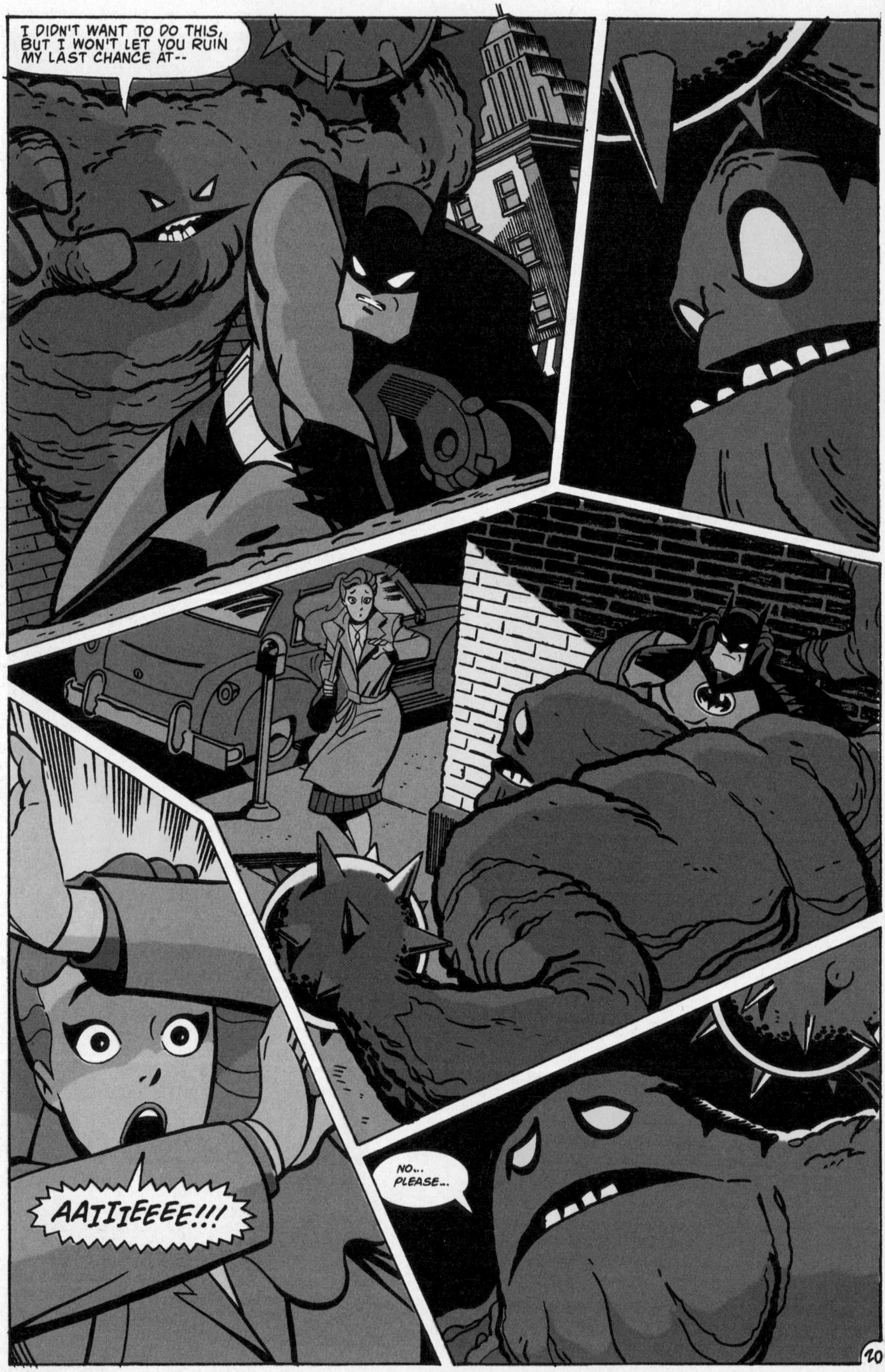
I DIDN'T WANT TO DO THIS, BUT I WON'T LET YOU RUIN MY LAST CHANCE AT--
AAIIIEEEE!!!
NO... PLEASE...
20

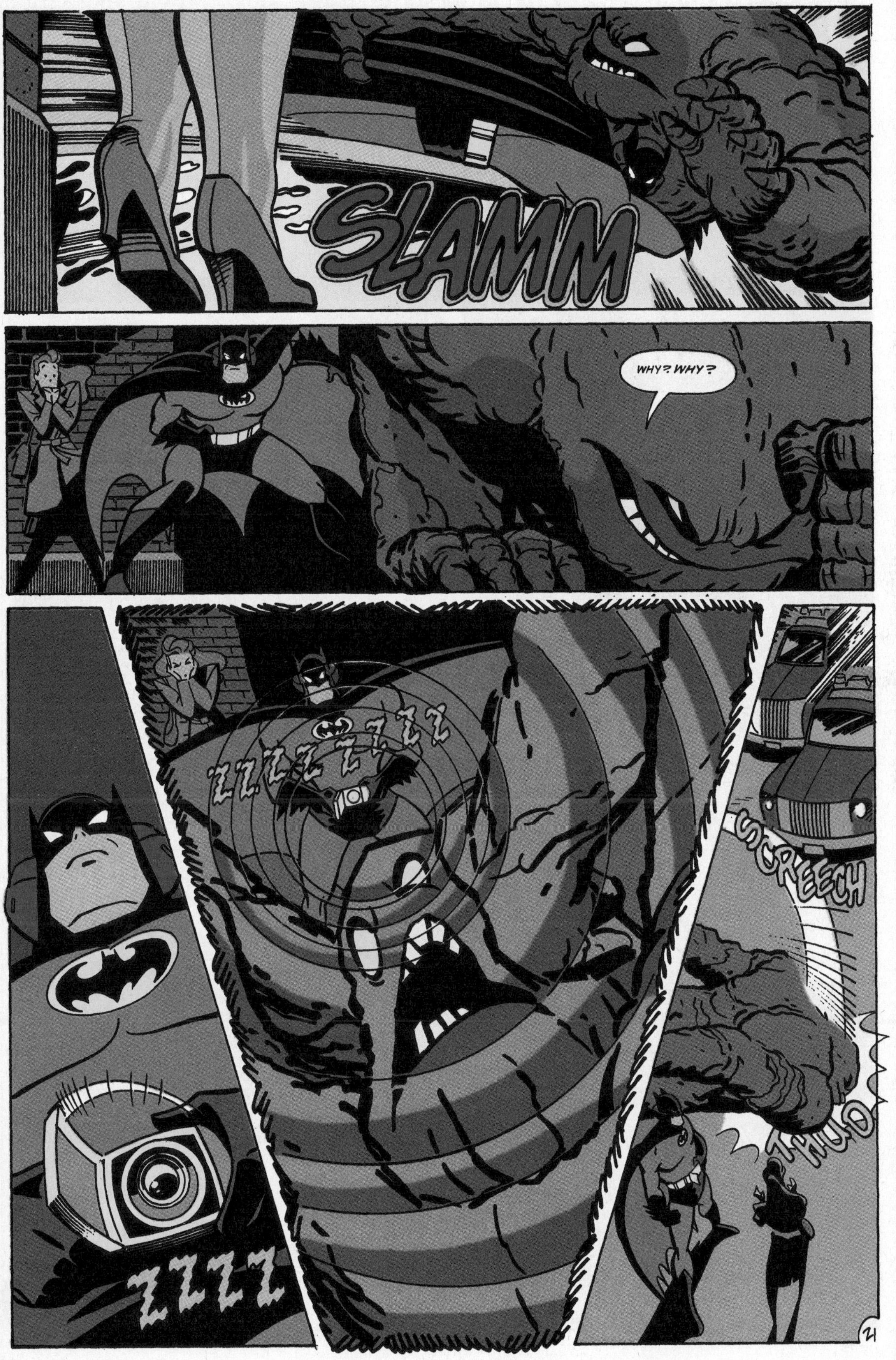
SLAMM
WHY? WHY?
ZZZZ
ZZZZZZZ
ZZZZ
SCREECH
THUD
21

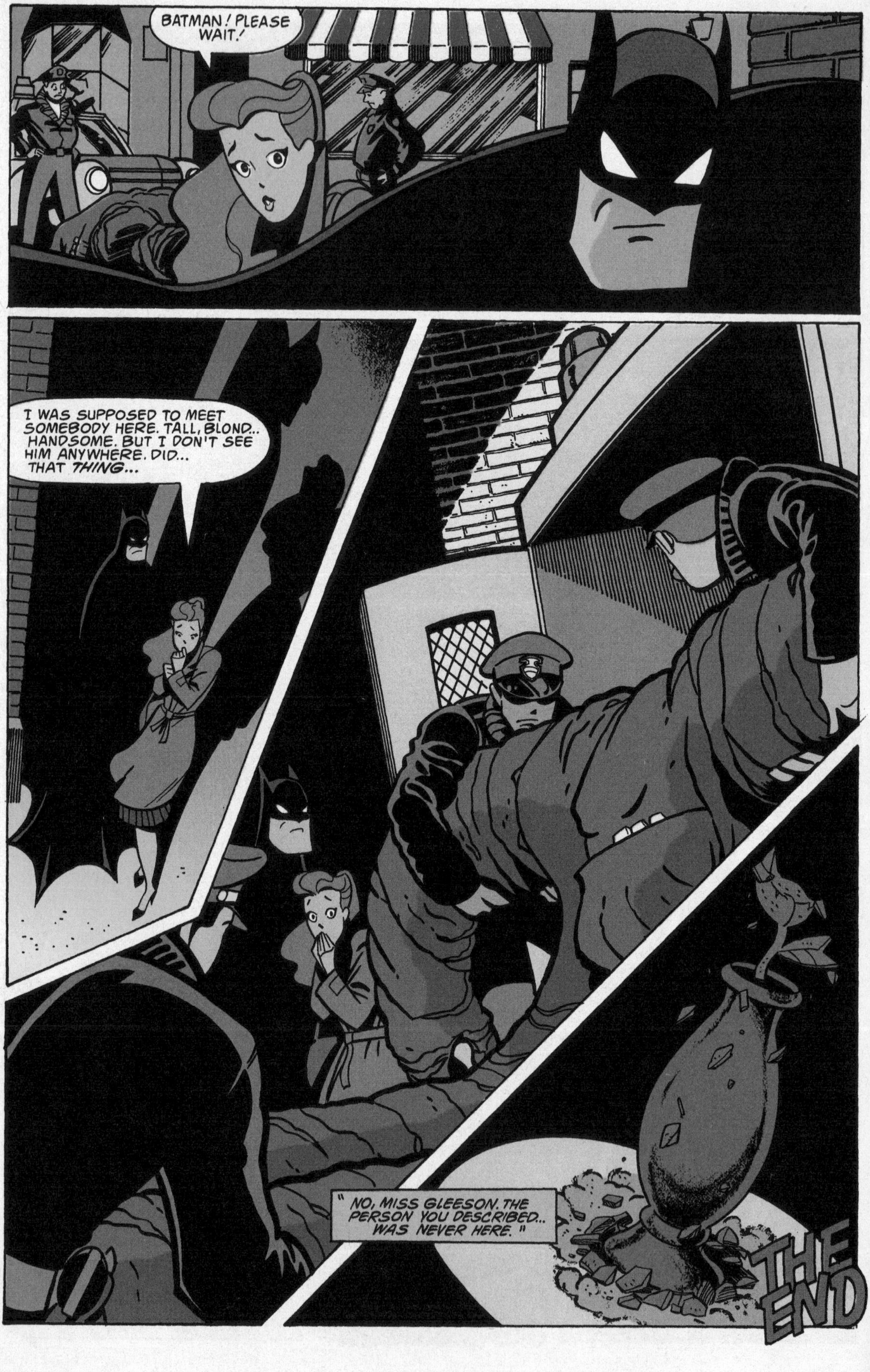
BATMAN! PLEASE WAIT!
I WAS SUPPOSED TO MEET SOMEBODY HERE. TALL, BLOND... HANDSOME. BUT I DON'T SEE HIM ANYWHERE. DID... THAT THING...
" NO, MISS GLEESON. THE PERSON YOU DESCRIBED... WAS NEVER HERE. "
THE END

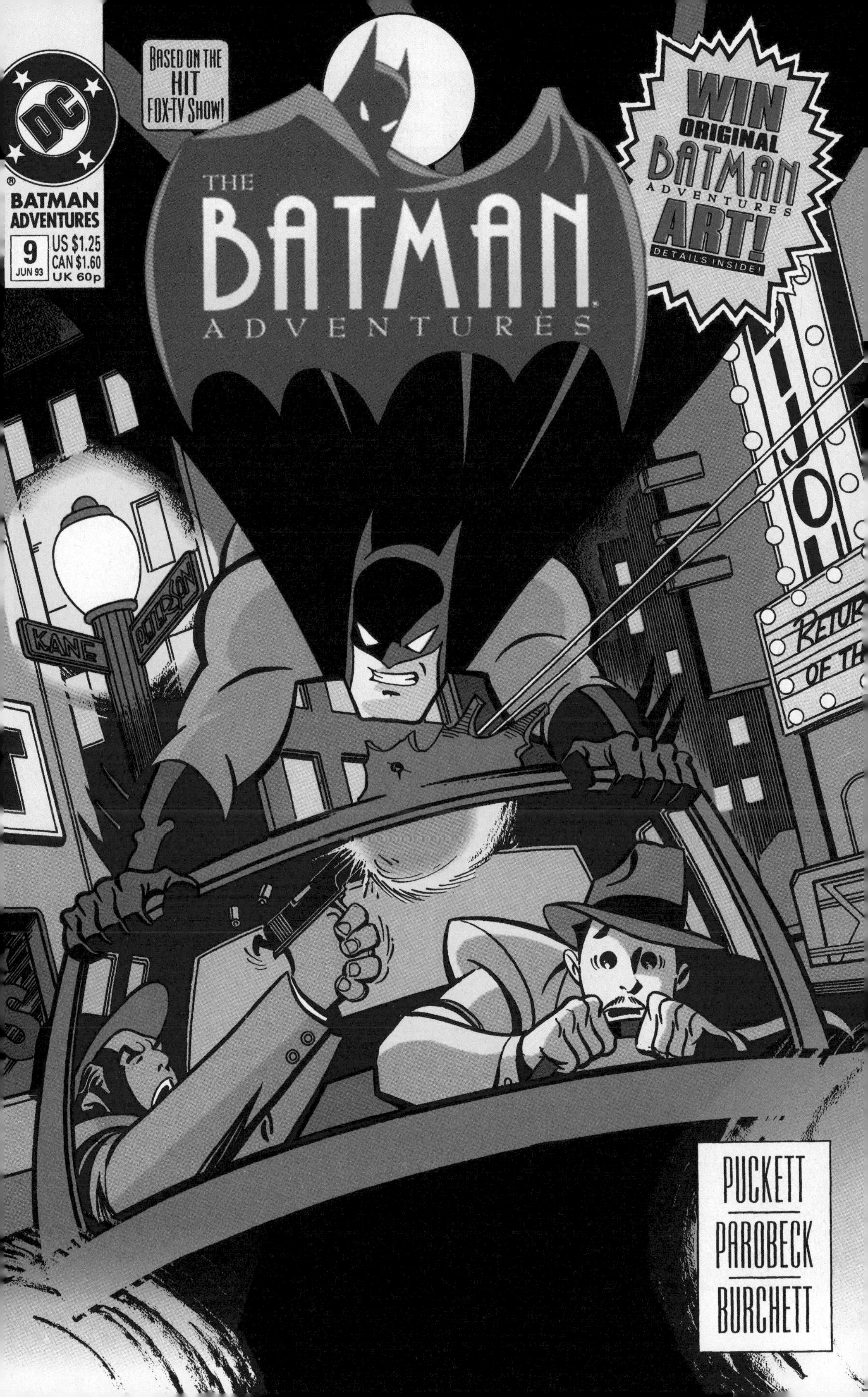
DC
BATMAN ADVENTURES
9
JUN 93
US $1.25
CAN $1.60
UK 60p
BASED ON THE HIT FOX-TV SHOW!
THE BATMAN ADVENTURES
WIN ORIGINAL BATMAN ADVENTURES ART!
DETAILS INSIDE!
KANE
PETERSON
RETUR
OF TH
PUCKETT
PAROBECK
BURCHETT

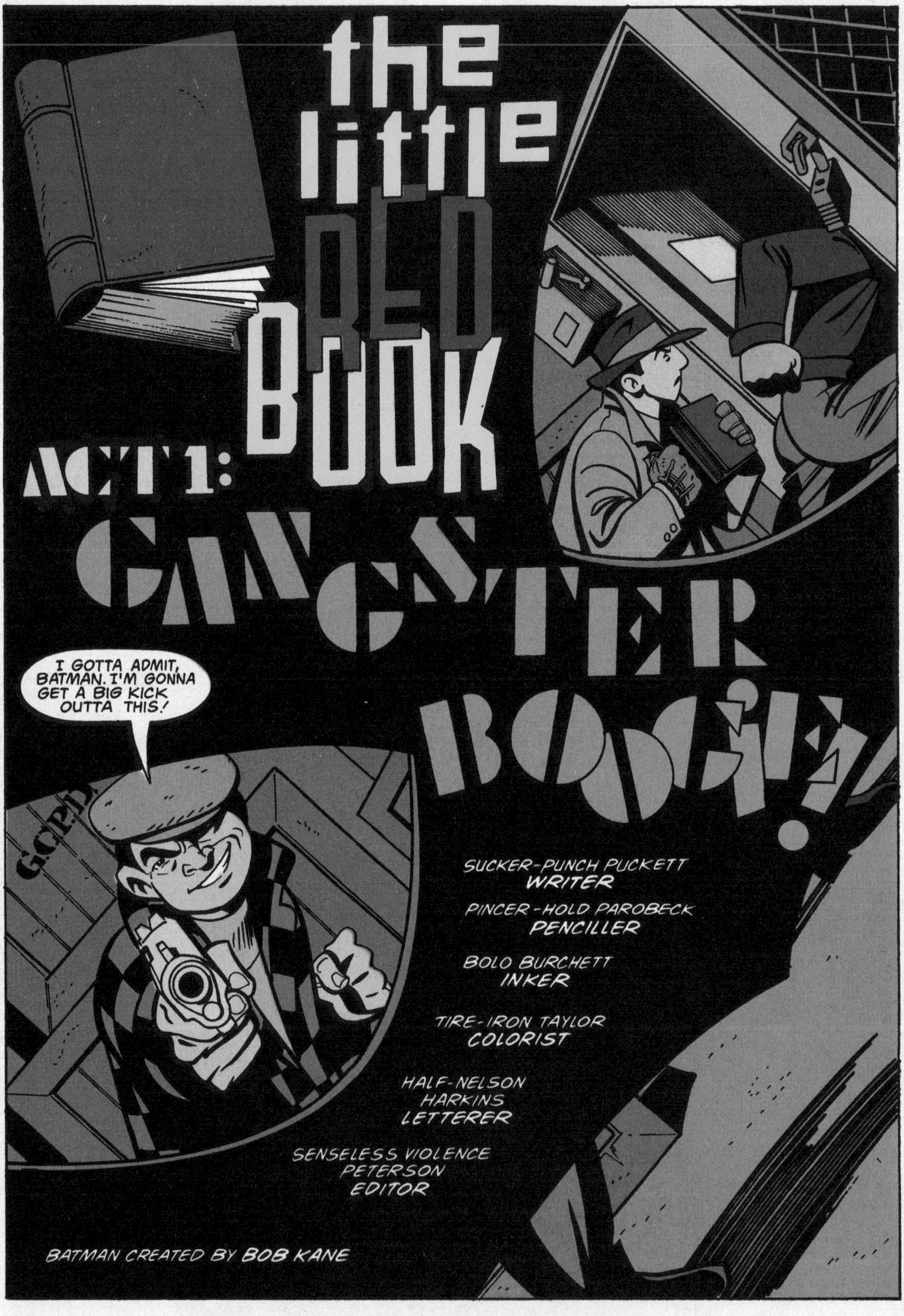
the little RED BOOK
ACT 1: GANGSTER BOOGIE!
I GOTTA ADMIT, BATMAN. I'M GONNA GET A BIG KICK OUTTA THIS!
G.C.P.D.
SUCKER-PUNCH PUCKETT WRITER
PINCER-HOLD PAROBECK PENCILLER
BOLO BURCHETT INKER
TIRE-IRON TAYLOR COLORIST
HALF-NELSON HARKINS LETTERER
SENSELESS VIOLENCE PETERSON EDITOR
BATMAN CREATED BY BOB KANE

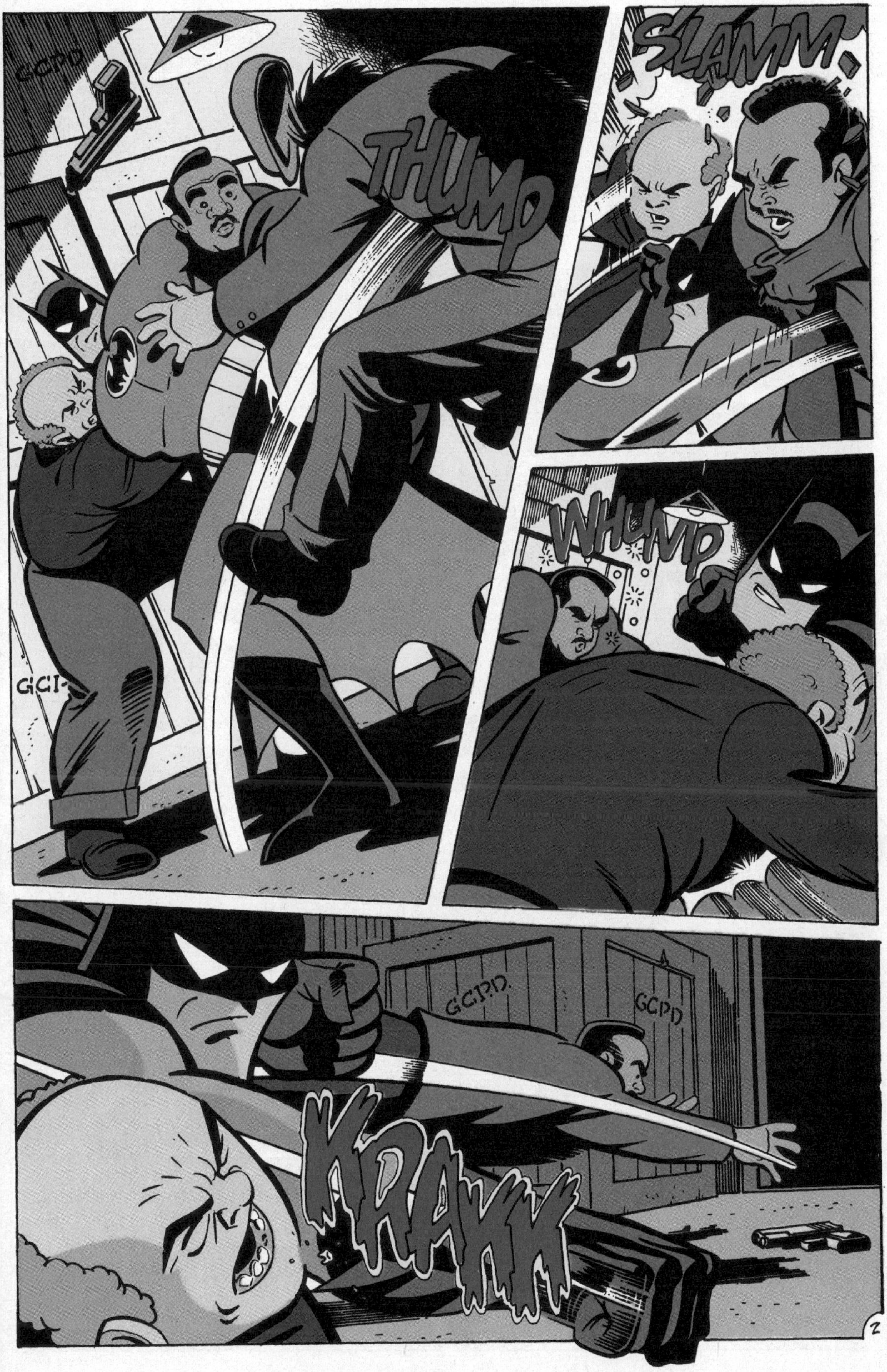
GCPD
THUMP
GCI-
SLAMM
WHUMP
GCPD.
GCPD
KRAKK
2

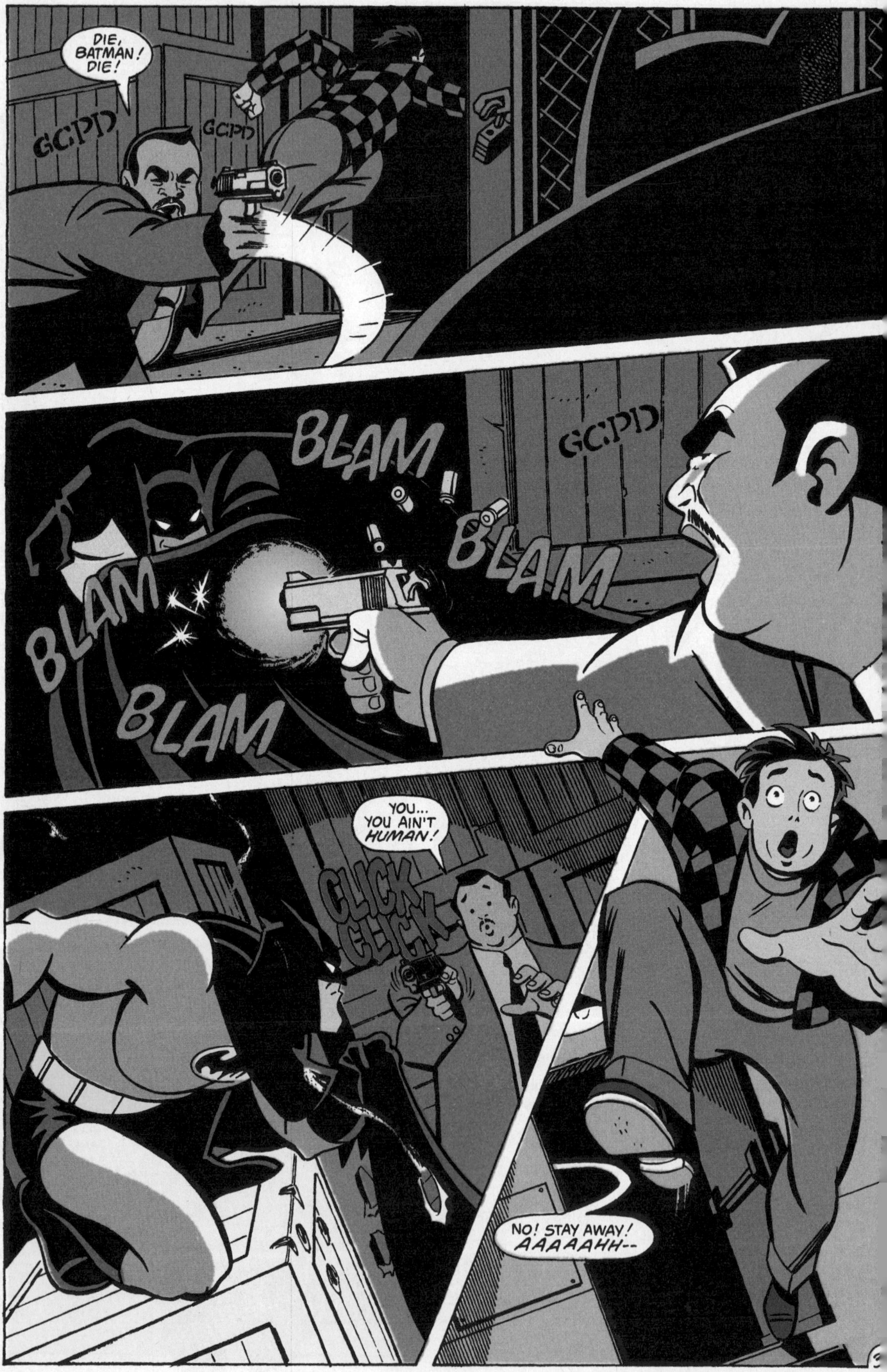
DIE, BATMAN! DIE!
GCPD
GCPD
BLAM
GCPD
BLAM
BLAM
BLAM
YOU... YOU AIN'T HUMAN!
CLICK CLICK
NO! STAY AWAY! AAAAAHH--

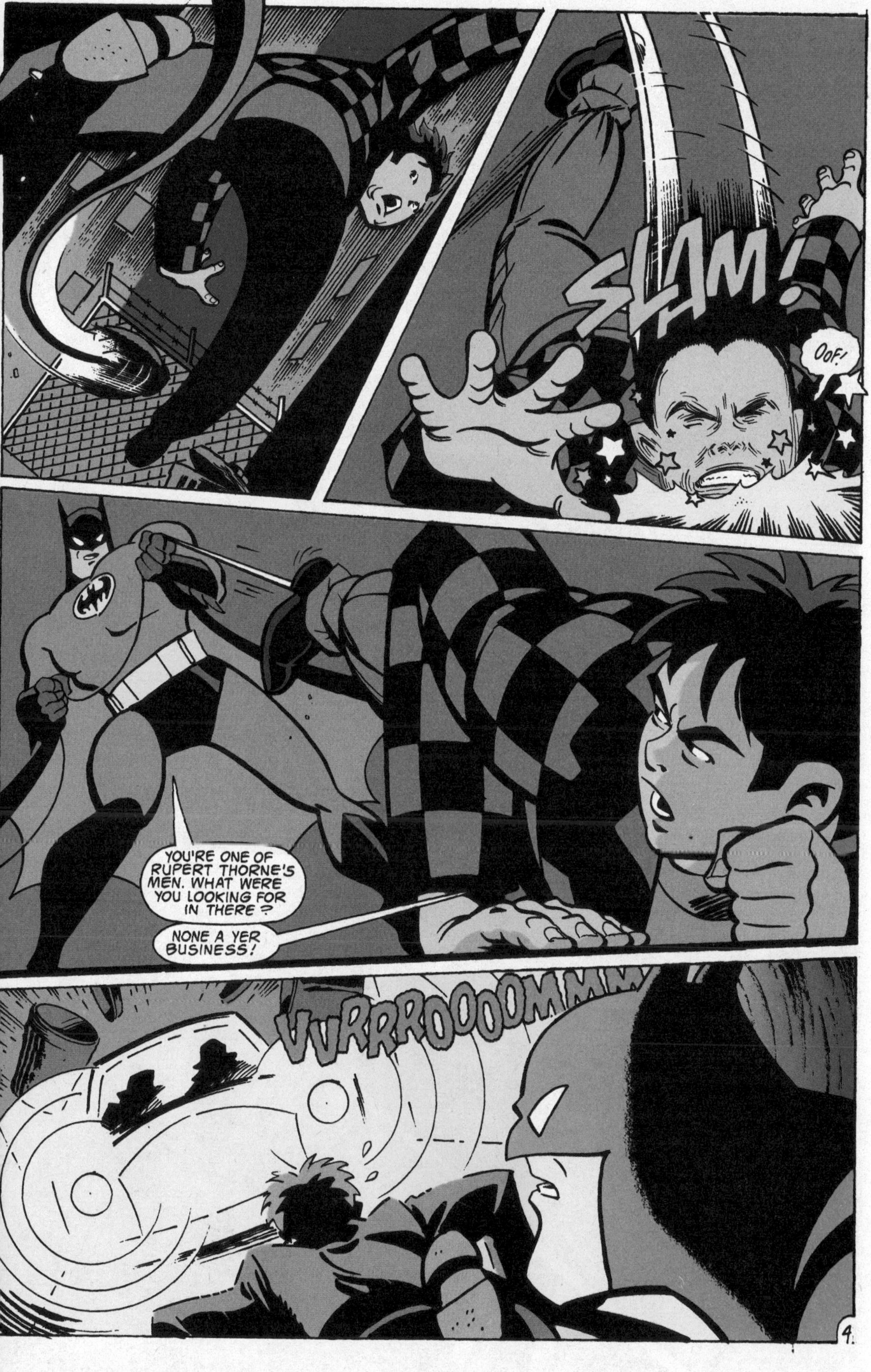
SLAM!
OOF!
YOU'RE ONE OF RUPERT THORNE'S MEN. WHAT WERE YOU LOOKING FOR IN THERE?
NONE A YER BUSINESS!
VVRRROOOOMMM
4

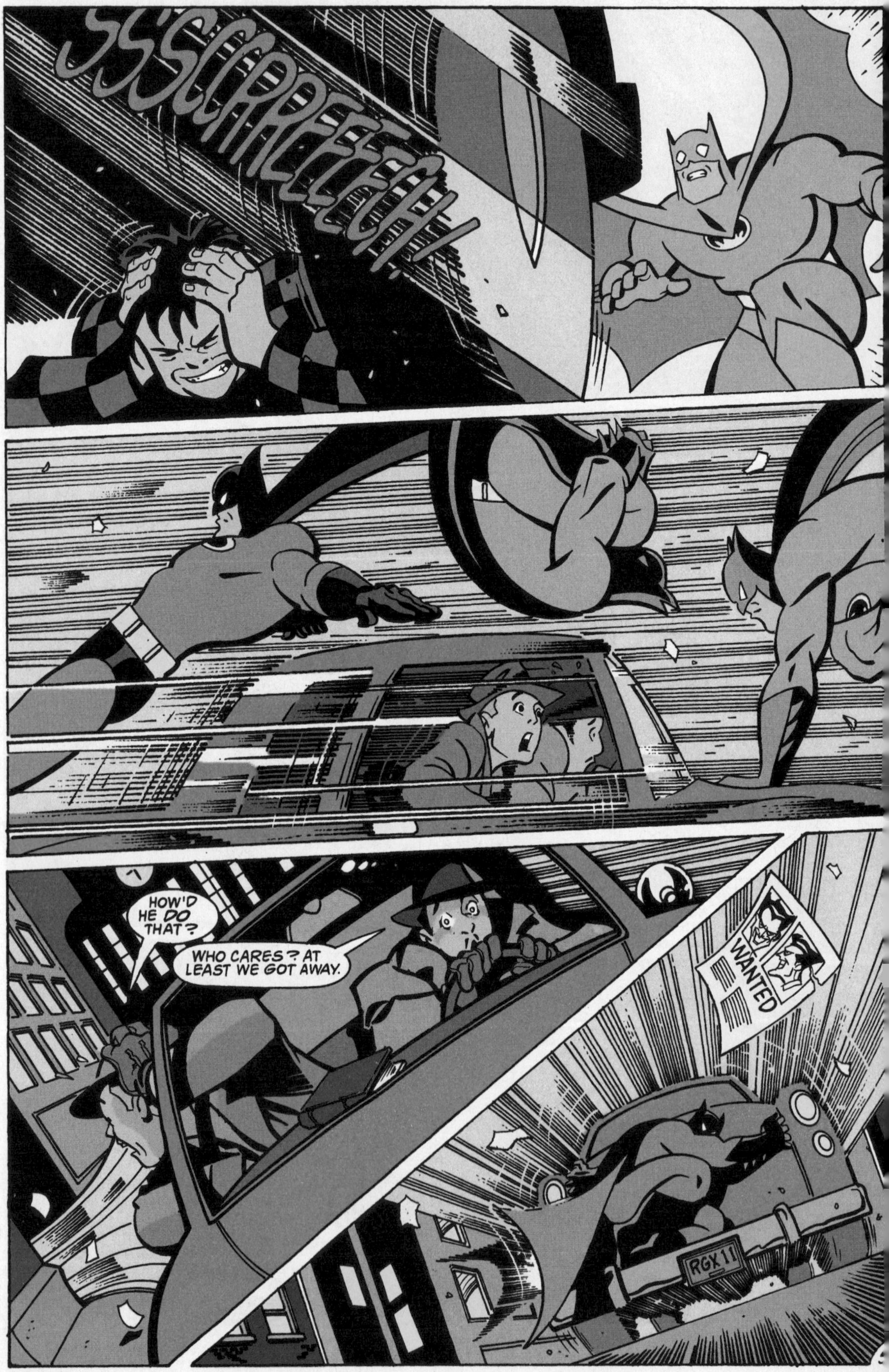
SSSCRREEECH!
HOW'D HE DO THAT?
WHO CARES? AT LEAST WE GOT AWAY.
WANTED
RGX 11

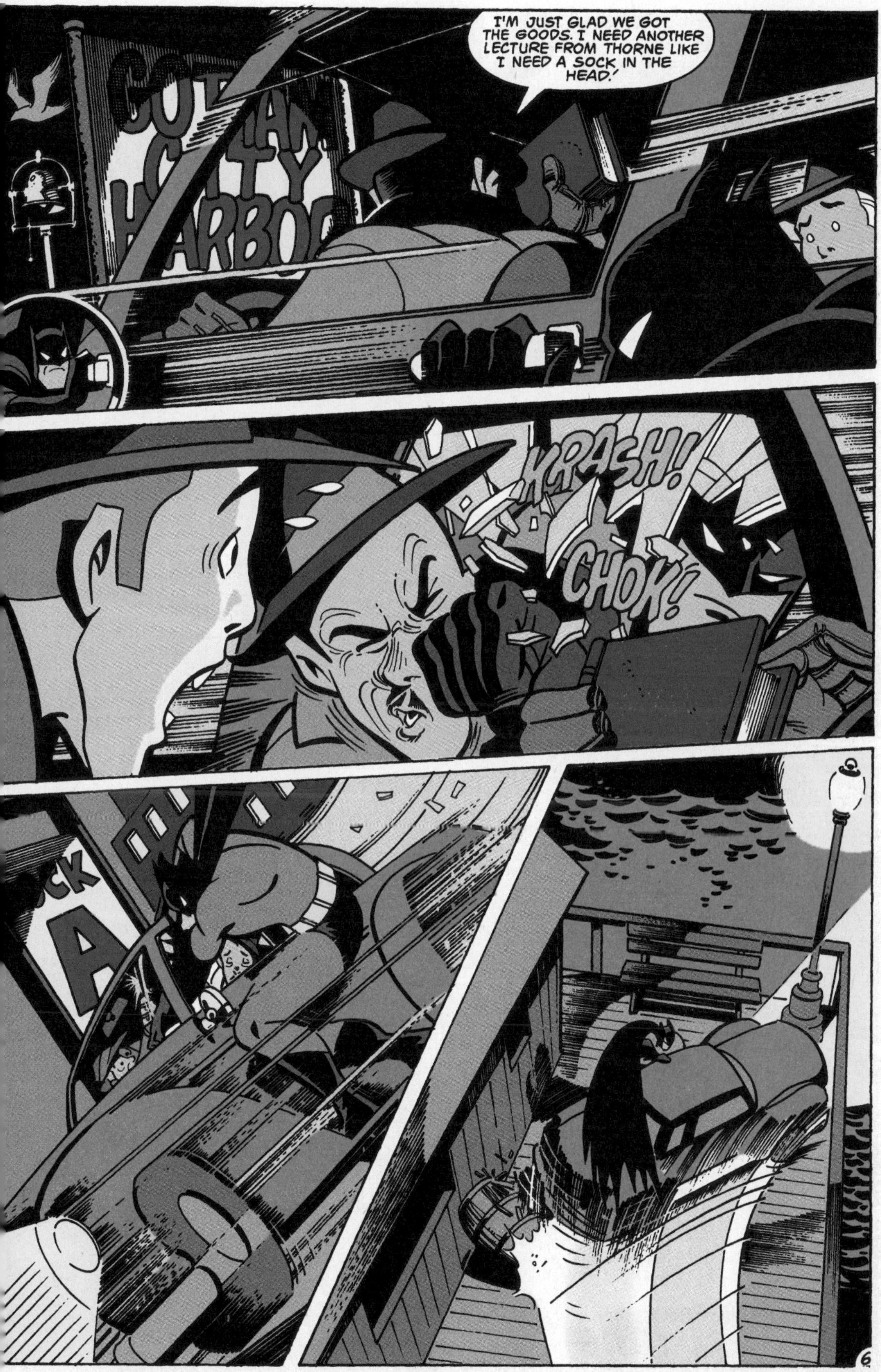

I'M JUST GLAD WE GOT THE GOODS. I NEED ANOTHER LECTURE FROM THORNE LIKE I NEED A SOCK IN THE HEAD.'
GOTHAM CITY HARBOR
K-RASH!
CHOK!
6

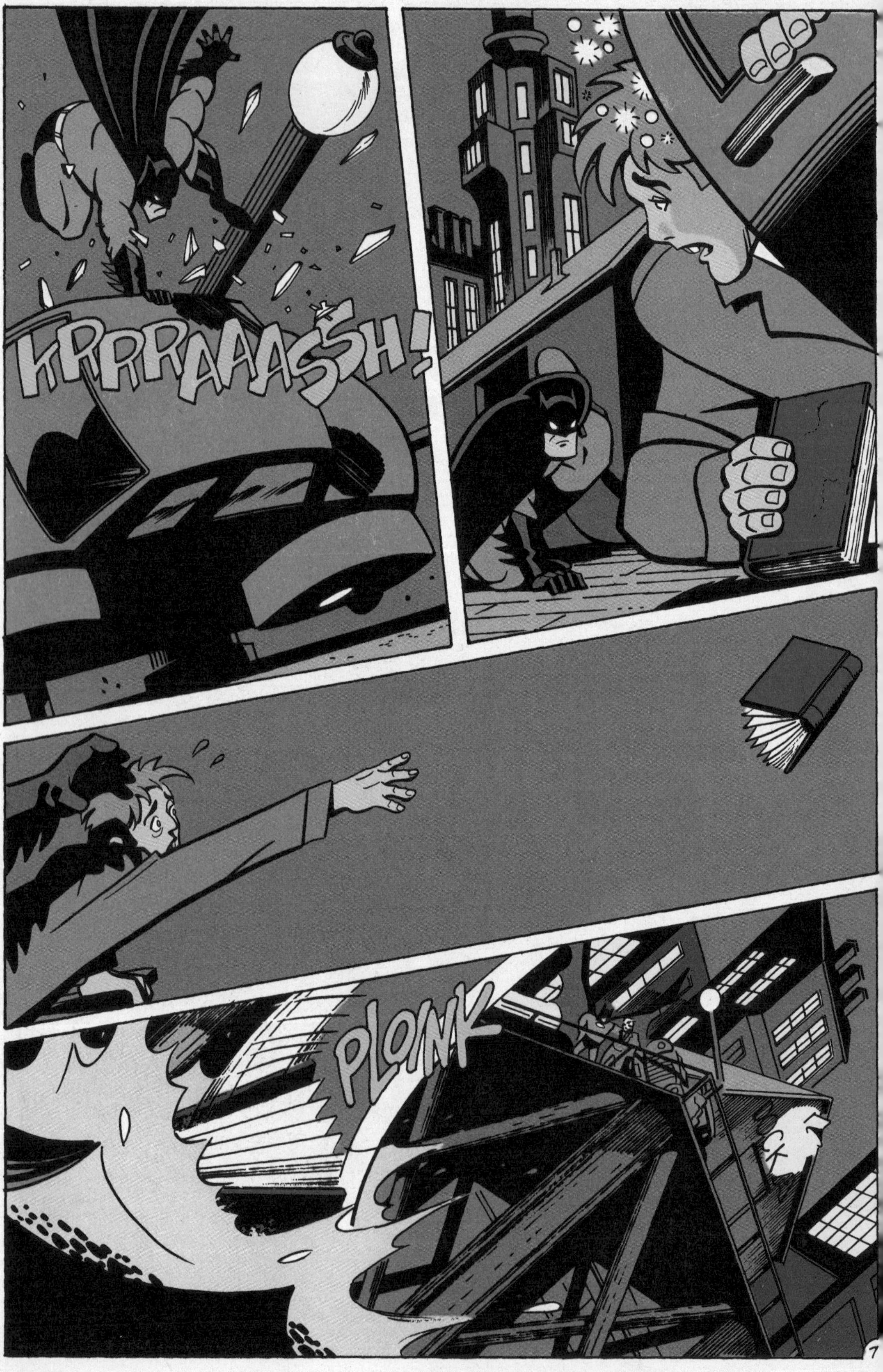
KRRRAAASSH!
PLONK

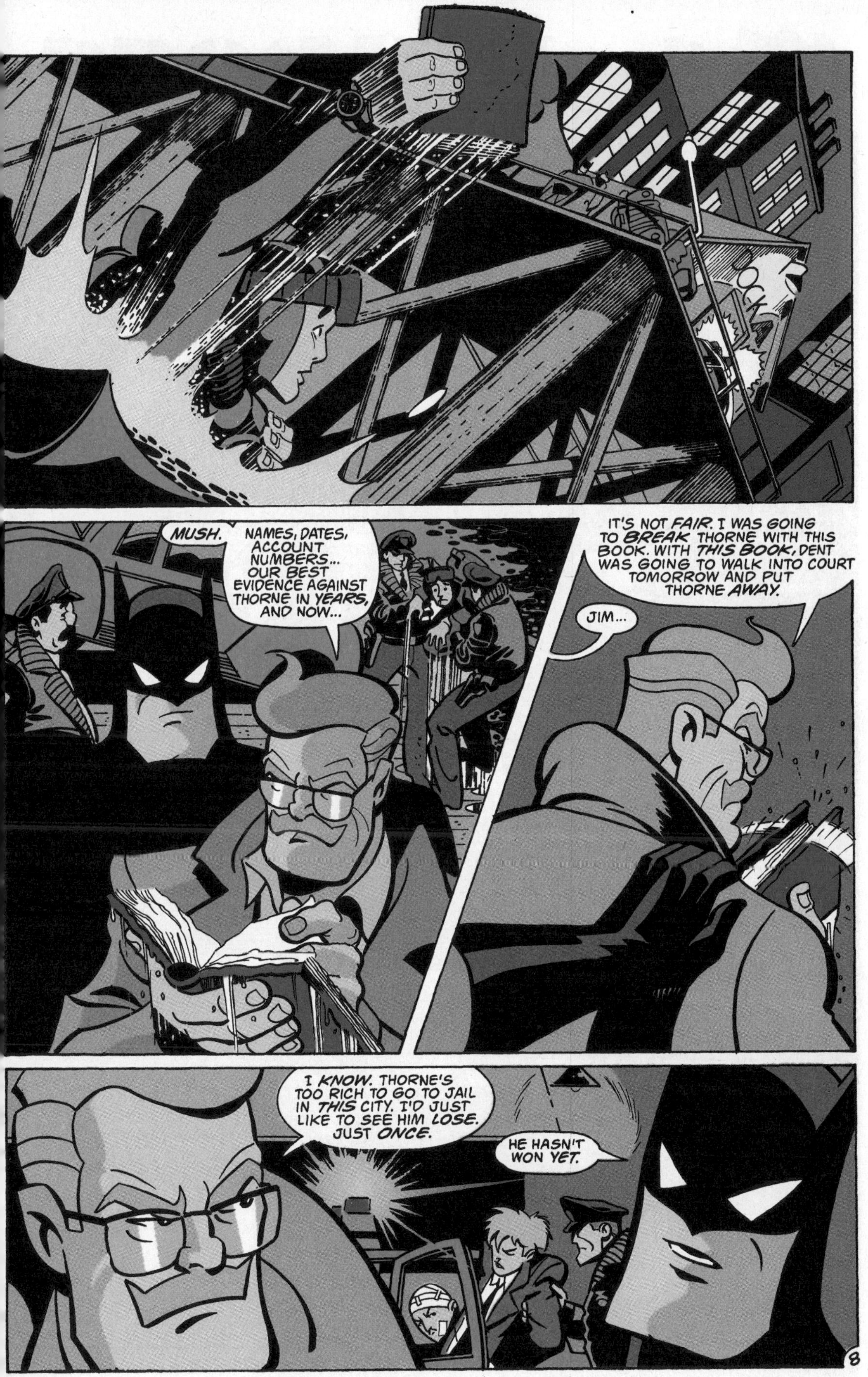
MUSH.
NAMES, DATES, ACCOUNT NUMBERS... OUR BEST EVIDENCE AGAINST THORNE IN YEARS, AND NOW...
IT'S NOT FAIR. I WAS GOING TO BREAK THORNE WITH THIS BOOK. WITH THIS BOOK, DENT WAS GOING TO WALK INTO COURT TOMORROW AND PUT THORNE AWAY.
JIM...
I KNOW. THORNE'S TOO RICH TO GO TO JAIL IN THIS CITY. I'D JUST LIKE TO SEE HIM LOSE. JUST ONCE.
HE HASN'T WON YET.
8

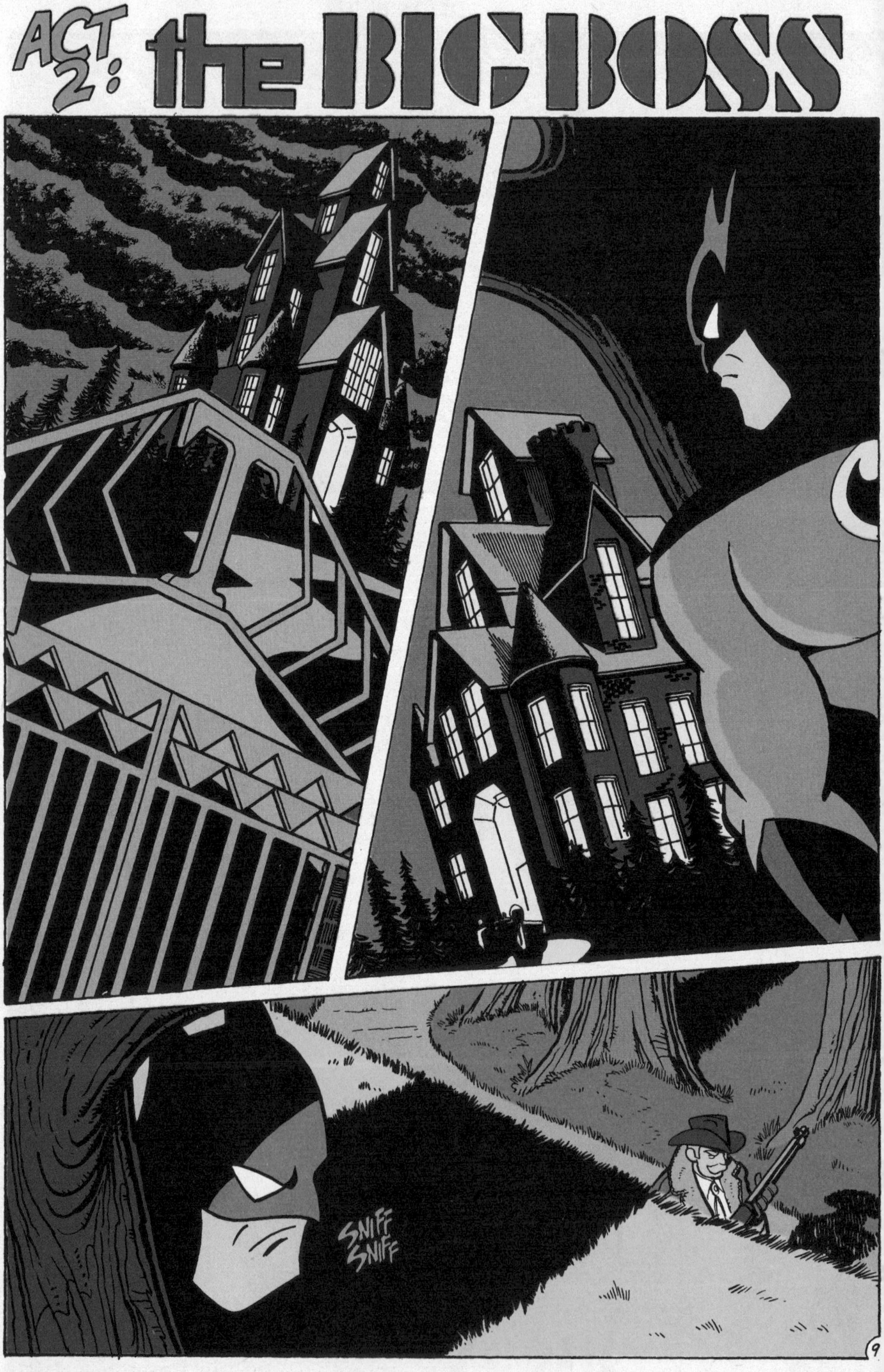
ACT 2: the BIG BOSS
SNIFF SNIFF
9

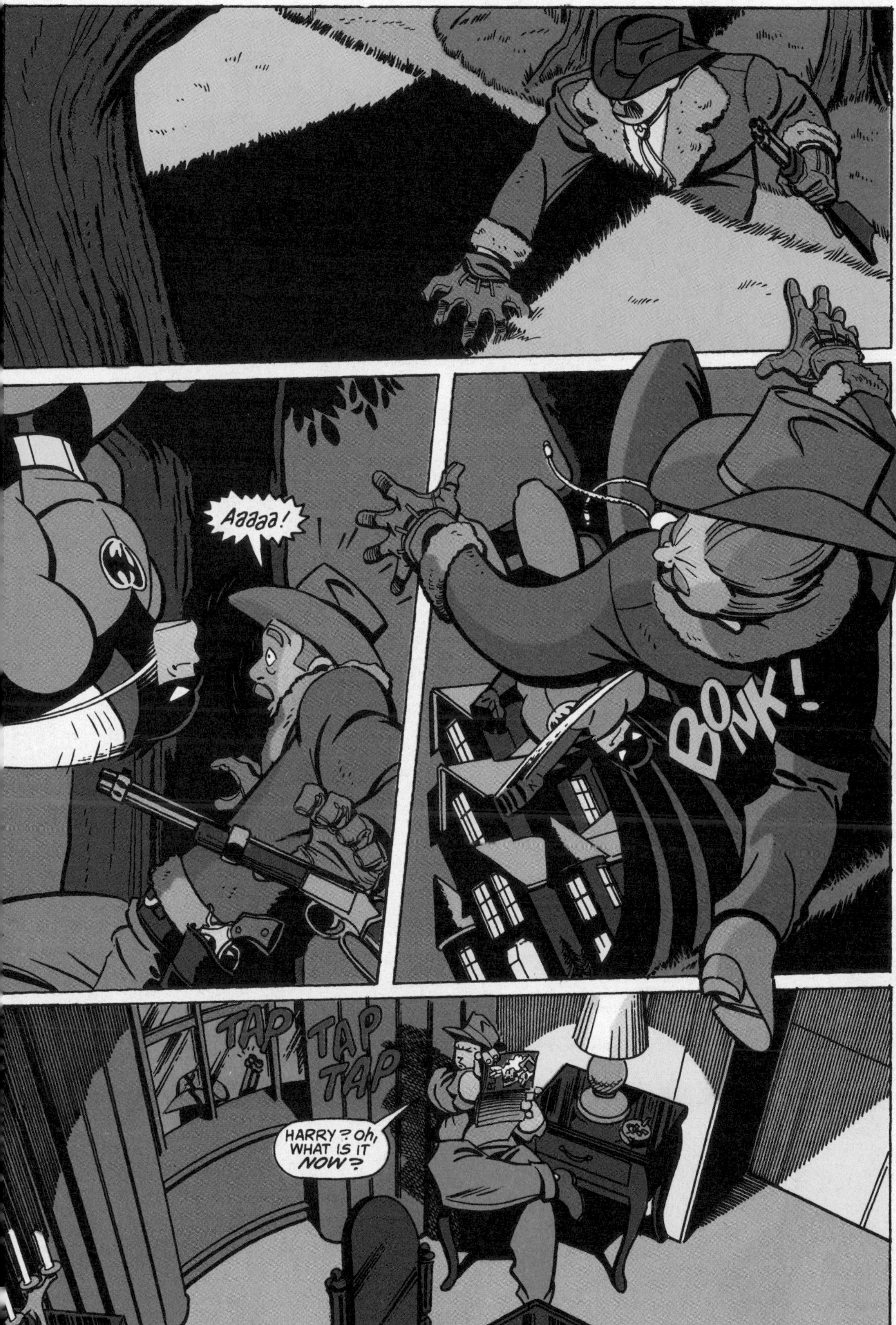
Aaaaa!
BONK!
TAP
TAP
TAP
HARRY? Oh, WHAT IS IT NOW?
10

DID LITTLE HARRY FALL DOWN AND GET A BOO-BOO?

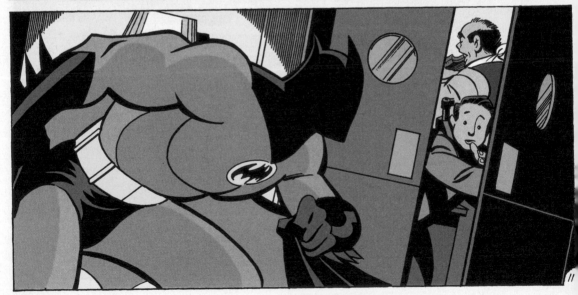

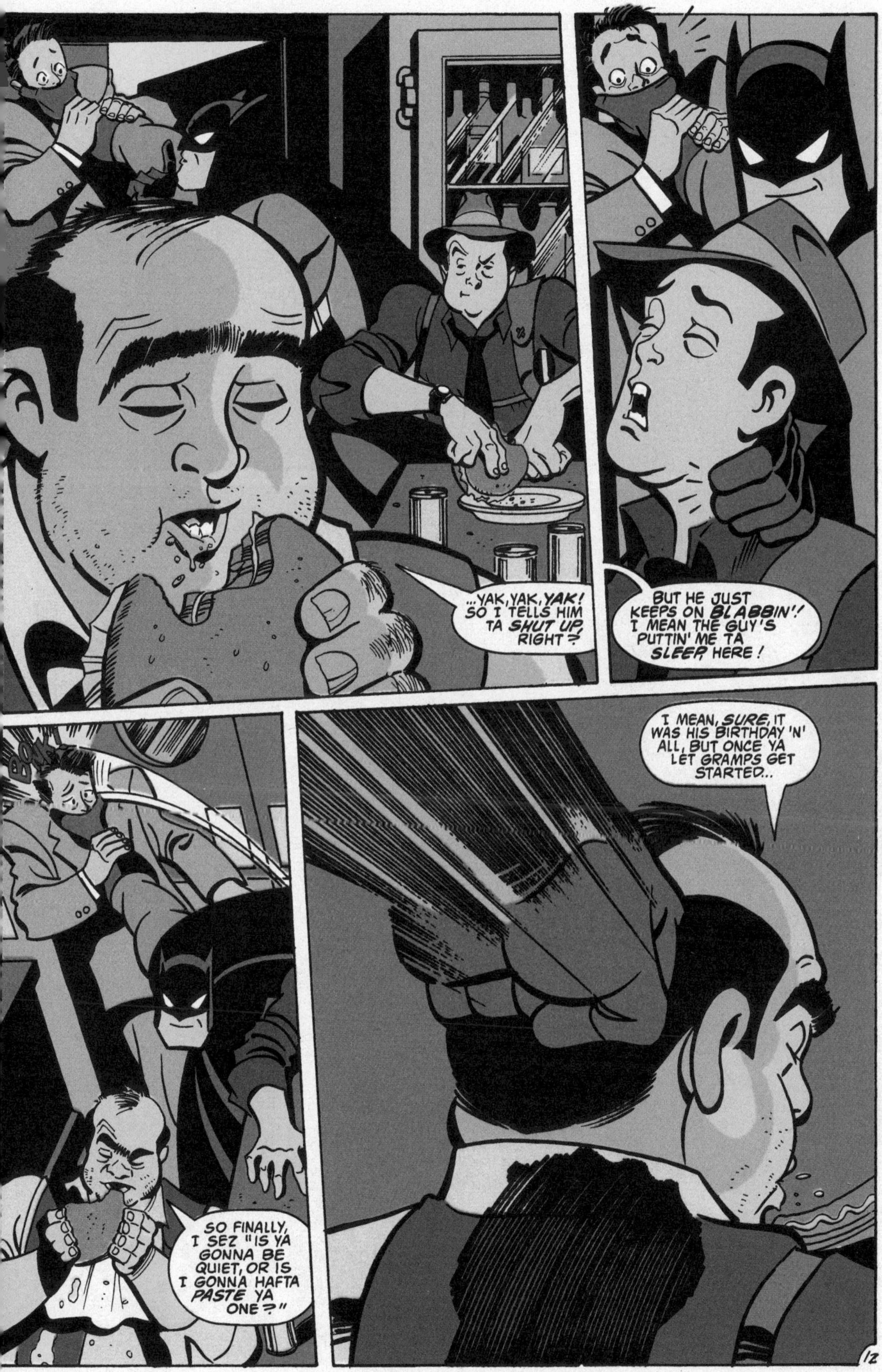
...YAK, YAK, YAK! SO I TELLS HIM TA SHUT UP, RIGHT?
BUT HE JUST KEEPS ON BLABBIN'! I MEAN THE GUY'S PUTTIN' ME TA SLEEP, HERE!
SO FINALLY, I SEZ "IS YA GONNA BE QUIET, OR IS I GONNA HAFTA PASTE YA ONE?"
I MEAN, SURE, IT WAS HIS BIRTHDAY 'N' ALL, BUT ONCE YA LET GRAMPS GET STARTED...
12

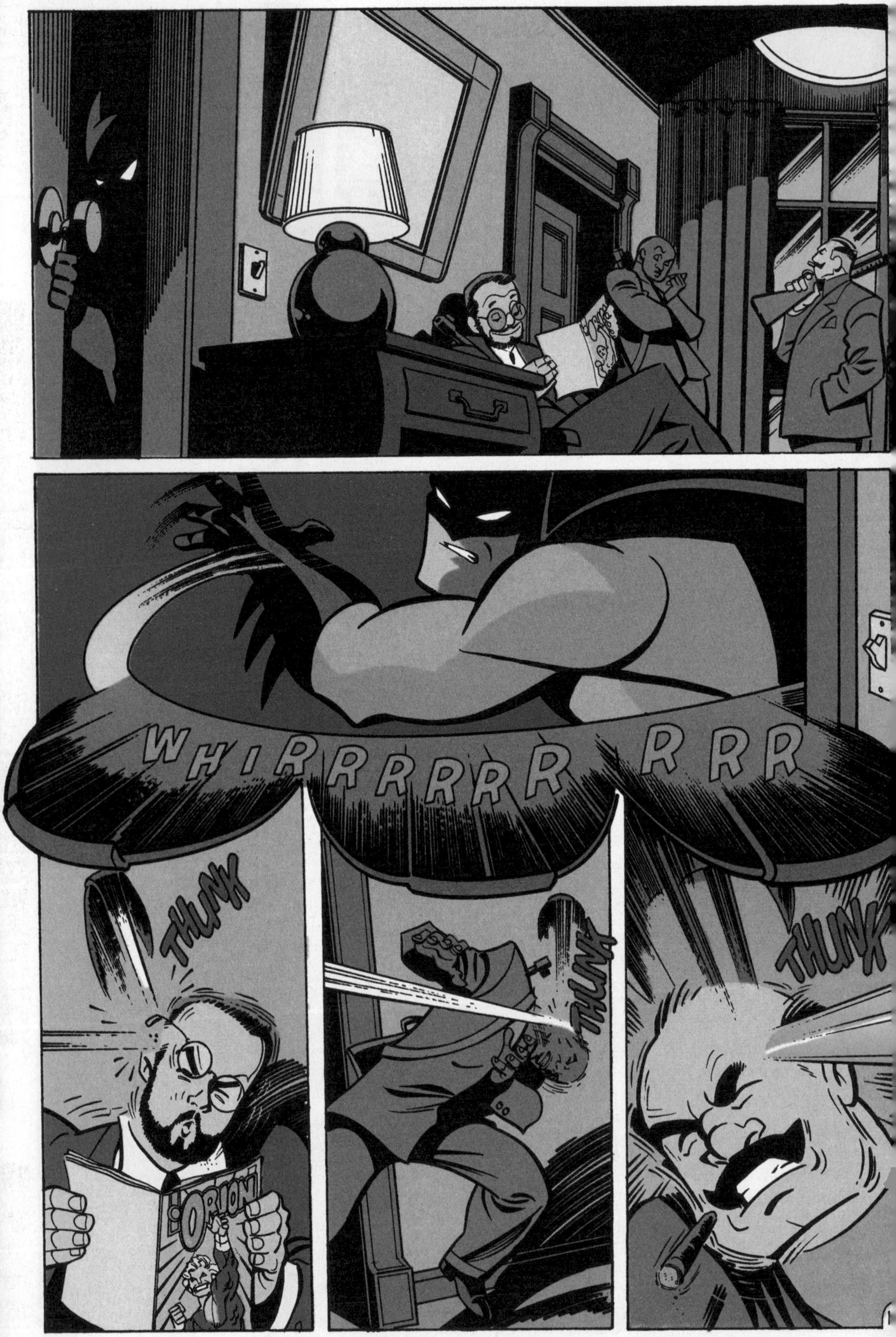
WHIRRRRRR RRR
THUNK
THUNK
THUNK
ORION

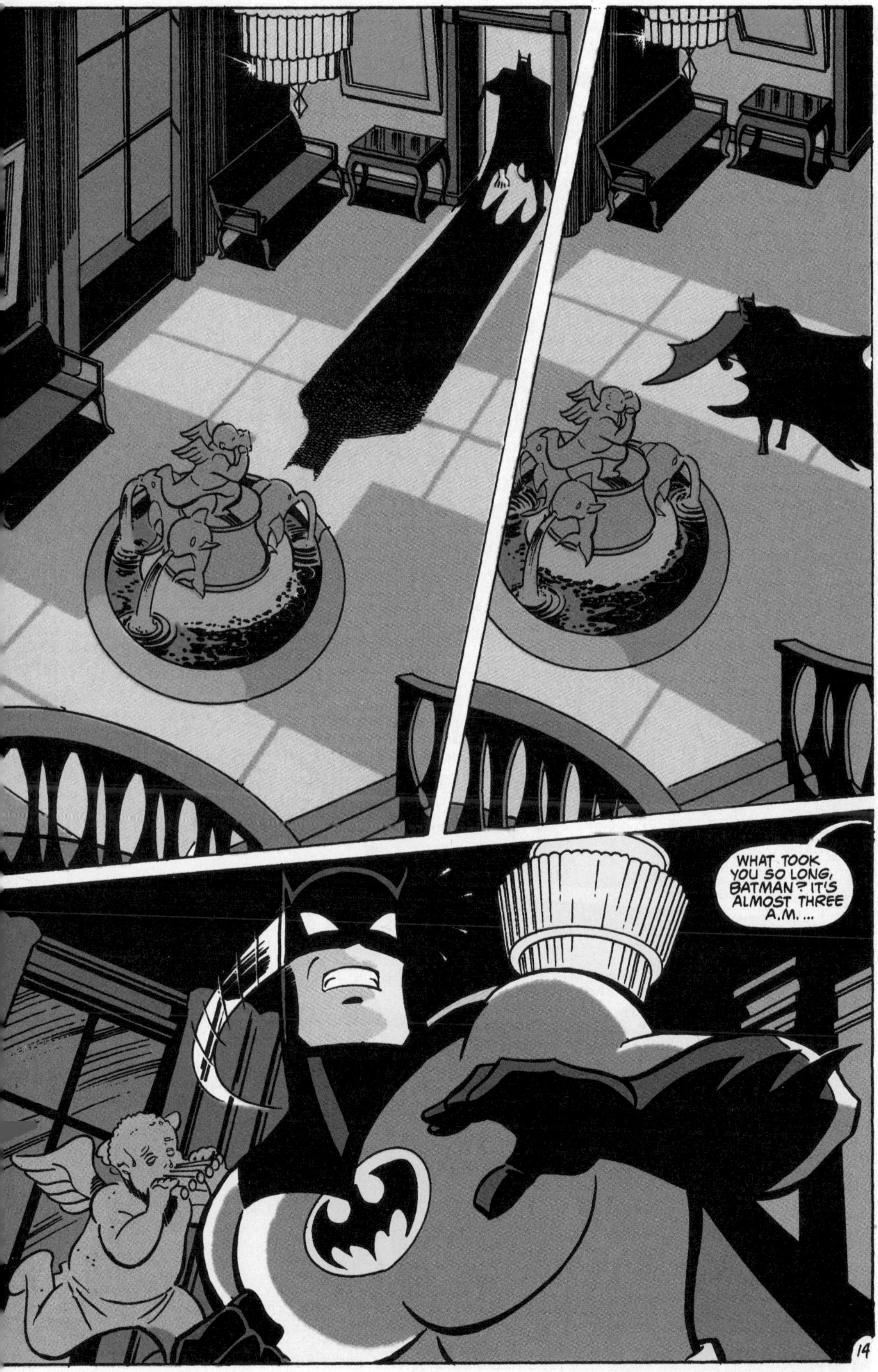
WHAT TOOK YOU SO LONG, BATMAN? IT'S ALMOST THREE A.M. ...
14

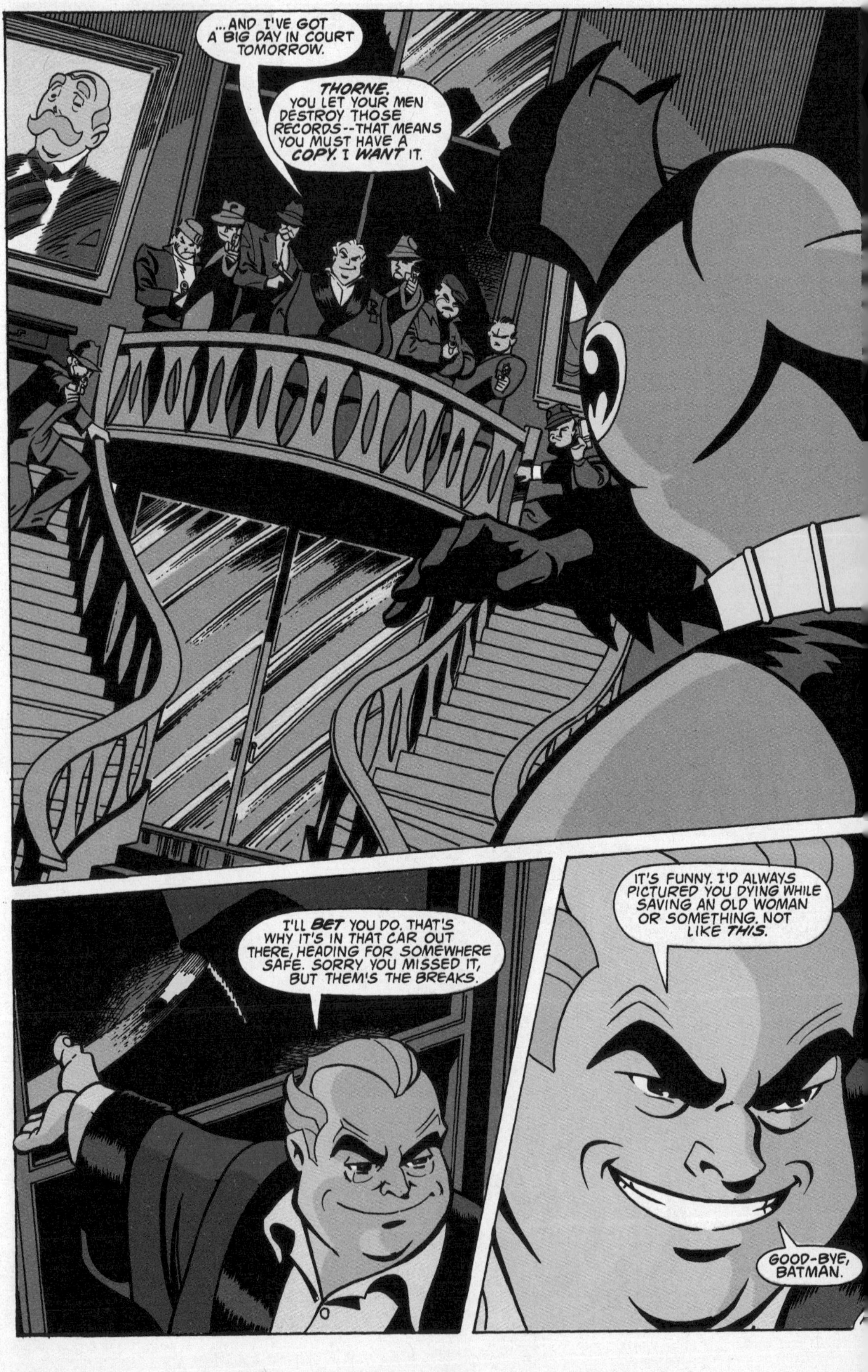
...AND I'VE GOT A BIG DAY IN COURT TOMORROW.
THORNE. YOU LET YOUR MEN DESTROY THOSE RECORDS--THAT MEANS YOU MUST HAVE A COPY. I WANT IT.
I'LL BET YOU DO. THAT'S WHY IT'S IN THAT CAR OUT THERE, HEADING FOR SOMEWHERE SAFE. SORRY YOU MISSED IT, BUT THEM'S THE BREAKS.
IT'S FUNNY. I'D ALWAYS PICTURED YOU DYING WHILE SAVING AN OLD WOMAN OR SOMETHING. NOT LIKE THIS.
GOOD-BYE, BATMAN.

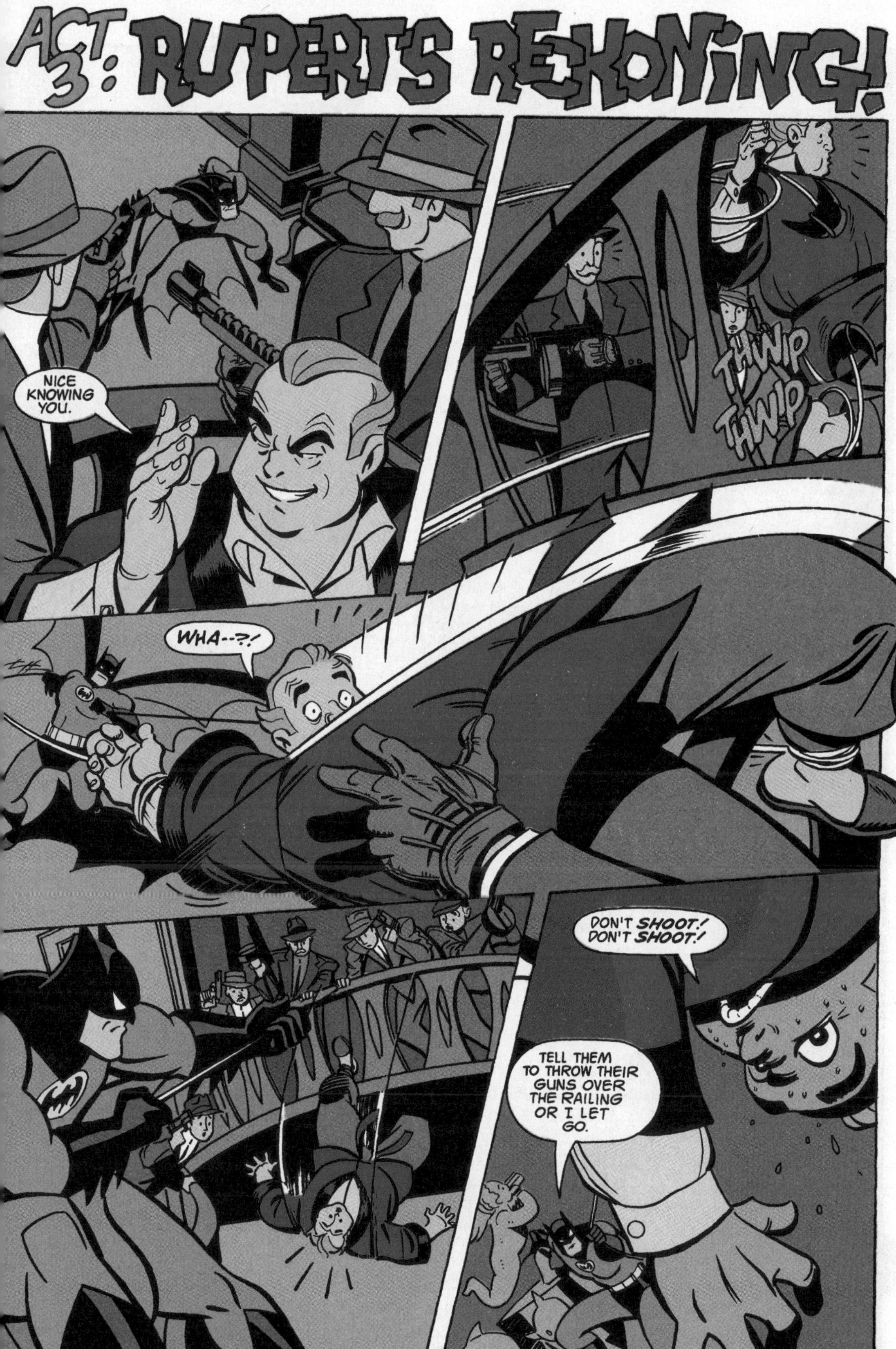
ACT 3: RUPERT'S RECKONING!
NICE KNOWING YOU.
THWIP
THWIP
WHA--?!
DON'T SHOOT! DON'T SHOOT!
TELL THEM TO THROW THEIR GUNS OVER THE RAILING OR I LET GO.
16

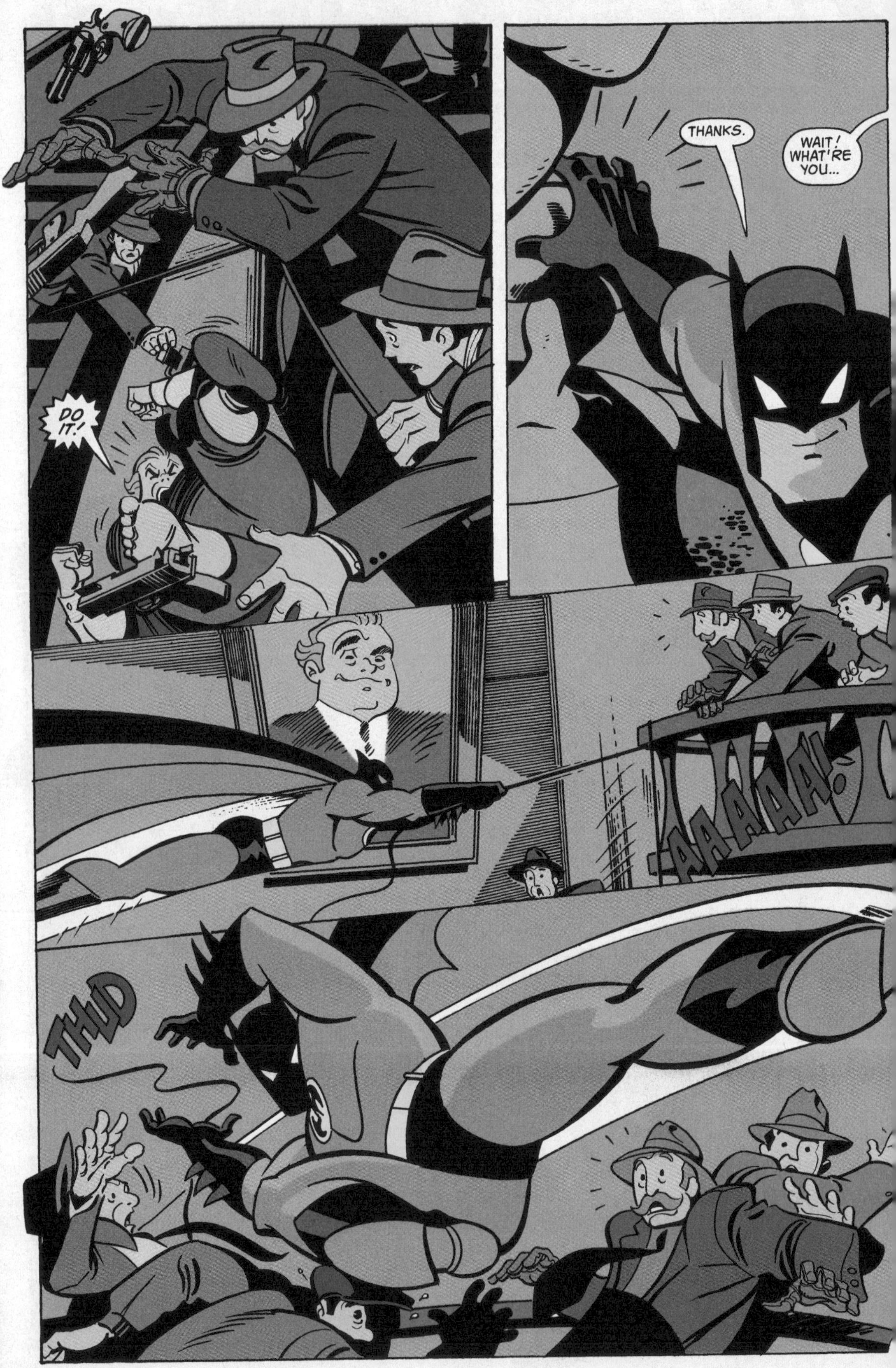
DO IT!
THANKS.
WAIT! WHAT'RE YOU...
AAAAAA!
THUD

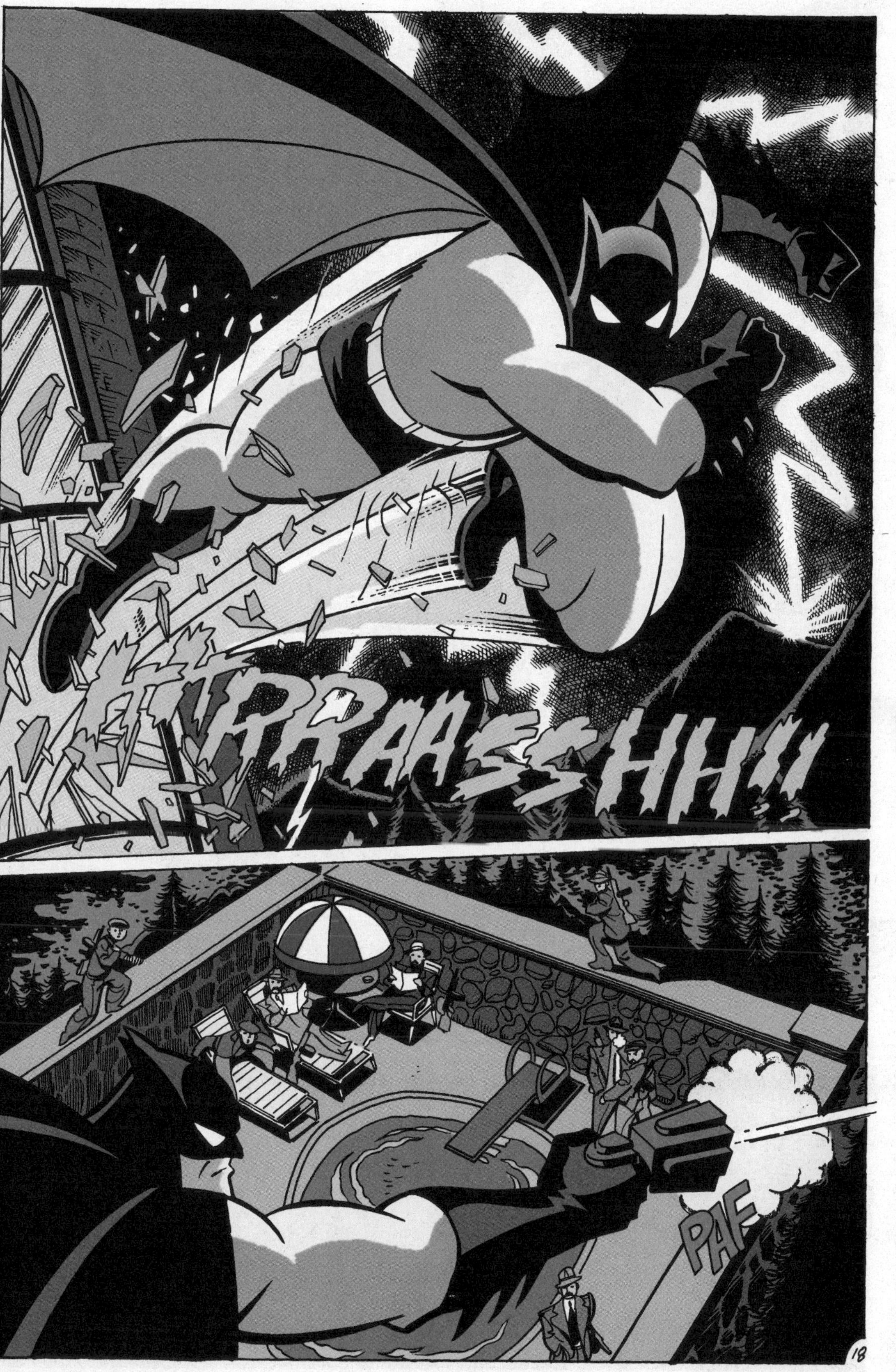
KRRAASSHH!!
PAF
18

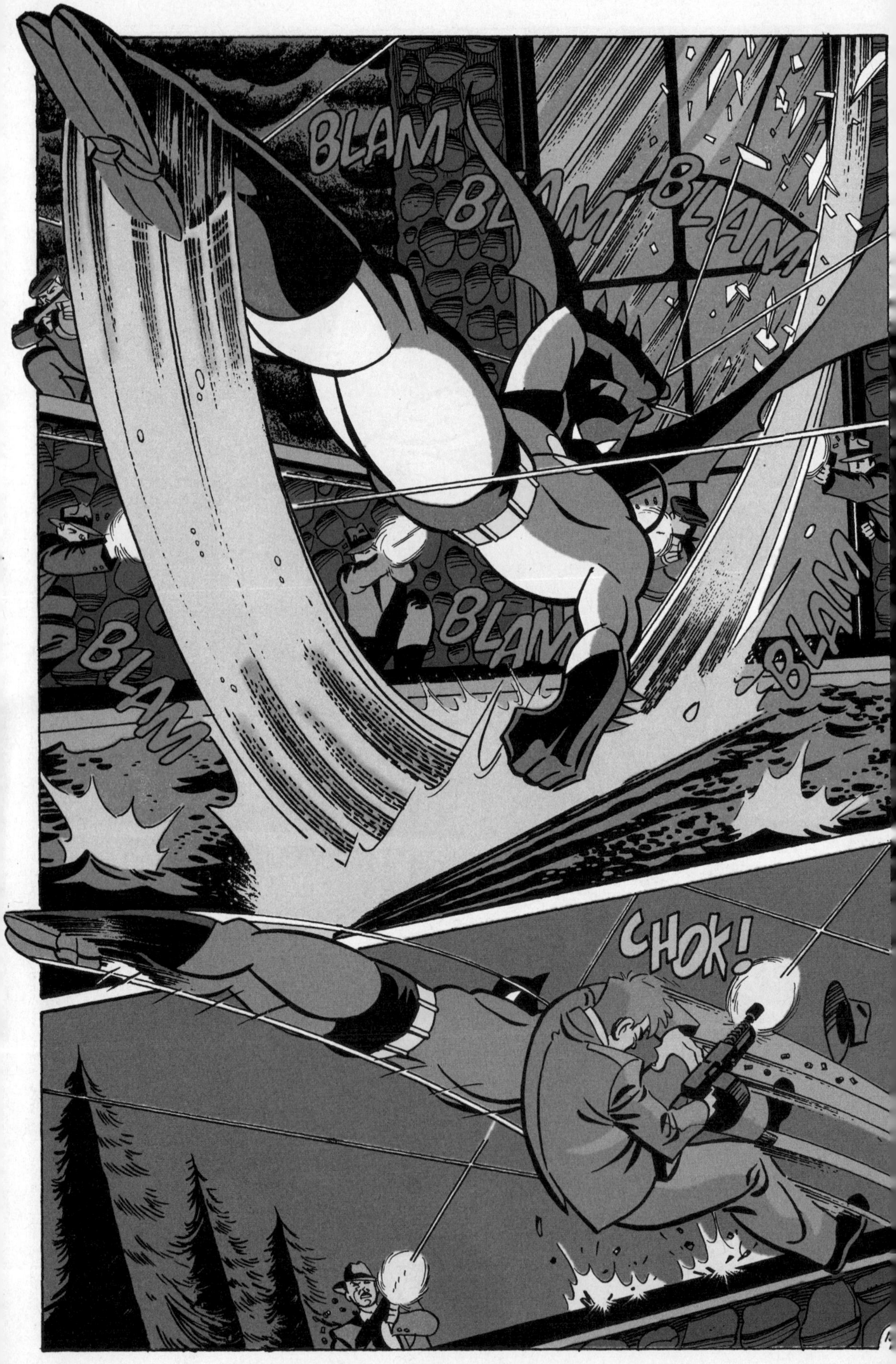
BLAM
BLAM
BLAM
BLAM
BLAM
BLAM
CHOK!

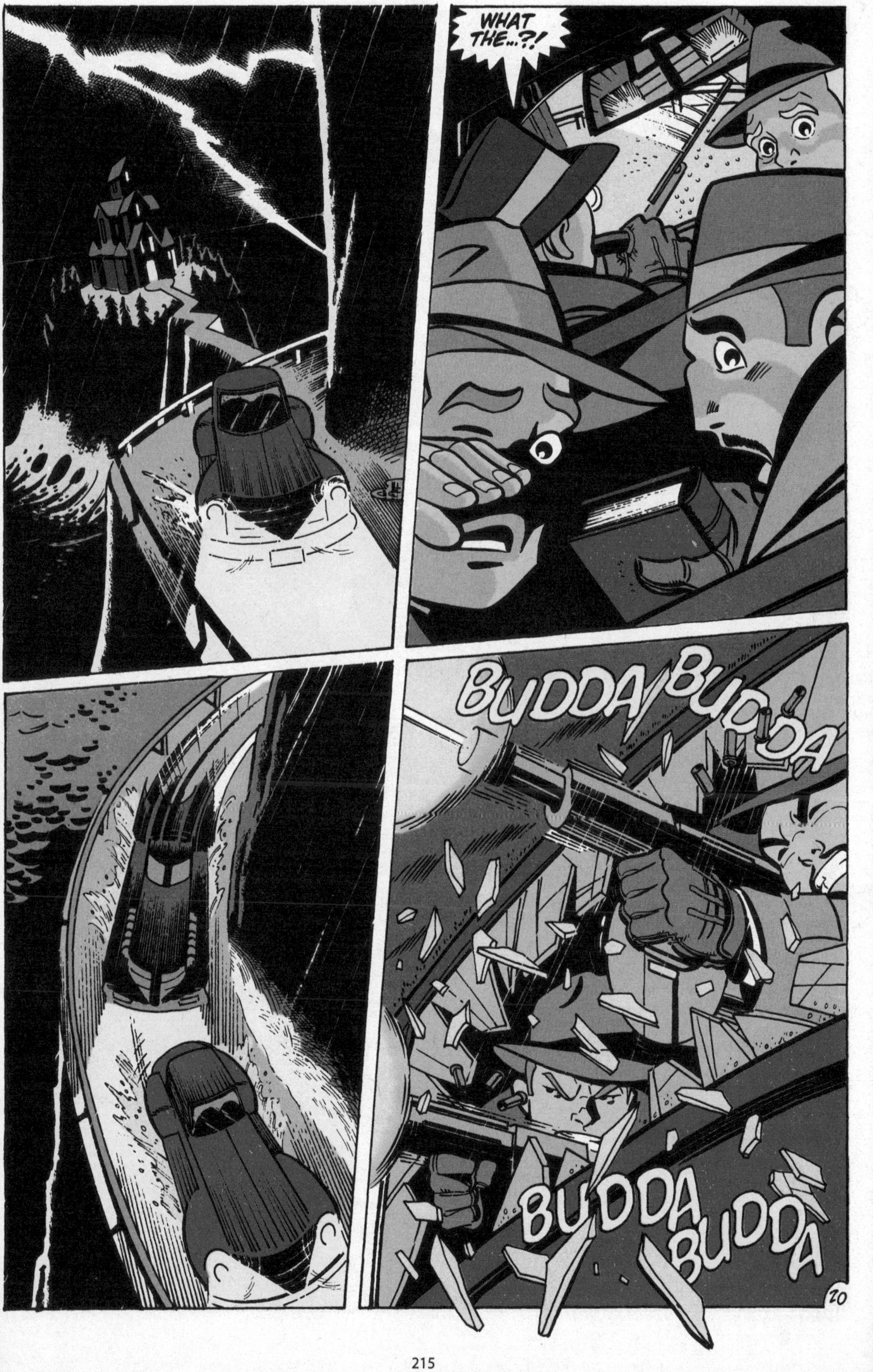
WHAT THE..?!
BUDDA BUDDA
BUDDA BUDDA
20

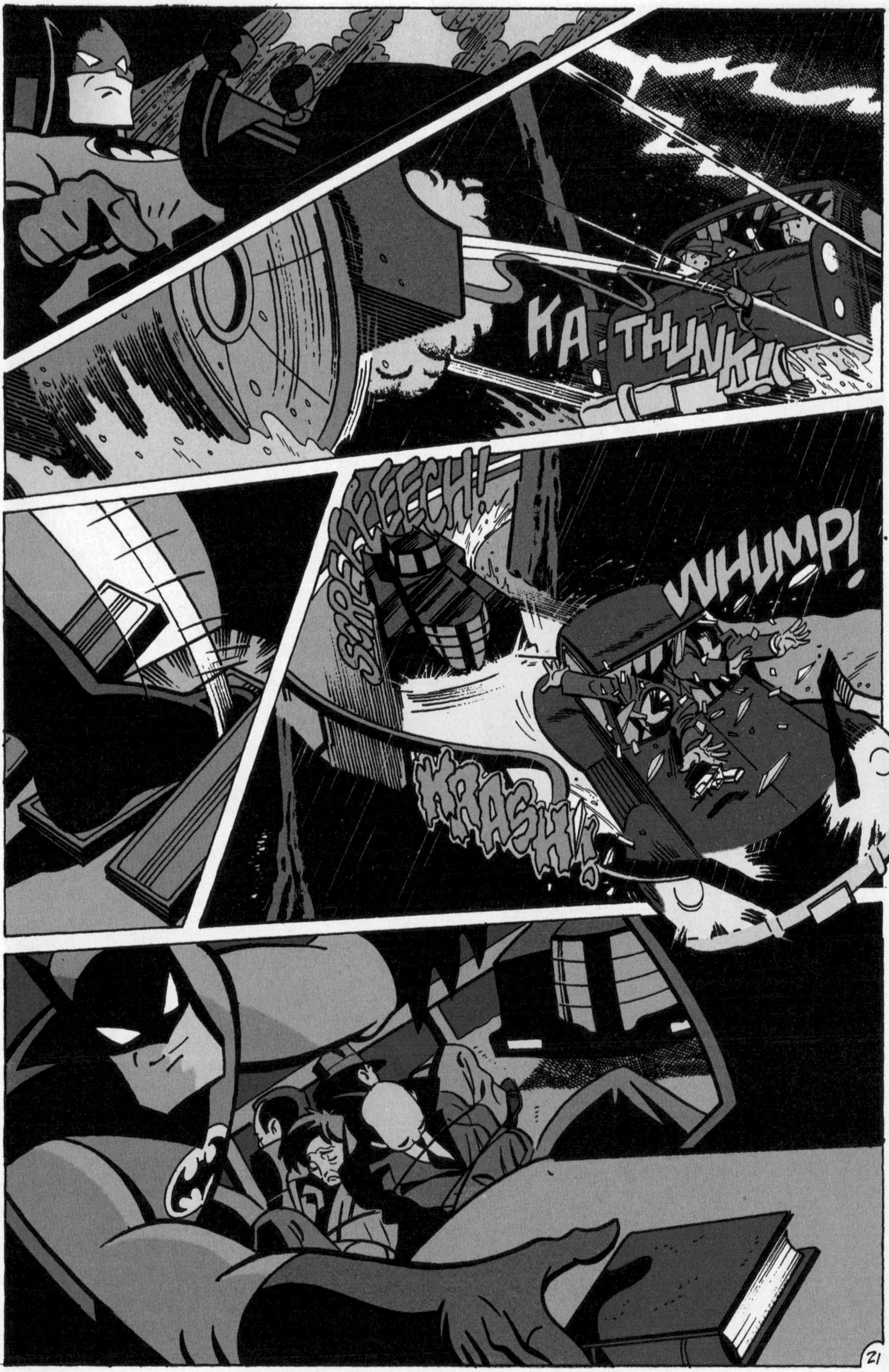
KA-THUNK!!
SCREEEEECH!
WHUMP!
KRASH!!
21

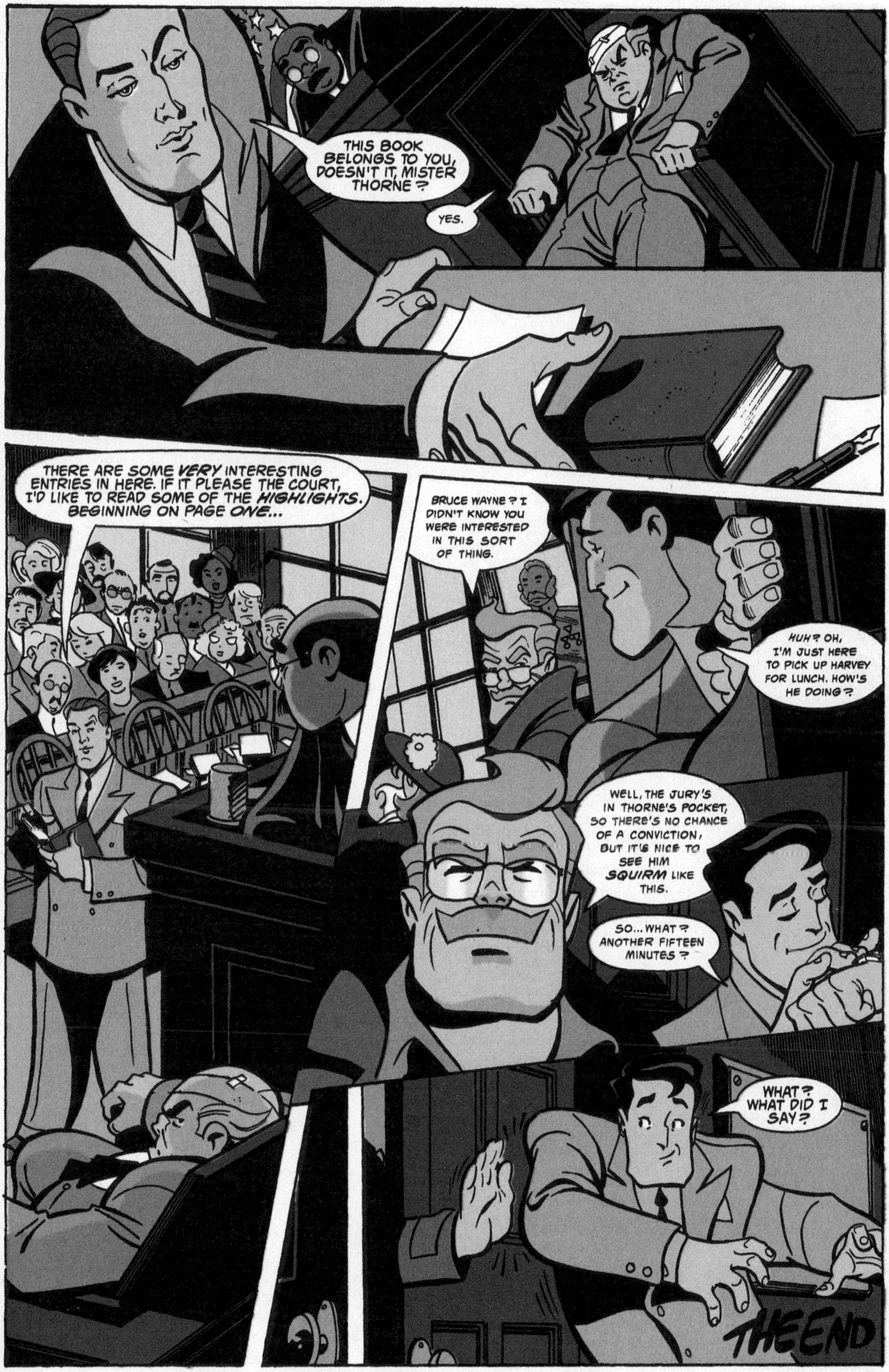
THIS BOOK BELONGS TO YOU, DOESN'T IT, MISTER THORNE?
YES.
THERE ARE SOME VERY INTERESTING ENTRIES IN HERE. IF IT PLEASE THE COURT, I'D LIKE TO READ SOME OF THE HIGHLIGHTS. BEGINNING ON PAGE ONE...
BRUCE WAYNE? I DIDN'T KNOW YOU WERE INTERESTED IN THIS SORT OF THING.
HUH? OH, I'M JUST HERE TO PICK UP HARVEY FOR LUNCH. HOW'S HE DOING?
WELL, THE JURY'S IN THORNE'S POCKET, SO THERE'S NO CHANCE OF A CONVICTION, BUT IT'S NICE TO SEE HIM SQUIRM LIKE THIS.
SO... WHAT? ANOTHER FIFTEEN MINUTES?
WHAT? WHAT DID I SAY?
THE END

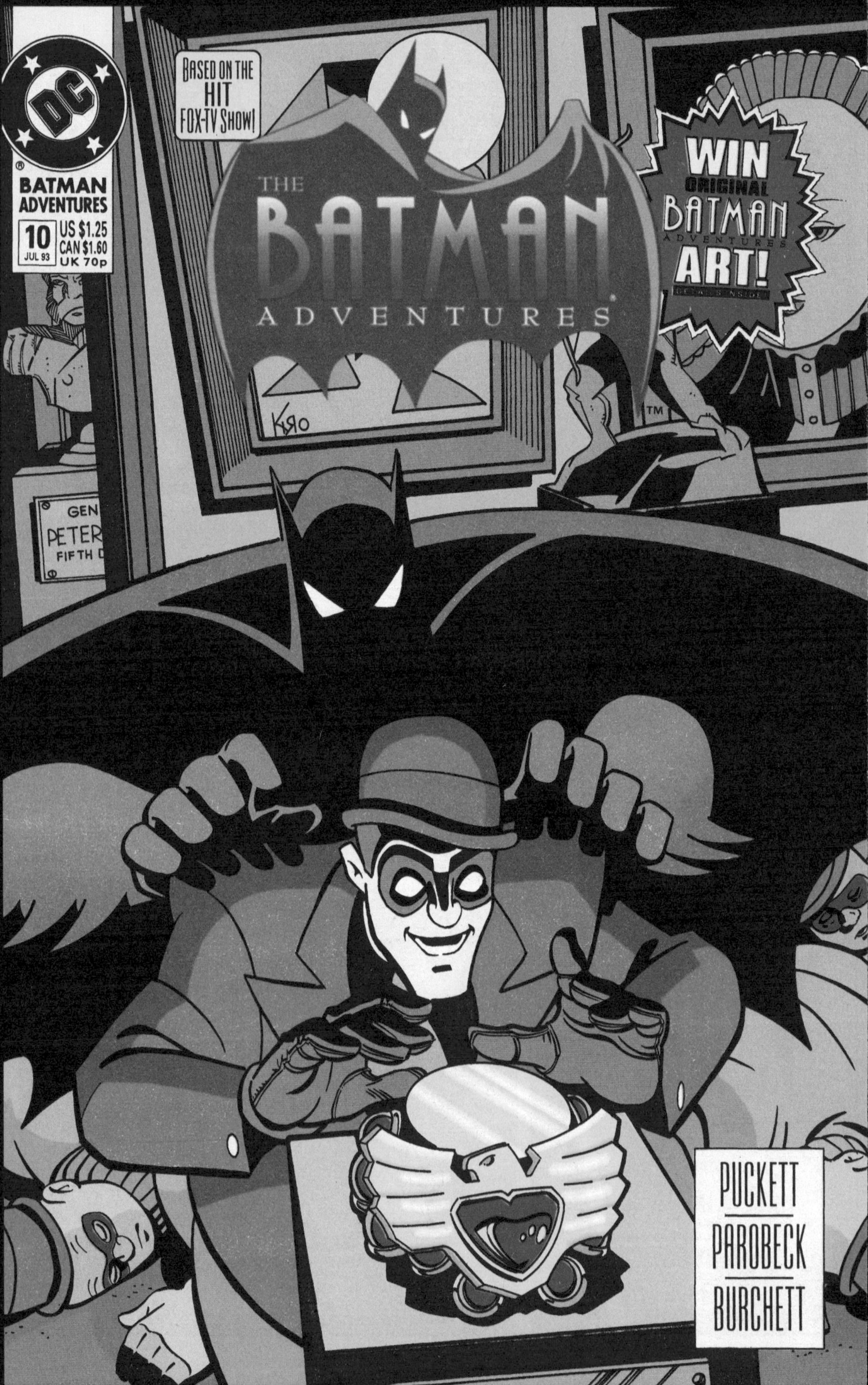
DC
BATMAN ADVENTURES
10
JUL 93
US $1.25
CAN $1.60
UK 70p
BASED ON THE HIT FOX-TV SHOW!
THE BATMAN ADVENTURES
TM
WIN ORIGINAL BATMAN ADVENTURES ART!
KIRO
GEN
PETER
FIFTH
PUCKETT
PAROBECK
BURCHETT

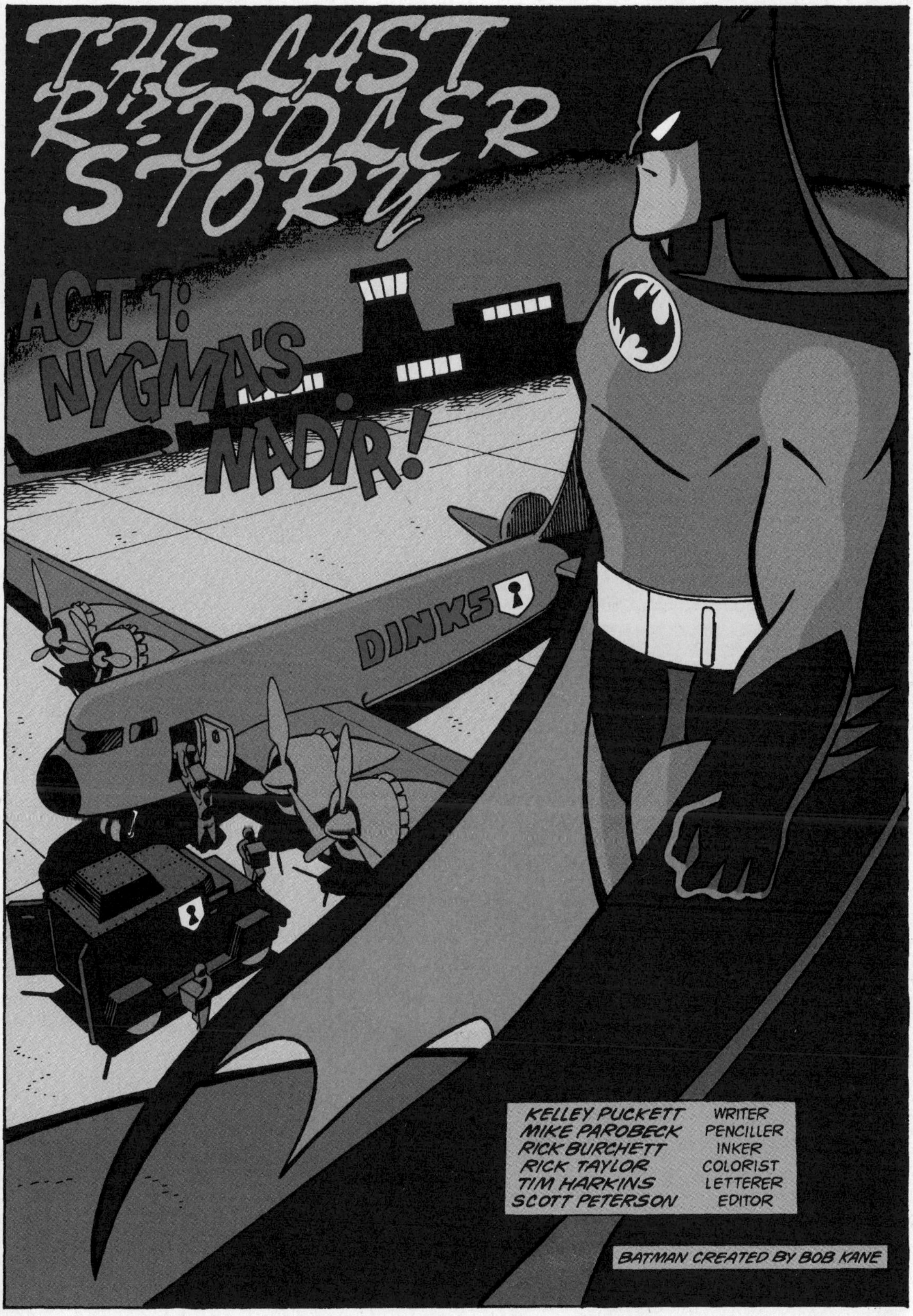
THE LAST RIDDLER STORY
ACT 1: NYGMA'S NADIR!
DINKS
KELLEY PUCKETT WRITER
MIKE PAROBECK PENCILLER
RICK BURCHETT INKER
RICK TAYLOR COLORIST
TIM HARKINS LETTERER
SCOTT PETERSON EDITOR
BATMAN CREATED BY BOB KANE

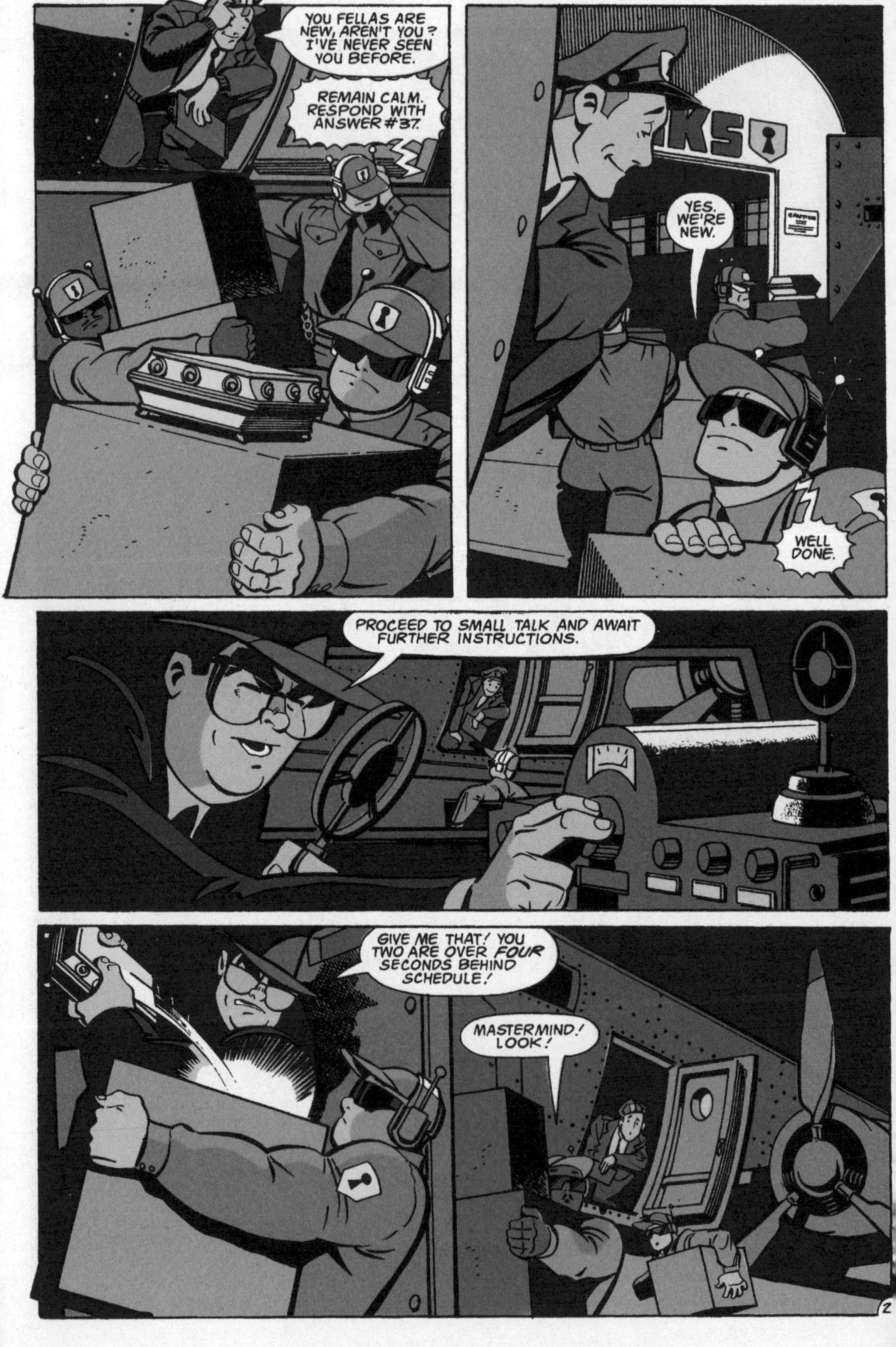
YOU FELLAS ARE NEW, AREN'T YOU? I'VE NEVER SEEN YOU BEFORE.
REMAIN CALM. RESPOND WITH ANSWER #37.
YES. WE'RE NEW.
WELL DONE.
PROCEED TO SMALL TALK AND AWAIT FURTHER INSTRUCTIONS.
GIVE ME THAT! YOU TWO ARE OVER *FOUR* SECONDS BEHIND SCHEDULE!
MASTERMIND! LOOK!
2

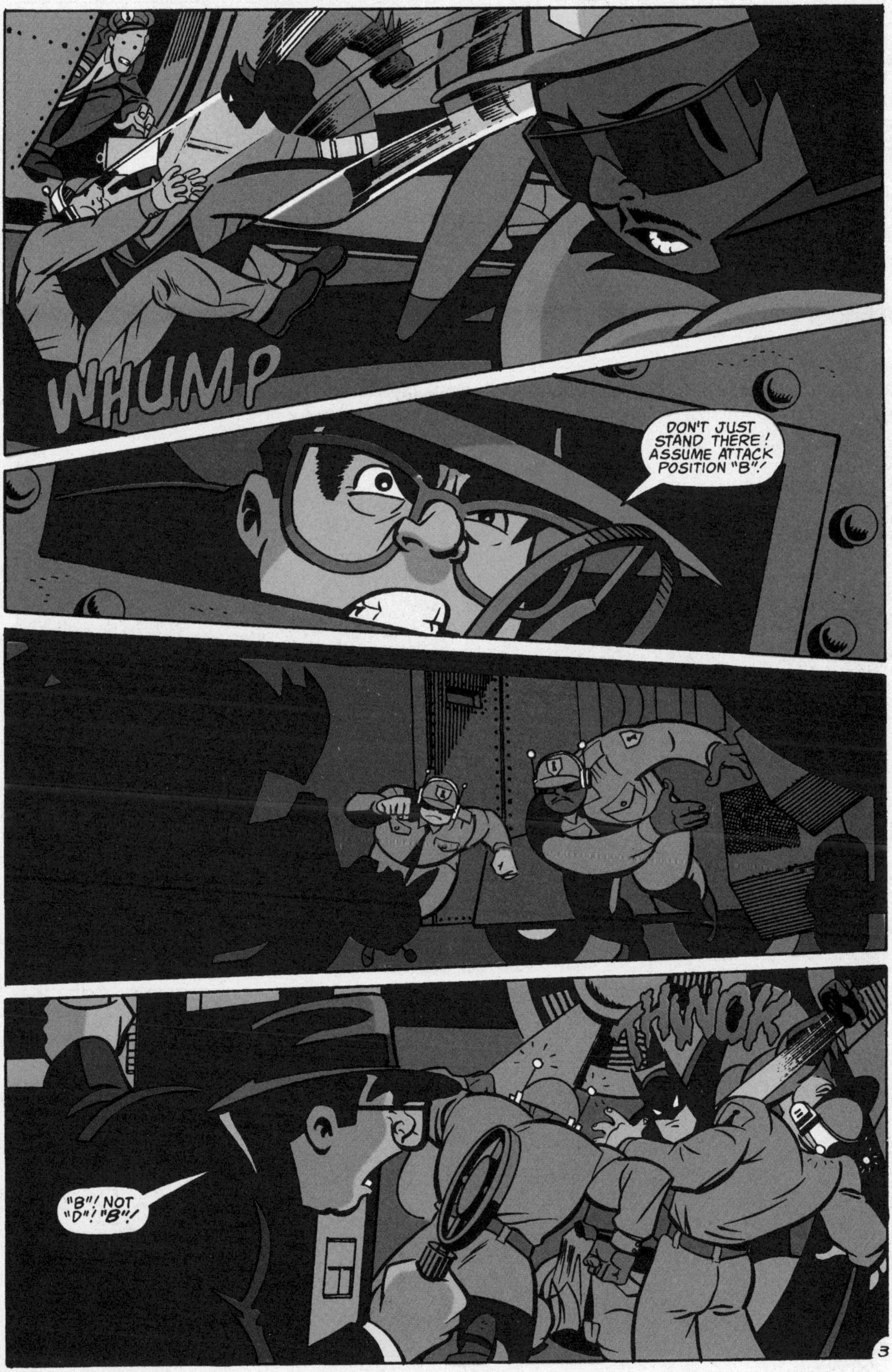
WHUMP
DON'T JUST STAND THERE! ASSUME ATTACK POSITION "B"!
THWOK
"B"! NOT "D"! "B"!
3

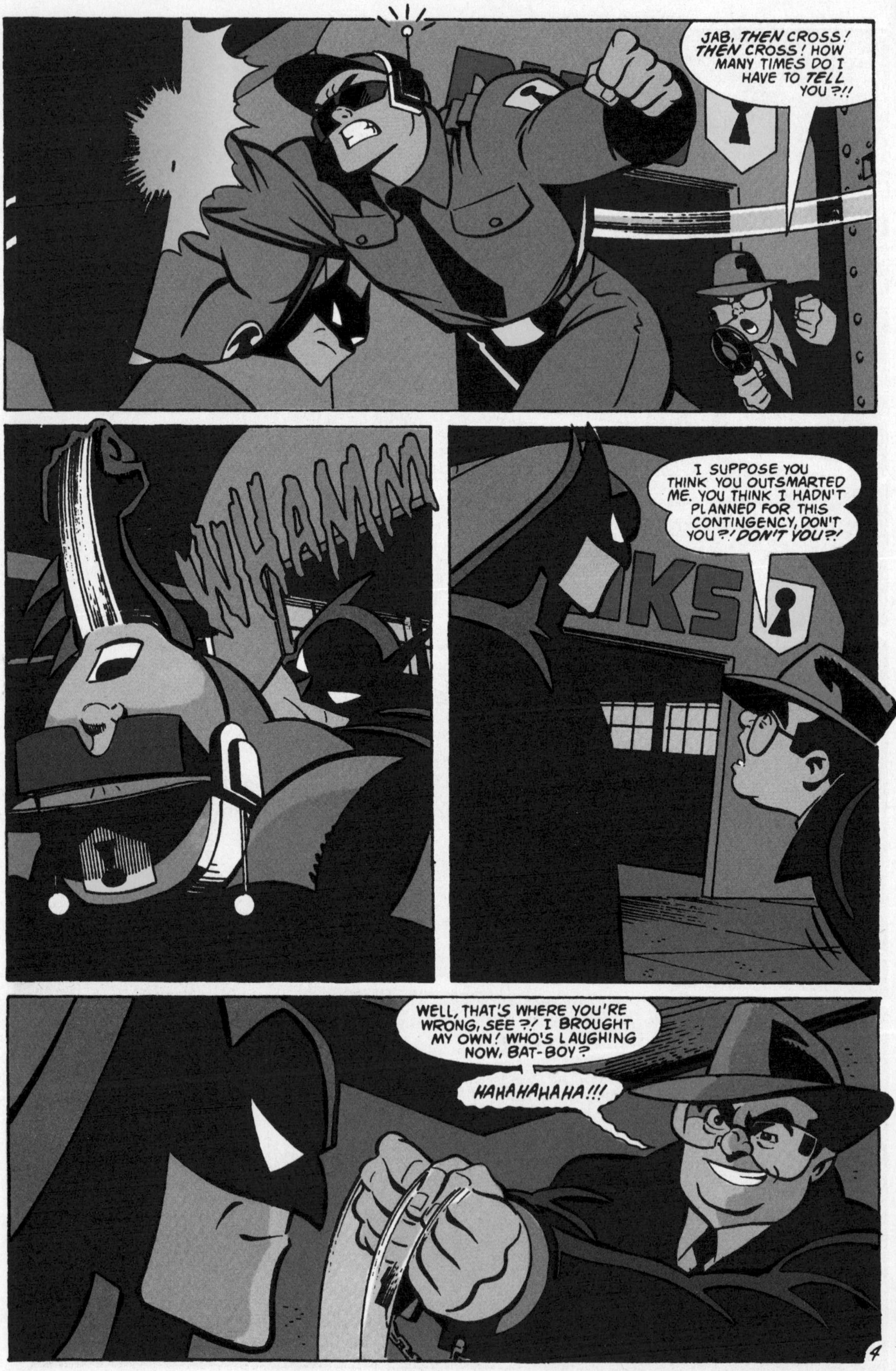
JAB, THEN CROSS! THEN CROSS! HOW MANY TIMES DO I HAVE TO TELL YOU?!!
WHAMM
I SUPPOSE YOU THINK YOU OUTSMARTED ME. YOU THINK I HADN'T PLANNED FOR THIS CONTINGENCY, DON'T YOU?! DON'T YOU?!
KS
WELL, THAT'S WHERE YOU'RE WRONG, SEE?! I BROUGHT MY OWN! WHO'S LAUGHING NOW, BAT-BOY?
HAHAHAHAHA!!!
4

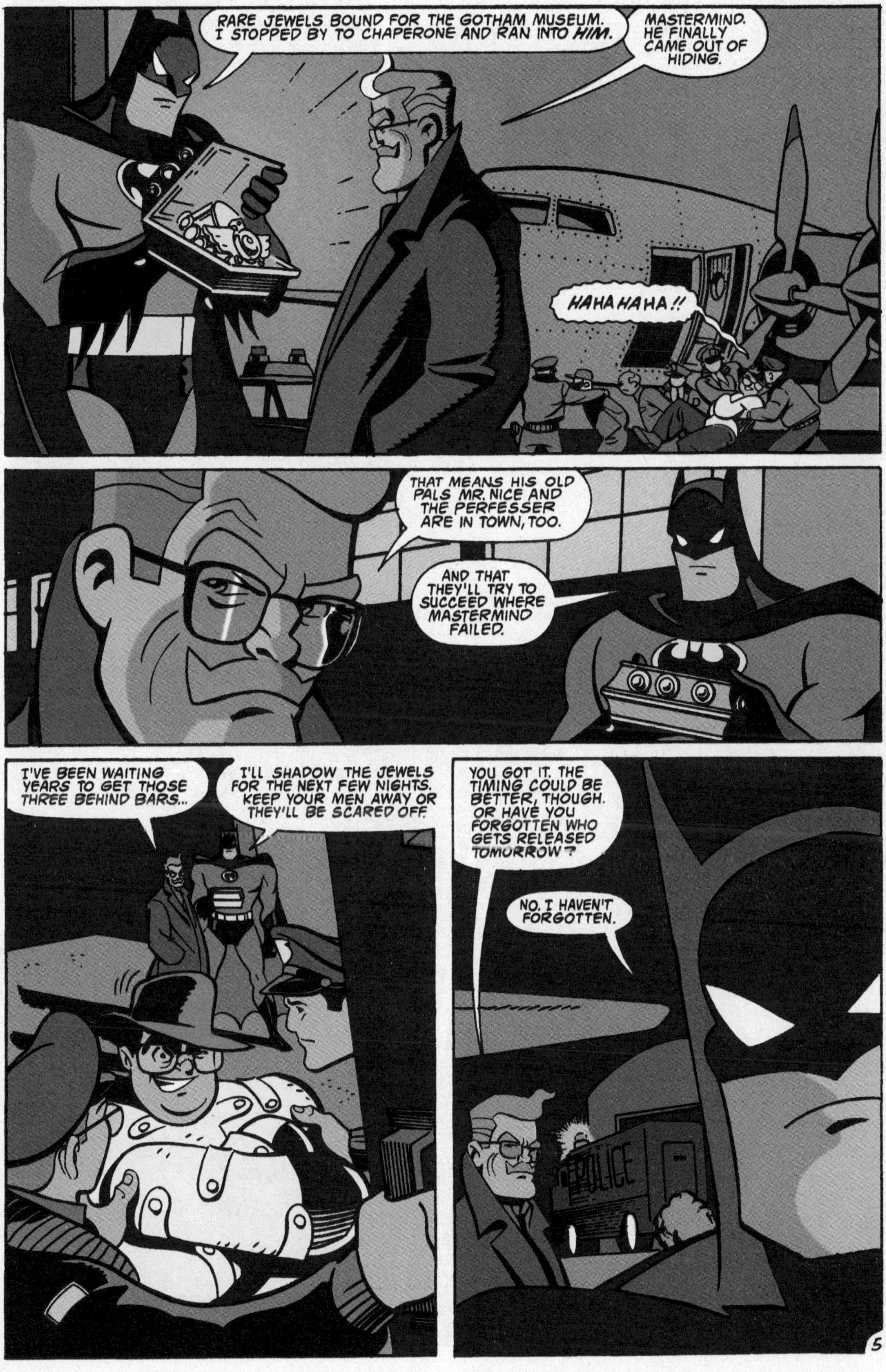
RARE JEWELS BOUND FOR THE GOTHAM MUSEUM. I STOPPED BY TO CHAPERONE AND RAN INTO *HIM*.
MASTERMIND. HE FINALLY CAME OUT OF HIDING.
HAHAHAHA!!
THAT MEANS HIS OLD PALS MR. NICE AND THE PERFESSER ARE IN TOWN, TOO.
AND THAT THEY'LL TRY TO SUCCEED WHERE MASTERMIND FAILED.
I'VE BEEN WAITING YEARS TO GET THOSE THREE BEHIND BARS...
I'LL SHADOW THE JEWELS FOR THE NEXT FEW NIGHTS. KEEP YOUR MEN AWAY OR THEY'LL BE SCARED OFF.
YOU GOT IT. THE TIMING COULD BE BETTER, THOUGH. OR HAVE YOU FORGOTTEN WHO GETS RELEASED TOMORROW?
NO, I HAVEN'T FORGOTTEN.
POLICE
5

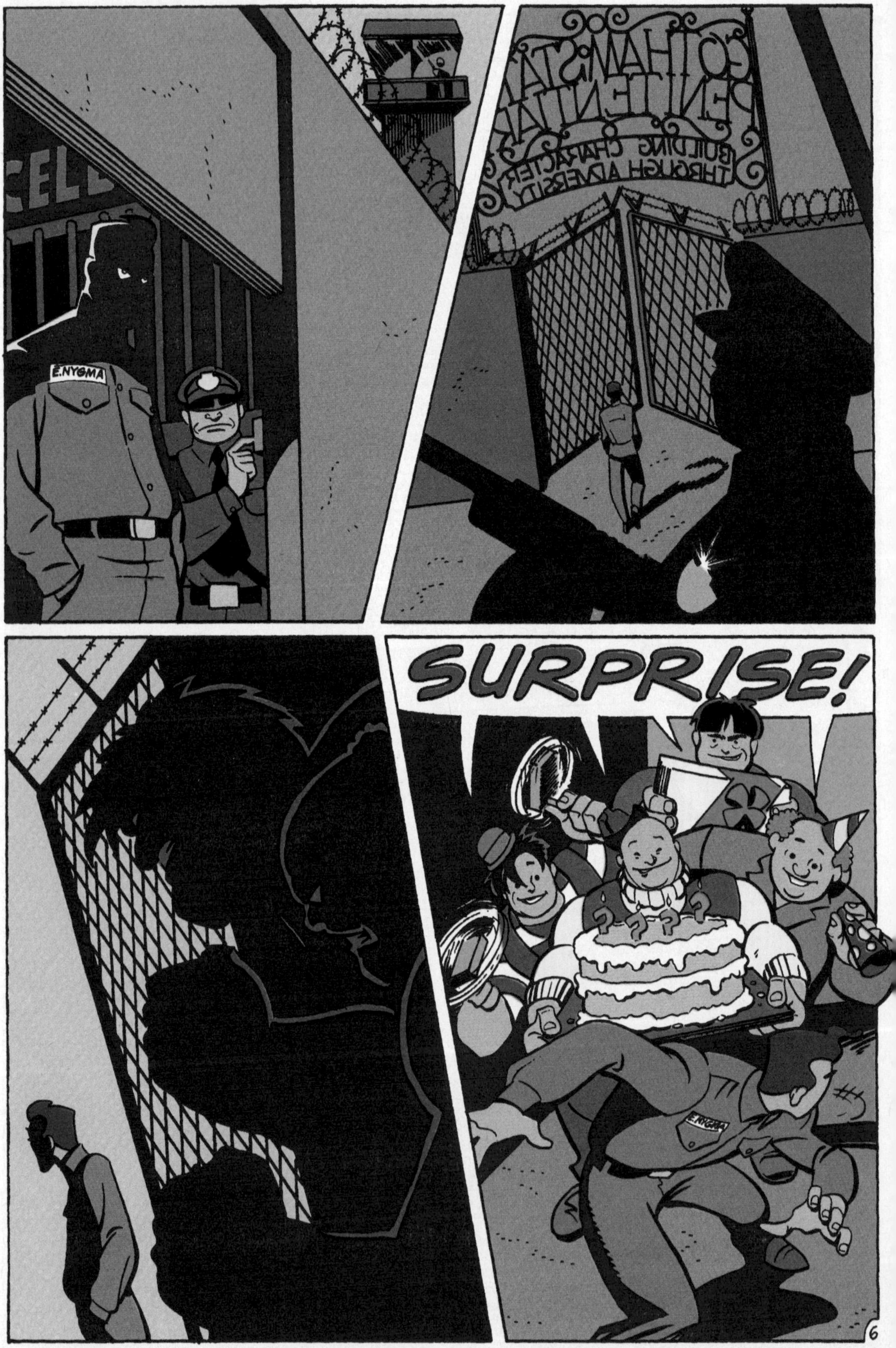
E.NYGMA
SURPRISE!
E.NYGMA
6

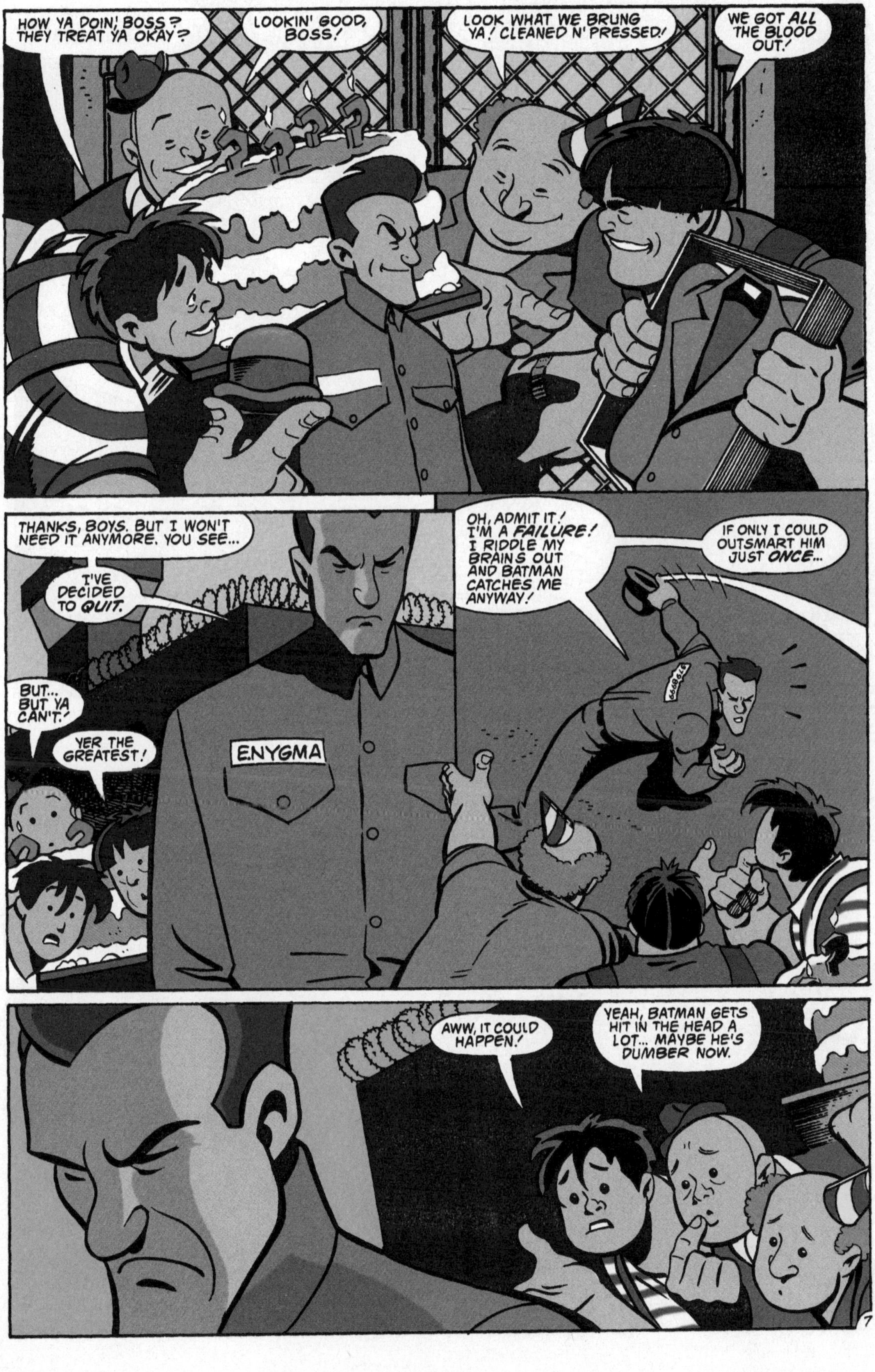

HOW YA DOIN' BOSS? THEY TREAT YA OKAY?
LOOKIN' GOOD, BOSS!
LOOK WHAT WE BRUNG YA! CLEANED N' PRESSED!
WE GOT ALL THE BLOOD OUT!
THANKS, BOYS. BUT I WON'T NEED IT ANYMORE. YOU SEE...
I'VE DECIDED TO QUIT.
BUT... BUT YA CAN'T!
YER THE GREATEST!
E.NYGMA
OH, ADMIT IT! I'M A FAILURE! I RIDDLE MY BRAINS OUT AND BATMAN CATCHES ME ANYWAY!
IF ONLY I COULD OUTSMART HIM JUST ONCE...
AWW, IT COULD HAPPEN!
YEAH, BATMAN GETS HIT IN THE HEAD A LOT... MAYBE HE'S DUMBER NOW.
7

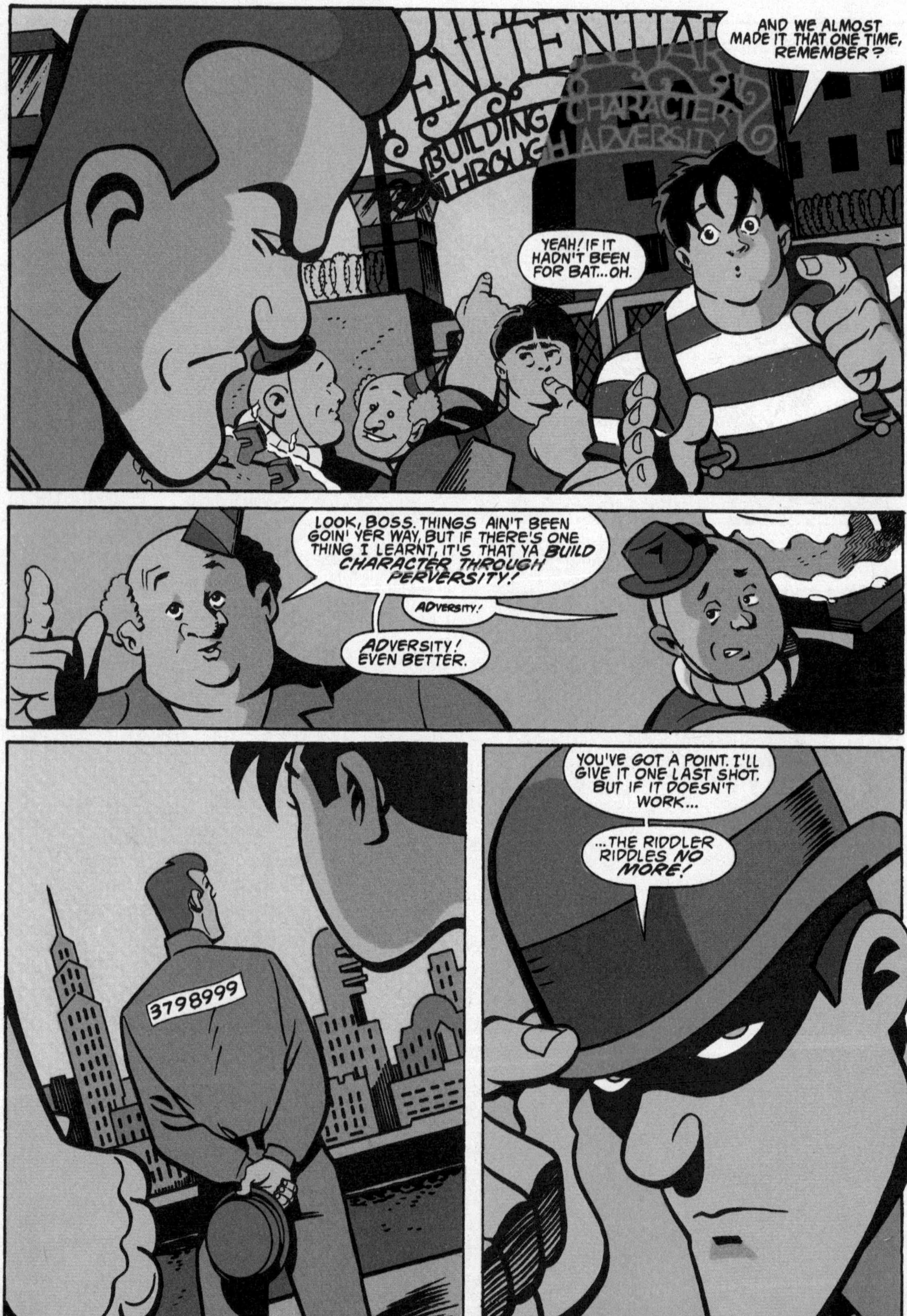
PENITENTIARY
BUILDING CHARACTER THROUGH ADVERSITY
AND WE ALMOST MADE IT THAT ONE TIME, REMEMBER?
YEAH! IF IT HADN'T BEEN FOR BAT...OH.
LOOK, BOSS. THINGS AIN'T BEEN GOIN' YER WAY, BUT IF THERE'S ONE THING I LEARNT, IT'S THAT YA BUILD CHARACTER THROUGH PERVERSITY!
ADVERSITY!
ADVERSITY! EVEN BETTER.
3798999
YOU'VE GOT A POINT. I'LL GIVE IT ONE LAST SHOT. BUT IF IT DOESN'T WORK...
...THE RIDDLER RIDDLES NO MORE!
8

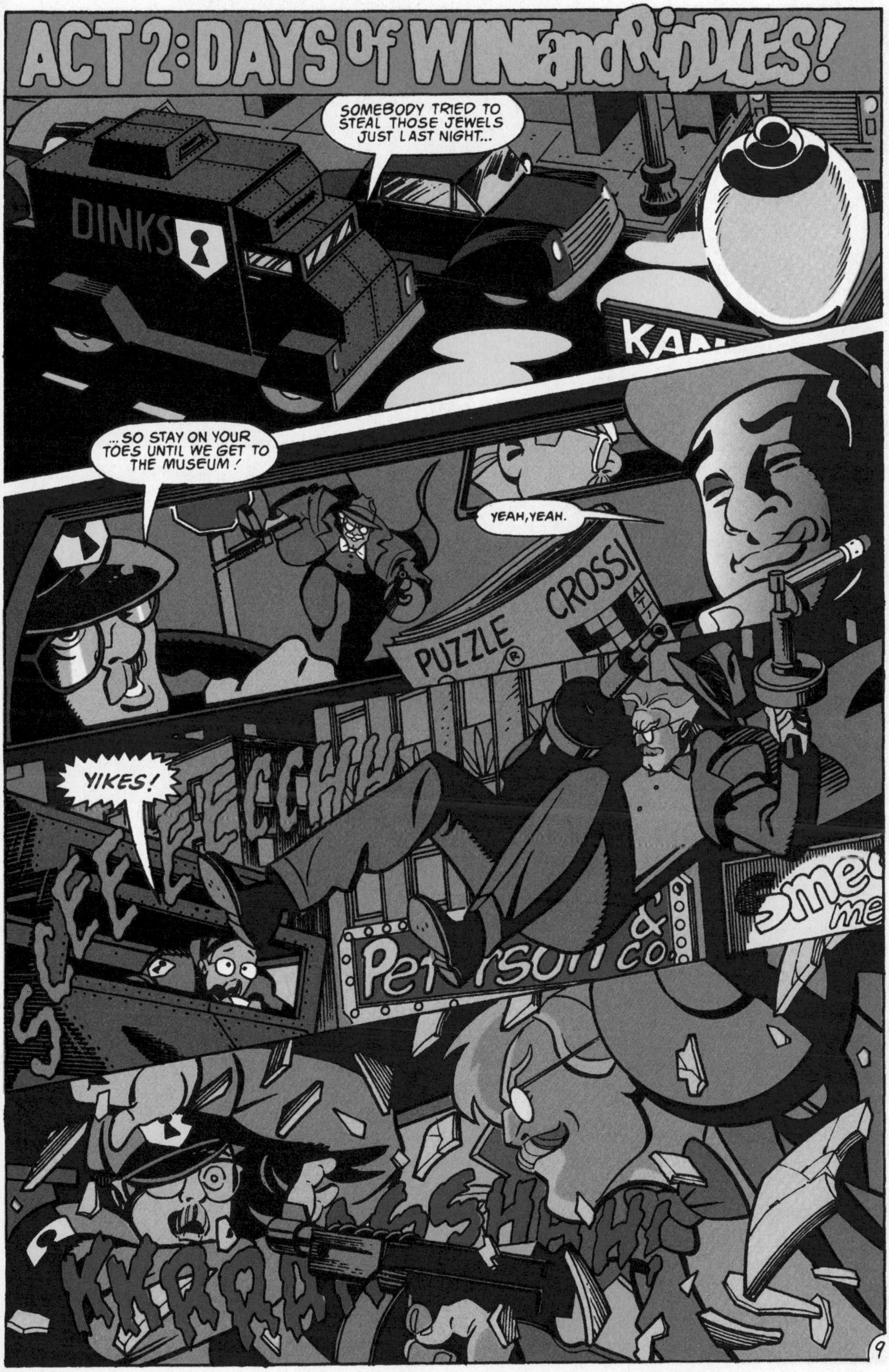
ACT 2: DAYS of WINE and RIDDLES!
SOMEBODY TRIED TO STEAL THOSE JEWELS JUST LAST NIGHT...
DINKS
...SO STAY ON YOUR TOES UNTIL WE GET TO THE MUSEUM!
YEAH, YEAH.
PUZZLE
CROSS
YIKES!
SCREEECCHH
Peterson & co.
KKRRAASSHH
9

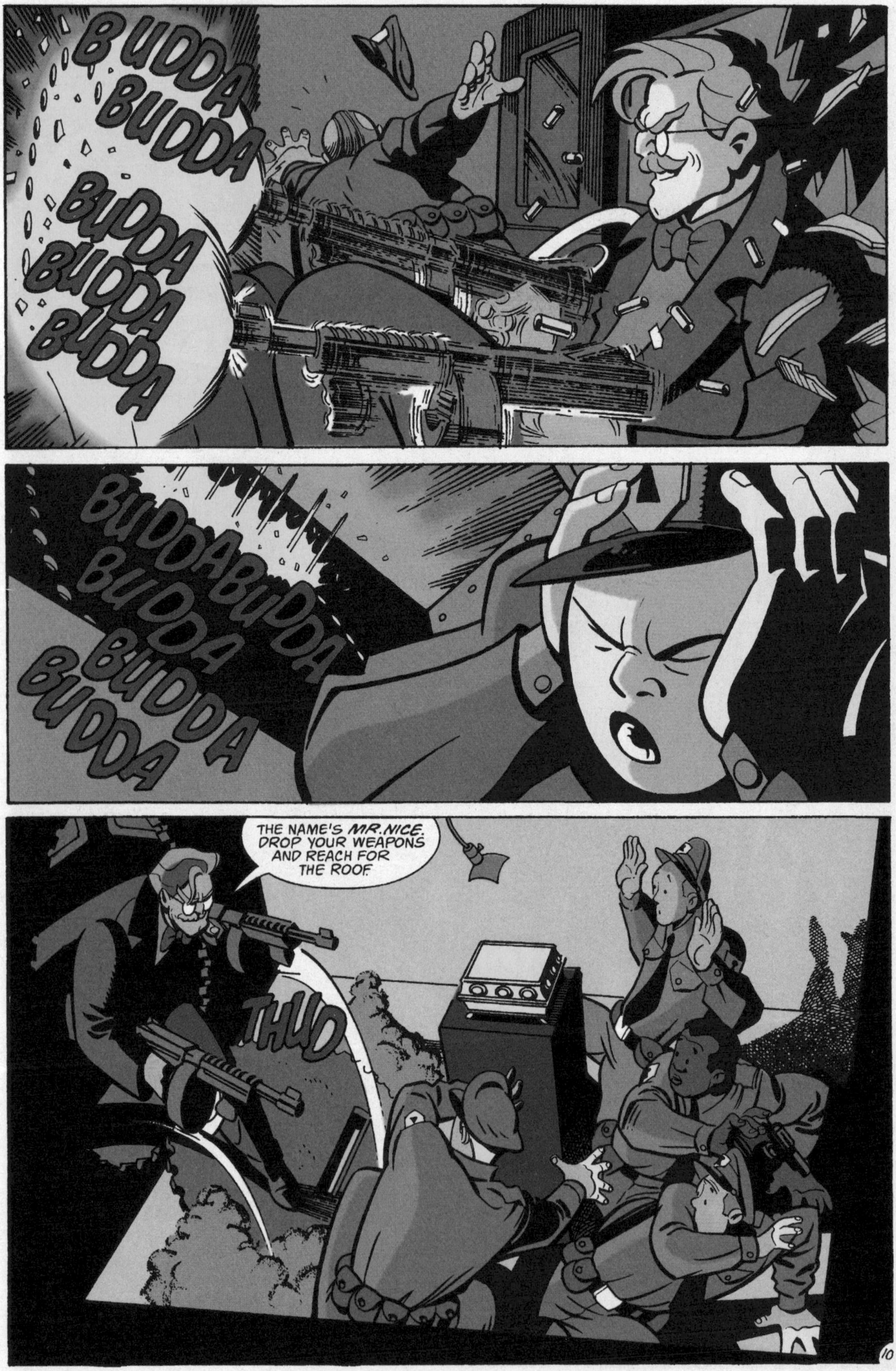
BUDDA BUDDA
BUDDA BUDDA BUDDA
BUDDABUDDA BUDDA BUDDA BUDDA
THE NAME'S MR. NICE. DROP YOUR WEAPONS AND REACH FOR THE ROOF.
THUD
10

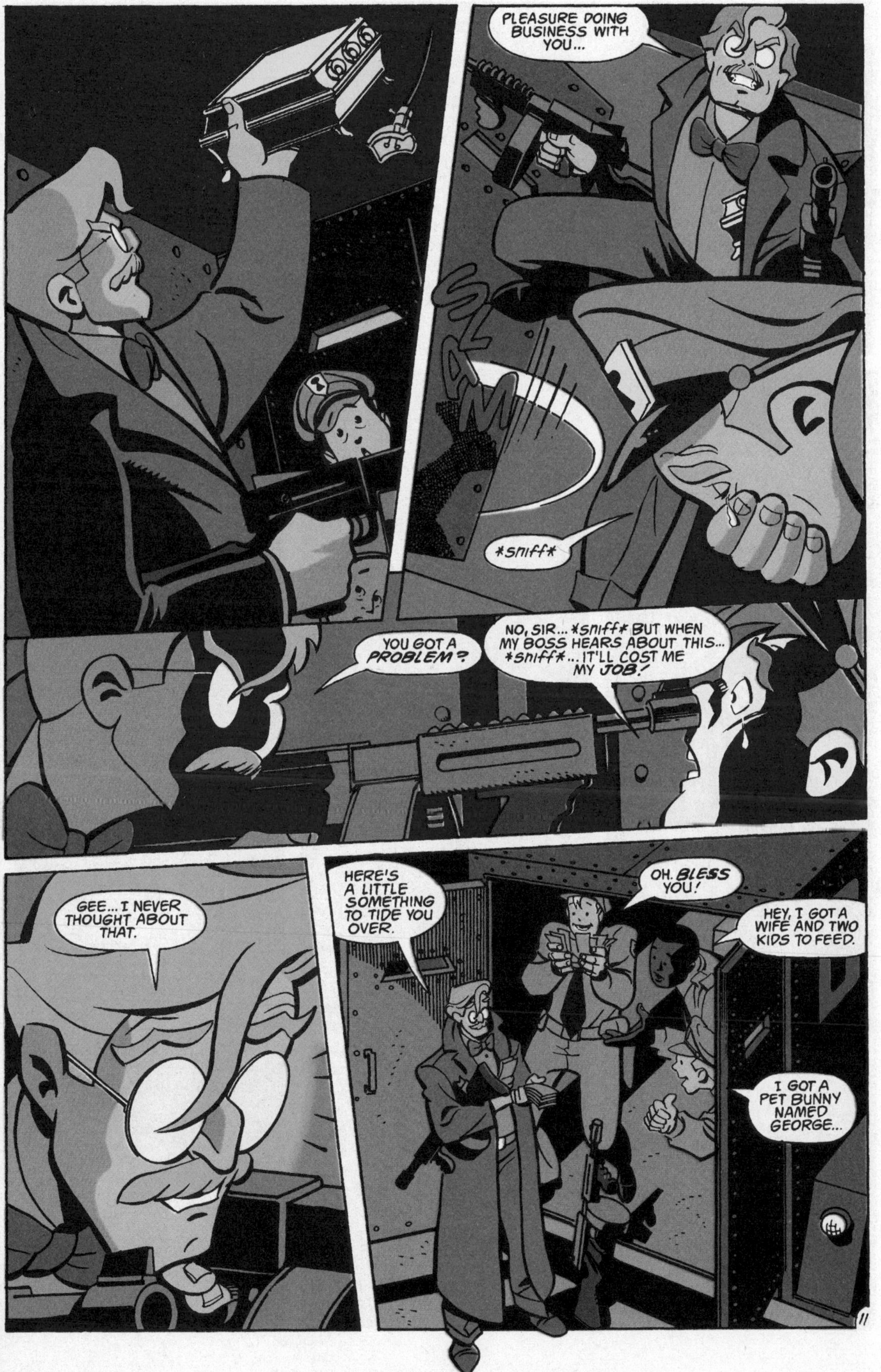
PLEASURE DOING BUSINESS WITH YOU...
SLAM
sniff
YOU GOT A PROBLEM?
NO, SIR... *sniff* BUT WHEN MY BOSS HEARS ABOUT THIS... *sniff*... IT'LL COST ME MY JOB!
GEE... I NEVER THOUGHT ABOUT THAT.
HERE'S A LITTLE SOMETHING TO TIDE YOU OVER.
OH. BLESS YOU!
HEY, I GOT A WIFE AND TWO KIDS TO FEED.
I GOT A PET BUNNY NAMED GEORGE...
11

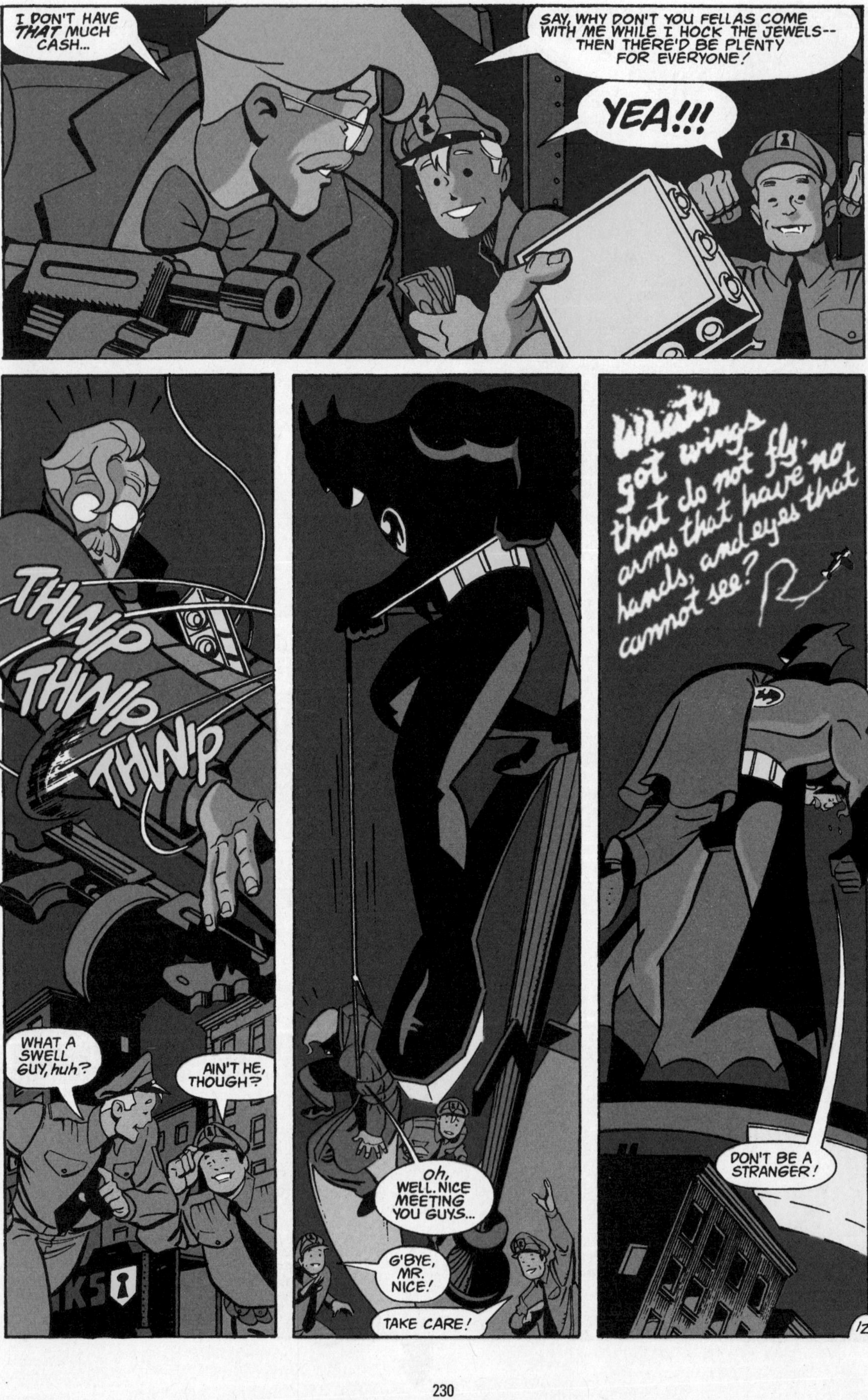

I DON'T HAVE THAT MUCH CASH...
SAY, WHY DON'T YOU FELLAS COME WITH ME WHILE I HOCK THE JEWELS-- THEN THERE'D BE PLENTY FOR EVERYONE!
YEA!!!
THWIP THWIP THWIP
WHAT A SWELL GUY, huh?
AIN'T HE, THOUGH?
Oh, WELL. NICE MEETING YOU GUYS...
G'BYE, MR. NICE!
TAKE CARE!
What's got wings that do not fly, arms that have no hands, and eyes that cannot see? R
DON'T BE A STRANGER!

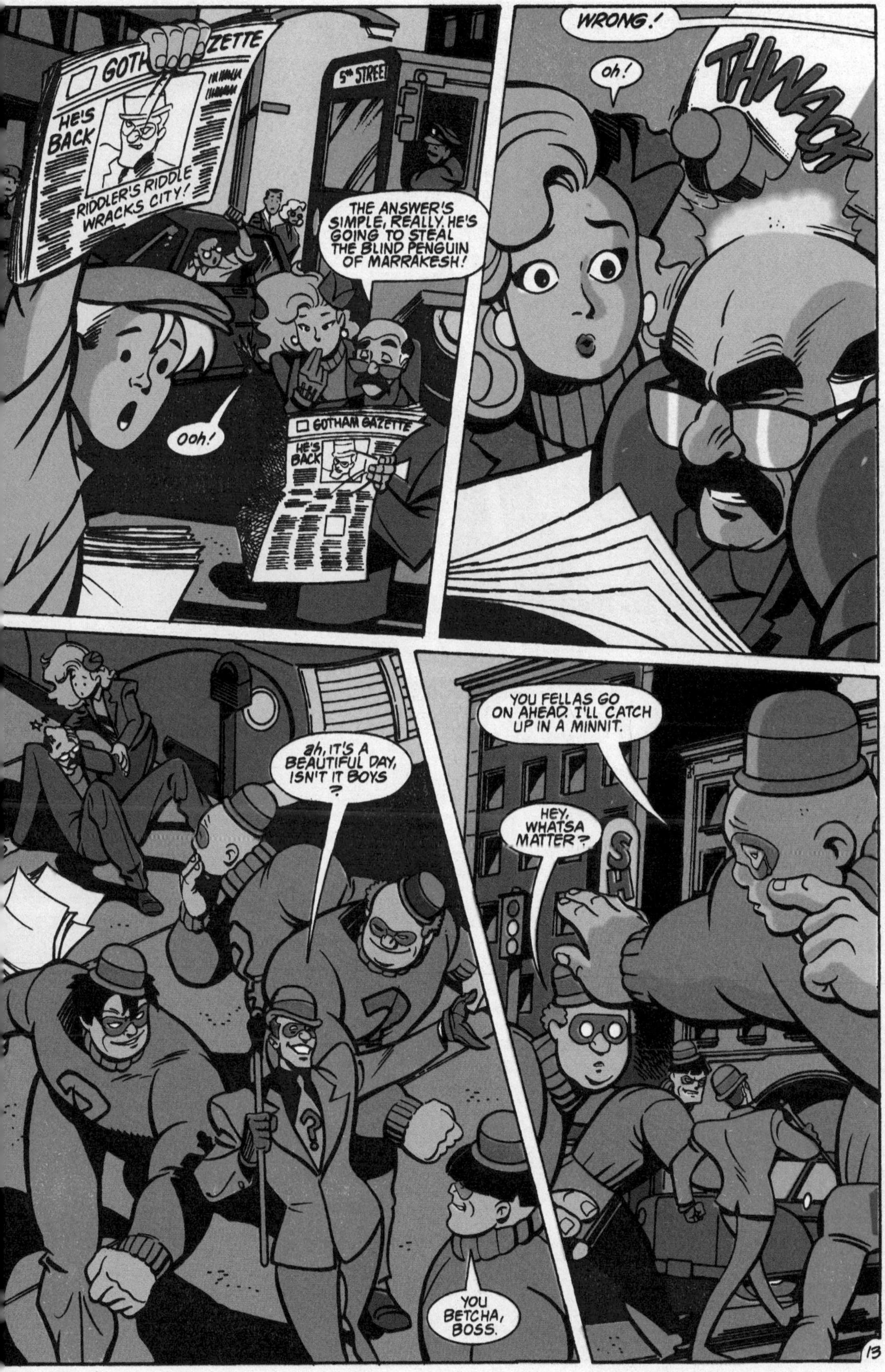
GOTHAM GAZETTE
HE'S BACK
RIDDLER'S RIDDLE WRACKS CITY!
5th STREET
THE ANSWER'S SIMPLE, REALLY. HE'S GOING TO STEAL THE BLIND PENGUIN OF MARRAKESH!
Ooh!
GOTHAM GAZETTE
HE'S BACK
WRONG.!
oh!
THWACK
ah, IT'S A BEAUTIFUL DAY, ISN'T IT BOYS?
YOU BETCHA, BOSS.
YOU FELLAS GO ON AHEAD. I'LL CATCH UP IN A MINNIT.
HEY, WHATSA MATTER?
13

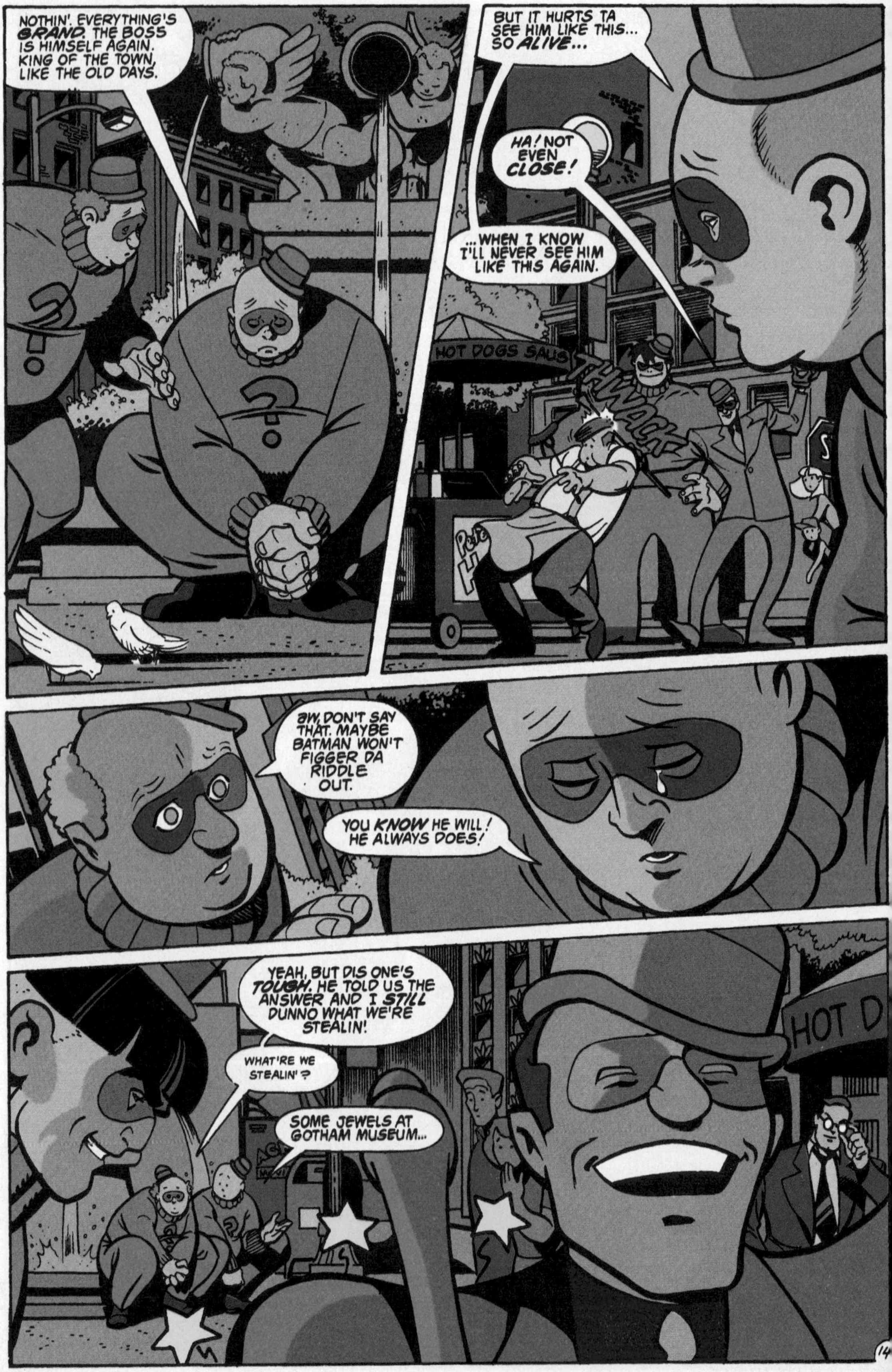
NOTHIN'. EVERYTHING'S GRAND. THE BOSS IS HIMSELF AGAIN. KING OF THE TOWN, LIKE THE OLD DAYS.
BUT IT HURTS TA SEE HIM LIKE THIS... SO ALIVE...
HA! NOT EVEN CLOSE!
...WHEN I KNOW I'LL NEVER SEE HIM LIKE THIS AGAIN.
HOT DOGS SAUS
THWACK
AW, DON'T SAY THAT. MAYBE BATMAN WON'T FIGGER DA RIDDLE OUT.
YOU KNOW HE WILL! HE ALWAYS DOES!
YEAH, BUT DIS ONE'S TOUGH. HE TOLD US THE ANSWER AND I STILL DUNNO WHAT WE'RE STEALIN'!
WHAT'RE WE STEALIN'?
SOME JEWELS AT GOTHAM MUSEUM...
HOT D
14

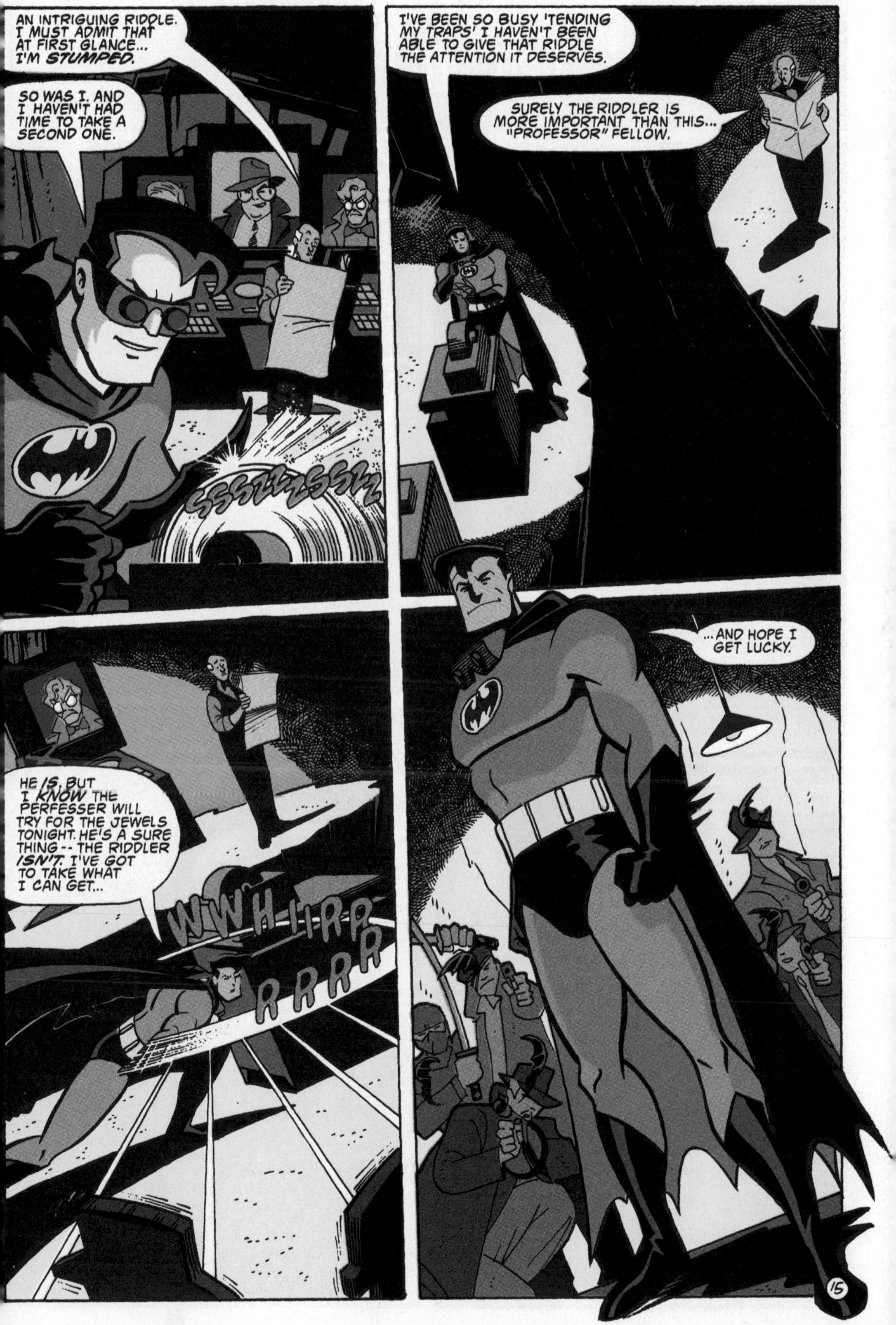
AN INTRIGUING RIDDLE. I MUST ADMIT THAT AT FIRST GLANCE... I'M STUMPED.
SO WAS I. AND I HAVEN'T HAD TIME TO TAKE A SECOND ONE.
SSSZZZZSSSZZ
I'VE BEEN SO BUSY 'TENDING MY TRAPS' I HAVEN'T BEEN ABLE TO GIVE THAT RIDDLE THE ATTENTION IT DESERVES.
SURELY THE RIDDLER IS MORE IMPORTANT THAN THIS... "PROFESSOR" FELLOW.
HE IS, BUT I KNOW THE PERFESSER WILL TRY FOR THE JEWELS TONIGHT. HE'S A SURE THING -- THE RIDDLER ISN'T. I'VE GOT TO TAKE WHAT I CAN GET...
WWHIIRRRRRRR
...AND HOPE I GET LUCKY.
15

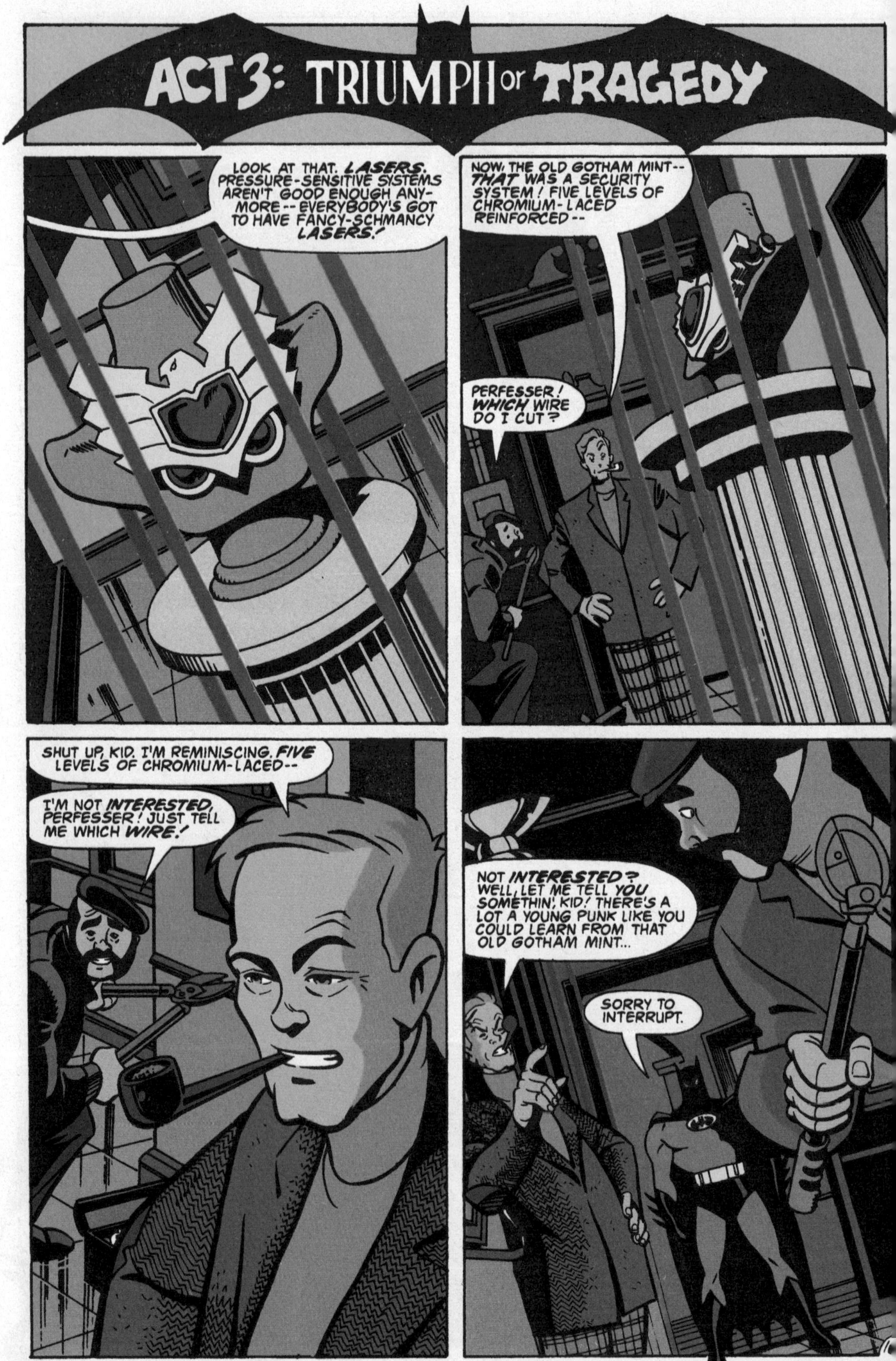

ACT 3: TRIUMPH or TRAGEDY
LOOK AT THAT. LASERS. PRESSURE-SENSITIVE SYSTEMS AREN'T GOOD ENOUGH ANY-MORE -- EVERYBODY'S GOT TO HAVE FANCY-SCHMANCY LASERS!
NOW, THE OLD GOTHAM MINT -- THAT WAS A SECURITY SYSTEM! FIVE LEVELS OF CHROMIUM-LACED REINFORCED --
PERFESSER! WHICH WIRE DO I CUT?
SHUT UP, KID. I'M REMINISCING. FIVE LEVELS OF CHROMIUM-LACED --
I'M NOT INTERESTED, PERFESSER! JUST TELL ME WHICH WIRE!
NOT INTERESTED? WELL, LET ME TELL YOU SOMETHIN', KID! THERE'S A LOT A YOUNG PUNK LIKE YOU COULD LEARN FROM THAT OLD GOTHAM MINT...
SORRY TO INTERRUPT.

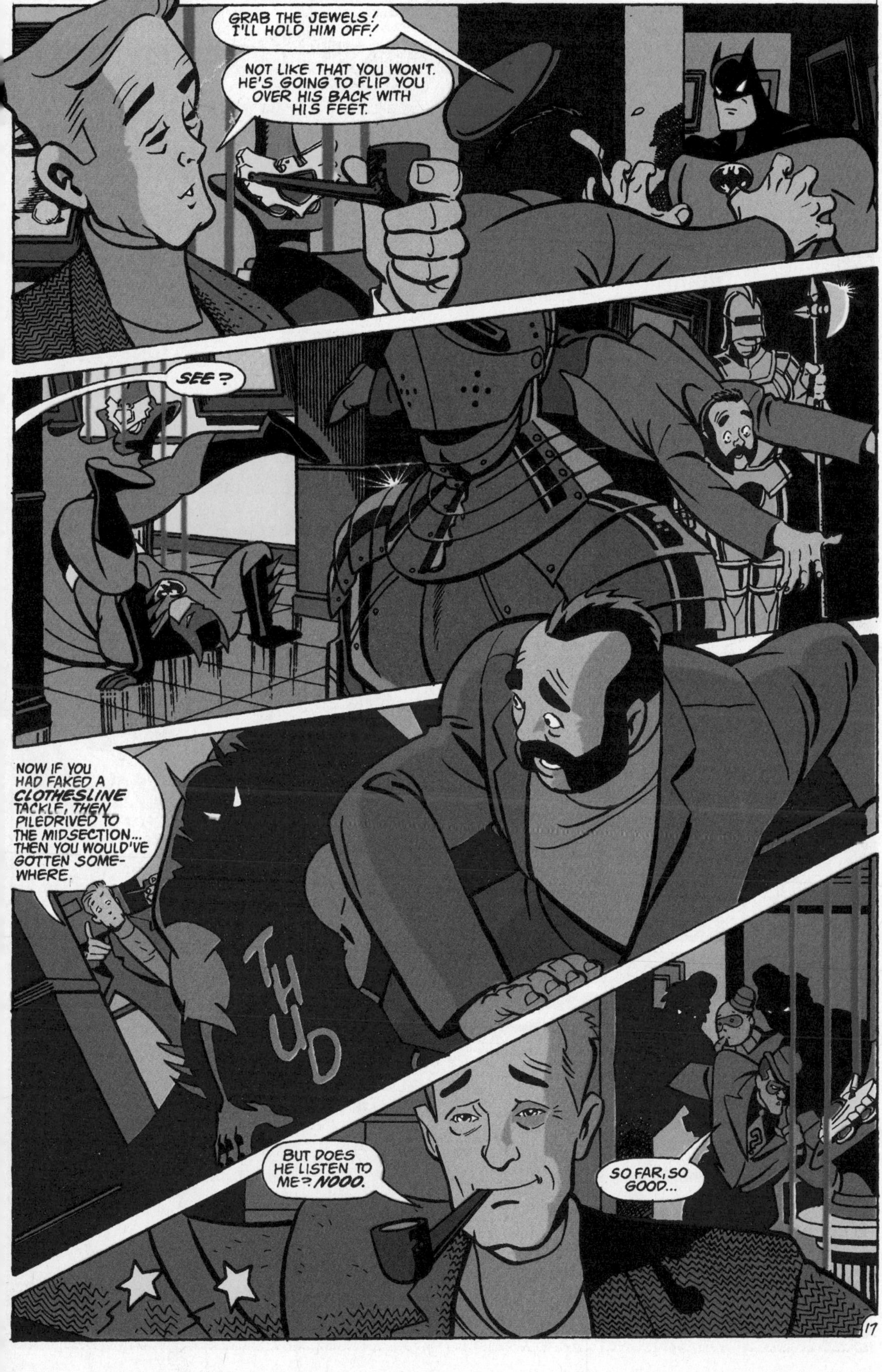
GRAB THE JEWELS! I'LL HOLD HIM OFF!
NOT LIKE THAT YOU WON'T. HE'S GOING TO FLIP YOU OVER HIS BACK WITH HIS FEET.
SEE?
NOW IF YOU HAD FAKED A CLOTHESLINE TACKLE, THEN PILEDRIVED TO THE MIDSECTION... THEN YOU WOULD'VE GOTTEN SOME-WHERE.
THUD
BUT DOES HE LISTEN TO ME? NOOO.
SO FAR, SO GOOD...
17

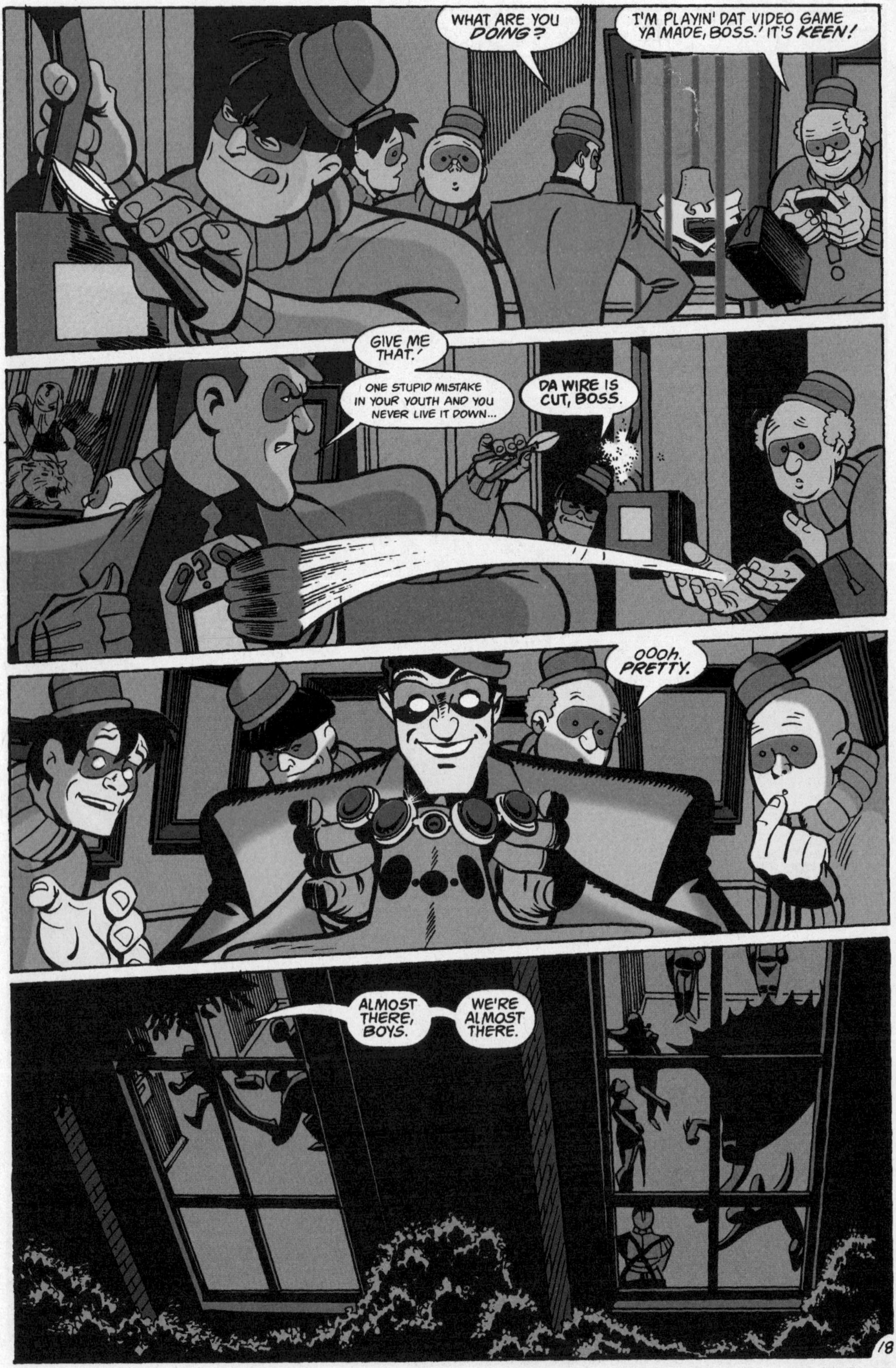
WHAT ARE YOU DOING?
I'M PLAYIN' DAT VIDEO GAME YA MADE, BOSS.' IT'S KEEN!
GIVE ME THAT.'
ONE STUPID MISTAKE IN YOUR YOUTH AND YOU NEVER LIVE IT DOWN...
DA WIRE IS CUT, BOSS.
oooh. PRETTY.
ALMOST THERE, BOYS.
WE'RE ALMOST THERE.
18

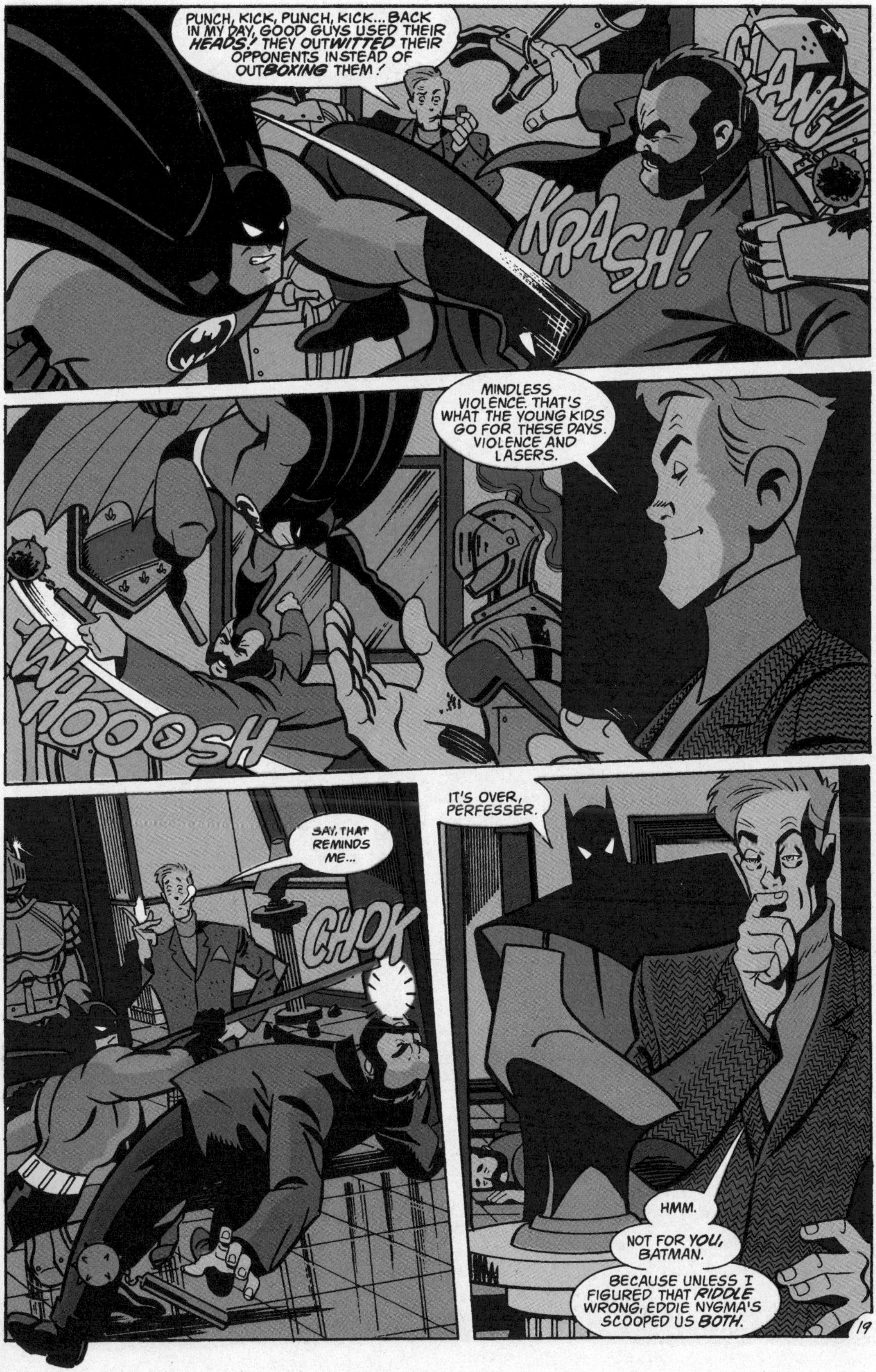
PUNCH, KICK, PUNCH, KICK... BACK IN MY DAY, GOOD GUYS USED THEIR *HEADS!* THEY OUT*WITTED* THEIR OPPONENTS INSTEAD OF OUT*BOXING* THEM!
CLANG!
KRASH!
MINDLESS VIOLENCE. THAT'S WHAT THE YOUNG KIDS GO FOR THESE DAYS. VIOLENCE AND LASERS.
WHOOOSH
SAY, THAT REMINDS ME...
CHOK
IT'S OVER, PERFESSER.
HMM.
NOT FOR *YOU*, BATMAN.
BECAUSE UNLESS I FIGURED THAT *RIDDLE* WRONG, EDDIE NYGMA'S SCOOPED US *BOTH*.
19

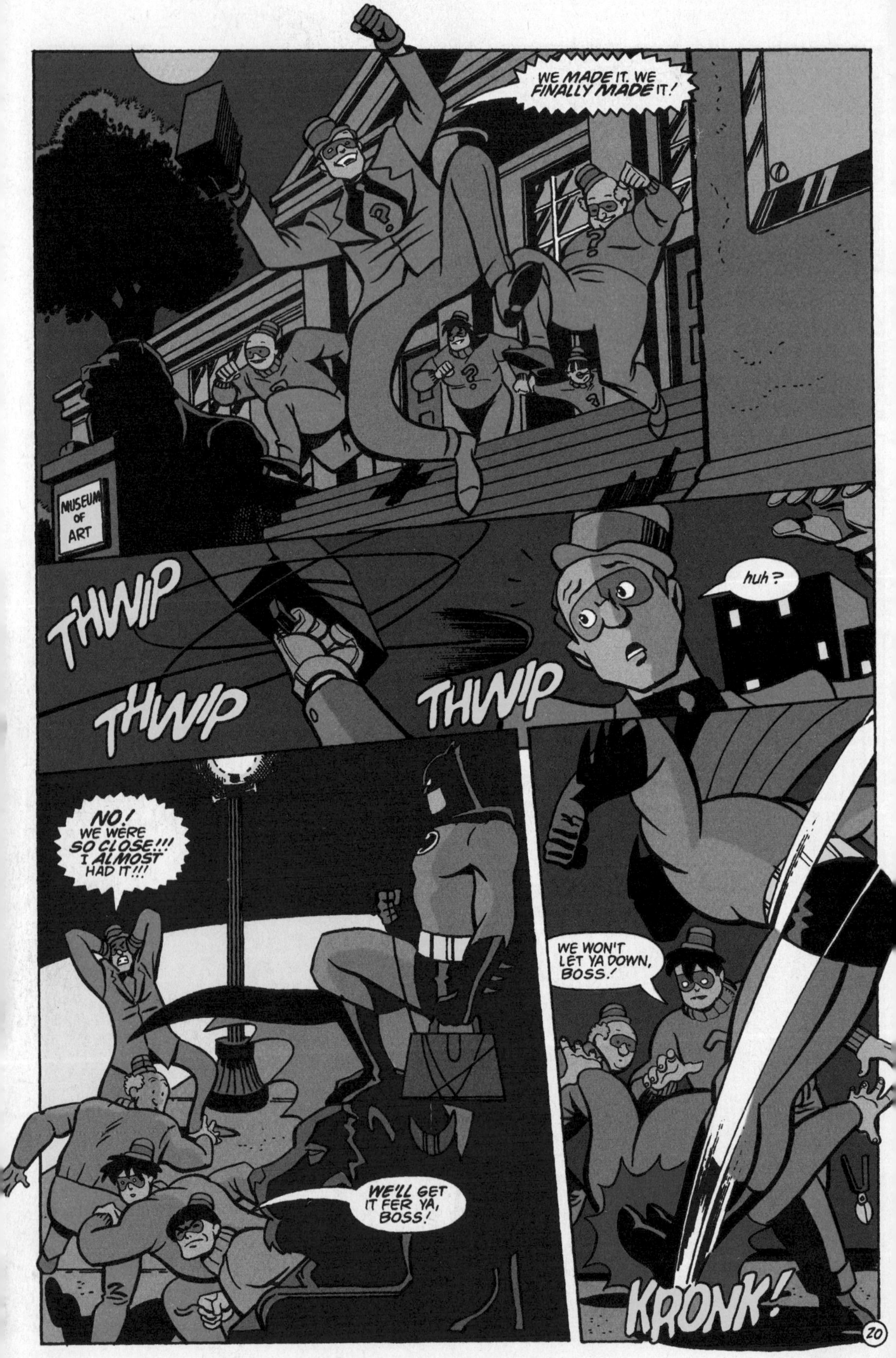

WE MADE IT. WE FINALLY MADE IT!
MUSEUM OF ART
THWIP
THWIP
THWIP
huh?
NO! WE WERE SO CLOSE!!! I ALMOST HAD IT!!!
WE'LL GET IT FER YA, BOSS!
WE WON'T LET YA DOWN, BOSS!
KRONK!
20

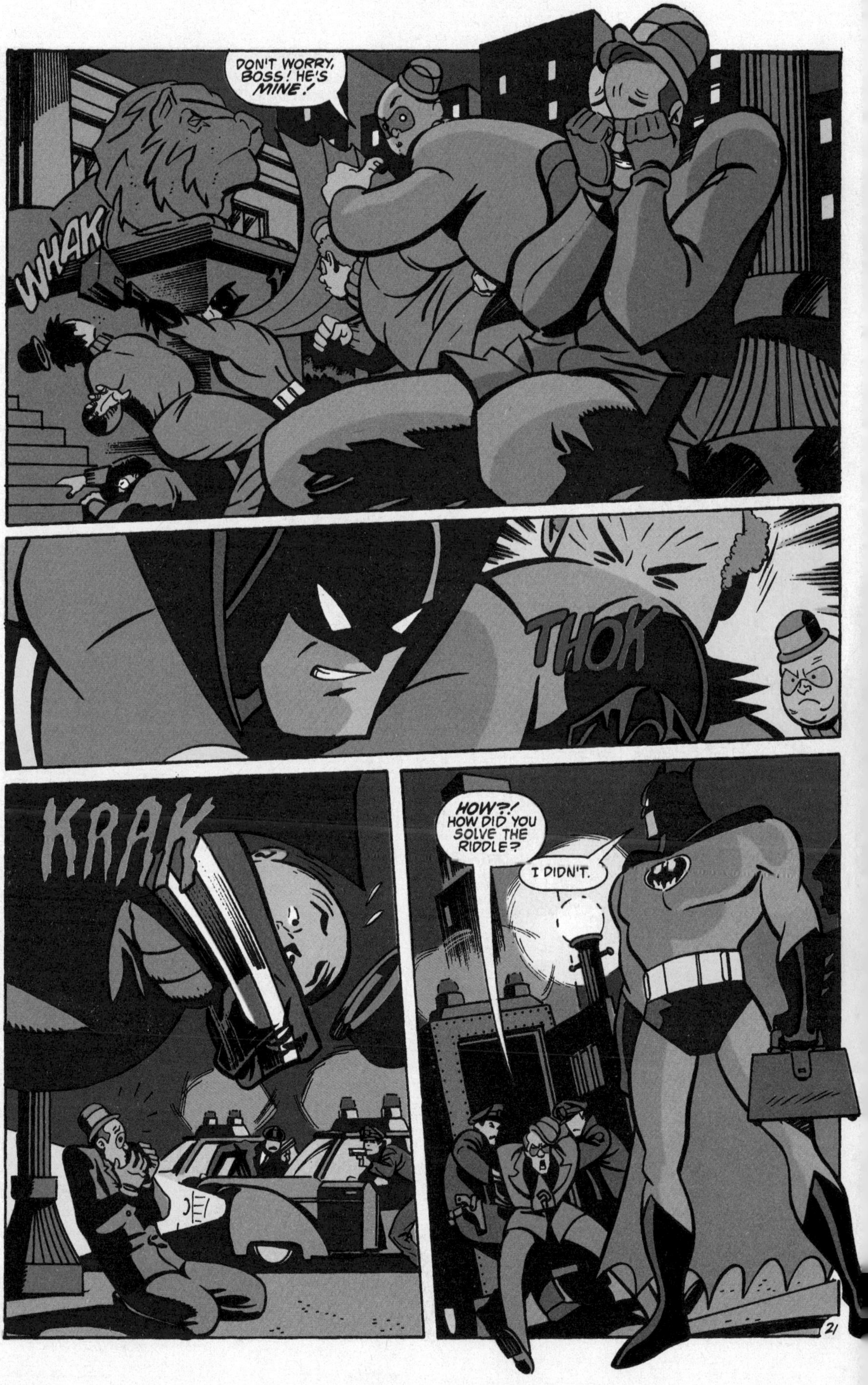
DON'T WORRY, BOSS! HE'S MINE!
WHAK
THOK
KRAK
HOW?! HOW DID YOU SOLVE THE RIDDLE?
I DIDN'T.
21

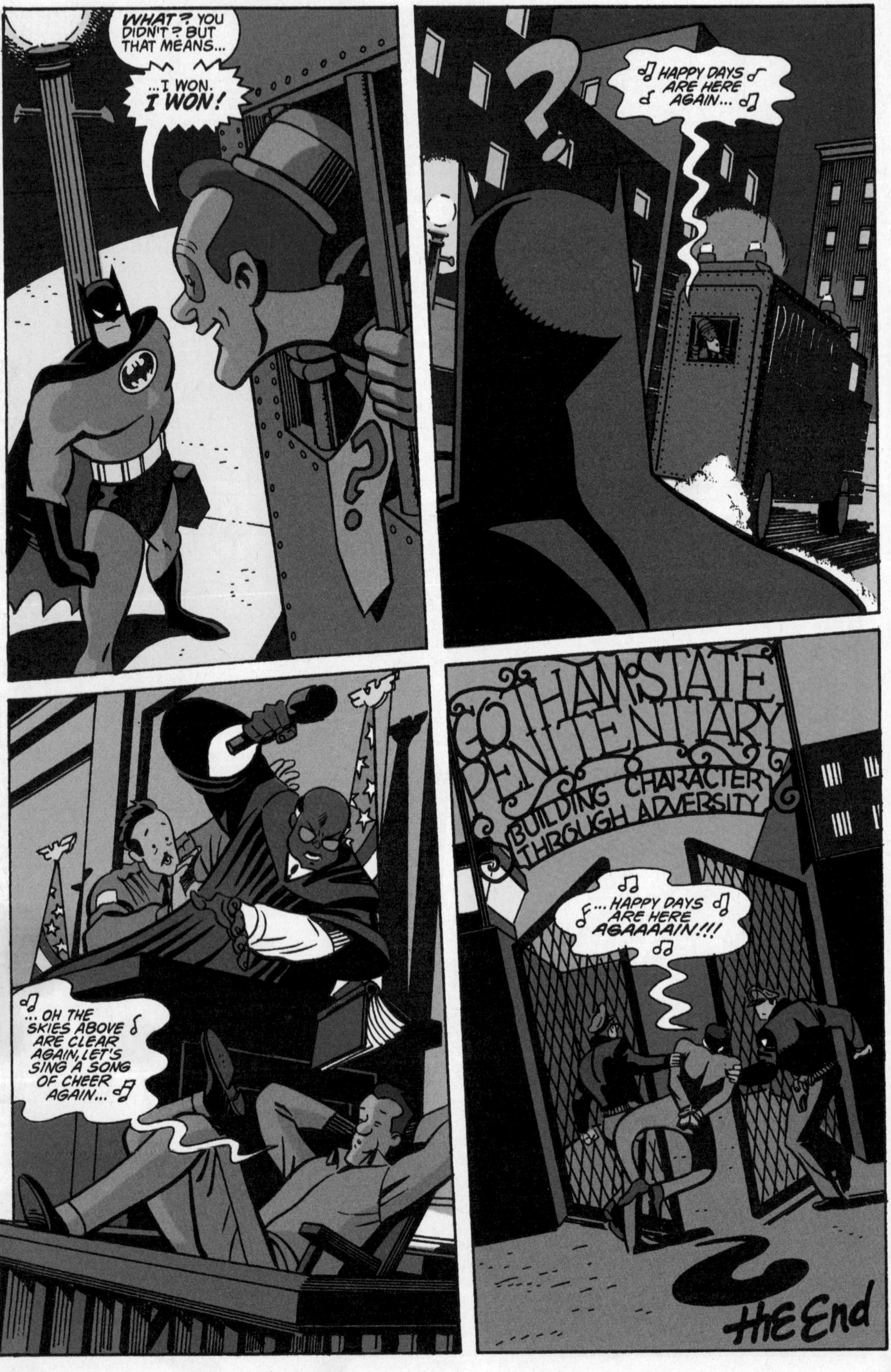
WHAT? YOU DIDN'T? BUT THAT MEANS...
...I WON. I WON!
♫ HAPPY DAYS ARE HERE AGAIN... ♫
GOTHAM STATE PENITENTIARY
BUILDING CHARACTER THROUGH ADVERSITY
♫ ...OH THE SKIES ABOVE ARE CLEAR AGAIN, LET'S SING A SONG OF CHEER AGAIN... ♫
♫ ...HAPPY DAYS ARE HERE AGAAAAAIN!!! ♫
THE End